CANADIAN
POLITICS
THROUGH
PRESS REPORTS

CANADIAN POLITICS THROUGH PRESS REPORTS

Donald C. Wallace
Frederick J. Fletcher

Toronto
Oxford University Press
1984

Canadian Cataloguing in Publication Data

Wallace, Donald C.
Canadian politics through press reports

ISBN 0-19-540456-4

1. Canada — Politics and government
2. Press and politics — Canada.
I. Fletcher, Frederick J.   II. Title

JL65 1984 W34 1984   320.971   C84-098330-1

40,323

Cover photo: courtesy *The Toronto Star*
Designed by Margaret Kaufhold

1 2 3 4 — 7 6 5 4   Printed in Canada by Webcom Ltd.

Acknowledgements

BAIN, George. Columns from *The Globe and Mail*, Toronto, of 17 May 1982; 4 October 1982; 1 November 1982; 20 December 1982. Reprinted by permission of Professor Bain. BAUCH Hubert. 'Inside Ottawa's Inner Sanctum', *The Gazette*, Montreal, 3 January 1981. Reprinted by permission. BISSONNETTE, Lise. 'On our last gasp' appeared originally as 'De notre agonie' in *Le Devoir*, 17 September 1982. Reprinted by permission. BLISS, Michael. 'Are the Conservatives Living in Canada?', *The Financial Post* 5 February 1983 and 'The Once and Future King', *Saturday Night*, October 1982. Reprinted by permission of Michael Bliss. BRAID, Don. 'Ya-hoo! West Rides Again', *The Toronto Star* 20 February 1982 and 'Western Separatists Have Birthday Blues', *The Toronto Star* 20 February 1983. Don Braid is the Edmonton Journal's political columnist. Reprinted by permission. BULLOCK, Helen. 'Red Tape + Red Ink = Bureaucracy Blues', *The Toronto Star*, 6 March 1982. Reprinted with permission — The Toronto Star Syndicate. CARRIERE, Vianney. 'Bullock Means Business on Budget' *The Globe and Mail*, Toronto, 13 May 1982. Reprinted by permission. CHAPUT-ROLLAND, Solange. 'Two nationalisms within a single state' appeared originally as 'Deux nationalismes au sein du même État' in *La Presse*, 15 June 1981. Reprinted by permission of La Presse, Ltée. 'A Federalist No More', *Today*, 10 July 1982. Reprinted by permission of Solange Chaput-Rolland. CHRONICLE-HERALD. 'Canadian Newspapers Editorialize on Election Outcome', *The Chronicle-Herald*, Halifax, 21 February 1980, reprinted by permission of The Canadian Press News Limited. 'Straighter Shooting', The *Chronicle Herald*, Halifax, 28 August 1982, reprinted by permission of The Halifax Herald Limited. CRANE, David. Reprinted with permission — The Toronto Star Syndicate: 'How Powerful is the Man Who Sits in Office 307-S?', *The Toronto Star*, 23 August 1980 and 'Frenzy Over Pitfield: What Silly Nonsense!', *The Toronto Star*, 26 December 1982. CROOK, Farrell. 'Bertha Wilson: Champion of the Underdog', *The Toronto Star*, 10 March 1982. Reprinted with permission — The Toronto Star Syndicate. DOBELL, Peter C. 'The West Can Be Won and No Reforms are Necessary', *The Calgary Herald*, 22 May 1980. Reprinted by permission of Peter Dobell. DOUGLAS-HOME, Charles. 'What Will Mr Trudeau Do With His Power Now?, *The Times*, London, 3 March 1980. Used by permission of Times Newspapers Limited. DRANOFF, Linda Silver. 'Override: Menace to Basic Right?, *The Globe and Mail*, Toronto, 23 December 1981. DUFFY, Robert. Reprinted with permission — The Toronto Star Syndicate: 'Is Budget-Making Process in Need of Streamlining?', *The Toronto Star*, 31 January 1982; 'Premiers' Talks Were Useful', *The Toronto Star*, 28 August 1982. FALARDEAU, Louis. 'The Halifax conference: A public-relations operation' appeared originally as 'La conférence de Halifax: une opération de relations publiques' in *La Presse*, 28 August 1982. Reprinted by permission of La Presse, Ltée. FERGUSON, John. 'Affable Whiz Kid is Ottawa's New Top Mandarin', *The Globe and Mail*, Toronto, 22 September 1981, reprinted by permission of The Canadian Press News Limited. FISHER, Douglas. 'Accountability', *Toronto Sun* 26 July 1982, reprinted with the permission of the Toronto Sun Publishing Corporation. FOTHERINGHAM, Allan. 'Lack of Strong People Led to Clark's Defeat', *Winnipeg Free Press*, 19 February 1980. Used by permission of Southam News. FOX, Bill. 'Sober Second Thoughts From Members of the Other Place', *The Toronto Star*, 30 May 1982. Reprinted with permission — The Toronto Star Syndicate. FRASER, John. 'The Bagman: No More Taint of Backrooms' *The Globe and Mail*, Toronto, 15 February 1980. Reprinted by permission. FULFORD, Robert. 'The Night of the No Vote: A Very Canadian Occasion', *Saturday Night*, June 1980 and 'Disorder in the Court' *Saturday Night*, September 1982. Reprinted by permission. GHERSON, Giles. 'Premiers Edge Towards Alliance of Necessity', *The Financial Post*, 4 September 1982. Reprinted by permission. GLOBE AND MAIL, The. Reprinted by permission of The Globe and Mail, Toronto: 'Bank Act Successes Won by Guerilla Lobbyists', 28 October 1980; 'On April 17, 1982 . . .', 17 April 1982; 'Order in the House', 20 December 1982; and 'His Great Reward', 23 December 1982. GOAR, Carol. 'An Uneasy Move Toward Reform', *The Toronto Star*, 20 March 1982. Reprinted with permission — The Toronto Star Syndicate. GOLDBLATT, Murray. 'Media Notebook: Record on Issues Still Below Par', *The Globe and Mail*, Toronto, 8 February 1980. Reprinted by permission. GORDON, Charles. 'Media Watch: TV Can Be Fast, Newspapers Thorough', *The Citizen*, Ottawa, 13 February 1980 and 'Media Watch: Has Election Coverage Been Fair to Clark?' *The Citizen*, Ottawa, 18 February 1980. Reprinted by permission. GRAY, John. Reprinted by permission: 'Parties Richer but Democratic Dreams Fading', 'Flesh Going Unpressed but Mails a Bonanza', and 'Parties Find Money Rolling in, Control of Ridings Trickling Out,' *The Globe and Mail*, Toronto, 29 November 1980; 'Clout is a Numbers Game the West Can't Win', *The Globe and Mail*, Toronto, 20 April 1981; 'Envelope System is a Bid to Make Sense of Federal Spending', *The Globe and Mail*, Toronto, 21 September 1981; 'A Dual-Paternity Brainchild Controls the Federal Purse', *The Globe and Mail*, Toronto, 22 September 1981; 'Grit Policy Awaits PM's Parting', *The Globe and Mail*, Toronto, 22 November 1982; and 'Joe Clark: Tory With True Grit', *The Globe and Mail*, Toronto, 22 January 1983. GWYN, Richard. Reprinted with permission — The Toronto Star Syndicate: 'Ottawa's Overfed Bureaucracy a Sign of Decadence', *The Toronto Star*, 27 April 1982 and 'The Good, the Bad and the Ugly of Federalism', *The Toronto Star*, 28 August 1982. HANDELMAN, Stephen. 'New "Hidden Government" Grips Ottawa', *The Toronto Star*, 28 June 1980. Reprinted with permission — The Toronto Star Syndicate. HAYES, David R. 'A Word From the Wise', *The Globe and Mail*, Toronto, 12 February 1983. Reprinted by permission of David R. Hayes. HEPBURN, Bob. Reprinted with permission — The Toronto Star Syndicate: 'How Your Tax Dollars Are Spent', *The Toronto Star*, 21 August 1982 and 'NDP Running Hard Just to Stay Even', *The Toronto Star*, 18 December 1982. IRVINE, William P. 'The Need for Election Reform' *The Globe and Mail*, Toronto, 14 January 1980. Reprinted by permission of Professor Irvine. JACKSON, Robert. Reprinted with permission — The Toronto Star Syndicate: 'The Cabinet-Making Ritual', *The Toronto Star*, 12 September 1982, and 'Parliament Takes Giant Step', *The Toronto Star*, 5 December 1982. JOHNSON, Bryan. 'Self-Promotion Ottawa Style: Spend Money', *The Globe and Mail*, Toronto, 8 May 1982. Reprinted by permission. KLIFF, Barry. 'Can Public Good Be a Bottom Line?', *The Gazette*, Montreal, 24 July 1982. Reprinted by permission. LANCASHIRE, David. 'The Last Word — Legally', *The Globe and Mail*, Toronto, 6 June 1981. Reprinted by permission. LANGER, Inge. '''Female Ghetto'' Still Reigns in PS', *The Citizen*, Ottawa, 9 July 1982. Reprinted by permission. LATOUCHE, Daniel. 'Autopsy of a Crisis' appeared originally as 'Autopsie d'une crise' in *Le Devoir*, 5 December 1981. Reprinted by permission. LAVOIE, Gilbert. 'The charter will not prove to be a miracle cure' appeared originally as 'La charte ne deviendra pas une solution miracle' in *La Presse*, 28 November 1981. Reprinted by permission of La Presse, Ltée. LESAGE, Gilles. 'Agreement tragic for Québec' appeared originally as 'Une entente tragique pour le Québec' in *Le Soleil*, 6 November 1981. Used by permission. LEWIS, Robert. 'The Deals Behind the Commons' Back', *Maclean's*, 22 March 1982. Reprinted by permission. LONGPRÉ, Paul. 'Trudeau Starts Again with a Free Hand' appeared originally as 'Trudeau repart les mains libres' in *La Presse*, 17 February 1980. Reprinted by permission of La Presse, Ltée. LYNCH, Charles. Used by permission of Southam News: 'Trudeau May Be Around a Long Time', *The Citizen*, Ottawa, 19 February 1980 and 'Premiers' Gabfest Must Go', *Calgary Herald*, 14 August 1981. MCCALL, Christina. 'Women and Political Power', *Chatelaine*, December 1982. Reprinted by permission of Christina McCall. MCDONALD, Kenneth. 'Bureaucracy Remote from Business Reality', *The Globe and Mail*, Toronto, 13 April 1982. Reprinted by permission of Kenneth McDonald. MCGREGOR, Deborah. 'Business Lobby Splits on Strategy', *Financial Times of Canada*, 22 March 1982. Reprinted by permission. MAGNET, Joseph. 'The Deadly Muzzling of the Public Servant', *The Globe and Mail*, Toronto, 26 October 1982. Reprinted by permission of Professor Magnet. MOLONEY, Paul. 'Touring with Trudeau (But Why?)', *Winnipeg Free Press*, 14 February 1980. Used by permission. MONOPOLI, William. 'The Court: Politics Invaded Legality', *The Financial Post*, 3 October 1981 and 'The View From Inside the Supreme Court', *The Financial Post*, 27 March 1982. Reprinted by permission. NEWMAN, Peter C. 'Requiem for a Featherweight', *Maclean's*, 7 February 1983. Reprinted by permission. NEW YORK TIMES. 'Mr. Trudeau, Too, Has to Save Gas', *The New York Times*, 20 February 1980. © 1980 by The New York Times Company. Reprinted by permission. O'DONNELL, Joe. 'Pollsters Set Priorities for the 1980s', *The Toronto Star* 15 August 1982. Reprinted with permission — The Toronto Star Syndicate. PARÉ, Jean. 'Scorched-earth policy' appeared originally as 'La stratégie de la terre brulée' in *L'actualité*, February 1983. Reprinted by permission. PÉPIN, Marcel. 'The Death of Separatism', *Saturday Night*, October 1980. Reprinted by permission of Marcel Pépin. PICARD, Jean-Claude. 'Fiscal accords: another duel between Ottawa and Québec' appeared originally as 'Les accords fiscaux: Un autre duel Ottawa-Québec' in *Le Devoir*, 8 August 1981. Reprinted by permission. PRINCE, Vincent. 'Does the Electoral System Need Review?' appeared originally as 'Un système électoral à repenser?' in *La Presse*, 27 February 1980, and 'Towards a summit on the economy' appeared originally as 'Pour un sommet sur l'économie' in *La Presse*, 27 August 1982. Both are reprinted by permission of La Presse, Ltée. ROWAT, Donald C. 'Can Lid be Lifted on Ottawa Secrecy?', *The Globe and Mail*, Toronto, 9 April 1981. Reprinted by permission of Professor Rowat. ROY, Jean-Louis. 'Our rights and freedoms in the constitutional turmoil' appeared originally as 'Nos droits et libertés dans le tourmente constitutionelle' in *Le Devoir*, 30–31 October 1981; 'Building Canada Without Québec' appeared originally as 'Construire le Canada sans le Québec' in *Le Devoir*, 4 December 1981. Both are reprinted by permission. ROY, Michel. 'Requiem for an unfinished country' appeared originally as 'Requiem pour un pays inachevé' in *La Presse*, 19 April 1982. Reprinted by permission of La Presse, Ltée. RUSK, James. 'Joel Bell: ''Policy Activist But Not Political Activist''', *The Globe and Mail*, Toronto, 26 November 1982. Reprinted by permission. RUSSELL, Frances. 'Provinces Will Rule Canada', *Winnipeg Free Press*, 10 November 1981. Reprinted by permission. RUSSELL, Peter. 'Legally Right, Ethically Wrong', *The Globe and Mail*, Toronto, 1 October 1981. Reprinted by permission of Professor Russell. SALLOT, Jeff. 'Loss of Political Clout Final Straw for Some

in West', *The Globe and Mail*, Toronto, 24 January 1982, and 'Judges Reject Liberal Views in Charter Cases', *The Globe and Mail*, Toronto, 7 January 1983. Both reprinted by permission. SCOTTON, Lindsay. ''Ottawa's Advertising: Persuading Us With Our Own Money', *The Toronto Star*, 27 March 1982. Reprinted with permission — The Toronto Star Syndicate. SEARS, Val. Reprinted with permission — The Toronto Star Syndicate; 'Minority Rule, Like Hanging, ''Concentrates the Mind''', *The Toronto Star*, 9 February 1980; 'Ottawa: Where Power is the Fascination', *The Toronto Star*, 5 September 1981; and 'Who is Running the Country?', *The Toronto Star*, 13 November 1982. SHERMAN, Paddy. 'Pierre Killed It', *Vancouver Province*, 7 February 1982. Reprinted by permission of Paddy Sherman. SIMPSON, Jeffrey. 'Short-changed Even in Civil Service, Alberta Feels', *The Globe and Mail*, Toronto, 22 April 1981. Reprinted by permission. SMITH, Roger. 'Patronage: Is it Blatant Corruption or a Necessary Evil?' *The Toronto Star*, 12 June 1982. Reprinted by permission of The Canadian Press News Limited. SPEIRS, Rosemary. 'Tracking the Voters Right to the Polls', *The Globe and Mail*, Toronto, 17 April 1982. Reprinted by permission. STAR-PHOENIX. 'Premiers Far From Impressive', 28 August 1982. Used by permission of the *Star-Phoenix*. STEED, Judy. 'Warming Up for Senate Reform Again', *The Globe and Mail*, Toronto, 8 February 1983 and 'Canada's NEP: The Beauty or the Beast?', *The Globe and Mail*, Toronto, 19 March 1983. Both reprinted by permission. STEVENS, Geoffrey. 'A Case of Image Over Reality', *The Globe and Mail*, Toronto, 23 February 1980, and 'Controlling the Public Purse: There's No More Urgent Need Than to Restore Accountability', *The Globe and Mail*, Toronto, 21 June 1982. Reprinted by permission. STEWART, John. 'Tories' Unprecedented Use of Bells Undermines Purpose', *The Toronto Star*, 18 March 1982. Reprinted by permission of John Stewart. STRAUSS, Marina. 'Charting a New Course for the Bench', *The Globe and Mail*, Toronto, 14 September 1982. Reprinted by permission. THE TIMES, LONDON. 'The Return of Mr Trudeau', *The Times*, London, 20 February 1980 and 'A Canadian Celebration', *The Times*, London, 17 April 1982. Reprinted by permission of Times Newspapers Limited. THOMSON, Dale. '''Rep-by-Pop'': Prescription for Minority Government', *The Gazette*, Montreal, 26 February 1980. Reprinted by permission of Professor Thomson. TIERNEY, Ben. 'Joe, the Journalists' Gaff, But Had it Been Pierre . . . ?' *The Citizen*, Ottawa, 29 January 1980. Reprinted by permission of Southam News. TORONTO STAR, The. Reprinted with permission — The Toronto Star Syndicate: 'A Gutted Constitution', 6 November 1981; 'Lifting Budget Lid, Slightly', 24 April 1982; and 'A Short-Sighted Consensus', 27 August 1982. TOWNSEND, Hugh. 'Carving His Signature Into History . . .', *The Chronicle-Herald*, Halifax, 29 September 1981. Reprinted by permission of The Halifax Herald Limited. URQUHART, Ian. 'War No. 3 With Provinces', *The Toronto Star*, 11 April 1981. Reprinted with permission — The Toronto Star Syndicate. VALPY, Michael. Reprinted by permission: 'MPs at Their Best: The System Does Work', *The Globe and Mail*, Toronto, 6 April 1982; 'A Rare Case', *The Globe and Mail*, Toronto, 4 September 1982; and 'For the Record', *The Globe and Mail*, Toronto, 27 January 1983. VANCOUVER SUN, The. 'The Canadian Way', 6 November 1981 and 'Now Let's Work For Tomorrow', 17 April 1982. VIENNEAU, David. 'New Rights Charter Paves the Way for Changing Way of Life', *The Toronto Star*, 19 April 1982. Reprinted with permission — The Toronto Star Syndicate. WALKOM, Thomas. 'Fiscal Arrangements: Like Chinese to Most People', *The Globe and Mail*, Toronto, 28 November 1981. Reprinted by permission. WALL STREET JOURNAL, The. 'The Bullet Bites Back', 20 February 1980. Reprinted by permission of The Wall Street Journal © Dow Jones & Company, Inc. 1980. All rights reserved. WHITTINGTON, Les. 'Lobbying Ottawa', *Financial Times of Canada*, 22 June 1981. Reprinted by permission. WILLIAMS, Blair. 'The Decline of Political Parties', *The Globe and Mail*, Toronto, 4 July 1980. Reprinted by permission of Blair Williams. WILSON, W.A. 'Power Delusions', *Vancouver Province*, 14 January 1982 and 'Pass the Dagger', *Vancouver Province*, 28 September 1982. Both reprinted by permission of W.A. Wilson. WINNIPEG FREE PRESS. 'Agreement at Last', *Winnipeg Free Press*, 6 November 1981. Reprinted by permission. YOUNG, Christopher. Reprinted by permission of Southam News: 'Accept Verdict of the Voters', *The Citizen*, Ottawa, 25 February 1980 and 'Messing With the Mandarins', *The Gazette*, Montreal, 3 January 1981.

Contents

Preface

It is now widely accepted that much of the information about the political process that is available to citizens in modern democratic societies comes to them through the news media. Television news reaches the greatest number of people, but those interested in politics, including the decision-makers, are most likely to read newspapers for information. In fact, broadcast journalists themselves tend to rely on newspapers for news and, above all, for analysis and comment on public affairs. Essential for the student of the political process, therefore, is the capacity to use newspaper articles effectively — in other words, the ability to identify key assumptions, evaluate the reasoning and the conclusions, and place these elements in the larger context of the political system.

Political science instructors have traditionally asked students in introductory courses to read a daily newspaper as an informal requirement. Few, however, have had the resources to equip their students with the skills necessary to exploit the newspaper to good effect. *Canadian Politics Through Press Reports* is intended to fill that gap: to help students enhance their knowledge of a wide range of political phenomena by examining the coverage given them in the press. Each of the thirteen chapters presents a selection of news reports, preceded by a brief introductory essay, and then asks a series of questions related to the articles. These questions require the student to interpret each piece by drawing out its major arguments and assumptions and relating them to the discipline of political science. They are designed to draw the student's attention to the key components of the report (including omissions) without providing a pre-packaged interpretation.

The book covers three major areas of the political process usually dealt with in introductory courses: governmental institutions, the federal system, and political structures. Although the selections concentrate on Canadian politics, they are intended to clarify general principles. Obviously not all topics could be included, but the material provided ought to cover most of the major ones. Given the focus of contemporary journalism, areas relating to subjects such as the philosophical and ideological underpinnings of the system could be addressed only indirectly. Nevertheless, many of the articles offer the instructor the opportunity to raise fundamental issues.

In presenting our selection of newspaper articles, we have attempted to serve a variety of purposes:

1. The first is to provide real-world examples of textbook political science. Careful study of the selections will help the student grasp the specific applications of the general propositions presented in texts and lectures. In addition, these concrete examples can stimulate interest in the principles.

2. The workbook format requires students to think political problems through, rather than simply to reproduce imperfectly understood generalizations. Having to interpret a specific account will lead them to seek the necessary contextual information.

3. The articles, many of which are excellent in their own right, supply a useful set of supplementary readings. They illuminate a wide range of institutions and processes, with particular emphasis on actual political tensions and conflicts, and they bring into focus the gap between theory and practice found in many cases.

4. Even the deficiencies in the articles contribute to the goals of this volume. Students will become acquainted with the systematic biases that daily newspapers bring to their coverage of politics. The introductory essays and questions should sensitize students to the distortions inherent in political coverage, as well as suggest ways to discount them. (All the articles have been reprinted in their original style, and errors have not been corrected.)

The introduction to each section provides an overview of the political factors relevant to the topic at hand, identifies the major principles involved, and suggests the context and perspective necessary to interpret the material. These essays are intended to be used along with lectures and assigned readings in the course as a basis for dealing with the questions on the articles. To aid students who wish to pursue particular topics in greater depth, each section includes a short list of suggested readings. All fairly recent, these readings are listed in reverse chronological order.

In our view, this volume can be used successfully both in introductions to Canadian politics and in general introductions to political science. Since we have emphasized the *process* of news coverage as well as its *outcome*, it may also be useful in courses in journalism or political communication.

We would like to acknowledge gratefully the research assistance of John Finney, who helped locate materials; the many newspapers, magazines, and news services for permission to reproduce their articles; and the help of the kind people at Oxford University Press, especially Don LePan, Sally Livingston, and Richard Teleky.

DONALD C. WALLACE

FREDERICK J. FLETCHER

York University
January 1984

Introduction

The Press and Canadian Politics: A Consumer's Guide

Citizens in modern democracies rely heavily on the mass media for their political information, but few are equipped to be effective consumers of news. Although many students of politics recognize that the mass media perform essential functions in the political process, the standard textbooks in Canadian politics give them little attention. The present volume, by contrast, uses some of the best recent examples of Canadian political journalism to illustrate current issues and the strengths and weaknesses of their press coverage. In this introductory essay we will put that material in context by examining the role of the mass media, particularly newspapers, in the political process, describing the central features of the Canadian mass media system, setting out the major factors that influence what becomes news, discussing the most important biases and patterns of political coverage in the press, and suggesting ways in which citizens can become more effective consumers of news. As Dennis K. Davis and Stanley J. Baran have pointed out, 'Adulthood . . . involves developing our ability to make conscious, rational choices about what we will and will not accept and believe. Understanding media genres and their codes can help us . . . make these choices.'[1] The working codes of political journalism are essential knowledge for active citizens.

The Mass Media in the Political Process

If it is true that the quality of public debate is a measure of democracy, then the mass media constitute a vital political institution. The news media provide not only most of the information upon which political discussion must be based, but also the interpretive frameworks that shape the debate. While providing information and commentary, as Anthony Westell has put it, 'the media . . . define what is normal and respectable in a society, what is debatable and what is beyond discussion by decent, responsible citizens.'[2]

Most observers agree that the issues treated as priorities by the media tend to be accepted as such by the public. Thus it appears that the media have a good deal of influence on the agenda of public debate, even though when forming their opinions people also respond to direct per-sonal experience as well as perspectives gained from relatives, friends, co-workers, and specialized publications.

The media also have a direct influence on government decision-makers, an influence that citizens should be aware of. Research shows that newspapers in particular are a major resource for top decision-makers in both business and government, providing them with information on reactions to policy initiatives and the activities of other agencies, and with useful summaries of complex reports that they would not otherwise have time to digest. On technical matters the direct policy influence of the news media is limited, but they can influence the development of government priorities on moral issues and concrete problems that affect individual citizens. The decision of the Ontario Progressive Conservative government to impose rent control in 1975, for example, appears to have been a direct result of pressures generated by media coverage. By keeping watch over government activities, the news media can make officials more prudent. From time to time they can also bring unpopular government plans to light early enough for public reaction to stop them.[3]

Although television news has become the primary source of current-affairs information for most citizens, the daily newspaper remains the crucial element in the Canadian news system. Newspapers continue to supply much of the coverage, especially with respect to political and economic issues, upon which other news services draw. They also generate most of the commentary and a good deal of the probing investigative reporting. The major dailies not only provide the broadcast media with background information, but help to set the agenda for television and radio news, especially news of longer-term significance. Moreover, the press tends to receive more attention from decision-makers than television does (except in election campaigns).

The continuing importance of the daily newspaper depends to a large extent on certain comparative advantages that it enjoys over its broadcast competitors. Newspapers can be read selectively at the reader's own speed; reports can be compared and kept for reference. Being primarily an information rather than an entertainment medium, the daily press also has a tradition of providing much more detailed and complex coverage than newscasts do, especially with respect to public affairs. Such coverage is possible in part because print reporting is simpler and cheaper than television reporting, allowing the newspapers to retain larger and more specialized staffs. Most important, perhaps, a newspaper can build circulation by appealing to an aggregate of minorities, members of which are free to read the items that interest them; it does not have to attract the lowest-common-denominator mass audience that television requires. It can therefore provide specialized political coverage, for example, without alienating those members of its audience with other interests, as television does when it displaces regular programming to cover political events.

The Canadian Mass Media System

Canadian newspapers have from their earliest times been political—and partisan. By the end of the nineteenth century, however, partisan loyalties had to compete with commercial considerations as publishers became more interested in profits than politics. Urbanization, increases in literacy, and new technologies—mechanized printing, cheap newsprint, the telegraph for rapid newsgathering—set the stage for a mass press that derived its revenues primarily from advertising. Partisanship declined as newspapers sought mass audiences, made increasing use of wire services—which supplied non-partisan copy to a wide range of clients—and became more business-like with the growth of newspaper chains. (The most important news service is the *Canadian Press* [CP], founded in 1917 as a national co-operative owned collectively by the daily newspapers. Today it remains the primary source of non-local news for most dailies. It endeavours to meet the diverse expectations of its clients by distributing materials derived from the member newspapers themselves, as well as from its own staff and the world's major news services.) The advent of radio news in the 1930s and television news in the 1950s strengthened the trend towards non-partisan journalism, since the broadcast media had to appeal to mass audiences and satisfy government regulators.

The Canadian mass media system is dominated by the national media, the major components of which are generally considered to be the following: three newspapers that tend to set the agenda for public affairs—*The Globe and Mail* (based in Toronto), *The Toronto Star*, and *Le Devoir* (published in Montréal); two news services—CP and Southam News (serving the fourteen dailies in the Southam chain); CBC radio and television (both French and English); *Maclean's*, a weekly newsmagazine; and *The Financial Post*, a weekly business newspaper. Apart from the fact they all reach large audiences directly, the distinguishing feature of these media is that they generate much of the news coverage and commentary on federal politics. The influence of *The Globe and Mail* derives mainly from its élite readership, although circulation of its national edition is growing. *Le Devoir* holds a similar position among francophone élites. *The Toronto Star*'s national stature, on the other hand, is based on the frequent re-printing of its material across the country through its syndication service. In distributing news across the country, the wire services obviously play a major role in determining the topics of public discussion. In a less direct way, *Maclean's* and *The Financial Post* also carry considerable weight, as does *Saturday Night*, a monthly magazine of politics and the arts that, while it does not present news in the sense that the other national media do, offers some of the most penetrating commentary in Canada. The predominant role of the national media in serious political journalism is reflected in the articles reprinted in this volume. Although we have drawn on a wide range of sources—over two dozen in all—more than half the selections come from the national media.

The media system also includes such important regional papers as *La Presse* in Québec, *The Winnipeg Free Press* in Manitoba, *The Edmonton Journal* and *The Calgary Herald* in Alberta, and *The Vancouver Sun* in British Columbia. Together with the major regional television networks, these dailies help to shape public-affairs coverage in their regions, but their national influence is limited because they are not regularly seen in the national power centres. Even when their work is excellent, as it often is, their influence depends on the national media's picking up the material. The media system is completed by local dailies and broadcasting stations, and local and suburban weeklies. All of these outlets play a role in the preparation and dissemination of public-affairs news and commentary. But the national media are dominant, and usually determine the topics the others will cover, especially with respect to national politics.

The parliamentary press gallery in Ottawa is the major source of news and commentary on national affairs. As such, it is a vital institution in the democratic process: without media coverage the safeguards in the parliamentary process that exist to hold government accountable are largely empty ritual. As one study for the Royal Commission on Newspapers put it, 'The gallery correspondents play an important role in deciding what aspects of the political process will be communicated to the citizenry, both by screening the information presented to them by government and the [opposing] parties . . . and by deciding which additional stories and features to pursue. They also provide . . . interpretations of events.'[4] By 1982 the gallery had about 240 members, more than double the number two decades earlier. The members include reporters, editors, syndicated columnists, broadcasters, and foreign correspondents. About 150 are employed by the press (newspapers, magazines, and news services); many of these writers are represented in our selections.

On the whole, the gallery provides more and better coverage of federal politics than it did twenty years ago. But there are still problems areas, the most important being the limited scope of coverage, insufficient behind-the-scenes examination of public policy, and a tendency towards 'pack journalism'. Most routine coverage of federal politics is based on government announcements (often with opposition-party reactions) and the verbal sparring that takes place in the daily oral Question Period in the House of Commons. Large areas of government activity are not covered adequately, especially the courts, regulatory agencies, and the public policy process within the civil service and cabinet. In addition, fundamental issues of ideology and political culture are rarely explored.

Most observers concede that the press gallery's work is competent but unimaginative, placing far too much emphasis on routine issues. Part of the problem is that most journalists are generalists expected to cover a wide spectrum of subject areas. As Robert Fulford has observed, 'Most [political] reporting, on TV or in the papers, is done by men and women who appear innocent of serious knowledge in the fields they describe. You have a sense, as you listen to them or read them, that all they know of the subject is what they heard from the last expert they met.'[5] A few political journalists specialize in such subjects as economic affairs, intergovernmental relations, energy, or social issues, but they are mainly concentrated in the larger bureaux and exercise a disproportionate influence on the coverage of their areas.

Although a greater number of journalists would allow for greater specialization and more attention to other aspects of the political system, tendencies towards superficial coverage and conformity are not purely a function of the numbers in the press gallery. In their unimaginative pursuit and filing of essentially the same stories carried by the wire services, reporters respond to a herd instinct; when a group of them get together to share information or inter-pretations on any particular story, deviations from the accepted view are uncommon. It is more important, for most, to avoid being scooped than it is to strike out on their own. By filing the same story as everyone else, they do not risk being asked by their editors why they 'missed' some routine item that is reported by the wire services, the late news, and all the papers the next day.

The quality of coverage is affected as well by the rapid turnover in gallery members. Some news organizations rotate their reporters out of the gallery after two or three years for fear of having them 'go native.' Consequently, few journalists are allowed the time necessary to perfect their skills at effective reporting in Ottawa. For some, the lure of money and security offered by government jobs proves to be a temptation they cannot resist. Another problem is that few English-speaking reporters strive to become bilingual, thus seriously impairing their ability to cover important aspects of Canada's basic dualism, or to report on developments in Québec.

Beyond these factors, the structure of Canada's media system itself militates against diversity in coverage. Chain ownership of newspapers means that in many cases national reporters or columnists based in Ottawa serve a wide variety of clients in many regions. The Royal Com-mission on Newspapers concluded that 'concentration of ownership appears to have produced concentration of news facilities in Ottawa, resulting in a centralization of national political coverage. . . . Regional correspondents in Ottawa traditionally helped to inform politicians of conditions at home as well as reporting Ottawa news from a regional perspective. Central news bureaus often tend to produce copy that even editors, let alone readers, find irrelevant.'[6] National wire services and national television networks reinforce a national rather than a regional perspective. In recent years more and more newspapers have closed their Ottawa bureaux and have come to rely on wire-service or chain news-service coverage. This problem has been most acute in newspapers outside Central Canada.

Ottawa correspondents must contend not only with inadequate time and resources, but also with a govern-ment that actively seeks to control information, set the

agenda for political reporting, and manage the news. Canada's highly secretive political tradition makes it easy for politicians and officials to create news by making speeches, issuing statements, holding news conferences, or leaking information. A phalanx of press officers provides a continuing supply of ready-made news for hard-pressed journalists. Although many reporters would publicly criticize managed news and perceived manipulation, the fact that they are required to turn in so many stories every working day often forces them to rely on government hand-outs. Of course, they also enjoy special access to government documents, parliamentary facilities, and the decision-makers themselves; at budget time, for example, reporters enter a 'lock-up' in advance of the document's release to study it and receive government briefings, in order to report intelligently on its contents. However, they have little opportunity to consult outside experts.

Political reporting, then, is characterized by the mutual dependence of reporters and their sources. Politicians need publicity to promote their careers and programmes, while journalists require facts and statements to include in their dispatches. Even the prime minister is not immune to the need for media attention to maintain his popularity or to persuade people to support particular government initiatives. He uses his high profile and control over the machinery of government to highlight or down-play certain issues. He can reward or punish certain reporters by grant-ing or denying them access, or bypass them altogether by making televised speeches to the nation. Other political figures obviously share some of these resources, but none can command the 'clout' of the prime minister.

Many of these criticisms must be tempered in the case of newspapers with larger Ottawa contingents—The Globe and Mail, for instance, or The Toronto Star. These papers place greater emphasis on the quality of their political reporting than most others do, and the scope of their coverage extends far beyond Question Period. They also exercise considerable influence because they are read by central decision-makers. In fact, Westell has commented of the Globe that its 'claim to be Canada's national newspaper rests less on national distribution than on the fact that it often writes the agenda for Parliament and for other papers which report on Parliament'.[7] It is only among the larger bureaux within the gallery that any real competition occurs. Full-scale journalistic competition arises when there are several bureaux of roughly equal size that can measure their accomplishments against one another. Smaller operations spend most of their time on routine coverage; their stories derive predominantly from specific events, releases, and news reports in other media. Smaller bureaux (especially single-reporter ones) have little opportunity for innovative reporting and are apt to be buried under the avalanche of government information. Only the major bureaux have the resources, the per-sonnel, and the willingness to develop alternatives to the items on the government's agenda and to provide the best coverage. There is a tremendous contrast between the excellent reporting and commentary offered by a few journalists and the great bulk of what is presented.

The News Services

The news services supply the hard core of political coverage upon which the system depends. The basic service provided by CP to its 110 member papers is supplemented by some special CP services and a variety of other news agencies: *United Press Canada*, a small, tabloid-oriented service; *Southam News*, with a staff of twenty-three in six Canadian bureaux and five abroad; *The Globe and Mail*, with eight bureaux across Canada and five abroad for its own use; and a variety of major foreign news services (such as the *New York Times* service), specialized agencies, and feature syndicates. Still, CP is the one service regarded as indispensable by most dailies.

CP[8] obtains its news from three major sources: (1) the member papers; (2) its own staff; and (3) foreign wire services with which it has an exchange relationship. Much of its routine coverage comes from the member papers. CP staffers collect items from local news-rooms, then select and rewrite the most news-worthy before distributing them over CP's 90,000 kilometres of leased wires to news-rooms across Canada. Most of its political coverage comes from its thirty-member Ottawa bureau and from thirteen other bureaux across the country. Foreign news is derived mainly from a few foreign news agencies, particularly CP's American counterpart, *Associated Press* (AP). CP transmits about 250,000 words a day on its main circuit—about ten times the news that a typical daily could print. Even so, CP editors in Toronto (English), Montréal (French), and the regional centres send out only a fraction of the news they receive.

By selecting the news to be transmitted and dispatching regular lists of the major national and international stories of the day, CP editors help to set the national news agenda. CP also sends out lists of the top stories from eight major Canadian dailies and the national television newscasts. Editors have considerable leeway in selecting among CP items, but most of the smaller dailies depend heavily on the agency's priorities. The larger ones have other sources of news as well, since they usually subscribe to several services. With respect to foreign news, however, it is almost impossible for editors to escape an American-oriented view of the world—CP relies substantially on U.S. sources, and the alternative services are mostly American. Only *The Globe and Mail* and the Southam papers can provide much in the way of foreign coverage prepared specifically for Canadian audiences.

The Manufacture of News

News is not simply an objective reflection of the world around us, as many journalists would have us believe. News is manufactured by organizations that are designed to seek out interesting stories to attract audiences. News organizations choose what they will report on the basis of certain widely accepted, but rather general, criteria of news-worthiness. In fact, news is as much created as it is discovered. Editors do not simply choose from what comes into their news-rooms from wire services, the staff writers covering various 'beats', and interested groups; they also send reporters to seek out stories based on ideas generated within the organizations. The editors and reporters who decide what will be reported or commented on are influenced by many factors, including community norms, journalistic traditions and fashions, news management by sources, pressures from interest groups and advertisers (rarely), internal politics, and the commercial concerns of management.

News selection depends on what is considered news-worthy. Although there is much truth in the old saying that the news is what the editors say it is, certain news values are widely agreed upon. Significance—importance for the political or economic system, especially if large numbers of people are affected—obviously plays an important role in the selection of political news. At the same time, however, journalists tend to seek out stories that contain some of the familiar elements of human interest: novelty, paradox, drama, incongruity, or shock value. Anthony Westell has argued that the conventional definition of news 'often values speed over completeness, brevity over explanation, sensation over sobriety, immediacy over perspective, conflict over co-operation, the event over the trend, the entertaining triviality over the difficult but important. . . .'[9] In the end, of course, news is the product of negotiations between reporters and editors over what should be covered (and how), between reporters and sources as they exchange information, and among editors over what should be published.[10] Many news organizations have distinctive traditions or 'sacred cows' that influence their coverage. Cases in point might include the economic nationalism of *The Toronto Star*, the anti-Trudeau bias of *The Toronto Sun* and its counterparts in Calgary and Edmonton, the pro-development viewpoint of the Irving dailies in New Brunswick, and the focus on language issues in the Québec dailies. Some sacred cows reflect the pet peeves of publishers; others stem from community norms and interests.

In most news-rooms key editors set the tone of coverage not so much by issuing orders as by selecting among submissions and awarding praise or blame. Generally, reporters are assigned 'beats' for which they are responsible. In a large Ottawa bureau an individual reporter may be assigned to cover a key department (such as Finance or Energy), an institution or agency (such as the Supreme Court or the Canadian Radio-television and Telecommunications Commission), or a subject area (such as constitutional reform). The beat is part of a general news net established by the organization to keep potential sources of news under surveillance. Beat reporters must cultivate contacts in the appropriate offices and organizations to keep themselves well informed. The paper's choice of the beats it will assign reporters to determines where it looks for news, while the news values of the beat reporter and his or her understanding of the relevant editor's requirements also influence news selection. The fact that most political news comes from expected sources and is processed in a routine manner produces systematic biases in the coverage.

In addition to internal factors, there are many external pressures on the news-selection process. Journalists creative enough to probe proposals still under consideration often run into difficulty. Governments want the public to know about their services and accomplishments, but not about their failures. Community norms and regional and cultural loyalties are also constraining factors. In Québec, for example, the French-language press tends to reflect a strong social consensus regarding certain culture and language policies. To depart from them would be to risk serious community protest in the form of decreased circulation and advertising. Another consideration is advertising. Surveys indicate that many readers suspect advertisers of having an unseemly influence on news content. In fact, direct advertiser influence on political coverage is quite rare on the larger established dailes. Newspapers do derive some 75 per cent of their revenues from advertising, however, and thus management generally seeks to keep newspaper content within the limits of tolerance of the business community. Together, the libel laws that inhibit investigative reporting, government secrecy, community norms, and a set of other factors related to the fact that newspapers are commercial enterprises can weigh quite heavily on a paper's content.[11]

Systematic Biases in Political Coverage

All institutions have certain built-in ways of approaching their tasks, and newspapers are no exception. As we have seen, news organizations operate in a complex world in which news judgements must be made rapidly. The organizational routines and established criteria necessary to cope in such situations lead inevitably to systematic biases in the coverage. These biases are not the result of some conspiracy; they simply reflect the various pressures on media personnel. From the point of view of the consumer, the essential thing is to understand—and thus be able to discount—the general biases in the system, as well as the idiosyncracies of particular newspapers.

At present the most common systematic biases in Canada's English-language press are these: reliance on official sources; a tendency to interpret politics almost exclusively in terms of electoral activity (accompanied by a certain cynicism about the motives of political actors); a focus on personal factors—for example, party leaders—in political life, rather than social or organizational ones; an unconscious acceptance of liberal ideology; and a preoccupation with the specific at the expense of the general. It should be noted, of course, that these biases are general

tendencies, not ironclad rules, and that exceptions occur regularly. What is important is that the coverage as a whole reflects and reinforces these patterns.

Much systematic bias derives from the fact that news organizations train their personnel 'to see and classify the world in terms of established images'.[12] Editors often appear to like nothing better than a cliché slightly twisted to give it interest. In fact, of course, mass communication is difficult without recourse to images with meaning to large numbers of people. The danger is that the symbols or metaphors needed for effective communication will come to have a life of their own: thus politics in British Columbia must always be portrayed as conflictual and bizarre, or Newfoundlanders as quaint (or on welfare). Such stereotypes help to determine which political matters the papers will cover and how they will do it. Once a politician has been tagged—as arrogant (Trudeau) or bumbling (Clark)—subsequent coverage is often presented in such a way as to reinforce the stereotype. Reports reinforcing existing images are generally subjected to much less scrutiny by editorial 'gatekeepers' than are those that challenge conventional wisdom.[13]

News coverage also tends to reinforce existing patterns of authority. For the sake of convenience as much as anything else, journalists rely on established institutions for public-affairs news. As a result, the perspectives of those holding institutional power are apt to predominate, and challengers have a difficult time getting a hearing. Thus, for example, certain myths about Canadian society are perpetuated by the media. Among these are the widely accepted notion that Canada is a class-less society—which ignores the significant disparities in wealth and power in our system—and the assumption that the federal government should be able to manage the economy, despite our dependence on the U.S.

An important limitation on political coverage is the propensity of journalists to see everything in terms of the clash between the government and the opposition. Indeed, the focus frequently narrows down to the electoral prospects of key political figures. Government policies are often poorly explained unless the opposition parties oppose them. The influence of individual political leaders is consequently exaggerated, and many subjects relevant to the political process escape media scrutiny. For example, critical or investigative journalism is likely to focus on public- rather than private-sector problems—such issues as auto safety, dangerous drugs, food additives, and environmental pollution were taken up by the media only after being raised by interest groups or opposition parties. It appears that the media's generally critical stance towards public institutions has worked to reduce their legitimacy and to perpetuate the largely unexamined myth that the private sector is more efficient than the public sector. Civil servants and politicians alike are subject to negative stereotyping.

With the exception of *The Globe and Mail*, Canada's newspapers are essentially regional in their orientation. The most striking differences, of course, are those between the English- and French-language papers, which reflect cultural as well as regional factors. But there are systematic regional differences in news emphasis and editorial perspective even within the English-language press. Both circulation and advertising come primarily from the area surrounding the city of publication, and one result is that the focus of newspaper coverage varies with regional priorities. Thus federal–provincial conflicts are reported quite differently in the various regions, while the treatment of issues involving the French language and culture or Québec's aspirations often depends on the location of the newspaper. More generally, the national media, controlled in Toronto and Montréal, show a clear Central Canadian bias. This bias emerges not only in a pattern of coverage that often neglects the Eastern and Western provinces, but also in a tendency to stereotype Easterners and Westerners. The national media are apt to equate Central Canadian interests with the national interest when regional conflict emerges. Although in recent years the national media have made a serious attempt to improve their cross-regional coverage, regional biases remain.

The general status-quo, middle-of-the-road orientation of the news media has important effects on political coverage. As Edwin R. Black has pointed out, 'The effective range of public debate is limited in even the freest of countries.'[14] The selectivity exercised by news organizations helps to ensure that public debate is confined within the framework of the dominant ideology. In Canada, this ideology could be labelled 'welfare capitalism'. Both private property and the welfare state are relatively sacred. Very seldom, according to Black, 'do arguments about public affairs involve even genuine socialist and liberal views let alone those as conflicting as Marxism and multinational capitalism'.[15] The majority of readers are thus rarely exposed to any thoroughgoing critique of their basic political assumptions. The news organizations tend to enforce the boundaries of 'legitimate' debate by labelling the holders of views that challenge the status quo, whether from the left or the right, as cranks. Neither Marxist nor libertarian parties get much coverage. Even the social-democratic New Democratic Party has received the editorial endorsement of a major daily newspaper at election time only four times. Most dailies are reluctant to challenge basic assumptions or the dominant interests of their communities. After all, to prosper they need broad community support in the form of circulation and advertising sales. To quote Black once more: 'No communications medium trying to win and hold the attention of a majority of people can do so by venturing very far outside the agreed set of values.'[16]

The Active Consumer

To use the mass media effectively it is necessary to learn their peculiar rules of communication. Although individual dailies have their idiosyncracies, there are common rules that govern their presentation of news. Some are obvious, such as the use of relative headline size and the placement of items on the page to indicate importance; but

others are less well known. Today, for example, many newspapers distinguish between (1) 'hard' news, which is reported impartially with little analysis or commentary; (2) 'soft' news or features, which may present more of the writer's reactions (but no partisan commentary); (3) analysis, which involves assessment and commentary on the feasibility or future prospects of a politician or party (but no personal opinion); (4) commentary, in which regular columnists are free to express opinions of all kinds in their signed columns; and (5) editorials, which in the English-language press are unsigned, expressing the corporate views of the newspaper, and in the French-language press are normally signed, representing the opinions of the individual editorial writers. Newspapers have slightly different ways of identifying the different types of content, but regular readers soon learn the signals.

The clear distinction between fact and opinion that the mass media attempt to make is unique to them. It is not made in normal conversation, and it is criticized by philosophers of knowledge, who argue that the objectivity journalism aspires to is in practice impossible, since to make sense all facts must undergo the subjective process of selection and be presented within some framework. Newspapers still use the 'inverted pyramid' style of presentation, with its emphasis on the straightforward delivery of 'facts' in order of importance, even though hard news has declined as a proportion of newspaper content in recent years. Fortunately, with more and more space devoted to signed analysis, commentary, and features, readers now have more opportunity to get to know the views and perspectives of individual writers, and can use this information to help them assess the material presented.

To approach political coverage with a critical eye, the reader must be aware of the standard techniques of propaganda—one-sided arguments, stereotyping, unsupported generalizations—as well as the more subtle signs of unconscious bias. These signs include the structuring of a report to lead the reader to a particular conclusion; the use of a limited range of sources; the juxtaposition of quotations to build meaning; the use of symbols or metaphors with specific ideological content; and the failure to consider alternative explanations. To add interest, journalists often employ rhetorical devices that identify heroes and villains. The critical reader must bear in mind not only the systematic bias in favour of institutional authority, for example, but also the areas of coverage that are usually underemphasized or omitted.

Having made an effort to spot the biases, the active consumer can move on to compare sources. A study for the Royal Commission on Newspapers concluded that 'citizens can get the full range of information they need to participate in the democratic process only by diligent effort, using a wide range of sources'.[17] The ideal mix of sources for most readers would be at least two daily newspapers (one national and one regional), Maclean's, selected radio and television programmes, at least two magazines of opinion (such as Saturday Night and Canadian Forum), and selected issues of alternative publications to obtain perspectives outside the mainstream. Those able to read French would be well advised to consult *Le Devoir*. While such a range is well beyond the time and resources of most of us, the need to compare reports and to look beyond conventional sources on issues of real personal importance should be evident. The extent of the search will depend on the individual's perspective on the political process: 'For those generally satisfied with the economic and political status quo, the information [and commentary] provided by the major outlets may be sufficient, since most provide a variety of points of view. For those not satisfied with reformist approaches, the range of options will inevitably be too narrow.'[18] Because 'news imparts to occurrences their *public character* as it transforms mere happenings into publicly discussable events',[19] as Tuchman has put it, students of politics cannot ignore the news media, even if they have more personal or specialized sources. For average citizens who care about the political realm, newspapers are indispensable, but they must know how to use them. Within its inherent limitations, Canadian political journalism is often excellent. The active consumer must develop the skills to identify the excellent work, understand it in context, and discard the rest.

Notes

1. Dennis K. Davis and Stanley J. Baran, *Mass Communication and Everyday Life: A Perspective on Theory and Effects* (Belmont, Calif.: Wadsworth, 1981), 108.

2. Anthony Westell, *The New Society* (Toronto: McClelland and Stewart, 1977), 73.

3. For a more detailed discussion of these issues, see Frederick J. Fletcher, *The Newspaper and Public Affairs*, vol. 7, research publications of the Royal Commission on Newspapers (Ottawa: Supply and Services, 1981), chap. 2.

4. *Ibid*, 50.

5. *Saturday Night*, October 1977.

6. Canada, Royal Commission on Newspapers, *Report* (Ottawa: Supply and Services, 1981), 142.

7. Anthony Westell, 'The Press: Adversary or Channel of Communication?' in H.D. Clarke *et al.*, eds., *Parliament, Policy and Representation* (Toronto: Methuen, 1980), 27.

8. For a detailed treatment of Canadian Press in operation, see Carman Cumming, Mario Cardinal, and Peter Johansen, *Canadian News Services*, vol. 6, research publications of the Royal Commission on Newspapers (Ottawa: Supply and Services, 1981).

9. Westell, 1977, *op. cit.*, 80.

10. Gaye Tuchman, *Making News: A Study in the Construction of Reality* (New York: Free Press, 1978), 31-8.

11. For a more detailed discussion, see Fletcher, *op. cit.*, chap 3.

12. Edwin R. Black, *Politics and the News: The Political Functions of the Mass Media* (Toronto: Butterworths, 1982), 137.

13. *Ibid*.

14. *Ibid*, 54.

15. *Ibid*.

16. *Ibid*.

17. Fletcher, *op. cit.*, 114.

18. Frederick J. Fletcher and Daphne F. Gottlieb, 'The Mass Media and the Political Process', in Michael S. Whittington and Glen Williams, eds., *Canadian Politics in the 1980s* (Toronto: Methuen, 1981), 162-3.

19. Tuchman, *op. cit.*, 3.

Suggested Readings

Arthur Siegel. *Politics and the Media in Canada*. Toronto: McGraw-Hill Ryerson, 1983.

Edwin R. Black. *Politics and the News: The Political Functions of the Mass Media*. Toronto: Butterworths, 1982.

John Hartley. *Understanding News*. New York: Methuen, 1982.

Frederick J. Fletcher. *The Newspaper and Public Affairs*, vol. 7, research publications of the Royal Commission on Newspapers. Ottawa: Supply and Services, 1981.

Frederick J. Fletcher and Daphne F. Gottlieb. 'The Mass Media and the Political Process', in Michael S. Whittington and Glen Williams, eds., *Canadian Politics in the 1980s*. Toronto: Methuen, 1981.

Elinor MacLean. *Between the Lines: How to Detect Bias and Propaganda in the News and Everyday Life*. Montréal: Black Rose, 1981.

Gaye Tuchman. *Making News: A Study in the Construction of Reality*. New York: Free Press, 1978.

1. Governmental Institutions

a. Parliament

The role of the Canadian Parliament does not conform to the classical notion of a flexible parliamentary system. Encompassed in this view are the tenets that Parliament acts in an independent manner, exercises a free will of its own, chooses governments, and freely dismisses them between elections. This perspective does not take into account the existence of political parties; it assumes that fluid groups or cliques will form around issues. But changes in the electoral system in the nineteenth century facilitated the formation of political parties. Today, structural features such as party discipline—MPs voting according to positions established by the parties to which they belong—ensure that government bills will be passed in the House of Commons. Even a minority government is usually able to get most of its legislative programme through by making modest concessions to gain the support of one or more of the opposition parties. The opposition no longer plays the part it once did; it is there to embarrass the government, not to assist it. Even more important, the prime minister has developed into the most significant figure in our political system.

Press coverage of Parliament—or, more particularly, the House of Commons—is simultaneously exemplary and deplorable. It is beyond dispute that the news media's treatment of Parliament far outpaces their handling of any other aspect of Canadian politics. The largest and most important group of political reporters and commentators in Canada (approximately 240) is found in the parliamentary press gallery on the Hill. At the same time, the very proficiency of these journalists distorts perceptions of the legislature's importance in the political system. Not all political activity takes place in Parliament or even in Ottawa, and with the growth and increasing complexity of modern government has come a range of official business that far exceeds the capacities of most in the gallery. Many government dealings go unreported as journalists scramble to cover stories arising from the daily Question Period or the activities of major party leaders. Reporters are provided with the *Sturm und Drang* of politics, and just enough content to pass for news, but they miss the real decisions made behind closed doors.

In the article by Val Sears, the familiar arguments about the value of minority governments reflect a more traditional view of Parliament. Even during periods of minority government, our executive-dominated system still sees decisions of importance being made outside the House of Commons. Opposition pressure becomes more significant, but it usually can only force or block decisions or affect their timing. In contrast to Sears's optimistic piece, George Bain's column concerning the effect of Parliament on the decision to test the cruise missile in Canada shows that exemptions from the rule of party discipline are rare. Party discipline is generally so strict in this country that back-benchers have almost never been afforded any genuine opportunity to affect legislation in recent years. Partisanship is a vital component of parliamentary government, and 'free' votes would simply mean that members would coalesce around factions other than the existing parties. Members vote with their parties out of loyalty to party and/or leader, hope of reward from the leader who controls important appointments, and fear of sanctions—for instance, loss of campaign support or, ultimately, expulsion from the caucus. And voters rarely elect independent candidates.

The inefficacy of the House of Commons and the frustration experienced by the opposition is best demonstrated by the 'bells incident' in the spring of 1982. Robert Lewis's overview of the inadequacies of Parliament amply illustrates both the difficulty it has in addressing issues and the paucity of weapons in the opposition's arsenal. Lewis alludes to the power of the executive, Cabinet's use of orders-in-council, the emasculation of committees, and the absence of controls on Crown corporations. On the other hand, when political scientist John Stewart (a former Liberal MP) examines the detailed procedural questions underlying the political manoeuvring, he blames the Conservatives for using flimsy grounds to launch their protest.

Carol Goar summarizes the stands of the three parties on parliamentary reform in the wake of the bells incident. She argues that the institution is out of date and in need of modernization. But this opinion fails to take into account the phenomenal growth in government over the past two decades, the introduction of so-called rational decision-making techniques, the accompanying ascendancy of central agencies, and the standardization of Cabinet committees—all of which centralize decision-making in fewer hands. In addition, governments indicate no willingness to surrender any control, which would be a prerequisite for substantial or comprehensive reform. Most of the suggestions made by the parties and cited in Goar's article are narrow and *ad hoc*. They also neglect the party caucuses (weekly meetings of all members of each party in the House and Senate), the only place where government back-bench MPs can really have any impact. In fact, caucus revolts do block government proposals occasionally, and governments must consider the limits of caucus tolerance in formulating their programmes.

The *Globe and Mail* editorial and the column by political scientist Robert Jackson outline reforms instituted in late 1982. The deficiency of these reforms lies in the fact that they do not introduce effective checks and balances within the central structures of government. The original checks and balances in the parliamentary system reflected the reality of the Crown's true power and the absence of disciplined parties; competition for power was between the Crown and Parliament. Opposition parties now have only one significant weapon: delay of government legislation. In the end the government usually gets its way, although exceptions do occur from time to time—remember the influence of the Conservative delaying tactics on the 1981 constitutional accord.

An important component of the parliamentary system is its network of committees and their variants, such as joint House and Senate committees, and task forces. The most important ones, of course, are the standing or permanent committees. Michael Valpy's article gives an excellent survey of one such body, the Standing Committee on Transport. A standing committee does more than advise on policy; it is responsible for the detailed review of bills after second reading. (Since they have been approved in principle by the time they reach the committee, however, only minor amendments are normally entertained.) As well, each standing committee examines the government's estimates or spending plans for its particular sector of government. The committee uses this stage to seek information about the operation of various departments on a wide range of issues and to solicit the views of expert witnesses. It is this activity that Douglas Fisher describes so accurately in his column 'Accountability'.

Questions continue as to whether the Canadian Parliament is truly democratic. Not only is it largely ineffective in holding the government accountable, but it seems that the institution itself is losing legitimacy in the public's eye. In the excerpts from her long article printed here, Christina McCall-Newman relates in detail how unrepresentative the House of Commons continues to be, especially for women. Among the considerable obstacles that face women running for Parliament are many that also stand in the way of certain minority groups. Part of the problem, which McCall-Newman neglects to point out, is that MPs have almost always come from the affluent groups in society, the ones with the easiest access to the resources required to run for office.

Parliament, of course, is not only the House of Commons but the Senate and Governor General as well. The Senate has been the focus of attention in recent years as a potential source of enhanced regional representation, but it currently performs other functions. Bill Fox illustrates the body's limited legislative function; the Senate is occasionally the site of debates of importance, usually on moral issues that the government does not at that particular time wish to present to the House. Judy Steed also summarizes the functions and activities of the Senate and the potential for its reform. Her article, though informative, makes some errors—the most serious is the quotation of a tongue-in-cheek remark by Senator John Godfrey about the reason he was appointed to the Red Chamber. Yet Steed clearly shows that the body's legislative function is not significant when placed beside its other crucial activity: patronage. Perhaps the most controversial Senate appointment in recent years was that of former Clerk of the Privy Council Michael Pitfield. The indignation that this appointment aroused in most of the writers here is aimed at patronage in general and at the Senate as the prime minister's principal instrument of reward. David Crane, however, presents a distinctly contrary view. He does not advocate the abolition of the upper chamber: instead, he argues in favour of the creation of an elected body. His perspective is a sensible one: if the Senate is the repository of partisan political appointments, then we should not inject a false sense of morality into its functioning. On the other hand, having an elected Senate, which would compete for legitimacy with the House, might create more problems than it would solve.

THE TORONTO STAR, FEBRUARY 9, 1980

Minority rule, like hanging, 'concentrates the mind'

By Val Sears Toronto Star

OTTAWA — There are Liberals — constitutional guru Eugene Forsey says so — who think of it as a nameless horror, a political fate worse than death.

The Progressive Conservative government of Joe Clark died because they couldn't control it.

Most of the time the New Democrats like it — even if it means getting into bed with people who don't respect them in the morning.

It's called minority government.

Five out of our last nine governments have had to rule peeking over their shoulders, working out deals with opposition parties, worrying all the time that one false move and their enemies would combine to vote them out of office.

The Clark government put up with it for two months and then, confident the leaderless Liberals would not combine with the NDP and Social Credit to defeat them, put their minority position on the line with a budget that was bad news for everyone.

Cold, cold world

The nameless, faceless horror struck and the Tories were out in the cold, cold world, probably with the cabinet doors closed firmly behind them and the Liberals back in power, perhaps as a minority.

If the pollsters are right, either the Liberals or the Conservatives may form another minority government after Feb. 18; that is, no party will have more than 141 seats and will have to govern with the agreement of at least one other party.

Not surprisingly, the government party regards this as undignified, untidy and downright undemocratic but the opposition sort of likes it.

Jim Gillies, Clark's chief policy adviser, argues that any sort of radical change is impossible in a minority situation.

"The essence of minority government is compromise," he says. "You wind up with the lowest common denominator of legislation. But you can't always compromise if you really believe in something. That's why we fell on the budget."

Gillies insists that the budget was radical in that it abandoned the Liberal belief in spending to create prosperity and replaced it with the conservative theology that unless the national deficit was reduced there would be bad times forever.

Liberals and NDP don't agree. For them the budget was simply bad economics and worse social policy and could not be supported.

"If you want continuity of policy," Gillies adds, "which the civil service always does — then minorities are fine. But try to shift direction and you're in trouble."

Prime ministers and government policy advisers always talk this way. And whether their government is in danger or not, they tend to take the most serious risks in an effort to win a majority.

Walter Gordon, who was finance minister and campaign chairman in the government of Lester Pearson during two minority administrations in the '60s, recalls it as a time when everyone in cabinet had the jitters.

'Jumping around'

"Everyone was jumping around, changing stances," he says. "There was a sort of continuous terror.

"Under the circumstances I thought we ought to call an election in 1965 and try for a majority. We didn't get it and I offered to resign."

Gordon, out of government now, has changed his own stance about minorities. He believes that a Liberal minority after the next election — with the NDP in the catbird seat — would be just fine.

One of the most dedicated, long-term defenders of minority government is former senator and constitutional expert Eugene Forsey.

Writing in the Canadian Journal of Economics and Political Science during the period of the Pearson minorities, Forsey says the number and success of minority governments in other Commonwealth countries suggests "it can scarcely be maintained, rationally, that minority government is something monstrous and unnatural, foreign to the whole spirit of British parliamentary government.

"The idea that 'doing something' is always good, doing nothing always bad, that action is always better than inaction, is a strange, but apparently powerful delusion. A government with a clear majority may go lickety-split in the wrong direction."

Nothing like hanging

Just as other minority defenders do, Forsey calls Dr. Samuel Johnson to his side. "Depend upon it, when a man knows he is to be hanged in a fortnight, it concentrates his mind wonderfully."

Indeed, there are strong arguments that some of the best legislation ever to emerge from Parliament was a result of minority pressure.

John McLeod, professor of political economy at the University of Toronto, says: "We got old-age pensions in Canada in 1927 as a result of J.S. Woodsworth and the Ginger Group using their balance-of-power position to force the Liberal government to act."

A national contributory pension plan, medicare, unification of the defence forces and a national flag were all products of the Pearson minority government between 1963 and 1968. History will likely confirm the NDP claim that the Liberals would never have established PetroCan without NDP pressure on the minority government of 1972-74.

But if there is passionate argument about the virtue of minority government, there is hardly any about the desirability of allowing a minority government to go about governing without gambling an election on every piece of legislation.

Some time ago, Lord Balfour remarked: "No constitution can stand a diet of dissolutions."

In 1972, a joint committee of the House of Commons and the Senate recommended a mandatory four-year term for the House except when the government is defeated on a specific "want of confidence" motion or when the House itself resolves to dissolve.

Senator Gildas Molgat, who co-chaired the committee, now says that if Parliament had accepted the report's recommendations "we would have fewer problems today.

Freedom to vote

"Private members would have more freedom to vote against their party," Molgat says. "There would have been a strengthening of regionalism because members could vote their region's interests without worrying about bringing down the government."

Forsey calls the fixed-term concept "nonsense, cockeyed," preferring to rely on the traditional means of stabilizing Parliament including the threat of an election. But if the government should be defeated on an important vote, there is always the wisdom of the Governor-General to fall back on if an election is clearly not in the public interest.

That is almost certainly the case today, all parties agree. It was widely reported, when Clark called on Governor-General Ed Schreyer and asked him to dissolve Parliament after the budget defeat, that the pair discussed delaying dissolution until the election weather was better or even calling on Liberal Leader Pierre Trudeau to try to form a government.

Not true. Insiders say the two "new boys" simply had to figure out the forms of dissolution ("whom do I call?") and that took time.

But there's no doubt that if Clark was elected again in a minority position and re-introduced the same budget and was defeated again, Schreyer would not entertain a request for dissolution but would exercise his royal prerogative and ask Trudeau to try to form a government.

He's not crazy

Of course, despite his campaign protestations, Clark would not introduce the same budget. Some people may call him a wimp, but he's not crazy enough to court defeat a second time.

Top Tory contacts say that in a new Conservative minority Parliament there would be much more consultation between House leaders of the various parties before any legislation is introduced.

"Certainly (Tory House Leader Walter) Baker will be in on our strategy sessions," said a Clark adviser. "I'm not saying he didn't do a good job last time but everyone is going to be a whole lot more political in the next Parliament."

Canadians are going to have to learn to live with minority parliaments, Forsey says.

He writes: "If we use our brains we can survive any amount of minority government, even thrive on it.

"If we do not, we may have to resign ourselves to an almost continuous performance of listening to campaign speeches, watching campaign TV and trudging through polling booths 'til, in sheer weariness or despair, we scrap parliamentary government and summon some Canadian de Gaulle to rescue us from the consequences of our failure ..."

THE GLOBE AND MAIL, DECEMBER 20, 1982

HALIFAX

GEORGE BAIN

The Prime Minister said in effect last week that he'd be happy to have a debate on the testing of the Cruise missile in Canada so long as it was understood it couldn't be allowed to change anything.

In the ordinary course, our parliamentary debates almost never do; that's a large part of what's wrong with them. The MPs, sometimes loosely referred to as the representatives of the people, have almost no weight.

The difference in the Cruise matter was that NDP leader Ed Broadbent was asking for a free vote, which is to say, a vote in which party discipline would be suspended and every member of every party would be confined only by his or her conscience.

The Prime Minister presumably knows his caucus, but what he seemed to be saying was that if the pack were let off the leash many more would desert the Government and its commitment to permit the testing than could be expected to come over from the other side.

Funny, that. The NDP has a pacifist streak. But the Tories are supposed traditionally to be the main custodians of the Canadian military interests. In a free vote on the testing of a U.S. weapon designed to be deployed in Europe, they could be counted on to provide compensation for any Liberal defections.

(It is possible, of course, that Mr. Trudeau was loath to trust himself to a free vote. In the mid-1960s, before he caught that tide in the affairs of man that leads on to fortune, or at least the East Block, he excoriated his predecessor, Lester B. Pearson, for accepting nuclear warheads, the equivalent military decision of the day.)

In any case, Mr. Trudeau declined Ed Broadbent's invitation to a free vote. And he took the occasion to say that debates launched by opposition parties were defined as non-confidence motions and, though not quite in so many words, that in circumstances as crucial as those, he wasn't leaving decisions to anything so chancy as democracy.

But it would have been a useful exercise if the Government, and the Prime Minister himself, had had to get out among the MPs and scrape together as best they could a majority for the approval to which they are committed in principle. A system in which a majority government of some 30 persons rules very nearly absolutely, on the strength of imposed discipline, has very little to recommend it.

Early in its recent report on changes to be considered in the practices of the House of Commons, the Special Committee on Standing Orders and Procedure said two things:

It said the committees should be given powers to initiate investigations — which is to say, on their own. But it noted that, while there was general agreement on this, "caution was expressed ... on the basis that any additional powers given to committees should not detract from the fact that the Government must maintain the confidence of the House."

Then it said that, "the plight of the private member received considerable attention" and that "it was argued that a private member could be more effective and be seen to be exerting some influence if political party discipline were relaxed and more free votes were held."

But, as the Prime Minister couldn't have illustrated better if he'd tried, relaxation of party discipline and more free votes, which would enable the private member to be more effective and be seen to be exerting influence, are in direct conflict with the necessity of a government's maintaining the confidence of the House.

A government can't (or won't) risk *not* dictating, not laying on the whip, if there's the remotest danger of it being proved fallible. And that means that debate in the House will continue always to be to a known conclusion — which is, as someone once said in remarkably different circumstances, like washing your feet with your socks on.

The really fundamental reform needed is a fixed term, four years, after which the country will decide the only question of confidence that matters.

MACLEAN'S, MARCH 22, 1982

The deals behind the Commons' back

Newfoundland MP Jim McGrath, the former Conservative minister of fisheries and oceans, paces his elegantly refurbished East Block office, reflecting aloud on the perks of Opposition. There is the controversial $64,900 salary and tax-free expense allowance, a staff of four, a free Air Canada pass, the latest electronic word processor, no postage or telephone bills and free trips abroad. But McGrath's voice wells into an angry roar as he concludes the litany of largess: "They've given me all that — and taken my power away."

Histrionics aside, McGrath's misgivings about the impotence of Parliament are shared by a growing number of MPs and experts. The frustration, in part, fuels the Tory stand on the Long Division that has paralysed Parliament. By their lights, the massive energy bill that produced the Ottawa stalemate is only the latest example of legislators being the last — and least equipped — to approve major changes in the course of the nation.

There is an impressive body of evidence to support their case. Canadians now fuel their cars at flashy Petro-Canada pumps, owing to the $1.5-billion takeover of Petrofina, but the elected members still must retroactively sanction the tax that pays for the purchase. Each year thousands of decisions — 53 last week alone — are not even placed before Parliament but issue forth from the cabinet in the form of orders-in-council which authorize everything from judicial appointments and bureaucrats' salaries to company takeovers and spending by Crown corporations. When cabinet decided to abolish 20 per cent of Via Rail's passenger service, it first had to reject the Canadian Transportation Commission's (CTC) rulings that service be maintained, then barred the CTC from reviewing the new policy.

Pierre Trudeau once said that MPs were nobodies when they left Parliament Hill, but former Tory prime ministerial adviser James Gillies submits that Trudeau was wrong. "What is correct," Gillies observes, "is that 20 miles from Parliament Hill MPs are somebodies, but on Parliament Hill they are nobodies."

In fact, in committees of the House, they are virtual eunuchs. The rules of Parliament and overriding party discipline consign most ordinary MPs to the status of political pygmies. Committees, for example, are barred from initiating investigations, a responsibility that resides with government. Accordingly, while a Canadian commission of inquiry on the sinking of the oil rig Ocean Ranger is organizing its probe, a televised congressional hearing in Washington last week brought embarrassed Canadian MPs the first public evidence on the tragedy off Newfoundland — provided by company officials. Senator John Godfrey, Liberal cochairman of the committee charged with reviewing government regulations, observes, "We have no power — or anything else." As if to prove the point, last week the committee had to *order* a transport department official to appear after he said last month that he was too busy to break off from departmental duties.

In theory, committees now have more scope for detailed scrutiny of departmental spending estimates. But the Lambert royal commission on financial management in the public service concluded in 1979, "The review of estimates is often meaningless." Only a small dedicated group of MPs consistently submits to the drudgery of committee work on estimates, while the press corps chases simpler stories elsewhere. At the same time, committees are understaffed and ill-equipped to deal with the mysteries of national accounting. Even though committees customarily fail to scrutinize spending by all departments, the estimates automatically are deemed to have passed on May 31 each year. The tab that awaits the rubber stamp this spring is $76.3 billion. Even tighter limits are placed on budget bills: they are heard in the House, where outside experts cannot be called.

Not only that, billions of dollars are spent on programs that do not even come before Parliament for approval. Of the estimated 460 Crown corporations, 16 of the most powerful submit their capital budgets, but no multi-year plans, to the cabinet for approval. Parliament eventually gets the figures, but in approving the appropriations MPs have so little information that they never really know how the money will be spent.

Parliament's public accounts committee, typically after the fact, did haul Eldorado Nuclear Ltd. to account last month for closing the Uranium City, Sask., mine with a loss of 830 jobs. In the past five years the company spent $115 million from its capital budget sprucing up the town and improving the mine site. The firm now acknowledges that the closing will cost an additional $130 million.

Eldorado and other Crown corporations argue that their business is not Parliament's affair. Yet a deal made between the cabinet and Eldorado last May belies the claim to corporate independence. The government turned over $300 million worth of uranium yellow-cake from stockpiles accumulated during a world price slump. The terms amount to a four-year gift: the company will "pay back" the loan by issuing Ottawa $100 million in common shares and $200 million in preferred shares, with a 10-per-cent dividend. While Eldorado gets to use proceeds from the sale of the yellow-cake, it doesn't have to pay dividends to the sole shareholder — the government — until 1986.

Auditor General Kenneth Dye, Parliament's official spending watchdog, is especially concerned that Eldorado refuses to submit to a comprehensive audit of the books. "They're not playing with *their* money," he observes. "They're dealing with your money and my money as taxpayers." Like Joe Clark's government before, the federal Liberals are actively reviewing ways to tighten the reins on Crown corporations. But instead of an omnibus bill, the government is leaning to administrative changes that would force more disclosure of corporate plans. Dye concludes, however, that the cabinet's plan "doesn't seem to be moving anywhere."

Parliament is at a standstill of a different sort. Even when the current siege is over, the institution will have to deal with reform of its rules. The consensus of concerned MPs on both sides of the House is that MPs need more freedom—to start their own inquiries and to obtain more expert counsel. Government House Leader Yvon Pinard is committed to House reform too. The real problem, however, is that the Commons has ceased to function as a chamber of the national interest. The ruling Liberals, by House tradition, force their members to vote for government bills. That practice tends to stifle legitimate regional objections on the government side, already bereft of members from Western Canada. The Conservatives, in turn, have never accepted their 1980 defeat and conduct House business as if the latest poll were an election result.

In the celebrated phrase of onetime Social Credit leader Robert Thompson, "Parliament is being turned into a political arena." That's as it should be, and always was. But, like an endangered pro hockey league, the political game needs some new rules. It needs less slashing and better stickhandling. Above all, it needs some respect, which the players alone can regain by cleaning up their acts.

— ROBERT LEWIS

THE TORONTO STAR, MARCH 18, 1983

Tories' unprecedented use of bells undermines purpose

by John Stewart
Toronto Star special

ANTIGONISH, N.S. — Parliamentarians in other Commonwealth countries must be incredulous: The Canadian House of Commons stood frozen for 16 days. On March 2 a Progressive Conservative member, Harvie Andre, moved, "That this House do now adjourn." The Progressive Conservatives then requested a recorded vote on Andre's motion, and from March 2 they refused to heed the bells summoning them to vote on that motion.

No rule or precedent

The Speaker found herself powerless to rescue the House from the impasse. She had taken the position that a Speaker cannot complete a formal division — in which the vote of each member is recorded — until the two whips, one for the government and one for the opposition, had indicated that the two sides were ready. This is done by a little ceremony in which the whips enter the chamber together, bow to the Speaker, and then take their seats. She has stated publicly, but not from the Chair, that there is no rule or precedent that would have authorized her to conclude the vote.

The Canadian practice of ringing the division bells until the whips have had a reasonable time to round up their supporters is wonderfully leisurely by British standards. At Westminster the bells formally rang for only five minutes, but this has been increased to eight minutes. At Ottawa the limit on a vote at a prescribed hour, such as those during the budget debate or on supply business, is 15 minutes, but there is no standing order that states how long the bells are to ring for votes on questions put at unpredictable times, such as the vote on Andre's motion. However, in recent years they rarely have rung much more than an hour. For example, on Feb. 19, 1968 after the bells had rung for about an hour, the whips proceeded with the vote even though it meant the certain loss of a very important financial measure and endangered the life of Lester Pearson's minority Liberal government.

The purpose of the bells is to call the members to the chamber to vote; it is not to permit either side to stop the work of Parliament. My view is that once it has become obvious — a few hours should be more than sufficient—that the practice is being used, not to round up members, but to stop the House, the Speaker has the power to complete the interrupted vote.

The only way a House of Commons properly sitting can lose the right to carry on with its work is by losing its quorum, and even then it meets for business as usual on the next day. The British North America Act sets the quorum; it is the Speaker and 19 other members. After the bells have rung unanswered for over two weeks nobody will contend seriously that the House is proceeding with business.

Constitutional implications

Consider the constitutional implications of the recent impasse. If what had been going on were proper, hereafter any opposition or any minority government when confronted by the prospect of a defeat in the House might avoid defeat by the simple tactic of moving the adjournment and then absconding.

John Diefenbaker and his Conservatives could have done this on Feb. 5, 1963. Pierre Trudeau's Liberals could have done this on the afternoon of May 8, 1974, instead of letting the House reject John Turner's

□ **A leading expert on Parliamentary procedure, Prof. John Stewart teaches in the political science department at St. Francis Xavier University in Antigonish, Nova Scotia. He is the author of The Canadian House of Commons: Procedure and Reform, and was a Liberal member of the House of Commons from 1962 to 1968.**

budget that evening. Joe Clark's Progressive Conservatives could have resorted to this kind of pre-emptive strike on the afternoon of Dec. 13, 1979. While the bells rang and rang efforts could be made to win over the support of third-party members. The argument that this is unthinkable is hollow: Desperate politicians are likely to employ whatever tactics are available. The present ploy was unthinkable in 1963, 1974, and 1979, but it may well be used again and again in the future.

The Speaker had ruled that Bill C-94 was in order. As a result of a change in the standing orders made unanimously by the House on Dec. 20, 1968, there is no appeal from the Speaker's rulings. However, Andre stated that his motion to adjourn was a direct response to the Speaker's ruling. Hereafter is this kind of punitive action against the House to be the standard form of protest against Speakers' rulings?

Evidently the government had agreed for weeks that Bill C-94, although in order, should be divided for reasons of style and convenience. But both the government and the opposition have been posturing and bargaining. The official opposition demanded that the bill be divided into a whole fleet of bills, while the government asked in return for an agreed time limit because it suspected that the real reason for the Progressive Conservative request was that they were determined to prevent important parts of the energy policy from becoming law, or at least to stage a new version of the pipeline debate of 1956. The Progressive Conservatives at first refused to agree to a program for debate and consideration of the bills, as Conservative House Leader Erik Nielsen's letter of March 15 shows.

No standing order

The Speaker had said that there is no standing order that would have authorized her to complete the vote. There is no standing order because what we are dealing with is a practice. If there were a rule, the rule would state both a minimum and a maximum time for the bells. She had said that there is no precedent bearing directly on the present situation. If Speakers never dealt with procedural situations except on the basis of exact precedents, there would be no precedents.

Sometimes impartiality requires no action, and sometimes it requires action. Every day the bells rang tended to confirm the propriety of the tactic being used. As long as we enjoy the constitutional system known as responsible government, the House of Commons should be protected from those who would disable it by procedural arrest. The Governor-General, of course, may prorogue a session or dissolve a Parliament, but neither the government nor the opposition should be permitted to arrest the House of Commons by a walkout.

THE TORONTO STAR, MARCH 20, 1982

An uneasy move toward reform

All sides agree that something must be done in the wake of the bells fiasco, trouble is the parties don't seem to agree on what must be done

By Carol Goar Toronto Star

OTTAWA — Canada's Parliament, its ear drums battered and its ego bruised, has finally survived the incident of the bells. But mere survival is not enough.

It is now up to Canadians to decide whether the schoolboy antics which paralyzed the House of Commons for the first half of this month will go down in history as a burst of March madness, or as the catalyst for a genuine campaign to make Parliament work better.

Many will be tempted to dismiss the whole noisy episode as just silliness. And, looking back at the event of the last two weeks, they can hardly be blamed.

The bells drama began on March 2, with an opening act sadly lacking in sophistication. The Conservatives proposed that the Commons be adjourned for the day. When the Speaker turned on the bells to beckon MPs to vote on the motion, the Tories simply refused to show up.

It was a clever, but an essentially schoolboyish trick that went on for an unprecedented, nerve-jangling 358 hours. As the stand-off evolved from a brief lark into an unbelievable marathon, both sides grew ever more eloquent in insisting that they were protecting important democratic principles.

The Conservatives said they could not go back to the House of Commons until the Liberals agreed to split up their massive, controversial energy bill. "The government will use this as a dangerous precedent to steamroller legislation through the House," Conservative Leader Joe Clark warned darkly.

Meanwhile, the Liberals argued with equal vigor, that they could not split up their energy bill until the Conservatives returned to the House. "The Opposition will use this as an unacceptable precedent to wrench control of Parliamentary business out of the government's hands," predicted Government House Leader Yvon Pinard.

Little wonder the public yawned, or snickered.

Then came the third and final act. On Wednesday, at 2:30 p.m., the bells stopped ringing. Merciful silence.

The clanging had barely died away before Clark and Pinard had piped up to tell Canadians they had, at last, found something they could agree upon. It was time to change Parliament to make sure this kind of trouble didn't erupt again.

The $174-million bastion of democracy was getting a little out of date. Its rules needed to be streamlined, its procedures modernized. Jaded by two weeks of posturing and pettiness on Parliament Hill, many observers treated the final act as skeptically as the first two.

Where the parties stand

LIBERAL PRESCRIPTION	TORY PRESCRIPTION	NDP PRESCRIPTION
Speeches be limited to 20 minutes instead of 40 minutes.	Same	Same
Votes be held at predetermined times.	No position	No position
Commons committees be chopped to 14 members from the current 20.	Committees be chopped to 11 members.	No position
No position	Committees be allowed to launch an independent inquiry into any matter of public concern, without formal Commons go-ahead.	Same as Tories
No position	Committees be allowed to hire expert researchers to guide politicians through complex issues.	Same as Tories
Commons work week be cut to 4 days — but same number of hours (27).	No position	MPs be given every 4th week off to work in their ridings.
Speaker be allowed to adjourn Commons if MPs don't show up to vote after the bells have rung for 10 minutes.	No position	No position
No position	Commons should fix its Christmas, Easter & summer breaks well in advance.	Same as Tories
More limits on debate should be studied.	No position	All legislation, with the exception of 2 or 3 controversial bills chosen by the Opposition should be debated with time limits.
Budget secrecy should be reconsidered.	Budget secrecy should be lifted. Instead the Finance Minister should consult all those affected before tabling the budget.	No position
No position	MPs should be free on all but a few issues to vote as their conscience, not their party allegiance, dictates.	No position
Further reforms should be explored by an all-party committee of MPs or former parliamentarians.	Further changes should be explored by the Commons and its committees.	Further changes are needed.

One well-placed Ottawa watcher accused the country's politicians of embarking on a great Parliamentary reform crusade to fool the public into thinking there had been some point to their bickering.

Another scoffed at the idea that new rules would do any good with the same old crew in the Commons to bend and manipulate them. A third actually suggested that it would be dangerous to outfit the House of Commons with shiny new rules because people would be fooled into thinking they were getting a Parliament that would provide them, and their MPs, with a meaningful role in the governing of the country.

So act three ended, without applause.

One doesn't have to dig through many layers of silliness to find real Parliamentary troubles at the root of the bells incident.

Push aside the Tories' mischievous tactics, and one discovers an official Opposition so powerless that it feels the only way it can stop the government from doing anything it likes is by closing down Parliament altogether.

Ask taxpayers what the two-week stalemate proved, and many will reply that it was just one more demonstration that Ottawa is an ivory-tower world, out of touch with the concerns of the average person. Not only is Parliament incapable of doing anything about Canada's deteriorating economy — it can't even manage to keep itself in business.

Delve into Pinard's accusations that the Tories are trying to wrench control of Parliament out of Liberal hands, and one finds a government frustrated by an ever-growing pile of legislation that it can't jam into Parliament's agenda.

Hamstrung by rules that allow MPs to speak for 40 minutes apiece, by procedures that allow opposition MPs to suggest dozens of amendments to every bill, and by a Canadian reluctance to cut off debate, the government constantly finds itself bogged down in long, directionless debates.

Ask any backbench MP how much real power he or she has in running the country and the answer is likely to be a sad shrug.

As long as politicians can use the Commons to grab headlines by exposing scandals, screaming about the unemployment rate and tantalizing taxpayers with juicy stories of government waste, no one thinks much about the shortcomings of the institution. As an issue, Parliamentary reform is no barn-burner.

If it did nothing else, the two-week shutdown of Parliament prompted many of the country's 279 MPs to sit in their offices and reflect on how the institution is failing them and their constituents, and how it could be made to work better.

"A good side of all this, if there is a good side, is that it will have sensitized public opinion to the need to modernize this institution, which is ruled by an old archaic procedure that makes Parliament unable to cope with reality," said an exhausted Pinard, as he returned to the Commons.

Joe Clark agreed: "We believe now that there is a very broad public interest in the question of the reform of our Parliamentary institution."

So saying, they headed into the Commons on their first day back at work to discuss the best prescription for a new, revitalized Parliament. What rapidly emerged in the debate was that Parliamentary reform is easy to agree on in theory and virtually impossible to work out in practice.

To the Conservatives, Parliamentary reform means giving back to ordinary MPs the power which has fallen, bit by bit, into the hands of the prime minister, his tight circle of advisers, a few key bureaucrats and a handful of powerful cabinet ministers.

"Our system has been changing for a long time, gradually giving more power to governments and parties and gradually limiting the rights of Parliament," Clark said: "If that continues, we will waste the talent of the members who serve here, lose the trust of the people who sent us here and gradually erode our democracy. We cannot let that happen.''

But Parliamentary reform means something quite different to the Liberals. As the party in power, they want the system streamlined to allow faster passage of legislation. They want a more predictable agenda so members can avoid last last-minute foul-ups every time they plan a trip home.

And they see no reason votes should not be scheduled well in advance, so the bells episode need never be repeated.

''Democracies can be destroyed because Parliaments are made unworkable,'' Prime Minister Pierre Trudeau warned. He said the bells incident should be taken as a danger sign that Canada's House of Commons can be made to look impotent to the public.

''I just ask Canadians to be objective and look at the reforms that do take place in Britain,'' Trudeau urged, adding that the Parliament at Westminster ''is a devil of a lot more efficient than ours.''

In Britain, he pointed out, debate on the second reading stage of any bill — during which the House approves the legislation in principle and sends it on to a committee for detailed study — normally lasts one to three days. In Canada; the norm is 20 to 50 days.

The New Democratic Party falls somewhere between the other two on the question of Parliamentary reform. Like the Liberals they feel that valuable time is being wasted because of inefficient procedures and outdated rules. But, like the Conservatives, they worry that ordinary MPs are losing their role in decision-making.

To NDP Leader Ed Broadbent it all boils down to a question of trust.

''My own sense of the reality of Canada right now is that cynicism about politicians and about political institutions is growing. We, in the House of Commons have to be concerned about the growing state of cynicism in the country about politicians and about the House of Commons.''

There is some common ground among the three parties, however. All agree it would be useful to limit speeches to 20 minutes, all MPs would like to be able to predict, with some assurance, when they will be home at Christmas and Easter and all concede that 20-member Parliamentary committees are too big.

But there are vast areas of disagreement.

The Conservatives are hardly likely to go along with any Liberal-inspired plan to limit debate when they are already convinced that their power to influence the

course of decision-making is already woefully inadequate.

The Liberals, for their part, are unlikely to go along with any plan to give opposition MPs more of a role in the House, when they believe the Tories are capable only of obstruction.

For many Canadians, there is something even more disturbing than the squabbling and finger-pointing that erupts every time politicians try to discuss Parliamentary reform. They fear the biggest questions are simply not being asked by any of the parties:

☐ Can a Parliamentary system, designed for two strong parties, work when one of them, the Liberal party, has been in power for 20 almost uninterrupted years?

☐ How long can Parliament continue to function when the men and women in charge of it appear to have lost respect for one another and for the traditions of the institution?

☐ Now that the bells have been silenced, how many more tricks does the opposition have in its bag? Parliament weathered this crisis, but what about the next one? And the one after that?

No, the House on the Hill is not a happy place this week.

☐ **Carol Goar is a member of The Star's Ottawa bureau.**

THE GLOBE AND MAIL, DECEMBER 20, 1982

Order in the House

The House of Commons is bristling with procedural reform. It has voted unanimously to change the way it conducts its business and to regroup at the end of 1983 to see whether the changes worked.

For example: The length of the parliamentary calendar has depended on a wild and woolly contest between the Government, which tries to pass several bills by session's end, and the opposition, which tries to debate them thoroughly before passage. The calendar will now be set in advance, with three semesters and adjournments on specified dates; the Government will announce its legislative intentions at the start of each semester, giving the opposition a chance to concentrate on the more controversial bills.

Members are used to speaking for a maximum of 40 minutes. The limit

will now be 20 minutes, which may deprive us of the odd impassioned flight of oratory but will, in turn, spare us a good deal of verbal woolgathering. Colleagues will have 10 minutes after each speech to discuss the speaker's point — an innovation which may either spur debate or allow a single MP to exhaust the time (and the House) with a 10-minute rebuttal.

There will be no more Standing Order 43. The order was designed to let MPs make motions of ''urgent and pressing necessity'' before the start of Question Period; too often, they used it to josh with other MPs and note their constituents' birthdays. In its place, members will have 15 minutes a day in which to make 90-second remarks.

The procedure for calling quorum will be changed. If an MP notes that

there are fewer than 20 MPs in the House, the Speaker won't count heads until the bells have rung for 15 minutes — a courtesy to MPs who may have left the chamber to make a telephone call or grab a sandwich. The new rule will not, however, prevent the repetition of last March's ''bell-ringing'' affair, when the Conservatives, in an effort to prevent the Government from passing a ghastly omnibus energy bill, boycotted the Commons for 15 days and brought business to a halt. This boycott is a drastic step, one which allows the minority to dictate to the majority, but the Commons is wise to keep it available as a last resort. If a party is foolish enough to misuse it, the voters can tell it so at the polls.

Standing committees will be smaller, with 10 or 15 members, and will gain the automatic right to consider all reports tabled before Parliament under a statute, including bills and estimates. As Conservative House leader Erik Nielsen notes, this power won't amount to much unless the government majority on each committee calls the group into session and agrees to consider a particular report. The question is one of trust; without it, rule changes alone won't improve Parliament's operations.

Mr. Nielsen says his party is agreeing to these changes, many of which limit the opposition's already limited power, as a gesture of good faith. He wants the Special Committee on Standing Orders and Procedures, which proposed these changes, to go further — to spell out criteria to govern the use of omnibus bills and to find a way to restore Parliament's control over government expenditures, a control whose loss has been deplored by a succession of auditors-general.

We're not sure good faith is the Conservatives' only motive; as a party hoping to form the next government, they may have a certain vested interest in streamlining the process. But what the special committee recommended, and what the House has adopted, is an encouraging set of rules. Like Mr. Nielsen, we can't wait for the sequel.

THE TORONTO STAR, DECEMBER 5, 1982

Parliament takes giant step

ROBERT JACKSON

OTTAWA — At last there has been a breakthrough in parliamentary reform. Changes recommended by the reform committee in its third report will go into effect on an experimental basis for one year beginning in January. They represent a giant step toward updating the antiquated rules of the House.

Any gleeful self-congratulations are premature, however, until more fundamental reforms are instigated. The recommendations of the third report are important but relatively uncontentious.

The real test will be whether headway can be made with reforms which will cause the government to lose some control over Parliament. Reforms dealing with the Speaker of the House and even more difficult issues, such as reducing government power over the budget and the committee system, will be the real test of success.

Reasonable period

The experimental period of one year to try out the new procedural reforms is reasonable given the complex nature of the changes and the practical difficulties that are likely to be encountered.

The adoption of an annual calendar and daily timetable for Parliament is warranted not merely for the convenience of officials and MPs. Meeting at regular hours every waking day will make Parliament more accessible. An annual calendar will remove the familiar government ploy of threatening to extend the parliamentary session through holidays such as Christmas in order to force legislation through Parliament.

Reducing the length of speeches from 40 minutes to 20 and dispensing with the ludicrous standing order 43 should also be welcomed by all. Most members do not have 40 minutes worth of systematic thought to divulge, and even fewer can listen to 40 minutes of monologue.

The truly significant reform of this experimental package, however, pertains to committees. Reducing the membership to not less than 10 and not more than 15 will make for more coherent behavior in committees.

The efforts to make substitution less available could be tightened further, but the new rules will at least help to reduce the roving bands of replacements that now lurk about the House of Commons.

The only dramatic reform for committees is that they will be given the power to initiate inquiries through the automatic referral of annual reports by departments, crown corporations and other agencies. The fact that a committee can request the government to table a response to their report within a fixed period will strengthen the surveillance function of MPs over the bureaucracy.

The committee decided, after a long, raucous meeting, to separate their recommendations on the Speaker from their first reform package. Their report on the Speaker is quite contentious, and the committee was intent on achieving unanimity on their basic proposals so that they would be implemented in January.

Now, in its fourth report, the committee recommends that the Speaker be elected much like the Pope is. They suggest secret ballot in the House, without a government nomination. It is a good reform that would legitimize the impartiality of that position.

The Speaker's job is to ensure that the democratic assembly operates effectively and fairly without regard for which party is the government. A Speaker elected by the House and unwhipped by political parties would provide the best candidate.

Spending study

In future months the committee intends to investigate several other subjects, particularly supply proceedings — that is, how the government spends its money. Members will visit Britain in January to study their procedures. There is no doubt that a revision of the public accounts committee is needed and at least a new expenditure committee similar to the one in Britain.

As Ron Huntington and Claude-Andre Lachance point out in their paper to the committee on accountability, government expenditures are currently approved at the staggering rate of $150 million per hour. That process should be made as systematic and responsible as possible.

One would hope the final reforms would be as complete as the auspicious beginning suggests.

☐ **Robert J. Jackson is head of the political science department at Carleton University.**

THE GLOBE AND MAIL, APRIL 6, 1982

MPs at their best: The system does work

BY MICHAEL VALPY

Mr. Valpy is Ottawa columnist for The Globe and Mail.

OTTAWA

THIS AFTERNOON, following the House of Commons Question Period, Maurice Dionne is going to unveil a piece of political produce that should give Canadians positive feelings about how their Parliament can work.

Mr. Dionne is chairman of the Commons' Standing Committee on Transport. At about 3:30 p.m., the 45-year-old former New Brunswick high school principal, and now Liberal member of Parliament for Northumberland Miramichi, will table in the House his committee's report on domestic air policy.

There is so much good karma surrounding the preparation of the committee's report that it merits having a stage set for it before it appears.

It has elements of parliamentary democracy, of backbench MPs being given an opportunity to shape Government policy, of conflicting bureaucratic concepts being publicly debated, of major policy issues being publicly debated, of the public interest being seen to be served.

In other words, it comes close to being a textbook example of how most Canadians would like to think their Parliament and their legislators operate — but which far too seldom is reality.

In the wake of the bells affair, the closing down of Parliament for two weeks, and all the speeches and articles about what is wrong with Parliament, it is nice to see something right about the institution.

And it poses the question: Why does it not happen more often?

Let's start with the issue.

Canada has two national airlines, four regional airlines, 82 local airlines and one airline — Wardair — that doesn't fit any of those categories.

All want a profitable and, at the very least, stable share of the domestic market. Most of them also want a chance to grow. The Canadian public, for its part, wants efficiency, affordable rates and good service.

Last summer, Transport Minister Jean-Luc Pépin put out a white paper on domestic air policy. It was accepted by most of the major airlines. But it was criticized elsewhere as excessively restricting competition through regulation, particularly when the Americans were having success with deregulating their airlines.

The Transport Minister's policy ran into the same problems in Cabinet. Some ministers liked it; others said it came nowhere close to the Cabinet's desire to deregulate what could be deregulated.

Therefore, Mr. Pépin referred the policy to the Transport Committee. He said to the committee, in effect, "We'll make the details of our policy and all our expert public servants available to you. You call your own experts as well. And you come up with some advice for me."

Keep two things in mind:

First, the Government does not often do that — ask an all-party committee for advice before it slaps legislation before Parliament. Second, this is the same minister who only a month before had completely restructured the nation's passenger-rail system by executive regulation; that is, without any reference to Parliament at all.

That is the first positive act: the referral of a policy issue to an all-party committee.

Ministers are reluctant to do that because they are afraid of losing control of an issue. The argument has been that if a committee rejects a minister's policy, it makes it harder for the minister to continue pushing it through.

Yet whenever it has been done, good, constructive things have resulted. Five recent examples:

— A Senate-Commons committee held hearings across the country in 1975 on the Government's green paper on immigration. The very fact that it went out and listened to the people helped ease public concerns about immigration. And its report eased MPs' concerns and led to smooth passage of what otherwise would have been undesirably contentious legislation.

— The Commons subcommittee on penitentiaries, under the chairmanship of Mark MacGuigan, now External Affairs Minister, produced a superb report in 1977. It cooled tensions in the federal prison system and successfully pressured the Government into passing needed reforms.

— The Senate-Commons committee on the Constitution in the winter of 1980-81 probably did far more to interest and involve the Canadian people in the Constitution than all the millions of dollars spent by the Canadian Unity Information Office on advertising geese and whatnot.

— The parliamentary task force on federal-provincial fiscal arrangements reported a few months ago. It got in the way somewhat of Finance Minister Allan MacEachen's plans. But federal and provincial politicians of all parties have praised it for its objectivity and its quality of information on a complex subject.

— The Commons subcommittee on Canada's relations with Latin America and the Caribbean has been providing thoughtful, if provocative, options for Canadian foreign policy-makers in one of the world's most troubled spots. Perhaps more than that, it has strengthened the Government's hand in devising an independent Canadian foreign policy toward the region.

The second positive aspect to what has gone on at the Transport Committee the past few months touches on the openness of the senior officials who have appeared before it.

That openness is not often seen in public.

Canadians seldom have any idea what information is placed before Cabinet ministers for decision, or whether there is conflicting information. If there are conflicts, they are almost always hidden from view.

Not in this case. Two fundamental concepts were placed before Mr.

Dionne's committee.

The first, from the Ministry of Transport goes like this: The domestic air transport industry is relatively well off under the Government's existing policy and regulations. This policy basically carves up the country for the various national, regional and local carriers, giving everyone a stable share of the market — something like Pope Alexander VI's 1493 Bull of Demarcation that divided the Americas between Portugal and Spain.

Canada is a big geographical area with low population density. That makes it too fragile a market to follow the U.S. lead of wholesale deregulation — or wide-open competition. Moreover, relatively little traffic growth is predicted throughout the decade.

Thus, Transport says, opening the doors to free competition would destabilize the entire industry. What is needed is simply fine-tuning.

The ministry's officials think the best kind of fine-tuning would be to have an over-all policy preserving various markets for various carriers. At the same time the Canadian Transport Commission would have the discretion to bend the rules where it thinks the interest of the public and the industry would be best served.

The second concept was presented to the committee by Lawson Hunter, the newly appointed director of the Bureau of Competition Policy. Mr. Hunter's argument can be summed up in one quotation: "If we want to live in a market oriented economy, then some people are not going to be successful and they are going to have to go out of business."

Mr. Hunter thinks the Transport policy would serve the major players in the industry but not the public or those innovative airlines keen to grow.

He pointed out to the committee that the two national and four regional airlines together account for 98.3 of domestic passengers, leaving only 1.7 per cent for the 82 designated local carriers. He said excessive regulation has meant no

price competition between carriers (fares are set by the CTC). The only competition has been in inflight service quality which adds to the airlines' costs, and therefore to ticket prices.

(One example given by his staff was the price of a meal on a Toronto-Montreal or Ottawa-Toronto run. The meal is given "free;" in fact it costs about $50 to serve, because of staff and cooking arrangements required.)

The Transport Committee met about a dozen times between Jan. 28 and March 2. It heard public servants, academics and regulatory experts from Canada and the United States.

It has produced a report that people who have seen it call an imaginative, innovative approach to both deregulation and protection of the industry.

Most important, one would think, the backbench MPs who sat on the committee will be able to feel they've done something more worthwhile than simply voting at their party's call when the division bells ring.

THE TORONTO SUN, JULY 26, 1982

DOUGLAS FISHER

Accountability

Most hearings of House committees are tedious, even to the MPs who make the forum and, too often, not a quorum. But such committees have significance now, and much potential.

More and more, the best work of MPs is done in committees. They are becoming the stuff of Parliament; if it is to be saved from obsolescence forced by the extending reach of the executive, the future must lie with committees.

There is so much committee activity that no one in the government, in the party leadership's cadre, among House officials, and in political journalism, has an intelligent overview of it all.

Work done in private

At most committee hearings, there's rarely more than a couple of the public present. It's unusual if more than one reporter attends (normally from Canadian Press). Sound or TV recording is not allowed. (The constitutional committee was an exception.) There are too few committee rooms and none of them is attractive. (Several are dour, low-ceiling boxes with atrocious acoustics.)

The hearings are usually very informal. There's much chafing and needling. MPs have a penchant for statements, often musing aloud during their five or 10-minute stints, rather

than for incisive questioning. The qualities of the chairmen vary incredibly, so do the moods and the 'esprit' of the memberships.

Many ministers (and their deputies) are cavalier about the number of times and length of time they'll spend in a committee which is examining their legislation or spending. Most of the bureaucratic witnesses tend to be cautious. So often they have to be pried open, or they eat away a hearing's time with long, flat obfuscations.

There's much substitution of MPs on committees, playing hell with continuity and guaranteeing repetition of argument and questions.

Each committee hearing gets a Hansard-type of record — it's usually printed and available a week or so later. The accumulated pages of the committee hearings for this marathon session would likely be more than double the 20,000 pages of print that Hansard has piled up.

Only a scattering of people across the country or, indeed in Ottawa, read Hansard. Just a small portion of that scattering reads committee hearings — mostly the MPs on the committees, the representatives from particular interest groups touched by a committee, or the aides of deputy ministers vetting a committee.

Despite all this, committees have importance and most MPs, even many who curse at their meandering, believe that the rescue of Parliament has to come through them.

They must be improved: Better staffed and located, with more authority; with guarantees of attention or action by the executive; with genuine rewards within the parties; and through greater credit with the public.

Such optimism must be hinged on a matter which is dicey at best, a matter which few MPs want to address openly.

One veteran Liberal MP, Keith Penner, is presently in the ministerial doghouse. He chaired the Indian affairs committee which reamed the departmental bureaucracy and almost got away with slashing its budget. Penner has touched on the great "no-no."

"Somehow, we have to distance the legislative branch a bit from the executive," he said.

There's the rub! In theory, the parliamentary system sets out that the government is "accountable" to the House. Not just once in a while, but at any time.

On the other hand, the executive of the government is in the House and so long as it can command a majority of the MPs, it should have its way.

To use a pop phrase, in principle there should always be a "creative tension" in Parliament between the executive's need to have its way and Parliament's right to keep it accountable. The latter right is implicit in the title "Her Majesty's Loyal Opposition."

The most important House committee in years — that on standing orders and procedure — is now engaged in the res-cue of Parliament as a workable, credible institution.

Last week, it decided to hire one Alistair Fraser, clerk of the House from 1966 to 1979. In an oral, unprepared 'tour de force' at the committee on July 13, Fraser blew open every problem of Parliament, from the pettiest to the grandest.

Credits in Liberal Party

Fraser has credits in the Liberal Party. He was an aide in the '50s to Jimmy Sinclair, Mrs. Trudeau's dad. He ran unsuccessfully as a candidate. He orchestrated the Coyne hearings (in the Senate) which so undermined the Diefenbaker hegemony.

Here's how he raised the prime issue before the committee.

"It is time for somebody to attempt to write a charter of rights for the Parliament of Canada and for its members … first and foremost there should be an assertion of the position of Parliament vis-a-vis the executive of the country."

Fraser then sketched a dozen other issues which should be addressed in the "charter of Parliament."

His romp through the problems, great and small, electrified the MPs. They questioned him at length (and later decided to hire him).

What was discouraging, indeed almost devastating, was that not one of nine questioners took up the "first-and-foremost" point he made: "The assertion of the position of Parliament vis-a-vis the executive."

CHATELAINE, DECEMBER 1982

Women and political power: What's holding us back?

Christina McCall-Newman

For most of the men at the centre of [the political] world — the politicians, businessmen and media managers who make up the great combine of elites that runs this country — women still exist at the periphery, inconsequential guests at the feast of the mighty, largely unheeded voices at the councils of the powerful.

How can you say that? I hear you asking. After all, there is a record number of women now sitting in the House of Commons, and two of them are in Cabinet. Every provincial legislature has its quota of female members, as do most city councils. The major parties boast women presidents in their riding associations and women members on their national executives. Surely, the millennium's approaching. How can you say that women are only at the periphery of power still?

I say it because these portents so widely hailed as important continue to smack of tokenism. I say it because I don't think women have anything even approaching the real political power that's their due as people with the legal right to parity in a democratic state. (And I'm using power in the sociologists' sense as the ability to mobilize resources, to lead people, to effect change, to deliver to your followers what they need and expect.) I say it because I've spent more than 15 years watching from a front-row seat the way power politics — what Pierre Trudeau once described to me as "the great game" — is really played in this country. What I learned from observation, conversation and reportage in that time has been reinforced further by my experience in the last few years spent researching and writing a book that involved a detailed analysis of the power game based on hundreds of interviews with its chief players, attendance at dozens of political meetings and journeys of thousands of miles — a book about the denizens of the federal Liberal Party, the people who have held power in Canada for all but 12 of the last 60 years. What I've learned has lead me to the inescapable if sobering conclusion that, even with all the advances women have made — and I'll grant straight off that it's a lot better to be heading up a riding association or sitting on the back benches of a provincial legislature than to be typing the letters in an MP's office or cutting the sandwiches in a candidate's headquarters — we are still amateur players in politics, still serving on the second-string teams or, more often, sitting on the sidelines as spectators, cheering hoarsely (or booing fiercely, in the case of the confrontationist feminists) while we wait to get into the game.

We may have a record number of women in the House, but it's only 16 out of 282 — that's something less than 6 percent, although we're more than half the population. And there are two women in Cabinet now along with the 34 men, which means we're twice as well off as we were in the late '50s and early '60s when only one woman was allowed in at a time. Rumors abounded in Ottawa then that the two who followed each other as the single female voice in the Privy Council chamber (Ellen Fairclough under the John Diefenbaker regime and Judy LaMarsh under Lester Pearson) had proven so overly "emotional" that there might never be another.

In fact, there wasn't a woman in Cabinet at all during the early Trudeau years when we were first governed by a prime minister who was on the record as an appreciator of women's beauty and off the record as a depreciator of their brains. (He liked to call women "the babes" in those days before he married his own.) It wasn't until 1972 that Jeanne Sauvé became the first woman in a Trudeau Cabinet. Later in the decade, under pressure from the women's movement and from the evidence of the opinion polls, when the Liberals' declining popularity showed an attrition of their traditionally large female vote, the cabinet contingent of women actually went up to three. (Iona Campagnolo as Minister of State for Fitness and Amateur

Sport joined Monique Bégin, who was then Minister of National Revenue, and Jeanne Sauvé, who was by then Minister of Communications.) But after the 1980 election, when the Liberals got back into power, the number of women was cut back to two. (Campagnolo had been defeated, and Sauvé had been sidetracked into the arduous if powerless job of Speaker of the House.)

In this government, Bégin's continuing presence has been bolstered by Judy Erola, although neither of them has a first-tier portfolio since Erola was given a junior job as Minister of State for Mines (with responsibilities for the status of women thrown in for when Lloyd Axworthy wanted out from under them), and Bégin is still in the ministry of health. You might even say that women are downwardly mobile in Cabinet. LaMarsh headed health and welfare nearly 20 years ago, when the economy was expanding and what could be accomplished in terms of pensions and Medicare was more dramatic than anything any minister can aspire to in the recessive climate of the 1980s, even so gutsy and philosophically committed a minister as Bégin.

Younger working women gather regularly to exchange information and make contacts. What they don't discuss is how to get political power for women.

To be short, sharp and blunt about it, at the rate we're going it will take several hundred years for women to achieve political parity in Canada, to move out from being the support staff who organize men's campaigns, run men's offices, prepare men's briefing papers or, as the rare MPs scattered on the back benches, applaud the important male ministers during televised Question Periods, to become the candidates who get the plum "winnable" ridings, the key jobs in Cabinet and in the Prime Minister's Office, the ones that bring real power with them and real impact on the government's direction.

It's as though, some 60 years since women were enfranchised, politics is still a sport whose rules we don't precisely understand. Or to use an analogy more pertinent to our situation as a politically underrepresented group, we are in a position similar to that of the French

Canadians before the ferment of the Quiet Revolution led to dramatic social and political change.

We back the ruling federal party loyally (the women's vote has been disproportionately higher for the Liberals than for either the Tories or the NDP) as French Canadians did (and do). In return, we get two or three acceptable portfolios to keep us happy, appointments to a few key boards, some token high positions in the public service, not quite up there at the top, and several seats on the party's executive, where the power definitely isn't. But for the really important jobs, as the anglophone male power group used to say soothingly of French Canadians (and the francophone/anglophone male power group now says soothingly of women), they "aren't educated for the big portfolios or the crucial decision-making roles; they're not interested in exercising power since they're too caught up in their own rich culture/church teachings/ provincial hierarchy (read families/ love life/career) to go for broke to the top."

I don't believe those statements about women any more than Pierre Trudeau and his friends in the '50s believed them about Quebecers. I think women are educated for and capable of political power now. But if we are to alter our political lot radically in the next 30 years, as French Canadians have altered theirs, then we're going to have to change the way we behave. . . .

I get it, I hear you saying, she's talking about networks. Well, women have networks too now. Yes, I know they do. But from my observation, and from the observations of several women who view the three major federal parties from within, they're not the same as male networks. The bulk of them are comprised of "supportive" or "survival" groups that grew out of the women's movement and that still operate outside the mainstream of political life, gathering their forces periodically for the occasional guerrilla raid, like the two mounted in 1981 with so much publicity and so little effect over the question of the Constitution and then falling back without consolidating their gains.

Younger working women of the kind who have been pouring out of the universities in the last six or seven years with degrees in law, economics and business administration are gathering regularly in big cities to exchange information and make contacts, to talk about bond issues or new wrinkles in the real estate laws. What they're not talking about is how to get and wield political power for women. Most of them are too busy learning the intricacies of the business world to have time left over for the intricacies of politics. Even women who do have time to join the ranks of the major parties find discussions there are rarely concerned with the large questions of women's advancement or even the specific questions of concern to themselves, such as the horrific widespread poverty among the elderly that our pension policies exacerbate. Women rarely make common cause in the parties even now. Certainly, there is no deep belief among Liberal women, for instance, that Monique Bégin could become the party leader (although, if her name were Marcel, left-wing Liberals would have been talking up her prospects for the last two years); or no groundswell among the Tories to make Flora MacDonald the new head of the Conservatives; no movement among the social democrats to make Pauline Jewett a rallying point in the NDP. Political women are too engrossed in how to keep their individual footholds on the shifting beachheads that have already been established, how to decide who is the male figure with whom they should throw in their political lot, how to circumvent the worst of the male chauvinism that still surfaces occasionally like an oil slick from a submarine.

Sometimes, this chauvinism is subtle, as it was when Flora MacDonald was the Secretary of State for External Affairs and all Ottawa whispered that she wouldn't make a move without the advice of her very own male brain trust, a hapless professor from Queen's in Kingston, Ont. Sometimes, it's insidious, as when it's pointed out that Bégin is chronically late, a habit that drives her officials to distraction and her executive assistants to tears. Sometimes, it's simply sexist.

A prize story in this category, still being told in political circles three years after it occurred, involved a very well-known Liberal who was representing the government at an important international function. She was standing talking in a circle when a prominent member of the interest group she was meant to lobby lurched up, grabbed the bodice of her dress and, peering down the front, said accusingly, "Hey, I heard you had big tits, and they're really not big at all."

The woman who recounted this anecdote to me shivered a little as she talked; she was one of several people representing all three major parties that I talked to at length this fall trying to unravel once more the whole question of the general alienation of women from the masculine world of power.

Interestingly, the reasons given for our backwardness concentrated far less on the antagonisms of men, as they would have in the '70s, and more on the limitations of the way women view themselves within the political process.

"Women are held back by their own fears," said an NDPer. "They wind up in the sacrificial lamb seats because they're afraid to go after the winnable ones. They expect the party to be a 'fathering' institution, to provide them with workers, money, policies, everything, whereas men are aware of the need to look after themselves and to aggress from dawn till dark."

"Women don't seem to realize they need an independent base, if they're to move away from the support roles," said a Tory who was lamenting the fact that, despite her leader's interest in fostering women, there is no solid woman candidate emerging for the party's presidency at its January convention. "What we have is many more women in the middle but no more women at the top. Men move on from being acolytes, they learn from their mentors and eventually become mentors themselves. But women either cling or quit. Ever since I read Colette Dowling, I see so many political women's careers in terms of the Cinderella Complex—the need to be rescued by a strong male."

"I sometimes have the feeling that it will be another generation before women really catch on to team playing," said a Liberal who's adept at the art herself. "Something goes wrong at a level below the rational. We haven't been taught accommodation or turf-sharing. Women can be supportive of each other emotionally on an egalitarian level, but once a woman moves out ahead of the pack, other women get nervous about supporting her. *Why isn't that me?* they start thinking, instead of *How can that help me?*—which is the equivalent response of the male. Women even have trouble using male networks if they're lucky enough to work their way into one. They either fall back on occasional confrontations, which get them precisely nowhere, or they are so anxious not to offend, they do a self-effacing fade."

Despite the general puzzlement about why women haven't moved further faster, all the political activists could see some cause for hope. Most cited the sheer numbers of women working in the professions, law and business, which traditionally provide the parties with the bulk of their candidates. Once these young women reach the partnership level over the next 10 years, the reasoning goes, they're bound to be drawn to politics. Once in politics, they'll be able to benefit from the advice of the women now at the middle level of the party structures. The executive assistants and members of the research staffs in the Prime Minister's Office and the depart-

ments are getting a solid education in how government works, how reputations are made and broken, how combines form and win.

Each of the parties can point to two or three women, most of whom aren't currently in office but who know their way around. The Liberals have Lorna Marsden, 40, a sociologist who's been Associate Dean for the Social Sciences in the School of Graduate Studies at the University of Toronto and the party's most effective ever policy chairperson, and Kathryn Robinson, 33, a lawyer who belongs to the same powerful network as Keith Davey and James Coutts and will be heavily involved in Donald Macdonald's campaign if he decides to go for the leadership. The Tories have Libby Burnham, 44, another lawyer, who was the organizing brains behind Richard Hatfield in New Brunswick for half a dozen years and has the attentive respect of Joe Clark, and Jean Pigott, 58, an Ottawa businesswoman who was briefly an MP, even more briefly in charge of Tory patronage and is now one of the party's biggest draws on the speaker circuit. The NDP has Alexa McDonough, 37, a former social worker who's the party's leader in Nova Scotia and could eventually be a formidable federal MP, and Lynn McDonald, 42, a sociologist who, by sheer aggressive organizational know-how, with the help of a female network of her own, won the nomination for the plum NDP riding of Broadview-Greenwood, in Toronto, taking it away from Gerry Caplan, the kind of experienced, male party insider who in the past would have had any woman spooked.

In trying to weigh where women are politically now, one woman shrewdly summed up: "What we're doing in the '80s isn't always exhilarating. These are times for retrenchment, for carefulness and cunning, for making minor gains. No woman in any party has the positive power of the men. But there are two women who have something women never had before. Flora [MacDonald] and Monique [Bégin] haven't a hope in hell of winning a leadership race. But all the years of battling and hanging in have brought them enough respect among women and the more liberal-minded men that they have a kind of negative power, the power to stop someone else. Come the conventions, the candidates will have to court their support."

Then, she leaned forward to deliver the clincher: "*That means the men will have to listen when the women get up to talk.*" Looking back eight years, I had to agree that represents progress of a sort. □

THE TORONTO STAR, MAY 30, 1982

Sober second thoughts from members of 'the other place'

By Bill Fox Toronto Star

OTTAWA — The Senate — the words on a page are sometimes enough to persuade a reader to move on to the next item.

With its image as a place peopled by geriatrics and political party hacks, the Senate is an institution many Canadians find easy to ignore.

Yet every once in a while, the men and women who serve in "the other place," as it is referred to in the House of Commons, get our attention long enough to remind us they do fill an important and useful role as a chamber of sober second thought.

Last week's debate on the controversial issue of ownership of Newfoundland's offshore resources is a case in point.

Quit party

Echoing the debate in the Commons, several senators denounced the federal government's decision to refer the question directly to the Supreme Court of Canada — despite the fact the Newfoundland Supreme Court is already seized of the issue — as an insult to the province and its judiciary.

Indeed, Senator Eric Cook was so incensed at the Trudeau government's action that he resigned from the Liberal party.

But the Commons debate was in the main restricted to the rather narrow, albeit important issue, of whether Justice Minister Jean Chretien misled the House about the federal government's intentions.

The Senate debate, by contrast, dealt with the larger and more significant issue of the danger in governments at

The Senate

any level using the nation's courts to resolve essentially political problems.

"For the last several years, there's been an increasing tendency to somehow abandon the process of political negotiation of political problems opposing the federal government and the provinces," said Senator Martial Asselin who served in the Diefenbaker and Clark cabinets.

"We have the impression that the federal government is progressively attempting to shift its activities and its relations with the provinces towards legal solutions, rather than trying to find political answers through negotiations.

"The federal government should not be perceived by the Canadian people as constantly using the Supreme Court of Canada as an instrument to settle its political differences with the provinces," Asselin concluded.

Senator Daniel Lang of Toronto was even more outspoken in his criticisms — both of his fellow Liberals and Newfoundland Premier Brian Peckford's Conservative government.

"I am not going to blame the federal government nor am I going to blame the provincial government but I can say to both of them that they are incompetent," Lang said; once again making the point that the ownership of offshore resources is essentially a political question.

Lang said the patriation of Canada's constitution "dangerously politicizes our judicial system."

"The methodology involved — which involves federal-provincial con-

frontation — has been nearly disastrous. Does this government intend to go further, until we have confrontation between provincial courts and the federal courts?

"Once we start to pit our federal and provincial courts against each other, we shall start to see the breakup of the judicial system we have known in Canada," Lang said.

According to Lang, the present danger inherent in the Peckford government's decision to refer the ownership question to Newfoundland's courts and the federal government's decision to go directly to the Supreme Court is that both actions might "give a public perception to the notion our courts can be manipulated — the provincial courts by the provincial governments and the federal courts by the federal governments."

Sharply critical

Retired senator Eugene Forsey was also sharply critical of the Trudeau government's decision to refer the case directly to the Supreme Court.

In a telex to Peckford, Forsey states: "It (the reference) interferes with the normal judicial procedure . . . it is highly improper . . . it is a tactic that undermines the whole judicial system."

The views of Senators Asselin, Lang and Forsey obviously are not shared by all of their colleagues in the red chamber, but their views are not the issue.

What is important is that the Senate has addressed a crucial question — the use of the courts to resolve political problems — that our elected representatives in the House of Commons have so far ignored.

THE GLOBE AND MAIL, FEBRUARY 8, 1983

Warming up for Senate reform again

BY JUDY STEED
Miss Steed is a feature writer for The Globe and Mail.

MICHAEL PITFIELD'S appointment to the Senate caused a furor, but it may be the best thing that's ever happened to the Red Chamber. "Let's face it," said Senator George McIlraith, 74, "the best thing that could happen is for people to pay more attention to us." Senators complain that they are ignored and Canadians respond with a nonchalance born of the deeply held conviction that the Senate is little more than a bridge club of old fuddy duddies who worry incessantly about irrelevancies and cost the country a fortune.

But Michael Pitfield's presence will change all that, at least in the short run. In the political hothouse of the nation's capital, his every move is followed with obsessive interest. Known as Prime Minister Pierre Trudeau's closest confidant, Mr. Pitfield was the secretary to the Cabinet, the clerk of the Privy Council and the top civil servant in the country. Add to those credentials an upper-crust WASP upbringing in Montreal and an overachieving temperament that made young Pitfield ready for university at 14, and you have a uniquely Canadian superstar.

Interesting, then, that this youthful 45-year-old lawyer who is not lacking in ambition should choose the Senate. "What's he doing here? Why that's just what I've been wondering," said Senator Daniel Lang with a wicked glint in his eye. Mr. Lang, who sits as an independent and who terms Mr. Pitfield's appointment "scandalous," believes that the mirage of Senate reform may be on the brink of realization.

Certainly it has been a long time coming. Reform has been talked about since 1869, two years after the Upper House was created. Former senator Eugene Forsey writes that the major impetus behind its birth was that hoary old chestnut: regional conflict. Because members of Parliament were elected on the basis of representation by population, and Ontario was the most populous and fastest growing province, other provinces feared Ontario would dominate Confederation. "Neither Quebec nor the Maritimes dared leave their economic interests at the mercy of Ontario," Mr. Forsey writes. "They had to be protected by equal representation in the Senate."

A second consideration, according to Mr. Forsey, "was to protect the country against radical or revolutionary legislation. The Fathers of Confederation distrusted democracy, 'mob rule' . . . Against this danger, a Senate made up of mature men, with a substantial 'stake' in the country, with an absolute veto, would be an insurmountable barrier."

In practice, however, democracy evolved in favor of elected representatives. Fear of "mob rule" dissipated and the value of senators' "sober second thought," in John A. Macdonald's words, was debased to the point where "we're just a bunch of pussycats and the House of Commons doesn't worry about us," according to Senator Royce Frith. It's not surprising that Mr. Frith is keen to strengthen the Senate's role by transforming it into an effective forum for regional interests. And that can only be achieved, he says, by having senators elected.

The traditional objection to the Senate, as expressed by NDP MP Stanley Knowles, is that "the recipients of patronage appointments have no right to a position of authority in a democracy. Who are these people who have never been elected to tell us what we should do?"

NDP leader Ed Broadbent points out that the Fathers of Confederation distrusted democracy from the vantage point of a small, privileged elite that believed only its own members could govern society. He notes that this theme is carried out on the Senate walls of the Speaker's chamber, where "some extremely anti-democratic quotes are displayed." One, from Cicero, says: "It is the duty of the nobles to oppose the fickleness of the multitudes."

An elected Senate would obviously be more democratic, but it would also upset the balance of power that has evolved in relation to the House of Commons. At present, the Senate is a helpful body, whose primary practical function is to study and improve legislation from a purely technical point of view. But it lacks real power. In theory, it has an absolute veto over ordinary legislation and a suspensive veto of 180 days on constitutional amendments. In practice, the Senate has not used its veto power since the 1930s. Even if an extreme circumstance had arisen in which it was felt the Senate should oppose the Government, it would not likely happen. As Mr. Forsey points out, "Canadian governments have usually been so long-lived and so partisan in their appointments that most have been able to build up a massive majority in the Senate . . . Since 1943, there has been a perpetual Liberal majority in the Senate." (There are at present 58 Liberals, 24 Conservatives, 4 independents, 1 independent Liberal, and 1 Social Credit.)

Senate reform, as Mr. Frith sees it, will involve "a massive shift of political power,'' requiring the House of Commons to give up some of its authority in order to afford the Senate real clout. "We've got a lot of good people, but they could be better used," Mr. Frith says.

Many Senators admit that the way things are, the majority of their colleagues are not pulling their weight. George McIlraith figures that out of 88 senators (there are currently 16 vacancies in the 104-seat chamber), there are about 30 who do most of the work. The rest, he says, "are too old to work, or too sick, or too lazy."

Nevertheless Canadian taxpayers pay dearly for their services. In this era of mass unemployment and soaring government deficits, it is hard not to stare rudely at lists of the ample sums earned by senators who work part-time, often maintaining jobs in the private sector, and are rarely heard from.

The post pays $48,600 a year plus a tax-free allowance of $7,900. It includes a senate office, secretarial and security services, free mailing services, free rail transportation, and a limited amount of free air travel for themselves and their dependents. The money and services are all available unless a senator is absent for two consecutive sessions. The current session has been running for nearly three years, so a senator can stay away for a few years without forfeiting his seat or his salary — and some do.

In contrast, the British House of Lords pays a daily attendance fee of about $96 to peers. The House sits four days a week for about 35 weeks a year, and "if you just sit on your country estate you won't get any money," according to Richard Evans, a press officer with the British Treasury.

In Canada, you get paid if you stay at home, and the longer term values of a Senate post are even more impressive. For instance: Senator Peter Bosa, a former ministerial assistant, faces a Senate pension conservatively estimated at $82,903 a year; in the meantime, his appointment is worth an accumulated $2,684,521 until retirement. Alasdair Graham, party worker, will receive a pension of $95,244 a year; by the time he retires he will have earned $3,278,645 for his senatorial en-

deavors. What do they do?

The Senate sits in the Chamber three days a week: Tuesday evening, Wednesday afternoon and Thursday afternoon. Senators, however, can spend twice as much time in committees that also sit Tuesday, Wednesday and Thursday. As a rule every piece of legislation that goes through the House of Commons comes to Senate committees for study. At present there are some 16 committees: the most prestigious is Banking Trade and Commerce, headed for years by Salter Hayden, who is now ill; George McIlraith currently is chairman. Among the busiest are Legal and Constitutional Affairs, Health Welfare and Science, Regulations and Other Statutory Instruments, and Agriculture. One of the newest is the Special Joint Committee on Reform of the Senate, which will start work in a few weeks and is expected to re-

fairs and Regulations committees and is an adamant advocate of reform. He makes no bones about how he became a senator: "I got drunk at the '68 Liberal convention and hoisted a Trudeau sign and embarrassed my wife who supported that nice man John Turner. I guess I was the first person in the Toronto business establishment to come out for Trudeau."

Although Mr. Godfrey concedes that Mr. Trudeau has made some "imaginative appointments," including people like Eugene Forsey, he says, "Everybody knows Trudeau has nothing but contempt for the Senate. He doesn't like making appointments to it, and in my view, if it's going to survive, it has to change radically. It's possible Pitfield will work on the reform committee, and he'd be good, but naturally he'll be seen as an enemy by senators who want to maintain the status quo."

A special committee on reform will start work in a few weeks

port by the end of the year.

Hard-working, out-of-town senators like John Godfrey and Daniel Lang travel to Ottawa from their Toronto base every Tuesday, returning home on Thursday night or Friday morning. (George McIlraith, who lives in Ottawa, criticizes the schedule as wasteful. "Better to meet the full week when there's work to be done.") When they are not in meetings in Ottawa, they are inundated with reading material. And they defend many of their colleagues from the West and from the Maritimes whom they say spend a lot of time in valuable discussion in home territories, doing constituency work, finding out how the other half thinks.

"It took me years to figure out how the system works," says Mr. Godfrey. "Some senators still don't know how the hell it operates. We make amendments to bills before they go to Parliament, we work behind the scenes helping to reach compromises . . ." A Liberal bagman and corporate lawyer now retired from practice, Mr. Godfrey works on the Legal Af-

Many of the appointees, he says, look on the post "as a straight payoff for services rendered in the past." Some of the committees are jokes: "The joint committee on the Parliamentary restaurant — it meets at least once every four years. Then there's the Library committee that has never met, to anyone's knowledge." In terms of amendments to legislation, "50 per cent of the time we achieve our objectives, but we have no clout. The whole thing depends on good will."

Mr. Lang is more critical. "As it presently functions, the Senate is legislatively impotent." He cites, as "a classic example," what he calls "the Dominion Day bill — a fiasco. Here was a piece of legislation that came from the House of Commons as a private member's bill, incomplete, poorly considered, hasty, and there was nothing we could do to stop it. The Government rammed it down our throats. During the last 10 years the Senate has turned from a workplace to a theatre — and pretty poor theatre at that. It's a pale mimicry of the

House of Commons. We used to function as a quasi-judicial review body; the atmosphere was of a court rather than a political arena.''

Nowadays, he feels, parliamentary procedures are being ignored and a claustrophobic partisanship has interfered with important Senate functions. Mocking the trained seals who toe the party line, the ''donkeys'' as he calls them, he stands and salutes: ''Ready, aye, ready . . . '' He grins. ''That's a naval expression. It means, 'whatever you say, boss.' '' The good boys do what they're told, he suggests, and

he deplores such behavior. And though he is a Liberal appointee, he sits with the independent group and votes according to his conscience, not according to the party whip. One critic has likened Mr. Lang and his fellow travellers to ''a gang of naive, idealistic teen-aged anarchists.''

Appointed to the Senate by Lester Pearson and no fan of Pierre Trudeau, Mr. Lang blames the Prime Minister for part of the problem. ''Trudeau has an authoritarian nature. When coupled with the most powerful office in the land, this can be dangerous to our par-

liamentary institutions and their historical roots.'' He implies that Mr. Trudeau's impatience with or distaste for certain procedures or institutions, such as the Senate, have contributed to its demise. Yet like most of his colleagues, he insists that ''we must have a bi-cameral structure. The Senate is absolutely necessary to redress the regional imbalances that plague this country. I only hope that the result of the reform process on which we're embarking will be to give us a clearer role.''

THE GLOBE AND MAIL, DECEMBER 23, 1982

His great reward

Lord Acton's dictum has been proved again. Absolute power corrupts absolutely. Pierre Trudeau's appointment of Michael Pitfield to the Senate is cynical enough to make a stone weep.

Mr. Pitfield has not been appointed to the Senate because of the skill and experience he possesses. He has been appointed because he has worked as the right-hand man to the Prime Minister, hand-picked and hired as Clerk of the Privy Council to advise Mr. Trudeau on running the nation. The coy ''independent'' label attached to Mr. Pitfield's seat does not obscure the close working relationship he has had for years with the top Liberal, the man who has now rewarded him for services rendered with the choicest plum of all.

Mr. Pitfield has had other plums. There was the time the Conservative Government dropped him as Clerk of the Privy

Council in 1979 with severance pay of $107,800 — only $10,000 of which he returned when the Liberal Government hired him back as clerk nine months later. There was the $4,191.41 the taxpayers gave him to fly first-class between Ottawa and Boston 13 times in early 1980 for visits to his family and teaching chores at Harvard University. Last month the Trudeau Government saw to it that he was made a Companion of the Royal Victorian Order by the Queen at a dinner in Windsor Castle, as an award for public service.

But the Senate beats all — and Mr. Trudeau's timing was incredible. He announced the appointment even as the Commons mulled over the pension arrangements made for Mr. Pitfield, who officially resigned as clerk on December 10. (Now that he has the prospect of *two* pensions, Mr. Pitfield has graciously promised to reimburse the Government for

any contribution it makes to his Senate pension. For this small favor he has the thanks of a grateful nation.)

Funny thing: in July, 1981, Mr. Trudeau appointed Liberal MP Peter Stollery to the Senate, thereby creating a vacancy in the Spadina riding. It was the Prime Minister's gift to James Coutts, until then his Principal Secretary and chief political adviser, and its only redeeming feature was that Mr. Coutts did not, in the end, win the by-election. Until this week, we thought Mr. Trudeau could never surpass the arrogance of that disgraceful episode.

We were wrong. Mr. Trudeau has appointed his principal adviser to the Senate. It is the crowning argument for the sweeping reform, if not the total abolition, of the Upper Chamber, a body which has become the shameless repository for the Prime Minister's friends. The whole episode leaves a foul taste in the mouth.

THE TORONTO STAR, DECEMBER 26, 1982

Frenzy over Pitfield: What silly nonsense!

By David Crane Star economics editor

I don't know whether I'm in a minority group or not. But I am one Canadian who isn't the least disturbed by the fact that Prime Minister Pierre Trudeau has named his longtime aide, Michael Pitfield, to the Senate.

I don't know Pitfield personally but I of course know who he is. And I can't see how his appointment to the Senate is any worse than other Senate appointments. And, in fact, he may turn out to be a much better senator than most of those who get appointed because of his long experience in the inner circles of government and public policy.

I have a different quarrel — I don't think anybody should be appointed to the Senate. If we are to have such a body, it should be elected.

But as for the Pitfield appointment, what is most remarkable is the frenzied foaming-at-the-mouth reaction of Trudeau's critics, including Opposition Leader Joe Clark and New Democrat MP Ian Waddell.

Clark has denounced the appointment as "clearly a partisan appointment — a reward to a friend," adding, "I consider it a contemptuous act by the Prime Minister."

What silly nonsense! What hypocrisy!

Most appointments to the Senate have always been partisan, to political and even personal friends of the prime minister. And when Clark was prime minister in 1979-80 his appointments were clearly in this category.

One of Clark's first appointments was of Lowell Murray, a longtime personal friend who also happens to be godfather to Clark's daughter. Murray's main claim to fame is that he is a leading backroom boy of the Conservative party.

Opinion

Rewards to friends

Other appointees to the Senate by Clark included onetime Tory MPs James Balfour and Heath Macquarrie, Quebec Tory fundraising chairman Guy Charbonneau, onetime Alberta provincial Tory candidate Martha Bielish, Richard Donahoe, a Nova Scotia Conservative lawyer, former PC party president Nathan Nurgitz, defeated PC federal candidate Bob de Cotret, former New Brunswick PC leader Cyril Sherwood, and former Newfoundland provincial PC cabinet minister William Doody.

If these appointments weren't partisan, what were they? And if they weren't rewards to friends, what were they? Of course they were partisan, reflecting Clark's choices. And nobody begrudged him that right.

So he is the one who really sound partisan in this entire silly dispute.

Waddell has resorted to one of the most commonly used adjectives in political life today to attack the Pitfield appointment. He has called it obscene. It's too bad he doesn't own a dictionary.

Yet if anyone has come up with an even worse version of the current Senate made up of political appointees, it is Waddell's own party. In 1980 the federal NDP proposed that the Senate be replaced by a provincially appointed Council of the Federation which would have the power to veto federal legislation and federal appointments.

The idea of a handful of people appointed by provincial premiers being able to veto the decisions of a democratically elected House of Commons is surely far more frightening than any amount of damage that Pitfield could conceivably do as a senator.

The real problem with the Senate is not the appointment of Michael Pitfield or Lowell Murray or any other partisan figure. The real problem is that it has no real standing or legitimacy with the Canadian people so long as it is appointed instead of elected.

Its members are appointed to age 75 and are accountable to no one. That surely is objectionable in a democratic society. If people are to have power and influence over the country's laws, policies and spending, then surely the public should have the chance (a) to elect them and (b) to throw them out if they don't do a good job.

And there's another question as well. Even if the Senate were elected, what do we really want it to do? The main role that is widely discussed today is that of a body to give greater voice to the regions, as the U.S. Senate does with the election of two senators from each state state regardless of population.

Veto power?

But how much power would we want to take from the House of Commons to give to an elected Senate? Veto power? The power to defeat an elected government?

These are the real issues. Pitfield's appointment is objectionable only in the sense that an appointed Senate is objectionable.

People like Clark and Waddell would win more respect if they would tackle the real question of Senate reform rather than engaging in shrill and self-serving harangues.

Discussion Questions

1. By what means does the Cabinet dominate the House of Commons? Are sufficient opportunities to criticize, evaluate, and inform provided in order to challenge Cabinet's control? Should we be concerned about this issue, or should we be content to know that the public is adequately informed to make its judgement at election time?
2. What is meant by the 'fusion of powers' between the executive and legislative branches of the Canadian political system? Examine the consequences of this fusion in terms of Val Sears's article on the advantages of minority government.
3. In December 1979, the House of Commons played a decisive role as a legislature by defeating the Progressive Conservatives on their budget. Later, as explained in some of the articles above, the Tories succeeded in forcing the government to alter its energy legislation by prohibiting the House from meeting for several days. How do these actions fit within the context of Parliament's usual role? Are they legitimate instances of Parliament's exercising its right to intervene and call a halt to an executive action?
4. What is the relation between the responsiveness and legitimacy of the House of Commons and its representativeness? Discuss in the context of McCall-Newman's article.
5. In the articles by Goar and others, it is implied that Big Government has overtaken Parliament. Have the instruments of parliamentary control kept pace with the growth of government? What reforms would address this question? Would these reforms not simply make the business of governing more difficult?
6. How well do the two Houses of Parliament perform their traditional functions?
7. Does the presence of Cabinet ministers in the Senate undermine the principles of responsible government, or does it make that body more relevant? How do the proposals for the reform of the Senate deal with the issue of ministerial responsibility?

Suggested Readings

Paul W. Fox, ed. *Politics: Canada*, fifth edition. Toronto: McGraw-Hill Ryerson, 1982, 483–549.

Michael M. Atkinson. 'Parliamentary Government in Canada', in Michael S. Whittington and Glen Williams, eds. *Canadian Politics in the 1980s*. Toronto: Methuen, 1981, 260–73.

J.R. Mallory. 'Parliament in the Eighties', in R. Kenneth Carty and W. Peter Ward, eds. *Entering the Eighties: Canada in Crisis*. Toronto: Oxford University Press, 1980, 120–34.

Robert J. Jackson and Michael M. Atkinson. *The Canadian Legislative System*, second edition. Toronto: Macmillan, 1980.

H.D. Clarke *et al.*, eds. *Parliament, Policy and Representation.* Toronto: Methuen, 1980.

Denis Smith. 'President and Parliament: The Transformation of Parliamentary Government in Canada', in R. Schultz, O. Kruhlak, and J. Terry, eds. *The Canadian Political Process*, third edition. Toronto: Holt, Rinehart and Winston, 1979, 302–13 *or* in Thomas A. Hockin, ed. *Apex of Power: The Prime Minister and Political Leadership in Canada*, second edition. Toronto: Prentice-Hall, 1977, 308–25.

Jean-Pierre Gaboury and J.R. Hurley, eds. *The Canadian House of Commons Observed*. Ottawa: University of Ottawa Press, 1979.

W.A.W. Neilson and J.C. MacPherson, eds. *The Legislative Process in Canada: The Need for Reform.* Montreal: Institute for Research on Public Policy, 1978.

b. The Prime Minister, Cabinet, and Leadership

To say that the prime minister and his Cabinet are at the centre of Canadian politics is to state the obvious. A day does not go by when some of these people are not prominently featured in the nation's media. Moreover, it is on the basis of these personalities that many people form their judgements about politics in general. A continuing problem in press coverage of the prime minister and the Cabinet is that, although extensive, it is remarkably superficial at times. In this area more than in others, reporters tend to react to events — controversies in the House, Cabinet shuffles, scandals, speeches, or announcements — rather than probe the issues surrounding decision-makers. Political coverage usually focuses on interesting or controversial individuals. Reporters, therefore, rarely examine the bases of power or ideologies of high officials. The sources of power often go unexplored as well.

One exception to this rule is the first article here, David Crane's reflections on the nature of prime-ministerial powers (it is interesting to note that this piece is largely derived from the thoughts of former Clerk of the Privy Council Michael Pitfield). Crane details some of the practical aspects of the office, the consequent human limitations (such as scarcity of time), and the institutional constraints on the exercise of power. He does not provide a complete list, however; he could have noted that the key central agencies of the Prime Minister's Office (PMO) and the Privy Council Office (PCO) report directly to the prime minister.

The coverage in this section does not reflect average press treatment of the prime minister and Cabinet; the typical daily paper very rarely includes articles on prime-ministerial decision-making styles, Cabinet organization, or the role of Cabinet committees. Little emphasis is placed on the extremely powerful Priorities and Planning Committee of Cabinet chaired by the prime minister. This committee, called the 'inner cabinet' by Joe Clark when he was in office, sets broad objectives and long-term priorities, determines overall expenditure plans; directs federal macro-economic policy; and oversees the personnel policies for senior civil servants. Part of the reason the press provides so little information on such matters is that these bodies operate behind an almost impenetrable curtain of secrecy. With, generally, enough drama in the daily activities on Parliament Hill to satisfy journalists and their editors, there is little imperative for the difficult behind-the-scenes probing needed to unveil the real decision-making process.

The next group of articles addresses the prime minister-ship of Pierre Elliott Trudeau. The first three illustrate foreign perspectives on his overwhelming dominance of the Canadian political scene for a decade and a half. *The Wall Street Journal* saw the 1980 Trudeau resurrection in clear ideological terms, a view most Canadians would not easily share. Nor would most of us accept the American paper's version of Canadian priorities. The London *Times* editorial, while it demonstrates a firmer grasp of the reasons for the Trudeau victory and the nature of Canadian politics, also makes certain statements that might seem jarring to domestic audiences. The assertion that Trudeau appears to be a puppet of his party reflects more on the conduct of that particular election than on the realities of the office. Nevertheless, the editorial does pick up on two key issues that faced Trudeau on his return: the price of oil and the separatist challenge from Québec. Charles Douglas-Home's article takes a tack quite different from that of the American editorial. It down-plays the importance of economic issues for Trudeau and emphasizes the centrality of the constitution. Unlike the *Times* editorialist, Douglas-Home is inclined to interpret the lack of a clear mandate from the election as licence for Trudeau to carry out his vision.

The next trio of articles reflects on certain other aspects of Trudeau's leadership. The first of the two by W.A. Wilson discusses the overall impact of Trudeau's leadership on the country. This type of article is rare for the press; it resembles academic discussion. Underlying the actions it describes is a clear philosophy on the appropriate use of state power. Wilson offers some excellent insights into the extent to which a prime minister can set the direction and decision-making style of government, and into the central-izing trends within the federal government since the 1960s. His second piece is a brief discussion of the nature of prime-ministerial (particularly Liberal prime-ministerial) dominance of the parliamentary party in power. Moreover, Wilson does not succumb to the inevitable temptation to measure accomplishments in the Canadian parliamentary system against the lax but different British system. His thesis that Trudeau, in asserting absolute control over the Liberals, reduced a national party to a regional one, is profoundly disturbing. The Canadian Press story by Roger Smith reviews the patronage practices of the Trudeau government. Although the article tries to balance its dis-cussion between opposing viewpoints, it provides little continuity between historic accounts and the modern con-text to judge these activities. The contemporary morality that lies at the root of some of the outrage of those quoted is not explicitly spelled out, and is subject to change.

The four pieces on Joe Clark's leadership were largely provoked by the challenges posed to it throughout 1981 and 1982, which were to culminate in the June 1983 convention, when Clark lost the leadership to Brian Mul-roney. The two articles by Professor Michael Bliss and the column by Michael Valpy stress the accomplishments of the Clark government in office. Bliss, an historian, draws some intriguing parallels between Clark and previous incumbents, carefully assessing his strengths and weak-nesses as party leader. His second article elaborates on the destructive challenges that the Conservative party posed for Clark's leadership. Valpy attempts to jog what Bliss refers to as 'our historical memory' by detailing many of Clark's accomplishments in office. This perspective is poignantly counterbalanced by Peter C. Newman's scath-ing indictment of Clark's leadership. In stressing the under-lying crisis in Canadian leadership, he sounds a familiar media theme.

The pieces by Val Sears and Stephen Handelman on the blurring of responsibility between the senior bureau-cracy and members of the Cabinet are exceptions to the general run of articles about Cabinet. Both describe the difficulties that ministers have in trying to get their policy initiatives put into effect. They support the thesis that it is the senior bureaucrats who stymie the duly elected min-isters' efforts to carry out the public will. However, both also neglect to examine a number of other constraints facing ministers. One enormous constraint, which is driven home in the Sears article, is time—ministers are extremely busy people, constantly having to deal with a multitude of demands.

The next two articles are atypical examples of press treatment of Cabinet selection. After each Cabinet shuffle, reporters usually seek to divine clues to the government's ideological position. George Bain, however, suggests that there is little use in attempting to discern much about the thrust of overall government policy by identifying the occupants of particular positions. Political scientist Robert Jackson, for his part, gives a brief summary of the restric-tions faced by every prime minister in choosing a Cabinet. Not only is the field from which to choose narrow, but talent is tempered by other factors, which Jackson lists. An ideal Cabinet minister is someone with overall intel-lectual ability who can quickly absorb what experts recom-mend, make decisions, and communicate complicated policy issues effectively.

THE TORONTO STAR, AUGUST 23, 1980

How powerful is the man who sits in office 307-S?

By David Crane Toronto Star

Prime Minister Pierre Trudeau works a 52-hour week, most of it in his panelled third-floor office in the Centre Block of the Parliament Buildings.

We think of the man in office 307-S as the most powerful man in Canada. He's boss to 350,000 civil servants who will spend $60 billion of our tax money this year. He's the godfather of federal political patronage, personally handing out more than 250 of the most senior government jobs to men and women who came to the aid of their party. He speaks with the full authority of the government of Canada, and his 147 Liberal MPs owe their majority in Parliament largely to his personal appeal.

Now, however, a document has surfaced which suggests that Trudeau really isn't as powerful as we seem to think he is. It's an academic paper written last year by Michael Pitfield, current secretary of the cabinet, a close friend of Trudeau's and probably the most powerful civil servant in Ottawa.

Pitfield, who was fired as Privy Council president when Joe Clark's Conservatives won power in May, 1979, wrote the paper during his six-month interregnum at the Harvard School of Public Administration. He was recalled to Ottawa last February after Trudeau had regained power.

In it, Pitfield argues that changes in the structure of government have curbed certain presidential-style powers that might have emerged due to the growth and complexity of bureaucracy. Whereas a U.S. president spends a great deal of time initiating policy, Pitfield argues that the prime ministership under Trudeau has become managerial.

Using power

This doesn't mean a prime minister holds back from using what power he does have, Pitfield says. "It can be said with some certainty that every prime minister, facing the constraints surrounding him, has at one time or another felt himself required to use the full armory of his office."

Pitfield sees the prime minister operating as a kind of orchestra conductor, directing his power back and forth to suit circumstances. "His authority is fundamentally founded on the willingness of his followers to accept his lead," Pitfield writes. This means he must "never lose the confidence of three groups regularly meeting and passing judgment on him: His cabinet, his caucus and the House of Commons."

If the prime minister seems more powerful today, Pitfield argues, it is because the reforms in the PMO during the past 20 years have put more emphasis on the collective responsibility of the cabinet. Cabinet ministers have less leeway to speak independently on government policy but, Pitfield argues, have a greater chance to get their views heard in cabinet.

At the same time, he argues, the improved efficiency of the PMO may make Trudeau seem more powerful within the government. Changes in the operation of the PMO and of the Privy Council Office, which works closely both with Trudeau's office and the cabinet, have "added considerably, to the efficiency and effectiveness with which a prime minister can use the powers he has always had. He is unquestionably better informed than before. He can use his time better and is more certain to achieve the results he seeks."

According to Pitfield, the prime minister has three basic roles. They are to: Maintain the unity of the government; lead the general direction of the government; and be responsible for national security.

Trudeau has six principal powers to do his job, Pitfield says. These powers are:

☐ The appointment of key members of the executive, including cabinet ministers, deputy ministers, the chairmen and presidents of crown corporations and government agencies, and parliamentary secretaries to cabinet ministers. Of about 2,500 appointments, including about 1,000 part-time appointments, that go through the cabinet, the prime minister personally makes about 250.

☐ Setting the terms of reference of cabinet ministers and altering the make-up of government departments and agencies. But such changes are usually discussed in cabinet and may also have to be approved by Parliament, Pitfield says.

☐ Presiding over cabinet meetings; this includes the power to set up cabinet committees and appoint their chairmen and members. The prime minister also has the power to sum up a consensus out of a cabinet discussion.

☐ Making direct recommendations to a government department. But, says Pitfield, "the closest thing to the use of this power today is the occasional letter that a prime minister sends to explain his understanding of policy or his position on an issue to one or another of his colleagues."

☐ The convocation and dissolution of Parliament. This is restricted both by the British North America Act, which limits the term of office of a government, and by the rights of the Crown. Thus the prime minister can use the threat of an election against the opposition but is unlikely to use it to keep his own followers in line, Pitfield says.

☐ His more informal role as "the" national leader, which is displayed mainly in times of public ceremony or during a crisis. But, Pitfield argues, this is offset to some extent by "equal time" rules which he says are "more and more insisted upon by the media."

Although the constitution limits the powers of a prime minister, Pitfield says: "The concepts of collective and ministerial responsibility are the most constant

How Pierre earns $32.17 an hour

Prime Minister Pierre Trudeau makes $32.17 an hour.

That's what his total income of $87,000 — or $1,673.07 a week — works out to when divided by the 52 hours Privy Council president Michael Pitfield says Trudeau works in an average week.

In the first public accounting of how the Prime Minister spends his time, figures provided by Pitfield show Trudeau spending only 5 hours working at his desk alone during a typical week. Here's the breakdown:

40% government

Governor-General and foreign visitors (2 hours, 5 min.).
House of Commons (4 hours, 40 min.).
Cabinet and cabinet committees (6 hours, 45 min.).
Ministers (3 hours, 38 min.).
Outside visitors and delegations (2 hours, 36 min.)
Special events, ceremonies (1 hour).

9% political

MPs, senators and party officials (2 hours, 5 min.).
Political cabinet, caucus and constituency (2 hours, 36 min.).

4% press
10% staff

Senior staff (2 hours, 5 min.).
Senior appointments, planning and speech preparation (1 hour, 34 min.).
Personal office staff (1 hour, 34 min.).

10% work at desk

Policy matters, reading (5 hours, 12 min.).

3% private time

Private visitors, doctors, haircuts (1 hour, 34 min.).

3% non-scheduled
15% travel in Canada

Riding business, speeches, appearances (7 hours, 48 min.).

6% foreign travel

Conferences, official visits abroad (3 hours, 7 min.).

and pervasive of the constraints on a Canadian prime minister's powers."

Collective responsibility means that cabinet ministers must present a united front to Parliament; ministers who disagree with what the prime minister says must resign. This means the prime minister is under pressure to achieve consensus within his cabinet.

Ministerial responsibility means that individual cabinet ministers are directly responsible to Parliament since most of their powers and responsibilities are the result of laws passed by Parliament. This means that the prime minister cannot order a cabinet minister to do something if it is in conflict with his legal responsibilities and powers.

Other constraints on the prime minister include the regional nature of the country as well as its religious and racial diversity, all of which complicates the appointment of the cabinet and leads to the emergence of strong regional leaders.

Another constraint is the prime minister's dependence on his political party.

It gave him the leadership and it is the party's organization that enables him to win elections. The party has the power to review his leadership and he must deal with party executives that party members.

The media, as critics of the prime minister, also constrain his powers, according to Pitfield.

But "scarcity of time is the most pervasive circumstantial limitation on a Canadian prime minister's freedom of action." Only about 25 per cent of his time is available to run the administration, and half of that, Pitfield says, "is heavily occupied in fighting fires and resolving disputes among ministers."

No new powers

While there has been considerable effort to improve the scope and depth of the prime minister's supervision of the government, use time more effectively, give ministers greater control over the bureaucracy, improve the ability of the decision-making process to set priorities and plan for the future and generally upgrade government performance, this has not increased the power of the prime minister, according to Pitfield.

For example, he argues, cabinet committees have been given more decision-making powers, new cabinet posts have been created, a cabinet committee on priorities and planning has been established and certain responsibilities in such areas as federal-provincial relations, science and technology, management of Parliament's legislative timetable and much of the handling of internal security, have been taken from the prime minister and given to other cabinet ministers.

He blames the image of Trudeau as a presidential prime minister on a number of factors, including "the strength of Trudeau's media image and intellect; partly from the increased role of Canadian prime ministers as international figures; partly from their changed lifestyle and the expense of facilities supporting them; partly from a failure to understand the administrative changes that have taken place."

The ability of the prime minister to persuade others to follow him is what gives him his real influence, according to Pitfield.

"Few things are more nebulous than influence yet it is the glue that provides the cohesion of leadership in Parliamentary government," Pitfield argues. "Influence, no less than power, is a necessary thing and, in the final analysis, since the real power of the prime minister is so political so also must be the checks upon his use of it."

THE WALL STREET JOURNAL, FEBRUARY 20, 1980

The Bullet Bites Back

Conservatives often see it as their political role to force the electorate to bite bullets, or accept the discipline of budget-balancing and other forms of self-denial. Canada's voters responded to that message this week by retiring a nine-months-old Conservative government and restoring Pierre Elliott Trudeau and his liberals to power. There no doubt is a political lesson to be learned here somewhere.

Some pessimists would read the Canadian results as a symptom of the malaise of the Western democracies, a public demand for welfare state services without a corresponding willingness to foot the bill. We would not want to undervalue such readings but neither can we fully accept them or the element of despair they contain.

It is true that the conservatives in Canada, attempting to govern with a slim plurality, were faced with a monumental fiscal problem when they came to power last May. The budget deficit they inherited from 16 years of Liberal

rule was the equivalent of a $100 billion deficit in the United States. The conservatives felt it was their first duty, from the point of view of Canada's economic health, to attempt to reduce that deficit. Their route to that goal was, in large part, heavy additional taxes on energy, including an 18-cent-a-gallon increase in the tax on gasoline.

By returning the liberals to power with a clear majority, Canada's voters demonstrated that the conservative program was not to their liking. The big swing back to the liberals occurred in Ontario, the province that consumes the bulk of the energy Canada's Western provinces produce.

Now it may well be that Canada's voters understand the nation's priorities better than the conservative government did. There can be little doubt that the country's deficit is dangerously high, but a fiscal deficit is only part of a larger equation. The realistic way to reduce the deficit and put the government and the monetary system on a sounder foot-

ing is to hold down the growth of government while at the same time expanding incentives for investment and production. Sharp increases in the tax on energy, a resource that Canada has in some plentitude, is not a very good way to encourage investment and production.

There is no certainty that Mr. Trudeau's born-again liberals will do any better than the conservatives. Mr. Trudeau has run a tight-lipped campaign on the assumption that the conservatives had done enough to hang themselves without further help. Now that he has won, he seems to think that his first order of business should be mediating between the U.S. and U.S.S.R., rather than confronting Canada's serious economic problems.

But the lesson for conservatives should be clear: The government's first priority should go not to bullet biting, but to economic development and growth.

THE TIMES, LONDON, FEBRUARY 20, 1980

THE RETURN OF MR TRUDEAU

The Canadian electorate has registered an emphatic vote of no confidence in Mr Joe Clark and the policies of the Progressive Conservatives. It was unimpressed by his performance in office; it did not feel that his success in Iran outweighed his failures and fumbles elsewhere; it disliked his budget which, whatever might be said against it in detail, was strikingly honest in its strategy. Above all, the electorate rejected his energy policy. In a sense, what it has really voted for is petrol and oil at half world prices sustained by subsidised imports. Since Canadians use more petrol per capita than any other people, this piece of democracy need not have been unexpected — Mr Clark was naif to introduce his dose of realism while still in a vulnerable minority. Also, he fatally misread Mr Trudeau's resignation of the Liberal leadership, so readily re-

scinded when the Party wanted him back, as giving the Conservatives time to make their unpopular reforms.

Mr Trudeau, discredited nine months ago, now finds himself restored to power on exactly the terms on which he left it. He has a working majority, and he heads much the same party in parliament as that from which he had, over his eleven years of office, eliminated nearly all the talent which could challenge his supremacy. Moreover, the opinion polls made clear that the electorate sees him by far as Canada's best leader. This reassertion of his indispensability after his rejection in favour of Mr Clark, gives Mr Trudeau an unchallengeable position, no matter what his party officials and backers may say.

He campaigned more as the party's puppet, than as its leader. He put for-

ward no striking policy proposals. He remained vague or ambiguous on the great issues that face the country. He returns to office comfortably uncommitted, unless his promise to stand down in three years (when he will be 63, young for politicians) is held to limit his dominance and to give incentive to new contenders for the leadership to sprout from underfoot. All in all, Mr Trudeau must be awed by his new authority.

He lost office in May because he seemed to have run out of ideas, expedients and men to deal with the problems that he must again face. But he is now free to use some of the solutions which brought his predecessors down — indeed his very strength in eastern Canada may enable him to make deals with the western interests. He can, and surely will, ignore the motorists' vote by putting up the price of oil, no doubt calling it the "blended" price. He will hardly try socialist controls of wages and prices. He will keep, but control, the state oil corporation. He in no way depends on the New Democrats, who failed to become the balancing party. Even nine short months out of power can teach a politician useful lessons. But the key issue, the issue which destiny seems to have reserved for Mr Trudeau to resolve, is the unity of Canada, the coming confrontation with the secessionist forces in Quebec. At the end of the campaign, scenting victory, the old Mr Trudeau spoke out for a strong federal government and for one Canada as a blend of two cultures.

Mr Levesque, perhaps ominously, welcomed the renewal of his struggle with federalist Mr Trudeau. He has his worries. The referendum in which he will ask Quebec voters to agree to negotiations for the so-called sovereignty-association is a few months off. But the resurgence of the provincial Liberal Party under Mr Claude Ryan has made a difference. Mr Ryan's own scheme for a new relationship between Quebec and Canada, which carefully retains federal unity, is evidently liked by Quebeckers, who are enjoying a new sense of self-confidence as both French and Canadians. This is the upshot of many factors. But it is one on which Mr Trudeau and Mr Ryan could build constructively — if they worked well together and with the other provinces, especially the west. It is the nub of the problem: for Mr Trudeau's will be the decisive role.

THE TIMES, LONDON, MARCH 3, 1980

What will Mr Trudeau do with his power now?

Charles Douglas-Home on the return of Mr Trudeau with a blank cheque

Mr Pierre Trudeau will be sworn in again today as Canada's Prime Minister. For this, his fourth government, he has a good working majority, which will be only Canada's fourth majority government in the past 10 administrations. He has personally dominated Canadian politics for 12 years; yet after a wasted and desultory period of nine months in opposition he comes back into office now giving few clues as to what he intends to do with his power. We may be able to draw certain conclusions from his past record, but as far as the future position of Canada is concerned Mr Trudeau is in the astonishing position of having been returned to office with the equivalent of a blank cheque and a majority to cash it.

The record of previous

> It is on Canada's constitutional future that Mr Trudeau's record leaves some important questions unanswered. . . . It would be a tragedy if his return reactivates the mood of separation and division

Liberal governments under Mr Trudeau suggests that on economic matters the rate of inflation, the size of the national debt, and the foreign exchange deficit will all rise; and that his response to these trends may be to attempt further accretions of federal economic power by asserting the primacy of centralizing policies as the only means to cope with Canada's problems.

Although the Liberals precipitated last month's election by voting against the Conservatives' plans to increase petrol tax, Mr Trudeau's Government might soon find itself having to adjust to the same economic realities in much the same way. There is a precedent. In 1974 the Conservatives fought the election on a campaign for wage and price controls, which Mr Trudeau rejected at the time. He introduced them the following year.

However, it is on Canada's constitutional future that Mr Trudeau's record leaves some important questions unanswered. There is no manifesto commitment to go by, since there was no manifesto. Mr Trudeau, long recognised as an almost triumphalist exponent of federal supremacy, has been curiously silent on the subject. Less than two years ago he introduced major constitutional proposals which set alarm bells ringing in every provincial capital; yet during the election campaign he was asked why he had not made constitutional reform an issue and replied that the English speaking media had declared it to be a 'non-issue', showing uncharacteristic readiness to be told what and what not to say by the press.

When he calls the next first-ministers meeting, he will have to face 11 provincial premiers, who, whatever their different political viewpoints (and eight of them are Progressive Conservatives) are more or less united in their desire to prevent any reforms which add to federal power over the provinces.

Canada has no formal constitution. An Act of the British Parliament is all that there is of Canada's constitution, and no constitutional change can be achieved without amendment to the British North America Act (1867) being passed through the House of Commons in London.

The BNAA was designed for a largely rural society of four million people. Its crucial sections 91 and 92 define the area of jurisdiction between federal and provincial governments. The founding fathers of Canada intended, in the words of John A. Macdonald 'a powerful central government, powerful central legislation and a decentralized system of minor legislatures for local purposes'. But the past 113 years have seen the pendulum of power swing between periods of strong centralization — notably in the war and post war years — and periods of strong provincialism in the late nineteenth century and in the past 20 years.

With a more leisured political pace than is now tolerable, these swings of the pendulum may have been adequate for Canada to overlook the fatal flaw in her constitution: the absence of any procedure for amending it. There is no court to arbitrate between jurisdictional disputes (let alone a bill

of rights), and the difficulty of achieving a point where all parties in Canada can agree on the terms of a request to the British House of Commons to amend the Act, has meant that the pendulum would have to swing very far one way before Canadians think that it is not coming back; and then, as many have feared with the case of Quebec, it might be too late.

So for 50 years Canada has tried and failed to agree on amendment procedures. Meanwhile two developments more recently have marked a trend away from centralized power, though both have been resisted where possible by federal governments in Ottawa. One is the growing power of the western provinces based on their mineral wealth; the other is the increased nationalism of governments in Quebec.

The gradualism of Canada's constitutional argument received a sudden and nasty shock in November, 1976, when Quebec returned a government dedicated to a referendum on the question of separation from the rest of Canada. In the wake of several abortive constitutional initiatives during the 1960s and 1970s Mr Trudeau then decided to force the pace, once it had become clear that his introduction of bilingual laws, rather than constitutional reforms, had failed to draw the teeth of Quebec nationalism.

He did not wait for the report of a task force on Canadian unity which he himself set up in 1977 — it reported in January 1979 — but instead surprised Canada in June, 1978, with a sudden constitutional package.

The package was in two parts: a White Paper called ''Time for Action'' proposing

a set of principles for a renewed federation; and a Bill C-60 which was immediately tabled in Parliament and contained those changes which he said could be unilaterally introduced by the Federal Government. This claim was made on the questionable basis of an amendment to the BNAA which had been passed in 1949, without the consent of the provinces, but which purported to give Ottawa the unilateral right to establish a house of federation instead of a senate, and a restructured supreme court to rule on the constitution.

The provincial premiers unanimously rejected this agenda, which Mr Trudeau had said was to be completed by July 1981. Nevertheless Bill C-60 remained on the table, the subject of much discussion, until his government was defeated last May.

Mr Clark, the incoming Conservative Prime Minister, approached the constitutional impasse in an entirely different way from Mr Trudeau. Perhaps because Mr Trudeau came from Quebec his Government seemed to have created a disproportionate obsession with the Quebec issue, when the other provinces in their different ways also had profound criticisms of Canada's constitution. Mr Trudeau had had a brilliant career as a professor of constitutional law, which led him to challenge and provoke the Canadian body politic, in a way which, in spite of his Quebec origins, tended to aggravate the crisis rather than defuse it.

Mr Clark being neither an intellectual nor a Quebecois approached the question altogether more modestly. He dealt with all provinces on an

equal footing much to the frustration of Quebec's premier who found that his heroic dialogue with Mr Trudeau had turned into a much less dramatic but more practical discussion with his fellow premiers, none of whom were disposed to be impressed by his claim for treatment so much more special than they expected for themselves.

Mr Clark's intention was to demonstrate not that the structure of provincial-federal relations was perfect, but that any change would have to come about as a result of multilateral discussion among colleagues rather than as a bilateral matter between Quebec and Ottawa. Though everybody, then as now, awaited the result of Quebec's referendum this June, his technique made it clear that the future of Quebec was a matter for all the other provinces as well. Mr Clark was criticised in some quarters for what was called 'executive federalism', for attempting to bypass the House of Commons by trying to govern through a cabinet of provincial chief executives. Nevertheless the atmosphere in which constitutional reform was to be discussed became much improved compared to the high temperature of the years which had gone before, and this led to the prospect of a defeat for Quebec's separatists in the referendum.

Now Mr Trudeau is back; with his blank cheque. It would be a tragedy if his return reactivates the mood of separatism and division and postpones again the chance that Canada's provinces, for all their diversity, might now at last join with Ottawa to renew their constitution in a spirit of unity.

THE FINANCIAL POST, MARCH 20, 1982

Ottawa/Column by William A. Wilson

The steady progress toward remaking Canadian society

DURING the past couple of years the Trudeau administration has attempted a series of changes bearing on the nature of government, the power of the state, important aspects of our economic system and on certain principles which our society has viewed as fundamental.

It is not yet clear whether this is part of a long-term trend toward a far more active and somewhat arbitrary state, partially freed from traditional constraints on the use of power, or an aberration of politics brought about by a particular Prime Minister's impatience with existing barriers to action. If it is indeed a trend that will continue in one way or another, the state in the future could be greatly changed.

It would have characteristics in common with earlier versions of the state before Parliament had first curbed the power of the Crown, and then entirely taken it away. We may be witnessing a contemporary renewal of that old contest, but this time between a government with presidential overtones and a legislature to which it is ostensibly responsible, but where in reality the true function of the majority under party discipline is simply to sustain and protect the power of the executive.

Basic change

Whether we are witnessing trend or aberration, there are actual and attempted departures from established patterns of parliamentary government and the intergovernment relationships. These are coupled with significant changes in our economic system and the revision of values habitually accepted in our society. Some examples:

• The concentration of power in the hands of a small number of ministers and officials, replacing its normal diffusion through the cabinet as an entity, more akin to presidential than prime ministerial government.

• The attempted destruction of important constitutional convention through the unilateral effort to alter provincial powers without consent. Although the attempt was unsuccessful, it was followed by the announced death of co-operative federalism implying more arbitrary central action to replace past efforts at intergovernmental consensus.

• The effort in the Energy Security bill to secure power to increase taxation without further references to Parliament.

• The attempt in the same bill to establish new legislative methods through piggy-backing four completely new acts onto a mass of amendments to existing legislation.

• The advanced interventionism of the National Energy Program, a radical change in one segment of the economic system.

• Restoration of the principle of state confiscation of property, discredited since Magna Carta in 1215, through the 25% government back-in on petroleum developments under federal jurisdiction as it originally stood in the NEP, although modifications followed.

• The removal of normal property rights belonging to certain classes of minority shareholders and their exposure to unscrupulous as well as officially approved action if the proposed amendments to the Corporations Act are passed in their present form.

The government has failed in certain of these efforts, accomplished others, and currently faces determined opposition to some. But in combination they establish a pattern touching important aspects of our national life.

Each would lead to a much more powerful state, subject to fewer constraints upon its actions and would be in accord with the Prime Minister's earlier statement that the nation faces more, not less, exercise of authority over its affairs. The case of the proposed changes affecting minority shareholders in oil and gas companies is worth examination because of the way it illustrates a changing emphasis between the rights of the individual and the powers of the state.

At least since the Great Depression, the regulations of securities commissions, and some legislation, has had as a primary aim the protection of minority shareholders. The proposed legislation would remove important protections, permitting directors, with approval of two thirds of the shareholders, to constrain shares and then sell out holdings of nonresident Canadians and nonCanadians. (Shareholders who object could go to court.) The purpose is to further the official Canadianization policy. The emphasis is entirely on the achievement of state policy, regardless of damage and injustice to individual investors.

Policy shift

There are clearly very important ethical problems involved both in the initial proposal for state confiscation of 25% interest, later modified, and in the treatment of minority shareholders that is now contemplated. The issue of ethics has barely been discussed and in both cases the government view appears to be that normal ethical considerations do not apply to actions by the state.

There would be nothing wrong in itself with a move toward presidential government in Canada. The hazard in the present direction lies in the partial nature of the move: the expansion of executive power without the constraints imposed by an independent legislature.

The current movement exploits, in effect, the weakness inherent in the parliamentary system since power was removed from the Crown in favor of the legislature. While true power rested with the monarch, Parliament was an effective counterweight. When power resides in a Parliament composed of disciplined political parties, the counterweight against abuses consists only of the minority in opposition.

In the Canadian federation, a fairly effective system of checks and balances has existed through the division of powers between federal and provincial legislatures, but this constraint is now under attack through the central government's renunciation of intergovernment consensus in favor of unilateral action.

Against the pattern that has developed since the 1980 election, the Conservative strike which brought Parliament to a halt has an historic dimension which separates it from ordinary partisan action. Both the unprecedented scope of the latest omnibus bill and the exceptional powers sought under it are outside established parliamentary practice in this country.

The Energy Security bill as presented to Parliament is exceptional and it provoked an exceptional response. But the questions surrounding the nature of the state that will exist in future remain unanswered.

W.A. WILSON *is a columnist and television commentator.*

THE VANCOUVER PROVINCE, SEPTEMBER 28, 1982

Pass the dagger

By W.A. WILSON
Special to The Province

OTTAWA — The great weakness of the parliamentary system of government lies in the way the function of the parliamentary majority has evolved over the years, a development that has radically altered the system.

The role of the majority in Parliament has become limited to maintaining the power of the prime minister where it used to be to serve as a constraint on the use of power. The change came about with the development of disciplined political parties and it is this difference that gives rise to complaints that the elected representatives of the people have lost their power.

Except for the requirement for periodic elections, our system of government now accords one man far more unfettered power over the country than the president has in the U.S. And now another constraint has been removed by the stated determination of the prime minister not to lead his party in the next election and by the indications that he feels little concern for the Liberal Party once he has finished using it.

Lynda Sorenson, co-chairman of the party's impending policy convention, has stated with considerable bluntness the role of the Liberal Party: "You have to trust that those to whom you have given power will make the right decisions. That's how we have to run the country."

In the narrow context of policy resolutions her view is unexceptional for a sound reason: the delegates to a convention are narrowly selected by their own party where members of the House of Commons are broadly elected by the country. Convention delegates should not be able to bind the country's elected representatives. Mrs. Sorenson went beyond this, however, by adding that her party takes pride in not turning on a leader or government.

Even given the servility the system demands of the majority in Parliament, there are reasons why Liberal Party delegates might question the present leadership of their party. The most pressing political one would be the great damage the party itself has suffered under its present leadership. Prime Minister Trudeau inherited a great national party and has reduced it to a regional party.

There is an even more fundamental reason why Liberal delegates should think the unthinkable about party leadership: there has been a serious decline in public confidence in government during Mr. Trudeau's tenure of office.

In actual fact, Mrs. Sorenson is less than accurate in her view that Liberals never turn on leaders. Louis St. Laurent could have corrected her after he had received the party delegation that warned him the time had come to move aside. That was after the party's 1957 defeat. He responded by retiring. The dagger was shown to the defeated leader so discreetly that most party members never knew of it.

It is by the exercise of great discretion, not lemming-like servility, that great national parties not only protect themselves from leaders who have run the course but build reputations for undying loyalty to leaders, regardless of performance. But while that happens in great national parties it may not occur in weakened regional ones.

THE TORONTO STAR, JUNE 12, 1982

PATRONAGE:
Is it blatant corruption or a necessary evil?

"Patronage is power. Our men won the victory and they are entitled to the prize money."

—Letter to Robert Baldwin, Upper Canada reformist leader, in 1843.

By Roger Smith Star special news services.

OTTAWA — The Canadian political pork barrel is richer and more contentious than ever.

Patronage may be less prevalent now than in days when every federal government opening was filled with a friend of the party in power, but political stripes still mean as much as merit in thousands of top federal and provincial jobs and contracts.

Rewards range from high-paid plums reaped by senators, ambassadors and heads of Crown corporations down to jobs as census-takers and toll collectors on government docks.

Even invitations to meet the Queen during her recent visit were used to pay off loyal Liberal workers.

Despite its long history, patronage outrages critics who want the practice ended and touches off debates about whether it is blatant corruption or a "necessary evil." Some say the focus on party connections obscures the blue-ribbon credentials of many appointees.

"If you said: 'Listen, there's no way we can appoint anyone who's been a Liberal,' surely that would be insane," said Multiculturalism Minister Jim Fleming. "Patronage is legitimate, if indeed you also appoint people who are competent."

Norman Ward, a political scientist at

the University of Saskatchewan, agrees, saying unfairly negative connotations have been linked to patronage. "It's become almost a dirty word," he said.

But critics argue party service is too often the overriding factor in filling key jobs and say the public can't be blamed for cynicism when they see:

☐ Former cabinet minister Jack Horner, defeated in the 1979 and 1980 elections after switching to the Liberals from the Progressive Conservatives, named chairman of Canadian National Railways at an annual salary of about $100,000.

☐ Arthur Erickson, Prime Minister Pierre Trudeau's friend, chosen to design a new embassy in Washington over four other recommended architects.

☐ Peter Stollery appointed to a $56,500-a-year Senate seat so Jim Coutts, formerly Trudeau's principal secretary, could run for Parliament. Coutts lost the Spadina by-election last summer.

Horner follows a long line of Liberals who have found greener and richer pastures, thanks to the federal cabinet's power, through order-in-council appointments, to fill almost 2,000 jobs. More than one-third of Trudeau's original 28-member cabinet in 1968 have already cashed in.

Defeated candidates

Leo Cadieux, then Gerard Pelletier, were ambassadors to France and Paul Martin became Canadian High Commissioner in London. One minister became a judge, two went to the Senate and several were named to head Crown corporations or agencies — Mitchell Sharp at the Northern Pipeline Agency, Edgar Benson at the Canadian Transport Commission, Bud Drury at the National Capital Commission and Bryce Mackasey, briefly, at Air Canada. Jean-Pierre Cote became lieutenant governor of Quebec.

Federal Liberals also look after defeated candidates, provincial allies and party workers by doling out order-in-council appointments as deputy ministers, judges, directors of Crown corporations, members of federal regulatory agencies and a host of lesser posts.

Ministers also decide who gets key contracts and where major projects should go. For example, a planned uranium refinery in Northern Ontario was switched to a Liberal riding from a Tory one after

the 1980 election. The same things happen in the provinces. The new Tory government of Saskatchewan is presently busy purging New Democrat appointees to make way for its own supporters.

Joe Clark's administration made several patronage appointments but was criticized within the party for not making more, a sign the Tories have a cleaner record on patronage at least partly because they have been in power only seven of the past 47 years. Nonetheless, the Conservatives railed against the choice of Horner and Erickson.

The rhetoric in such instances tends to blur the fine line between legitimate appointments and abuse of power. Even outside observers are uncertain where it should be drawn.

Several acknowledge there is merit in the defence of Horner's appointment on the grounds he is a westerner with experience as chairman of the Commons transport committee and as Tory transport critic.

But J.E. Hodgetts, a political economist from the University of Toronto, says the choice of Erickson is "corrupt behavior." Ward, however, defends political allegiance as a valid factor in such choices.

And Kenneth Gibbons, a University of Winnipeg political scientist, thinks patronage falls somewhere in the grey area between outright corruption such as bribery and "little white lies" such as trying to fix a parking ticket or stretching the truth at income tax time.

It is still accepted because many politicians contend "our party system wouldn't work without it, that it's a necessary evil." Equating elections to wars, he says party workers are motivated by the belief: "To the victor goes the spoils."

In other words, bagmen don't raise money and canvassers don't knock on doors purely out of dedication to party philosophy. Many expect a payoff.

Scramble for food

By more than one account, the term "pork barrel" originated on southern United States plantations where owners trotted out a barrel of salt pork for slaves on special occasions. The similarities between their scramble for food and the bitter scrap for jobs and contracts was not lost on observers who began applying the term to the U.S. politics in the late 1880s.

In Canada, the pork barrel was used to

fill almost every job in earlier days when government was smaller and less complicated. Writing about Sir Wilfrid Laurier's Liberal government at the turn of the century, O.D. Skelton observed: "The distribution of patronage was the most important single function of government."

With the establishment of the Civil Service Commission in the early 1900s and the growing complication of government after World War I, patronage was used less. But it was never eradicated.

One of its greatest defenders was James Gardiner, Saskatchewan premier 1926-29 and 1934-35 who later joined the federal cabinet and became czar of Liberal patronage in his province.

"He made no bones about the fact he felt the patronage way was the right way," said Ward, who is writing Gardiner's biography. In Gardiner's view, all jobs — from Christmas work in the post office to cutting grass in national parks — should go to Liberals.

When bodies of Canadian soldiers were sent home during World War II, for example, he saw to it that Liberal undertakers got first crack at the work.

When the Tories came to power in 1979, they tried to balance the need to reward workers with a desire to put competent people in key jobs. But it boomeranged.

Former MP Jean Pigott carefully assembled "yellow books" listing order-in-council positions and set about finding the needed talent. Clark made about 125 appointments, including controversial moves which put defeated Tory candidate Robert de Cotret and party strategist Lowell Murray, a Clark crony, in the Senate. Another 150 planned appointments were cancelled when the Liberals forced an election.

Clark was criticized both for the appointments he didn't make and some of the ones he did. But Pigott defends Clark's approach. The only thing that should be done differently next time is better preparation so the Tories can move more quickly.

"I don't mind if the Arts Centre is filled with every Liberal organizer when the Queen comes, that's how you reward your people," she said.

"But not when it comes to the president of regulatory bodies that affect people's lives. Those should be based on who is the best damn person."

CANADIAN PRESS

SATURDAY NIGHT, OCTOBER 1982

THE ONCE AND FUTURE KING

Before long the Conservatives must decide what to do with a leader who offers many of the strengths and some of the weaknesses of the man who kept his party in power longer than any prime minister in Canadian history

BY MICHAEL BLISS

IF MACKENZIE King reappeared in Canadian politics, and even if his personal quirks were kept under wraps, he would be unelectable, disdained by voters as a colourless wimp. The country would be poorer, for it would have chosen not to be served by the man who was perhaps our most successful prime minister.

It's not totally fanciful to suggest that Mackenzie King has been living at Stornoway for most of the past six years, disdained by many Canadians as a colourless wimp. As the Tories wash their leadership linen this winter, they have to decide what to do with a man who offers many of the strengths and some of the weaknesses of the leader who kept his party in power longer than anyone in Canadian history. Do they stick with the superficially unimpressive Joe Clark? Or do they turf him out to get the strong personality and strong views of a good-looking, good-talking outsider?

Clark resembles King in two important ways: his sense of the country and his leadership style. The sense of the country has been the most difficult of Clark's positions for even members of his own party to understand. Most Canadians, Conservatives included, are suckers for emotional nationalism on such issues as constitutional change. They have sympathized almost instinctively with Trudeau, the self-proclaimed spokesman for Canada, in his struggles against provincialism and regionalism. Clark's attempts to talk about Canada as a "community of communities," in which provincial and regional interests have to be respected, seemed pathetic, incoherent, irrelevant, or downright unpatriotic.

Mackenzie King would have understood what Joe Clark was driving at with his endless talk of our diversity, the need to conciliate the provinces,

the need to find consensus. Like it or not, the Canadian nation is the sum of a collection of provinces or regions whose unity is little more than the sum of national politicians' ability to find a practical common denominator. King made the preservation of national unity a primary political goal, and, like Macdonald and Laurier before him, was endlessly patient in courting the West, Québec, and the Maritimes (plus any other interest group he could accommodate within the Liberal Party). During the Tories' short period of government in 1979, Clark attempted to practise King-like conciliation. He didn't have time to succeed or fail on specific issues (partly because Peter Lougheed and Bill Davis were proving about as statesmanlike as William Aberhart and Mitch Hepburn had been in negotiations with King); but even in political defeat Clark has maintained the Tories as more of a national party than the Trudeau Liberals. This is an achievement King probably would have applauded, just as he probably would have recoiled in horror at what Trudeau's confrontational style has done to the Liberal Party. Maintain-

ing unity used to be seen as the essence of Canadian politics, a task ignored by only a handful of mavericks (Arthur Meighen, R.B. Bennett, Diefenbaker, and Trudeau), usually at their peril.

King also understood that no one could lead Canada who was unable or unwilling to surround himself with strong lieutenants. His governments were characterized by powerful cabinet ministers – C.D. Howe, Jimmy Gardiner, Ernest Lapointe, Louis St. Laurent, and a dozen others, many of whom had as high a profile and as much ability as the prime minister. Less colourful than many of his ministers, not really liked by more than a few of them, King was content to be a kind of shrewd chairman of the board. His personal peculiarities did not make him unable to work with other strong personalities. The evidence from Clark's six years of Tory leadership suggests a similar ability to work with strong men and women, whether they like him or not. His 1979 government was on its way to looking somewhat like a King government – star cabinet ministers carrying the ball and a quiet, low-profile quarterback handing it off.

THE Tories fumbled disastrously, of course, and the man who had lost his luggage lost the country. An accident-prone leader? All of Canada's great prime ministers made mistakes early in their careers of the same magnitude as the miscalculations of Clark. King himself got caught in the muck of a customs scandal that brought down his short-lived second government in 1926. The conventional wisdom about Sir John A. Macdonald in the early 1870s was that he had destroyed his party's future and his own in the Pacific Scandal. Perhaps Wilfrid Laurier's apprenticeship as an opposition leader after 1887 most resembled Clark's. Young Laurier was widely seen as a shallow, stop-gap leader, likely to give way after a few years to someone with more substance. His disastrous misjudgements on economic policy led the party to humiliating defeat by Macdonald in the 1891 election and to the brink of dissolution immediately afterward. No one would have dreamed in, say, 1892, that four years later Laurier would begin the first of four terms as prime minister.

Laurier learned from his mistakes. He was also helped by the thoroughness with which the Tory governments of the day destroyed themselves and their party. From the time of his government's defeat in the House in December, 1979, Clark appeared to learn from his mistakes. He ran an excellent, albeit losing, election campaign. Since February, 1980, he has led one of the most effective oppositions in recent memory, scoring repeatedly and heavily against a government sliding into disarray. His handling of the endlessly tricky constitutional issue through 1980 and 1981 was as fine and useful a piece of opposition statesmanship as Laurier's classic finessing of the Manitoba Schools Question in the mid-1890s. These would be substantial achievements by a leader fully in control of his party; that Clark has managed them while under constant, brutal harassment from his critics within and without the party is remarkable. It used to be said that Clark had not proven himself, had not shown his mettle. If he survives through the 1980s, it will be said that he won his spurs between 1980 and 1982.

Mackenzie King's lady friends and his spiritual interests did not handicap him as a politician because they were not publicly known. His "image" problem was that he was not very likable as a person (he was fussy, vain, and smarmy); not very effective as a public speaker, especially in the House; and distinctly unimpressive to look at. Clark does better than King on two of these three counts. Almost everyone who knows him likes him; the real Joe Clark is friendly, witty, self-deprecating, articulate, and well-informed. He has become a fair-to-middling public speaker, often a very good House of Commons man. His facial appearance, hairstyles, physique, and athletic skills are no more impressive than King's, and this may be a fatal handicap in a television age. On the other hand, Clark's grace and good manners are evident and shine by comparison with Trudeau's. One of Clark's paradoxes is that while media exposure has almost destroyed him, media people tend to like and respect him. Watch how many political columnists finally find a few kind words for him this fall.

When Mackenzie King wanted his way with his ministers he often threatened to resign, daring them to find an effective replacement. One cannot imagine Joe Clark having yet dared even to threaten. If he does resign this fall or winter, or is forced into a leadership fight, Tories will be surprised to realize just how short they are on effective replacements. The media, for example, would have a field day grilling aspirants for the prime ministership of Canada who cannot speak one of its official languages. For comic relief there would be the bilingual businessman who has never been elected to anything. Like the Liberals in King's time, the Conservative Party is long on credible cabinet ministers, short on credible prime ministers. (Whether or not there is a credible Tory alternative to Clark seems to depend on the quality of David Crombie's French.)

A shrewd Toronto businessman, thought to be an anti-Clark Tory, told me recently that he was personally satisfied with Joe Clark's leadership. "He's an ordinary guy, but who needs a genius? We've seen the genius screw up the country. The trouble is that while I think Clark's okay, ordinary people out there still think he's an asshole. And what can you do about that?" His suggestion was a leadership convention that Clark might well win and, in winning, clear the air. Perhaps. Perhaps the government has been destroying itself so thoroughly and the economy collapsing into such a mess that a Tory leadership fight will seem a pointless blood-letting. As this was written, Clark's showing in the polls – against Trudeau, Turner, or any other Liberal – seemed to make him unassailable.

If Canadians understood their politics and their history, Mackenzie King would not be the figure of fun he appears in our ahistorical memory. King's low standing in our political rating-game actually says more about our own failure of understanding than it does about King as a politician. Joe Clark's reputation and political future are snarled in the same web of trendy ignorance. The prospect of his being cut down by the demands of our system, or by the looniness of his party, suggests that in the 1980s we may have lost even the capacity to give ourselves the leadership we deserve. ◄

THE FINANCIAL POST, FEBRUARY 5, 1983

Are the Conservatives living in Canada?

By Michael Bliss

JOE CLARK was brought down by people with the political sense of a turnip. Here is why:

1. Canada is officially a bilingual country. Many Canadian institutions, including the federal government, are officially bilingual. Most top jobs in the civil service require the ability to speak both of Canada's official languages. We are in the 1980s now, not the 1960s. It has become unthinkable that a man or woman who is unable to talk or understand one of its official languages should hold the highest office in this country.

Anachronism

The unilingual candidates for the Conservative leadership will be grilled unmercifuly by the media on this subject. Rightly so, for the very candidacy of someone who has not cared enough to become even moderately bilingual would be an anachronism and an affront to millions of his countrymen. This is only the most obvious reason why Peter Lougheed and William Davis, to name only two of the unilingual leadership aspirants, are unsuitable as candidates to be Prime Minister of Canada.

2. It is ridiculous to think that the Canadian people would select as Prime Minister a man who has cared so little for public life that he has never run for any elected office.

A party so desperate that it has to bypass *all* of its elected members to bring in a totally inexperienced outsider would be held in contempt by all Canadians with a political IQ over 50. A party that has to take a Brian Mulroney candidacy seriously is admitting it is unfit to form a government. A Conservative Party led by Brian Mulroney would be lucky to win 70 seats in a federal election.

3. There is a world of difference between dumping Diefenbaker in 1967 and ousting Joe Clark in 1983. Diefenbaker had lost two elections (three counting 1962), had lost the allegiance of the young, was going nowhere in the polls, and was blindly clinging to personal power. He would never have gone voluntarily, and the party would have died with him. Clark, by contrast, was young, moderate, learning from his mistakes, miles ahead of the Liberals in the polls. Dalton Camp and those like him who opposed Diefenbaker then and supported Clark now have been utterly consistent in defending the welfare of the party against personal ambitions and primitive ideology.

4. If Clark stays firm in his decision to run for the leadership, the most likely result of the race will be the destruction of his opponents' political careers. If those who fomented the disloyalty to the leader do not declare themselves now, their cowardice will destroy their credibility. If they come into the arena and lose, they will not be forgiven for having put the party through such pointless trauma. The odds are that Joe Clark will be firmly entrenched as Tory leader 12 months from now.

So much blood may have been spilled by then — or, more likely, so much ridicule and laughter directed at the hapless Tories — that the Progressive Conservative Party will be crippled for at least another decade. And we will continue to be a one-party state, our democracy itself crippled because there is no alternative to the Liberal Party. Crippled because of the alliance of right-wing ideologues, second-rate power mongers, and feather-brained Torontonians who stabbed the Conservative Party in Winnipeg just as it was returning to life and health.

Mindless chroniclers

It should be noted that they were helped along in their wrecking effort by the low level of political analysis which is a consistent feature of our media's coverage of national politics. There are a few honorable exceptions, but by and large our political journalists, who ought to have been helping to clarify, sharpen and forecast our political options, chose instead to serve as mindless chroniclers or cheer leaders of the lemming instinct in the Progressive Conservative Party. The Canadian media make about the same contribution to wise political discourse as Pac-man does to computer science.

MICHAEL BLISS *is an author and Canadian historian.*

THE GLOBE AND MAIL, JANUARY 27, 1983

For the record

BY MICHAEL VALPY

WINNIPEG

Today some memory-nudges for the Conservatives, milling in the Winnipeg Convention Centre. If they're going to review Joe Clark's leadership, they might try to do a thorough job.

Specifically, they might review Mr. Clark's record as chief executive officer of the national Government in 1979. That's an excellent yardstick of his leadership ability.

The record shows that during his brief months in the Prime Minister's Office (PMO), he created a remarkably bright, zesty and open-sunshine atmosphere in political and bureaucratic Ottawa.

He was praised by senior officials of the Privy Council Office (PCO) — including Michael Pitfield, whom he fired as secretary to the Cabinet — for his quick grasp of government's complexities.

Bureaucrats and former aides recall how speedily after Mr. Clark took over the dynamics changed in the Langevin Block, the building housing the PMO and PCO.

PCO professionals who had become frustrated either by inactivity or by being ignored by Pierre Trudeau and his staff suddenly found in their presence a warm, inquisitive, intelligent, energetic man, genuinely seeking their suggestions and showing interest and enthusiasm in their ideas.

One of Mr. Clark's first acts was to meet with the Government's most senior public servants and spell out what his relationship with them was going to be. Many of them, once they got his measure, made no secret around town of how much they liked and respected him.

Treasury Board was delighted when Mr. Clark adopted significant revisions to controls over government spending — in particular, the envelope system which compelled ministries to work within fixed expenditure perimeters, a reform the Liberals kept when they returned to power.

He tried to simplify the work of government and of governing, from the Cabinet level on down. He tried (with commendable success for the short period he held office) to make the whole process of government more open.

Journalists who were not satisfied with his answers at press conferences frequently found themselves called by PMO officials and invited over to the Langevin Block for further explanations and backgrounding (unheard of with the Liberals).

Mr. Clark promoted the new atmosphere of openness at the Cabinet table — and remember that he was the manager of the Government's timetable, its priorities and its tone.

His ministers tried to give straightforward, responsible answers in Question Period. His Government introduced freedom of information legislation after years of stalling by the Liberals.

It produced a white paper on parliamentary reform. It introduced legislation to make Crown corporations more accountable to the public — proposals far and away more substantial than those contained in the bill that the Liberals now have brought in.

Mr. Clark was eager to get more women appointed to senior bureaucratic and patronage posts — Jean Wadds to the Canadian High Commission in London, for example.

He strove to build good relationships with the provincial premiers. British Columbia's William Bennett once recalled how Mr. Clark would call him just to chat, or to ask his advice on issues. "Pierre never did that," said Premier Bennett.

Mr. Clark put Pierre Trudeau's battleship limousine up on blocks and travelled in a much humbler car. He and his wife, Maureen McTeer, opened up 24 Sussex Drive to Canadians as it has never been opened before or since.

The list goes on.

Square all that with his critics' claim that he can't be marketed.

Requiem for a featherweight

By Peter C. Newman

There was a kind of oldtime radio rhythm to Joe Clark's crucial speech at the Conservative convention in Winnipeg last week as he kept insisting that he is everything his scrapbooks claim him to be.

His cheeks made brave attempts to become jowls as he chewed his thoughts, calling on the tricks of a lifetime in politics to rescue him. The appeal didn't rouse the doubters because the speech—and the man making it—failed to comprehend what Canadian politics is all about. It is not, as Clark kept repeating, about such bunkum as "beating the Liberals" or "fulfilling Canada's destiny," whatever that is. Nor does successful statesmanship in this country flow from the elegant droppings of computers or the Tories' $200,000 worth of audiovisual equipment. Political leadership in these frigid latitudes ultimately is an exercise in magic. It has to do with a party leader's capacity for filling his followers with enchantment, a sense of mission that goes beyond partisan name-calling: the leader's ability to turn himself into the embodiment of the nation he hopes to govern.

This, Joe Clark can never do.

He has, after all, been campaigning since the 1981 leadership review, stumping the country, making countless "do not reject this man" speeches about himself. Yet he has managed to raise his approval rating by a stunning half per cent.

All politicians are haunted, not by their enemies but by their former selves. It is seven years now since Joe Clark was chosen to lead the Conservatives into power. He did it, ending a 16-year streak of Liberal rule, only to be humbled back into opposition by a combination of miscalculation and just plain stupidity. The memory of his brief fling in office is not that of a maker of decisions or dispenser of favors to power-starved Tories but of a frightened creature retreating from his own

policy clinkers, such as moving the Canadian Embassy to Jerusalem and dismantling Petro-Canada. Last week's convention demonstrated that Clark has come dangerously close to wearing out his welcome. Just as few TV comedians now have a viewing expectancy of more than a couple of seasons (though they could go on for 20 years on the vaudeville circuit), a politician must succeed or be replaced.

Clark's failure to impress the Conservative party was caused by at least three self-inflicted wounds. He suffered from poor intelligence from Quebec, listening to the discredited hacks left over from the Union Nationale era while ignoring the outriders of the new political army Brian Mulroney was mobilizing east of the Ottawa River. At the same time, Clark discarded too many of his former alliances. Of the five key organizers who had masterminded his original bid for the leadership in 1976, for example, only two (Harvie Andre and Jim Hawkes, who became MPs) were in Winnipeg. The others (the campaign's national co-chairman, Montreal lawyer Pierre Bouchard; Dave King, an Alberta Tory who is now Peter Lougheed's minister of education; and Ralph Hedlin, a Saskatchewan-born energy expert) weren't officially invited.

The preconvention tussle with Peter Worthington hurt Clark badly because he was perceived as being unable to handle one renegade delegate—at a time when he was applying to resolve the country's complex economic problems. (The Liberals would have had no trouble soothing Senator Worthington's feathers.)

Watching the Tory party in conclave was a sobering experience, even if the delegates themselves drank enough booze to pickle a pharaoh. They were all there, the bushy-tailed Mulroney people, with smiles on their faces and mur-

der in their hearts; the defrocked zealots from the Age of Diefenbaker, worn out by years of political outrage; the prime-time guys who had jetted in from Toronto, scrutinizing Clark through slit eyes, like pawnbrokers trying to calculate the downside risk of sticking by him. The charmers came from British Columbia, and the heavy breathers from rural Saskatchewan and Alberta, sipping Styrofoam coffee out of Styrofoam cups, cursing a world they never made.

What these and other delegates had in common—what unites the Conservatives into a political movement—is that no true-blue Tory recognizes any statute of limitations in the party's internal feuds. Conservatives' hatreds for one another don't fade like sorrow or fizzle like anger. They just keep growing. It's not a new phenomenon. Between 1887 and 1948, for instance, the Liberals stayed loyal to two leaders: Sir Wilfrid Laurier and Mackenzie King. The Tories, on the other hand, managed to inflict on themselves no fewer than 12 new chieftains who kept them out of power during most of those same 61 years. (Even the party's official label—Progressive Conservative—seems a contradiction in terms, like military intelligence or Canadian humor.)

What Canada lacks at the moment is a government with moral authority. We have at the helm of our political parties an odd couple of used-up hoofers with no prospect of rescuing themselves. Now, at least, the process of succession has begun, and, with the Tories launched into a leadership contest, the Liberals cannot afford to be far behind.

Joe Clark may have guts to burn, but as a national leader he has nowhere to go but out. The only thing that saved him from an even worse humiliation in Winnipeg was that most of the other contenders for the Tory crown were relative strangers to the party's rank and file. Even so, for Joe Clark, familiarity did not breed consent.

THE TORONTO STAR, SEPTEMBER 5, 1981

Ottawa: Where power is the fascination

Is it in the hands of the ministers or mandarins?

By Val Sears Toronto Star

OTTAWA — Henry Kissinger called it "the greatest aphrodisiac of all."

Politicians hunger for it.

Bureaucrats contrive, conspire, even work very hard to win it.

Power.

And yet in these last damp days of summer — as Ottawa waits for Parliament to open — power hangs as limply over the capital as the flag on the peace tower. It is diffused, uncertain, lacking in focus.

Jim Coutts, the prince of power brokers, is gone, broken by the voters of Spadina as he sought to leap from advice — as the prime minister's principal secretary — to action as a minister in the cabinet.

Prime Minister Pierre Trudeau, once all powerful, is a lame duck, preparing to leave office, while his ministers jostle to replace him.

The other party leaders, Joe Clark of the Progressive Conservatives and Ed Broadbent of the New Democrats, are beleagured losers, threatened and increasingly isolated.

And the Rideau Club, court of the bureaucratic mandarins for decades, has burned down, leaving the ambitious to conspire at the austere Cercle Universitaire or huddle over the lasagna at Mama Teresas.

As one Ottawa hostess lamented: "It is so difficult to give a party these days. No one seems to fit anywhere anymore."

Nonetheless, power, even more than money, is the mothers' milk of politics. It nourishes ambition, and so, endlessly, it is discussed, haggled over, written about in learned political journals.

From the bars of Lowertown to the dance floor at Bob Campeau's mansion out in the horsey country at the edge of the city, everyone wants to know: Who is doing what to whom? Who has it? Who is losing it?

And perhaps most fascinating of all: Who really runs the country? Is it the ministers who come and go? Or is power really in the hands of the civil service mandarins who stay on forever?

Mitchell Sharp, who has been both a deputy minister in the civil service and a minister under Lester Pearson and Pierre Trudeau, asks: "To what extent are we being governed by a back-room bureaucracy? This is a serious question."

Profoundly deferential

Sharp is not sure he has a complete answer. Much depends, he says, on the strength of the minister and the skill of his deputy.

But he is prepared to argue that the Canadian experience is not like that of some British ministers, particularly Richard Crossman who serves under the Labour Party's Harold Wilson. Crossman wrote in his diaries:

"My minister's room is like a padded cell, and in certain ways, I am like a person who is suddenly certified a lunatic and put safely into this great, vast room, cut off from real life and surrounded by male and female trained nurses and attendants.

"When I am in a good mood, they occasionally allow an ordinary human being to come and visit me; but they make sure that I behave right and that the other person behaves right; and they know how to handle me.

"Of course, they don't behave quite like nurses because the civil service is profoundly deferential — 'yes, minister, no, minister.'"

Still . . . Flora MacDonald, who was external affairs minister in the brief Clark government, has written bitterly of her experience in the hands of senior bureaucrats: "I think that resistance resides almost entirely among those who really have their hands on the levers of power — the senior mandarins."

She says they tried to thwart her designs by (breathlessly) forcing decisions on her in a corridor; by long, unreadable memos, by preparing her submissions to cabinet too late for her to appraise them properly and by "one-dimensional" opinions offered her.

Novice ministers must necessarily place themselves in the hands of their deputies at first. Whether they ever get out of that control — acting as little more than salesmen for the programs their managers have devised — depends on their own confidence and strength.

Paul Cosgrove, former mayor of Scarborough and now Minister of Public Works in the Trudeau cabinet, says he was so green when he arrived in Ottawa a year and a half ago that, told he would have to "carry legislation into the House", he had visions of "totting a large book down the centre aisle."

"Fortunately," he says, "my deputy is rather my type, no back-slapping extrovert. He has a sense of humor and he's a diplomat. I depend upon him for a great deal of the work. But when I say 'no,' he does it my way."

The principal mandarins in Ottawa are the deputy ministers, appointed at the pleasure of the prime minister. They are powerful, envied men who earn up to $78,800 a year and work their heads off.

Once, in simpler times under St. Laurent and Pearson, they were the administrative heads of government, meeting over gins at the Rideau Club or the Gatineau fishing club to run the country, while their masters fiddled with the lesser business of politics.

When Trudeau was elected he set out to break their power. Whether he has succeeded is what makes the debate so interesting.

Trudeau made no bones about the need to "do away with the sluggishness and resistance to change of entrenched bureaucracies."

Almost as soon as he became prime minister, he told his ministers it would not be good enough for them simply to bring their deputy's programs to cabinet for approval. They must understand them, do their homework and be prepared to defend their sponsorship before their colleagues at the cabinet committee table.

There would be a principle of "collegiality", he said. Everyone must agree or the program goes back for more work.

But the deputies would have their own forum, as well — The Mirror Committee.

These meetings of deputies would "mirror" their masters' committee, for a final co-ordinating look at programs before the politicians got at them.

Some ministers argue that these mirror committees increase deputies' power by giving them an all but final word on legislation. They can stall, argue and advise more study if the program does not suit them.

And the deputies know how to apply a touch of the whip. In their book, The Super-Bureaucrats, authors Colin Campbell and George Szablowski tell of one deputy who was out of town when a meeting he should have attended was held.

Social dynamics

Immediately upon his return, he sent a memo to his minister. "During my absence and without my knowledge a cabinet-committee meeting was held and a decision taken against which I had no opportunity to speak. This must not happen again."

Some deputies are privately contemptuous of the ministers they serve and of the documents they must prepare for cabinet.

Doug Hartle, now a political science professor but once a senior official in treasury board, wrote a fictional essay on the mandarin approach to ministers that is widely circulated in Ottawa as close to the truth.

Hartle's not-so-fictional mandarin has to prepare a memo:

"To give and not to give; to be weak while appearing to be strong; to be obscure while appearing to be forthright; to be inconsistent while appearing to be infinitely reasonable. The hallmarks of a successful Memorandum to Cabinet."

Veteran politicians here agree there are standouts among the 32 deputies who move from ministry to ministry: Mickey Cohen in Energy; Al Gottlieb of external (soon to be ambassador in Washington); Bob Johnstone, Industry Trade and Commerce; Ian Stewart in finance and Gordon Smith in Social Development.

Just behind them in the social dynamics of power are such comers as de Montigny Marchand in External and, in the prime minister's office, Joyce Fairburn and her husband Mike Gillan, who bring people together for parties in their garden.

Jack Manion, secretary of the Treasury Board and veteran mandarin, Gordon Osbaldeston in Economic Development, are high up on the scale.

As the government grows and governing grows more complex, it is argued, the power of individual deputies diminishes. There are 100 movers and shakers in Ottawa now where there were not two dozen a decade ago.

Others, Sharp among them, insist governing has become so complex and individual ministers are so harried and consumed by work that some ministries are virtually "out of control." (Cosgrove works weekdays from 8 a.m. to midnight in an effort to keep on top.).

Robert Bryce, former clerk of the privy council and thus chief mandarin, says ministers have to cut back on constituency work, depend more on the polls to advise them of the feeling in the country and thus add another set of professionals to government.

Find sinecures

Bryce notes, incidentally, one of the chief mandarin's worries is to find sinecures for incompetent or incompatible deputy ministers.

The complexity power argument is circular: If government is more complex, doesn't that give the bureaucrats even more power over their amateur and overworked ministers?

Before any obvious power centres can be re-established in the capital, the questions of party leadership have to be settled.

Trudeau is such a commanding figure that his retirement will leave a vacuum.

Sharp put Trudeau's power role in perspective: "At Pearson's cabinet table, we ministers could say: 'He's here because we're here.' But with Trudeau we had to say: 'We're here because he's here.'"

Tom Axworthy, Coutts' successor, is more policy oriented than manipulative, and his role as a broker is still to be established.

And sometime there has to be a new Rideau Club.

Meanwhile, Ottawa's fascination with power flourishes, fuelled by such stories as that of Winston Churchill speaking to his Permanent Secretary — corresponding to a deputy-minister in Canada:

"I know, Sir Edward, that you are the Permanent Secretary, and I am only the Minister, but at least I think that you should give some consideration to my views."

THE TORONTO STAR, JUNE 28, 1980

Ministers are showered with lengthy memos and rushed into decisions by bureaucrats pushing their projects

New 'hidden government' grips Ottawa

By Stephen Handelman
Toronto Star

OTTAWA — An aide to a senior minister in the last government was startled to get a telephone call from a civil servant preparing a policy memo.

"Do you want to hear both sides of the argument?" the civil servant asked.

Most people outside government probably assume a minister makes a decision after getting all sides of an issue. And that a cabinet minister, as an elected politician, makes the decisions that count.

That's not always true. In fact, there's virtually a "hidden government" at work in Ottawa these days.

The man or woman who can keep paper moving smoothly through endless government channels holds the key to power. In the new era, civil servants supply more than just the answers; they're in charge of the questions.

Disturbing trend

The trend is disturbing many people both inside and outside government. Observers have already noted the existence of an influential group of senor civil servants — some have called them "super-bureaucrats" — who make the choices that keep the system running regardless of who's in power.

The system is now firmly locked in place, helped along by some little-known changes in the structure of bureaucracy during the past year.

☐ A short while ago, one Liberal minister was violently opposed to plans to spend $100 million on a certain federal building in Ottawa. Civil servants in his department wanted the project to go ahead. So they smuggled the plans out to another sympathetic minister . . . and the recommendation presented to cabinet was positive.

☐ Certain officials of a crown corporation who were sending their cabinet minister all the documentation necessary to keep a multi-million-dollar project afloat made a habit of delaying everything until the last minute. The minister never really got a chance to examine the details, and when he balked, he was reminded the deadline was pressing.

The spread of federal agencies and services has created a new decision-making process in Ottawa which gives top priority to efficiency.

Powerful committees of anonymous civil servants now map out the agenda and set the priorities for overworked cabinet ministers. They can be responsible for decisions ranging from whether to locate a government installation up the block from your house to whether to impose a new tax regime.

"It's an obvious danger to a democratic system," says one former top assistant to several Liberal cabinet ministers.

"The people you want to make decisions are the people who are supposed to be accountable to the public, the politicians, not a bureaucratic elite."

The assistant and others who are concerned about the situation are quick to say there is no sinister plot on the part of the public service. Many, in fact, insist that without the new management systems, government just couldn't work.

"It's just not right to say we are all working together in some sort of cabal," says another insider who has served under both the Tories and Liberals.

"But I guess it's true to say there are a lot of ways we can put the minister under pressure to accept something: if he says no to something you propose, you can make it sound like the Third World War is about to happen, and what can he do?"

Thrives on secrecy

Not the least of the system's dangers is that it thrives on secrecy.

The people who know what's going on are often the same people who stand to lose the most by blowing the whistle. Many of the past and present civil servants and minister's aides interviewed by The Star insisted their names not be used. "I still have to work with these people," explained one.

That's why it was something of a shock when former External Affairs Minister Flora MacDonald decided to go public this month with the frustrations she felt as minister — and in the process lifted the curtain for a rare look at the secret life of government.

She complained in a Montreal speech that her job was made more difficult by the red tape thrown up by a bureaucracy intent on preserving its own interests. She warned of a "looking-glass jungle" of civil servants and high mandarins who know how to keep an unwary politician on the outside looking in.

"Too many bureaucrats, I fear, have the mistaken impression that vigorous debate of policy options by cabinet ministers is an indication that they — the bureaucrats — have somehow failed to properly channel and co-ordinate views before the cabinet meeting takes place," she said.

Miss MacDonald noted the problems are also common to senior bureaucracies in Great Britain and the United States. And she listed some "entrapment devices" used by Canadian civil servants to influence ministers:
☐ The "crisis corridor" technique in which a civil servant races up to his minister demanding an important decision without leaving any time to think about it;
☐ Floods of lengthy memos which bury the minister in a mass of often irrelevant verbiage, such as the measurements for an External Affairs booth at the Canadian National Exhibition;
☐ Eleventh-hour delivery of mammoth background papers for cabinet on which recommendations will have to be made without any chance of checking other opinions;
☐ The technique of giving "one-dimensional options," in which the minister is forced to pick the one supported by his own bureaucrats.

Miss MacDonald is sensitive to any objection that she's conducting a one-woman revenge on the people who worked for her.

"I'm not saying it's me against them," she insisted later in an interview. "Ministers in other administrations are confronted with the same thing."

Only hope

But she points out the only real hope of changing it is to use a broader range of views in the making of government policy, with special advisers independent of the civil service and public hearings and debates on major issues.

"The biggest problem for a minister is how do you get independent advice," she says. "Otherwise, the system can be structured against you; the greatest growth rate in the civil service now is at the very top."

According to the Public Service Commission, the number of senior executives in the top echelons of government departments has nearly tripled in less than a decade, from 618 in 1971 to 1,790 in 1979.

While many people agree with Miss MacDonald's recommendations, they take issue with parts of her analysis, suggesting that if civil servants are allowed to get the better of a minister, the blame must be laid at the feet of the minister or his staff.

"A department will always try to capture a minister," says one former executive assistant. "Once you let a deputy minister schedule the minister's time, that's it."

"The problem with the Tories was that they just didn't have the experience of managing power when they got in," says another civil servant. "After all, it had been 16 years since they had been in government.

"When the Liberals took office in February, every would-be minister got at least 18 calls from potential assistants who came out of the woodwork from Toronto and Ottawa and Montreal — all good people who knew the ropes, who in fact were almost a farm team. The Tories couldn't command that kind of farm team."

Deeper problem

But the problem goes deeper. Even the most skillful Ottawa politician can't hope to master all the details of a complicated portfolio, and he can find himself rapidly indebted to the "experts."

"One of the amazing things I discovered after I'd been in office for a while was how well things carried on without me," recalls former energy minister Ray Hnatyshyn. "It meant that I didn't have to be overwhelmed by all the technical details and decisions that they kept pushing in front of me."

Hnatyshyn has seen the change happen over a generation. When he first came to Ottawa in 1958 as a young executive assistant to the government leader in the Senate, government was comparatively easy.

"I knew everybody that I had to liase with in my job and I knew everybody's name," he says. "You could almost contain everybody in a single room."

But as government progressively got involved in expensive social programs, and as domestic and international relations grew more complicated, a new system had to be developed.

A decision taken by the Ministry of Transport could also affect Industry, Trade and Commerce. If the agriculture minister wants to transfer funds from a milk subsidy, he may now need the advice of the Treasury Board to know the full impact of his decision.

The result of these complex new interrelationships has been the creation of two "super-ministries" which group together departments to make decision-making more efficient:
☐ The Ministry of State for Economic Development, headed by Alberta Senator Bud Olson, which co-ordinates the work of 16 senior government departments;
☐ The new Ministry of State for Social Development, under Jean Chretien, which is intended to group together 10 government departments involved in the making of social policy.

Under a system first introduced by the Tories under Joe Clark last year and effectively adopted by the Liberals, these giant ministries act as powerful cabinet subcommittees, allocating resources within their separate departments — a function once held by the cabinet acting as a whole.

A new bureaucracy has been created to serve these ministries, formed partly from the deputy ministers and executives of each of the departments grouped together, and from bureaucrats working for the two super-ministries.

Lobby ministers

Since the individual ministers now face an even more imposing array of decisions and policy problems, the bureaucrats do most of the initial groundwork.

"Quite often the deputy ministers responsible for the departments brought together under economic development will decide together what issues need to be brought up, and then lobby each of their individual ministers to get them to vote in committee for the compromise they have worked out,'' explains one insider.

''It used to be true that whoever had information had power; now it's also true that whoever gets the agenda in government has power.''

The system has obvious flaws. Bureaucrats, meeting in what some have called a ''mirror committee of deputies'' have no need to be sensitive to the political impact of various decisions.

But it can also fundamentally un-dermine the independence of ministers, and aides are full of the resulting ''horror stories.''

''I would get a letter marked 'for minister's eyes only,''' remembers one former Tory assistant. ''And then I would discover that the entire group of them already knew what was in it.''

Miss MacDonald lamented the tendency to create bureaucratic structures which become as powerful as ministers.

''One wonders how many such mirror committees of deputies a cabinet minister can cope with before he or she ends up surrounded by a wall of mirrors,'' she said. ''Even Alice in Wonderland might have difficulty in finding her way through what is likely to become a looking-glass jungle, presenting the illusion of ministerial control.''

The new Liberal ministers also have some misgivings about the system, but they are keeping an open mind.

''It can be a danger for a new and inexperienced government,'' says Multiculturalism Minister Jim Fleming. ''But I think it's a system that allows for tough interchange of views.''

THE GLOBE AND MAIL, OCTOBER 4, 1982

GEORGE BAIN

HALIFAX

Joe Clark persists in letting on — he can't believe it; there is too much evidence against it — that Pierre Trudeau acts according to some consistent political philosophy.

Clark was at it again after the cabinet shuffle when he said, evidently against the suggestion that there had been a rightward shift, that ''there can be no shift to the right in a government that has Pierre Trudeau as prime minister and Marc Lalonde as his minister of finance.''

That seemingly was to say they are anchored, on the left. But what the record shows is that Pierre Trudeau, and the whole crew with him, Marc Lalonde included, has flitted across the spectrum as the spirit (and/or Martin Goldfarb) moved him.

Take away official bilingualism and incorporation of a charter of rights in the constitution and the one thing he has been steadfastly intent on doing with public office is keeping himself in it.

Joe Clark must remember — he couldn't not — the night of Dec. 11 and the afternoon of Dec. 12, 1979.

His government's one budget has just been presented. Herb Gray is on his feet as Liberal finance critic. He gives the Tories hell. He calls up visions of the Great Depression and a government which, he says, ''had the same fixation with the deficit.''

He speaks of the ''doctrinaire Conservative fixation with the Government's deficit,'' the health of the economy deserving not to be ''looked at primarily in terms of the Government's deficit,'' of the Government's ''bizarre fixation with the deficit.''

Come forward to Sept. 30, 1982. The chairman of the Economic Council of Canada gently chides the Government — Herb Gray's government now — ''not to be spooked by the deficit numbers.'' Deficit or no, the council thinks the Government — Herb Gray's government now — should risk $2-billion more to create jobs.

When Gray spoke in 1979, unemployment was 7.3 per cent. Now it's 12.2 per cent. The Economic Council says it will stay above 10 per cent until at least 1987 if present policies continue.

Who is being shunted off at this moment to the presidency of Treasury Board, the pruning post of government, certainly not an initiating one? Herb Gray.

Who is moving up in the cabinet hierarchy? Donald Johnson, late of Treasury Board, who promptly dismisses the Economic Council's suggested $2 billion of tax cuts. He cites the deficit, which he calls ''stimulation enough.''

Not by the Liberals' own (election) standard. Not with more than a million unemployed. Nor is it the case that concern for unemployment exceeding concern for the deficit was just an amiable quirk of Herb Gray's in 1980. It was policy.

For one of many examples, consider Pierre Trudeau (Kamloops, Feb. 6, 1980): ''My answer is that our government ... would not make the reduction of the deficit into a fetish ... It's a matter of using the deficit to make sure that jobs are created ...''

The administration of the Foreign Investment Review Agency (FIRA) is something else for which the cabinet shuffle is supposed to have significance; it has been given to Ed Lumley, who is lukewarm, from Gray, who is a believer.

Compared with the record on foreign investment, even a swing from stimulative to contractionary budgeting as the prescription to unemployment becomes a model of constancy.

When Walter Gordon was promoting economic nationalism in the Sixties, Trudeau was cold. He found U.S. economic domination, he said in a 1968 interview, ''somewhat inevitable.'' It didn't worry him.

He was opportunistically for regulation — FIRA came into being then — when the NDP, which wanted it, let his government live for two years in the 1972-74 minority parliament. He was against it when he appointed Jack Horner, an avowed foe, to administer it. He was for it — FIRA was to be strengthened — when that seemed likely to yield Ontario votes in 1980. Now? Cool again.

Joe Clark runs the risk of having people think he hasn't been paying attention, talking as if he detected some guiding principle in all this.

THE TORONTO STAR, SEPTEMBER 12, 1982

The cabinet-making ritual

OTTAWA — Rumors and speculation about imminent cabinet changes have temporarily been satiated by the Prime Minister's announcement of senior portfolio shuffles. Some observers, disillusioned by the scope of the changes, are already looking forward to the second round of changes to be announced later this fall.

They will, however, notice a familiar pattern in this traditional ritual which often precedes a new session of Parliament. Each time, regardless of which party is in power, there is an implicit public criticism of the Prime Minister and his ability to choose wise and appropriate ministers. The charge is invariably accompanied by a notion that major cabinet changes are necessary, but that only a few cosmetic adjustments will be made.

Senior faces

There is some justification for this widespread public scepticism. Once again the most senior faces remain the same, only the titles have changed. In Trudeau's defence, however, it should be noted that Canadian prime ministers are in straitjackets when it comes to choosing their cabinet ministers. Regional demands must be met before all others. Criteria such as intelligence and expertise may not be primary considerations. In fact, sometimes one wonders if they are even on the list.

This widely recognized fact is illustrated by the true story of an MP who was told he would not be

ROBERT JACKSON

selected for the cabinet because he was not talented enough. The unfortunate soul replied that he was not asking to be made a deputy minister, only a cabinet minister.

All prime ministers since confederation have encountered the same restrictions in choosing their teams. In fact, Sir John A. Macdonald once described his occupation as cabinetmaker to show how much energy had to go into the selection of personnel.

In spite of the popular wisdom that Pierre Trudeau is an intellectual who constantly breaks with tradition, there has been little evidence of this in his selection of cabinet ministers. He has been just as handicapped as his predecessors in balancing personal characteristics and merit with the need to select a cabinet which is representative of the regions, provinces, cities, occupations and sexes of Canadians.

The major traditional constraint, of course, is regionalism. When the second stage of cabinet changes is announced it can be expected that they will be within the traditional guidelines. So far Trudeau has religiously followed the principle that there must be at least one minister from each province. When he had no MPs west of Manitoba, he assigned four senators for that region.

On the east coast he assigned Newfoundland, Prince Edward Island and New Brunswick each a cabinet minister. Nova Scotia is slightly over-represented with two. Traditionally, Ontario has had more cabinet ministers than Quebec, but since Trudeau's tenure Quebec has had as many or more than Ontario.

Such historical constraints prevent most dramatic shifts in cabinet personnel. To remain with tradition, for example, Trudeau cannot drop ministers from the west or east of Canada. This leaves him only Ontario and Quebec in which to manoeuvre.

Wait in droves

Meanwhile, however, eager young MPs — and often not so young — wait in droves to replace junior cabinet ministers who might have been less than outstanding in their job, or who have offended the Prime Minister. Some, anticipating promotion, have already conditionally promised jobs to staffers.

The cabinet maker's straitjacket was conceived and put into place while Canada was a very different country than it is today. Perhaps, in this era when specialization is so important, we should consider removing the traditional restrictions and allowing the Prime Minister a wider selection of cabinet material.

☐ **Robert J. Jackson is head of the political science department at Carleton University.**

Discussion Questions

1. In the past few years, it seems that people have increasingly come to identify the government with the prime minister. In light of the articles in this section, how has this personalization affected the course of Canadian politics? Has it contributed to the inevitability of the prime minister's pre-eminence? How can the prime minister exercise his power as spokesman more effectively? What are the constraints on his effectiveness?

2. It has been argued that in relation to his country's political system, Pierre Elliott Trudeau is one of the most powerful chief executives in the Western world. If so, does he derive his power from his personal attributes, his office, or both?

3. Were Joe Clark's leadership difficulties a result of his shortcomings as leader (Newman's argument) or of the contradictions in the Conservative party (Bliss's argument)?

4. On the basis of the articles here, compare the leadership styles of Pierre Trudeau and Joe Clark.

5. Among the assumptions of the Westminster model of parliamentary government are that Parliament is the focus of political attention, that Cabinet is chaired by a prime minister who is merely first among equals, that the government's policies reflect public opinion as expressed by Parliament, that ministers are responsible for the activities of their departments, and that an impartial civil service carries out Parliament's will. How do these assumptions measure up to the trends observed by Crane, Sears, and Handelman?

6. Is Sears's description of the dominance of central agencies in Canada true of all government decisions? Would it be more accurate to say that officials prevail when matters of detail are important, whereas the prime minister and his Cabinet do when large matters of political importance arise?

7. Does the power of the prime minister emasculate Cabinet and Parliament, or has the growth of government merely brought all these bodies increased work, responsibilities, power, and influence?

Suggested Readings

Walter D. Young. 'Leadership and Canadian Politics', in John H. Redekop, ed. *Approaches to Canadian Politics*, second edition. Toronto: Prentice-Hall, 1983, 267–91.

Paul W. Fox, ed. *Politics: Canada*, fifth edition. Toronto: McGraw-Hill Ryerson, 1982, 460–82.

E. Colin Campbell. 'Political Leadership in Canada: Pierre Elliott Trudeau and the Ottawa Model', in Richard Rose and Ezra N. Suleiman, eds. *Presidents and Prime Ministers*. Washington: American Enterprise Institute, 1980, 50–93.

Richard Gwyn. *The Northern Magus: Pierre Trudeau and Canadians.* Toronto: McClelland and Stewart, 1980.

Jeffrey Simpson. *Discipline of Power: The Conservative Interlude and the Liberal Restoration.* Toronto: Personal Library, 1980.

David Humphreys. *Joe Clark: A Portrait.* Toronto: Totem Books, 1979.

George Radwanski. *Trudeau.* Toronto: Macmillan, 1978.

R.M. Punnett. *The Prime Minister in Canadian Government and Politics.* Toronto: Macmillan, 1977.

Thomas A. Hockin, ed. *Apex of Power: The Prime Minister and Political Leadership in Canada*, second edition. Toronto: Prentice-Hall, 1977.

W.A. Matheson. *The Prime Minister and the Cabinet.* Toronto: Methuen, 1976.

c. Bureaucracy

We cannot understand modern government without understanding something of the state's administrative component—the civil service, or bureaucracy. Technically, bureaucracy is defined only by the two characteristics of merit selection and hierarchical organization. In fact, however, the civil service is the permanent part of government, a key source of continuity. Its members are in a strategic position to advise political decision-makers—a position not shared by other actors in the political system—and make up the most powerful lobby in the country. The bureaucracy is also the primary point of contact with government for most members of society. Whatever the issue—an income-tax audit or a complaint about garbage collection—it puts the citizen in touch with government on a systematic basis through interactions with civil servants. Most important, the civil service in Canada has grown so substantially that the sheer size of this 'permanent government' gives it considerable significance. At present some one million people are directly employed by various levels of government, and hundreds of thousands more are employed in the so-called para-public sector.

The articles in this section share several characteristics. First, they demonstrate the closed and secretive nature of Canadian politics. Little is known about how the bureaucracy functions; consequently, the press devotes little attention to it. Journalists rarely examine critically important bureaucratic institutions, perhaps because few are fully aware of their significance. As a group, moreover, these articles are remarkably superficial. Very few of them examine the techniques of government, the policy-making process, or the question of why bureaucracy is powerful. Each assumes that power is derived either from position or from proximity to key politicians, but none clearly demonstrates the sources of power. Above all, these writers stress personality. The press and the mass media in general have great difficulty in dealing with grey, anonymous institutions and therefore rely on the inadequate substitute of describing the individuals who occupy offices with arcane titles.

One article that tries to summarize many complicated issues in a brief space but does not quite succeed is Helen Bullock's 'Red Tape + Red Ink = Bureaucracy Blues', which mixes popular maxims about bureaucracy with scattered references unearthed by various Auditors General. Regrettably, most reporters choose to describe only the defects of bureacracy or, more accurately, the symptoms of modern government. This is not to advocate ignoring scandals and bureaucratic problems, but simply to recommend setting them in a more readily comprehensible framework. A perfect example of this failing is Richard Gwyn's column, which emphasizes the increase in the number of senior officials in the upper reaches of the Department of External Affairs without considering the overall growth of government or the expansion in that particular department. Nor does Gwyn recognize that the pressures of accountability to Parliament have required more senior managers, and that the department has adopted many new duties and absorbed parts of other departments.

The next four articles deal with specific issues relating to the civil service. Kenneth McDonald looks at business–government relations and concludes that bureaucracy imposes a substantial burden on business activities. He accurately describes several bureaucratic excesses, but ignores the fact that many of the functions the civil service performs are the implementation of Parliament's will and enjoy great public support. Inge Langer writes about the continuing concern that women are not adequately represented in the public service, particularly in the senior categories. It is troubling to note that while no one challenges the principle of equal representation any more, the pace and means of actual reform have not kept up. Professor Joseph Eliot Magnet raises the issue of the rights of public servants to question the policies of the government they work for. Provoked by the firing of civil servant Neil Fraser for criticizing

Ottawa's metric conversion and bilingualism policies, the article points out the incongruity of an archaic principle restricting the freedom of expression of public servants. Instead of upholding an unassailable position, the government appears to be merely sensitive to fundamentally innocuous criticism. Professor Donald Rowat gives an excellent account of the nature of freedom-of-information legislation prior to its final adoption at the federal level in 1982. Although the passage of this legislation seemed in doubt at several points, the government did move forward with it and introduced a new era of bureacratic responsibility, the consequences of which are not yet clear.

A related issue is the politicization of the bureaucracy and the growth of mechanisms to hold the bureaucracy accountable. Neither Christopher Young nor George Bain alleges that senior officials are openly partisan; however, both make the exception of Michael Pitfield, former Clerk of the Privy Council, whose partisan position was implicitly confirmed by his elevation to the Senate by Prime Minister Trudeau in 1982. Young details the difficulties faced by the Clark government in trying to put its programme into force. In his first column, Bain explodes the myth of the political neutrality of deputy ministers. In his second, he dwells on the demise of this long-standing doctrine and comments on the greater visibility of 'political administrators', the centralization of activities within the federal government, and the apparent decline of accountability to Parliament. Although several matters are muddled together here, his thesis is a powerful one: senior bureaucrats more and more owe their allegiance to the prime minister of the day, which further enhances his pre-eminence.

Val Sears provides a much more conventional account in 'The New Power Behind the Trudeau Throne'. He briefly describes the functions of the office of the Clerk of the Privy Council, but concentrates most heavily on the personal background of the new incumbent, Gordon Osbaldeston. Unfortunately, Sears tells us little in any precise way of his work at the PCO. Hubert Bauch's atypical article provides more information, although it does make some small errors. The Federal–Provincial Relations Office (FPRO) is not a branch of the PCO but a central agency in its own right. Moreover, it was the FPRO, not the PCO, that was responsible for drafting and implementing the government's constitutional strategy. Nevertheless, Bauch accurately describes both the history of the PCO, and the powerful and persistent forces that have concentrated at the centre.

Apart from the increasing refinement of the Cabinet committee system in the past two decades, the structure of Canadian government has probably been altered most by the growing power and control of the so-called central agencies. These mechanisms provide executive support to the Cabinet and involve civil servants at the highest levels of policy-making. Although both are graced by misleading headlines, the two final articles in this section, by Val Sears and John Ferguson, exhibit traditional fascination with the powerful and shed light on previously seldom-seen back-room figures. As well, their discussions reveal the pivotal role played by the PMO as a key political instrument for the prime minister, especially in the Trudeau era. Sears presents a short history of the principal aides or advisers to a succession of Liberal prime ministers but gives little detail on the operation of the PMO or its growth in recent years. John Ferguson fills in the background since 1968 and examines many of the office's contemporary activities.

THE TORONTO STAR, MARCH 6, 1982

Red tape + red ink = bureaucracy blues

By Helen Bullock Toronto Star

When people were asked in an 1980 survey to identify the civil service with an animal, they chose the amoeba and the turtle — amorphous and slow. That's an awful lot of action, but not much motion.

In a word it's bureaucracy, control by organization where the process of organizing overshadows the reason the organization was formed in the first place. We suspect it's growing. We're right. We suspect our money's being wasted. We're right. We suspect there's a better way to manage our affairs. Right again. But it's hard to get that across to a computer print-out.

Six out of every 100 federal employees get paid for administering government regulations; 30 cents out of every dollar of this country's output is from activities covered by government regulations; 16 cents out of every $10 of federal spending is used to administer regulations.

Bureaucracy, with its clubby, secretive tone, its emphasis on cases rather than individuals, has robbed us of much of our feeling of individual strength and determination. Ralph Hummel, in his book The Bureaucratic Experience, points out that bureaucracy reflects the basic conflict between what people need to survive and be happy in society, and what the bureaucratic machine needs to grow, expand and survive in society.

Bureaucracy has become entrenched deeply enough to develop its own protective language. In The Institutional Imperative, Robert Kharasch notes that the truth-telling ability of bureaucracy, especially government bureaucracy, is sorely limited by the maxim that no institution can admit error. The language is corrupted to cover-up. A failure becomes a "shortfall," a depression, "a slowdown in the growth rate," a lie becomes "an inoperative." The meanings have become detached from the message.

The tidy maxim

Or, in the tidy maxim that one bureaucrat posted on his wall: "Don't fix the mistake — fix the blame." And there's a lot of it around.

Every year the auditor-general's report lists cases of wasteful government spending and mismanagement that would freeze the blood in the veins of a private sector executive. Every year the Opposition, government critics and the cringing public lament the dollar drain on obsolete or half-completed projects, enquiries, commissions and other government hobby-horses. And every year taxpayers send Ottawa more money so the government can spend it as foolishly.

Two months ago, Canada's new auditor-general, Kenneth Dye, singled out some examples
☐ The federal government's 6,250 photocopying machines churn out more than $50 million worth of paper a year;
☐ The consumer and corporate affairs competition branch investigations, alleged to take about 18 months, actually drag on in almost half the investigations from three to five years;
☐ More than 93,000 students have defaulted on their student loans leaving the government to pay $173 million.

This latest report comes as no surprise to James Macdonnell, Canada's recently retired auditor-general who spent seven years as a super-detective among the bureaucrats. In one of his last reports he told Canadians they were paying $9 billion a year for a waste-riddled civil service in which many employees worked at 60 per cent efficiency.

Among the scandalous nuggets he dug out and still talks about with relish are:
☐ Internal accounting controls so lax that in one region Environment Canada spent $159,000 twice on the same item;
☐ The Canadian Transport Commission spending $350 million a year in the last decade on rail subsidies without checking to see whether the loss claims made by companies are true;
☐ The Canadian International Development Agency (CIDA) pumped $1.5 million into a fishing training vessel for Colombia that wasn't seaworthy.

"I saw a total lack of accountability in government and it was close to losing control of the public purse,' Macdonnell told Insight. 'There was no one of top financial calibre in control, although a comptroller-general has since been appointed. But not until they'd had a royal commission, that the public paid for, to see if it was necessary. To see if it was necessary!"

Macdonnell said when he became auditor-general "the idea of getting good value for money was completely foreign to the government. The idea didn't exist. Public servants had no idea of accountability." Much of the blame, he said, must be borne by the system of bureaucratic government that wants to spend money for reasons other than to make money, as private industry would do.

"The government knows that certain programs are obsolete but that doesn't stop them pouring money in if the programs are popular or politically expedient. The system is destructive and wasteful by nature. We elect politicians to spend money and we pay bureaucrats to administer the programs effectively, but in the civil service there are no rewards for good management and no penalties for bad management," said Macdonnell, now chairman of the non-profit Canadian Comprehensive Auditing Association.

Civil servants are under pressure to spend every cent they get. If they don't, the "saved" money in their program or department's budget lapses or expires. "Coming in under budget is a sin," Macdonnell said bluntly. "At the end of the fiscal year they are running around in Ottawa with wheelbarrows full of money trying to dump it somewhere so they can say they've used up their budget.

"When I took the job in 1973 government expenditure was $16 billion. When I left in 1980, the *deficit* was about $16 billion, the expenditure had blown up to $60 billion. It's an incredible rate of increase and I think it's fair to say that most of the provincial governments have mirrored that huge increase. When there is such a lot of money being spent, it has an inevitable tendency to get away from you."

An added irony was the salary of the auditor-general himself. When Macdonnell retired he made $62,000. When Kenneth Dye took over, a series of raises in Parliament boosted the salary to $86,600. But payroll for all had jumped ahead. In 1970 the federal government employed 492,785 people with a payroll of about $998 million. Ten years later the employees had only increased to 586,383 but the payroll had jumped to almost $3 billion.

Experienced politicians, civil servants who like their jobs and a long-suffering public seem inured to the financial vagaries of spending public money, but every once in a while a green, fledgling politician is so bowled over by the callousness and carelessness of the government shop, he or she speaks out.

Scott Fennell, the 54-year-old MP for the federal riding of Ontario, a riding in the Ajax-Pickering area who has been two years in Ottawa, is one of them. "I was a total innocent when I came here," he confessed. "I'm still dazzled by the terrible inefficiency and weakness in central management. The government has grown out of control with no guidelines."

Fennell's condemnation of the government is interspersed with tidbits of thriftlessness. "Did you know there are more civilians than soldiers in National Defence? Did you know that for every fish dollar of salmon landed, it cost $12.60 in government research and supervision money? Did you know that government Xeroxes make 900 million copies of things — memos, reports and all that — every year. There are only 24 million people in Canada. Where's all the paper going?"

But spending isn't the only thing that's mushroomed over the years. The civil service has blossomed into a power in its own right. "We're into third and fourth generation civil servants," Fennell said. "People get their children in and the power lines are hard to penetrate. We're totally governed here by civil servants. The individual MPs don't have that much power. Everything is written by civil servants and MPs rubber-stamp it.

"A prime example of that, in my humble opinion, is that I don't think (Finance Minister Allan) MacEachen read that budget until he gave it in Parliament. It was composed by an "inner circle" of experts. A minister just gets a portfolio and has to depend on his staff of civil servants. We're at their mercy. I feel sorry for some of the ministers. They end up defending in the House policies they didn't originate or form."

Fennell said a deputy minister, always a civil servant, is more powerful than the minister. "Only a prime minister can choose his deputy and they're the real politicians," Fennell said. When Flora Macdonald was briefly a cabinet minister she found dealing with the civil servants a trial and complained of it after.

Among the many techniques they used to control a minister, she said, was "crisis corridor" rushing, in which a civil servant races up to his minister and demands an important decision without giving the minister time to think, flooding the minister with lengthy memos of largely irrelevant verbiage and last minute delivery of massive background papers.

Part of the strength of any bureaucracy is the veil of secrecy in which it shrouds itself. What people don't know, they can't criticize whatever they might suspect. It heightens the public sense that bureaucrats are doing some of their finest work behind closed account books.

THE TORONTO STAR, APRIL 27, 1982

Ottawa's overfed bureaucracy a sign of decadence

RICHARD GWYN

OTTAWA — Two decades ago, the strip of carpeted corridor outside the offices of the top officials of the Department of External Affairs was known to all junior officers as "Killers' Row."

The individuals inside each of these offices were magisterial, almost mythical. There were just five of them, an under-secretary, comparable to the deputy minister at the head of all other government departments, and four assistant under-secretaries.

Today, Killers' Row no longer exists. If it did, it would now have to be called Killers' Phalanx. At the top of External Affairs there are now 42 assistant under-secretaries or officers with equivalent rank. Also nine assistant deputy ministers and two deputy ministers. And, as the last tier of the wedding-cake, a single, solitary under-secretary.

The work being done two decades ago by five senior officers now is being done by 54. A bit more work, to be fair, since although External Affairs has lost much of its old glamor and influence within government its jurisdiction recently was expanded to encompass that of trade.

Once, this process by which civil servants advanced up a ladder they had built for themselves was known as "grade up-creep." A better description today would be "grade uprush." In the entire civil service, for instance, there are now 114 individuals with the rank, and pay and perks, of a deputy minister.

Of itself, this debasement of civil service titles is a matter of no great consequence. More people make more money than they should. To fill up their time they fight each other for territory more than they used to, much in the manner of underemployed university professors.

The phenomenon matters instead because it is a symptom of a deep, deep sickness that now afflicts the federal civil service. It contains, still, many dedicated and diligent individuals; but as an institution, it is decadent.

The nature of this decadence has nothing to do with corruption, as conventionally might be assumed to be the case. Civil servants have done exceedingly well for themselves in all those highly-paid positions.

The decadence of the civil service today is more subtle, and far more consequential. It no longer serves us. It rules us. It's become Canada's equivalent to the "military-industry complex" in the U.S., a self-generating, self-sustaining, self-directing force.

It's easy to blame the civil servants for this. Even easier, and more satisfying, because he is a visible target, to blame Pierre Trudeau.

But it is we ourselves, not Trudeau nor the bureaucrats, who created the kind of government that we've got, an all-embracing government.

Each time we need money, we run to the government, with businessmen these days being the first in queue. Each time a problem arises, all the special interest groups, and lobbyists, and editorial writers, demand that government solve it.

As decisively, we have become psychologically dependent upon government. Last fall, in a paper deploring the lack of involvement by ordinary Canadians in drafting the constitution, Gail Stewart, an Ottawa consultant, wrote that 'Outside the sphere of government, discussion about our situation seems peripheral, inconsequential, somehow wistful, futile.'

Government, today, though, no longer means — as our textbooks taught us it meant — parliamentarians and cabinet ministers. It means the civil servants. They've become the cuckoos in the national nest.

Conservative leader Joe Clark, wise if also sadder now after his experience of six months in office, raised the issue in a recent speech in which he said that, "our system has changed to the point where most policy decisions are taken by the public service."

Last November's budget is the best-known example. Tax changes that decisively affected the financial lives of tens of thousands of Canadians were engineered in absolute isolation by, at most, two dozen officials in the Finance Department.

The real point about the examples is that they are endless. The $125 million poured by civil servants into now-bankrupt Consolidated Computer to save the faces of their colleagues, and of themselves. The 3,500 orders-in-council issued each year and each affecting Canadians, most spectacularly so in the instance of metrification.

Orders-in-council bypass Parliament. The funds to Consolidated Computer bypassed the cabinet. The tax changes even bypassed the minister, Finance Minister Allan MacEachen, who himself, until last November, had never used nor knew about tax loopholes.

To end what he called, "the abuse of power by senior public servants," Clark suggested two reforms. A shift of power to Parliament and adoption of the American practice of new governments appointing new, senior civil servants.

In fact, the decadence now is too entrenched to be amenable to reform. To effect real change will take a revolution, a revolution that is in the attitude of Canadians.

"We have over-burdened our governments," Stewart wrote in her paper, "and the frustration of those expectations breeds our anger."

The problem really isn't with the civil servants. They exercise power all right, but by default. Government today is so complicated that most issues demand an expertise that only bureaucrats, rather than the politicians, whether in the cabinet or in the Opposition, can command.

The problem is with ourselves. We expect too much of government. Only by lowering our expectations of government itself can we master it again, and turn bureaucrats back into being, literally so, civil servants.

The dominant political fact in Canada today is the widespread, and deep-seated anger at "Ottawa." Perhaps that is only anger at ourselves for acting like servants, if still occasionally uncivil ones, toward our own government.

THE GLOBE AND MAIL, APRIL 13, 1982

Bureaucracy remote from business reality

KENNETH McDONALD

"A large fraction of what passes for human folly," wrote Stuart Chase, "is failure of communication."

Anyone who has served in a staff appointment, as distinct from a line appointment, will recall how hard it was to write a directive that meant the same to the recipients as it did to the writer.

The staff deals in generalities, the line with specifics; hence Mr. Chase's insistence upon the referent, so that people can focus on an "object or situation in the real world to which the word or label refers."

As a staff grows in size, the gap in communication widens. In the private sector, the market supplies a remedy. An overgrown bureaucracy rots the whole enterprise, profitability declines and the resultant streamlining trims the staff.

In the public sector, there is no such check. C. Northcote Parkinson, in his book The Law, cited the example of the British Admiralty of 1914, which had 4,366 officials administering the world's largest navy, in contrast to the Admiralty of 1967, when "over 33,000 civil servants are barely sufficient to administer the navy we no longer possess."

Bureaucratic tangle

In Canada, the largest Cabinet in our history uses Orders-in-Council to cut through the bureaucratic tangle. Still, it must come to Parliament for major events, where it risks exposure of what the bureaucracy has forced upon it.

The bill introduced by the Minister of Energy, Mines and Resources on Feb. 26 exemplifies Mr. Chase's warning in its title: "An Act to amend and enact provisions related to the Petroleum Administration Act, the National Energy Board Act, the Foreign Investment Review Act, the Canada Business Corporations Act, the Petro-Canada Act, the Energy Supplies Emergency Act 1979, and the Oil Substitution and Conservation Act; to repeal the Energy Supplies Emergency Act; amend an Act to amend the Petroleum Administration Act and the Energy Supplies Emergency Act; to amend the Adjustment of Accounts Act; and to enact the Petroleum Incentives Program Act, the Canadian Ownership and Control Determination Act, the Energy Monitoring Act and the Motor Vehicle Fuel Consumption Standards Act."

That particular example provoked a parliamentary uproar.

Members of opposition parties balked at the prospect of voting a single yea or nay to such a host of provisions.

Yet it was the inevitable outcome of an assumption, common to western governments these 50 years, that the staff knows best, and that the farther one is from the scene of the action the better able one is to direct it.

Another example erupted six weeks earlier, when the Prime Minister's Office announced a "reoganization for economic development." Replete with acronyms and sub-paragraphs and annotated organization charts, it supplied the connoisseur with such gems as this:

"The regional offices of MSERD will provide feedback to the CCERD on the implementation and effects of government economic programs in the regions and on the development of regional strategic overviews for the administration of the new regional fund or for plans for program tailoring."

Having announced the creation of a ministry, a cabinet committee, a regional fund and a department, the release declared: "The reorganization will be achieved without increasing the size of Government or the cost of operations."

The officials who compose these obscurities betray their remoteness from the "situations in the real world" they presume to direct. The business people who must try to cope with them are less fortunate.

The contrasting circumstances of the two groups reveal both the failure of communication between them and the damaging effects upon the economy that result.

The officials are secure in their jobs. In fact, the PMO's release assured any doubters that the reorganization would proceed "in such a way that present indeterminate employees of those departments directly affected will not, as a direct result of the reorganization, be laid off, reduced in classification level, or, as far as possible, be subjected to unacceptable geographic location."

Business people must live every day with the risks of their occupations: competition, financing, shortages of material and skilled workers, taxes, paperwork and survival.

In settled conditions, with a stable currency and a familiar framework of taxes, the daily risks can be faced. But conditions are unsettled. The risks are compounded by man-made difficulties. Business's

judgment in the investment of its earnings gives way to the judgment of officials, who determine whether some of these earnings, after submission, consideration and possible approval of the necessary applications, may be returned.

Two-fold effect

The effect of bureaucratic growth is two-fold. First, by increasing the number of officials, all with the impulse to justify their appointments and authority, it adds complexity and delay to endeavors whose success depends upon quick decisions.

Second, by exchanging business's judgment for that of officials, it limits the tax concessions, grants and subsidies to those companies that have the profit against which to apply them. Concentration is reinforced, the smaller businesses that employ 75 per cent of the work force are frozen out and there is even less incentive to start new ones.

Unless the two groups can bridge the communication gap, the outlook for Canada is scarcely encouraging. Yet Parliament, which should be the bridging agency, concerns itself with the effect instead of the cause.

Kenneth McDonald is a Toronto writer.

THE CITIZEN, OTTAWA, JULY 9, 1982

'Female ghetto' still reigns in PS

By Inge Langer
Citizen staff writer

The issue is still simmering.

Since the Royal Commission Report on the Status of Women in 1970, the battle cry for women's rights has been echoing through the Capital. The focus of the outrage was, and is, Canada's largest single employer of women, the federal government.

The report had come on the heels of

discrimination which, some felt, was blatant and discouraging. Until the mid-1950s, for example, female public servants who married were required to resign. And it was only in 1967 that women were guaranteed legal protection against sexual discrimination.

More than 10 years have passed since the commission report urged equality in the public service, and yet organizations dedicated to eradicating discrimination say there hasn't been much improvement.

The recently released Public Service

Commission annual report tells the tale. Only 4.3 per cent of the public service's executive category, and 3.1 per cent of those in the $50,000-a-year and up income range, are female. Since the previous year, that's an increase of 0.2 per cent and a drop of 0.5 per cent respectively.

And it's only a slight change from the 1970s. In 1974, there were about three per cent fewer females in the executive category than now, and there were no females in the higher income ranges.

Other things have changed even less. Women have been consistently over-represented in the low wage jobs. To date, almost 70 per cent of all public service jobs paying less than $10,000 per year are held by women. Some call it the "female ghetto."

"The results show absolutely no improvement, or very little improvement," said Bonnie Carroll, equal opportunities co-ordinator for the Public Service Alliance, of which more than half the members are women. "Equal opportunities hasn't gone far enough. As a matter of fact, it hasn't gone anywhere. I mean, there's been no teeth to it. It's been a rather polite program.

". . . Basically, the program is more or less a suggestion to the different departments that, hey, if you want to, you can hire a woman. You don't have to or anything. You don't have to actively fight discrimination."

But Carroll emphasizes she's not as pessimistic as she sounds. "Like anything else, things take time to get started and to get off the ground . . . The question we have to ask is why are women low paid? They're low paid because that's the kind of price-tag society has put on women . . . It's an attitudinal problem."

Judging by the statistics, attitudes aren't much different in the provincial public service. Out of 649 top managerial positions available in Ontario in 1981, 41 were held by women. In 1980, about 80 per cent of the provincial clerical staff were women.

Women are also under-represented in the executive levels of the private sector. More than 78 per cent of all the clerical workers in Canada in 1980 were women. In Ontario, in the same year, about 28 per cent of all supervisors, managers and executives were women. Some of the consequences of these statistics are wages for women which have been consistently lower than those for men. In 1979, full-time female workers in Ontario earned

63.5 per cent of what full-time males earned.

Carroll said she thinks it's the responsibility of government to set an example for the private sector by using fair hiring practices. "Women need money for the same reason as anyone else. The price-tag we place on their work should be that of another man's work of equal value. And they should be able to progress as easily as other men. Right now, it's just not happening."

Carroll said she thinks most people would like to see a fairer public service, but the problem is that "people are complaining, but not as one unified voice. Women have to show that they're behind this."

One woman who's reluctant to agree with Carroll's position is Jill Stern, acting director of the management services branch for the Supply and Services Department — one of the relatively few women to make it to the top in the public service.

"I think the government is an excellent employer. I have absolutely no complaints about the public service . . . I have encountered very little, if any, discrimination," Stern said.

Stern, 44, has been working for the government for less than six years, and has risen quickly in the ranks from her first job as a planning officer. "I'm very happy in my work. It's very interesting and challenging.

"I can't fault the government in one instance. I've been advised, people here have shown an interest in my career advancement and I've received career counselling. I've had to work hard, but no harder than anyone else, to get ahead. I've never seen men more quickly promoted than women."

Stern said she thinks any woman who wants to get ahead in the public service can. "I can't see that they're not being accommodated. It's assumed that everyone's got the same ambitions and I just

don't believe that . . . I've found that many women have no career ambitions, they're happy where they are. If they want to get ahead, then they've got to express their ambitions and work hard."

Carroll disagrees. She said she thinks women are barred from higher positions in the public service because of barriers present in the employment practices of government and the attitudes of society.

"It goes back to the way women see themselves and the way society sees women," Carroll said. "Girls get screened out of math programs (in school) and they don't end up qualified technically for some of the higher level jobs. The barriers are there because the qualifications (the government) is asking for are ones that women just don't have. But then again, they aren't always necessary for the job."

Carroll added she hopes the new affirmative active program, started in 1980 and being tested in three departments, will eliminate the barriers of unfair testing and unnecessary qualification demands for hiring. She is the sole union representative on the steering committee for the program.

"The affirmative action strategy is systematic. It's no longer piecemeal like the equal opportunities program. We're looking at the system itself, at training, staffing."

Johanna Hickey, director of the PSC's Office of Equal Opportunities for Women for the past six years, also has her fingers crossed for affirmative action.

"We've got to push ahead and push harder . . . Things just haven't moved ahead as quickly as we had hoped or would have liked. It's a fact of life . . . but at least it hasn't been at a total standstill."

Jack Donegani, president of the Professional Institute of the Public Service of Canada, agrees the changes will take some time. "It's an evolutionary process, not a revolutionary process."

THE GLOBE AND MAIL, OCTOBER 26, 1982

The deadly muzzling of the public servant

VIEWS OF TALENTED PEOPLE ARE LOST TO THE COUNTRY

BY JOSEPH ELIOT MAGNET

Mr. Magnet is professor of law at University of Ottawa.

AMONG THE civilized nations of the world, Canada imposes the severest restrictions on political activities of civil servants. Alone among democratic countries, Canada forbids all political comment on government policy by public officials. As the Government of Canada successfully argued this year in the case of Neil Fraser, a Revenue Canada employee fired for criticizing metrication, "public servants should remain the silent members of society."

One of six members of the labor force works for the public service at all levels of government in Canada. Among these are the best educated and brightest talent in the nation. Canada's public administration includes those who are most knowledgeable about the functioning of the administrative machine. From their perspective inside, public officials have relatively greater opportunity to distinguish promising growth issue from dead wood in government activities.

The political sterilization of this large and important block of citizens must be a source of concern. It lowers the quality of Canadian political debate by silencing those best qualified to discuss fundamental policy. The political community loses input from those constituents eminently able to formulate party policy. A significant social group forfeits the right to an equal voice in the political process which affects its interests. Such debilitating effects on Canadian political life cry out for the Government to identify what higher values require a muzzle on one-sixth of the polity

The Government of Canada has been quick to enforce the prohibition on employee political activity by firing or suspending civil servants who write letters to the editor critical of Government policy, speak at political rallies, or hold offices in political pressure groups. The resulting arbitration reports reveal, in the arguments of Government lawyers, official justification for a public service gag.

The leading cases delineate four rationales: (1) Employees must be faithful to their employers. The duty of fidelity is breached if an employee criticizes employer actions. (2) Unlike other citizens, civil servants may claim no freedom of speech under the Bill of Rights, since they voluntarily renounce it on entering government service. (3) Tradition requires that public servants manifest reserve when expressing views publicly. (4) The public administration must be impartial to escape patronage appointments and insure professionalism; it must also appear impartial to maintain public trust.

The official justifications are hollow. They fall far short of that compelling demonstration necessary to warrant draconian intrusion into the political freedom of the community. To begin with, the Government's line has swelled the employee's duty of fidelity beyond all hitherto recognized juridical limits. There is nothing in the legal doctrine of fidelity that restrains a post office clerk from complaining publicly about interest rates. Nor can it be said that the clerk is employed by the partisan government of the day. In reality, his employer is Canada Post; the clerk's duty of fidelity ends with the activities of the post office corporation. The view that civil servants voluntarily surrender their constitutional right to free speech hardly deserves serious comment. The Constitution is the supreme law of Canada. The rights it enshrines cannot be abridged by private agreement, or even by legislation.

Nor is it correct that tradition requires neutralization of public servants. Depoliticization of Canada's civil service is a relatively new idea, first emerging in the Civil Service Amendment Act of 1908 and finding fuller expression in the Civil Service Act of 1918. Even then, only specific partisan activities were prohibited, such as working in an election campaign. Restraint on criticism of government policy outside of departmental responsibility is entirely novel. It was first suggested in arbitrations of the 1970s, but the principle did not crystallize into law until Neil Fraser's case in 1982. Mr. Fraser, a Revenue Canada accountant, was dismissed for criticizing metrication and the Charter of Rights — government activities utterly unrelated to his job or department.

As a statement of law, Mr. Fraser's case is not only rigid — it is without precedent. Tradition cannot require this draconian attack on free speech because the incursion itself is altogether original.

No one seriously disputes the need to maintain an impartial and professional civil service. But it is open to urgent question whether the best way to attain the goal is by blunt and undiscriminating prohibitions on political expression. "Man," Aristotle rightly told us, "is a political animal." To hack away blindly at the political instinct will make it increasingly difficult to attract the best and brightest to public service careers. We risk being governed by the frustrated few — by a corps of sheep.

Twenty years of British research has examined whether contraventions of the more relaxed British rules on political activity have caused embarrassment or difficulty in public administration. The research is conclusive that activities such as canvassing, service on political committees, criticism of policy beyond departmental responsibilities, or local government activity cause neither difficulty nor embarrassment. Based partly on that research, retrictions on public servant political activity in Britain have been all but eliminated. Sixty-two per cent of British public employees labor under no political prohibitions; 22 per cent are restrained only in running for Parliament; a mere 16 per cent of the higher officials have political restraints remotely similar to Canada's.

An innovative approach recently was legislated in Saskatchewan. Saskatchewan Government employees are free to engage in off-duty political activity, unless the activity "impairs his usefulness in the position in which he is employed."

A man encumbered with an idea has a pressing need to express it. In a free society, it is crucially important that we hear what he has to say. Unconditional debate about public affairs and public leaders is the fundamental safeguard against irresponsible political power. A self-governing citizenry cannot exercise wise and informed political judgment unless exposed to all varieties of ideas, criticism and counter-criticism; to the fullest and freest analysis from every point of view of political proposals. Full public debate exposes false doctrine. That is why our Charter of Rights begins with constitutional protection of conscience — of ideas — and moves immediately to guarantee the freedom to express them.

It is intolerable in this age of mammoth and expanding government that the reins choking public servant political activity should be drawn even tighter. The full energy and talent of this capacious multitude needs to be released to the advantage of the political commonweal. I propose that a civil servant should be subject only to such political restraints as bind the rest of the community: a restriction on activities which prejudice interests of his department, or which impair his ability to perform conscientiously the tasks required of him.

THE GLOBE AND MAIL, APRIL 9, 1981

Can lid be lifted on Ottawa's secrecy?

EXEMPTIONS LET CABINET GO ON HIDING

BY DONALD C. ROWAT

Mr. Rowat is professor of political science at Carleton University and editor of the book The Right to Know.

PARLIAMENT IS considering a bill that could have been a revolutionary move toward open government. It is Bill C-43, the Access to Information Act, which provides for a right of public access to the administrative records of the federal Government.

The bill has such a long and broadly worded list of exempted matters that the Government will be able to go on hiding what it wants from Parliament and the public. In fact, some exemptions reverse the bill's stated objective of greater openness by requiring certain classes of records to be kept secret, thus turning it into an extension of the Official Secrets Act.

The outstanding example is the exemption for Cabinet documents, which prohibits access to any type of record remotely connected with policy-making by the Cabinet, including "any record that contains information about the contents" of such a record. Whereas such records were kept secret entirely at the discretion of the Government, under Bill C-43 this secrecy will now have behind it the force of law.

Other weaknesses in the bill

The bill has other serious weaknesses. One is its blanket exemptions for certain classes of records, with no test of the harm that might be done by their release. Another is that fees to be charged for searches and copies of records and the cost of appealing to the Federal Court could be prohibitively high. So, if the bill is really going to promote open government, it must be made stronger by amendments to reduce the scope of exemptions and costs of access.

The Government will no doubt oppose such amendments, however. It likes the convenience of deliberating secretly and wants to protect itself from politically embarrassing disclosures. Also, it is supported by a bureaucracy that enjoys the freedom of its anonymity and the power of its near-monopoly of knowledge. Clearly the Government won't accept a strengthening of the bill unless public opinion becomes strong enough to force its hand.

But even if the Access Act is strengthened, this will not meet our need for greater openness in government. The reason is that the apex of power in our system of government — the Cabinet — conducts its affairs in secret. This results in serious limitations not only on the Government's accountability to Parliament, but on its ability to make publicly acceptable policy; the public is frozen out of its deliberations. The cabinet system is seriously deficient in its ability to provide for public participation in policy-making, because all major legislative measures are decided in secret by the Government before they are presented to Parliament, which only dots the Is and crosses the Ts.

A government will rarely alter the main features of a bill once it is presented to Parliament and affected groups have little prospect of significantly changing a measure at this stage. New techniques for public participation in policy-making are needed to overcome this disability.

Not only the Cabinet's decisions on proposed laws but orders-in-council, ministerial regulations and decisions affecting individual persons or corporations are made in secret. Indeed, the Cabinet's practice of secrecy has permeated the whole administrative system to such a degree that most independent regulatory bodies make their rules and decisions in secret. One of the great advantages of such bodies is that they can be freed from the influence of cabinet secrecy without altering the cabinet system of government. We should immediately avail ourselves of this advantage by requiring that their deliberations be open to the public.

If we are to overcome the crippling effect of governmental secrecy on public participation in the affairs of government, much needs to be done on all these fronts. We need to invent (or explore experience elsewhere for) new techniques for public participation in all three areas of executive decision-making — decisions on proposed legislation, on regulations and on individual cases.

Regarding proposed legislation, the federal and provincial cabinets, as a result of secret deliberations, suffer from a lack of communication with the public and especially affected interest groups. So, they don't have adequate opportunities to garner proposals for legislative measures from relevant groups in society and must rely on the bureaucracy for such proposals. Nor do they have an adequate way of gauging the public's reaction to proposed measures or of receiving proposals to improve these measures. There may literally be no public opinion on an issue or proposed measure because the public has inadequate knowledge about it and has had no opportunity to discuss it.

This is in sharp contrast to the situation in the United States, where under the congressional system all bills are introduced by individual members of Congress and are studied and discussed publicly by congressional committees and interest groups — sometimes for years — before they reach the floor of one of the houses in the form of a legislative measure. Even then they must undergo a long period of congressional consideration, and frequently major amendments, before they are finally approved.

Under the cabinet system, a traditional method of trying to meet the disability of insufficient public discussion of policy problems has been the use of royal commissions to hold public hearings, stir up public interest in an issue, receive proposals from interested groups and make recommendations. Another method has been the publishing of a white paper as a statement of government policy to get a public reaction before a bill is drafted. A more recent technique has been the release of a green paper on an issue to present alternative proposals and receive views from the public before the Government is committed to a particular policy.

Chance for public to study bills

Another device that ought to be adopted is the release of draft bills on important measures before final bills are presented to Parliament, so the public and affected groups will have time to study and react to them and make proposals for major amendments. The Cabinet would then have an opportunity to accept proposed amendments that would improve the bills and make them more acceptable, since it is unlikely to accept major amendments after bills are introduced. This device is already used in several parliamentary countries in Western Europe, notably Switzerland and Sweden.

In making regulations, the Cabinet, departments and regulatory bodies should likewise release draft orders and regulations for public discussion, possible objection and proposed amendment before their adoption. A similar procedure should be followed for decision-making in individual cases. Where administrative decisions will affect individuals or corporations, provision should be made for a public hearing to receive the views of interested parties, especially those whose interests will be directly affected.

A few departments and several regulatory bodies, notably the Canadian Radio-Television and Telecommunications Commission, the Canadian Transport Commission and the National Energy Board, are already following these procedures and they are used generally by departments and regulatory commissions in the United States.

Although one could not expect the secret precincts of the Cabinet to be invaded immediately in this way, there is no reason why such practices should not be demanded at once of most regulatory bodies. If they work well there, they should then be adopted by ministers and their departments, and finally by the whole Cabinet in making important orders-in-council. Only by such devices as these will the pernicious way in which cabinet secrecy prevents public participation in decision-making be overcome.

THE GAZETTE, MONTREAL, JANUARY 3, 1981

Messing with the mandarins

CHRISTOPHER YOUNG

OTTAWA — When Pierre Trudeau came to power in 1968, he set out to bring the public service under political control. He failed.

Today the bureaucracy is more powerful than ever. Its top leaders, aptly known as mandarins, run the country. They not only run the machinery of government, as they are supposed to do, but to a very great degree they set the policies, as they are not in theory supposed to do.

When Joe Clark became prime minister, he served notice at his first press conference that he would brook no obstruction from the public service to the policies set by his new government. He failed utterly.

Clark unwisely chose the promise to shift the Canadian embassy in Israel to Jerusalem as the issue on which to stand against the resistance of the bureaucracy. A terrific campaign was launched against the Jerusalem policy, and Clark was forced to back off.

The same thing happened with his plan to dismantle Petro-Canada.

It happened in department after department, particularly in external affairs, energy and defence. In finance, John Crosbie seems to have climbed willingly into bed with his officials, even though a new deputy was appointed.

Flora MacDonald was the first to go public with a denunciation of her public service advisers in the external affairs department, whom she said had tried to prevent her from boning up on complex issues and had tried to force her into snap decisions in order to leave no alternative to the actions they recommended.

MacDonald tried to persuade Prime Minister Clark to transfer her deputy minister, Allan Gotlieb, to another post, but Clark refused. It seems he had decided that by firing the clerk of the Privy Council, Michael Pitfield, and the deputy minister of finance, William Hood, he had made enough waves in the public service. He did not not want to be seen as conducting a purge.

The Conservative defence minister, Allan McKinnon, has now spoken out along similar lines. In an interview published in *The Gazette* last Saturday, McKinnon has described how his deputy, C.R. Nixon, and the chief of the defence staff, Admiral Robert Falls, ignored or blocked ministerial orders that did not accord with their views of what should be done.

"They take great umbrage if you don't consult them and push their policies or if you express a policy that doesn't turn out to be the one they've briefed you on or in the manner they've briefed you," McKinnon said.

Admiral Falls went so far as to attack his minister publicly in the middle of last winter's election campaign on a statement McKinnon had made during the course of the campaign. This highly improper move by the chief of the defence staff was made at a time when the polls showed the Liberals well in the lead.

(Ironically, the Tories arranged to get rid of Falls by having him promoted to the prestigious job of chairman of the NATO military committee in Brussels. The government changed before Falls left Ottawa, and it was the Liberals who had to face the minor political storm that followed when the admiral lined up housing for himself at a rental rate of about $8,000 a month, courtesy of the Canadian taxpayer.)

McKinnon, mentioning no names, said several of his colleagues "had a far worse time than I" in dealing with their officials. But another member of the Clark cabinet believes only a small minority of mandarins resisted the policies of the new government.

"Many were waiting for a change of direction and welcomed it, but others had wielded so much power for so long that they wanted no change. There was nothing personal in it," said the ex-minister.

McKinnon thinks about 10 of the 30 deputy ministers should have been fired, although he says it was not a matter of partisan politics.

"I don't think they cared a whit whether they had a Liberal or a Conservative minister provided he didn't try too much to change the policies they'd gone to so much trouble to put in."

Given the offhand manner in which Prime Minister Trudeau had treated the defence portfolio and department during his first 11 years in office, it seems remarkable that the bureaucracy there did not welcome the change to the Conservatives, who are traditionally more respectful of the military.

One ministerial staffer concluded that the mandarins were not fighting for any particular policy or for more billions to spend on defence, but just "for the right to call the shots."

But not all the mandarins are so nonpartisan. Michael Pitfield, who tried desperately to impress Joe Clark favorably with his performance during the transition period in the hope that he would be retained, was very close to the Liberal establishment and to Trudeau in particular.

Just how close he was politically is demonstrated by Richard Gwyn in his recent book on Trudeau, *The Northern Magus*. Gwyn shows that in 1968, when Pitfield was a deputy minister, he was deeply involved behind the scenes in the campaign to win the Liberal leadership for Trudeau.

This involvement not only in partisan politics but in factional politics within a party was highly improper in a senior official. The wonder is not that Clark sacked him but that Pitfield seriously believed he might be spared.

If the Tories come back to power in the lifetime of the generation who served in the 1979 cabinet, you can bet your last Gerald Bouey dollar they will be a lot less squeamish next time.

Christopher Young is general manager of Southam News

THE GLOBE AND MAIL, MAY 17, 1982

GEORGE BAIN

HALIFAX

That sound heard faintly over Ottawa last week was the sound of coffee cups chattering against teeth as mandarins read the news from Saskatchewan that the new government of Grant Devine was saying goodbye to one third of the province's top civil servants.

In Ottawa, where the bureaucracy's grown fat under the governments of Pierre Trudeau, so much so as to form a caste separate from and above ordinary Canadians, nervousness is in order. What the bureaucracy sees in Saskatchewan is the future.

Jeffrey Simpson, in Discipline of Power, subtitled, The Conservative Interlude and The Liberal Restoration, said: "The civil service became more politicized under Trudeau than it had ever been before."

Richard Gwyn, in The Northern Magus, published at the same time, said the same thing, although he fudged it a little by placing the blame on Michael Pitfield and ("at least by passive consent") Gordon Robertson, as clerks of the Privy Council.

Said Gwyn : "During the Pit-field-Robertson era the top ranks of the civil service became indistinguishable for all practical purposes from the Liberal Party. Trudeau's political aides moved into top civil service positions, and vice versa . . .

"Down the line, civil servants took their cues from Pitfield: It was all right to bend the rules, provided you didn't get caught. Liberal Cabinet ministers took their cues from Trudeau: It was all right to fill civil service posts with Liberals (Bill Teron at Central Mortgage and Housing Corporation; Pierre Juneau at the National Capital Commission and, later, Secretary of State) provided the election was sufficiently far away for voters to have time to forget."

The Liberals, after they lost the 1979 election, put it about that the incoming Clark Government brought with it "a hit list," an opprobrious term for what would have been, had the new Government chosen to remove more of the flagrant politicals from a supposedly neutral civil service, not just warranted but desirable.

To its discredit, a considerable part of the parliamentary press corps uncritically swallowed the term and the implications that de-politicizing the public service (as distinct from politicizing it) would be somehow dirty pool and un-Canadian. If the new government had any extensive list of mandarins to bid farewell to — it's not clear that it had — it didn't go far with it.

The principal victim, if that's the word for it, was Pierre Trudeau's friend and loyal servant, Michael Pitfield, of whom Gwyn, in what must be the most scathing footnote ever written about a Canadian public functionary said:

"When Pitfield left the civil service in 1979, after turning down an offer from the new Conservative Government to become ambassador to the Organization for Economic Co-operation and Development (OECD), he wangled for himself an unprecedented termination settlement $107,800. When he returned to his old job he repaid just $10,000 and when reporters questioned him about the propriety of this, said: 'It's goddamn unfair.' "

Since the Liberal restoration in 1980, the planting of Liberals has resumed undiminished. The most recent such appointment, which passed with surprisingly little comment, was that of Pierre Juneau to the presidency of the CBC. It is in no way to disparage Mr. Juneau's intelligence or industry to say that the appointment of a former Liberal Cabinet minister designate to the headship of the national broadcasting system is, at best, an act of gross insensitivity. Before that there was the appointment of Michael Kirby, the author of the Liberals' political strategy for the constitutional wars, to become deputy minister of fisheries when he finishes a fisheries task force duty.

Patently, where a bureaucracy permits itself to be politicized, or to be suborned by perks and privilege, it must also expect to be affected by elections. That was the Saskatchewan message.

THE GLOBE AND MAIL, NOVEMBER 1, 1982

GEORGE BAIN

HALIFAX

Quickly, now, who was clerk of the Privy Council before Michael Pitfield — not Marcel Masse who barely had time to get the seat warm while the Tories were in power, but the last long-running clerk before that?

Gordon Robertson. Robertson occupied the post from 1963 to 1975 and, inescapably over that many years, he came to public notice from time to time. But, compared to Michael Pitfield, he could have been a hermit in a cave.

When Robertson ceased to be clerk of the Privy Council — he stepped sideways into the job of secretary to the Cabinet for federal-provincial relations — the movement was duly noted as being of probable intense interest at least to public servants and political scientists.

When Pitfield stepped down last week, it looked like the biggest thing since Kaiser William II sacked Bismarck, an event Punch celebrated with a cartoon showing the old boy being sent off, spiked helmet and all, in a rowboat, this over a caption reading: "Dropping the pilot."

At that, the edge had been taken off Pitfield's announcement by Ian Stewart's resignation as deputy minister of finance the week before. The Globe and Mail national edition, having flared Stewart's going across the top of page one, "PM's top economic adviser resigns," was left to mark the departure of Pitfield, also across the top of page one, with a flattish, "PM's top mandarin is latest to quit post."

Both these resignations were presented in all the media as news of high importance and, in most cases, the main stories were backed with potted biographies of the two men and analyses of their philosphies, accomplishments and awesome influences.

The attention given to these voluntary, amicable departures of two members of what once was thought of as the anonymous public service says something about the degree of acceptance there has been of the great change in government in the Trudeau years, namely, the accelerated development of the presidential prime ministership.

The main reflection of the change has been in the enlargement and the concentration of power in the Prime Minister's Office; Michael Pitfield has been very much the man with all the strings in his hands, more important in the Government of Canada than all but two or three ministers (and perhaps only one, Lalonde) whose importance derives mainly from their relationship with the Prime Minister.

Secondary reflections of it have been in the diminution of Parliament — the three call-all-ye-sinners evangelical broadcasts were a symptom of that — and the corresponding rise in the standing of the permanent machinery of government, the department, where the mandarins, increasingly politicized, flourish.

Both Pitfield and Stewart are said to resent suggestions that they, or any of them, have become subject to political influence and are anything but the committed, non-partisan advisers of parliamentary song and fable.

It may, in fact, be that Michael Pitfield is that icy cold. But he has been for a long time not just a prodigy and close associate of the Prime Minister, but a friend, and the worse slander on him than to say he could not equally well serve a friend and a stranger, as Joe Clark in effect said in inviting Pitfield to go in 1979, would have been to say that he could.

As for Stewart, even while insisting that the public service had not allowed itself to be seduced from its traditional role of dispassionate advice-giving, he perhaps unthinkingly performed a political service for the government in tendering his resignation. He accepted the responsibility for the advice given the then finance minister, Allan MacEachen, in the formulation of that great dud, the Nov. 12, 1981, budget. But, as the public servant does not accept praise for the accomplishments of government, neither is he called upon to offer himself as a target on which criticism of government for his failures may be deflected. The parliamentary system does not need public service martyrs; the presidential system sometimes find them handy.

The new power behind Trudeau throne

By Val Sears Toronto Star

OTTAWA — A former colleague, wishing to say something nice about Gordon Osbaldeston, newly appointed as Ottawa's top bureaucrat, thought a moment and said: "He's the Vicar of Bray."

The good vicar was a Roman Catholic under Henry VIII, a Calvinist under Edward VI, a Papist under Queen Mary and a Protestant under Queen Elizabeth.

"It doesn't matter to Gordon what minister or governing party he serves," his colleague mused. "He does the same competent, non-partisan job."

Osbaldeston, a 52-year-old native of Hamilton, was named clerk of the privy council — the most powerful civil service job in Ottawa—to succeed Michael Pitfield, who announced last week he was quitting.

The two men's styles are significantly different and official Ottawa has been digging into Osbaldeston's past performance for clues to how the nation's bureaucracy—and perhaps even ordinary citizens — are likely to be affected.

The clerk's job is pivotal in the capital. Around him moves almost every facet of government policy, from the decision-making of cabinet to the shape of the civil service.

The clerk briefs the prime minister every day and that alone is enough to give him enormous leverage. In effect, he decides what the prime minister ought to know, whom he should see, what his options are.

The clerk also heads the cabinet secretariat which writes the agenda for cabinet meetings. Again he may decide what items are to be discussed, when and in what order. He is the cabinet gatekeeper.

Finally, he advises the prime minister on all senior appointments in the civil service. And it would be a rare occurrence for the chief executive to reject a man or woman whom the clerk favors.

Pitfield had the additional advantage of being a close friend of Prime Minister Pierre Trudeau. He had his ear not only in the office but when they were putting on their gear for scuba diving. Osbaldeston is cut differently.

He is, by most accounts, the capital's most astute bureaucrat, moving smoothly through trade and economic portfolios, stroking the minister, staying in the background.

"He has very little concern with policy matters," says a fellow mandarin. "He's like Dolly Levi, he 'arranges things.'"

"He can also charm the birds out of the trees."

When he moves into the $100,000 a year job, Osbaldeston will inherit a civil service much criticized for both its size and cumbersomeness. The top levels are also under fire — as they have been for 50 years— for being dependent servants of the long-ruling Liberal party.

Osbaldeston's appointment may go some way to shatter this image. He is distinctly non-partisan, concerned only with making things work.

Even when they don't, his peers admire the style and innovation he brings to the job.

One example were the so-called "sectoral studies" he organized for the Department of Industry, Trade and Commerce when he was deputy minister in 1979.

Osbaldeston arranged for representatives from business, industry and labor to draw up papers that talked about how their sector could be aided by government, what their goals were and how they might be achieved.

It was a tour-de-force in government management of the private sector. Unhappily, the project came and went leaving hardly a trace.

Osbaldeston graduated from the University of Toronto with a bachelor's degree in 1952 and with a Master's Degree in Business Administration from the University of Western Ontario in 1953.

First posting

His first job was as a marketing man for the advertising firm of J. Walter Thompson. But he decided his future lay with government. He joined the foreign service as a commercial officer in 1953.

His first posting was to Sao Paulo, Brazil where he picked up cigar-smoking and working knowledge of the bossa nova.

Back in Ottawa, after working in the Canadian consulates in Los Angeles and Chicago, Osbaldeston was moved through the Department of Trade and Commerce, to the top civil service job in Consumer and Corporate Affairs and to the Treasury Board as Secretary.

His last job before being appointed clerk was as undersecretary of state for External Affairs.

He had the massive job there, barely started, of integrating trade commissioners into the foreign service.

His friends say it was typical of Osbaldeston's style that he had—so far anyway — managed to ease the fears of the diplomats that they were being turned into a sales department for Canadian industry.

But there are already unhappy rumblings from some departments that their offices are being dismantled and replaced with shoulder-high partitions and rubber plants.

Friends say Osbaldeston is a straight-arrow family man, vacationing in his camper with his wife Geraldine. He has four grown children. He's devoted to them and to the Hamilton Tiger-Cats.

"Gordon is a very smooth operator," said a ministerial aide who worked with him in an economic portfolio. "I was awed by the kind of groundwork he lays before bringing a proposal to the minister.

"He also seems to be able to give the top guys in the department their orders about a policy they didn't support and make them like it."

Probably the most significant of the changes the bureaucracy can expect when Osbaldeston takes over is the form of decision-making.

More policy options

Under Pitfield, orders flowed from the prime minister's office to the deputy ministers. Osbaldeston's style would be to restore some of the authority of the deputies with a great many more policy options reaching the cabinet committees from them.

He may also be expected to reach out to the business community with which he has been associated for most of his life.

Ottawa's bureaucracy is likely to be in for a cooler governing style from the Vicar of Bray than from Michael Pitfield.

But no one in the capital doubts that by the time Osbaldeston piles into his camper for a summer vacation next year, the bureaucracy will be working better and smiling more.

Inside Ottawa's inner sanctum

The Privy Council Office is the hub of the federal government. How does it work and who runs it?

By HUBERT BAUCH
of The Gazette

OTTAWA — There is no such thing as a messy desk in the Privy Council Office.

Each evening the day's paperwork goes under heavy lock and key in the office's filing cabinets, or else into "secret waste" boxes, the contents of which are later fed into a paper shredder.

The shredder is in the basement of the Langevin Block, a massive sandstone hulk of an edifice that looks like it was designed less for beauty than to withstand rocket attacks. It squats on Ottawa's Wellington St. just across from Parliament Hill.

What gives the Langevin its high-power cachet, apart from the fact that it is where the prime minister hangs his hat (in the prime minister's office, or PMO) is that the Privy Council Office is there. Little-known outside Ottawa, this operation is the clearing house for the government's most important work, and indeed for most of Ottawa's decision-making.

(A distinct branch of the PCO, the Federal Provincial Relations Office, an innovation from the Trudeau years, advises the government on the conduct of federal-provincial affairs.)

National incident

The Privy Council Office (just "PCO" to insiders) is the secretariat, or support staff, for the highest level of Canada's federal government, the cabinet. Every sensitive issue in the capital winds up here for consideration and processing. On the rare occasions when something escapes the paper shredder, there's a national incident.

That happened twice near the end of last summer. First there was the memo to Prime Minister Pierre Trudeau from Michael Pitfield, clerk of the Privy Council and secretary to the cabinet. The memo advised Trudeau to proceed with constitutional patriation with or without agreement from the provinces at September's conference of first ministers. That one wound up on the front page of the Ottawa *Citizen*.

Then, on the eve of the conference, an elaborate paper outlining a divide-and-conquer strategy to be used on the provinces made its way into the hands of the Quebec delegation, and from there to practically everyone else at the meeting.

The conference failed. It might well have failed even if the PCO documents had remained secret. But there is no denying that the leaks served to poison the atmosphere and harden provincial attitudes.

From the Privy Council point of view, those leaks demonstrate the need for the shredder and the heavy-duty locks on the filing cabinets. For the rest of us, they were rare insights into the mysteries of the Langevin Block.

The memo and the discussion paper were prime examples of the PCO's routine function, which is to give the prime minister and cabinet clear and decisive advice on sensitive and complex topics. On the basis of that advice the cabinet makes decisions, which the PCO then feeds back into the bureaucracy as government policy.

In effect, the PCO takes care of "details" for the cabinet — co-ordinating the policies of various departments, keeping track of what has been decided and making sure that everyone in government who needs certain information can get it.

To do this, the PCO obviously must have universal access to the government apparatus; and this closeness to the centre of decision-making, plus the veil of anonymity and secrecy behind which it operates, give the PCO its clout and mystique among Ottawa insiders.

The PCO's influence on the order of government priorities has given rise to the notion that it has come to dominate the governmental process, and the inordinate amount of time it has worked under Liberal administrations has created the widespread impression that it functions as an appendage of the Liberal party.

'We can give advice but if it doesn't jibe with the government's political considerations we don't get listened to'
— former PCO official

A major contributing factor to this notion was the appointment five years ago of Michael Pitfield, a longtime Trudeau intimate, as head of the PCO operation and hence the senior bureaucrat in the country.

Contributing to the suspicion has been Pitfield's innate aloofness and his obsessive insistence on anonymity and secrecy by his officials. (Some PCO people will talk, in guarded terms, about the way their office operates. But none of them will talk for attribution, or allow themselves to be quoted directly by name.)

In theory the PCO should function as a purely apolitical advisory body. But in practice, it has to be keenly political, without becoming politized. "We have to be political as hell," said a former PCO official.

"We can give the best technical advice in the world, but if it doesn't jibe with the government's political considerations, we don't get listened to."

Proof that the PCO somehow manages the balancing act of being at once apolitical and politically sensitive lies in the relative smoothness of last year's transfer of power from the Liberals to the Conservatives.

Prepared the ground

Pitfield was summarily dismissed, but the dismissal was absorbed not so much as a shock to the system as a fact of life. Indeed, in the months leading up to the Conservative victory, Pitfield had prepared the ground for what happened by appointing his eventual successor, Marcel Masse, to one of the most senior posts in the PCO.

Since the Liberal restoration, several Conservative ex-ministers have complained that they were pressured by their departmental officials into making decisions they weren't altogether comfortable with. (Allan McKinnon, defence minister in the Conservative regime, made that point in an interview in *The Gazette* last Saturday.) But no-one has gone so far as to impugn the professional integrity of the Privy Council Office.

"You tend to hear complaints about the PCO from people who have had pet projects sidetracked," said Bill Neville, chief of staff to former Conservative Prime Minister Joe Clark.

"But I never detected any partisan motivations in the PCO while we were in power," he goes on. "They're first-rate mechanics above all, and I never had any indication that they were giving us any less than 100 per cent."

As a rule, PCO staffers do not become public figures. The rare exception are those like Marc Lalonde and Pierre Trudeau himself who go on to active politics. Or its leading figures like Pitfield, his predecessor Gordon Robertson, and Michael Kirby, the current head of the federal-provincial relations office and the man to whom the notorious constitutional strategy paper has been attributed.

But then the government decision-making process is rooted in the principle of cabinet responsibility and unanimity. If civil servants were to voice their opinions and preferences in public, the process would fall apart. Hence the rule at the PCO is keep your mouth shut, particularly within earshot of reporters.

Apart from abiding by the rule of silence, PCO staffers are advised from the outset that their careers in the Langevin Block will be fleeting. The practice is to rotate bureaucrats through the PCO so as to minimize dependency on individuals and the bureaucratic instinct for empire building.

The theory, as Gordon Robertson put it, is to maintain "a small and discreet staff, constantly changing to avoid the formation of a ruling elite." There are exceptions to the rule that a PCO tour of duty should not extend beyond four or five years. Pitfield is a case in point as was Robertson who served as cabinet secretary from 1963 to 1975.

But even so, during the time they do spend in the Langevin Block, PCO staffers are very much aware of being part of an elite guard. They have access to everybody, from the prime minister on down. They also have access to the widest possible range of information, and rare indeed is the bureaucrat who ignores a phone call from the PCO.

PCO officers don't make any more than other civil servants, so it's not money that holds the attraction. Pitfield, as top man — his post makes him head of the civil service, not a title which means much but an indication of his status — earns about $85,000, which is peanuts compared to top-level salaries in business. Canadian Pacific Chairman Ian Sinclair makes about $600,000, and even Bob Bandeen, president of the Crown corporation Canadian National, makes about $190,000.

Most of the people working in the policy field at the PCO — the rank-and-file guys who do the thinking — tend to be in the $40,000 to $60,000 a year range.

The real lure, as most people who have worked there will readily admit, is the proximity to power. "What makes it an exciting place to work," says a PCO staffer nearing the end of his tour of duty, "is the perception of being at the centre of things.

"It's nonsense to say that we run the country. But when you work here you know what's going on."

● ● ●

There was no Privy Council Office as we know it at Confederation. It has grown up during the past 40 years from less than a dozen civil servants to its present complement of more than 300 bureaucrats and support staff.

The modern PCO was created in 1941 by then Prime Minister Mackenzie King, who borrowed the idea of a "cabinet secretariat" from Britain to cope with the unprecedented demands that the Second World War was imposing on the government.

For its first years it did little more than serve the cabinet's war committee; only after 1945 did King feel the need for cabinet agendas and formal records of decisions, the maintenance of which became central to the PCO's role.

From those humble beginnings, the PCO has become the motor of the government decision-making process. If the earth were to open up along Wellington St. today and swallow up the Langevin Block, the governing apparatus would be thrown into chaos until something approximating the PCO could be set up again.

Part of the mystery surrounding the office stems from its name.

The Privy Council itself is a formal body assigned by the constitution to advise the Governor-General. Membership includes all cabinet ministers, present and past, who are still living. As well, it includes a number of prominent Commonwealth figures and others appointed at the discretion of the Prime Minister.

The Duke of Edinburgh, for instance, is a member. And in 1967, Prime Minister Lester Pearson had all the provincial premiers appointed to the council to mark the centennial of Confederation.

But just as the Governor-General has only nominal power, so the Privy Council does little more than grace the annals of Parliament. It meets only on formal occasions as part of the pomp and pageantry — there was a gathering of Privy Councillors for the Coronation of Queen Elizabeth for instance. The most recent meeting was back in 1956, when the Queen came to Canada to open Parliament.

In fact, the real power is exercised by a small committee of the Privy Council, which is the cabinet. You won't find the cabinet in the British North America Act at all, though the

Privy Council is there.

The PCO is so called because Mackenzie King wasn't sure what he wanted to do with his new secretariat. So he simply grafted it on to the small staff that administered Privy Council formalities.

Together with the Prime Minister's staff of political appointees, which constitutes the Prime Minister's Office (PMO), the PCO has experienced a more dramatic growth in importance than any other branch of the public administration in recent times.

But then the PCO is only the tip of the bureaucratic iceberg that has formed during the past 40 years. Just as the office was created in response to the growing complexity of governing the country, so its importance has increased in proportion to the bureaucratic sprawl in Ottawa.

A more precise yardstick of the PCO's rise lies in the growth of the cabinet committee system, another of Mackenzie King's tentative innovations which only came into its own several administrations later.

King's idea of how to run cabinet meetings when he first assumed power, was to get his ministers to-

'It's nonsense to say we run the country. But when you work here, you know what's going on'
— PCO official

gether and introduce topics for discussion off the top of his head. No one would be present to take notes of the discussions, and after the meetings each minister would transmit to his departmental officials what he thought had been decided at the meeting.

Later King hit upon the notion of creating cabinet committees for each ministry, so that preliminary discussion of issues could take place before the full cabinet met.

Exhaustive detail

Today, according to a system initiated by Pearson and further refined by Trudeau, these committees of ministers handle most of the day-to-day decision-making. The whole cabinet, at its weekly meetings, concerns itself only with the major and most controversial questions.

The kind of advice cabinet gets from the PCO is concise and unequivocal, but backed up by exhaustive detail. Because all of this is highly-sensitive and secret material, specific examples are hard to come by.

But that leaked memo last summer is a good example. (Leaks from the PCO-PMO are few and far between, and some people still suspect that the federal side leaked that memo on purpose, to serve some unfathomable purpose in the federal-provincial bargaining.)

"The challenge," the memo told the cabinet, "now lies with the federal government to try to bring out the agreement on a package which appears to be within reach and, failing this, to show that disagreement leading to unilateral federal action is the result of an impossibly cumbersome process or of the intransigence of the provincial governments, and not the fault of the federal government."

That was written in the PCO last August and it remains the most concise summary of the arguments that Pierre Trudeau has marshalled in support of his constitutional initiative ever since.

THE TORONTO STAR, NOVEMBER 13, 1982

Who is running the country?

"(There are) masterminds who, behind the scenes, are formulating our . . . policies. These men have responsibilities, they have great power; but they are not answerable to anybody."

— **Conservative leader W. B. Hanson, 1942**

"(This convention) condemns the view that non-accountable, non-legitimate, non-elected members of the party should have direct informal roles in advising the government which totally bypass the democratically accountable executives of the party."

— **Liberal convention, 1982**

By Val Sears Toronto Star

OTTAWA — For more than 40 years, Canada's elected politicians have worried

It used to be civil servants, now aides are wresting power from elected politicians.

that power was slipping from their legitimate hands to some Rasputin whispering in the prime minister's ear.

In Hanson's day it was the gray, faceless civil service who were taking control, the Ottawa Men, the Superbureaucrats, hypnotizing ministers with their Queen's University erudition and Rideau Club plots.

Today, the Liberal party worries about a different breed, men and women in the

Prime Minister's Office who amuse him, guard his gate, energize his jaded wits and write briefing memos that can kill a ministerial recommendation.

Many political scientists, and even some ex-advisers, agree there is cause for concern.

Jack Pickersgill, the first of the extra-parliamentary advisers, once wrote of his relations with prime minister Louis St. Laurent: "I had very great influence on Mr. St. Laurent. He had more confidence in me than any cabinet minister or anyone else."

From Pickersgill's time — he was assigned to prime minister MacKenzie King's office from External Affairs in 1937 — to the present, a remarkable collection of courtiers have sat by the throne, offering their views on everything from elections to ecology.

They have had different titles, "principal secretary," "chief of staff," "chief policy adviser."

But their various roles are not greatly different from the description for the office offered by Gov.-Gen. Lord Tweedsmuir to King: A permanent principal assistant to head the Prime Minister's Office, to serve as an "intelligence officer" ready to advise the prime minister on anything he deemed important, and to serve as liaison officer with the departments of the government.

The present "villains," Senator Keith Davey and former principal secretary Jim Coutts, began their apprenticeship with prime minister Lester Pearson.

But most Ottawans would say a far more significant role was played by policy adviser Tom Kent.

"I've often thought," said former bureaucrat Doug Hartle, "that if the statues on Parliament Hill are meant to represent important men, there ought to be one to Kent, taller than all the rest."

It was Kent who fashioned for Pearson such landmark legislation as Medicare, a National Pension Plan and regional economic policy.

More important

This tall, angular, pipe-smoking English immigrant was far more important to Pearson's political decision-making on social matters than any deputy-minister and probably most of his cabinet.

Pierre Trudeau has had Marc Lalonde as well as Coutts and Davey in their ascendency.

Conservative prime minister Joe Clark, in his brief stay at 24 Sussex, had ex-wire serviceman Bill Neville, academic Jim Gillies and New Brunswick politico, Senator Lowell Murray.

With Coutts gone to try to find political legitimacy in Spadina riding, the principal secretary's job for Trudeau has been taken over by Tom Axworthy, a shrewd and merry intelligence officer.

A superbureaucrat who has served a number of prime ministers says the influence of advisers can be seriously overrated.

"No man becomes prime minister," he said, "without a very secure sense of his own identity and the rightness of his views.

Offer advice

"What he wants around him are men who feel the way he does and will offer him advice that meets with his own directions.

"Some, Pearson was perhaps one, were influenced more than others by advisers. But Pearson was tougher than most people thought. No one pushed him where he didn't want to go."

In fact, it was in Pearson's day that advisers began to proliferate around ministers as well as the prime minister.

Mitchell Sharp, who has been both a deputy-minister and a member of the Pearson cabinet, writes in the magazine Policy Options this month:

". . . I see no objection if ministers decide to appoint aides in their offices to assist them in dealing with policy questions or anything else for that matter.

"My personal experience leads me to observe only that it does not help relations between the minister and the department if ministerial aides attempt to assume more authority than they possess when dealing with department officials."

Most observers suggest, however, it is exactly this assumption of power that has led party people to resent and attack the role of advisers.

Doug Rowland, an ex-Member of Parliament who now works for an Ottawa think tank, says when Trudeau took power there was a concern that the deputy-ministers had too much power.

He, under the direction of Privy Council Clerk Michael Pitfield, undertook to re-allocate it to the politicians, by establishing cabinet committees and a countervailing power in the Prime Minister's own office.

Worried Liberals

"It didn't work very well," said Rowland. "The deputy-ministers were simply replaced by men in the prime minister's office or the federal provincial relations office.

"It's difficult to conceive of a system that doesn't have a powerful, non-accountable set of advisers.

What worried the Liberals at their recent convention was the ancient problem of getting party policy up to the cabinet instead of having decisions handed down to them.

"One way it used to be done," said Rowland, "was for the party president to be a senator. He then sat in the caucus of elected members to represent party views.

"Perhaps it is an indication of Trudeau's attitude to the party that he never made the past Liberal party president a senator."

The Progressive Conservative party has caucus members who sit on the party's executive committee but the party president only attends caucus by invitation.

The New Democrats have the party's federal secretary as a regular member of caucus.

Rowland says the role of advisers is continually changing.

"There is talk around town now," he says, "that the power of the Prime Minister's Office is weakening. Their power is passing to the superministries, the ministries of economic and social development.

"These have so much authority and such large staffs that they are the inheritors of power."

But there is still the political work to be done and civil servants are not always the best choice for this sort of thing.

Pickersgill, although he came from External Affairs, apparently had no qualms in serving King as a political man. King wrote in his diary that he had been discussing the 1939 election campaign with his new aide.

"I found him very willing to do anything that he could do, and would fit in anywhere," King purred. "He has first class ability."

Liberals may "condemn the view that elections and party life should revolve around polls, propaganda and patronage orchestrated by a small elite."

But the past 40 years in Ottawa suggest the party will have a hard time separating any prime minister from friends who orchestrate the kind of music he likes to hear.

THE GLOBE AND MAIL, SEPTEMBER 22, 1981

Affable whiz kid is Ottawa's new top mandarin

By JOHN FERGUSON

OTTAWA (CP)—While the verbal war with the United States over "Canadianizing" the oil industry was growing in intensity over the past few months, the nationalist whiz kid who played a big role in promoting that policy was quietly taking over as head of Prime Minister Pierre Trudeau's political staff.

Bright, affable, roly-poly Tom Axworthy, PhD, at 34 (the youngest ever to hold the post of principal secretary, thus has become the backroom boy of all backroom boys in Canada, with access to levers of power that most can only dream about.

He heads a staff of about 60 in Mr. Trudeau's office — known in Ottawa simply as "the PMO" — where the political and bureaucratic sides of Government come together. Most are political appointees, whose fortunes rise and fall with that of the Government, and their job is to help keep Mr. Trudeau and his Cabinet out of trouble by ensuring they get detailed political intelligence from a variety of sources, including polls, the media, the party and the caucus.

"We are the radar of the ship of state," Mr. Axworthy says.

"It's not our job to say where the ship will go — that's the politicians' job. It's being able to say whether there is clear sailing ahead or whether there are storms or shoals."

The younger brother of Employment and Immigration Minister Lloyd Axworthy was born in Manitoba, obtained his master's and doctorate in political science at Queen's and is an ardent nationalist of the Walter Gordon school. His first job in Ottawa in 1967 was as a researcher for Mr. Gordon's task force on the economy.

He joined the PMO in 1975 and worked his way up to senior policy adviser, second in command to principal secretary James Coutts, and moved into the top spot when Mr. Coutts left for his ill-fated run in the Spadina by-election.

The Ax, as he is known to some around the PMO, wrote nearly every speech Mr. Trudeau delivered in the Liberals' nationalistic 1980 election campaign, including the one in Halifax in which he unveiled the policy of making the Canadian oil industry 50 per cent Canadian-controlled by 1990.

The Canadianization policy had its origins in a party platform committee, but Mr. Axworthy was one of a few key advisers who helped defend the idea with Mr. Trudeau, who "saw the implications . . . immediately and asked some pretty penetrating questions," Mr. Axworthy says now.

He calls it an "absolutely massive change" in the ownership of the economy, and notes with satisfaction that it has tremendous support from the public and his Liberal Party.

"Canadianization is here to stay. It's the most popular, perhaps the most significant — the constitution aside — one of the most significant actions the party has taken since the Second World War."

If Mr. Coutts's image was that of the fixer with a telephone growing out of his ear, Mr. Axworthy's is that of the bookish policy man whose fun is reading weighty political and economic tomes. "Have you read the Harvard Energy Report," he once asked a reporter on the 1980 campaign. "No, I missed it," came the reply.

But Mr. Axworthy is also a child of the Sixties. He has a Beatles poster in his office, he likes rock-and-roll concerts, and his heroes include John F. Kennedy and retired pitcher Catfish Hunter.

He places great emphasis on research, and took offence at news stories that the new Ottawa-Alberta energy deal violated the Liberal election promise of cheap oil. At his behest, Energy Department officials churned out graphs and charts with which Mr. Trudeau attempted to refute the charge of broken promises.

Lorna Marsden, chairman of the Liberal policy committee, says she's impressed by Mr. Axworthy's ability to think things through, by his concern for expressing ideas in terms of Liberal philosophy, and by the fact that although he "commands the knowledge," he "draws people out in debate and never puts people down."

Soon after he took over the new job, Mr. Axworthy called the 22 members of her committee to tell them: "I'm still here, and I'm still interested in policy."

Asked what he likes best about his job, he grins and replies: "I don't want to sound too drippy here, but I still think politics is the best avenue for achieving reform. Aristotle defined politics as 'the honorable profession,' and I believe that."

At the same time, he acknowledges that the Liberal Party, after so long in power, is often accused of a somewhat more cynical view of the "profession."

Although Mr. Trudeau has said he won't run in the next election, Mr. Axworthy thinks his chief will stay Prime Minister for another year or two to complete some of the jobs left undone.

At the top of the list are new fiscal arrangements with the provinces to restore the balance that Mr. Axworthy believes has tipped too far away from Ottawa, and major legislation overhauling the pension system to relieve poverty among the elderly.

There will also be a new thrust in economic development, with the federal Government taking on a more visible role rather than being relegated to the role of signer of cheques.

Discussion Questions

1. How does the massive growth of the bureaucracy in the past two decades relate to the issues raised by Helen Bullock?
2. Is Richard Gwyn correct in contending that the problems of bureaucracy have hobbled the country? Have elected politicians lost control of the bureaucracy?
3. Should the bureaucracy be representative of the population at large, especially in terms of gender and language?
4. In several of the articles above, it is suggested that Canada adopt the American practice of replacing many of the senior bureaucrats when the government changes.

What would the advantages and disadvantages of this scheme be for government in Canada?
5. Has the introduction of many new central agencies in the 1970s enhanced bureaucratic accountability, or has this accountability become bogged down in extensive growth and reorganization?
6. Should bureaucrats be accountable to Parliament and the public? Has the rise of central agencies contributed to the decline of Parliament as an effective institution for political control and accountability?

Suggested Readings

R.F. Adie and P.G. Thomas. *Canadian Public Administration: Problematical Perspectives.* Toronto: Prentice-Hall, 1983.

Canadian Public Administration, vol. 25, no. 4, Winter 1982.

Paul W. Fox, ed. *Politics: Canada,* fifth edition. Toronto: McGraw-Hill Ryerson, 1982, 550–90.

W.D.K. Kernaghan, ed. *Public Administration in Canada: Selected Readings,* fourth edition. Toronto: Methuen, 1982.

D. Butler and B. Macnaughton. 'Public Sector Growth in Canada: Issues, Explanations and Implications', in Michael S. Whittington and Glen Williams, eds. *Canadian Politics in the 1980s.* Toronto: Methuen, 1981, 84–107.

Richard J. Van Loon and Michael S. Whittington. *The Canadian Political System: Environment, Structure and Process,* third edition. Toronto: McGraw-Hill Ryerson, 1981, 550–615.

V.S. Wilson. *Canadian Public Policy and Administration: Theory and Environment.* Toronto: McGraw-Hill Ryerson, 1981.

Audrey D. Doerr. *The Machinery of Government.* Toronto: Methuen, 1981.

Richard D. French. *How Ottawa Decides.* Toronto: Lorimer, 1980.

E.C. Campbell and G.J. Szablowski. *The Superbureaucrats: Structure and Behaviour in Central Agencies.* Toronto: Macmillan, 1979.

d. Crown Corporations

Barry Kliff, 'Can Public Good be a Bottom Line?' *Montreal Gazette,* July 24, 1982 : *69*

'Crowns Need Scrutiny', *Financial Post,* February 5, 1983 : *72*

Judy Steed, 'New Post Office Faster', *Globe and Mail,* November 24, 1982 : *72*

James Rusk, 'Joel Bell: "Policy Activist But Not Political Activist"', *Globe and Mail,* November 26, 1982 : *74*

The Crown corporation is an aspect of Canadian government that has been largely neglected in political science literature. Recently, however, several events—the unrealized plans of the Clark government to 'privatize' (or sell to the private sector) several Crown corporations, the transformation of the Post Office from a department to a Crown corporation, the controversial establishment of the Canada Development Investment Corporation (CDIC), and the huge losses associated with Canadair's Challenger executive jet programme—have shot public enterprise dramatically onto the public agenda. It is not surprising that the whirl of these developments and the wide diversity of public enterprises leave reporters and citizens puzzled. The bulk of press coverage in recent years has dwelt on financial control and accountability, and, as a consequence, there is a widespread perception that public enterprises are grossly inefficient and mismanaged. (A pleasant exception is Peter Foster's article, 'Battle of the Sectors'—see Suggested Readings.) This idea seems to fly in the face of the general confidence displayed by Canadians in a relatively activist and interventionist government. It may be explained in part by the fact that the scope of public enterprise has only been fully examined in the past few years; data indicate that there are more than 500 federal Crown corporations accounting for one-fifth of the government's revenues.

The first article, by Barry Kliff, gives a fine analysis of these corporations, particularly as regards the tension between their public-service mandates and the profit imperative. Although he does not address the question of why some corporations are successful and others are not, he does note the difficulties some enterprises have in identifying public goals and the possible benefit that could accrue to some through stricter application of business principles. The editorial from *The Financial Post* directs itself squarely to the accountability of Crown corporations. That taxpayers deserve the greatest value for their money is not controversial, but the overall question of the appropriate use of public enterprise is rarely considered. Judy Steed provides an insightful account of the problems associated with the Post Office's first year as a Crown corporation. Finally, in his profile of the new head of the CDIC, James Rusk casts some light on the government's economic strategies. Joel Bell stands out as one of the leading exponents of government intervention and is a veteran of many years in service with a succession of Crown firms.

THE GAZETTE, MONTREAL, JULY 24, 1982

Can public good be a bottom line?

Crown corporations are part of the Canadian way

By BARRY KLIFF
of The Gazette

Shortly before it became part of Petro-Canada last year, the market value of Petrofina Canada Inc.'s equity was about $515 million. The federal government, however, wound up paying $1.46 billion for the oil company.

When Dominion Steel and Coal Corp. Ltd. decided in 1967 to shut down its aging and unprofitable Sydney Steel Corp. (Sysco) mill, Nova Scotia and Ottawa were faced with the prospect of what to do with 3,000 unemployed steelworkers.

Rather than let the plant close, the provincial government took it over, and Ottawa kicked in $77 million to help rehabilitate the aging structure.

But, even with federal and provincial assistance, Sysco's accumulated debt is about $275 million and annual losses have jumped from $20 million to at least $50 million.

Petro-Canada and Sysco, along with 460 other organizations engaged in everything from manufacturing airplanes (Canadair Ltd.) to raising oysters (Crane Cove Oyster Farm Ltd.), are owned wholly or in part by the federal government.

Some make money

Some are called Crown corporations, others are labelled "mixed-enterprise" corporations. But, whatever their labels, these businesses have mushroomed over the years into an integral — and expensive — sector of the Canadian economy.

And every Canadian taxpayer, like it or not, is a partner.

Some of these businesses actually make money. But every time you mail a letter or take a train, you're paying twice — once when you actually use the service and again when you file your federal income-tax return.

The $475 million in combined profits earned last year by the five most successful government-assisted corporations was more than offset by $2.7 billion in subsidies and other financial aid needed to keep the five least-profitable ones afloat.

This fiscal year, Ottawa will have to spend an estimated $2.4 billion to support the five biggest losers — more money than is spent on culture and recreation, educational assistance, or foreign affairs.

Government involvement in business, particularly in the transportation and communications sectors, has been a fact of life in Canada since Confederation. And, in a country with a relatively sparse population strung out across a vast continent, few would argue against the need for at least some involvement from Ottawa.

Nor are you likely to hear much griping from the thousands of Montrealers who earn their daily bread from Air Canada, Canadian National Railway Co., VIA Rail, Canadair, the Canadian Broadcasting Corp. and other large federally controlled employers.

Privately, however, some business leaders, economists and politicians are again questioning the depth of government involvement in the economy.

20 or 30 per cent

These critics estimate that many government-assisted corporations must add 20 or 30 per cent to the price of their product or service to cover the costs of serving "the public good."

"Who can tell how much something would have cost if Crown corporations were run for business and not political considerations?" wonders Michael Walker, director of the Vancouver-based Fraser Institute. "Trying to put a figure on that is nearly impossible."

Unlike private corporations, which exist solely to produce a profit, government-assisted corporations are supposed to place the public good first and profits second.

Sometimes it's possible to do both.

Air Canada and Teleglobe Canada, for example, earned profits of $40.1 million and $36.6 million, respectively, in 1981, while still providing for the public good.

"Just because a corporation is owned by the government doesn't mean it will be run any differently," said Robert Morrison, a professor of management at Montreal's McGill University. "The same people who run Air Canada could just as easily run CP Air. They all speak the same language and travel in the same circles."

But the balancing act hasn't been so easy for some other Crown corporations.

Last fall, when VIA Rail wanted to trim its projected $490-million deficit for 1981-82 by reducing the number of routes by 20 per cent, public reaction was both swift and predictable. Even though the federal subsidy for each passenger is about $70 per trip, most members of Parliament called on VIA officials to increase the service and lower the cost.

As part of its mandate, the CBC must provide television programming to every person in Canada, no matter where he or she lives — a policy that requires the expenditure of millions of dollars to purchase transmission equipment that will reach only several thousand people.

"Because the government is footing the bill, people think there's no limit to what can be done," said consulting economist Marsha Gordon, a former staff member at the C.D. Howe Institute.

"People want more, but aren't aware of what it actually costs them," added Gordon, who last year wrote a book entitled *Government in Business*, which criticized many government-assisted corporations for being inefficient, misguided and wasteful.

"Because they know the federal government will back them up in almost anything they do, these corporations don't worry about piling up big debts that would scare private companies," said the Fraser Institute's Walker. "Debt is not a bad thing, but it should be balanced by other forces."

Afford loss

Morrison, a member of the advisory committee for the McGill Centre for the Study of Regulated Industries, countered that a business should not be measured by the balance sheet alone.

"Sometimes the cost of keeping a plant open is less than the welfare and unemployment payments that would follow its closing," he said. "Governments can afford to take a loss easier than private industry."

MP Walter Baker, chairman of the federal Progressive Conservative caucus committee on government operations, is worried about the number of people working for government-assisted corporations.

With approximately 200,000 employees, 60,000 in the post office alone, government-assisted corporations are now referred to as the second public service, because they employ almost as many people as the 300,000 working directly in the federal civil service.

Room for improvement

While conceding he hasn't conducted any efficiency studies on government-assisted corporations, Baker said his personal experiences suggest there is room for improvement.

"When the CBC comes here for an interview, they usually have four or five people and no one helps anybody else with the equipment," he said. "But when CTV (the private network) does an interview, it's usually two people, a reporter and a camermen. They help each other with the equipment.''

Morrison, however, said most government-assisted corporations operate in the same manner as private industries. "I'd say 98 per cent of decisions in a Crown corporation are made for the same reason as in any other business — economics.''

"Sure, there are some cases where a decision is made to please the government,'' Morrison added. "But there are a lot of decisions made in private industry that have nothing to do with economics. What about the CEO who builds a plant in Montreal because he wants to be away from his in-laws in Ontario?''

Peter Von Ond, vice-president of research for stockbrokers Nesbitt Thomson Bongard Inc., has expressed concern about government-assisted corporations' competing with private companies for the limited amount of money available in capital markets.

In 1958, according to Statistics Canada, there were 28 government-assisted corporations on the federal level. Twenty years later, the number had reached 50 — more than half of which compete directly with private-sector companies.

As they've grown in numbers, government-assisted corporations have also increased dramatically in size.

In 1958, for example, federal government corporations controlled assets valued at $6.5 billion. By the end of 1978, the figure had grown to $35.1 billion.

What's most alarming to Von Ond is that, by 1979, corporations controlled by Ottawa and by provincial governments accounted for almost 15 per cent of total investment in Canada.

"Both their losses and investments are underwritten with our money, which takes away from the amount of money that could be used for other purposes,'' Von Ond said. "The money has to come from somewhere and more often than not it's out of our pockets.''

While few politicians or business leaders would do away with government-assisted corporations

OTTAWA'S FIVE BIGGEST LOSERS

Fiscal year 1981–82	Subsidies ($ Millions)
Canada Mortgage & Housing Corp.	1,100.6
Canadian Broadcasting Corp.	663.9
Canada Post	300.0
Atomic Energy of Canada Ltd.	286.0
National Research Council	271.5

OTTAWA'S FIVE BIGGEST WINNERS

Fiscal year 1981–82	Profits ($ Millions)
Petro-Canada	203.8
Canadian National Railway Co.	193.2
Air Canada	40.1
Teleglobe Canada	36.6
Export Development Corp.	2.0

altogether, most would like to see some changes in the way these companies operate.

Most popular among the suggestions is enacting so-called "sunset" legislation, which would require government-assisted corporations to justify their existence every few years or be abolished. This approach already has been applied in the United States to some state and federal government agencies.

Better control

"Once an organization gets funded, it tends to stay funded whether it's needed or not,'' Walker said. "By requiring these organizations to justify themselves, we'd have better control over where the money is spent.''

Even though the post office recently was converted to a Crown corporation in an attempt to improve its efficiency, the Tories' Baker wants all government-assisted corporations reviewed to determine whether some should go the opposite route and be

absorbed into government ministries.

"If the government wants to accomplish something, than it should be part of the government,'' Baker reasoned. "I'm sure some corporations would be better off this way.''

Such suggestions might save the taxpayers money and improve the efficiency of some government assisted-corporations. But it seems doubtful that anything more than cosmetic changes will be made in the foreseeable future.

In fact, Morrison expects to see a greater number of government-assisted corporations over the next few years.

"We're all looking for a better society and I don't think it makes a difference whether we get there via government-assisted corporations or private enterprise,'' he said.

Gordon, dropping her critical role for a moment, concluded "there are some Crown corporations that don't make economic sense. But there are some people who would say the same thing about Canada.''

THE FINANCIAL POST, FEBRUARY 5, 1983

Crowns need scrutiny

AUDITOR GENERAL Kenneth Dye has forcefully reiter-
ated his call for closer financial scrutiny of federal Crown
corporations. Dye devoted considerable space in his 1982 report (The Post, Dec. 18) to the need for such scrutiny by
Parliament. This week, Dye told the Canadian Club in Toronto
that although his role isn't to go around in public second guessing the government or elected representatives, "this doesn't mean
that I should lose my voice once my report is published."

Neither should he. Especially when he has such an important
message.

Although Dye acknowledged that proposed changes to the
Financial Administration Act may make Crown corporations
more accountable to the government, the changes still won't
give *Parliament* the proper look-in.

"Parliament's involvement both in establishing and over-
seeing Crown-owned corporations is essential for effective
accountability," Dye said. "We have found that the present system is open to abuse. There is the potential for invoking a crisis
atmosphere and bypassing parliamentary authorization."

Dye is not engaged in some sort of vendetta against Crown
corporations. "By calling for increased accountability, I am in
no way questioning the original decision to establish these
corporations, or their continued existence," Dye said. But "as

Parliament's auditor," he added, "it's my job to see that where
Parliament's funds are used by these organizations, there is adequate accountability for them."

The government should indeed consider these recommendations made by Dye to strengthen the accountability framework:

• There should be a clear authority and mandate for the Crown
corporation when it is established.

• A minister should report to Parliament on how the corporation is carrying out its activities. The government should assess
these reports and evaluate progress.

• The government should assess the corporation's financial needs
and set out for Parliament the form of financing, be it equity,
loans or appropriations. The government should demonstrate
the need for additional financing from the public purse, and let
Parliament know the form, amount and timing of such financing.

• Before voting on the financing proposals, Parliament should
be informed in a clear manner as to how the proposed financing
is going to affect the public purse.

These are not onerous conditions, considering that the Crown
corporations Dye is talking about last year took in $32 billion
and spent about $34 billion. As Dye said, "That's a lot of money,
and in the final analysis, it's public money."

THE GLOBE AND MAIL, NOVEMBER 24, 1982

New post office faster, leaner, but not everyone is happy

By JUDY STEED
Globe and Mail Reporter

OTTAWA — Can the post office
survive and prosper?

The fifth-largest employer in
Canada with more than 60,000 people on the payroll, a $2.2-billion
budget and an annual deficit that
typically topped $600-million, the
national mail service is celebrating
the first anniversary of its transformation into a Crown corporation.

Its image of blundering incompetence has been overtaken by a new

aggressive stance, supported by a
restructured organization that is
riddled with service improvement
groups and in-house task forces.
The post office, one hears, is determined to make money doing what
it's supposed to do: deliver the mail
on time.

The new management team,
headed by Michael Warren (who
was lured from Toronto's transit
system for a reputed $150,000 sala-
ry), rode into office with high expectations. It promised to improve

service, improve "the human relations climate," and attain financial
self-sufficiency within five years.

It has succeeded in cutting the
deficit by $200-million, slashing the
overtime budget by $25-million, and
incurring the wrath of the 23,000-
member Canadian Union of Postal
Workers.

CUPW president Jean-Claude
Parrot has not been seduced by Mr.
Warren's conciliatory talk. Mr.
Parrot says that labor-manage-
ment relations are worse than ever

before, that Michael Warren's only real focus is money — spending less of it — and that service is deteriorating.

His latest charge, denied by management, is that stacks of first-class mail are being held up by the corporation's campaign to cut its overtime bill.

Canada Post's own records show on-time delivery improvements of up to 10 per cent: this means that almost 90 per cent of all mail is being delivered accurately across the country in a specified number of days. A letter sent from Vancouver to Halifax takes three days, Montreal to Toronto two days, and local mail reaches its destination the next day in 95 per cent of all cases.

One independent organization that has measured the post office's performance is the Canadian Direct Marketing Association, which represents 260 corporate members doing business of more than $2-billion a year. "We're impressed with the improvements," says association president Frank Ferguson. "We measured the number of days it takes to get the first response in after a mailing has gone out, and we're finding a reduction from 11 days to six to eight days. That's very good."

The post office is happy about these findings, because the key sector it's hoping to attract is business, which accounts for more than 80 per cent of all mail — a figure that has not changed in decades.

Almost 60 per cent of the 6.1 billion pieces of mail that travel through the postal system every

company pre-sorts to letter carrier routes, it can get a 21-cent rate.

CUPW leaders don't like the scheme because it means less work for their members, but management argues that incentives are necessary to increase volume. Since a 45-day CUPW strike in the summer of 1981, followed shortly thereafter by a rate increase from 17 cents to 30 cents for a first-class letter, volume dropped from a high of 6.5 billion pieces to the present level of 6.1 billion — a drop that the post office would dearly love to recover.

Canada Post is not shy about its ambition to compete with the private sector. Larry Sperling, vice-president of corporate planning and business development, believes Priority Post, now in third place, will outstrip its rivals within a few years. The real trick, he says, is to overcome the "negative image" left from the Seventies, when the introduction of mechanized equipment in postal stations added to labor problems and resulted in unreliable service.

Mr. Warren likes to point out that when more than 6 billion pieces of mail are being moved each year an error rate of even 1 per cent can mean 60 million horror stories.

That perhaps explains the results of a recent survey on postal services done by the Canadian Federation of Independent Business. "Out of 10,000 members, only 10 per cent felt there was an improvement," says James Bennett, the federation's director of national affairs. "The majority — 64 per cent — said

inside workers, has come under new Government legislation limiting public sector employees to wage increases of 6 and 5 per cent over the next two years.

"The post office is an industrial enterprise that for years was miscast as a government department," says Mr. Sperling, who is busy dreaming up money-making ventures for the corporation to explore.

Inevitably, there are objections. The Canadian Federation of Independent Business doesn't appreciate the public sector "horning in on the private sector, using legislative fiat to protect its operations," Mr. Bennett says. And the unions increasingly worry about a post office obsessed with the bottom line and failing to accommodate the human factor.

"We're a hard-driving merchandising operation and we're willing to talk business," Mr. Sperling says. "Our 8,200 locations gives us more outlets than all the banks combined and makes us the largest retail chain in the country. We can add to our product lines. We can sell traveller's cheques, we can operate catalogue sales offices."

Mr. Sperling would like to see more imaginative use made of his trucks, for instance. "We've got 3,700 vehicles that hit just about every street in every city every day. We're saying to retailers, 'Maybe you can utilize our equipment'; after all, it makes no sense having five different sets of trucks travelling the same routes. And look at all the fuel we'd conserve."

But the final message is that no

Quality of labor relations tough to assess

year is first class and 22 per cent comes from large-volume mailers like the telephone company, electric utilities and banks. The second-largest category is third-class (at 13 cents a letter), which accounts for 31 per cent of volume and comes from advertising and direct-mail companies.

The post office is trying to woo its corporate customers into using the mails more often by offering new incentive rates: large-volume mailers who send in 20,000 pieces postal-coded and machine-sortable get a discount rate of 24 cents; if the

service was the same and 25 per cent said it was worse."

It is equally difficult to assess the quality of labor relations. Despite the complaints of CUPW, Mr. Warren and his managers point with pride to the total of man-days lost due to work stoppages, which is lower than it's been for 10 years. Absenteeism also is down slightly, although the 18 days lost per employee each year is still twice the national average.

No strikes are looming: the letter carriers recently signed a new contract and CUPW, which represents

matter how slick and efficient the post office becomes it's never going to deliver mail faster until more people use postal codes.

Almost 87 per cent of the mail is properly coded, of which 80 per cent comes from business, which means that only 7 per cent of personal mail is coded so that it can be machine-sorted.

The machines digest 28,000 letters an hour, but improperly addressed or uncoded letters act like slugs in the system. They take longer and cost more to process.

THE GLOBE AND MAIL, NOVEMBER 26, 1982

Joel Bell: 'Policy activist but not political activist'

By JAMES RUSK
Globe and Mail Reporter

OTTAWA — In choosing Joel Bell for the sensitive job of managing the federal Government's holdings in a number of companies, Social Development Minister Jack Austin turned to one of the strongest economic nationalists and most activist public servants in the capital.

After Mr. Bell's appointment as president of the Canada Development Investment Corp. was announced this week, Opposition Leader Joe Clark described Mr. Bell as a Liberal henchman. However, those close to the economist-lawyer said yesterday the description is not quite fair.

In an interview, Mr. Bell said he is not a political activist but a policy activist. That characterization is supported by those who have been close to him during his career.

With the Liberals in power during all but nine months of his career in the public service and with the Crown oil company PetroCanada, policy activism has put him close to the Liberals.

He has been close enough to the party to have been consulted when it was writing its energy policy during the 1980 election campaign and close enough to be seconded from his vice-presidency at PetroCanada to help draft the national energy policy.

But to be consulted on energy policy does not make him a Liberal. One long-time associate said that "he's never considered himself as a Liberal as such."

And Mr. Bell, whom associates describe as passionately interested in public policy and public policy formulation, said

he is quite ready to discuss his views on policy and the pros and cons of policy with anyone who seeks his advice. "If someone calls me, I say what I think."

What emerges from interviews with associates is a picture of a very bright professional who chose a career in the public sector, whose support for intervention and economic nationalism has fostered a close relationship with Liberal governments since he first came to Ottawa in 1969.

In short, it is a case of congruency of views and approach with a number of prominent Liberals around whom he built a meteoric career in the public service and Petrocan — with Ronald Basford when competition legislation was first being drafted, with Herb Gray when Mr. Bell was the principal author of the controversial Gray report on Canadian economic nationalism a decade ago, with Jack Austin as principal secretary to the Prime Minister and as deputy minister of energy, with Marc Lalonde as energy minister, and now with Jack Austin in Senator Austin's role as minister responsible for the CDIC.

Conservatives and Conservative governments probably would have had a less easy relationship with Mr. Bell and he with them than he has enjoyed with the Liberals. Indeed, during the Tory interregnum, Mr. Bell attended none of the meetings with then energy minister Ramon Hnatyshyn and Petrocan executives and Mr. Hnatyshyn has yet to meet Mr. Bell.

Mr. Bell's major achievement

at Petrocan was putting together the financing for the acqusitions of the Canadian operations of Pacific Petroleums and Petrofina and the refining and marketing operations of British Petroleum, the deals that have rapidly made Petrocan one of the big three among Canadian oil companies.

In this he has been a conduit between Ottawa and the Petrocan head office in Calgary, sometimes spending more than half his time in Ottawa. Whether he was the Ottawa's establishment's man in Petrocan or Petrocan's link to a lot of the key players in Ottawa was not clear.

While oil industry critics have argued that Mr. Bell's role in the formulation of the national energy policy was to make certain that the policy favored Petrocan, Mr. Bell said: "That's nonsense. I worked on a narrow segment of the policy and all I did was give the benefit of my views to the minister and his colleagues."

One former official who was close to the formulation of the NEP said that Mr. Bell's role has been overblown by the oil industry. What was not understood was that Mr. Bell was an outsider to the bureacratic machine in the Energy Department and that "a lot of people spent a lot of time trying to make sure that what Joel was doing would not upset what they were doing."

But his Petrocan career leaves doubts that he will take the various enterprises the Government has thrown into the CDIC — Canadair, de Havilland, Eldorado Nuclear, Teleglobe Canada, the Government share of Mas-

sey-Ferguson and the Canada Development Corp. — operate them to best commercial advantage and sell the winners to the private sector. After all, he did oppose the privatization of Petrocan by the Tories and bought up three major blocks of oil industry assets for the Government.

One Ottawa lobbyist suggested that under Mr. Bell the CDIC will become an acquisitor of industrial companies as Ottawa embarks on an interventionist industrial policy.

Mr. Bell argued that there is no better training to be a seller of a companies than to have been a buyer of companies and that the proof of his and the Government's intentions will have to be in the record he builds at CDIC.

However, he has no apologies for government involvement in commercial enterprise in Canada. There are broad national interests to be served by commercial enterprises, he said , and it is inconceivable to him that the CDIC would operate without regard to public policy.

At the same time, he said, public goals are not well served if commercial enterprise is not conducted according to the rules of efficiency and economic advantage — if, as has often been the case, government ownership of enterprise is a shelter for the uneconomic and the unsound.

Mr. Bell said that the managers of businesses into which the Goverment has gone for sound national reasons, such as the desire to preserve an airframe industry in Canada, will benefit from a corporate structure such as the CDIC.

Discussion Questions

1. Kliff's article alludes to the sometimes heavy burdens placed on Crown corporations in the way of public mandates. Does a clear mandate help or hinder the possibilities of success for public enterprises? What are the effects of other factors—the degree of political interference, for instance, or the strength of the management?
2. It is often charged that Crown corporations have unfair advantages (for example, access to govern-ment revenues for borrowing purposes) in competing with private firms. Is this the case with the Post Office?
3. Will proposals for greater accountability of Crown corporations destroy the flexibility and independence from political control that made them such an attrac-tive mechanism for implementing public policy in the first place?

Suggested Readings

Peter Foster. 'Battle of the Sectors', in *Saturday Night*, March 1982, 23–32.

D.P. Gracey. 'Federal Crown Corporations in Canada', in W.D.K. Kernaghan, ed. *Public Administration in Canada*, fourth edition. Toronto: Methuen, 1982, 59–70.

Allan Tupper and G.B. Doern, eds. *Public Corporations and Public Policy in Canada*. Montreal: Institute for Research on Public Policy, 1981.

Marsha Gordon. *Government in Business*. Montreal: C.D. Howe Research Institute, 1981.

A. Gelinas, ed. *Public Enterprise and the Public Interest*. Toronto: Institute of Public Administration of Canada, 1981.

J.W. Langford. 'The Identification and Classification of Federal Public Corporations: A Preface to Regime Build-ing', in *Canadian Public Administration*, vol. 23, no. 1, Spring 1980, 76–104.

J.W. Langford. 'Crown Corporations as Instruments of Policy', in G.B. Doern and Peter Aucoin, eds. *Public Policy in Canada: Organization, Process and Manage-ment.* Toronto: Macmillan, 1979, 239–75.

e. The Expenditure –Budgetary Process

W.A. Wilson, 'Power Delusions', *Vancouver Province*, January 14, 1982 : 77

John Gray, 'Envelope System is a Bid to Make Sense of Federal Spending', *Globe and Mail*, September 21, 1981 : 78

John Gray, 'A Dual-Paternity Brainchild Controls the Federal Purse', *Globe and Mail*, September 22, 1981 : 80

Bob Hepburn, 'How Your Tax Dollars Are Spent', *Toronto Star*, August 21, 1982 : 81

Geoffrey Stevens, 'Controlling the Public Purse: There's No More Urgent Need Than to Restore Accountability', *Globe and Mail*, June 21, 1982 : 83

Robert Duffy, 'Is Budget-Making Process in Need of Streamlining?', *Toronto Star*, January 31, 1982 : 84

'Lifting Budget Lid, Slightly', *Toronto Star*, April 24, 1982 : 86

How governments spend tax dollars is a critical question in political science. The tabling of the Estimates Blue Book (the government's spending plan) reveals detailed information on the government's priorities and the nature of relations among its various programmes, departments, and agencies. Examining the expenditure–budgetary process also affords us the opportunity of learning more about public-sector management and the structure of government decision-making. These questions, of course, are related to the overall scrutiny to which the size of government has been increasingly subjected. Critics have contended that government has lost the ability to handle financial matters effectively. Indeed, the scope of public expenditure has expanded substantially. In 1970, the federal government spent some $12-billion; by 1983, the federal expenditure budget almost reached $90-billion. Even though growth has been greater at the provincial and municipal levels than at the federal one, Ottawa has received the most criticism for the lack of expenditure contróls and excessive growth.

Apart from the expenditure budget, governments confer hand-outs, incentives, or investment opportunities upon particular groups or interests. These are often referred to as tax expenditures, because they result in the government's foregoing tax revenues. W.A. Wilson reflects on the implications of this terminology, including the perception that tax expenditures are roughly analogous to actual expenditures. That is not to say that tax expenditures are unimportant: in recent years, the growth in these 'indirect' expenditures has outpaced that in direct expenditures.

An innovation in the expenditure–budgetary process introduced by the ill-fated Clark government was the so-called envelope system, or Policy and Expenditure Management System (PEMS). In his two-part series examining this new structure, John Gray outlines many of the reasons behind its adoption. He also shows how expenditure demands are balanced within a particular envelope or sector by Cabinet committees rather than by the President of the Treasury Board. In short, the system is designed to draw priority-setting and resource-allocation closer together to induce programme trade-offs. It is probably premature to evaluate fully the effectiveness of the new system, but many have already suggested that it has helped clarify priorities, improved interdepartmental co-ordination, enhanced long-range planning and policy analysis, and introduced genuine choice among competing policy initiatives.

The article by Bob Hepburn gives a detailed break-down of the 1982–83 Estimates. Although the press always provides extensive coverage of the government's spending plans, the sheer mass and complexity of the information baffle most journalists. Many are forced by circumstance to rely on government press releases to handle the story. Hepburn's article differs in several respects. First, it is a feature story on the issue, and not a next-day news report on the tabling of the Blue Book. Second, it summarizes a large body of information by means of two simple graphic presentations. Third, it relies on material from other sources to provide a balanced interpretation. In a similar vein, Geoffrey Stevens's discussion of accountability in public expenditure benefits from a more leisurely perspective. Stevens, however, tends to accept the capabilities of Parliament and the Auditor General uncritically. Although the process could benefit from greater parliamentary scrutiny, Parliament itself is not without defects: it often construes the allocation of public monies as a political matter alone and neglects the crucial management issues involved.

The final two articles in this section are included to contrast the reform of the expenditure–budgetary process with proposed reforms of the 'economic' budgetary process. The two are obviously closely related to one another, and the latter has also been subjected to extensive scrutiny and criticism. Robert Duffy presents a litany of criticisms levelled at the process, including the inadequate consultation imposed by the blanket of budget secrecy, the short length of the budgeting cycle, and the lack of access to expert consultants. This image of a system of great complexity and difficult priority management reappears in the *Toronto Star* editorial, which also stresses the need for greater openness. These articles implicitly suggest that the budget is the result of bureaucratic bargaining relations that threaten the legitimacy of the process itself.

THE VANCOUVER PROVINCE, JANUARY 14, 1982

POWER DELUSIONS

BY W.A. WILSON
Special to The Province

OTTAWA — A few years back the department of finance adopted a change of terminology that, on the face of it, seemed so trivial and unimportant that no one noticed or thought of it twice.

It adopted the term "tax expenditures" for provisions in the tax system that until then had been known as deductions, exemptions, credits, incentives and so on. It still has to fall back on the conventional terms when it sets about explaining what it means by its new phraseology.

This looks like the most innocent example of bureaucratese but in fact it is significant because there is an implication in the new terminology that the state owns the money and this is simply not true, although both politicians and senior officials constantly forget that reality.

On odd occasions, and not very recently, the prime minister has put matters accurately — the state has no money. The money belongs to the people who worked to get it and who then necessarily contribute some of it to the official operation of the country. The public funds are just that — public, owned by the people of the country, not by the state itself.

In this matter, the state is only an agent and a trustee, albeit given to practices for which the citizen would be sent to prison if he attempted them and were caught.

This is not just a nit-picking point because the psychology behind it is important. When a very senior official not long ago insisted upon having a hand-carved, black walnut desk specially made for his use at a cost just below $10,000 he probably did not think of the money involved as belonging to other people. He presumably fell into the trap of thinking of the public funds as something that belonged to the state and decided that he would use some of the state's money to satisfy his personal taste for luxury in office.

That is why the finance department's small change of terminology reflects an unhealthy psychology among the extraordinarily privileged men who wield power at the national level.

In a recent publication the department claims that exemptions, deductions and so on "are equivalent to spending programs" by government and again it is the psychology behind the words that is important. They imply that money left with the man or woman who earned it is in some way the same thing as the government spending money on him.

One example in the department's study shows how far this sort of thinking goes. The finance officials have spent some time calculating that if everyone who owns his own home and lives in it were forced to treat the fact that he is not paying rent as a taxable benefit and then paid tax on that, the state could collect another $4.5 billion annually.

Most people would dismiss ideas of this sort with impatience but a good deal of time and money is spent developing them. The officials who work on calculations of that sort are well-paid. Yet their thinking has become wholly detached from realities that no finance minister would attempt to impose their schemes unless he were certifiably insane.

These little examples involving terminology and theoretical tax exercises are just minor signs showing how far men in power in Ottawa have drifted into the undemocratic idea that they are masters of the public.

THE GLOBE AND MAIL, SEPTEMBER 21, 1982

Envelope system is a bid to make sense of federal spending

By JOHN GRAY
Globe and Mail Reporter

OTTAWA — Those within the federal Government regard it as a minor revolution, but a senior official explains it best in the bland, everyday terms of buying a new car.

It's fine if you decide you want a Lincoln Continental, he says, but the choice by itself doesn't really mean anything if you don't have enough money to go out and actually buy it. What it boils down to, for Lincolns and Government programs alike, is that you have to match what you want against the money you've got.

Nothing could be simpler. But, oddly, until quite recently, the Government — and those of other countries as well — never managed to work out a system that achieved that kind of match-up.

Among those who use the official bureaucratese of Ottawa it's called the Policy and Expenditure Management System. Less officially it's known as the envelope system. And it has, indeed, been something of a revolution.

Those in Government take satisfaction from the fact that officials from other Western countries have started arriving in Ottawa to inspect Canada's attempt to achieve the kind of system that has so far eluded them.

In the simplest possible terms, the concerns of the federal Government are divided into 10 broad areas, and in the autumn of each year, each area is allotted a budget, or "envelope," to cover all spending in that area.

The beauty of the system is that there is flexibility within each of those 10 envelopes; the Cabinet committees responsible for each of the envelopes may juggle and rearrange their spending priorities as circumstances change during the year.

But the size of each envelope is fixed for the year. Whatever the internal rearrangements of program priorities, the total spending in each envelope must not change and, by extension, neither must the Government's total spending for all envelopes combined.

So if spending for one program goes up, spending must go down for another program in the same envelope. This means, for example, that a social program is not sacrificed to expand an economic program; instead, economic programs are measured only against each other, and social programs only against other social programs.

In terms of the household budget, you can't cut into the grocery money to buy that Lincoln.

For those not in government it may all seem like the most common of common sense, but successfully combining policy priorities and spending within a single system had previously escaped the best minds among bureaucrats and politicians.

Nobody would suggest that the federal Government previously enjoyed a reputation for rational planning. It was not for lack of trying, but the various efforts never seemed to work.

Going back to the time when Pierre Trudeau first came to power, the federal Cabinet has tried various systems by which the desires of politicians could be co-ordinated, decided, implemented — and then controlled.

The Priorities and Planning committee of Cabinet was created to sift through the policy proposals of the bureaucracy; at a later stage, bureaucrats laboriously interviewed individual ministers to divine their broad goals.

Treasury Board made major decisions

The hitch was that the eventual decisions were effectively made by the Treasury Board where, as one official put it, "their policy guys took a look at a program, decided they didn't like it and announced there wasn't enough money to finance it.

"Then they would decide on their own a program they liked, and they would direct the money toward that, whatever the Cabinet decided."

If it was not the Treasury Board making policy, it was the Minister of Finance who, through his budgets, instituted policy decisions that had ramifications, social as well as economic, throughout Canadian society.

The mystery surrounding the budget was such that finance ministers and their deputies refused for years even to provide the other Cabinet ministers with a statement on the Government's financial and economic position.

To this day, one highly respected Ottawa mandarin lays the blame for his sour relations with a former deputy minister of finance on a bitter argument in a Cabinet committee over whether or not anyone else could get some idea of the Government's accounts.

Ministers of finance had power of secrecy

This secrecy gave ministers of finance an impressive power around the Cabinet table. As one official explains it, such secrecy meant that the Finance Minister alone could decide whether there was more money to be raised or perhaps a little to spread around. And he could raise or spread that money without regard for the policy concerns of his Cabinet colleagues.

The essential fault lay not with the whims of individual ministers but with the whole traditional structure of Ottawa decision-making. The royal commission on financial management and accountability neatly defined the problem in its complaint: "We cannot accept that priorities and objectives can continue to be set without full awareness of the financial implications of attempting to achieve them."

Perhaps the final grand gesture under the old system came in August, 1978. Mr. Trudeau had just come back from the Western economic summit at Bonn determined to cut Government spending dramatically. And whatever else they may have been, the cuts certainly were dramatic. Most of the Cabinet, including the Finance Minister, Jean Chretien, found out about them by watching Mr. Trudeau on television.

The cuts had been made by a team of public servants. They had done what they were told, but their decisions were based primarily on what could be done most easily; there was little or no concern about the Cabinet's broad policy commitments.

As a result of that exercise, one senior public servant recently acknowledged, "we decided there had to be a better way." And in the months that followed, the task of finding that better way fell largely to three senior officials in the Privy Council Office: Gordon Smith, Robert Rabinovitch and Ken Stein. It was they who came up with the envelope system.

The proposal was greeted enthusiastically by Michael Pitfield, then and now Secretary to the Cabinet and Clerk of the Privy Council, and by Marcel Masse, then the new deputy secretary who had tried out a similar kind of system when he was the senior public servant in New Brunswick.

Such was the enthusiasm that the outline of the new system was contained in the transitional briefing books handed over to Joe Clark short-ly after the 1979 election that put in a new Conservative government.

Perhaps the most important change is that the decision-making process has shifted dramatically toward the politicians and away from the public servants. Some public servants miss their power; some ministers complain that they are now fighting with other ministers.

Instead of the vital decisions on spending being left to the Treasury Board, the priorities are argued out in Cabinet committees. Decisions are no longer written in stone. If new money is needed for one program, it can be taken away from another program in the same envelope.

How tax dollars are divided

Priorities and Planning Committee

1. Financial Arrangements Envelope

Finance:
Subsidies under BNA Act; Federal-Provincial fiscal arrangements; Utilities income tax transfers; Reciprocal taxation.

Public Works
Municipal grants.

2. Public Debt Envelope

Finance
Public Debt: interest and amortization.

Economic Development Committee

3. Economic Development Envelope

Agriculture:
Department; Canadian Dairy Commission; Canadian Livestock Feed Board; Farm Credit Corp.

Communications:
Department.

Consumer and Corporate Affairs:
Department.

Economic Development — Ministry of State.

Energy, Mines and Resources:
Minerals; Earth sciences.

Environment:
Forestry.

Fisheries and Oceans:
Department.

Industry, Trade and Commerce:
Department; Canadian Commercial Corp.; Export Development Corp.; Federal Business Development Bank; Foreign Investment Review Agency; Standards Council of Canada.

Labor:
Department; Canada Labor Relations Board.

Regional Economic Expansion:
Department; Cape Breton Development Corp.

Science and Technology:
Department; National Research Council; Natural Sciences and Engineering Research Council; Science Council of Canada;

Supply and Services:
Unsolicited proposals for research and development.

Transport:
Department; Air Canada; Canada Transport Commission.

4. Energy Envelope

Energy, Mines and Resources:
Energy budgetary; Energy non-budgetary; Petroleum Compensation Program; Sarnia-Montreal pipeline; Canadian Home Insulation Program; Atomic Energy Control Board; Atomic Energy of Canada Ltd.; National Energy Board; Petro-Canada.

Economic Development:
Northern Pipeline Agency.

Social Development Committee

5. Social Affairs Envelope

Communications:
Arts and culture; Canada Council; CBC; Canadian Radio-Television and Telecommunications Commission; National Arts Centre Corp.; National Film Board; National Library; National Museums of Canada; Public Archives; Social Science and Humanities Research Council.

Employment and Immigration:
Department; Advisory Council on Status of Women; Immigration Appeal Board; Status of Women — office of the co-ordinator.

Environment:
Environment Programs.

Indian Affairs and Northern Development:
Department; Northern Canada Power Commission.

Labor:
Canadian Centre for Occupational Health and Safety; Fitness and Amateur Sport.

National Health and Welfare:
Department; Medical Research Council.

Public Works:
Canada Mortgage and Housing Corp.

Secretary of State:
Department.

Social Development — Ministry of State.

Treasury Board Canada:
Student, youth and other employment.

Veterans Affairs:
Department.

6. Justice and Legal Envelope

Justice:
Department; Canadian Human Rights Commission; Commissioner for Federal Judicial Affairs; Law Reform Commission of Canada; Supreme Court of Canada; Tax Review Board.

Solicitor-General:
Department; Correctional Services; National Parole Board; RCMP.

Foreign and Defence Policy Committee

7. External Affairs Envelope

External Affairs:
Department; Canadian International Development Agency; International Development Research Centre; International Joint Commission.

Finance:
Official development assistance — loans and investments.

8. Defence Envelope

National Defence:
Department.

Government Operations Committee

9. Parliament Envelope

Parliament
The Senate; House of Commons; Library of Parliament.

10. Services to Government Envelope

Finance:
Department; Auditor-General; Insurance; Tariff Board; Governor-General and Lieutenant-Governors.

National Revenue:
Department.'

Post Office:
Department.

Privy Council Office:
Canadian Intergovernmental Conference Secretariat; Chief Electoral Officer; Commissioner of Official Languages; Economic Council of Canada; Public Service Staff Relations Board.

Public Works:
Department; National Capital Commission.

Secretary of State:
Public Service Commission.

Supply and Services:
Department; Statistics Canada.

Treasury Board Canada:
Comptroller-General.

THE GLOBE AND MAIL, SEPTEMBER 22, 1981

A dual-paternity brainchild controls the federal purse

By JOHN GRAY
Globe and Mail Reporter

OTTAWA — In a town where almost everything takes its legitimacy from politics, not many of the major changes in Government can claim a shared paternity.

A surprising exception is the envelope system, which for the past 2½ years has determined how Ottawa sets its policy priorities and spends its money. It was conceived by the Liberals, first saw the light of day officially under the brief Tory administration, and now is being carefully nurtured by the Liberals again.

The system was the brainchild of senior officials in the Privy Council Office in late 1978, after a decade in which the first Trudeau government tried a succession of ways to integrate policy and spending.

Despite its various efforts and its commitment to rational planning, that government alternately spent and saved money in its first 10 years without any real regard to the effects of that spending or saving.

Bizarre though it may seem, Cabinet committees ignored the financial implications of their policy decisions leaving the money problem to the Treasury Board. Policy and spending were quite separate concerns.

So a team from the Privy Council Office devised a system in which the total amount of all Government spending is fixed every autumn, and divided among 10 broad policy areas, known as "envelopes," in shares that are also fixed. There is nothing new in establishing limits, of course, but the beauty of this system is that there is flexibility within each envelope, so money can be taken from one program and added to another in that same envelope as priorities change during the year.

The first chance for the system came when Joe Clark led his Conservative Party to power in 1979, and the man in charge of implementing it was Marcel Masse, who became Clerk of the Privy Council, the most senior public servant in Ottawa, after Mr. Clark dumped his predecessor, Michael Pitfield, who was regarded as too close to Pierre Trudeau's Liberals.

Mr. Clark's decision to adopt the envelope system was the source of some unhappiness among those members of his new Cabinet who regarded any idea of either the Privy Council Office or the Liberals as the work of the devil.

The reward for the Conservative Leader's determination was that in the eyes of many the envelope system came to be regarded as a great Clark contribution to the process of Government and a clever Conservative innovation.

The new system was perfectly suited to a new administration that had made financial responsibility and spending cuts central planks in its election platform. As Mr. Clark said of the new system at the time:

"We are ending the era where several ministers were interested in spending and only the President of the Treasury Board was concerned about restraint. We have a system in place now that imposes an obligation to pursue restraint upon each minister and each department."

The next surprise came after the Tories' defeat. To the consternation of many of his own ministers, who regarded the envelope system as a vile Conservative instrument, Mr. Trudeau agreed it was the solution to the problems that had bedevilled his earlier government.

In the 18 months since his return, all has not been sweetness and light with the envelope system. Some public servants and even some ministers have been suspicious, especially because decision-making has become more the concern of politicians than public servants. Some public servants miss the power, and some ministers complain they now are fighting with their ministerial colleagues.

Instead of the vital decisions on spending being left to the Treasury Board, the priorities are argued out in Cabinet committees. And decisions are no longer written in stone; if new money is needed for one program, it can be taken away from another program in the same envelope.

"That's why our meetings are well attended," says Senator H.A. Olson, who was minister of agriculture between 1968 and 1972 and is now Economic Development Minister. "The ministers come. If they want any more, they've got to get the authorization there for the allocation of the funds and for the policy to deliver it.

"If they don't show up, first of all they don't get their oars in for whatever they might want to do. And they also, I guess it's fair to say, have to defend the ongoing viability of their priority to keep the funds they've got."

For Senator Olson, the envelope system has not been totally painless. But his experience with controlling expenditures in his early months as economic development minister was a powerful introduction to the system.

After he was sworn in he discovered that the Clark government had overspent the economic development envelope by $80-million, and Liberal campaign promises had added another $250-million in commitments from it. This meant that priorities in the envelope, covering 12 different Government departments, had to be juggled to come up with $330-million from other economic development programs. "I don't want to kid you that it was easy, but it was fun."

Most other ministers don't regard cutting programs as fun, because if they are not having their own programs cut they're doing it to someone else. The fun part comes on days when the Cabinet committees decide they must dispose of some of the slush funds saved for discretionary spending in case of some national or regional crisis. On the economic development committee they call the parcelling-out of such funds "the auction" and in the social development committee they call it "banking day."

The odd lapse aside, in the 2½ years since the system was instituted two governments have stayed within its strictures to a degree that has surprised both bureaucrats and ministers.

Bruce Doern, director of Carleton University's School of Public Administration, says the crucial test is whether the Cabinet holds the line on the allocations for each envelope, and does not allow appeals. "If the line is held, the system has a chance of working. If it is not held, the system will be little different in practice than the one which preceded it."

So far, people in Ottawa believe the system is indeed working. As Senator Olson says, with a tone of some surprise: "I think we've got this expenditure thing under control, at last."

THE TORONTO STAR, AUGUST 21, 1982

How your tax dollars are spent

By Bob Hepburn Toronto Star

OTTAWA — When Finance Minister Allan MacEachen announced in June that the federal deficit would hit almost $20 billion, it was a bombshell to the Canadian investment and business community.

It was a whopping and dramatic increase from the $10.5-billion deficit MacEachen initially forecast in his November budget. What's worse, some private economists said the deficit could go as high as $23 billion.

Immediately, Conservative Leader Joe Clark, his finance critic Michael Wilson and a stream of business leaders and economists denounced the Liberal government for its failure to control the deficit and curb Ottawa's seemingly insatiable thirst for tax dollars.

Denounced Liberals

But how easy is it to cut back? In reality, it's easier said than done.

And the question left unanswered by Clark and other critics is just what cuts in government spending they would make that would significantly reduce the bulging deficit.

Despite the political rhetoric of Clark and others, there's little Ottawa can do to lower the deficit in any major way. That is unless the Liberals, Conservatives and New Democrats are prepared to approve massive cuts in social programs such as old-age pensions, medicare or baby bonuses or are ready to incur the wrath of the provinces by slashing transfer payments.

And there's no sign any of them are willing to do so.

Ottawa is locked into spending the bulk of its tax revenue to help the elderly, the poor, the unemployed; or to finance national defence, education, medicare, or ship money straight back to the 10 provinces in the form of transfer payments.

The federal government is left with very little room to make discretionary spending cuts that will have a dramatic impact on the budget.

Right now, out of every dollar Ottawa receives from taxpayers, almost 40 cents is returned to individuals in forms such as pensions or baby bonuses or to provin-

cial and municipal governments as the federal government's share of such programs as medicare, welfare and post-secondary education.

Also included are transfer payments, which are the equalization payments to help the poorer provinces. Another 23 cents is spent to pay interest costs on the public debt.

Ottawa will only spend 16 cents out of every dollar on operating and capital expenditures for all its departments, except defence, in the 1982–83 fiscal year. That leaves little room for cuts.

"Even if the government eliminated all its waste and boondoggles, there would not be much affect on the deficit," says Bruce Doern, a professor at Carleton University's School of Public Administration and editor of a series of annual books titled How Ottawa Spends Your Tax Dollars.

Doern, one of the leading private authorities on government spending policies, told Insight "The acid test for any government or party claiming to be serious about cutting spending would be to eliminate a big, universal program such as family allowances."

Other areas might include the issue of indexing of social benefits such as old-age pensions or welfare payments. Or Ottawa might slash grants under the Department of Regional Economic Expansion (DREE), he said.

Spending plans

"All these areas are political dynamite. This is not Reagan country," Doern said, referring to the sweeping cuts in social programs championed by U.S. President Ronald Reagan.

"I don't think the Liberals have the stomach for it. I don't think even the Conservatives do. What they say when they are in opposition may be a far cry from what they would do if they were in power."

An examination of Ottawa's spending plans indicates the narrow extent the government has to trim costs in a dramatic fashion.

In the current fiscal year, the federal government will spend $17.8 billion just paying interest charges on its huge debt. That amounts to 23 cents of every dollar spent. Another $14.9 billion (or 20.5 cents per dollar) is returned directly to

How Ottawa divides your dollar

Defence	Transfer payments to provinces municipalities, etc.	Subsidies to railways, agriculture, fishing, oil exploration, etc.
9.5c	19.3c	7.6c

Interest payments on public debt	Other federal departments	Old age pensions, baby bonus, etc.	Subsidies to some Crown corporations
23c	16c	20.5c	4c

Canadians in programs for old-age pensions ($7.05 billion), guaranteed income supplements to the elderly poor ($2.6 billion), family allowances or baby bonuses ($2.26 billion), veterans' pensions ($597 million), war veterans' allowances ($394 million), home insulation grants ($252 million), Indian and Inuit payments ($57 million), training allowances ($91 million) and scores of minor plans.

While Ottawa's contribution to unemployment insurance is slated at $1.25 billion, there are strong indications that the amount may rise by another $2 billion because of Canada's high jobless rate. When unemployment eases, the contributions will fall.

Governments of all levels receive $14.07 billion, or 19.3 cents out of every dollar from Ottawa and any move by the federal government to curb the rate of increase of these payments is certain to raise another round of federal-provincial confrontation just as last year, when MacEachen announced that the growth of some payments would be eased.

Fiscal transfers are the biggest item flowing to the provinces, accounting for $4.8 billion. Welfare contributions under the Established Programs Financing Plan amount to $2.58 billion, hospital insurance $2.36 billion and post-secondary education $1.5 billion.

Extra payments going to other governments include $382 million to the running of the Northwest Territories and the Yukon, $200 million to municipal governments, $130 million for crop insurance, and $47.6 million for vocational rehabilitation of disabled persons.

Two other major areas also receive huge chunks of federal dollars, including subsidies and other transfer payments that encompass items such as $352 million to railway and transportation companies, $314 million for grain stabilization, $246 million for oil substitution programs, $114 million for western grain stabilization and $75 million for commercial and fishing vessels. Neither the Conservatives nor the New Democrats have suggested slashing any of these programs.

Items such as foreign aid ($955 million), DREE ($663 million) and transfers to Indians and Inuit ($547 million) fall into this category.

The other area is payments to crown corporations, notably $941 million to Central Mortgage and Housing, $737 million to the Canadian Broadcasting Corp. and $506 million to Via Rail.

That leaves the operation of the federal departments themselves. Their budgets total $11.7 billion, excluding defence which the Tories probably would not touch and in fact might increase.

Conservatives claim that during their short nine-month reign in 1979–80, then Treasury Board President Sinclair Stevens ordered a full review of where spending could be cut. When Stevens reported, the study showed that 10 per cent could be trimmed from the operating budgets, he was tagged with the nickname "The Slasher."

Famous report

However, the Tories have never produced the famous report, complete or incomplete, to support the 10-per-cent claim.

Even if the claim were true, the savings would amount to $1.1 billion, barely a 6-per-cent reduction in the $19.6 billion deficit.

Despite constant reports of questionable spending, Doern believes federal bureaucrats are now much more cost-conscious than they were four years ago. Indeed, many federal officials have pleaded with elected politicians to abandon plans for expensive projects. Construction of the "white elephant" Mirabel airport near Montreal is a classic example of bureaucrats being overruled by politicians.

As the Liberals and Conservatives move slowly toward the next election, expected in less than two years, the pressure to justify government spending and proposed spending cuts will grow.

Doern says in his analysis of 1982 spending patterns that "there is an inexorable pressure building within the cabinet to increase social spending. As the 1984 election draws closer, social spending will undoubtedly increase. The Liberals' election bid will be hinged to a social package containing any one or all of increased pensions, another increase in the guaranteed income supplement and an expanded child tax credit."

If the recession lingers, the end result may be a deficit that stubbornly refuses to come down.

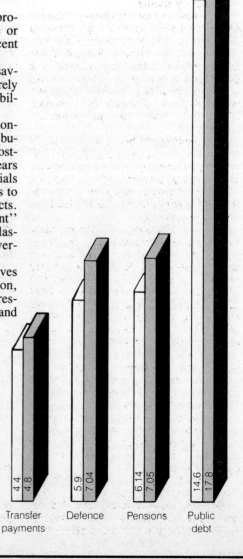

The big spenders

All figures in billions of dollars

1981–82
1982–83

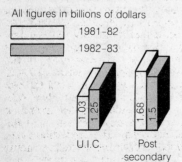
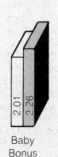
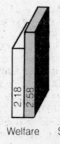
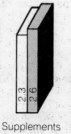

| 1.03 1.25 | 1.68 1.5 | 2.01 2.26 | 2.18 2.58 | 2.3 2.6 | 2.64 2.36 | 4.4 4.8 | 5.9 7.04 | 6.14 7.05 | 14.6 17.8 |
| U.I.C. | Post secondary education | Baby Bonus | Welfare | Supplements to elderly | Medicare | Transfer payments | Defence | Pensions | Public debt |

THE GLOBE AND MAIL, JUNE 21, 1982

Controlling the public purse:

There's no more urgent need than to restore accountability.

BY GEOFFREY STEVENS

Mr. Stevens is national editor of The Globe and Mail.

A LARGE share of the blame must be laid squarely at the door of Beardsley Ruml.

Beardsley Ruml?

Mr. Ruml was the treasurer of Macy's department store in New York when, in 1942, he had the bright idea that the war effort would be greatly assisted if the United States introduced income tax deductions at source for individuals. He wrote to President Franklin Roosevelt who, delighted, promptly implemented Mr. Ruml's idea. Canada, naturally, followed suit.

The result might be known as Ruml's Syndrome — a lingering malaise characterized among governments by a certain casualness toward the husbanding of taxpayer monies and among the public by a sense of inevitability about government spending.

James J. Macdonell, the former auditor-general, speculated in a speech three years ago on what it might be like if wage-earners had to make quarterly income tax payments as self-employed individuals do. "The accountability level of politicians to taxpayers would double over night. And so would the accountability level of bureaucrats to politicians. Nothing could sharpen more quickly the taxpayer's awareness of government spending than the painful process of writing a cheque every three months to pay his personal share."

Impractical? Of course.

Yet there is no more urgent need in our parliamentary democracy than to restore accountability. The system of legislative regulation of Government spending doesn't work.

It wasn't working in 1962 when the Glassco Royal Commission on Government Organization found that federal operations had outgrown the controls. It wasn't working in 1968 when MPs, thoroughly alarmed by their inability to influence Government spending, embarked on one of the most spectacular failures in Canadian parliamentary history — new procedures for dealing with annual spending estimates.

It wasn't working in 1976 when the auditor-general warned the Commons that, "Parliament — and indeed the Government — has lost or is close to losing effective control of the public purse." And it wasn't working in 1979 when the Lambert Royal Commission on Financial Management and Accountability reached this sombre verdict:

"After two years of careful study, we have reached the deeply held conviction that the serious malaise pervading the management of government stems fundamentally from a grave weakening, and in some cases an almost total breakdown, in the chain of accountability, first within government, and second in the accountability of government to Parliament and ultimately to the Canadian people."

In the provinces — nine of which are forecasting deficits this year — as in Ottawa, accountability is (in theory) achieved in two ways. The first, the pre-expenditure audit, comes when legislators consider and vote on the Government's spending estimates. The second, the post-expenditure audit, comes in the form of an annual report of the auditor or auditor-general and in the review of the annual statement of public accounts by a legislative committee.

Although post-expenditure auditing has become a big business — governments across Canada spend $60- to $70-million a year on auditing their accounts — its application is uneven. In Quebec, for example, the National Assembly's standing committee on Finance, Public Accounts and Revenue has not met for six years to consider the auditor's report or provincial public accounts. But even a zealous auditor and a determined public accounts committee can do only so much; by the time they come on the scene, the money has long since been spent.

If accountability is to be restored, it must be by reforming the pre-expenditure audit, the process of examining the annual spending estimates, known in Ottawa as the Blue Book. Here, ironically, MPs are the authors of their own considerable misfortune.

Until 1968, the estimates were debated by the full Commons, sitting as Committee of Supply. These debates were generally a farce, an excuse for the most shameless partisan posturing. Between 1962 and 1968, the House cut only three items — a total of $8,850,000 — from expenditures totalling more than $60-billion.

In 1968, embarrassed MPs adopted new procedures that came into effect on Jan. 1, 1969. The estimates were taken out of the Commons. Instead, they are automatically referred to standing committees which have March, April and May each year to give them detailed study. At the end of May, the estimates must be reported back to the House, which has until the end of June to pass them.

This revised system has proved an unleavened disaster. MPs have neither the time nor the interest to do the homework to probe details of complicated expenditure programs. The Government protects itself by controlling the choice of committee chairmen and exerting tight discipline over its supporters on each committee. Because examination of the estimates is tied now to the calendar, the Opposition can no longer use delay as a tactic of persuasion. In the old days, the Opposition could withhold approval of the estimates until the Government ran out of money. Now, failure to meet a deadline means automatic approval of the expenditures. And the rules do not permit the Opposition to try to reduce individual spending items when a department's estimates are reported back to the Commons from committee.

The abject failure of the new system is documented in a study by Peter Dobell, director of the Parliamentary Centre for Foreign Affairs and Foreign Trade. Mr. Dobell found that in 13 years of the new, "improved" system MPs have managed to slash Government spending by a grand total of $1,000. That's $1,000 from expenditures totalling $465-billion. (The $1,000 was a wrist-slap reduction in CBC spending during the minority Parliament of 1973-74.)

It is not only the magnitude of federal spending that hamstrings MPs. There's also the complexity of the spending. It is one thing, for example, for an MP to assess the investment of public monies in construction of a stretch of railway track (assuming there would be trains to use the track). It is another thing to measure the probable return on money spent on, say, incentives to encourage research in Canada. A third complication is the profusion of spenders in the federal firmament. The last time anyone bothered to count (in January, 1979) no fewer than 426 federal departments and agencies were hard at work spending taxpayer dollars.

Members of all parties are frustrated by their impotence. No fewer than 50 Liberal backbenchers applied for 11 Government seats on the 20-member Special Committee on Standing Orders and Procedure that was struck last week to review all aspects of procedural reform. With the committee scheduling hearings through the summer, many proposals for change are being brought forward. But most have been advanced so often they've become threadbare.

They include: smaller committees; a single, highly expert, estimates committee to deal with all departments' spending; more subcommittees; less use of the whip; more time for committees to work; full or partial return to pre-1969 procedures; professional staff for committees; greater continuity in committee assignments; introduction of sunset laws.

Inevitably, however, all proposals run up against the reality of the parliamentary power structure: there is no way Canadian MPs are going to be given authority to determine final appropriations, as the U.S. Congress does.

And whatever system is devised, the central dilemma will remain. Allen Lambert put his finger on it when he released his royal commission report three years ago: "Only if Parliament has the will and the means to exact a full accounting from government for its conduct of the nation's affairs will there exist the pressure within government to ensure that those affairs are being managed in a way that most efficiently and effectively serves the national interest. . ."

The *will* and the *means*.

Parliament can vote itself the *means*. But the *will* is more elusive. Politicians are spenders, not conservers. They gravitate to committees covering policy areas in which they or their constituents are interested and their natural desire is to secure more money, not less, for these endeavors.

More important, there is no political pay-out in this post-Beardsley Ruml age for an elected representative who assumes the duty of calling governments to account, item by item, dollar by dollar. Such drudge work brings no attention from the press, no advancement within his party, no thanks from his electors.

Until it does, the system, "reformed" or unreformed, will continue to offer an illusion of accountability where none exists.

THE TORONTO STAR, JANUARY 31, 1982

Is budget-making process in need of streamlining?

By Robert Duffy
Toronto Star

Few federal budgets in living memory have raised as big a political storm as the one Finance Minister Allan MacEachen brought down in November. Not only has the parliamentary opposition reacted with unprecedented hostility, but some Liberal members of Parliament have joined in the condemnation.

And Canadians still don't know exactly what the budget will mean to them in terms of the taxes they will have to pay this year.

Some of the major changes proposed by MacEachen have been withdrawn or delayed. Tax accountants are still waiting for Revenue Canada to spell out all the regulations for a much-heralded crackdown on employee perks and other special privileges scheduled to be included in taxable income.

While the main debate centres on the specific actions, or lack of action, in MacEachen's budget, the uproar points to a more fundamental question: Is the whole process of government budget-making adequate to deal with the problems of our complex modern economy?

Fundamental changes

It has become increasingly clear that MacEachen and his officials, confined as they were by the tradition of budget secrecy and therefore unable to consult widely, didn't fully appreciate the consequences of the changes they tried to make in the taxation system.

Some tax experts regard these changes as the most fundamental since the introduction of inflation indexing in 1973.

The Joint Taxation Committee of the Canadian Bar Association and the Canadian Institute of Chartered Accountants have attacked MacEachen for introducing "a major reform of the Canadian tax system without any prior public discussion of the impact of the changes on Canadian taxpayers."

The main problem is not the competence or lack of it in the finance department — though that question has been raised lately — but the whole process of preparing national budgets of expenditure and taxation.

Small group

Through a tradition inherited from British parliamentary practice, the budget is top secret until the finance minister rises to deliver his speech in the House of Commons. (Reporters get to study the budget documents several hours before in a budget "lockup" but are prohibited from communicating with the outside until the minister begins speaking.)

Hence only he and a small group of senior finance department officials know what goes into it. On their expertise and judgment depends the impact of $76 million (for the next fiscal year) of government taxation, borrowing and expenditure — about 20 per cent of Canada's gross national product (GNP).

Many people — including former Liberal finance ministers Donald Macdonald and Walter Gordon and members of the Canadian Tax Foundation, a non-profit organization for the analysis of taxation policy — suggest Canada should rethink the rules by which fiscal policy is achieved.

"The custom that the finance minister, probably with some consultation with the Prime Minister, sets the budget of the day in isolation is all wrong," says Gordon, whose 1963 budget came under bitter attack.

In his May, 1976, budget speech, Macdonald questioned the secrecy and procedural rules surrounding the budget and later asked the tax foundation to study the problem.

The essential conclusions of the foundation's 1977 report: The budget process needs to be opened up to public consideration and debate, both in Parliament and the country as a whole; and, while advance secrecy with some budget decisions is necessary, the present rule is far too rigidly comprehensive.

The budget-making process involves a one-year cycle — beginning with the kind of feedback the finance department is getting now.

In April and May, information is starting to emerge from the government's data collecting systems and work begins on developing ideas for the "fiscal stance" the government should take for an October or November budget.

For instance, MacEachen's basic fiscal stance this time was the need to reduce the federal deficit.

Over the summer and early fall the finance department's view of the economy and what to do about it goes to the cabinet. During the same period, revenue needs and priorities are set for the so-called spend-ing "envelopes."

Meanwhile, the tax policy division of the finance department is coming up with possibilities for generating government revenue as well as working out problems or anomalies that have surfaced in the system.

Then the hard work begins for the finance minister and his top officials.

He has first of all to find the money to carry out the spending programs agreed on earlier in cabinet. Then he has to relate taxing and spending with the proposed "fiscal stance," whether restrictive or expansionary.

From this point on, there are no more cabinet discussions or talks with other individual ministers on budget matters. The finance minister is alone with his officials in assessing the options for revenue generation and deciding the precise direction of fiscal policy.

As budget night approaches, the number of officials involved falls away steadily. In the final two weeks of preparation of the actual budget speech, the minister works virtually in seclusion with his deputy minister.

Virtually all Canadian finance ministers in modern times have stumbled at one time or another over the effects of the narrowness of this budget-making process and the limited range of expert judgment that it allows. Most have questioned whether the rigid code of government secrecy is necessary.

MacEachen, in a telephone interview from Ottawa, told The Star the government is considering changes in the method of budget preparation, though no conclusions have been reached. "We're considering the problem," he said. "I think the time has come to find ways for a meeting of a broader range of minds."

Ironically, it was MacEachen's attempt to undo some of what are now regarded as past mistakes in federal budget policy that has contributed to his present problems.

Given the primary objective of reducing the government deficit, he had a choice of either raising tax rates or broadening the tax base, John Evans, MacEachen's parliamentary assistant, explains.

Raising the rates would be damaging to the fragile economy and also could increase the problem of the so-called "underground economy" — non-cash transactions of goods and services which escape the tax net, as well as unreported cash deals that are almost impossible to catch.

Weedy field

So MacEachen plowed up the weedy field of "tax expenditures," the wide range of reduced rates, cost deductions and special allowances that have been brought into taxation policy in recent years.

"Most Canadians find our tax system unfair, and I agree with them," he said in the budget speech. "Over $47 billion of personal income escaped tax in 1979. If these preferences were eliminated, rates of tax could be halved without reducing federal revenues."

But the changes MacEachen made, without warning and without consultation, brought howls of protest from the individuals and businesses. The minister has had to yield on several fronts to this onslaught, evidently unforeseen by his advisers.

Tax experts are almost unanimous in calling for a better way of arriving at national fiscal and taxation policy.

The 1977 Canadian Tax Foundation report, commissioned by Donald Macdonald, "is the best analysis of the budget process that's ever been done," says foundation director Douglas Sherbaniuk.

Among the report's observations: " . . . The public has little real assurance that budgetary decisions are being made with a full appreciation of all the relevant circumstances. By and large, the budget policy options available to the minister of finance are those presented to him by a very small group of officials in the Department of Finance.

"The minister is unlikely to have the background and train-ing necessary to question seriously the recommendations made by his officials or to develop independent policies."

Walter Gordon knew what he wanted to do in his 1963 budget. But his nationalistic proposal for a 30 per cent tax on the sale of Canadian businesses to foreign buyers proved politically impractical and had to be withdrawn. "It provoked an absolute furor," Gordon recalls.

Macdonald, finance minister from September, 1975, to September, 1977, agrees mainly with the findings of the tax foundation's report.

'With today's complex fiscal and economic problems, it is very difficult for any single group of individuals to know how to handle them.'

Prof. Richard Bird, director of the University of Toronto's Institute for Policy Analysis, thinks both the finance and revenue departments in Ottawa are unwilling prisoners of the rule of secrecy and the tradition that a budget is a statement of government policy by which at least the finance minister, if not the government, must stand or fall.

"What was missing, and what has never really existed in Canada, is a good documentation and justification of the government's position. I would have liked to see four or five papers on different policy areas published some months before the measures were brought in."

Prof. Roger Smith, dean of the Faculty of Business Administration and Commerce at the University of Alberta and an expert on the "underground economy" and the use of tax expenditures in government fiscal policy, agrees on the need for advance discussion of major structural changes in the tax system.

"What one has in the recent budget is a situation where that did not occur adequately before the budget was brought down," he says.

"And unfortunately the finance department did not have the in-house expertise to identify some of the likely problems with the new policies."

THE TORONTO STAR, APRIL 24, 1982

Lifting budget lid, slightly

Finance Minister Allan MacEachen's green paper of proposals for opening up the budget-making process in Canada is a somewhat faltering step on the path towards the important goal of ensuring more public and parliamentary discussion of proposed fiscal and taxation measures.

MacEachen acknowledges the need for reform in the system, and declares himself to be in favor of lifting the veils of secrecy that currently surround an incubating budget. But he seems more interested in setting up groups of tax experts to consult with government officials in camera than he is in ensuring that the government's budget ideas get full scrutiny at an early stage from the public and from appropriate parliamentary committees.

MacEachen's green paper suggests that each finance minister should be free to establish "whatever consultative arrangements he thinks necessary" in order to get advice on budget proposals from the private sector.

MacEachen himself seems particularly enamored of the idea of a permanent advisory committee to the finance minister, made up of tax specialists from the private sector, which would regularly advise the government on tax matters under consideration. The input of such a group would undoubtedly be useful — but MacEachen makes it clear that the tax advisory committee he envisions would report in confidence to the minister, and would not make its findings public.

MacEachen does outline scenarios for public input through ad hoc committees on specific fiscal or taxation initiatives — committees that would be empowered to hold public hearings, accept briefs, and make recommendations to the minister. Another idea that has merit is a suggestion that white or green papers on budget ideas be used and circulated more widely, and be used as the basis for hearings and conferences.

Indeed, MacEachen is much more amenable to the idea of setting up consultative bodies outside the parliamentary process than he is to the idea — recommended by the Canadian Tax Foundation in 1977 and again in 1982 — of referring tax bills and fiscal initiatives to the House finance committee, made up of MPs from all sides of the House.

In this, he appears to put his emphasis in the wrong place. Surely the elected representatives of the people of Canada, in a committee setting where they can make their constituents' views known, should participate fully in pre-budget discussions, if pre-budget discussions are to be tried.

Committees of the House traditionally draw a wide variety of representations from all sectors of the economy. Farmers, ordinary taxpayers, consumers associations and small business groups can expect to be heard as witnesses on the same basis as legal experts, taxation wizards, and high powered corporate executives. The same assurance might not be available in a conference setting, or at sessions of an ad hoc committee set up to look specifically at a fine point of taxation policy.

It's encouraging that MacEachen has, like many other finance ministers before him, recognized that the tradition of budget secrecy can be destructive and counter-productive. Let's hope that this time we actually get some action.

While certain information that could allow individuals or businesses in the know to turn extra profit or gain an extra advantage in the marketplace should naturally be kept from public view, there is much that goes into a modern budget that can and should be discussed by the widest possible range of interest groups.

Discussion Questions

1. In light of Wilson's article, what are the advantages and disadvantages of direct spending and tax expenditures?

2. What is the relation between changes in the Cabinet committee system and the introduction of the envelope spending control system? Does Gray adequately explain the origins of the envelope system?

3. What can we learn from an assessment of the government's annual expenditure plan along the lines of Hepburn's article?

4. Is the current system of expenditure accountability to Parliament adequate, or are the changes advocated by Stevens necessary?

5. Outline the criticisms of the current economic budgetary process. Are the pressures for reform outlined in Duffy's article and the *Star* editorial greater than the recent pressures to reform the expenditure–budgetary process?

Suggested Readings

W.D.K. Kernaghan, ed. *Public Administration in Canada: Selected Readings,* fourth edition. Toronto: Methuen, 1982, 156–89.

G.B. Doern, ed. *How Ottawa Spends Your Tax Dollars: Federal Priorities, 1982.* Toronto: Lorimer, 1982 (annual publication since 1980).

Richard J. Van Loon. 'Stop the Music: The Current Policy and Expenditure Management System in Ottawa', in *Canadian Public Administration,* vol. 24, no. 2, Summer 1981, 175–99.

Peter Aucoin, ed. *The Politics and Management of Restraint in Government.* Montreal: Institute for Research on Public Policy, 1981.

Richard D. French. *How Ottawa Decides.* Toronto: Lorimer, 1980.

Canada, Royal Commission on Financial Management and Accountability. *Final Report.* Ottawa: Supply and Services, 1979.

Hal Kroeker. 'The Expenditure–Budgetary Process', in G.B. Doern and Peter Aucoin, eds. *Public Policy in Canada: Organization, Process and Management.* Toronto: Macmillan, 1979, 132–57.

f. The Judicial Process

The process of patriating the Canadian constitution in 1981 and 1982 turned the spotlight more than ever before on the Supreme Court of Canada (SCC) and the political functions of the entire judicial system. The Supreme Court performs a number of crucial functions, for it sits at the apex of a single integrated judicial system for the country. This structure contrasts with the separate state and federal court systems in the United States. The Canadian court system is further integrated by the existence of only one criminal code with uniform application across the country. The Supreme Court acts as political arbiter when it settles constitutional disputes among the provinces and Ottawa by striking down laws outside the particular jurisdiction of one level or the other. In short, the SCC gives the country a judicial focus in much the same way that Parliament provides a legislative focus. This last activity is likely to intensify in the near future as challenges to laws are made on the basis of the new Charter of Rights and Freedoms.

Press coverage of the SCC and the judiciary in general is mixed. Since few papers have full-time legal correspondents assigned to the SCC, most have to rely on the haphazard reporting of major decisions. With the notable exception of coverage of the SCC's September 1981 ruling on the constitutionality of the federal government's constitutional package, the press has generally ignored the internal dynamics of court operations and decision-making. A fine example of reporting on the Supreme Court is David Lancashire's feature which, although it concentrates on the physical trappings of the Court bench and building, also discusses how cases arrive at the Court and are heard, the Court's record on civil liberties, and its constitutional functions. Similarly, William Monopoli's interview with retired justice Ronald Martland stresses the constitutional importance of the SCC. In addition, Martland deals with many of the changes affecting the Court and suggested reforms of the institution.

The article by Marina Strauss provides an interesting look at the political role of the judiciary. She emphasizes the point that judges are not particularly well equipped to deal with the important public-policy decisions that the courts must make. Her article reflects a growing controversy over the political aspects of the courts. These concerns were raised again by the famous SCC decision in September 1981 distinguishing between the legality and conventionality of the Trudeau government's unilateral move to patriate the British North America Act and to impose an entrenched charter of rights. As political scientist Peter Russell and journalist William Monopoli indicate in their articles, the decision is complex and somewhat confusing. Monopoli discusses the internal workings of the decision and shows how participants in the constitutional revision process could read their own conclusions into the judgements. Russell explores the question of how the participants could all find some dignity in the Court's rendering. Hugh Townsend concentrates less on the substance of the decision than on the implications for the SCC itself. He draws special attention to the educative function of the Court and the sense of legitimacy that it must maintain in order to be effective. The other two articles on the decision are selected from the veritable avalanche of opinion following its release. Given the ambiguity of the decision, the press can hardly be blamed if its reporting of such subtle and intricate political manoeuvring comes out slightly garbled.

The appointment of justices to the SCC always attracts considerable media attention, even though the average citizen would be hard pressed to name one of the justices. The elevation of the first woman to the Court received even greater coverage than usual. Farrell Crook gives an excellent account of the background of Justice Bertha Wilson, but falls into the trap of trying to classify her ideology. This is a risky venture, given judicial independence, the collegial factors involved in decisions, and the mixture of fact, law, and personal viewpoints reflected in judgements. It is interesting to note that while the article celebrates the end of a male stranglehold on the highest court, it makes no comment on the elitist nature of the judiciary in general.

The final two articles in this section address the question of judicial independence. More specifically, they discuss the conduct of one outspoken judge, Thomas Berger, and his criticisms of the constitutional accord of November 1981. Robert Fulford gives an excellent critique of the handling of the matter by the government and the Judicial Council. Michael Valpy chooses to note the special circumstances surrounding Berger's intervention in a political debate. Valpy does not mention the fact that judges cannot be held accountable in any political or legal way. The immunity they enjoy, which ensures judicial independence, applies to their actions on the bench, but the public has no avenue through which to hold judges responsible for their political actions.

THE GLOBE AND MAIL, JUNE 6, 1981

THE LAST WORD - LEGALLY

BY DAVID LANCASHIRE

Law is the wisdom of the old...
Law is the senses of the young...
Law is the clothes men wear.

W.H. Auden

There are no witnesses, no theatrics, yet the judges of the Supreme Court make decisions that affect everyone

OTTAWA

CANADA'S CHIEF Justice Bora Laskin takes comfort in reciting that poem from time to time. And supreme court judges need comfort, for hidden beneath their robes, he says, "there is something of the loneliness of the long distance runner." Other judges can depend on higher authority to correct their mistakes, but a judge of the highest appeal court in the land is on his own. As Chief Justice Laskin says, a supreme court judge "who looks over his shoulder for any comfort will find no one there."

Never has that lofty isolation — or that weighty responsibility — been more evident than now, as the Supreme Court of Canada's nine judges deliberate in secret on Prime Minister Pierre Trudeau's constitutional proposals.

The constitution is simply another case

Settling constitutional skirmishes between Ottawa and the provinces is routine work in the walnut-walled, red-carpeted courtroom. ("We are the umpire — the only umpire," Mr. Laskin notes.) Nine such cases were handled last year alone. Today's battle over bringing home the constitution, however, is the most important case in the 106-year history of Canada's court of last resort.

Yet for the chief justice and his colleagues, the historic test is simply business as usual. Minutes after the lawyers packed up their briefcases from five days of constitutional argument in early May, the judges cleared their desks in routine fashion and started hearing details of their next case, a criminal break-and-entry appeal from British Columbia. They have taken on more cases almost daily since then, and despite the importance of the constitution issue they have given no sign of hurrying to pronounce judgment on it. "As far as procedure is concerned," says court registrar Bernard Hofley, "the constitution is just another case."

Just another case in the Supreme Court of Canada covers a wide range of legal territory. From their high, red leather-backed chairs behind the bench, the judges deal with cases involving anything from a pothole in a Vancouver street (it threw a man from his bicycle) or the damages awarded to an injured Alberta bus driver, to whether a rape victim can be asked about her sexual past (yes), whether Manitoba can make Air Canada charge tax on drinks served aboard jetliners passing over the province (no), or whether a common-law wife deserves half her partner's property (yes).

The common-law judgment last December was a landmark advance over 1928 when the court ruled that women were not legally "persons" and therefore could not be appointed to the Senate. Now another advance is on the way, according to some reports that claim a woman judge may be appointed to the court next year, for the first time. Supreme court judges are appointed by the prime minister.

Judgments from the Supreme Court of Canada may take weeks, months or more than a year, but the judges handle cases with almost assembly line speed. They disposed of 113 last year. The usual case is heard in half a day "or a day at most," says Mr. Laskin. Lawyers are given unlimited time to argue — "We have a secret weapon known as sleep" against long-winded presentations, says Mr. Justice Willard Estey — but most keep it brief.

When the arguments end, the judges retire to their inner sanctum, a private conference room where the bookshelves are filled with rare manuscripts. There they discuss the case for only 10 minutes or so over a big, round oak table.

"We all sit around and furtively glance about to see who might know the answer to the argument," says Mr. Estey. "We speak in the reverse order of seniority. The old guys would never miss a chance to get the young ones to explain it all. (The oldest judge is Ronald Martland, 74. The youngest is Antonio Lamer, 47. Chief Justice Laskin is 68 and Mr. Estey is 61.) The chief has the last say." Then Mr. Laskin immediately assigns one judge, or himself, to write a draft judgment. If the judges disagree on the case — "We dissent about half the time," says Mr. Estey — two of them are asked to write dissenting opinions.

Within 15 minutes the judges are back at the courtroom bench, opening the next case. In their off-bench hours they finish the drafts, wandering in and out of each other's chambers to discuss them, and eventually they reach a final decision in later conferences. Then the judgments are handed down.

Legal expenses of getting a case through the supreme court may run anywhere from $3,000 to $200,-000.

In the past 18 months the court has made judgments on banking, trucking, labor strikes, surgical operations, drug trafficking, taxation, a rate increase by Bell Canada, pollution, Indian affairs, fire damage, computer use, beer, and the composition of the Senate.

Because the cases it hears are appeals of verdicts already reached in provincial supreme courts, or are questions referred by the federal Government, it lacks the melodrama of an ordinary court. There are no witnesses, no live testimony, no theatrics — only the shuffling of pages and dry, complex, legal manoeuvring. "You could never put it on television," shrugs one court official. "People would be bored out of their minds."

Still, says Mr. Laskin, all cases accepted by the court involve matters of "national or public importance. . .conflicting decisions on some point of law," and their outcome can affect the day-to-day life of Canadians "as husband or wife, as businessman, corporate executive, shareholder, policy holder, union member, civil servant, teacher, student, policeman, as a person accused of an offence, a member of any government."

"And people are becoming more aware of the supreme court," says registrar Hofley. "We get almost 10,000 visitors a year. Some of them even ask Mr. Laskin for his autograph." (There is no use asking the chief justice for a chat, however. He and his colleagues are refusing to give interviews until the constitution case is disposed of; all quotes appearing here are taken from their writings, speeches and previous interviews.)

The court refuses to handle mere disputes between individuals. It concentrates instead on molding legal standards to today's needs, bit by bit. "We nibble, so to speak," Mr. Laskin has said. The aim is to "build up a body of law."

It wasn't always so. Until 1975, the court was not allowed to pick and choose the cases it would handle, and it was forced to hear time-wasting "bumper cases" — automobile accidents and private disputes. Any argument involving $10,000 or more could be taken to Ottawa. (The amount of money at stake no longer counts in the right of appeal.) For many years, in fact, the judges had no final say about anything much, because lawyers could go over the supreme court's head to the House of Lords in England, which in those days was the court of last resort for Canada. That changed only in 1949.

Today the court meets in its own imposing, grey stone building on a bluff above the Ottawa River. Its beginnings in 1875 were less impressive. For years there were attempts to abolish it. Even now the supreme court's existence is not guaranteed in the constitution, and Parliament can overrule its decisions. At its first session — held in a railway committee room in the House of Commons — nobody bothered to appear before it.

Despite its growing stature in recent years, critics complain that the Supreme Court of Canada is still weaker, more docile and less creative than the U.S. Supreme Court. The U.S. court virtually makes law; the Canadian court follows the law and interprets it. While the U.S. court champions social issues, the Ottawa judges have appeared reluctant to tackle civil liberties and social questions. This "judicial restraint," as Mr. Justice Brian Dickson calls it, is because Canada's Bill of Rights is not part of the constitution.

Prime Minister Trudeau's constitutional proposal for a built-in charter of rights could change that. The supreme court would acquire a new prominence as the interpreter of those rights. If rights are firmly embedded in the constitution, says law professor Walter Tarnopolsky of the University of Ottawa, "the supreme court will have wider powers to invalidate legislation. The court won't knock down legislation right and left," but instead of being limited to legal technicalities, the judges may challenge Parliament by deciding "whether legislation is unwise, whether it is too arbitrary, whether it is discriminatory."

"The possibilites of a wider role are there, no question about it," Chief Justice Laskin told an interviewer last year, but "one cannot gauge in advance what (the effect) would be." (One effect might be the appearance of some curious appeals. Mr. Estey notes that the U.S. Supreme Court has been asked to consider a student's demand to fire his college football coach, and a prisoner's complaint that his rights were violated by a warden who refused to serve him toast for breakfast.)

Constitutional decisions made by the court are not always popular. On provincial rights, Quebec Premier Rene Levesque has complained, "The Supreme Court of Canada is like the tower of Pisa — always leaning in the same direction."

"Do we lean?" retorted Chief Justice Laskin. "Of course we do. . .in the direction in which the commands of the constitution take us according to our individual understandings."

Mr. Laskin also denies any suggestion that he or his fellow judges lean in favor of the provinces from which they come. He is against the many proposals that have been made to change or enlarge the court's structure. It works well as it is, he says. This doesn't mean the judges always agree with each other. "We have differences of opinion all the time. . .We are individually independent of each other as well as of the outside world."

A high-paid job, but only time for work

For this impartiality and for their abilities, supreme court judges are handsomely paid. Mr. Laskin earns $94,000 a year. The eight "puisne" (born later, or junior) judges get $86,000, with generous pensions.

The job circumscribes their lives, however. Most are usually kept too busy to indulge much in hobbies or get away for lunch; they eat sandwiches from the court's basement cafeteria. They cannot vote in federal or provincial elections. And they must live within 40 kilometres of Ottawa, a condition Mr. Justice Estey calls "capital punishment."

Less than a decade ago, a study of the supreme court, In The Last Resort by Paul Weiler, said "our judges share an outmoded and unduly narrow conception of the role of law in courts."

The appointment in 1973 of Bora Laskin as Canada's 14th chief justice has done much to change that. The gaunt, silver-haired former professor, former judge of the Ontario Court of Appeal and son of a Thunder Bay furniture dealer, was seen as a bold and liberal legal craftsman who broadened and improved the court's whole performance.

Time and again Chief Justice Laskin has stood up for civil liberties, dissenting from the judgments of his court's conservative majority. "In the 1970s the majority of the court was very conservative indeed," says Prof. Tarnopolsky, director of Ottawa University's Human Rights Institute. The court's present direction is uncertain, he says, because "the newest members — Justices Estey, William McIntyre, Julien Chouinard and Antonio Lamer, all appointed since 1977 — haven't yet had the opportunity to show clearly where they stand."

The question now, for the power of the provinces, of the federal Government and of the Supreme Court of Canada itself, is where the court stands on the constitution issue. And that depends not on power or on politics but on law. Law is all that matters for the court, as Chief Justice Laskin underlines by quoting from W.H. Auden's poem: "Law, says the judge as he looks down his nose. . . .Law is The Law."

Mr. Lancashire is chief features writer for The Globe and Mail.

THE FINANCIAL POST, MARCH 27, 1982

Interview with Mr. Justice Martland

The view from inside the Supreme Court of Canada

ONCE CANADA's new constitution is in effect, more attention than ever will be focused on the Supreme Court.

Although the Court for years has made judgments affecting every part of Canadian life, its power has never been more evident than in its decisions last fall in the Constitutional Appeals. Separate majorities of the Court held that the Trudeau government's constitutional proposals were legal but violated convention.

As a direct result of those decisions, the federal proposals were modified, and the support of every province except Quebec was obtained.

No member of the Court has had a better vantage point from which to observe the increasing public importance of the Court's work than Mr. Justice Ronald Martland.

Martland, who retired from the Court last month upon reaching 75, has served longer than all but six judges in the Court's history. Appointed by Prime Minister John Diefenbaker in 1958, Martland has been a witness to — and a participant in — the Court's power during a critical period.

In an interview with William Monopoli, The Post's Senior Editor for Legal Affairs, Martland reflected on his years as a member of the Court.

He was one of two members of the Court who held that provincial agreement to the federal patriation proposals was constitutionally required and that by proceeding without sufficient provincial consent, Ottawa violated convention.

The Post: What would you characterize as the most important work the Court did during your tenure?

Martland: I would rate the constitutional cases as being the most important and having the great impact. One of the last cases I sat on, the constitutional reference, was to me the most important that was dealt with during my time. It had implications that were serious, and it had consequences that were of importance, I think, to Canada. I put that at the top . . .

When I first came here, a good deal of time was spent on very ordinary litigation, because at that time any person who had more than $10,000 involved in a judgment had an automatic right to appeal to this Court. It's only relatively recently that we have instituted the leave-to-appeal right across the board.

Your judicial philosophy, as you know, often has been characterized as a conservative one. How do you characterize it yourself?

I have seen that very frequently — the small-c conservative philosophy and being a mainstay in that school of thought. I am troubled with the idea of a judicial philosophy. I can't say that after 24 years I have ever formulated one. I tried to deal with cases as they came along and to apply what I saw to be the rules of law . . . But each individual who comes here has a certain number of traits, background, and they have been accumulating generally for a period of nearly 50 years before the man gets here.

But what conclusions can be drawn from the fact that the Court has divided with some predictability on, say, issues involving the Canadian Bill of Rights?

(Editor's note — *R. v Drybones*, a 1970 case, is the only one in which the Court found that the Bill of Rights overrode a federal law inconsistent with it.)

Of course. *Drybones* wasn't unanimous at the start, and I would hesitate to embark on a dissertation on subsequent cases in which *Drybones* has been cited . . . I think one distinction — you might call it a distinction of view — is the extent to which individual judges feel they are clothed with a measure of legislative power and whether they have a license by means of judicial decision to create law . . . I rather share the view that it is not the task of judges to make law, but essentially it's to apply it as it exists, and leave it to the people's elected representatives to determine whether or not they want change.

This leads to the question of what happens when the popular will is manifestly unfair. If the judge's primary role is to adjudicate the case before him and not to adopt a sort of legislative approach, how are minorities protected?

Under the British Parliamentary system, of course, if the legislature of the day enacts legislation that may be unfair to the minority, or that fails to protect its position, our task is to deal with that legislation. It has to be applied, and we can't refuse to apply it merely because we don't like it.

U.S. Supreme Court Justice William Douglas wrote in his autobiography that when he joined that court, Chief Justice Charles Evans Hughes told him that at the constitutional level, 90% of any decision is emotional — and that the justices' rational sides supplied them with the reasons for supporting their predilections. Douglas said that although he was surprised by that, he later found it to be true. Can you compare that view to your perspective in the Supreme Court of Canada?

I think it's an overstatement. On the other hand, it certainly has to be recognized that as a great many jurists have recog-

nized you can't scrap entirely your background, your training, your temperament, and so on. They all have an influence on the way in which you may look at a problem.

I think it's an overstatement in that there is a great deal of research that goes into any constitutional issue. On the other hand, you may have certain ideas about what is proper in a federal constitution that have a bearing on your reaction to the arguments.

Constitutional cases, of course, do lend themselves more than others to the possibility of making new law, because you are dealing with situations that haven't arisen before, and so it's brand new and you have no precedent. You have some leeway there, and must have in a growing constitution.

Over the course of your tenure, how has the Supreme Court's role in Canadian society changed or evolved?

As I have observed it, one phase is the increase in the number of cases involving what we might call public law. The number of cases involving strictly the application of the common law has dwindled. More and more, we are involved in interpretation of statutes — and even more troublesome than statutes, interpretation of badly drawn regulations. That's the factor I've noticed most.

I think there has been an increase in the number of constitutional cases coming here, and there has been some increase in the number of criminal cases coming up, which may, in part, be the result of the advent of legal-aid systems.

The U.S. Supreme Court has for years been the subject of much attention by scholars and by the press. Even some of the justices themselves have written accounts of their work. Why has relatively less attention been paid to this Court? Why have the judges here not written about their work? Perhaps you have plans . . .

I have no present intention of trying to emulate Mr. Justice Douglas's efforts, or to accomplish anything like *The*

Brethren (a book on the U.S. Supreme Court's inner workings). Perhaps they are more tempted to do it because there's a bigger market for book sales there than in this country, and I assume that the profit motive applies even to retired American Supreme Court judges.

Certainly, we haven't got anybody tempted so far to undertake legal autobiography . . . I think there's been a certain feeling — and I am only guessing now — among people who have been judges on this Court that they prefer to let the judgments of the Court stand and speak for themselves.

There's a certain measure, perhaps, of loyalty to the Court, and it's a collegiate system and you don't wish afterward to try and justify to the public your position as compared with somebody else's. You wrote at the time, the score was taken, and that's the end of the game, I think, as far as most of us are concerned.

The Court has been dealing increasingly with matters of great public importance. Has the decision-making process changed in light of that?

No. I don't think there has been any observable change in that regard . . .

The big problem is volume. I think to a degree the Court will have to prune even more in the future to cut down to a reasonable workload, because with too many cases, certainly, the quality of the writing won't be as good. And there's a tendency then to hasten decision, which is not desirable.

Is the Court's workload too heavy?

The workload has increased very substantially over the years since I came here. The work involved for the individual judges has increased in the past eight or 10 years, because the practice has developed — and I think a proper one — of trying to seat the full Court of nine judges in practically all the cases that come up, the theory being that if leave (to appeal) has been given, it must be a matter of importance and, therefore, warrants a full Court. When I first came here, most of the cases were heard

with a quorum of five, and that meant that you were sitting only approximately five ninths of the time.

So we have a situation in which the workload has increased substantially, and there is much speculation that the crush to try to get in the door, just in requests for leave to appeal, will be even greater in the future.

You are quite right.

What is the remedy?

There you can turn to the United States' practice. They have carried on throughout with a court of nine. The volume of cases involving leave to get to that court has certainly not diminished. You have to evolve some techniques that will do even more culling. That's a sad thing, because it means that a number of cases that otherwise might warrant being heard here, cannot be heard. But as a practical matter, you are going to have to adopt some guidelines to have a cutoff point and limit the number and return to a reasonable workload.

There has been speculation that the new Charter of Rights invites the judiciary to take on overtly political tasks. Do you anticipate that the courts will have a different role in the future because of that invitation?

It's not a different role, but as I see the impact of the Charter, to a degree you might say it's a political role or legislative role which is really placed on the Court. The consequence of a Charter of Rights is that certain areas are removed from the control of Parliament and the provincial Legislatures. Their powers have been diminished, and any legislation which is enacted has to be scrutinized to see whether it trespasses on (the Charter). That becomes the job of the Court.

Does that not suggest a changed role? Your own approach has been that judges should not get involved in legislating. Does not the Charter require in certain instances that judges do adopt that role?

I don't know. It is very hard and, of course, all of these things will start at the trial level and work their way up. Just what the reaction will be is a little hard to foretell. Does the very able 15-year-old girl goalkeeper have the constitutional right now to play goal for a team that heretofore had been a boys' team? These are the kinds of issues that come up, and that's a different process from interpreting a tax statute or something of that kind.

Because of that, will the Canadian judiciary be forced to look at the U.S. model?

I think the Court will be bound to be deluged with American authorities as these cases arise. The big problem as I see it in relation to any Charter of Rights is that you are bound to make some pretty fine hairline distinctions as between one case and another, and judgments become more and more difficult to interpret . . .

There are certainly going to be a lot more civil rights cases. At the outset, I would imagine, any lawyer would be looking to see if he is dealing with a piece of legislation where there isn't some way of finding whether it reaches some of the guaranteed civil rights under the Charter. There's bound to be a lot more of that type of litigation.

Is the type of task the judiciary would be called upon to undertake, because of the Charter, compatible with the tradition of parliamentary supremacy?

I would put it this way: the whole idea of evolving a Charter of Rights as we have now done, and removing from legislative bodies areas of power they formerly had, is in itself an invasion of the idea of parliamentary supremacy. Our basic doctrine was that between them, the federal Parliament and the provincial Legislatures could legislate on any subject under the sun, the same as the British Parliament. The fact of the Charter of Rights is that they can't, because they are not permitted . . . I add the rider that the protective (notwithstanding) clauses are in there to give Parliament and the Legislatures some leeway as in comparison with the rule in the United States . . .

THE GLOBE AND MAIL, SEPTEMBER 14, 1982

Charting a new course for the bench

BY MARINA STRAUSS

Marina Strauss covers legal affairs for The Globe and Mail.

WHEN JULES Deschênes, Chief Justice of the Quebec Superior Court, handed down his controversial ruling affecting English-speaking children attending English schools, he was in effect taking a political stance. That is something judges in Canada have been very reluctant to do, but something they may find an increasing part of their role under Canada's new Charter of Rights and Freedoms.

Canadian judges are not accustomed to fashioning public policy. They tend to stick closely to giving strict interpretations of statutes, which is why many rulings read far more like technical documents than policy statements. Judge Deschênes is an exception among judges. His most recent ruling tells the Quebec Government very clearly that it is violating the Canadian Constitution's charter by restricting anglophone parents who are educated outside the province from sending their children to English schools.

Judges do not like to be in the limelight. A strong ruling can make a judge the target of a storm of protest to which he or she cannot reply. At the same time, judges are reminded constantly that they must remain impartial and removed from the political sphere. Many judges are former politicians; they are cautious, realizing they tread on dangerous ground.

This lengthy tradition of judicial independence was driven home once again earlier this month when Chief Justice Bora Laskin of the Supreme Court of Canada made a rare — and pointed — public speech. "A judge has no freedom of speech," he said, "to address political issues which have nothing to do with his judicial duties."

Still, the new rights charter now invites judges more than ever to rule on political issues that call into play value judgments previously made by elected representatives. The charter is putting judges on the spot by asking them to answer fundamental social questions, and the public will come to look more and more to the courts for their answers.

Under the charter, the judges can be asked whether women should be able to have abortions, whether someone should be able to earn his or her living in another province, whether a film should be censored or whether a homosexual can be refused certain jobs.

It may become increasingly difficult for judges to draw the line on what is fair comment from the bench, and what is fair comment outside the courtroom. The result could be that, in dealing with the charter, judges will be more apt to shy away from policy-setting and, instead of following Judge Deschênes' recent example, opt for decisions based on the technicalities.

Yves Fortier, president of the Canadian Bar Asociation, is among many lawyers conscious of judges' more visible role with the advent of the charter. "Justices of the Supreme Court of Canada will be perceived as being much more activist in the life of citizens," he said. "That's the nature of enshrining the charter in the constitution.

"As events unfold you're going to find, as in the United States, that the Supreme Court of Canada is going to be seen as being much more present in the life of citizens than it is now."

Mr. Fortier's observation would suggest that in the future Canadian judges may be taking on a role similar to their American counterparts. At the U.S. Supreme Court judges tackle such high-profile political issues as school busing and other race-related matters in crisp judgments.

'The U.S. system gets a lot of bad blood out of the public arena'

The U.S. high court judges, however, can feel more confident in taking stands because their presidential appointments must be approved by the elected senators. For example, last year, when President Ronald Reagan chose Sandra O'Connor as the first woman Supreme Court judge, the Senate quizzed her on her views on everything from abortion (she believes it's repugnant and offensive "for myself") to the death penalty (she favors it).

In Canada, there is no comparable process to approve the Prime Minister's judicial appointments. When Pierre Trudeau recently appointed Bertha Wilson as the first woman member of the Supreme Court of Canada, the public got only a scanty glimpse into the person behind the decision-maker.

Edward McWhinney, a constitutional expert at Simon Fraser University, says that, with the judges' expanded role in charter-related policymaking, it's time

Canada, too, have its prospective judicial appointees scrutinized by elected officials, ideally Parliament.

"The U.S. system gets a lot of bad blood out of the public arena . . . Constitutionalism is more and more participatory democracy," he said, adding that, during the Richard Nixon administration, for example, the Senate weeded out a number of choices put forward by the president.

"It may mean that many people will not accept an appointment to the bench," Mr. McWhinney explained. "It will change the type of judges we get . . . A lot of people won't like the heat."

However, once the judge has undergone the screening, "he's been through the fire and he says, 'I'm entitled to give a policy ruling.'"

With the advent of important decisions on the charter, all the various special-

interest groups will be geared to lobby the prime minister and justice minister to try to get certain judicial appointments. Allowing legislators to veto these choices would serve as a safeguard to any undue pressure.

The legislative endorsement of appointees would also give the public some input into who will be rendering decisions and could provide judges with the confidence to forge new directions in policymaking.

THE FINANCIAL POST, OCTOBER 3, 1981

The Court: Politics invaded legality

By William Monopoli

A GOOD judicial decision ordinarily resolves a dispute, states the applicable law, and provides specific guidance for the determination of future cases.

Against that standard, the Supreme Court's decision on the federal government's constitutional patriation plan is a kind of legal patch-work quilt, attempting to reconcile two seemingly distinct and inconsistent lines of thought, each of which persuaded a majority of the Court.

Canadian courts normally eschew political and policy-making roles. Most judges prefer to leave such matters to politicians and see their own task as interpreting the law in specific cases. But in this case — in public importance, the most significant decision the Supreme Court has ever been asked to make — that was not possible. The result is two decisions: one, an essential legal victory for Ottawa; the other, a gratuitous political victory for the eight provinces which oppose the patriation plan.

The Court's response to the three questions addressed to it was the basis of four unsigned opinions — two majority and two in dissent — reflecting but not reconciling divergent views.

Only one of the questions was crucial to the patriation plan: Is provincial agreement to the federal package

constitutionally required? In a seven-to-two decision, the Court held that it was not. But having reached that conclusion, a six-member majority went on to find that by proceeding without sufficient provincial consent, Ottawa violated a convention or unwritten understanding. That latter finding is without legal effect: conventions are not judicially enforceable, because although they are based on custom or historical tradition, they are not law.

Detract

Indeed, the only apparent effect of the finding that Ottawa breached custom or offended the federal principle is to detract from the real importance of what the Court did in deciding that the law does not require provincial assent to the federal patriation plan.

On the first question put to the Court, the parties to the dispute had no disagreement: yes, the federal package would affect the federal-provincial relationship. On the other two questions, the parties went in different directions, and, unfortunately, so did the Court.

The legal key to what the Court did is found in the strongly worded, seven-member judgment that Ottawa may proceed with the patriation plan, without provincial agreement.

The Court took apart the provinces' principal legal arguments. The assertion that provincial consent to constitutional amendment was a convention that had "crystal-

lized into law," and had become a rule of law, was denied. The provinces, the Court said, had not produced a single example of such a custom or practice having matured into a law. The Court characterized as an "overdrawn proposition" the provinces' contention that a host of cases give legal force to conventions.

The provinces had cited the 1980 Senate reference, in which the Court held that under the British North America Act, the federal government could not abolish the Senate, as an example of judicial enforcement of convention. The Court found that argument "baffling" and added that the Senate reference was decided on an entirely different basis.

The provinces' other arguments fared no better. The Court found clear authority for the House of Commons and the Senate to pass the patriation package. To decide otherwise, the Court said, would be to enact by judicial legislation a formula of unanimity to initiate the amending process, binding not only Canada, but also Britain.

Noting that Canada's "essential federal character" is preserved under the federal package, the Court said: "The law knows nothing of any requirement of provincial consent, either to a resolution of the federal House or as a condition of the exercise of United Kingdom legislative power."

What is central, the Court found,

is the "untrammeled authority . . . of the two federal Houses to proceed as they wish in the management of their own procedures . . ."

In dissent, the two members of the Court most often characterized as conservative and traditionalist, Mr. Justice Ronald Martland and Mr. Justice Roland Ritchie, defined the question not in terms of legality or illegality of the federal position, but as a matter of whether unilateral patriation was within federal power. They found that it was not and that the federal action violated the federalism that they described as the dominant principle of Canadian constitutional law.

Significantly, Martland and Ritchie were the only members of the Court persuaded by the provinces' primary arguments. But the importance of this is obscured by the Court's separate findings, by six to three, that it is a constitutional convention that the House of Commons and Senate not request that the British parliament amend the constitution without first obtaining provincial agreement, and that as a (legally unenforceable) matter of convention, agreement of the provinces is required before the constitution can be amended.

Anomalous

In this, Martland and Ritchie were joined by Justices Brian Dickson,

Jean Beetz, Julien Chouinard, and Antonio Lamer—placing those four judges in the somewhat anomalous position of having participated in one majority opinion endorsing Ottawa saying that provincial agreement is not required by law, and another saying that provincial consent is required by constitutional convention.

Although seven of the eight provinces opposing the federal position had argued that unanimous provincial consent was required, the six-member majority on this issue interpreted the question addressed to the Court as whether there is a convention requiring provincial agreement—not whether that agreement must be unanimous.

The majority moved on to find that such a convention does exist and requires a "measure of provincial agreement." No amendment changing provincial legislative powers has been made since Confederation when agreement of a province whose legislative powers would have been changed was withheld, the Court said.

The opinion acknowledged that Canada would remain a confederation if the federal package becomes law. "But it would be a different federation, made different at the instance of a majority in the Houses of the federal Parliament acting alone," the Court said. "It is this process itself which offends the fed-

eral principle."

Illustrating the deep division in the Court on this issue, the dissent to that opinion, by Chief Justice Bora Laskin, Mr. Justice Willard Z. Estey, and Mr. Justice William R. McIntyre, began with a different interpretation of the question. Following from the arguments of the provinces and based on "plain English," the dissent said, the question was whether consent of *all* the provinces was required.

Unlike the majority, the dissenting judges chose to look at all amendments to the constitution, rather than just those that directly affected provincial rights, and found that only in four cases was full provincial consent obtained and that in many cases, "the federal government has proceeded with amendments in the face of active provincial opposition." The dissent went on to specifically reject the argument that preservation of the principles of federalism requires the recognition of a convention.

Neither the parties supporting the patriation proposals nor those against them had seriously expected — or wanted — the Court to divide as it did. And although each of the four opinions is thorough, taken together they perhaps are best evidence of the view that Canadian courts do not excel at resolving such intensely political issues.

THE GLOBE AND MAIL, OCTOBER 1, 1981

Legally right, ethically wrong

BY PETER H. RUSSELL
Mr. Russell is a professor in the department of political economy at the University of Toronto.

ON MONDAY THE Supreme Court of Canada ruled that while there is no legal bar to the Trudeau Government proceeding unilaterally with its constitutional proposals, such unilateral action would be "unconstitutional in the conventional sense." Some Canadians find this difficult to understand. How, they ask, can something be legal yet un-

constitutional at the same time?

The answer to this riddle is not as puzzling as it may seem. We all know in our personal relationshps that our behavior may be legal yet wrong — ethically, or morally wrong. And we know that the fact that there is no chance of our being hauled into court for doing what is wrong does not relieve us of the obligation of doing what is right.

Constitutional conventions are the ethical side of our political relationships. They constitute that part of our constitu-

tional system which expresses our society's evolving understanding of how the legal powers of government are properly used. In a sense they embody our conception of political justice. In the Supreme Court's words "The main purpose of constitutional conventions is to ensure that the legal framework of the Constitution will be operated in accordance with the prevailing constitutional values or principles of the period."

Prime Minister Pierre Trudeau's first response to the Supreme Court's decision had the great merit of recognizing the importance of constitutional conventions. He acknowledged that in the past the principle of federalism had required his government to observe the convention of obtaining the provinces' consent for constitutional changes affecting their rights. As he pointed out, that is why the federal Government had tried for more than 50 years to reach an accommodation with the provinces on constitutional reform. If he had any argument with the Court it was that the convention of provincial consent should no longer be observed precisely because that prolonged effort at accommodation had failed — and failed primarily because of provincial obstinacy. In effect, Mr. Trudeau was suggesting that Canadians are living in a new period — a post-accommodation period — which must be governed by conventions that will not forever permit selfish provinces to prevent us from taking charge of our constitutional destiny.

For Canada's sake, I hope Mr. Trudeau will take another look at the Court's decision and the invitation to accommodation it holds out. The Court has increased the likelihood of accommodation by removing the requirement of unanimity from the convention of provincial consent. In the Court's view "a substantial degree of provincial consent is required" for amendments directly affecting provincial powers, but not the consent of all the provinces. The Court should not be castigated for "ducking" the question of precisely how many or which provinces need consent. We should, instead, welcome the legitimacy the Court's judgment lends to a process which would free us from the tyranny of unanimity. Here is where Mr. Trudeau and all of us have an opportunity to achieve patriation soon — something we all want — but in a manner that will not leave our body politic bloodied and divided.

Taking advantage of this new opportunity will require major concessions on both sides. On the provincial side, several provincial governments — at least six or seven — will have to accept an amending formula that does not give every province a right to opt out of constitutional changes which have substantial support in all regions of the country. If there is to be accommodation, these provinces must not insist on additions to provincial powers as the price for their agreement to an amending formula.

There must be a similar movement on the federal side. The federal Government must be willing to untie its package and drop its insistence that its constitutional priorities be implemented in the process of patriation.

This probably means that to reach an agreement with a substantial number of provinces the federal Government will have to postpone its attempt to add a charter of rights and freedoms to the Canadian constitution. This will not be an easy concession for Mr. Trudeau and his colleagues to contemplate. For the past few months they have wrapped themselves in the charter. To yield on some or all of it now, even for a while, may appear to entail what for politicians is sometimes the roughest medicine to swallow — a loss of face.

But the Trudeau Government cannot, with reason, maintain that the rights and freedoms of Canadians are in jeopardy if the Charter is not established in the process of patriation. Remember only three years ago that Government told us it was content to undertake the first stage of constitutional reform without a charter of rights binding on the provinces. Nothing has happened since then to demonstrate that freedom and equality and due process of law are in peril without a char-

We have an opportunity for patriation without a bloodied and divided body politic

ter. Nor is immediate action on a charter required to honor the commitment Mr. Trudeau made to Quebeckers in the referendum campaign to reform the constitution. That was a commitment to a renewed federalism, not to a charter of rights. Most Quebeckers will forgive Mr. Trudeau if for now he does not go forward with the entrenchment of minority language school rights.

The federal Government, like the provincial governments, must be willing to take its chances with the amending system embodied in a patriated constitution. After all, that is the whole point of patriation — to be self-governing in our constitutional affairs. To argue that the constitutional changes one cherishes must be made before patriation or they will never

be made at all is to abandon faith in the capacity of the Canadian people and their governments to take charge of their own constitution.

What will happen if this judicial invitation to a renewed effort at accommodation is not accepted? The federal Government could legally go ahead against the wishes of most of the provinces and most of the people and override the Supreme Court's understanding of constitutional convention. Legally it might be successful. After a terrible political storm here and a humiliating row in London, Mrs. Thatcher might well be able to marshall her troops and push the federal package through Westminster.

The Constitution would be home, but what a home!

If this happened, the constitution would be home — but what a home! Our nation might well survive. We are, after all, a law-abiding people so that most of us, including our unhappy provincial leaders, would probably obey the law of the new constitution. But just as personal relationships which survive serious ethical breaches are sometimes never quite the same again, the political relationships which enable this country to function reasonably well would suffer serious, if not irreparable, damage. For a long time to come our capacity to do things together as a people would be weakened, our energies drained by discord and distrust.

I cannot see why it is necessary to put this country to such a test now. Now is the time for our political leaders, those who care about the future of Canada, to make concessions of the magnitude of those made by the political leaders who founded this country. Confederation became possible when leading politicians on both sides agreed to set aside commitments to strongly held political positions. In doing so, they may have lost some political face, but we revere them as statesmen for their magnitude. Let us hope that enough of our political leaders, federal and provincial, will have the courage to accept the invitation which the Supreme Court, in its wisdom, may have given them, to achieve a similar stature.

THE CHRONICLE-HERALD, HALIFAX, SEPTEMBER 29, 1981

Carving his signature into history...

by Hugh Townsend

Regardless of what direction the federal government's constitutional package takes following Monday's decision by the Supreme Court of Canada, Chief Justice Bora Laskin has signed his name to Canadian history. Regardless of whether the ruling leads to the patriation of the British North America Act in the form proposed by the Pierre Trudeau government, or whether the provinces will get another opportunity to make an input into the amendments, Chief Justice Laskin, chairman of the nine-member court that rendered its judgments, was carving his signature into the nation's history in the decision delivered by live television to Canadians from coast to coast.

It is more than fitting that Chief Justice Laskin, whose father was a refugee from the imperial Russian army before settling in Winnipeg in 1904, was in the spotlight as the television cameras and lights focused on the proceedings. The chief justice, who will celebrate his 69th birthday next Monday, has often suggested wider media coverage of the Supreme Court's work.

Yesterday, perhaps more than ever before, the court was in the national limelight.

Let's, because of the significance of this occasion, take a closer look at Chief Justice Laskin, a controversial but respected and popular figure since he was appointed to head the high court in December, 1973.

As the country's 14th chief justice, his approach to the Supreme Court position has been seen as simply more liberal and perhaps slightly more in tune with the thinking of Canadians as a whole. In the days following his appointment, he often found himself in dissent, arguing against the views of the conservative majority. But more recently he has received support for his way of thinking.

One of Chief Justice Laskin's greatest concerns was that Canadians had insufficient knowledge and understanding of the legal system.

Just months after his appointment, he told an Atlantic Provinces Law Conference in Charlottetown the public's understanding of the Supreme Court's work would be helped by more complete coverage by the media of court decisions. He said at the time he had no doubts about the understanding of the legal profession, but wondered about public comprehension.

"With a jurisdiction that is as wide as the range of the legal questions that can arise in Canada, the court's centrality is well understood by the legal profession and well understood by the law schools of the country. But how well is it understood by the public and I would add in what sense? There are two measures I can apply to supply an answer: the response to the court's decisions in the daily press and on radio and TV, and by the numerous letters that the chief justice receives from throughout Canada . . . .

"What is missing is in-depth assessment. Unless the press develops or engages reporters that can paint in the background of important cases or see them as part of an evolutionary process and explain this in their stories or a review column, the coverage is bound to be episodic and lack continuity."

Three years later, addressing The Canadian Press annual dinner in Toronto, Chief Justice Laskin spoke in a similar vein.

On that occasion, he asked: ". . . Will we see the day when The Canadian Press, or some of Canada's leading newspapers, put law-trained reporters on the Supreme Court beat and, if not, then as a second best, will they allow an assigned reporter to develop experience on the job, reinforced by a modicum of law training in special courses which can be provided in some of our law schools?"

Perhaps, with the extent of media emphasis on the court's constitu-tional judgments yesterday, the chief justice has, to his satisfaction, garnered the attention he believes decisions should receive.

It was Chief Justice Laskin, as well, who three years ago put to rest allegations of bias toward federalism by the high court.

Speaking to a meeting of journalists, judges and lawyers in Ottawa — an historic event in itself when he chose to "go public" with his views — Chief Justice Laskin warned of the dangers of political pressures on his court.

He emphasized the bench must be kept free of such pressure, explaining he was not a "spear carrier for the federal prime minister in Ottawa-versus-province cases, nor was he acting for his home province of Ontario.

Said he: "I represent no one but myself."

Earlier, he said allegations of court bias were reckless, accusing academics, excluding lawyers and law professors, of lending their credentials "to a poisonous proposition" which has never been true in Canada.

"I have to be more sad than angry to read of an insinuation that we are acting as spear carriers for the federal prime minister,"he said.

Earlier this year, Chief Justice Laskin, and his eight fellow jurists on the Supreme Court bench, found themselves in the midst of a history-making drama in this country. A long and bitter road to constitutional reform began in earnest 16 months ago when Prime Minister Trudeau pledged a renewal of federalism as he openly challenged the proposals of the Parti Quebecois government in Quebec for sovereignty-association.

Now, whether the Supreme Court's judgments force an election, a national referendum, appeals to the British House of Commons or another round of federal-provincial negotiations, Chief Justice Laskin has completed his work—and earned a page in Canadian history.

THE TORONTO STAR, MARCH 10, 1982

Bertha Wilson: Champion of the underdog

By Farrell Crook Toronto Star

The Supreme Court of Canada's first female judge is a keen legal analyst who supports the rights of the individual against government officialdom, big business and sloppy lawyers.

Madam Justice Bertha Wilson would give wider legal rights to Canadians facing sexual and racial discrimination.

And in family law, the 58-year-old jurist is among the few judges who believe that, if at all possible, estranged spouses should share jointly the custody of their children.

That's been her track record during her six years on the Ontario Court of Appeal where she was a frequent dissenter in the company of some of the most able judges in the land.

She heads to the Supreme Court of Canada with a reputation as a practical, moderately liberal judge.

Wilson had no experience as a trial judge. As an appellate judge she read legal briefs, trial transcripts, listened to lawyers' courtroom arguments, researched the law and wrote judgments.

It's about the same job she'll be doing in the Supreme Court of Canada, except that her decisions could have a far wider impact: If she leads the majority or is with it, the judgment is binding on all courts and all citizens in Canada.

In criminal law, her approach during her years on the Ontario Court of Appeal has been cautious, seldom speaking out during the hearing of criminal appeals, and always siding with the majority.

But in other areas of the law, she's written well-researched dissenting judgments, exposing her judicial philosophy. On other occasions she's led the court with her opinion, leaving others to agree or dissent.

In the area of sexual and racial discrimination, Wilson was involved in four reported cases. She came out in favor of the complainant in all four.

☐ Wilson delivered the appeal court's judgment giving a Hamilton-area woman the go-ahead on her suit for wrongful dismissal from her warehouse job. The woman's boss had decided he wanted a man for the job, but the appeal court ruled that the situation appeared to be sexual discrimination and rightly the basis for a civil suit.

Wilson overruled

☐ Wilson held that 9-year-old softball player Debbie Bazso of Waterford and 10-year-old hockey goalie Gail Cummings of Muskoka were victims of sexual discrimination because league officials banned them from playing on boys' teams. But Wilson was overruled by other judges who held that the Ontario Human Rights Code against sexual discrimination didn't apply because the playing facilities for the children were not open to the general public.

Wilson thought the judges were off base when they decided that just because the public generally couldn't tread upon the baseball diamond or the ice surface, then the park or arena wasn't open to the public generally.

☐ Two years ago she delivered the appeal court's judgment that broke new legal ground in allowing an East Indian woman in Metro to sue Seneca College for racial discrimination.

Over a four-year period the woman, who has PhD in mathematics, made 10 applications to Seneca for teaching jobs but she was never granted an interview.

The Supreme Court of Canada overturned Wilson's decision, ruling that the woman's legal remedy was to complain to the Ontario Human Rights Commission, which could award her compensation.

In other cases of individuals up against the system, Wilson has ruled:

☐ The courts can step in and adjust penalties imposed by statutory professional bodies against their members.

An Ottawa pharmacist should not have been kicked out of business because it was not proved, as alleged, that he used false pretenses to overcharge welfare authorities for prescriptions for welfare recipients, Wilson held. Cancelling his licence was far too severe a penalty, she said, agreeing the case should be returned to the disciplinary body for reassessment.

☐ A female picture-framer factory worker, claiming she was a victim of sexual discrimination because she was paid less than men doing the same job, was entitled to know upon what information the government's employment standards officials rejected her complaint, Wilson ruled.

☐ She was overruled in her attempt to give a "fair, large and liberal" construction to the law so that a 19-year-old London youth, crippled in a car accident, could collect $57 in weekly benefits from an insurance company.

But the other appeal court judges wouldn't go for Wilson's interpretation that he was entitled to the benefits because he was "employed" on the date of the accident.

The accident happened at 3:30 a.m. The youth's would-be employer called his home six hours later to tell him that he had a job and to come into work. The other judges held that he wasn't "employed."

☐ Wilson agreed with Mr. Justice Charles Dubin that the Royal Canadian Mounted Police should be required to disclose the names of doctors and hospital employees who gave them confidential information on patients. The patient's right to privacy is paramount, they held. But the Supreme Court of Canada ruled the disclosures shouldn't be made.

☐ Because a lawyer made a slip-up and didn't sign his name on a notice that he was going to sell a woman's Mississauga property from under her, Wilson ruled, the woman won the chance to pay mortgage arrears and redeem her property.

In the area of family law, Wilson has suggested wider use of joint custody orders and broader powers for the courts to intervene when a parent snatches children away from the other parent.

☐ In a 1979 dissenting opinion, Wilson said courts in child-custody orders should pay more attention to hurt inflicted upon a child by the severance of his relationship with one of his parents.

Child's best interests

"Our courts have tended, while purporting to award custody on the basis of the child's best interests, to overlook that in some circumstances it may be in the child's best interests not to choose between the parents but to do everything possible to maintain the child's relationship with both parents," Wilson said.

She blamed the justice system's adversarial process which, by its nature, she said, "requires each spouse to attack the other in order to protect his or her economic interests. This has caused an undue emphasis to be placed at trial on the deterioration of the husband-and-wife relationship and not enough on the parent-and-child relationship."

Wilson said the courts should assess the ability of the parents to co-operate on the upbringing of their children.

☐ In the case of a Burlington mother, whose two boys were abducted and hidden by their father, Wilson said the court should intervene and seize relatives' telephone records so that the children might be located. But she was overruled by two other judges.

SATURDAY NIGHT, SEPTEMBER 1982

DISORDER IN THE COURT

Thomas Berger, who publicly criticized the constitutional agreement, isn't the first judge to voice a political opinion. Why was he the first to be rebuked?

BY ROBERT FULFORD

PIERRE TRUDEAU has somehow acquired a reputation as a politician whose career is dominated by cool logic — too much so, some of his critics say. Certainly he *looks* logical, and the humourless coldness of his manner suggests to many people a careful thinker. In fact, however, he's as capable of inconsistency as anyone in Canadian politics. Nothing demonstrates this so clearly as the appalling affair of Mr. Justice Thomas Berger, a controversy in which Trudeau took a self-contradictory position in the beginning and stuck with it to the end.

Last November 18 *The Globe and Mail* published Berger's critique of the constitutional agreement that the federal government and the English-speaking premiers had arrived at. Berger criticized the omission of a veto for Québec and the failure to protect native rights. That same day, in a press conference, Trudeau expressed annoyance: "So far as Berger is concerned, where was he when we were fighting? . . . I didn't see him writing the newspapers then." As everyone who follows these matters knew, Berger had done better than write to the newspapers, he had written a book, *Fragile Freedoms: Human Rights and Dissent in Canada* (Clarke, Irwin), which described the need for a charter of rights and endorsed Trudeau's attempt to get one — the book was in the stores as Trudeau spoke. Moreover, Berger had given a speech to the Canadian Bar Association on September 2 to the same

effect. Nevertheless Trudeau was offended, and his feelings were to have widespread consequences.

Six days later he was in Burnaby, B.C., talking to Jack Webster on television. When asked about Berger, Trudeau replied: "I do not think it's the purpose of a judge to get in and discuss an accord that was reached or a bill before parliament, and I take strong exception to that." Trudeau had apparently moved from his original pique to high principle: judges shouldn't meddle in politics. But in his next sentence Trudeau cut the ground from under himself: "If he [Berger] had wanted to do this, I wonder why he didn't support the bill when it was there and when it gave Québec the veto and it gave the Indians aboriginal rights. He didn't support us then. He saw fit to get off the bench and enter the political arena at a very inopportune time. I just regard that as the judiciary getting mixed into politics. I hope the judges will do something about it."

In other words, it would have been acceptable for Berger to speak out on Trudeau's side (as he had, though Trudeau still apparently didn't know it), but it was unacceptable for Berger to criticize Trudeau, particularly at an inopportune moment. Trudeau has never heard, or perhaps never agreed with, the saying that you can't have it both ways. His remarks make it clear that there is no issue of principle involved: what is involved is Trudeau's annoyance at an uppity judge. That annoyance

should have been quickly forgotten, as Trudeau's illogical responses to journalists usually are. Instead it was solemnly endorsed by the senior judges of Canada and the justice minister; now it is close to being the law of the land.

IN THE broadest sense, Canadian judges have always been involved in political issues. A truly apolitical judiciary would be forbidden to speak outside the courtroom and forbidden to conduct royal commissions or otherwise utter opinions on public issues. But that's not the Canadian system: we use our judiciary as a public resource. Throughout history we have turned to judges for advice on hundreds of policy questions; in general they have enriched public discourse by their knowledge and, on occasion, their wisdom. Moreover, as citizens judges have views about the direction of the country. Berger's article was part of a tradition that stretches a long way back — and so were *Fragile Freedoms* and the speeches he gave in support of his royal commission report on the Mackenzie Valley pipeline. "I believe," he has said, "that a judge has the right — a duty, in fact — to speak out on an appropriate occasion on questions of human rights and fundamental freedoms."

Once elevated to the bench, judges refrain from partisan comment. (Most, in the nature of things, are ex-Liberals.) But for as long as I can remember, they have been making statements that touch on political problems. In 1970, Mr. Justice Samuel Freedman, one of the country's most admired jurists, publicly supported the use of the War Measures Act. Mr. Justice Donald Thorson was famous as an enthusiastic supporter of nuclear disarmament. In the 1960s, after Mr. Justice Emmett Hall ran a royal commission on health services, he made speeches elaborating his point of view — speeches that by any definition were political. A judge who makes a comment on separatism, abortion, or pornography is making a political statement.

But the Canadian Judicial Council, when it finally dealt with the Berger matter in June, chose to ignore this tradition and establish what is in effect a new gag rule on judges. After an investigation by three judges, the council rebuked Berger, called his comments ''unwise and inappropriate,'' and declared that he had contravened the fundamental rule that judges must be ''divorced from all politics.'' The council claimed that Berger's comments would ''support a recommendation for removal from office'' but declined to make that recommendation. Instead it warned Berger and all other judges: ''It is possible that Justice Berger, and other judges too, have been under a misapprehension as to the nature of the constraints imposed upon judges. That should not be so in the future.''

Justice Minister Jean Chrétien greeted the report with approval and understood immediately what it meant for the bench: ''In my judgement any guys who will become judges will be well advised to read that report . . . . if they do not follow it their fellow judges will ask them why they didn't read it . . . .'' The effect of the Canadian Judicial Council's report will almost cer-

tainly be a tamer judiciary.

NO DOUBT about it, Mr. Justice Thomas Berger is a prickly fellow. He doesn't fit comfortably in the judges' club, and he apparently doesn't want to. He expresses a stern moral sense that stops just short of smug self-righteousness. He clearly sees himself not as a disinterested interpreter of the law but as a kind of national conscience, or at least a conscience for the white and English-speaking parts of Canada.

He's admired by the bar in British Columbia as an efficient legal technician, but that sort of accomplishment doesn't satisfy him. When the Trudeau government assigned him the Mackenzie Valley pipeline commission, he enlarged what could have been a narrow, legalistic inquiry into a national exercise in consciousness-raising. By the end of it, we all knew a good deal about the condition of natives in the North and a good deal about Tom Berger's thrusting, inquisitive, humane personality.

The *Globe* article that piqued Trudeau concerned not some picayune controversy of the moment but an issue close to the heart of Canadian democracy. And it was delivered on an appropriate occasion, i.e., when the matter was still open. But Berger's view of the constitution-making process as a failure was unacceptable to those politicians who had staked their reputations on it.

Berger has acquired a confidence that sometimes runs away with him, and perhaps that's what bothered Trudeau most. (Berger sounds like the young Trudeau.) In the newspaper article, Berger at one point turned to the question of the provincial override on fundamental freedoms. He opposed the agreement the premiers had reached, but he grandly acknowledged that ''this is a philosophical question on which

reasonable men and women can differ.'' The Québec veto and native rights, on the other hand, are apparently *not* questions on which reasonable men and women can differ.

Implying that most of the premiers of Canada are unreasonable is an everyday habit in journalism and politics, but it isn't the most tactful way for a supreme court justice to make his point. Elsewhere in the article Berger again sounded like a newspaper columnist — ''I don't know whether the Prime Minister and the premiers ganged up on Mr. Lévesque, but the amending formula they agreed upon makes it possible for English-speaking Canada to gang up on Québec in future.''

But while his writing is forceful, it isn't always persuasive or even notably intelligent. *Fragile Freedoms* is for the most part woolly-minded, unimaginative, and predictable. Reviewing it for the *Canadian Forum*, A. Alan Borovoy of the Canadian Civil Liberties Association remarked that ''the effective struggle for civil liberties and human rights requires not only a soft heart but also a hard head.'' He went on to demonstrate that Berger has the first but not the second.

Berger served in parliament and as New Democratic Party leader in the B.C. legislature before he became a judge. This academic year he will probably be on leave from the bench to teach at the University of Victoria — and, presumably, to contemplate his future. He may decide to remain a judge, rebuked but unrepentant; or he may return to politics to claim the national constituency that his activities in recent years have created. Whatever happens, he's already made a place for himself in the history of Canadian jurisprudence, though perhaps not the place he wanted to make.

THE GLOBE AND MAIL, SEPTEMBER 4, 1982

A 'rare case'

BY MICHAEL VALPY

OTTAWA

"My mention of the Berger case is not to reopen an issue which is closed." — *Chief Justice Bora Laskin of the Supreme Court of Canada.*

There is an axiom in journalism that communication takes place in the mind of the receiver, not the mind of the transmitter.

Whatever the Chief Justice intended in his address this week to the Canadian Bar Association, no one can speak for an hour on a controversial subject — and certainly not as forcefully as he did — without reopening it.

Mr. Justice Thomas Berger of the British Columbia Supreme Court spoke out against the shabby constitutional accord reached in November, 1981, by the Prime Minister and nine of the 10 provincial premiers. It was shabby, despicably shabby, because it was reached at the expense of Canada's Native peoples whose constitutional affirmation of the existence of treaty and aboriginal rights was dropped at the desire of some of the premiers.

For his outspokenness, Judge Berger was publicly criticized by Prime Minister Pierre Trudeau. He was the subject of an official complaint by Federal Court Justice George Addy. And he was investigated — and reprimanded — by the Canadian Judicial Council of which Chief Justice Laskin is chairman.

The Chief Justice, in his speech, said he only wanted to set the record straight on the council's mandate and its actions. He did considerably more than that.

First, in his criticism of Judge Berger's comments, he went well beyond the mild rebuke delivered by the Judicial Council (which said the judge's actions were "indiscreet" but constituted "no basis for a recommendation that he be removed from office").

The Chief Justice said that a judge who "feels so strongly on political issues that he must speak out is best advised to resign from the bench." He also said: "He cannot be allowed to speak from the shelter of a judgeship."

Those of us in the "ignorant" press (to use the adjective the Chief Justice applied to us and which received sycophantic applause from his audience) will be puzzled by the Chief Justice's public interpretation of his own council's ruling. We have always been told that a ruling should stand on its own, that we cannot ask for an explanation of what it means.

Second, there is the large chunk of the Chief Justice's speech that is an attack on the press.

He said that written complaints from Judge Addy were addressed to him on November 18 and 19, and that he referred the complaints to the Judicial Council's executive committee on November 20.

He then mentions the interview given by the Prime Minister on November 24 in which Mr. Trudeau criticized Judge Berger. "It is therefore mere mischief-making (by the press) to suggest that the Canadian Judicial Council was moved to action by the Prime Minister."

The Chief Justice should know that the Prime Minister's initial complaints against Judge Berger were made at a press conference on November 18.

Finally, the Chief Justice criticized those members of the press who defended Judge Berger's comments. Those of us who defended him agreed with what Tom Berger said — that there are some moral issues in society which transcend normal rules of conduct.

It was possibly, if you like, a rare case for civil disobedience.

Discussion Questions

1. The fact that the Supreme Court decides cases according to precedent is not discussed in Lancashire's article. How important is precedent?

2. Mr Justice Martland contends that one of the most significant matters concerning the SCC is its role in constitutional issues. Will the SCC come to carry more weight than political bargaining between levels of government in the future?

3. How important is the SCC? Assess this question in relation to the 1981 constitutional reference and the Court's role as constitutional arbiter.

4. Strauss illustrates how difficult it is for the SCC to maintain its independence in times of political change. Should or can the Court exercise greater self-restraint to avoid being drawn into political questions more appropriately left to other branches of government? Is the SCC likely to become more politicized in the future? Why?

5. Why is partisanship not an important factor in the appointment of Supreme Court judges? Is this desirable?

6. Can judges be divorced from politics? Does their independence suffer if they involve themselves in debates on public issues? Examine these questions in the context of the Berger case.

Suggested Readings

Peter Russell, ed. *Leading Constitutional Decisions*, third edition. Ottawa: Carleton University Press, 1982.

Paul W. Fox, ed. *Politics: Canada*, fifth edition. Toronto: McGraw-Hill Ryerson, 1982, 591–631.

Peter Russell. 'The Anti-Inflation Case: The Anatomy of a Constitutional Decision', in *Canadian Public Administration*, vol 20, no. 4, Winter 1977, 632–65 *or* in R. Schultz, O. Kruhlak, and J. Terry, eds. *The Canadian Political Process*, third edition. Toronto: Holt, Rinehart and Winston, 1979, 395–416.

Martha Fletcher. 'Judicial Review and the Division of Powers', in J. Peter Meekison, ed. *Canadian Federalism: Myth or Reality?*, third edition. Toronto: McGraw-Hill Ryerson, 1977, 100–22.

Peter Russell. 'The Political Role of the Supreme Court in its First Century', in *Canadian Bar Review*, vol. 53, no. 3, September 1975, 576–96.

Paul Weiler. *In the Last Resort: A Critical Study of the Supreme Court of Canada.* Toronto: Carswell–Methuen, 1974.

2. The Federal System

a. Mechanisms of Federal–Provincial Relations

The Canadian federal system has adapted to changing circumstances in the past two decades not only by judicial review (with the courts reinterpreting the division of powers as cases have come to them) and formal constitutional amendment, but also and most notably by political bargaining between the two levels of government. Prompted in part by a reluctance to place matters of dispute before the courts, which operate on a winner-take-all principle, these federal–provincial negotiations have permitted significant changes in the functioning of the federation without necessitating any alterations in the constitutional framework.

This process, which Professor Donald Smiley has called 'executive federalism', is characterized by ongoing negotiations between elected and appointed officials of the two orders of government. Executive federalism developed as governments recognized the degree to which their jurisdictions overlapped, the amount of conflict in their legislation, and the extent of their interdependence. At the same time, the development of the modern welfare state was creating a substantial financial imbalance and revealing the need for joint activity; the provinces held jurisidiction over the relevant policy areas but the federal government retained the spending capabilities to put the appropriate programmes in place. Co-operation was required, and thus out of extensive negotiations a unique network of formal consultation, joint co-operative programmes, and fiscal transfers was formed.

Pre-eminent among the mechanisms that sprang up as these discussions spread to a wider range of issues was the federal–provincial conference, in particular the first ministers' summit, at which the prime minister and the ten provincial premiers address the more intractable problems. These conferences deal with the major policy issues, including constitutional reform, and have been held with regularity from the 1960s on. Below the summit are a variety of other mechanisms, including ministerial meetings (such as the regular meetings between federal and provincial finance ministers), meetings of officials, and interprovincial gatherings. The most important of these are the premiers' conferences, where the provinces have in recent years endeavoured to arrive at common positions on federal–provincial issues. Meetings take place not only between the federal government and all the provinces, but also at the bilateral and regional levels (for instance, the Western Premiers' Conference and the Council of Maritime Premiers).

Coverage of federal–provincial relations is especially difficult for the press. Like an iceberg, federal–provincial activity is for the most part hidden from public view. Secrecy aside, federal–provincial relations are broad in scope and complex in character. Although it is difficult to state a precise figure, several hundred federal–provincial or interprovincial conferences of various sorts are held every year. Even specialist reporters find it a challenge to keep up with all the conferences within their particular fields. The general pattern in covering a major federal–provincial conference is for a large number of reporters to descend on participants as they emerge from private discussions. The respective governments use this opportunity to press their immediate causes, perhaps by selectively revealing the positions of other governments in order to put them at a disadvantage. Public conferences, some with television coverage, have been sporadic since the splashy Confederation of Tomorrow Conference in 1967.

The stated advantages of holding frank negotiations in private operate to the detriment of informed press coverage.

The prime consequence of these obstacles to full coverage of federal–provincial relations is that an embarrassingly small amount of newspaper space is devoted to the central organizing principle of government in Canada. Reporters try their best to cover the visible portions of the process, but they are rarely able to penetrate beyond the official communiqués and occasional leaks. As a result, our newspapers are remarkably lacking in discussion of the ongoing operation of these mechanisms.

The articles in this section have been arranged in three groups. The first two columns address particular aspects of the federal–provincial process. The second group of eight pieces provides a cross-section of commentary on one particular meeting: the annual premiers' conference held in August 1982. The final three articles deal with fiscal concerns and the renewal of existing tax-sharing arrangements in 1981.

Charles Lynch has been a persistent critic of the process of executive federalism. Here he takes aim at its deficiencies, including the extra-constitutionality of federal–provincial conferences, the lack of accountability, and the absence of any real activity. For his part, the then publisher of *The Vancouver Province*, Paddy Sherman, blames Prime Minister Trudeau for federal–provincial failures. Although there is considerable force behind Sherman's contentions, especially in recent times when Ottawa has sought to circumvent the provinces on the economy, the constitution, and fiscal issues, he neglects some of the deep-seated difficulties with the process. Above all, executive federalism in the 1970s and '80s has focused on a variety of seemingly intractable problems faced by most Western societies, such as energy and the economy. It is difficult to resolve these problems because they have different regional manifestations.

The strained operation of the process is well illustrated in the selection of articles on the 1982 premiers' conference. In a sense, interprovincial conferences have a different character from the federal–provincial variety. They are much less formal and provide for an exchange of information and consultation rather than solid negotiation. Moreover, the importance of interprovincialism fluctuates according to the state of the federal–provincial agenda. The extent of the provinces' unity among themselves and their propensity to confront the federal government, as Richard Gwyn observes, depend on Ottawa's intractability in dealing with

their concerns. Louis Falardeau goes one step further and characterizes the meeting as a well-orchestrated manoeuvre to counter federal policies.

These views are in sharp contrast to Robert Duffy's assessment. He frames his commentary within the limited context of past interprovincial meetings and concludes that the provinces had simply moved towards greater consensus on economic issues, without regard to federal positions. Similarly, Giles Gherson of *The Financial Post* interprets the outcome of the meeting as indicating a willingness on the part of the provinces to deal reasonably with Ottawa on economic matters. Gherson also comments, astutely, that federal–provincial relations may have begun a new phase of 'federal initiative/provincial response'. The editorials following the outcome dealt much less directly with the process than with the substance of the conference's final communiqué. *The Toronto Star* attacks many of the provinces' recommendations, and Vincent Prince, the editorialist from *La Presse*, takes a similar approach. The latter goes on to recommend that serious federal–provincial negotiations be undertaken to address the divergent viewpoints. The Halifax paper comes down more clearly on the provinces' side but criticizes the absence of a more detailed alternative to federal policies on restraint. The editorial from the West is not so charitable to the provincial complaints about economic ills.

The last three articles, which examine the fiscal negotiations between the two levels of government, detail the extent of interdependence. Clearly, the renegotiation of federal–provincial fiscal arrangements is the most significant intergovernmental issue in recent years after the constitution and energy-pricing. Always touted as a hallmark of co-operative federalism, the periodic renewal of the financing of hospital insurance, medicare, and post-secondary education became troublesome in 1981. Ian Urquhart's article reviews federal arguments for a reduction in payments to the provinces. Jean-Claude Picard picks up the same issue from a Québec perspective. Thomas Walkom describes the initial negotiations, revealing the intransigence at the federal level that led to the unilateral imposition of reduced payments. Underlying these three articles is the suggestion that federal–provincial relations, particularly in the financial area, have shifted into a new phase. Interdependence is accepted as a given, but there is a gradual readjustment taking place that sees the federal government asserting a greater degree of control.

THE CALGARY HERALD, AUGUST 14, 1981

All premiers' conferences should be scrapped

CHARLES LYNCH

OTTAWA — As a provincial voter you, dear reader, are represented at the conference of provincial premiers held this week in Victoria, B.C.

As a federal as well as a provincial voter, you are doubly represented at federal-provincial conferences, more grandly known as summit meetings of first ministers.

It has long been my impression that the federal-provincial conferences are rip-offs, and that the business of governing the country and its respective parts would proceed more efficiently if these gabfests were abandoned.

It has now become my impression that the meetings of provincial premiers serve no useful purpose and constitute non-events that could be axed, to the advantage of taxpayers.

If you read the dispatches from the Victoria meetings, you learn nothing you didn't know before about the views of various provincial premiers on the topics of the day, and you realize that when all the provincial premiers are laid end to end, the sum is no greater than its parts.

You discover, once more, the difficulties the premiers encounter in trying to reach a common front on anything, apart from the fact that Ottawa is a dirty word.

You find evidence that, as provincial governments get bigger, the provincial premiers become more and more preoccupied with the problems of their own turf, and the care and feeding of their own political reputations.

The premiers' meetings, like the federal-provincial conferences, have no status in law. The federal-provincial conference has a certain curiosity value, since it constitutes the only distinctively Canadian contribution to the democratic process (sovereignty-association would be another, should Quebec's Rene Levesque ever pull it off.)

The premiers' meetings are patterned on the meetings of the state governors in the United States, which tend to resemble Shriners' conventions because of the numbers involved and the showbiz atmosphere.

Our premiers tend to be more sombre, and they hew to the practice of holding their plenary meetings behind closed doors, a variation from legislative practice. In their legislatures, of course, opposition parties are represented, and hence a majority of voters have a voice, which is not the case when the first ministers gather.

It would behoove the likes of me, as an advocate of public business being transacted in public, to howl for the premiers to meet in the open, but the example of the federal-provincial conferences offers little encouragement.

The federal-provincial summits accomplish as little when they meet in public as when they meet in private, and when a group of the premiers came to Ottawa for an open meeting to air their constitutional views the show was the biggest flop since Jalna.

Therefore, we put the proposition that the interests of voters, which means taxpayers, would be served if no further meetings were held.

If the first ministers want to get together socially, let them do it on their own time and their own money, for the sheer joy of fraternizing the way the tycoons of big business do at their watering places.

If they have business to transact with one another, let them do it one-on-one, preferably over the telephone.

And if they have things to talk about or negotiate with the central government, the lines are always open and there's usually somebody home here in Ottawa, though it may not be the prime minister, who has more friends in Africa than he has among the Canadian premiers.

The only loss in the abandonment of these conferences would be the media attention the participants receive, upon which they place high value.

When was the last time you heard of a premiers' conference, or a federal-provincial summit, producing any solid results?

If total abandonment seems too extreme, could we not at least try a moratorium, or ceasefire, for a trial period of one year, or preferably two?

During this time, all first ministers could apply themselves to the tasks they were elected to perform, provincial and federal, and after the trial period an assessment would be made to determine whether the country was better or worse off for the lack of conferences.

(Lynch is chief of Southam News)

THE VANCOUVER PROVINCE, FEBRUARY 7, 1982

Pierre killed it

By PADDY SHERMAN

The most frightening prospect to emerge from the Economic Conference was not merely the realization that when you lock up all our leaders together to solve a crisis, they achieve less than nothing.

Nor was it finding out, again, that our national institutions themselves are feeble, unimaginative, and even unable to get simple arithmetic right within half a billion dollars.

To me, the tragedy was that federal-provincial co-operation as a way of running this strange country of ours is now dead. Prime Minister Trudeau killed it, and it will stay buried until he is gone from the political scene.

In the widest sense, it was deliberate sabotage. But for an understanding, we might better study textbooks on psychology/psychiatry than on political science.

Mr. Trudeau, the man of brilliant intellect, has become a man with an obsession. The constitutional battle hardened it. In short, it is that no matter how Canada used to do things, to hell with it. In future he will run the country. Premiers are intellectual pygmies out to destroy the country and only he can save it.

He stopped listening in the constitutional debate for things that a wise and honest man could stitch together into something new and consensual. He heard only the things he could snarl about. Only the Supreme Court's gun to his head changed his approach.

He struggled to put off the economic conference the premiers asked for. When it came he was interested in nothing more than showing that he ran the show, and that intellectual pygmies were cannon fodder to saviors.

It is fair to say that no prime minister in our history has so totally alienated all premiers. Mild-mannered Bill Davis of Ontario, his major prop in the constitutional brawl, used words about Trudeau's leadership that were for Davis the equivalent of knife and knuckleduster. New Brunswick's Richard Hatfield, so far the nearest thing to a prime ministerial stooge we've had, has angrily deserted him.

Rene Levesque, that consummate political actor, screamed "bloody rape" in frustrated agitation that went beyond acting.

None of these premiers had a clear and simple alternative to Mr. Trudeau's non-working plan to leave everything in the hands of the U.S. interest rate. But none expected to be treated as a half-witted child, there to be seen and not heard, then slapped and told to go home and play their village games.

That's why we need to study the psychology books not the political texts. Why would a man nearing retirement destroy all hopes of co-operation, and determine instead to put his own government, which has destroyed so much of what it touches, deeply into unilateral programs for changing the shape of the country?

His psyche urges him to fight rather than switch, to defend by insult rather than honestly seek consensus in a country that won't work without it.

Whatever those deep-seated needs may be, he came very close to satisfying them during the conference.

Even a village pygmy can see that from here on, no premier will take seriously a word he says. Regional forces are likely to get stronger. The talks to plan constitutional changes that must follow the patriation of our constitution will go nowhere, if indeed they start at all when Mr. Trudeau is there.

It has the makings of classical tragedy, since it springs from the seeds within him. We must hope that he doesn't wreak such damage that no successor can repair it.

THE TORONTO STAR, AUGUST 28, 1982

The good, the bad and the ugly of federalism

OTTAWA — Of all the various systems of government around the world, from left to right and through the various shades of the centre, federalism is at one and the same time one of the best and one of the worst.

For more cultural and social purposes, federalism is the best of all possible systems. The division of power between two levels of government allows people two chances to get what they want, such as to vote different ways in federal and provincial elections, or to be unilingual in their local affairs and bilingual in their national ones.

The initiation

It creates opportunities for initiatives, such as medicare by Saskatchewan, which, once established there, was transformed into a national program. The flexibility of federalism made it possible for Canada to become almost the only country — Sweden also has done so — to revise its constitution in peace time instead of during the crisis conditions of war or revolution.

For most economic purposes, federalism is one of the worst of all possible systems of governments. Economic decisions are usually hard ones these days, unlike during the easy years of the '60s and early '70s. Rather than take these hard economic decisions, the two levels of government can blame the other for not taking them, and equally can blame the other for the immediate consequences — the short-term pain for long-term gain phenomenon that is — of the decisions it does take.

This fault lies in the nature of federalism itself rather than in the personality

RICHARD GWYN in Ottawa

or political ideology of the national and provincial leaders at any particular time. At their conference in Halifax this week, the premiers not only ignored federalism's fault, but magnified it and made it almost into their guiding governing principle.

Repeatedly, in their statements in the press and in their final communique, the premiers declared that Canada suffered from a "crisis of confidence." True. A truism, even. Except that the premiers then amplified that crisis of confidence by opting for confrontation with the federal government rather than for co-operation with it.

Politics, almost entirely so, dictated the premiers' decision. They dislike Prime Minister Pierre Trudeau. They deeply distrust him. So they took collective aim against Trudeau's "six and five" program. They hit their political target all right, except that damaged as much by the fall-out will be the confidence of investors in the Canadian economy.

The premiers justified their refusal to go along with the federal program on that grounds that, as Conference chairman John Buchanan of Nova Scotia put it, "We already are exercising restraint."

Some provinces indeed are exercising restraint. Nova Scotia for one, B.C. for another. Quebec too; to cut back its budget deficit, actually cut civil service salaries.

Collectively though, the provinces are spenders rather than spendthrifts — during the five years to July 1 last, or to

the eve of the federal budget in which the "six and five" program was announced, provincial pay rises have each year outpaced those granted by Ottawa to its employees.

In Ottawa, examples of extravagances are easy to find, from free luggage for diplomats to language sabbaticals in the south of France. They are as easy to find in provincial capitals too, but they are less publicized.

Saskatchewan civil servants, for instance, stay home every second Friday. At up to $90,000, the top Alberta civil servants are paid close to twice as much as the highest-paid ones in Washington. Quebec civil servants, if their job disappears, by contract have to be offered another one, not just within the bureaucracy but within the community where they happen to be living.

Finger-pointing isn't the point. It is, rather, that the federal "six and five" program, for all its own faults, does point the way all Canadians could go together. Or more accurately, one way Canadians might go since, as the premiers pointed out, restraint on wages and prices, while it may help us to win the war against inflation, will do nothing to win us jobs and economic growth.

The signals

At their Halifax conference, the premiers huffed and puffed. And muffed it. They wanted to send out a signal of hope about the economy to investors, both foreign and Canadian. They succeeded only in reminding investors, whether here or there, that because of the politics of a federal system, the economic buck most times bounces from the desks of one government to that of another, and at other times drops to the floor between them.

LA PRESSE, MONTRÉAL, AUGUST 28, 1982

Louis Falardeau

The Halifax conference:
A public-relations operation

Journalists were sceptical at the end of the 23rd annual premiers' conference last Thursday in Halifax. They were trying to understand why the premiers were satisfied to aim once again at the federal level, this time under the high-sounding title 'An Economic Recovery Plan', a series of requests that the Trudeau government has firmly rejected several times.

Nova Scotia Premier John Buchanan, who presided over the conference, explained that the situation has gotten worse, that it is now clear the federal solutions are inadequate to handle the crisis. Therefore Ottawa has no choice but to agree to reopen discussions on the remedies proposed by the provinces, especially since the latter are prepared to negotiate in good faith and make some compromises.

And if Mr Trudeau refuses to call a federal-provincial conference, or if he shows the same inflexibility that he did last February, when the last such meeting took place? Then, the premiers answered unanimously, public opinion will be the judge!

Above all, it was a public-relations operation that the provincial leaders were engaged in at Halifax. Canadians are living through a very serious economic crisis, and all the polls prove that this has become their main concern. Thus they are waiting for those in government to take measures to correct the situation.

Look how serious we are

But the provincial government cannot do very much. It is Ottawa that controls the principal levers, and the Trudeau government has decided to act alone. All it expects from the provinces is that they will faithfully play the bit part it has left for them.

At the same time, the federal government is more unpopular than ever, and across the country the press is reporting both its mistakes and the citizens' demonstrations of their discontent. The provinces have thus taken advantage of the situation to send their constituents the following message: look how serious we are — we've spent two days discussing the economic crisis, and we have solutions to offer. If Mr Trudeau wants to meet with us, we are willing to do so during the week of Sept. 13.

Of course, these are 'old' solutions that Mr Trudeau wants no part of. But, the provinces say to each other, he is now so unpopular that, as the crisis continues to deepen, either he will have to give in or public opinion will make him pay for it. And the provinces will be the winners, since Canadians will tell themselves that they are doing all they can, and that Trudeau is the one preventing them from working effectively.

The Québec government more or less goes along with this analysis. Mr Lévesque, who has not forgiven the 'traitors' of Nov. 5, had no desire to go to Halifax. But Quebecers, as PQ polls show, would not understand it if their government did not become involved with a serious attempt to ease the crisis.

Québec made inquiries

So Québec made some inquiries, and when it seemed obvious that the crisis would be the number-one subject at the conference, and that the political will was strong enough for there to be a good chance the premiers would come up with a concrete agreement, Mr Lévesque resigned himself to the trip.

Oh, of course he made very sure his counterparts would understand that his anger had not abated. He stayed less than 24 hours in Halifax, missing the Thursday meetings and half of Wednesday afternoon.

He did go to the reception for delegates and journalists Tuesday evening — where they presented him with a cake and sang 'Happy Birthday' to mark his sixtieth — but he did not appear at the one given by Mr Buchanan for the premiers and their wives, later the same evening.

In the same way, he was not at the premiers' breakfast the next morning. 'I wanted to sleep', was the simple explanation he gave to journalists.

In contrast, the Québec delegation, headed by Jacques-Yvan Morin after Mr Lévesque's departure, worked in good faith, just like any other province. Furthermore, it was quite satisfied with the results.

Regarding, notably, the 6- and 5-per-cent policy, the other provinces stood firmer than had been hoped. They more or less adopted the Québec position, which in effect says governments must reduce their spending, and particularly the growth of their employees' salaries, but that each province must be free to do so in the way that best suits its particular case, and not by applying the federal dictates.

Above all, they are sending a clear message to Ottawa that this measure alone is not enough, and that the priority, on the contrary, should be job creation.

All Québec hopes for now is that this firmness will persist in Ottawa, when the federal-provincial conference on the economy eventually does take place. Once bitten, though, twice shy!

THE TORONTO STAR, AUGUST 29, 1982

Premiers' talks were useful

The first thing to remember about the annual conference of provincial premiers is that it has no constitutional status, no authority, no recognized leader, and not much common ground among its 10 government delegations.

Expectations of any firm consensus, let alone an action program, at last week's meeting in Halifax were therefore bound to be disappointed. The premiers have never formed a common front in any substantial issue — the constitution, energy policy, economic nationalism, language rights, or whatever.

This doesn't mean the meeting was a useless exercise — far from it. There ought to be more forums of the kind, allowing the 10 leaders as a group to assess each other's thinking and policies of their governments. Federal-provincial relations are not only a matter of provincial interaction with Ottawa, but also, and on a different basis, of relations between the provinces themselves.

National policy

But because the premiers are heads of government with their individual cabinets and legislatures to answer to, it is unreasonable to expect them to come up with national programs or declarations of national policy. That's Ottawa's responsibility.

This year's meeting was notable for the absence of fed-bashing, at least in public. However disappointed Prime Minister Pierre Trudeau may be that the premiers didn't dance to his six-five tune, he would be wise not to respond with any province-bashing.

There is a certain consensus now that Canadian's economic problems from coast to coast outweigh the political rancor the Trudeau government has generated in

ROBERT DUFFY Queen's Park Notebook

the past few years. It recognizes that Trudeau is the only prime minister we've got and so, because the problems won't wait until he decides to go, it's necessary — urgently — to find some kind of federal-provincial agreement on what needs to be done.

For Trudeau now to shrug off the provincial concerns expressed in Halifax, such as federal fiscal management, the effects of the national energy policy and the Foreign Investment Review Agency, and the arbitrary reductions in federal revenue-sharing, would be a disastrous failure of national policy.

The process of finding a way out of the economic mess we're in has only just begun. The Trudeau government will need all the federal-provincial co-operation it can get, as will Ontario Premier William Davis and his colleagues in attacking their provincial problems.

Having listened and said a few things in his usual equivocal fashion, Davis returned from Halifax and went off for a long weekend at his cottage. On Tuesday and Wednesday there will be an extended cabinet meeting at the Brampton Holiday Inn. This was originally planned as an end-of-session review meeting in July, then put off for lack of time. Now it will be dominated by economic issues.

The time for action is very near. Ever since federal Finance Minister Allan MacEachen's June budget, Davis has been "keeping his op-

tions open," while letting it be known through anonymnous senior aides that anything is posible — including wage and price controls for Ontario.

The cabinet is sharply divided on that issue, but Municipal Affairs Minister Claude Bennett dropped a brutal hint in another area of economic restraint when he told the annual meeting of the Association of Municipalities of Ontario not to expect any increase at all next year in the level of provincial grants to municipalities.

Fewer options

The range of options is narrowing as relentlessly as the fall weather in closing in.

Something else is happening. The Davis government's habitual bolt-hole — blaming bad times on Otawa policies — is crumbling. Outraged public reaction to Treasurer Frank Miller's extension of the sales tax last spring showed that people are increasingly ready to find a provincial scapegoat for their troubles.

Even though the next provincial election is a long way off, that means political worry for Davis and his Tories. He faces two new and vigorous opposition leaders, both commanding substantial electoral support. There can come a time when, rightly or wrongly, there is a public mood to "throw the rascals out" and try something new — as the Liberals in Ottawa have discovered.

It might be ironic, but it would be good for Canada's future, if Ontario Conservatism concluded that its best interest lay in helping rehabilitate federal Liberalism by supporting the measures that are needed to get this country back on the road to growth and prosperity.

THE FINANCIAL POST, SEPTEMBER 4, 1982

Premiers edge toward alliance of necessity

By Giles Gherson

HALIFAX

GATHERED AROUND the cabinet table at Halifax's Province House last week, Canada's 10 provincial premiers pasted together a policy program that is less a manifesto for action than an opening bid for serious economic talks with Ottawa.

For despite the visceral mood of alienation from the federal Liberals at their 23rd Annual Conference, the premiers appear to be edging toward an alliance of necessity. "Sure, there's plenty in the premiers' communique that is probably unacceptable to Ottawa. But among the somewhat platitudinous recommendations the feds have a provincial consensus they can build on," says Hugh Segal, top political aide to Ontario Premier Bill Davis.

It's all part of the ritual dance that now seems an integral part of the "new federalism" in Canada. The pattern of federal initiative/provincial response was established with Ottawa's energy and constitutional campaigns and could similarly yield a compromise federal-provincial economic recovery package possibly by late fall.

In the end, it may be that not all provinces will remain part of the common front forged last week. That could mean a series of bilateral deals with Ottawa; federal job-creation assistance, say, in return for a federally approved provincial wage- and price-restraint program.

Conversations with several Ontario delegates reinforced the impression in other provinces' delegations that Ontario is preparing a full-scale public sector wage- and regulated-price program but is coyly waiting on the sidelines to see what kind of leverage it can exact.

"If and when Ontario goes forward with restraint, I'd be surprised if apart from wages, we didn't have a strong framework on administered prices," Segal says.

Whatever the eventual price, that sort of talk is music to Ottawa's ears. To date, federal officials have been extremely discouraged by what they say is the provinces' reluctance to take the "hard political decisions" that controls on administered prices call for.

Not uncharacteristically, most premiers took pains to heap criticism on Prime Minister Trudeau's 6%-5% restraint program as a one-dimensional obsession insufficient to bring about economic recovery.

"The premiers see 6%-5% as primarily a Liberal tool designed more for political than economic salvation, and that makes them leery and skeptical," one senior Western adviser says.

Even so, Ontario's Davis and British Columbia Premier Bill Bennett consistently reminded their counterparts of the need to be flexible on restraint — if only to show a balanced posture that would attract Ottawa's interest. Aside from Quebec, which has asked its public servants to accept a three-month pay cut starting in January, British Columbia has adopted the toughest public sector wage restraint policy. Bennett came to the conference anxious to sell his wage "stabilization" scheme — which maintains collective bargaining within a four-percentage-point range above a 6%-5% basic pay raise ceiling.

Key concerns

One of Bennett's key concerns is that an indifferent approach to public-sector restraint in other provinces, particularly in neighboring Alberta, will undermine his efforts at home. So far, only Ontario has expressed a serious interest in British Columbia's program, while Alberta's Peter Lougheed, on the other hand, left the conference declaring himself quite satisfied with the 6% pay freeze he has imposed on the province's senior public service managers. (On the conference's final day, Edmonton firemen received a two-year 32% pay raise.)

Although no one knows what it really amounts to, both Davis and Bennett seemed reasonably pleased with the provinces' unanimous commitment to "exercise restraint on public-sector wages, prices and expenditures within their respective jurisdictions."

That restraint commitment should be enough for the federal government to call the provinces' bluff, Ontario and British Columbia officials say. "The provinces now have no choice but to show how serious they are about their intentions," one says.

Presumptuously labeled a dramatic economic recovery plan, the premiers' Halifax communique advocated, among other things, a series of federal policy U-turns which, if implemented, would give Ottawa's Liberal administration a decidedly Progressive Conservative complexion. But if Ottawa takes time to look at demands for abolition of Fira, a reversal of interest rate policy and substantial amendments to the National Energy Program, it should see that the premiers are, in essence, only asking Ottawa to repair the damaging impression at home and abroad that Canada is not a stable climate for capital investment.

In the end, Allan MacEachen's swift rejection of the premiers' demand for a Sept. 13 First Ministers' conference in favor of lower-level meetings to pave the way was no surprise. "If I were in the Prime Minister's shoes, I'd sift through the communique, choose a few promising areas such as Fira and interest rate policy, then write to Buchanan and ask him to explain precisely what he means," one senior provincial official says.

Annoyed at the few signs of provincial movement toward embracing the federal restraint package, this is precisely the course Ottawa seems to have adopted. Before a First Ministers' conference is called, federal-provincial officials will likely discuss:

● Tax changes to encourage equity investment. The provinces want the dividend tax credit reinstated, the corporate surtax removed, and changes made to the capital cost and resource allowance provisions.

● Further changes to Fira. Lougheed, for example, wants a two-year suspension of the act.

● How to achieve lower interest rates. Some provinces think the dollar could be buttressed by some form of interest equalization tax. This would reduce the possibility of capital outflows, because the interest-rate differential for a Canadian who invested in a foreign currency governed by higher interest rates would be eliminated.

● Joint federal-provincial targeting of employment-intensive capital projects that might be prodded to go ahead. Alberta's Heritage Fund's financing of British Columbia's Prince Rupert coal terminal facility is "a classic example" of what the premiers have in mind, Lougheed says.

THE TORONTO STAR, AUGUST 27, 1982

A short-sighted consensus

The Canadian premiers have emerged from their Halifax meeting with a cosy political consensus — but with no credible provincial program to help curb inflation and boost employment. Instead, the premiers have come up with a set of demands that would merely shift back the whole burden of economic recovery on Ottawa's shoulders, while considerably weakening our own control over our economic destiny.

For ordinary Canadians suffering from a painful 10.8 per cent inflation rate and an 11.8 per cent unemployment rate,

as we slide deeper into recession, the Halifax meeting shatters any hope that the provincial leaders will go boldly beyond Ottawa's lead in trying to sort out our economic woes.

The premiers have asked for a Sept. 13 economic meeting in Ottawa, and have served notice that they will be pushing — quite sensibly — for much-needed federal action to lower interest rates and to create jobs. So far, so good. But in exchange, the premiers seem willing to offer only vague pledges to put restraints on provincial employees' wages and on provincially-administered prices. That falls far short of what they might have resolved: Provincial wage and price controls applied uniformly, equitably and efficiently, and more provincial spending to create jobs.

If anything, the premiers have now made it clear that Ottawa would have been better advised to impose full, nation-wide controls from the start, rather than trying to rally support for largely voluntary controls.

But the short-sighted "Halifax consensus" hardly stops there. The premiers went on to call on Ottawa to seriously erode key federal programs to control foreign investment here, and to promote energy self-sufficiency. Let the foreigners in to invest and to exploit our oil, and jobs will be created for Canadians, the premiers argue seductively.

What the premiers are deliberately ignoring, in calling for a weakening of the National Energy Program and of the Foreign Investment Review Agency, is the heavy price foreign investment exacts from our economy. Foreigners already control 75 per cent of our energy sector, and 50 per cent of our manufacturing sector. The result is that billions of dollars annually in interest and dividends are siphoned out of the country; foreign investors decide when Canadian branch plants are closed and when Canadians are thrown out of work; and decisions are made abroad that have great repercussions on the fabric of our society.

With more than $50 billion in U.S. investment already in Canada — much of it doing less for us than it might — the premiers are now busy calling for even more, with fewer strings attached to ensure that future investment provides benefits by boosting our productivity, fostering competition and helping us sell more goods abroad.

Whatever their disclaimers, the premiers left Halifax determined indeed to "bargain and trade off" with Ottawa. What they are bargaining for is a chance to shift the whole difficult burden of economic recovery back onto Ottawa's shoulders; what they are willing to trade off for a short-term economic boost is our long-term prosperity.

LA PRESSE, MONTRÉAL, AUGUST 27, 1982

Towards a summit on the economy

It would be less than gracious of Prime Minister Trudeau to refuse his provincial colleagues the national conference on the economy they are asking him to call for September. The situation is dramatic enough to speed up such a summit meeting.

Furthermore, the generally positive attitude of the provincial premiers at the just-ended Halifax meeting suggests that the different levels of government could harmonize their policies regarding inflation and, above all, job creation.

Of course, the heads of the provincial governments did not fail to take Ottawa to task in Halifax. Fair enough. For instance, they attacked the Foreign Investment Review Agency. They maintained that the federal plan for a 6-and-5-per-cent society was unfair to low-wage earners, and claimed that Mr Trudeau's nationalist energy policy was bad for the country.

It must be recognized that, on the whole, these criticisms are legitimate. In a period of serious economic difficulties, screening foreign investments is hardly justified. You pretty well have to take whatever is offered. And if salary increases must be curtailed, arrangements must be made so that low-wage earners suffer less than those at the top of the scale. This objective cannot be achieved by means of percentages. Finally, Canadianization of the petroleum industry is swallowing up millions of dollars that could be producing jobs elsewhere.

Not every province is unblemished on these same issues. Québec, for example, is threatening to take back, through percentages, a good portion of the increases it granted its public employees. In so doing, it too is penalizing low-wage earners. As well, Québec has proceeded in the asbestos sector in the same way that Ottawa has done in the petroleum industry. The millions it has devoted to the purchase of the Asbestos Company have not created any new jobs, and would have been far more useful elsewhere. But it is always easier to recognize other people's mistakes.

Once again, however, one feels that this time the provinces did not want to be purely negative. They are ready to get involved. They have constructive suggestions to offer. Consequently they are demanding that they be listened to, and this is far from what has happened in the past.

The final communiqué from the Halifax conference also takes into account the promises already made by the provinces to limit their spending and thus fight inflation. These same provinces, of course, say they have more confidence in their own policy in this regard, and add that salary restraints should only be considered as one means among many of getting the economy moving again, but it is clear that they mean to continue practising austerity themselves.

For example, they want to focus, together with the federal government, on 'long-term plans aimed at reducing deficits, and to work at bringing the public debt under control'. Everyone recognizes that the enormous deficits of the various levels of government play a large role in keeping inflation high.

Finally, the provinces stress the importance of adopting bold programs to re-establish investor confidence. They are aware that the federal screening agency is not the only factor alienating the holders of capital. The labour-relations climate is another one, perhaps even more significant. This is an area in which provincial authority is stronger than Ottawa's. Thus there is reason to presume that here too they are ready to play a large role.

Vincent Prince

THE CHRONICLE-HERALD, HALIFAX, AUGUST 28, 1982

Straighter shooting

CANADA'S TEN premiers did come to one inescapable, but nonetheless valuable conclusion at the end of their three-day summit in Halifax this week. If they are not prepared to sign up for the federal program of pay and price restraint, then they had better have an alternative.

The alternative duly produced, the premiers' Economic Recovery Plan, has the shortcomings one would expect in the child of eight governments of varying shades of free-market conservatism, one socialist and one socialist-separatist. The premiers are not playing up their differences and inconsistencies in economic thinking, but it is readily apparent that they are there (on economic nationalism, interest rates, government deficits) and that the real absence of agreement has been glossed over rather than resolved. This makes for a political harmony that many Canadians are ready to welcome after what seems like a Hundred Years' War of intergovernmental, inter-regional struggle. But it does not necessarily lay the foundations for an economic recovery.

Thus the premiers have gone only part way toward what should have been their second conclusion — that their alternative recovery plan had better be able to stand up to critical examination by a public which is daily learning tougher habits of mind at the hands of the worst economic downturn in Canada since the Great Depression.

As their positions on major issues indicate, the premiers do have credible policies, which in some cases could be made stronger still. They also have their share of fudgy ones which will only weaken their case:

□ Economic nationalism. This is the premiers' strongest suit. The Foreign Investment Review Agency, which most want scrapped, and the National Energy Program, which all want changed substantially have unquestionably contributed to Canada's economic weakness. A few readily identifiable results are an unreasonable growth of debt in the Canadian economy and a concomitant weakening of both corporate balance sheets and the banking system itself; increased pressure on domestic interest rates; a virtual shutdown of new development in the West's oil and gas industry, particularly much planned-for megaprojects, which has translated into massive layoffs in Central Canada's industrial heartland. Still to come could be economic reprisals by Canada's trading partners, particularly the United States, upon whom Ottawa, paradoxically; is largely pinning its hopes of recovery.

Given these drastic consequences, it is surprising the premiers could not reach an unequivocal stand against economic nationalism. Watering down the majority feeling that FIRA should be abolished to one of tinkering with the agency or suspending it temporarily (a sop to Manitoba Premier Howard Pawley's ideology, and Ontario Premier William Davis' regional interests) was surely too weak. Why take off a hairshirt only to put it on again? The hold-out premiers might have been advised to defend their positions to the unemployed.

□ Interest rates and monetary policy. In calling for a simple lowering of interest rates, or a smaller gap between Canadian and U.S. rates, the premiers are barking up the wrong tree. Governor Gerald Bouey and the Bank of Canada have probably produced the lowest rates possible (if the alternative of hyper-inflation is ruled out) given the irresponsible growth of borrowing by Ottawa and the provinces themselves, the bleeding of $5 billion of foreign capital from our economy last year, and the resulting over-expansion of bank credit as foreign equity investment was nationalized or Canadianized with borrowed money and government blessing. Even with the current premium over American rates, it should be remembered, our dollar has managed nothing better than a hovering pattern around 80 cents U.S. Pulling down the last defence against a speculative run on our currency deserves no place in a recovery plan.

Instead, the premiers should be stressing the pressures which the National Energy Policy and record government deficits have exerted on domestic interest rates. Canada's monetary policy has become a slave of government debt and economic nationalism, and there will be no improvement in our interest rates relative to those in the U.S. while we continue to expel foreign investment, run proportionally bigger government deficits and make less progress against inflation. The provincial leaders are missing a major point in not driving home to the average Canadian the price he is paying — just in mortgage costs alone — for these policies.

□ Fiscal policy. Ten of the 11 guilty parties are taking the oft-heard vow to reduce government deficits and borrowing and are urging Ottawa to do likewise. Until the public sees something specific, it is likely to put little faith in these good intentions. Although recession has done what tax-revolters would like to do — reducing government revenues — there has yet been little resultant restraint on spending.

We can all welcome the fact that the premiers have not left Ottawa's limited recovery plan as the only game in town. But the ten will have still to shoot straighter if they are to win the draw against six-and-five.

THE STAR-PHOENIX, SASKATOON, AUGUST 28, 1982

Premiers far from impressive

The best way to react to this week's premiers' conference in Halifax is to paraphrase an editorial from the last century: Everybody talks about the economy, but nobody does anything about it.

Editorial

The nation's premiers, after thoroughly discussing the problem seemed only able to agree on two things—the economy is in bad shape, and somebody had better do something soon.

Oh yes, they did call for a meeting next month with the prime minister to discuss new economic measures for the country, including possible abolition of the Foreign Investment Review Agency (FIRA) and amendments to the national energy program; but in the absence of consensus, that meeting, if held, is unlikely to produce more results than the one just ended.

And to add bewilderment to disappointment, there was the statement of Nova Scotia's Premier John Buchanan, host and chairman of the conference, who said the premiers are willing to negotiate with the federal government on the package of economic recovery, but are not willing to "bargain and trade off."

Anyone appalled by the trading of fish for rights which haunted the constitutional talks last year should be downright stunned by this offer.

And, by the way, what's the difference between bargain and negotiate? "There's a big difference," says Buchanan, but he didn't explain.

More sensible was the observation of New Brunswick's Premier Richard Hatfield who said a consensus was impossible because the problem is too big for them.

The communique, that document that is supposed to sum up the deliberations and advance certain proposals, was actually quite vague.

In it, the premiers expressed concern "over the growing trend of the federal government to pursue and develop economic policies without adequate consultation with the provinces." After this week's performance, one is tempted to ask: Why should the federal government bother?

After all the noise about Ottawa's six-and-five formula for public sector wages, the communique was pointedly silent.

The communique called for an immediate change in monetary policy to "ensure that Canadians receive the full benefit of falling interest rates and that Canadian rates are not kept artificially high in relation to U.S. rates." But this position has been taken by the provinces on previous occasions. The problem with it is that it fails to include a suggestion as to what Ottawa might reasonably do without touching off more inflation. It is not responsible to demand a change in monetary policy without examining the consequences of that change or without proposing a workable alternative.

The communique also singled out FIRA as the culprit in the loss of investor confidence in Canada, and called for its abolition. Manitoba's NDP Premier Howard Pawley dissented. He fears that during a recession, a great deal more of Canada's economy would be bought up by Americans at bargain prices if FIRA were to go.

He may be right. But lest anyone believe that the case against FIRA is Conservative in origin because the other premiers are of that party or persuasion, Opposition Leader Joe Clark has come out for it. Reacting to the premiers' attack, Clark said he thought FIRA should undergo major changes, but should not be abolished.

Anyway, it's unlikely Ottawa is going to listen to the premiers on the matter of FIRA or monetary policy. And there's little reason why it should.

Simply put, the premiers did not come up with an intelligent analysis of Canada's economic situation, nor did they come up with any intelligent solutions.

As Hatfield said, the problem was too big for them.

THE TORONTO STAR, APRIL 11, 1981

War No.3 with provinces

Ottawa wants to slash subsidies on health care, education and some hospitals

By Ian Urquhart Toronto Star

OTTAWA — With battles still raging over energy policy and the constitution, the federal government is opening a third front in its war with the provinces that could prove more explosive than the other two combined.

Strapped for funds and saddled with a huge deficit, Ottawa is pressing the provinces to shoulder more of the burden of programs for which the two levels of government share responsibility.

At stake are the future of health care and post-secondary education in the country. If the federal-provincial conflict gets out of hand, some hospitals and universities may have to close or tuition and medicare fees might have to be tripled.

"The provinces and Ottawa are going to go to war and we are the victims," says a worried Donald Savage, executive director of the Canadian Association of University Teachers.

Ottawa will transfer $13.8 billion in cash to the provinces, territories and municipalities this year — some 21 per cent of the total federal budget. Finance Minister Allan MacEachen, desperate to save money, has said he wants to shave $1.5 billion from these transfer programs in the next two years.

Under the knife

The programs range from crop insurance ($99 million this year) to second-language training ($181 million) to equalization, the subsidization of the seven "have-not" provinces ($3.6 billion). MacEachen has not yet said which will come under the knife.

But it is no secret in Ottawa that the main targets for cuts are the so-called "established programs," government jargon for medicare, hospital insurance and post-secondary education. Together, these programs will account for $6.4 billion in federal spending this year, half of all transfer payments.

Ottawa and the provinces used to share the costs of the established programs on a rough 50-50 basis. The provinces literally submitted receipts for auditing by Ottawa, which sent back cheques.

Then, in 1977, at Ottawa's urging, that system was scrapped and replaced with "block funding," under which the federal contribution is tied to increases in the Gross National Product (GNP), not to actual costs. Federal officials felt this system would be an incentive to the provinces to hold down costs.

Before, if the provinces spent $1 on health or post-secondary education, they knew they would get 50 cents back from Ottawa. Under the new system, they get the same amount from Ottawa no matter what they spend.

The change worked, perhaps too well. The provinces restrained their spending to the point where Ottawa now contributes well over 50 per cent of the costs of the established programs. In some cases, Ottawa's share has run to absurd extremes. In Prince Edward Island, for example, it pays 110 per cent of the costs of post-secondary education. That means the provincial government actually makes a profit from running the University of PEI.

At the same time, Ottawa has been getting proportionately less tax revenue from the GNP pie, while provincial returns have been increasing.

Caught between a rock and a hard place, MacEachen decided to act. First, last fall, he introduced a budget that dramatically increased the federal share of resource revenues in an effort to reverse the recent trend that saw provincial coffers — notably Alberta's — swell while Ottawa's froze.

The next step is to come in April, 1982, when the existing federal-provincial financing agreement for established programs expires and Ottawa can begin cutting back the money it donates to provincial treasuries. The provinces will not give in without a fight.

Battle escalating

Skirmishes have already taken place between federal and provincial officials meeting privately over the last few months in Ottawa. And on Monday and Tuesday, the battle will escalate with a meeting between Ian Stewart, deputy minister of finance, and his provincial counterparts in Banff, Alta.

There has also been furious lobbying in Ottawa by groups that would be affected by cuts to the established programs, such as the association of university teachers. They will get a chance to make their case publicly before a parliamentary task force, which begins hearings on the issue later this month.

The task force, headed by MP Herb Breau (L-Gloucester) a MacEachen protege, is to report in June. MacEachen has said the federal government will make no firm proposals for cuts before then.

But his fellow cabinet ministers have already begun manoeuvring to protect their pet programs. Late last year, Health Minister Monique Begin boldly stated that the government would not touch the two programs under her sway — medicare and hospital insurance.

"But the third component . . . post-secondary education . . . is very elitist," she continued in an interview with CBC radio. "It does not provide for redistribution according to the poverty of a particular region in the country . . . This is a candidate for savings which will be rechannelled differently."

Begin was, as usual, speaking out

of turn. Cabinet has made no decision to spare her programs and axe post-secondary education. Secretary of State Francis Fox, minister responsible for the latter, is fighting a rear-guard action on behalf of the universities.

Both Begin and Fox want to retain cash grants to the provinces as levers to influence the management of health care and post-secondary education, which fall under provincial jurisdiction.

Another faction in cabinet, led by Justice Minister Jean Chretien, wants to see federal spending given more "visibility," Ottawa's latest buzz word. Chretien and his allies argue that it is no good transferring money to the provinces for them to spend on programs of their choice because Ottawa gets no credit for it. The money would be better spent on programs in which Ottawa's role is clear, such as old-age pensions, they argue.

As a substitute for grants to the provinces for post-secondary education, they offer a massive program of students loans and bursaries. The money would go directly from Ottawa to the students to pay for the higher tuition fees that would result from the withdrawal of the grants to the provinces.

MacEachen himself, from impoverished Cape Breton Island, is said

to favor an increase in equalization grants to the have-not provinces to offset the loss of revenues they would suffer from cuts in established-programs financing. The haves — Alberta, British Columbia, Ontario and, probably Saskatchewan — would be left to fend for themselves.

Budgetary deficit

This scheme might make sense in the three westernmost provinces, which are reaping the benefits of the resources in their ground and which, it must be noted, have no members on the government side in the House of Commons. But what about Ontario, which is limping along with its own budgetary deficit and has 52 Liberal MPs to speak up for it?

Ontario would have become a have-not province itself three years ago and has received more than $1 billion in equalization payments since then but for a retroactive change in the formula under which the grants are calculated.

The fact that Ontario, with the third-highest per capita income in the country, could be classified as a have-not province indicates how out of balance the whole fiscal system has grown.

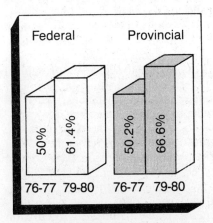

Hospital insurance

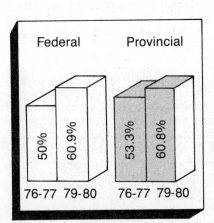

Medicare

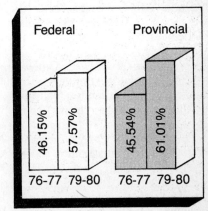

Post-secondary education

LE DEVOIR, AUGUST 8, 1981

Fiscal accords: another duel between Ottawa and Québec

by Jean-Claude Picard

QUEBEC—In addition to the constitutional issue, the negotiation of new fiscal accords between the federal and provincial governments will give rise to a major political battle between Québec and Ottawa in the next few months.

'I am getting ready for one of the most important struggles in my career. The cuts in financial transfers announced in the last federal budget are completely unacceptable, and Ottawa must understand that it cannot reduce its deficit by forcing the provinces to increase theirs,' said the Québec Minister of Finance, Mr Jacques Parizeau, in an interview Thursday with *Le Devoir*.

'It must be clearly understood that the negotiation of fiscal accords, which may at first sight seem very technical, is directly linked to the political future of Québec, to its ability to define its spending priorities and administer itself in an autonomous fashion within the federal system,' added the minister, who has declared his intention to fight the proposals announced last spring by his federal colleague, Mr Allan MacEachen.

Financial transfers between Ottawa and the provincial governments are the subject of elaborate federal-provincial discussions every five years, first at the level of the finance ministers, and then between the premiers and prime minister. It is more a matter of discussion, however, than of real negotiation, because in the end the decision rests with the central government, and is expressed in a bill presented to the House of Commons.

The last discussions of this kind go back to the winter of 1976–7, only a few months after the Parti québécois came to power. At the time, the Lévesque government said little about these matters, deciding essentially to accept what its Liberal predecessors had already agreed to.

Things will be entirely different this time, first because the current government has now been in place for close to five years, and is entering these negotiations in its own right, but also because Ottawa is going much further than last time in proposing to cut gradually the total amount of its financial transfers to the provinces.

In this respect, the intentions of the central government leave no room for misunderstanding. In the working paper it presented last April to the parliamentary committee responsible for examining the issue, Mr MacEachen in fact said that in this way he hoped to realize savings on the order of $1.5 billion in 1982–3 and as much again in 1983–4.

As the federal minister sees it, these cuts are necessary for three principal reasons:
• first, because Ottawa is grappling with serious financial problems and absolutely must reduce its deficit, a deficit that, Mr MacEachen explained, 'is roughly equal in size to the aggregate level of federal cash transfers to the provinces', that is, about $19 billion;
• second, the central government believes that these reductions, which will apply primarily in the areas of health and welfare, will release sums that can be invested in what has become its new priority, economic development;
• finally, the federal leaders are persuaded that they must end the current fiscal imbalance between Ottawa and the provincial governments. Thus Mr MacEachen explained that, taking into account the fiscal transfers in favour of the provinces, the central government's share of public revenue fell to 34% in 1979, compared with 52% in 1959. It is therefore time, in his view, to reduce the transfers in such a way as to re-establish this balance.

However that may be, these cuts in financial transfers will have a very important effect on provincial budgets as a whole, since most provinces are grappling with serious economic problems themselves and are committed to areas of responsibility that become more and more costly over the years — notably, all those health and education programs that in Québec, for example, represent close to 50% of expenditures.

In the last Québec budget, presented in March by Mr Parizeau, transfers from the central government represented slightly less than $4.3 billion, that is, nearly 30% of all the province's revenue.

This figure alone indicates how important the matter is. Any reduction in the rate of increase of these transfers or, worse still, any overall cut in the amounts transferred, will create a serious gap in the Québec budget, which must be filled.

Thus in 1980–1, these transfers will increase by only 3.8%, while inflation has been on the order of 12%; according to Mr Parizeau, this reduction has meant a loss of $230 million for Québec.

But these losses will be even more significant if the federal government applies last spring's proposal over the next five years. According to the finance minister, they would amount to $500 million this year and $800 million next year.

'To cause Québec to lose such amounts in the current context is to place it in genuine financial straits. It is impossible to see how a provincial government can function properly under such circumstances,' Mr Parizeau said in the interview.

To understand the scope of the question, it must be remembered that the reductions envisioned by Ottawa affect not so much equalization — although there too the central government has proposed several adjustments to the methods of calculation — as shared-cost programs in which the needs are urgent, and to which the provincial governments are deeply committed. These are the health and welfare programs, including health and hospital insurance, post-secondary education, and adult occupational training.

Before 1977, the costs of these programs were established by the provinces, and Ottawa paid 50% of them. In the spring of 1977, the central government passed a new law that changed this system profoundly. By virtue of this law and the regulations that followed it, federal contributions to these programs were no longer tied to their real costs but were supposed to follow the rate of growth in the Gross National Product, that is, approximately, 12% to 15% per year, taking 1977–8 as the base year.

This meant, in a way, obliging the provinces to develop programs whose increases in costs were not to exceed the increase in the GNP, which the great majority of them did, including Québec.

Now, at the moment of renewing these fiscal arrangements, the last of which comes due next spring, the central government wants not only to limit its contributions to the level of the last few years, but to reduce them in order to achieve the objectives defined by Mr MacEachen.

From this perspective, the provincial governments apparently have no choice but to raise their taxes or again make cuts in spending.

This is precisely what Mr Parizeau is refusing to do, explaining that the citizens of Québec already pay enough taxes and that it is difficult to go much further with budgetary cuts, those announced in the last provincial budget having almost provoked a revolution in the sectors concerned.

All the more so, he explained, since these are areas that might be deemed essential, and for which the province's constitutional responsibility is clear.

From this perspective, Mr Parizeau therefore believes that the central government has the duty to give the provinces the sums necessary for full exercise of these responsibilities.

Thus it is his intention to suggest that, in the framework of these discussions, his federal counterpart examine the two following avenues:
• either that the transfer payments continue to follow the rate of increase in the GNP;
• or that these payments be reduced on condition that the central government agree to withdraw from certain areas of taxation — for instance, tobacco and alcohol — so as to give the provinces more room for fiscal manoeuvre.

Certainly the Québec minister is aware that either route would mean a financial loss for the federal government, but he believes that the provinces should not have to pay for the federal budgetary deficit.

'Imagine the reaction if, in order to reduce its own budgetary deficit, Québec decided to reduce its transfer payments to municipalities. This is exactly what Ottawa is now proposing to do to the provinces,' he said.

In this spirit, Mr Parizeau says he is convinced that the provinces as a whole will fiercely oppose the federal plan. A first meeting of the provincial finance ministers has already been held, at the end of June, and another will take place next Tuesday in Victoria, just before the annual conference of provincial premiers begins.

Furthermore, the question of fiscal arrangements is on the agenda for this conference, and will probably give rise to a joint declaration by the heads of the provincial governments next week.

However, it is likely, as the Minister for Intergovernmental Affairs, Mr Claude Morin, indicated earlier this week, that for the moment this declaration will be no more than a statement of general principles, since the issue is still not completely developed.

For the rest, we will have to wait for the many meetings and conferences to come next fall and winter on a question that will determine the future of federal-provincial relations.

THE GLOBE AND MAIL, NOVEMBER 28, 1981

Fiscal arrangements: 'Like Chinese to most people'
Affect pocketbook of every Canadian

By THOMAS WALKOM
Globe and Mail Reporter

OTTAWA — It determines who can afford a doctor.

It can determine not only who is able to afford university, but what courses he would be allowed to take.

It will affect the ability of the nation to weather the current economic mix of recession and inflation.

It is a complex system of federal-provincial tax and money arrangements, and it is boring. Its very name —

fiscal arrangements — can provoke yawns from even the most dedicated aficionados of arcane constitutional practices.

"Nobody in Canada understands how this is set up," Finance Minister Jacques Parizeau of Quebec has said. "It is like Chinese to most people."

But as with so many aspects of Canadian life that seem dull — such as rocks, trees or fish — fiscal arrangements are profoundly important.

The current round of federal-provin-

cial wrangling — which lurched to a shaky start earlier this week in Halifax — has centred on Finance Minister Allan MacEachen's plan to cut back by $5.7-billion over the next five years the amount Ottawa transfers to the provinces.

But bound up in the debate over money are at least two other key questions: the effect of federal cutbacks on provincial economic policy (and hence the national economy), and the relationship between education and economic development in Canada.

The fiscal arrangements are based on three major principles: that provinces have relatively equal access to revenues for essential services, that individuals in distress across the nation have relatively similar access to welfare payments, and that tax systems be co-ordinated enough among the 11 political jurisdictions in Canada to prevent massive economic chaos.

In effect, the system works in a two-stage fashion. The federal Government raises tax revenue on its own, primarily from income and corporate taxes; then it bargains with the provinces over how much it is willing to give them.

Stage 1 for this round of negotiations included the protracted energy talks between Alberta and Ottawa, which ended with the federal Government's reaping an extra chunk of petroleum dollars.

Stage 2 — which is renegotiated every five years — began in earnest last spring when Mr. MacEachen announced he wanted to save the federal treasury $4.5-billion over the next five years. It accelerated this month when Mr. Mac-Eachen's budget revealed that in fact he has decided to save $5.7-billion over the period.

In Halifax, provincial finance ministers unanimously rejected the cutbacks. Mr. MacEachen insists that the savings will come from the elimination of a revenue guarantee program that he says has become redundant, and that nothing else will be affected. The provinces argue that a dollar is a dollar, and that if the federal Government cuts back on its contributions, health and education services must of necessity suffer.

A federal proposal that equalization payments designed to compensate poorer provinces with a small revenue base be recalculated also received a hostile response in Halifax. But there are indications that when the finance ministers meet again in December to continue negotiations they may be able to find an accommodation on this issue.

Not so with the cutbacks — in spite of Mr. MacEachen's soothing words to the provinces. He has told them not to worry, that with the extra tax revenue that they could generate if they go along with his budget they would lose a mere $1.9-billion over the five-year period.

Provincial officials found those figures suspicious. And Mr. MacEachen backtracked the night before his Halifax meeting began. An arithmetical mistake, he said; the federal Government now says the real loss would be $2.4-billion.

Mr. Parizeau, however, insists that the figure was still too low and that the cost to the provinces would be much higher. New Brunswick, Nova Scotia and Newfoundland have tended to agree.

Under the revised federal estimates, all provinces except Quebec would lose money right from the beginning. Next year, Albertans would on average get $23 less than they would have received under the old system; Newfoundlanders, where unemployment is the highest in the land, would lose $20 each.

Using Quebec estimates, Quebeckers would be the big losers next year at an average of $52 a head. Prince Edward Islanders would lose $45 each and New-foundlanders $41.

Whatever figures one uses, if the provinces do not replace lost federal money, the area hardest hit next year would include the traditionally have-not Atlantic provinces. And the effects across the nation could include higher medicare fees or premiums, fewer hospital beds, higher university tuition.

But even if the provinces do counteract these cutbacks somehow, there would be important economic effects. They provinces could, for instance, increase their own spending without raising taxes.

Such a move by shifting the federal deficit to the provinces would turn much of Mr. MacEachen's economic policy into a sham. It is debatable whether lower Government deficits actually do contribute to the fight against inflation. But even if this theory is correct, a deficit shift from one level of government to another would be more of an elaborate card trick than a blow against rising prices.

. . . as with so many aspects of Canadian life that seem dull — such as rocks, trees or fish — fiscal arrangements are profoundly important

If, on the other hand, the provinces want to keep health and education at their present levels by raising taxes, they will be reinforcing the chill wind that the federal budget of restraint is already sending through an economy marked by layoffs, bankruptcies, high unemployment and recession.

There is another element to the dispute, which is intimately tied in with Ottawa's so-called economic development strategy for the 1980s. The federal Government has served notice that it wants to restructure and co-ordinate the system of post-secondary education in Canada to promote its vision of resource-based growth, based on a skilled and mobile labor force.

A paper released with the budget puts it bluntly: "Canada's economic development depends increasingly on our ability to make the most effective use of our human resources . . . . Concerted and sustained efforts are required to avoid university and college graduates finding themselves unemployed because of an over-supply of their particular skills, while industrial expansion is hampered by a shortage of other skills . . . . Potential waste through duplication and wasteful competition could impede efforts to accelerate growth of the Canadian economy."

At the first level, that statement is telling students they may find themselves channelled increasingly into subjects such as engineering, economics or sheet-metal working rather than "wasteful" areas such as classics or political theory.

But more than that, the vision promoted by the federal Government runs directly counter to the role of education originally promoted at Confederation. Education was left as a provincial responsibility in 1867 because it was seen to be a service responding to local and regional peculiarities.

Under the federal view, education becomes tied less to local needs and more to the grand economic strategies of the country, which are in turn determined by the needs of the export market and the flows of capital.

Do the oil rigs of Alberta require pipe-fitters? Then the schools of Ontario or New Brunswick will provide them. It will be merely a question of efficiently using "human resources" to maximize gross national product under an over-all master central plan.

Should the federal Government decide to proceed with its plans to cut the transfers, or make its transfers contingent on drastic changes in the provincial education systems, there is little legally that the provinces can do about it.

After March 31, 1982, the federal Government will be able to alter unilaterally the contentious elements of the fiscal arrangements.

Ontario Treasurer Frank Miller is still optimistic. "Like the Pope, the provinces have no legions," he has said bravely.

Whether the provinces will have God on their side when they sit down to sup with Mr. MacEachen in December is an open question.

Discussion Questions

1. What do the articles on the 1982 premiers' conference indicate about the state of federal–provincial relations? What do they say about the future functioning of federalism in Canada?
2. How much has executive federalism contributed to our federal system's ability to adapt to changing circumstances? What are its successes? What are the weaknesses of the process? Has executive federalism contributed to the continuing problems of Canadian unity?
3. Could the decentralization of the 1960s and '70s accomplished by intergovernmental negotiation have been effected by judicial review? What was the role of the courts in adjusting the Canadian federal system to altered circumstances? Has the past pattern of judicial interpretation set a particular direction for the federal system?
4. Do the developments discussed in the articles on fiscal federalism indicate a trend towards a lower degree of federal–provincial integration? Are they moving Canada in the direction of classical federalism? What are the implications of these developments?
5. Has the reduction of Canada's problems to a discussion of federal–provincial relations helped Canadians avoid facing basic issues? Are there concerns that cannot be subsumed under federal–provincial relations?
6. Have the highly visible, almost constant federal–provincial conferences left Canadians with the impression that their national government is merely one of eleven equal participants? Has the process contributed to a situation of dangerous decentralization evidenced by an inability on the part of the federal government to control the economy and to formulate coherent policies even in its own area of jurisdiction?

Suggested Readings

J. Peter Meekison. 'Federal–Provincial Relations', in John H. Redekop, ed. *Approaches to Canadian Politics*, second edition. Toronto: Prentice-Hall, 1983, 169–203.

Paul W. Fox, ed. *Politics: Canada*, fifth edition. Toronto: McGraw-Hill Ryerson, 1982, 85–124.

Canada, Economic Council of Canada. *Financing Confederation Today and Tomorrow.* Ottawa: Supply and Services, 1982.

Canada, Parliamentary Task Force on Federal–Provincial Fiscal Arrangements. *Fiscal Federalism in Canada.* Ottawa: Supply and Services, 1981.

Richard J. Van Loon and Michael S. Whittington. *The Canadian Political System: Environment, Structure and Process*, third edition. Toronto: McGraw-Hill Ryerson, 1981, 524–49.

Garth Stevenson. 'Federalism and Intergovernmental Relations', in Michael S. Whittington and Glen Williams, eds. *Canadian Politics in the 1980s.* Toronto: Methuen, 1981, 275–91.

Milton Moore. 'Some Proposals for Adapting Federal–Provincial Financial Arrangements to Current Conditions', in *Canadian Public Administration*, vol. 24, no. 2, Summer 1981, 232–56.

Donald V. Smiley. *Canada in Question: Federalism in the Eighties*, third edition. Toronto: McGraw-Hill Ryerson, 1980.

Richard Schultz. *Federalism, Bureaucracy, and Public Policy: The Politics of Highway Transport Regulation.* Montreal: McGill-Queen's University Press, 1980.

Canadian Public Administration, vol. 23, no. 1, Spring 1980, 14–59.

Garth Stevenson. *Unfulfilled Union: Canadian Federalism and National Unity.* Toronto: Macmillan, 1979.

Richard Simeon, ed. *Confrontation and Collaboration: Intergovernmental Relations in Canada Today.* Toronto: Institute of Public Administration in Canada, 1979.

R.B. Byers and R.W. Reford, eds. *Canada Challenged: The Viability of Confederation.* Toronto: Canadian Institute of International Affairs, 1979.

Thomas Courchene. *Refinancing the Canadian Federation.* Montreal: C.D. Howe Research Institute, 1979.

b. Strains in Canadian Federalism

(i) Québec Nationalism and Independentism

(ii) Western Alienation

Within the Canadian federation two sets of conflicting relations have been of overwhelming importance: those between English and French, and those between East and West. The economic, social, and political implications of these ongoing conflicts have inspired countless debates regarding the fundamental nature of the Canadian political system and its structural deficiencies. Indeed, in the 1970s the dominant issue in our public affairs was the very survival of the Canadian political community. The discussion generally revolved around these two sets of relations, on which press attention focused even more closely after the election of the Parti québécois in November 1976. As members of the press became ever more intensely involved in the debate over Québec's continued presence within Confederation, political reporting often reflected very personal views.

If the volume of coverage concerning the strains on Canadian federalism has been great, however, the quality has for the most part been poor. Over and over, reports on these issues have used the same worn-out language, until the real sense of the debate has become lost. Rarely has any historical perspective been provided. As a result, press coverage has tended to leave the public cold; reporters, politicians, and constitutional experts have come to resemble a priestly caste reciting strange incantations that few outsiders can comprehend.

The continued salience of the Québec 'issue' testifies to the persistence of dualism in the Canadian political system. From the beginning, Canada has been composed of two ethnically and linguistically distinct communities, with the French component dominant only in Québec. However, the measures demanded by French-speaking Canadian leaders at the time of Confederation to ensure linguistic and cultural duality have not been fully implemented in the evolution of the federal system. French-speaking Canadians suffered numerous setbacks—Louis Riel, the schools questions, the conscription crises, etc.—in their quest for equality.

In more recent years, the election of the Parti québécois, dedicated to its vision of sovereignty-association, threw the country into another crisis. The PQ came to power with a promise to consult the population before taking steps towards independence, and the referendum held in May 1980 saw the defeat of its option by a 60–40 margin. The first two articles following deal explicitly with this event. Robert Fulford interprets it largely in the context of the Canadian political community. He also correctly catches the ambiguity of the debate: sovereignty-association was peddled to the public in an imprecise and unclear fashion, but the alternative of renewed federalism was presented in equally vague terms. Marcel Pépin of *Le Soleil* addresses the consequences of the referendum, particularly the dissipation of the momentum for genuine reform. A powerful coda to a sensitive political debate, his piece is saturated with a sense of sadness that meaningful constitutional change (i.e. increased powers for the Québec government, which would allow it to act more effectively in the interests of its

French-speaking population) was no longer possible. The tone here is in sharp contrast to the almost buoyant quality of Fulford's comments.

The remaining articles on Québec are drawn from a selection of French-speaking Québec writers. The French-language press has a remarkably different concept of itself and its societal role. Reporters and commentators are deeply engaged in social and political matters, and they focus overwhelmingly on Québec itself. The newspaper is regarded as more of a public service in Québec, and the fact that journalists see themselves as leaders of public opinion is reflected in the practice of signing editorials, which do not necessarily represent the views of management.

Solange Chaput-Rolland was an eloquent participant in the debate on Québec's future in the federation as a member of the blue-ribbon Pépin–Roberts Task Force on Canadian unity. Her two pieces here not only provide cogent insights into Québec politics but also reveal considerable emotional anguish over the outcome of the constitutional debates. In the article from *La Presse*, she comments vividly on the seeming paradox of the existence of two conflicting nationalisms within the Canadian polity. The competition between these two nationalisms, each of which has the resources of a powerful government behind it, is a defining characteristic of our federation. Indeed, the clashes between them have proven a great burden whenever they have become manifest in political demands and governmental actions.

In her second article, Chaput-Rolland laments the inaction of the Trudeau government when it came to fulfilling the expectations aroused by the referendum. Finally, after summarizing Trudeau's perspective on Canadian federalism and suggesting that he has betrayed Québec, she expresses her own disillusionment with trying to effect change in the Canadian federal system. Similarly, the publisher of *Le Devoir*, Jean-Louis Roy, lambastes Trudeau's vision, his resistance to developments in Québec, and the illegitimacy of the constitutional deal achieved with the nine other provinces. Lise Bissonnette examines the place of Québec in the federation in her two-part series on the fragility of the province's cultural identity in the larger North American context. Her approach is remarkably refreshing in that it avoids the rhetorical flourishes that so often permeate discussions of Québec's identity. In the same vein, Jean Paré of *L'Actualité* describes how the people of Québec have been victimized by both levels of government. His article is the logical conclusion to Chaput-Rolland's description of the two competing nationalisms. Paré issues a stinging indictment of the results of the federal system and concludes that it operates against the public interest.

The other critical theme of the Canadian federation mentioned above, East–West relations, has taken on a new character in the past decade with the growing economic power of the Western provinces, particularly Alberta. As Jeff Sallot explains in some detail, traditional Western grievances were economic in character and related to manufacturing, banking, and transportation. In short, Westerners perceived that many of the key institutions were controlled in Central Canada and operated against their interests. As Sallot observes, however, the grievances today are predominantly political in nature ('loss of political clout'). With economic prosperity, the West is no longer as troubled by economic concerns that may have been real at one time but now are mostly symbolic. Throughout the piece, and especially evident in Jeffrey Simpson's article on the civil service, is an underlying partisan distrust of the central government and the federal Liberals. Simpson advances the questionable assumption that the West's troubles with Ottawa hinge on representation—in other words, influence—in federal institutions (for example, the bureaucracy). In fact, it seems more realistic to view most of their differences as symptoms of a struggle between two bureaucratic empires attempting to exploit competing regional and national loyalties, even though real differences in economic interest and ideology do exist.

There is little sustainable evidence of deep-seated alienation from Ottawa in the West. Regional differences in economic interest or ideology are mobilized and intensified by political leaders to further their own goals. One consequence is that other cleavages, such as class, are downplayed. Political scientist Peter Dobell deals with the specific issue of Western representation on the government side in the House of Commons. Although the article is dated (for example, Michael Kirby is no longer Secretary to the Cabinet for Federal–Provincial Relations), the range of alternatives he canvasses is informative. What his discussion lacks is any consideration of proposals for adapting other central institutions to accommodate regional diversity. Many schemes have been advanced to alter the composition of the Supreme Court, the Senate, the Cabinet, political parties, and the bureaucracy.

The final two articles address the phenomenon of Western separatism, which appeared on the scene in the early 1980s. Although widely viewed as a fad or an expression of frustration at the combination of one-party dominance in Alberta and the lack of Western representation in the federal Liberal party, the movement did manage to elect a member to the Alberta legislature in 1981. Don Braid provides a profile of the Western Canada Concept party leader Gordon Kesler. Kesler's political platform is a confused one, and his discontent seems to be less that of a separatist than of a traditional right-wing populist. In a sense Western separatism was a media phenomenon. On the basis of a few protest meetings, these essentially frustrated people were accorded greater legitimacy than they deserved, primarily because of the Québec precedent and the West's long history of legitimate protest movements. In fact, one year after Kesler's victory the same columnist was drafting the party's obituary. Drawing most of its support from bewildered and angry rural voters who simply wanted to protest the erosion of traditional values and institutions in the face of Big Government, the WCC is not likely to survive for long.

(i) Québec Nationalism and Independentism

SATURDAY NIGHT, JUNE 1980

The night of the No vote: a very Canadian occasion

By Robert Fulford

It was "a great victory for Canada," the former premier of Nova Scotia told us on referendum night. And Knowlton Nash of the CBC, perhaps overcome by federalist emotion, declared at one point: "Quebecers have spoken with one voice and with that voice they've said No." Well, not precisely. In fact, quite a few more than a million Quebecers said Yes to the Parti Québecois' request for authority to work towards a separate Québec state, linked with Canada in customs and monetary union. Their votes indicated again the presence of a grave problem which had still not vanished on the bright and happy morning of May 21 and which likely will not disappear in this generation. Many, many Canadians are unhappy that they are Canadians: it is as simple and as appalling as that.

Still, for René Lévesque the defeat was real—and, in retrospect, surprising. There was a time, not long ago, when he seemed altogether in command, set on a course that would lead him to triumph. He and his colleagues had provided more than three years of good government for the province. On their side they had the intellectuals, the artists, most of the young, large parts of the media, much of the professional class. Lévesque himself, as he introduced the question in the National Assembly, still seemed the most attractive Québec politician of our time. For its part, English Canada helped: in particular, the intransigence of Ontario on the issue of French rights fuelled the separatist cause, as any reader of French-Canadian newspapers is all too painfully aware. And finally the question itself—market-tested, softened—was a masterpiece of reassuring understatement. There were even fools who said they would vote for it just to strengthen Québec's hand at the federal-provincial bargaining table. (Apparently they believed that was more important than the hardening effect a Yes vote would have had on public opinion in the nine provinces and the calamitous effect it would have had on the Canadian economy.)

The No vote will be attributed partly to hard times, to that global economic crisis which threatens us all and which discourages dangerous innovation. But it seems likelier that the French Canadians who voted for federalism simply recognized that Québec has already met many of its needs as a nation within Canada and can meet most of the others in the same way. It's clear to any student of Canadian history since the year 1960—when the election of the Lesage government in Québec began the transition period in which we still live—that the Canadian federation can change substantially as the demands of the people and their various governments change.

During the last twenty years most of that change has been the result of pressure from Québec. It was the Lesage cabinet, after all, that began the process which transformed the provincial governments from minor to major factors in the life of the country as a whole and changed the federal-provincial conference from an aimless tea-party into the real government of Canada. Others—in Edmonton, Toronto, Victoria, lately St. John's—learned a great deal from Québec.

Now Québec puts forward, through Claude Ryan, another idea: the provinces and the federal government, in a new constitution, will be equal partners, sharing responsibilities according to a new formula. If something like Ryan's proposals do indeed become the basis for the constitution, then that will not be a radical break with the past (as some federalists seem to believe) but rather the continuation of a process which began when Jean Lesage and his civil servants turned up at their first federal-provincial conference.

There was a comic side to the referendum which in our solemnity many of us tended to overlook. It proved, for one thing, that in political culture there's no essential difference between French Canada and English Canada. The referendum perfectly expressed the style of Canadians, those endlessly and inventively incoherent people, who never like to ask a straight question or answer one. Québec managed the whole thing just as an English-speaking province or indeed the federal government would have done. The PQ posed a question hardly anyone could understand, asking for authority it would be in no position to exercise. It did so, of course, with the maximum moral bombast, implying daily that its federalist opponents were vicious cheaters who wouldn't play by the rules the PQ had invented. The No forces, for their part, started out by arguing at tedious length about the wording of the question, then threw promises in all directions ("Don't worry, we'll have a new constitution ready for you in a minute or two") and concluded by singing *O Canada*. Mackenzie King, had he been on either side, could hardly have done the thing better.

In a more telling way the whole occasion was solidly within the Canadian tradition. Two colleagues of mine were talking about the crisis a few months ago. "What can you *do* with this country?" the younger one, in exasperation, demanded. The older one offered her years of accumulated wisdom in a few words. "You save it," she said. "That's what you do with Canada. You just keep on saving it."

SATURDAY NIGHT, OCTOBER 1980

THE DEATH OF SEPARATISM

The life went out of Québec's independence movement the night the referendum was lost

BY MARCEL PEPIN

THE REFERENDUM on Québec's future has been described by editorialists, TV reporters, and other giddy optimists as a turning point in Canada's history. Out of it will come, we have been told, a new constitution with a new sharing of powers – in fact, a new Canada. But the political realities, and the decision made by Quebeckers, dictate otherwise. May 20 was certainly a turning point in Québec history, but it was not the new beginning for Canada that has been so widely advertised.

For decades, nationalists in Québec worked toward a single goal: to increase the powers of the Québec government so that it could better protect the rights of the French population. This goal was opposed by those who believed French culture would be better protected if the French were strong in both the federal and provincial governments, even though this would mean remaining a minority in Canada forever. As those two views evolved, the nationalists grew more and more *souverainistes,* while the federalists grew more and more centralist. When the PQ government called the referendum, Quebeckers were finally given the chance to choose. On May 20, Pierre Trudeau won and René Lévesque lost. Quebeckers chose to *remain* a minority within the present federal system. The notion that Quebeckers voted for change is pure rhetorical fiction. That's why the referendum faded so quickly as a subject of conversation. When Quebeckers have spoken in the past of change in constitutional arrangements they have meant one thing: the strengthening of the provincial government. And Québec's government has been strengthened, steadily, during the past two decades. But with the referendum that movement stopped. After the No vote, Quebeckers realized they could not expect to achieve greater autonomy.

The atmosphere of emergency – accommodate Québec quickly and prevent a second referendum – faded just as quickly in Parliament. The danger was over. The referendum demonstrated that this was mainly a war between two schools of thought in French Canada – and between two Québec heroes. (English Canada was no more than a silent, helpless bystander.) The rest of Canada quickly realized there was no reason to change its priorities. Quebeckers, after all, had endorsed the federal system.

This is the reality of Québec – and therefore of French-English – politics for the foreseeable future. It will not be changed even if René Lévesque and the Parti Québecois win the forthcoming provincial election. Nor will it be changed if Claude Ryan and Pierre Trudeau never manage to resolve their numerous differences over the consti-

Marcel Pépin is editorial page editor of Le Soleil *in Québec City. He has been a parliamentary correspondent for* Le Droit *and* La Presse, *and has twice won National Newspaper Awards for reporting and editorial writing.*

tutional future of this country.

In Québec now there is no great interest in the constitutional debate. The great era of change that was discussed during the referendum campaign will not come to pass. Quebeckers, having chosen to remain Canadians, cannot now expect to weaken the main institution of their country, the federal parliament, in order to make their province stronger. Canada as a whole – including Québec – wants to develop as a prosperous and articulate industrial state, competitive in trade with other countries. To achieve that, Ottawa needs a *stronger* voice in the management of natural resources, and more control of public spending. It needs firm regulations to prevent the creation of closed regional economies. And it requires greater access to the taxation field so that it can redistribute wealth throughout the country.

A FEW DAYS after May 20, Pierre Trudeau stated that Quebeckers supported his own theory of a strong central government. At that point Québec's idea of enhanced provincial power was already dead. Trudeau then went on with his plan for constitutional reform – patriation of the BNA Act, entrenchment of civil rights (including linguistic rights for minorities), and a strong re-affirmation of Canada as a federal union. He mentioned that he is prepared to negotiate on redistribution of powers, but warned that he will not allow the provinces to weaken the federal government. The redistribution of powers will be possible only on a give-and-take basis, he said, which means that Ottawa intends to *increase* its own powers in the process.

Trudeau will patriate the constitution without serious opposition from the Québec people, provided he chooses to do it by referendum. Nor will Québec seriously oppose his charter of civil rights: that would be like opposing motherhood. There will be no power struggle, because Quebeckers with their No vote denied themselves the only bargaining tool available to them. At best there will be – after years of boring technical talk – a clarification of powers. This will be accomplished along lines dictated by efficiency; the process will completely ignore the idea of two associated states that Québec nationalists sought to impose on Canada.

QUEBECKERS have grasped this; we know that the goals of French Canada cannot be first on the national agenda. Canada has higher priorities: a national energy policy, a new economic deal for the Maritimes, the creation of a more important role for the West in the 1980s. The real issues now are the sharing of wealth and the development, at last, of a sound industrial strategy. The problem of Québec autonomy has been settled – by the French.

That doesn't mean, of course, that Québec nationalism will disappear. It will remain an underlying force in Québec society. But it will move into the background. In recent years, nationalism, instead of unifying Quebeckers, has been divisive. For most Quebeckers, the referendum was a torturous experience. Quebeckers wanted to show their attachment for Canada without at the same time hurting themselves. They knew from the beginning that they would emerge as losers no matter which side won. They were under heavy pressure and the pressure was painful. My belief is that

they will not allow politicians to impose such a violent choice upon them again – at least for a generation or two. Instead they will continue to protect, inch by inch, the autonomy Québec already enjoys, counting on favourable circumstances to improve this autonomy gradually. They will not risk weakening their own society by more emotional divisiveness.

Last summer, after it was over, the referendum became a sort of taboo subject in Québec. People began looking at other ways – non-political ways – to improve their society. And change *is* under way in many parts of Québec life. Hydro-Québec, for instance, is a huge success not because it is nationalized but because it is looked on as an ally of Quebeckers. Other institutions are growing stronger, particularly in finance. One-third of the business students in Canada are now in Québec: they know that the future for some of them holds jobs at the higher levels of both private and public corporations, jobs that in the past were rarely open to francophones. There have been more mergers in Québec in the past ten years than in the previous fifty. The co-op movement is playing a major role in building a strong French environment in business.

More and more, as Quebeckers become involved in the capitalist struggle – a part of life where they were so long the underdogs – the French are naturally banding together to improve their competitive position. And they are making great progress. In this world there will be more real change than any rewriting of the British North America Act can accomplish.

After the referendum, Québec discovered how mature a society it had

become. Despite dark prophecies, there was not a single violent incident. In this atmosphere pluralistic values will be looked on again in a favourable light. Québec will turn slowly away from the sharply focused ethnicity of the past few years – and away from government as the solver of all problems. Private organizations and individuals will accomplish what governments failed to do: build new bridges to link Québec to its neighbours, in Canada and elsewhere. Young people in Québec are showing an inclination to involve themselves in issues beyond nationalism; for instance, there seems to be a new and growing involvement in the problems of the Third World nations.

THE CANADIAN duality remains, of course, and will remain forever. Quebeckers want it to remain. Two societies will continue to shape their destinies in parallel ways. The referendum and all that went before it told us that these two societies need to talk more honestly and directly to each other. Both French and English Canada will remember that lesson – even if politicians take years to learn what the people already know.

The referendum was the end, not the beginning, of a moment in Canadian history. In the years ahead only an obvious and humiliating provocation on the part of Ottawa or the English provinces will rally Quebeckers behind the banner of independence. If relations between the two societies are treated with the proper delicacy, Québec will cease to be a threat to the Canadian order.

LA PRESSE, MONTRÉAL, JUNE 15, 1981

Solange Chaput-Rolland

Two nationalisms within a single state

Sociologists and historians have written numerous essays and learned studies describing the birth and rebirth of Québec nationalism. So it seems futile for me, as an amateur, to repeat the exercise when the experts have already done it. But nationalism does not live in books, or anywhere else outside of individuals; it is embodied in each of us, animating us with a variety of feelings whose source we often ignore, but whose intensity and emotional power we discover when our people and the surrounding society come under attack, both from without and from within.

For this Quebecer, who lives her nationalism sometimes bullishly, sometimes bearishly, according to the tide of political and cultural events, nationalism is a living fact that is the starting point for every step — social, political, or constitutional — that I take. I do not know if my nationalism will satisfy the jurists and sociologists; if it is of the right or the left, neo- or old-fashioned, traditional or innovative. But I feel that it has stirred at the core of my being ever since my ancestors staked their first colonial claim, in or about 1648.

If the French people of America, as Canon Groulx put it — or the French fact in Canada, as Mr Trudeau says, or the second half of Canada, as the Laurendeau-Dunton Commission put it, or the Québécois society of the Pépin-Robarts group, or the Québécois nation proclaimed by the Lévesque government, or the distinct society of Québec, as the Beige Paper calls it — does exist, it owes its longevity and its presence,

for more than three hundred years, on a hostile continent, to the vitality of a nationalism that has always expressed itself, though in different ways, according to the circumstances of its historic development.

To define nationalism is to run the risk of expressing it in words that correspond to the image envisioned by whoever is trying to describe it. The objectivity of the definition is severely compromised as a result. Hence it seems to me healthier to propose a definition of the object and *raison d'être* of nationalism as historian Ramsay Cook and Professor David Cameron, research director of the Pépin-Robarts Commission, see it. For the first, 'French-Canadian nationalism can best be seen as an attempt repeated in every generation to bring past, present and future into harmony.' For the second, 'There shall be no nationalism with a nation contented.' These two observations form the backdrop against which our nationalism — French-Canadian to begin with, then becoming resolutely Québécois under Jean-Lesage — has woven itself.

In this strange country, one open to all the freedoms prescribed in Canada's British constitution but closed to those who wish broader, more collective ones not inscribed in the supreme law of the land as it stands, nationalism has always existed, but its existence has been constantly decried by those who have made it indispensable. Mr Trudeau describes Québec nationalism as a vestige of old-fashioned tribalism, although he accommodates himself well enough to mani-

festations of tribalism in his favour, expressed as: 'Let's vote for one of our own, because he looks better to us than the rest.' The English Canadian fears what the French-Canadian of an earlier day called *l'achat chez nous*, but cultivates an economic nationalism to prove his confidence in products 'made in Canada' rather than those 'made in U.S.A.' In the same way a Québec nationalist will prefer 'made in Québec' to 'made in Canada', but he incurs the wrath of those he imitates, without understanding exactly why.

Our history contains many examples of nationalism that, though camouflaged under another name, encouraged individuals to experience and express the same feelings for different values. The Albertan of 1981 is a nationalist just as ardent in the defence of his natural resources as the Québec nationalist has become in the protection of his cultural heritage. And yet the two citizens are afraid of each other, because, not knowing one another, each blames the other for acting in exactly the same way, though no doubt for different reasons. Anyone who closely studies the rise of regionalism in Canada will simultaneously discover the fervent nationalism of individuals who are proud to display — in their ways and customs, their speech, their food, their reading, their products and crafts — the distinctive mark of their region. However, their nationalism will be contaminated, as ours was, the moment politics demands a presence in order to extract all the substance out of social, economic, or cultural conflicts.

In Québec, politics takes precedence over everything else, and thus corrodes the feelings that have inspired our people ever since the Lords of France returned to their native land, abandoning the poor folk and soldiers to the New Land they clung to, at first to keep from dying, and then to sow it with their labour and their loyalty. They embraced the rhythm, the climate, the rigours of winter, the absence of conventional food, and they dressed like Canadians, so as not to die like Frenchmen. Montcalm, in his journal, was astonished to discover the colonists' prejudice against the mother country. Without knowing it, for the word did not exist, the colonists, or Canadiens, had become nationalists to distinguish themselves from those who had abandoned them —and rare indeed, in 1981, are those who have not remained so.

Why? To make things uncomfortable for English Canada or the central government? Because David Cameron's observation is correct: our people-nation-society draws its strength from its experiences and its resistance; it is not yet 'contented'. Hence its heightened sense of belonging first to a land and territory, because this land and territory have allowed its descendants and our own to continue speaking French on an English-speaking continent.

Nationalism is not a feeling against the country or against a party; it is a persistent will to compel the country and perhaps some parties to respect the linguistic, cultural, judicial, denominational, and federal-provincial dualism prescribed in the constitution that has allowed our people to blossom no less than it has authorized the other people of Canada to harm them. Without the nationalism of the former, who knows where the others' will to dominate and assimilate would have led. In this sense nationalism as I see, feel, and understand it is not an adjunct to a political party or a trump card in the hands of a premier. It is a state of being resulting from a state of things. A Quebecer, especially a French-speaking one — is not a nationalist because he wants to be, or out of loyalty to a party or an ideology, but because he cannot *not* be a nationalist if his daily and collective life is preoccupied with the strength of his past, the fragility of his present, and the uncertainty of his future.

In its plan to repatriate the British constitution of Canada, the Canadian government has chosen to be more nationalist than federalist, since its desire to 'Canadianize' the Act of 1867 is stronger than its will to respect the very principle of the federal system. Disregarding the will of eight provinces, rushing to have done with the amending formula and the insertion of a charter of rights in the supreme law of the land, Prime Minister Trudeau puts his power and the powers of his government into the best seats of the constitutional theatre and relegates to the wings the powers of the provinces, without which, according to the very principle of federalism, he cannot govern.

Thus we find ourselves in the presence of two nationalisms, each as strong and plausible and necessary as the other: the desire to repatriate and Canadianize a British law suggests an open, healthy nationalism, but the desire to protect the rights that this constitution reserves for the provinces suggests a regional nationalism that is just as healthy, and even more plausible. Caught between these two desires to serve the interests of the country as a whole and those of the provinces, the citizens support Mr Trudeau, who, alleging that the provincial premiers are 'greedy', prides himself on that support. Now, in practice it is not the citizens who negotiate with the federal government but the premiers, who, strong in the powers accorded them by the supreme law of the land, seek to obtain as many rights as possible, to manage better the property of the people under their jurisdiction. I learned from John Robarts, former premier of Ontario, how frequent and urgent the conversations are between members of the provincial cabinets and those of the federal government, as well as between the civil servants of the two orders of government. The premiers are not aligning themselves against this unilateral move in order to demonstrate a narrow regional nationalism, but because their powers depend on the constitutional law; they are morally bound to defend the rights they have acquired and, most of the time, to demand more, to allow for the realities facing the people under their jurisdiction. Most of them would have liked to settle a new division of powers and jurisdiction before repatriating the constitution.

We are in the depths of a crisis that is not simply constitutional, even if it does shake the foundations of the federal form of government; we are torn between two orders of nationalism. Out of respect for the federalism in which 60% of Quebecers believe and to which all the provinces adhere, citizens should back the opposition of eight provincial premiers who know from experience that federal-provincial relations are strained, at present, and wonder how they will reach an understanding with the federal government tomorrow when it will not listen to them today. Professor Donald Smiley, of the department of political science at York University, cannot be suspected of being egocentric, and he writes in *Queen's Quarterly*, Spring 1981:

> The Federal strategy in respect to the constitution has made the two orders of government enemies . . . (. . .) The major defect of this strategy is that it forces citizens to choose between national and provincial loyalties.

The unilateral move thus risks making that tension official, and the crucial question is who, in six months or a year, will be capable of restoring some harmony to the power relations between these governments turned 'enemies'. The nationalism of both sides is once again at the heart of this debate, on which the stability of Canada as we know it depends.

TODAY, JULY 10, 1982

A Federalist No More

'We have had a French Canadian in power for almost 14 years, and French Canada has never been more estranged than it is today'

By Solange Chaput-Rolland

Solange Chaput-Rolland was a Liberal member of the Quebec National Assembly for two years. Her latest book is From Unity to Reality.

ON THE EVENING OF MAY 20, 1980, when the Canadian press informed the country that 60% of Quebec voters had refused secession and voted to remain Canadians, I was too weary physically and emotionally to celebrate. For security reasons I stayed at a downtown hotel close to my associates, who had helped me through a campaign whose poignancy and cruelty no one outside Quebec could grasp. Without knowing why, most of us partisans of the 'no' felt a curious empathy with the bitter disappointment of our Péquiste colleagues.

I have been involved in Quebec's evolution for almost 20 years; I knew that I had played a significant role in persuading my compatriots to remain attached to a country that did not love or respect or even understand Quebec. I had discovered during my stint with the Task Force on Canadian Unity that a majority of Canadians had no desire to become acquainted with our culture. They were not interested in regions other than their own. When on May 20 Canadians learned we had proclaimed our desire to retain our Canadian identity, all over the country it was business as usual. I felt that night like a woman who sacrifices her lover to return to a husband who does not really want her.

Since those hectic days we have witnessed patriation of the Constitution without the agreement of Quebec, the province without which the original Canadian Confederation of 1867 would never have been possible. In 1982, what kind of future are we facing? Are Quebecers reassured that we were right to assert our loyalty to our country? Has the referendum been a vast plot to diminish most of Quebec's powers by writing a new Constitution that the government of Quebec could not sign without denying our past, our Frenchness and our role as one of the two linguistic majorities?

These questions haunt me as I remember May 14, 1980. On that tumultuous night, Prime Minister Trudeau spoke before 10,000 Quebecers in the Paul Sauvé Arena in Montreal. I was on the platform with him. The crowd went wild as they heard his words: "I can make a most solemn commitment that following a 'no' vote we will immediately take action to renew the Constitution, and we will not stop until it is done."

That promise was never kept. The transformation of most of our political and legal institutions was at the very core of the renewal of our federation. Pierre Elliott Trudeau turned the referendum into a personal mandate to patriate our Constitution before negotiating a new division of powers between the provinces and the central government, and without attempting to transform the Senate into a House of the Provinces, to safeguard regional interests.

When we went back to the National Assembly after the referendum, Claude Ryan's Liberals, who had believed M. Trudeau's solemn words, were laughed at by our colleagues in René Lévesque's government. "Were you naive enough to imagine that Trudeau would give our society its distinctive character?" Some of us had said openly that patriation would come after a new division of powers. When it became clear that the federal Liberals were deaf to our wishes, that the Constitution would be patriated over the objections of Quebec, the stage was set for our electoral defeat in 1981.

One of the most tragic consequences of Quebec's referendum lies in the bitter confrontation between Quebec and Ottawa Liberals. The 74 Quebec members of Parliament in Ottawa convinced most Canadians that all of us in Quebec who dared to criticize M. Trudeau and M. Chrétien were nothing more than Péquistes in disguise. It is difficult to respect and trust this imperial government which haughtily rejects both friends and foes if they cannot accept its vision of Canada. As I watched M. Trudeau's performance during the patriation discussions and heard his arguments against the importance of recognizing the special status that was granted to Quebec in 1774 by the Quebec Act, I knew that never again would I trust his government with the fate of Quebec.

I WAS ONE OF THE EIGHT commissioners chosen by M.

Trudeau in 1977 to form the Pépin-Robarts commission. Our mandate was to advise him on ways to alleviate the problems between the provinces and the central government and among anglophones, francophones and ethnic minorities. We recommended giving the provinces more say in the central government's decisions and recognizing each province's distinctiveness by giving it ways to assert its individuality. I am still stung by M. Trudeau and M. Lalonde's refusals to accept or even to study our recommendations.

M. Trudeau's view of Canada reduces the provinces to a minor influence in the new federation, denies the historic role of Quebec, rejects the importance of regionalism, and transforms Canada into a country governed by a centralized administration. He has rejected all notions of cooperative federalism, and before he leaves Parliament, Canada will have become the unitary state that Sir John A. Macdonald wanted to create but could not because Sir George-Etienne Cartier pointed out that Quebec would never consent to be part of a country in which she would lose her identity.

In 1968, I, like many others,

strongly believed that M. Trudeau would help French and English-speaking Canadians understand each other. He did not. He imposed his Official Languages Act without bothering to explain its philosophy to his compatriots. He wanted to protect Quebec from separatism, but under his 'reign' the Péquistes have been elected twice, gaining popularity and seats in the Assembly the second time. He has pledged to further national unity and, according to Professor Donald Smiley of York University, has managed to transform the provinces into "enemies of the central government."

We have had a French Canadian in power for almost 14 years, and French Canada has never been more estranged from the federal government than it is today. And since he is a great man endowed with many fine qualities of mind, if he has failed to better our national life, who in Quebec can hope to succeed after him?

But a country is bigger than its leaders. I cling stubbornly to my ties to Canada, and I cannot join René Lévesque's party, though my life in Quebec would be much easier if I could accept his views.

To fight against both M. Trudeau and the Quebec Liberals because they support him is a difficult task. I am now discovering not two solitudes but one: my own. Yet, strangely, I have never been more at peace with myself, because now I am free to be myself without fear of damaging a political party or of losing votes. I am not a young woman anymore, and I have no one to flatter, no political ambitions to protect, and no favor to ask of any politician in Quebec or in Ottawa.

Ever since writing *Dear Enemies* in 1963 I have been trying to explain Quebec to Canada and vice versa. I have done my share of work for Canadian unity. I feel no desire to meet the same experts at the same universities to discuss the same problems all over again. I am now convinced that Canadians are more attached to their problems than to any man or woman who might suggest solutions. We cherish our problems so much that we have even enshrined them in our new Constitution so that our children may inherit them intact.

Now I am writing drama for television. For me fiction has become preferable to the Canadian reality. □

LE DEVOIR, DECEMBER 4, 1981

Building Canada without Québec

by Jean-Louis Roy

The vote on the constitutional resolution in the House of Commons confirms, for the moment, the thesis of Pierre Elliott Trudeau. Ever since entering federal politics, he has said that his surprising adherence to the Liberal party had to be understood as an attempt at restoring and strengthening the federal system that had been weakened by the assaults of Québec, and whose essen-

tial equilibrium was threatened by nationalist inflation, that less-than-sweet-smelling flower in the garden of the Quiet Revolution.

Invoking the theory of counterbalance, he proclaimed the necessity of Canadian resistance to the constitutional disorder, institutional upheaval, and conceptual perversion that pell-mell, in the actions and rhetoric of the Lesage government and the profoundly mistaken perspectives of the Laurendeau-Dunton Commission,

was obscuring the development and destabilizing the rationality and functionalism of the Canadian federal system.

Within a few months he had installed himself at the centre of the Liberal caucus and the Pearson government as the architect of this resistance to Québec, the originator and advocate of a certain vision of the unity of this country, then shaken and fragmented as never before. He will have consolidated a body of constitutional doctrine; established and deepened the scope and levels of discussion and political action; unified and respected — to the point of denying realities — a model of linguistic adjustment and constitutional development whose outcome we now know.

Pierre Trudeau will have destroyed everything, at the cost of an approach that has been authoritarian, violent, and on occasion unconstitutional, if it was necessary to dissolve and discredit concepts, groups, or persons who refused to yield to his seduction, his power, and his vision of the country's political future. He has practised powerful polemics, set traps, effected strategic retreats, seized on and exposed all signs of contradiction, real or apparent, in those who had the audacity to point out the fictitious nature and profound conservatism of his vision of the country. His political thought and actions have never been 'perverted' by those kite-builders in commissions of enquiry, parliamentary groups, or citizens' associations who dared to distance themselves from the political credo of the former editor of *Cité libre*.

Mr Trudeau has always treated with disdain those 'trouble-makers' eager to remake — hence, in his view, to destroy — the Canadian order. He has seen them all pass before him — naïve, courageous, utopian — only to disappear while he alone endured, ensconced there where the impossible would one day become possible, at the centre of power. In this context it matters quite little that Pierre Trudeau's opposite number at the last constitutional table was René Lévesque. Unless the head of the Québec government were someone with the mentality of a servile domestic, in one way or another he would have experienced a kind of exclusion. In fact, Mr Trudeau was not negotiating with Québec, but resisting Québec.

Resistance to Québec's self-assertion movement; conservatism; inflexibility — these are the three foundations of the constitutional action taken by the head of the Canadian government, and the explanation of the logic apparent in the man's survival and his power, both theoretical and political. Without diminishing his obvious qualities, it must nevertheless be stated that the apparent force of his reasoning can be explained in part by the narrow, repetitive range of his discourse. Without reducing the impact of his singu-

lar personality on the other Canada, it must nevertheless be stated that his constitutional leadership can be explained in part by the ignorance, psychological distance, and cultural and linguistic separation of the two societies.

Short of believing that words can wipe away deeds, and that force and domination have worn down and weakened the profound motives that have led more and more Quebecers over the past twenty years to want a revision in the bonds between Québec and Canada, the events of the last few days must be seen as a stage and not as an end. If Mr Trudeau has at last reduced the constitutional agreement to the narrow scope that has always been his, it is not in his power to force the country, Québec in particular, to accept his words and build its future on the constitutional skeleton that will travel to London. It has been possible to exclude Québec, reduce its historic traditional rights, and partially rebuild the country without it. However, this ultimate consequence of Mr Trudeau's initial political objectives leaves intact and even increases the need for profound changes in the relations between Québec and the regions surrounding it to the west and the east, as the results of the Québec elections of 1976 and 1981 — and, indeed, those of the referendum — eloquently attest.

While Mr Trudeau was dreaming of his final victory, the disenchantment of Quebecers was acquiring a breadth and depth unprecedented in our history. Camelot of the intellectuals, journalistic inflation, local political demagoguery — such invective is no longer sufficient to explain a movement that has thrice received the support of hundreds of thousands of Quebecers and carried a sovereignist party to power.

The constitutional resolution could have served as a powerful brake on Québec's secession movement. It would have been enough for the head of the Canadian government to adjust the essentials to the demands — all in all, fairly limited — of René Lévesque. In so doing he could have provided some powerful arguments for those in the future who will have the formidable task, in this society, of relaunching the debate on the reform of federalism. After the so-called historic vote in the Canadian

Parliament, the latter are no longer able to pick up the pieces of the hopes and plans destroyed by the implosion of constitutional reform. In a sense, Mr Trudeau has become as baffling and effective an adversary for them as Mr Lévesque is. It is not even the status quo, pure and simple, that has been sanctified by the Chrétien-Trudeau resolution. It is the reduction of Québec's rights, a radically unacceptable amending formula, a consecration of the federal government's quasi-absolute power of initiative in the constitutional area, that will be entrenched in the reformed constitution. Advocates of a third option are in a sense forced to unite and thus either consent to the Trudeau resolution or join the group headed by René Lévesque. Apart from these possibilities, they would need to invent a political space that is difficult to imagine at present.

However, the departure of Mr Trudeau could modify these prospects. In fact, his successor could put on the table, and swiftly, the genuine issues that must be negotiated, while proposing modifications to the various aspects of the Trudeau-Chrétien resolution that have been found insufficient or unacceptable.

Mr Clark and Mr Broadbent have raised some interesting perspectives on this subject in the last few days. They lack the power, and perhaps all of us lack the time.

Mr Trudeau has pushed resistance to Québec's self-assertion movement to the outermost limit. In so doing, perhaps he has given it its true scope, and provided the motives for its renewal.

Québec's political leaders must avoid taking hasty and dangerous chances. Their strength will come from the support of a people who will ultimately make their decision by free choice, in which lies their greatest security. The Trudeau-Chrétien initiative has not received the support of the legitimate government of Québec — this fact must go down on the record. Nevertheless, its illegitimacy is even more fundamental, for this people has been constitutionally bound without consultation, without elementary respect for democratic freedoms.

LE DEVOIR, SEPTEMBER 17, 1982

Lise Bissonnette

On our last gasp—1

'The question is whether, colonized as we are, now more than ever, it is still appropriate to live in French in an empire in which we apparently count for nothing' (Fernand Dumont, *Le Devoir,* 3 Sept. 1982).

'Here we are leaning on the enemy power, hanging on to the apron-strings of the United States. The satellite is uniting with the planet. And there is a kind of moral danger in this. Are we going to slide towards convenience, yield to the temptation of the South? Or will we brace ourselves against the wall, harden ourselves against destiny, and conquer our lands like a free people?' (André Laurendeau, autumn 1936, quoted by Guildo Rousseau in *L'Image des États-Unis dans la littérature auébécoise,* Éditions Naaman).

It would seem, then, that the question has not changed in close to forty years, and even more, for Laurendeau himself was drawing on Lionel Groulx and the whole post-1900 Laurentian school, who subscribed to the view that we could conquer corrupting America through a kind of purifying 'American Frenchness'. Resist the American peril, because we were different.

Search Mr Dumont's text as I may, including the conclusion we published on Sept. 7, all I can find in it is this repetition, which in itself is fatal. The sociologist, president of the Institut Québécois sur la Culture, has lost only one of the anxieties of the earlier period. He concedes that we will probably retain French as a tool. But, he adds, 'if that were our only difference, we would simply be using an idiom peculiar to us to translate something that has nothing to do with our true being.'

So the eternal existential question is posed once again. In Abbé Groulx's time, there was hardly any hesitation to define (or dictate) what our 'true being' was. Today one would search in vain for the words to express it, even from the quasi-official standard of our culture. The conclusion is even more distressing than the one introducing this discussion, bemoaning the imperialism of our neighbours: we must create things *Québécois.* Invent such institutions as, in the past, the *caisses populaires* and Hydro-Québec. Produce scientifically in French. Manufacture our own schoolbooks. Estab-lish our own research centres. Assist Québec creators in the 'free market' of the media.

But where is the famous 'difference' in all this, apart from the language? If Quebecers are proud of the *caisses populaires* and Hydro-Québec, it is because the *caisses* have succeeded, in French, in becoming as powerful as the banks, and because Hydro, while remaining French, is the fourth most important borrower on world money markets. If we were finally to succeed in conducting our own research and producing our own educational tools in French, it is the language we would help, and not the construction of some supposed ontological difference, that 'true being' whose smooth Québec-born imperialism scares me a good deal more than the cultural multinationals operating out of New York.

If living in French means travelling through this century with different values than living in American does, it's about time someone listed them for us. In Groulx's time they pointed to our catholicism, our order, our morality, against the materialism of the Anglo-Saxon continent. But what today? The discourse about values turns endlessly upon itself, a kind of mad missionary hope of intellectuals who notice an implacable uniformity throughout the world and rush at a few 'differences' in order to go on refusing to believe in it. Ireland, Poland, Québec, suggests Mr Dumont. The vocation of martyr for their destiny and specificity.

Last week, at a Harvard colloquium on the theme of Québec-U.S. relations, the director of the Centre d'Études Canadiennes-Françaises at McGill University, Mr Yvan Lamonde, presented an analysis of the American cultural influence here based almost exclusively on cultural products: film, theatre, periodicals, records — consumer goods. He nearly got himself torn apart by most of the university people there. According to them, he should have defined the concept of culture, shown how the 'values' of one people differ from those of another and therefore absorb 'The Little House on the Prairie' or the latest 'Rocky' in a different way. When the time came to take a closer look and define our inexpressible essence once and for all, they convinced us that the style of our suburban houses had a certain *je ne sais quoi* lacking in Minnesota. All to avoid facing the reality of an American-ness we share with a large part of this planet, without suffering any more for it than others do. We simply do it in French, and if that means 'dying in French', as Mr Dumont suggests, our last gasp is pretty lively.

What is sickening, literally, in this book, the reflection of so many others that have tried to explain us to ourselves, is the omnipresent fear of the other — for instance, that 'growing cultural empire' — that, it must be understood, is preparing to gobble us up the moment we let our guard down. 'We are one of those people in the world,' the sociologist said, again recalling Lionel Groulx, 'who, every morning in history, ask themselves whether they will see the sunset.'

This indeed is death, a paralysing anguish. It comes from a misreading of the facts. What do we know about the United States, apart from the clichés about imperialism so widely used in our universities, in which not a single specialized program in American studies is to be found? To speak of a cultural menace you must give it a face, see how it threatens you, measure it, understand it. Nothing of this kind has been done. We prefer to pick apart 'the liberating aspects of the popular environment', send our students to France, and continue our eternal discussions on the gender of our specificity.

That too is to 'die in French', and it's a good thing the Americans that we have become have developed a few antibodies, to prevent us from dying of fear.

On our last gasp—2

Scandalized letters accuse me of 'capitulating to the Americanism invading our culture' in my article 'On our last gasp' last Saturday, and, worse yet, of in some way betraying the cause of Québec in expressing doubts about our 'cultural specificity'. I will repeat the offence, more carefully, here.

Nothing is harder to kill than a

cliché, but all the same it is time to put an end to the one about Québec's 'cultural specificity' before it does us in. It's a handy cliché. Two peoples, two languages, two cultures. This perfect symmetry has served both the sovereignists and the nationalist school of Québec federalism. It was useful in the referendum crusade, useful for constitutional resistance, useful in fighting the folkloric multiculturalism officially imposed on Canada, useful to Robert Bourassa when he suggested his cultural sovereignty, and it is useful to René Lévesque, who is now left with nothing but the aforementioned cultural sovereignty.

All of which is to say that the Péquistes and their official ideologues have not invented anything new. Summer 1975. Under the apple trees in the garden of a village presbytery in l'Anse Saint-Jean, we were several journalists gathered to ask Mr Fernand Lalonde, minister in Mr Bourassa's government, what the motive for cultural sovereignty was. He was stammering. We're DIFFERENT. Yes, and then what? There's our language, of course, then our tradition. But now? As the other would be quick to point out, the words to express it did not come easily.

They have never come. Winter 1982. I again meet Clément Richard, Minister for Cultural Affairs, at Mr Lévesque's home, between a pine armoire and a bread-bin from a restaurant in Old Montréal, proud as a peacock before leaving on a provincial tour to oppose 'Canadian' multiculturalism. 'Québec will be cultural or it will be nothing at all!' Serious stuff, this: to be (or not to be—the great word has been pronounced).

I found the same existential anguish, minus the unbridled certainty, flowing from Mr Fernand Dumont's pen last week. It is not enough to speak French — one must say something in French that is different, something that expresses our 'true being', without which we are threatened with slow death. I therefore resumed my quest for that difference that ought to be staring me in the face, since everyone talks about it so much.

I found the beginning of an answer in a white paper on cultural development, volume I, pertinently titled *De quelle culture s'agit-il?*. Surely this would make everything clear. After numerous detours that the author or authors recognize as unsatisfactory (customs, recipes, language, civil law) we come to it finally on page 49: 'But it seems that Québec's originality lies

''within''.' There follows the enumeration, as official as can be: 'Something that values quiet strength and resignation, pride and hesitation, *joie de vivre* and protest and hope, conservatism and daring, a love for peace and fierce resistance, a sedentary spirit and a sense of adventure, the most pragmatic realism and the most utopian dream, all at the same time. This ''mentality'' manifests itself like an atmosphere, an air that we breathe.' Excuse me, but apart from the language once again, I breathed the same air not so long ago in Newfoundland, and not long before that in Iceland. And, come to think of it, in Vancouver too. If such is my 'own being', the one the white paper calls on me to 'defend' so as 'not to accept without examination the fashions and ideologies current in the world', it may be neat and pretty, but it is still not very specific.

Then by chance I came across a background paper on Québec published by Stock in 1979 to explain us to the French. A well-known sociology professor and deputy minister, Mr Guy Rocher, undertakes to make it better understood that we are North Americans, 'but different from other North Americans'. He too takes the unsatisfactory trip back to tradition, then returns to the present. The Quebecer, he says, 'brings to what he does, what he says, what he changes, a type of sensibility and emotion, a kind of intelligence, a humour, that set him apart.' At last the light goes out: we are inexpressible, and thereby specific. Along with common sense, that is no doubt one of the most widely shared characteristics on earth.

All the same, the reference to tradition and the past by the official standard-makers reminds me of the clearest, most intelligent remarks I have heard on the subject lately: 'Our roots are particular, but not the culture. Obviously, if we equate culture with roots, it comes down to the same thing.' That was Andrée Paradis, director of *Vie des arts*, in the interview she granted *Le Devoir* on May 22.

To try to define a cultural specificity beyond one's roots, to claim, on the eve of the twenty-first century, that the individual members of a collectivity must be careful not to betray a 'true being' that is presumed to be definable, these are political operations. And nothing stifles a culture more effectively or surely, as we have seen with the Péquiste theme. Neither Nelligan, Saint-Denys Garneau, Claude Gauvreau, nor Borduas would be found in today's world of subsidized navel-

gazing. They would be found in something like *Les Herbes rouges*, unclassifiable marginals who would be refused assistance in the name of 'quality' before being rediscovered a century later.

Despite murmurings about being open to 'foreign currents' and 'borrowings' — though not 'without examination' — as the white paper hints (to say the opposite would not appear scholarly), the consecrated culture still grows by its roots in Québec, which do not reach very far. They are glad to let us wander through the wide world, but on the leash.

That keeps us nice and cosy, and in good company. In July, at the world conference on cultural politics in Mexico, didn't the French Minister of Culture, Mr Jack Lang, denounce the cultural imperialism of the Americans, just as it is now fashionable to do in Québec City? According to him, this imperialism 'takes over consciences rather than territories . . . and constitutes a form of interference in the internal affairs of another country'. Our consciences, our 'true beings', become the internal affairs of a country. We must protect them, just as we do the footwear industry and other vulnerable sectors.

A vulnerable sector indeed, for not many people in creative circles are raising their voices against a profitable cocoon. Only a few, here and there. The magazine *Liberté*, for example, whose genuine cynicism is not managing to arouse a more organized refusal. Or a text-manifesto by François Charron in the magazine *Les Herbes rouges* (no. 99–100, 'Litterature et nationalisme'), which denounces that other kind of imperialism, 'the confusion of the I and the we', which 'forms the basis of the identity, the osmosis, the fusion, that rob us of our own inalienable breath'. Or, again, the work of two philosophers, Michel Morin and Claude Bertrand, *Le Territoire imaginaire de la culture* (HMH), which has become the object of a significant resistance.

A colleague, slightly alarmed, has asked me if I am not playing the game of Pierre Trudeau, for whom only language sets us apart. No indeed. There are death-bed repentances. In Ottawa, Canadian cultural specificity is preparing for the great battle against American cultural imperialism. This fall Mr Francis Fox, Mr Trudeau's minister, will come out with a plan for action that will no doubt have him in his turn stammering out our inexpressibility under the apple trees, this time stripped bare.

L'ACTUALITÉ, FEBRUARY 1983

Scorched-earth policy

by Jean Paré

We already knew about the cold war: Canada has invented the cold civil war. It has been raging for fifteen years between Québec and the government of Pierre Elliott Trudeau. It is the great disease of this country: Québec is suffering from it with record unemployment, deindustrialization, and financial crisis; so is Canada, with the worst economic performance in the West.

Last fall it was Bill S-31, which, in limiting the participation of provincial governments in 'national' ventures, sabotaged the role of the *caisse de dépôt* as an 'economic lever'. An action taken suddenly and in secret, in a special procedure before the Senate to conceal it from public view, put into effect retroactively to prevent any countermove . . . With a Québec that owns whole chunks of the Canadian economy, however, and an Alberta Heritage Fund investing here, this is a case not of 'balkanization', but of insurance against various separatist movements. But anti-nationalist hysteria does not see it that way. The initiative was so clumsy that it merely united Quebecers in opposition to it: the government, the Québec Liberal opposition, the press, the business community.

But we had already seen the irrational choice that Mirabel has proven to be, although it did show Montrealers and Quebecers who their real patrons are; the F-18 affair, which will facilitate the transfer to Toronto of the hub of the aeronautics and aviation industry; the Quebecair-Nordair crisis; all the decisions that have ruined Montreal's important pharmaceutical and petrochemical industries; the increasing scarcity of subsidies for scientific research; the laws permitting the expropriation of energy corridors in Québec territory; the politics of grain supply; the heavy-water installation at La Prade; the Guy-Favreau Complex . . .

This goes beyond simple incompetence. It is no longer a question of mistakes, but of a clique so blinded by its bias that it has made itself the tool of the Toronto establishment and a vengeful bureaucracy. 'You're going to hurt yourselves,' warned Pierre Trudeau, as early as 1968. *'Just watch me.'*

This French Power is fifteen years old. Fifteen lost years. For the first time, Quebecers have held considerable power in the federal government. But the experience remains merely a personal one; Quebecers as a whole have never been further from their goals. . . .

Major economic decisions are no longer made in their interests, but for the good of their political soul. Under the pretext of wiping out the separatist heresy and destroying the Parti québécois, the attack is really aimed at the citizens and the State of Québec itself, by those who do not see that Québec is half, if not more, of this French Power; its source; and, in any case, its sole justification.

Pierre Trudeau has claimed to be defending French-Canadians' rights by weakening, sapping the strength, of the only government in which they constitute a majority. By ridiculing the Daniel Johnsons and the Jean-Jacques Bertrands, by humiliating Robert Bourassa, by destroying even his ally Claude Ryan and the provincial Liberal opposition. With independence, he explained, French-Canadians will lose everything. After which he set about making sure they would have less and less to lose . . .

What is incomprehensible is that among the Liberal members there have not been ten willing to cross the floor of the House of Commons and demonstrate their opposition to this policy of destabilization, this scorched-earth strategy. Vague impulses, nothing more, though they showed that not everyone was unconscious. Yet these are brave people. Are they the last to be spellbound by the Trudeau myth? Do they think they would be betraying French Power, and be incapable of explaining why to their constituents?

No doubt they feel they are the representatives less of the people than of a party, a machine, that can unmake them at will, just as it created them out of nothing.

Yet they should see that their leader has created, in a good half of the citizens of Québec, such mistrust — even disdain — of the central State that after he has gone, when the ethnic vote no longer counts, there will be nothing left but a void. The Conservative party is, perhaps, already the image, the projection, of what the political scene will be when Quebecers no longer take any interest in it. A Québec that has psychologically separated.

Historians will show the contradictions in this brilliant but temperamental figure, who has always done the opposite of what he claimed: a social democrat catapulted into the Liberal party, a reformer who is basically conservative, a libertarian capable of invoking martial law, a destroyer of the federalism he hoped to strengthen, a dilettante incapable of giving up power, an antiduplessisist anxious to ensconce all his friends in the Senate, a defender of the French fact who has stripped Québec of its constitutional powers . . . Absolute powerlessness.

In any case, from Halifax to Vancouver, no one hopes for anything from this dying regime now, except that it will give way. The alternative is hardly inspiring, but politics, like nature, abhors a vacuum.

The problem is that the two Québec powers, each supporting the other, have found the formula for eternal life: we re-elect the Parti québécois to oppose Pierre Trudeau, and we re-elect Pierre Trudeau to neutralize the separatist tendencies of the other side. What can we say, except:

Leave! You have already hurt us enough. It will take us at least a generation to repair the damage.

(ii) Western Alienation

THE GLOBE AND MAIL, JANUARY 24, 1981

Loss of political clout final straw for some in West

By JEFF SALLOT
Globe and Mail Reporter

EDMONTON — On federal election night almost a year ago viewers in Saskatchewan and Alberta turned on their television sets to watch the returns come in as the polls closed in their provinces.

Few were prepared for the psychological jolt that was to greet them.

Westerners had a special stake in this election. Just nine months earlier Conservative leader Joe Clark, a native son from High River, Alta., had formed a minority Government, ending almost 16 years of Liberal rule.

The Liberals, who are thought of in this region as the handmaidens of Ontario and Quebec political interests, have dominated national politics for most of this century. But the 1979 victory of Joe Clark's Tories, —a victory made possible because of solid support from the West — had been a hopeful sign that in the national political arena the region had come into its own, and that newfound prosperity in the resource-rich provinces had found commensurate political weight in Ottawa.

Even the vanquished Pierre Trudeau, then the Opposition leader, had said so just a few months earlier at an appearance in Calgary. "You in the West have the power . . . ."

Now it seemed to be slipping away. The pre-election opinion polls indicated that the Tories were in trouble in Ontario. Their budget, which brought about this election when it was defeated by the Liberals and New Democrats in the Commons, was not going over well in Central Canada, where voters thought the Tories had caved in to Alberta's oil-price demands.

Yet few voters in Alberta and Saskatchewan were fully prepared for

what was to greet them at 8 p.m. Then, from studios in Toronto, the CBC's Knowlton Nash and CTV's Lloyd Robertson welcomed residents of the two provinces to the election-night telecasts with the news that it was all over with — before Western ballots had been counted.

Pierre Trudeau's Liberals were back on top. Joe Clark's Tories, the last best hope and choice of many Western voters, had gone down to ignoble defeat.

Even NDP voters in Saskatchewan, who almost equalled in numbers the Tory voters in that province, were astounded by how quickly the election had been decided — solely on the basis of returns from the East.

Manitoba voters had seen what was coming an hour earlier. They, at least, had the consolation of knowing that two of their MPs would sit on the Liberal Government benches. But British Columbia voters—those who hadn't already learned the results by phoning friends in the East or by monitoring U.S. radio stations in Seattle and Spokane — were to suffer the same psychological jolt — a sudden feeling of political impotence — an hour after their Alberta neighbors, at 8 p.m. Pacific Time.

A Westerner that night didn't need a political scientist or pundit to tell him that his vote, quite literally, didn't count when it came to electing a federal Government.

The two Manitoba Liberals from Winnipeg were the only elected political representatives from the West in the new "national Government." The Red River, where Louis Riel staged his unsuccessful rebellion against an Ottawa government more than a century earlier, became a demarcation point on the electoral map of Canada — a dividing line between the political interests of the

East and the West.

That, perhaps, is a simplistic interpretation of election night, 1980. After all, the NDP, a party that shares with the Liberals a generally centralist view of Canadian government, was well represented in three of the four Western provinces. Combined Liberal and NDP votes in the West were actually greater than those for the Conservatives, a party whose leader favors a "community-of-communities" decentralized approach to national government.

But raw vote totals don't count. It's seats in the Commons, on the Government side — MPs who can lobby for your interests, act as your representative in the two places where it really counts — the Cabinet room and the Government caucus room on Parliament Hill.

There were no elected MPs from west of Winnipeg in the Caucus and Cabinet rooms this fall when, from a Western perspective, two of the most important items of Government business — the national energy program and constitution change — were debated and decided upon.

In political terms, there have been few good times for the West in recent memory. Except for the few brief Diefenbaker years — and the Joe Clark months — a whole generation of Westerners has watched most of its MPs sit in opposition.

Yet that same generation has seen its region grow in economic importance as never before. With just 27 per cent of Canada's population, the West produces more than 31 per cent of Canada's gross domestic product —a fact that is accounted for more by increasing oil and gas prices than by an increase in worker productivity. Nevertheless, it's an economic turnaround unprecedented in the history of the West.

Take-home pay is up. Unemployment is down. With the exception of Manitoba, the economic picture has never been rosier. Westerners, however, sense that their economic well-being might be threatened, or at least constrained, by policies coming from Ottawa and a Government that is national in name only.

Public opinion polls conducted by the Canada West Foundation, a Calgary-based research and lobby group, indicate that there is a strong and potentially volatile feeling of alienation in the West. And the feeling is growing.

By and large, Westerners simply don't have much faith that Ottawa cares about them. An increasing number, but still a minority, are discussing independence — separatism — as an attractive alternative to the present economic and political arrangements of Confederation.

Litany learned at an early age

Some of the grievances of the West have grown into an entire mythology of discontent — a litany learned by many Westerners at an early age. Tariffs, freight rates, transportation woes, federal agricultural policies, cultural domination by Ontario. There is substance to many of the complaints. But, as with most mythologies, the time-honored stories of railroad, federal-government and Eastern bank villainies have been exaggerated in the telling.

Ontario Premier William Davis has called for a commission of inquiry to examine the grievances of the West. Western political commentators say the biggest problem is "fat-cat Ontario."

Meanwhile, many people living east of the Red River have come to believe the myth of the oil-rich, blue-eyed Alberta oil sheik, without ever learning the West's litany of woe.

The West is not a cultural, political and economic monolith. It is a vast, complex region. There are as many differences between Thompson, Man., and Centre Street in Calgary as one would find between

The haves and have-nots

Province	Population (% of total)	Seats in Commons (% of total)	GPP (1978) (% of GNP) per capita	Federal Income Taxes (1978)	Resource Revenues* (1977–78)		
B.C.	2,662,000 (11.1)	28 (10)	$27,891M (11.9%) $10,477	$1,939.1M (13.7%)	1. $ 137M	2. $ 405M	3. $ 35M
Alberta	2,113,000 (8.8)	21 (7.5)	$28,129M1 (12.0%) $13,312	$1,500.1M (12.0%)	1. $ 6M	2. $3148M	3. $ 20M
Saskatchewan	973,000 (4.1)	14 (5.0)	$ 9,661M (4.1%) $ 9,929	$ 454.7M (3.2%)	1. $ 3M	2. $ 228M	3. $ 109M
Manitoba	1,028,000 (4.3)	14 (5.0)	$ 9,300M (4.0%) $ 9,047	$ 504.5M (3.6%)	1. $ 1M	2. $ 7M	3. $ 5M
Ontario	8,587,000 (35.9)	95 (42.2)	$89,940M (38.3%) $10,474	$5,997.3M (42.2%)	1. $ 39M	2. —	3. $ 16M
Quebec	6,311,000 (26.4)	75 (26.9)	$56,181M (23.9%) $ 8,902	$2,873.7M (20.2%)	1. $ 35M	2. —	3. $ 44M
New Brunswick	709,000 (3.0)	10 (3.6)	$ 4,397M (1.9%) $ 6,202	$ 261.7M (1.8%)	1. $ 6M	2. —	3. $ 1M
Nova Scotia	855,000 (3.6)	11 (3.9)	$ 5,636M (2.4%) $ 6,592	$ 356.8M (2.5%)	1. $ 2M	2. —	3. $ 1M
P.E.I.	124,000 (0.5)	4 (1.4)	$ 634M (0.3%) $ 5,113	$ 37.3M (0.3%)	1. —	2. —	3. —
Newfoundland	583,000 (2.4)	7 (2.5)	$ 2,988M (1.3%) $ 5,125	$ 179.4M (1.3%)	1. $ 16M	2. —	3. $ 15M
Totals	23,945,000		$234,757M	$14,203.5M			

Notes: Resource revenues — 1. Forestry; 2. Oil-gas; 3. other minerals; total includes water power rentals.

North Bay, Ont., and Bay Street in Toronto.

Saskatchewean, with a firmly established NDP provincial Government, is an island of democratic socialism in a sea of small-c conservatism. But only seven years ago Alberta Premier Peter Lougheed headed the only free-enterprise capitalistic government in the West. The rest were NDP and there's a fair chance the socialists will be returned in the next provincial elections in Manitoba and British Columbia.

(There's a political joke making the rounds in Edmonton that has Mr. Lougheed as the opposition leader in the first parliament of an independent West, while Allan Blakeney, the NDP premier of Saskatchewan, is the prime minister.)

Even within staunchly Tory Alberta free-enterprise conservatism is a sometimes thing. The province owns the major telephone company and Pacific Western Airlines and is involved in petroleum projects through several Crown corporations.

Total	Provincial Income Tax revenue (1978)	Per capita Income (1978)	1980 equalization receipts (per capita)	1978 federal per capita income taxes (provincial)	December '80 Unemployed (rate)
	$1,058.2M	$12,196	—	$728.40 ($397.50)	82,000 (6.3%)
$ 592M					
	$ 676.8M	$12,237	—	$709.89 ($320.30)	39,000 (3.5%)
$3174M					
	$ 283.3M	$10,509	$ 49M (50)	$467.32 ($291.16)	19,000 (4.3%)
$ 341M					
	$ 343.9M	$ 9,515	$ 328M (319)	$490.76 ($334.53)	25,000 (5.1%)
$ 18M					
	$3,144.1M	$11,190	—	$698.42 ($366.15)	289,000 (6.6%)
$ 80M					
	$5,419.0M	$10,650	$1,641M (260)	$455.35 ($859.66)	295,000 (9.9%)
$ 85M					
	$ 183.3M	$ 8,922	$ 395M (557)	$369.11 ($285.53)	31,000 (10.1%)
$ 7M					
	$ 239.7M	$ 9,441	$ 453M (529)	$417.31 ($280.35)	37,000 (10.1%)
$ 5M					
	$ 25.5M	$ 8,430	$ 89M (717)	$300.80 ($205.65)	6,000 (11.2%)
$ 0.2M					
	$ 136.6M	$ 8,247	$ 381M (653)	$307.72 ($234.30)	29,000 (13.3%)
$ 31M					
	$11,510.4M		$3,336M		852,000

Agriculture and natural-resource exploitation have been the mainstays of the Western provincial economies since settlement and both sectors have been through boom and bust cycles.

Manitoba is the most heavily industrialized Prairie province. Its infant industries, like those of Ontario and Quebec, were the beneficiaries of the national tariff policy of the last century, a fact that's often overlooked in the other three Western provinces. Talk of free trade and the lifting of tariff barriers — one of the major selling points of Western separatist leaders — gives the jitters to many Manitobans.

Manitoba doesn't have major petroleum deposits like the other three Western provinces. Its continued economic development will depend on agriculture and small to medium-scale industry.

Not surprisingly, Manitoba is the province where separatist sentiments are weakest, the Canada West Foundation poll suggests. (They are strongest in Alberta and B.C., the wealthiest of the four provinces.)

Federal oil and natural gas policies are at the very heart of the new wave of alienation in Saskatchewan, Alberta and B.C. — the energy provinces. It was Ottawa's unilateral announcement of a petroleum-pricing-and-taxing regime last October, and Alberta's decision two days later to gradually reduce oil production in retaliation, that served as catalysts for the would-be separatists. Ottawa's unilateralism probably was more infuriating than the actual policy.

The price schedule set out in the federal budget is seen by many Westerners, particularly Albertans, as an Ottawa rip-off.

The new pricing regime keeps oil prices at 50 per cent or less of the world price for at least several years and perhaps for the rest of this decade. Alberta doesn't demand the world price, but would like to see Canadian prices move to within 75 per cent of the North American average price by 1984. That's a reasonable compromise and better than what Alberta demanded of the Clark government, Albertans say.

Constitution plans another irritant

Saskatchewan, the second-ranking oil-producing province, is also angry with the budget's price schedule. British Columbia seethes because it's the second-ranking natural-gas producer and gas prices are set in relation to oil prices.

Prime Minister Trudeau's unilateral plan for changing the constitution is the other new sore point in the West. Three of the provincial Governments — Manitoba, Alberta and B.C. — have strong objections and are joining with Quebec and some of the Atlantic provinces in a court challenge to Mr. Trudeau's plan.

Saskatchewan Premier Allan Blakeney has tried to keep a low profile in this federal-provincial battle by neither supporting nor condemning the federal plan.

The Western objections are numerous. The two major complaints are to the unilateral way in which Mr. Trudeau is proceeding, and to his proposed amending formula for future constitutional change.

In the past, it has been accepted practice that each of the 10 provinces could block constitutional changes that might alter the balance of power between Ottawa and the provincial governments. This has been the major stumbling block to major constitutional change.

The new amending formula would prevent any one province from vetoing amendments — except for Ontario and Quebec. They would have permanent vetoes because of the size of their populations. And they can keep those vetoes even if there are major population shifts away from Central Canada. Once again, Western politicians say, Ontario and Quebec are given first-class treatment while their provinces bring up the rear.

It's the same old story, Westerners say. Ontario and Quebec have always received special treatment, such as a tariff policy to protect Central Canadian manufacturing.

It's true that Westerners pay higher than world prices for manufactured goods from Ontario because of tariffs. But so do Ontarians. Economists say that tariffs don't determine where industries will be located in Canada. Tariffs only determine whether or not an industry will be established somewhere within the country. Once that's been settled, other economic conditions dictate where the industry will go. And manufacturing industries generally gravitate towards the largest markets — Ontario and Quebec.

'Market economy' proper target

But then there is the railway freight-rate question. Westerners, particularly those on the Prairies who do not have sea or lake ports, have to pay the transportation charges for manufactured goods.

Economists, such as Kenneth Norrie at the University of Alberta, say that many of the West's economic grievances are misdirected when they are aimed at federal policy. "The grievance is more properly directed at the inevitable operation of a (free) market economy where geographical distances are great, and in which regions are vastly different in size and proximity to other industrial areas of the world," he says.

What's often forgotten in the discussion of freight rates is the enormous economic benefit to grain farmers from the Crow's Nest Pass agreement of 1897. That low grain-transportation rate — known colloquially as "Holy Crow" because many farmers consider it sacred — is the same today as it was 84 years ago. The Crow rate kept many farmers in business. It is also blamed by the federal government, and even some farm groups, for discouraging the railroads from upgrading their grain-transportation system. Prairie farmers have lost millions of dollars in potential export sales as a result of outdated grain-transportation facilities and inadequate federal ports on the West Coast.

Federal Agriculture Minister Eugene Whelan says something has to be done about the Crow rate and Ottawa plans to announce its plans early this year.

Separatist leaders say that an independent West would be fabulously wealthy, that the standard of living would go up 30 to 50 per cent. There are no hard economic data to support such a claim.

Economists concede, however, that the four Western provinces could become a working economic unit on their own — a view that is shared by 60 per cent of Westerners, the Canada West Foundation poll suggests.

A common call for greater voice

Most economists caution that an independent West would not become highly industrialized, with a resource economy continuing.

Most thoughtful Westerners reject separatism, and they fear its potential popularity and the deep sense of alienation that is fuelling it.

But time and again during recent conversations and interviews with dozens of Westerners — politicians, businessmen, farmers, academics and others — people said that something must be done to alter the political system so that this region has a greater voice in national affairs. A reformed Senate that would provide equal representation from each province was one of the most frequent suggestions.

Others suggested the election of a constituent assembly to write a new constitution. Get the federal and provincial politicians out of the picture and let the people have a go at redrafting the terms of Confederation, they say.

There is strong criticism from most quarters for Mr. Trudeau. He doesn't understand the West, but what's worse is that he doesn't understand that he doesn't understand and that it is important for him to understand, says David Bercuson, a history professor at the University of Calgary.

Hu Harries, a former Liberal MP from Alberta, and one of the last (1968-1972), has formed a new political party to represent the West in Parliament and is setting up offices in Western cities.

Some Liberals and lapsed Liberals hope the situation will improve when Mr. Trudeau retires, for good.

Still others are counting on the apparent growing awareness in Ontario that there are legitimate grievances in the West to convince Ontario politicians, at the federal and provincial levels, that something must be done.

Mel Hurtig, the Edmonton book publisher who is trying to organize an anti-separatist group, says that one of the best things Ontario can do is to get its provincial election over with quickly. Premier Davis and Ontario Liberal Leader Stuart Smith have been using the energy-pricing issue to play politics at home, he says.

THE GLOBE AND MAIL, APRIL 22, 1981

Short-changed even in civil service, Alberta feels

By JEFFREY SIMPSON
Globe and Mail Reporter

OTTAWA — One Sunday morning in early 1979, Premier Peter Lougheed of Alberta was sitting in his hotel suite, criticizing the decisions of the Supreme Court of Canada.

The judges all showed a centralist bias, he argued. Even the ones from Western Canada were influenced by living in Ottawa. They no longer understood the regional nature of Canada. They had lost touch with their western roots, Mr. Lougheed said.

Ruminating further, the Premier extended his analysis to the civil service. Isolated in their Ottawa office buildings, the civil servants consistently misunderstood the country they served. They were insensitive and often arrogant in their dealings with the regions and the provincial governments.

Mr. Lougheed has always viewed the federal civil service with a mixture of contempt for its attitude and fear of its power. And his criticisms are shared by others in Western Canada, for whom the civil service is an extension of the "Central Canadian Establishment."

Of course, by Mr. Lougheed's analysis, anyone from the West working within smelling range of the paper mills on the Ottawa River is contaminated by the capital's corrosively centralist attitudes. But even purely from the point of view of representation, Mr. Lougheed has a point — his province has traditionally been under-represented in the federal civil service.

Only one deputy minister — Bruce Rawson of the Ministry of State for Social Development — and three of 198 civil servants at the level of assistant deputy minister or equivalent are Albertans.

Although British Columbia also suffers from lack of numbers in Ottawa, it is better off than Alberta. And the other two western provinces, especially Saskatchewan, have always sent plenty of talented men to the capital.

The most notable group of civil servants ever to arrive in a bunch in Ottawa was the so-called Saskatchewan mafia. They were refugees from the purge of provincial civil servants launched by the late Liberal premier Ross Thatcher, who came to power in 1964 after two decades of rule by the Co-operative Commonwealth Federation — now the New Democratic Party.

The refugee group included Thomas Shoyama, a former deputy minister of Finance; A. W. Johnson, now president of the Canadian Broadcasting Corp. and a former deputy minister of Health and Welfare; Donald Tansley, deputy minister of Fisheries and Oceans; Arthur Wakabayashi, assistant deputy minister in the Solicitor-General's Department; and William Haney, assistant secretary to the Cabinet for federal-provincial relations.

The members of the Saskatchewan mafia were accustomed to an activist Government. After all, they had worked under T. C. Douglas and Woodrow Lloyd, so they brought to Ottawa a belief in a Government role in solving social problems.

They arrived in the federal capital during the heyday of Gordon Robertson, then clerk of the Privy Council and the dean of the civil service. Born in Saskatchewan and a Rhodes Scholar from that province, Mr. Robertson had spent most of his career climbing to the top civil service job in Ottawa.

So no one could complain in the late 1960s that the voice of the West went unheard in Ottawa, if the number of westerners in the senior civil service was the yardstick by which influence was measured.

In recent years, however, that influence has waned. Mr. Robertson and Mr. Shoyama have retired. The West is prosperous, its provincial governments offering challenging opportunities to its native sons inclined toward public service. The private sector, booming everywhere in the region but Manitoba, lures talented university graduates, making recruitment by the federal Government more difficult.

"The Saskatchewan mafia was itself a product of the Ross Thatcher Government in Saskatchewan, which was foolish enough to make unwelcome a lot of brilliant civil servants," Mr. Robertson said recently. "We were bright enough to pick them up.

"Since then, the situation has been almost the reverse, and I think the change in the economic opportunities in the West has been the major factor. We tried to get people from the West, but it was often a matter of not being able to recruit them because of opportunities in the West rather than because of any dislike of Ottawa."

Mr. Rawson, the only federal deputy minister hired directly from a western provincial government (he was a deputy minister in Alberta), agrees that western prosperity has made recruitment difficult.

"It's awfully buoyant out there for many people in the West. There are lots of jobs with high salaries. In my own field, I've tried to get medical deans to come down to Ottawa, but I haven't had any luck. (He is a former deputy minister of Health and Welfare.)"

Stereotypes also inhibit westerners from moving, he said. "I had it — a sort of natural reluctance to look at this complex world down here where no one wants to talk straight and where no one goes around in shirtsleeves. It all seems so distant and complex."

Defining who is a westerner for statistical purposes is a slippery business. Who qualifies? Is it enough to have been born there? To have been educated or started a career in the West?

Using the criterion that having been raised and educated in the West makes a westerner, then Ottawa has five deputy ministers from the region. There are also 37 of 198 assistant deputy ministers (or equivalents) from the West. That's about 18 per cent of these positions in the civil service.

These numbers compare with 19 such positions held by Canadians from the Atlantic provinces, 80 from Ontario, 41 from Quebec and 19 born outside Canada. Indeed, there has never been a drive to recruit prominent westerners to compare with the one in the late 1960s and early 1970s to find French-speaking Canadians, most of whom came to Ottawa from

Quebec. Spurred by the Royal Commission on Bilingualism and Biculturalism and the Official Languages Act, the federal Government located and promoted French-speaking Canadians in a kind of affirmative-action program.

The lack of representation from the West is not as serious as was the dearth of French-speaking Canadians 15 years ago, but the numbers do point to a problem that neither the Government nor the Public Service Commission has addressed systematically.

Vaguely aware of the alienation in the region, the Government has appointed a handful of westerners to senior posts. After repeated complaints from British Columbia, the Government appointed Mr. Justice William McIntyre to the Supreme Court of Canada. More recently, Vancouver accountant Kenneth Dye was appointed Auditor-General of Canada.

Aware of western sensitivities in the volatile field of federal-provincial relations, both the Conservative and Liberal governments have gone

searching for westerners in this field. Joe Clark had persuaded Peter Meekison, Alberta's deputy minister of Intergovernmental Relations, to become secretary to the Cabinet for federal-provincial relations, but that appointment was scuttled when Mr. Clark's government was defeated.

Now, the Liberal Government has recruited Frances Russell, a Manitoba journalist, for the federal-provincial-relations office. The Government also tried unsuccessfully to land a senior member of Saskatchewan's intergovernmental-relations secretariat.

THE CALGARY HERALD, MAY 22, 1980

Change in Ottawa's attitude all that's required

The West can be 'won' — and no reforms are necessary

By Peter C. Dobell

(Dobell is director of the Parliamentary Centre for Foreign Affairs and Foreign Trade, Ottawa.)

For 50 years, Toronto has had a bad reputation in Western Canada.

The image of Scrooge began during the depression, when Toronto-based banks and trust companies foreclosed mortgages and seized property to cover loan defaults.

Recently, with oil and gas price increases fuelling a boom in the West, and many of Ontario's manufacturing industries marking time, animosity began to wane.

However, February's election has once again made Toronto, with its 23 seats — 2 more than Alberta's total representation — an object of resentment.

Western irritation was typified by the reaction of one voter: "Ontario thinks it has a divine right to rule the country."

On election day itself, frustration was heightened when Western viewers were told as they tuned in on their first election reports that the Liberals had a majority without them.

But these results only reinforced an already-strongly-developed sense of alienation. Even three years ago, polls revealed that 75.1 per cent of Westerners agreed that, because Ontario and Quebec had the majority of seats in Parliament, "the West usually gets ignored in federal politics".

A more imaginative use of Parliament by the government could reduce Western alienation.

Reactions to the Liberal shut-out differed in each of the three Western provinces where this happened.

More of the same

Alberta was the most composed, British Columbia the most distressed. Since 1972, Albertans have not sent a Liberal MP to Ottawa.

They are used to being unrepresented in the federal cabinet, and they have prospered in spite of it.

During that period, their interests have been defended by Premier Lougheed, and his support at the polls demonstrates the confidence he continues to enjoy. For Albertans, it is more of the same, and they are not worried.

By contrast, British Columbia has not previously been without strong elected representation in cabinet.

Moreover, Premier Bennett is far from enjoying general support in the province, and there is not the same confidence in his ability to defend the province's interests.

Saskatchewan is mid-way between: not previously unrepresented by an elected member in cabinet, but governed by a provincial premier with a proven track record in defending provincial interests.

However, it is in Saskatchewan that two prominent MLAs resigned from the Conservative party to sit as independents and to work for secession and ultimately union with the United States. They attributed their decision to the election results.

The results were as much of a source of concern to Trudeau as they were a disappointment to Western voters.

His remarks to TV viewers on election night indicated his desire to do something about the problem: "I will intend to seek the advice of the opposition parties in those areas of Canada where Liberals, in spite of all our efforts, we have remained weaker than we would have liked. I'm thinking of the Western provinces."

But while his reaction was genuine, this is not a role which opposition parties could or would play in our parliamentary system of government. Not surprisingly, nothing more has been heard of the suggestion.

In the days which followed the election, a number of ideas surfaced briefly, and then submerged as their deficiencies became apparent — a gaggle of mayors to deal directly with the federal government; the appointment to cabinet of ministers of state without portfolio who would not have to be MPs or senators; the nomination to the Senate of prominent defeated Western Liberals to hold ministries in the government.

The right decision

There has also been much advocacy of proportional representation, but even if such a system is eventually adopted, it will not occur soon enough to alleviate this current problem.

Eventually, the prime minister settled on the simplest, and least controversial approach — the appointment to cabinet of sitting Western Senators.

The decision was the right one. Each of the other ideas would offend some group.

The solution chosen will ensure a voice in cabinet for each of the three Western provinces which elected no Liberals.

Western concerns should now be taken account of, and cabinet should not act in ignorance of regional interests.

But the move is unlikely to diminish the sense of being excluded which now grips the West.

Cabinets meet in secrecy; differences among ministers are rarely revealed to the public; the process of compromise, not being perceived, has little credibility.

Jack Horner fought hard, and frequently with success, inside the cabinet.

A trivial example: an importer of cowboy boots, dear to the hearts of Westerners, was exempted from the quota placed on imported footwear. Yet, because the process occurred in secret, Horner and the Liberal government he had joined got no credit for it.

A shrewd move

Mistakes may have been avoided, but the image of an uncaring Ontario-Quebec-dominated government remained.

The consequence of the February election is that now, more than ever before, Westerners will look to their provincial governments to promote their interests.

In the next few years, there will be a series of major federal-provincial negotiations — on oil pricing, to renew the Fiscal Arrangements Act, on constitutional change, on offshore rights and boundaries — all of immediate concern in the West.

The appointment of Michael Kirby as secretary of the cabinet for federal-provincial relations is a shrewd move. Kirby is not a product of the federal bureaucracy; personal experience has made him sensitive to provincial concerns; and he has the trust of most provincial governments.

He will reduce the suspicion felt in Western provincial governments of Ottawa and ensure that negotiations are not complicated by false issues.

But no matter how well conducted the negotiations and how satisfactory their outcome as seen from the West, the credit will largely go to the provincial governments. Ottawa will seem no less remote.

Largely ignored

While direct federal-provincial negotiations adequately cover matters where provincial rights are involved, there are policy areas where the federal authority is sovereign.

Lloyd Axworthy and the Western Senators will undoubtedly put forward regional concerns in the confines of cabinet.

But Westerners will not witness their battles and will accord them little credit.

My contention is that Westerners will only begin to place confidence in the federal government when they can observe MPs whom they have elected pressing issues of concern to them, and the government subsequently adjusting its position to accommodate these pressures.

This is a process where Parliament can and should provide the forum.

The way Parliament traditionally operates leaves no room for these accommodations.

The normal practice is for a government to submit its bills for approval, using its majority to ensure their passage with only cosmetic improvement.

Only very occasionally is resistance so general that a government is forced to withdraw a measure and start again; legislation on gun control represented a rare instance.

More often, pressure for change comes from within the caucus.

Differential rates for unemployment insurance was pressed upon the last Liberal government by MPs from the Atlantic provinces.

But with no elected representatives from west of Winnipeg, corrective pressure within the Liberal caucus can only come from Senators, and their influence is not strong.

Normally, opposition criticism is taken for granted and, therefore, largely ignored.

The topsy-turvy path towards an incomes policy in 1974 well illustrates this phenomenon.

The Conservatives advocated controls during the election campaign, and Liberals attacked the whole idea.

Six months later, a Liberal government introduced just such a policy, almost every feature of which was attacked by the Conservatives.

The dynamics of parliamentary debate admit few exceptions.

When the government leads, the opposition instinctively counters.

And if they cannot attack the principle of the bill, they will object to some features of it.

Instances where Parliament has played an accommodating role of the kind which the country now needs, reconciling government and opposition positions, have occurred infrequently.

Unanimous report

Yet Parliament has occasionally done this, with committees representing the forum for finding common ground.

In 1963, the Diefenbaker government broke up over differences between ministers on nuclear policy.

Pearson took a unilateral position without consulting his colleagues. Continuing division over this issue seemed probable.

Not knowing how else to proceed, Pearson called for the appointment of an "ad hoc" defence committee.

Under a good chairman and with co-operation from the opposition, the members of the committee probed the delicate issue of policy on nuclear weapons without direction from their parties.

Their unanimous report healed the wound in the Conservative party and provided the government with guidance for close to a decade.

The special Joint Committee on Immigration Policy was pressed on a reluctant government in 1975 by its own caucus, which insisted that public consultation was the necessary business of Parliament.

The subject was highly political and potentially divisive.

The policy adopted in 1967 was in a shambles and the government needed help.

Constructive work

But the productive work of that committee was only possible after the opposition was persuaded by Bob Andras, then minister of manpower and immigration, that his mind was completely open and that he would await the committee's report before proceeding to draft a new bill.

That assurance allowed the opposition to focus on the real issues, freed government members from a mindless defence of the cabinet's position, and allowed each member of the committee to make up his own mind when voting on details of its report.

More recently, the subcommittee on penal reform undertook constructive work.

The challenge was thrown to the committee by a government embarrassed by incident after incident in federal prisons, yet afraid to reform for fear the situation might deteriorate still further.

The members rose to the challenge, and under a chairman, Mark MacGuigan, with a remarkable skill for achieving a consensus, produced unanimously an imaginative and hard-hitting report which has contrib-

uted to a better atmosphere in Canadian prisons.

The lesson in each of these illustrations is that Parliament is capable of making a constructive contribution to policy development even in areas which are politically sensitive and divisive.

The crucial factors have been an undertaking by the government to refrain from adopting a position until the committee has completed its report, and a committee chairman with the trust of both government and opposition and a talent for discreet leadership.

Parliamentary committees can help to reconcile regional differences.

If the government decided to take advantage of this potential, it should indicate its intention to turn to Parliament for advice.

This would require bringing legislation to the floor in a more tentative form; being prepared to consider significant changes recommended in committee; and greater use of white papers as a device for seeking policy advice.

Serious implications

This approach might be resisted by officials who prefer to control the advice their ministers receive.

It would be opposed by any ministers who believe Parliament's role should be limited to approving or rejecting the position taken by the cabinet.

Its principal virtue is that it would enable the government to do what Trudeau said he wanted to do on election night — to consult the opposition.

But the consultation would be taken in a way which would free the opposition to respond.

The process of accommodation would take place in the open, so the public could see for themselves that their concerns were being expressed and taken account of.

To the extent that the government accepted a committee's recommendation, MPs from all parts of the country who were involved would share in defending the government's action.

Opposition members naturally would not give the government credit, but those who participated could be expected to justify and support the policy adopted.

Finally, this approach could enlarge the opportunity for government backbenchers and opposition members to make personal contributions, and encourage good MPs to remain in Parliament.

The argument for electoral reform has been much strengthened by the results of the February election.

There are, however, serious implications of proportional representation which must be carefully considered.

Sense of exclusion

And even though each party would have something to gain from any such system, the Conservatives will not hasten to solve a problem which hurts the Liberals.

At best, changes may be worked out in time for them to apply in the next election.

But the Western sense of exclusion and alienation exists now.

A genuine resort to Parliament could mitigate the problem.

The beauty is that no reform would be needed.

A change in the government's approach is all that is required.

THE TORONTO STAR, FEBRUARY 20, 1982

Ya-hooo!
West rides again

Separatism is back — with a bang.
And winning MLA, rodeo rider
Kesler, says 'we're gonna lick 'em.'

DON BRAID
View from the West

OLDS, Alta. — Gordon Kesler, the first separatist rodeo rider ever elected to a Canadian legislature, ceased to be a Canadian the day he passed through Montreal's Mirabel Airport in 1975.

"Nobody could tell us where to find anything, at least not in English," he said while campaigning at the Olds Auction Mart. "I didn't feel like I was in Canada at all."

Kesler's resentment of central Canada, Ontario as well as Quebec, burned for seven years, until he finally used it this week to work the most remarkable by-election victory in Alberta history.

Under the banner of Western Canada Concept (WCC), the 37-year-old biology teacher, businessman and broncobuster, stole a riding the Socreds had held almost continuously since 1935, but nearly everybody expected the governing Tories to win this time.

The rural rage was so powerful that Kesler won 42 per cent of the vote, compared to 28 for the Socreds and 25 for the Tories. It was an amazing feat for a new group fighting against established, well-organized, well-financed parties.

Kesler won even though he lives in High River, Joe Clark's home town, more than 160 kilometres from the Olds-Didsbury riding he now represents.

Charges of parachuting didn't hurt him because his views were so appealing to voters that he often made his opponents seem like the intruders.

To boisterous cheers, and cowboy yells, he called for an end to "Socialist government" in Ottawa and Edmonton, the right to bear arms and recall bad politicians, an elected Senate, abolition of bilingualism and metrification and a referendum on the form of a free enterprise state.

At nearly every meeting, Kesler raised the roof by concluding: "If we are not to be allowed to have some control of those things that affect our lives each day, the answer will ultimately be independence for Western Canadians."

But he most powerfully moved his audiences of ranchers, farmers, oil-men and back-country cowboys when he charged that the new constitution robs them of the right to own property.

His Tory opponent, Stephen Stiles, argued angrily that Kesler was twisting the truth, but Kesler struck back by waving a copy of the document and claiming, "they can even take away your coat."

And he got a powerful boost when the British Parliament gave second reading to the Canada Bill just in time for the morning news on election day.

Kesler succeeded in linking Prime Minister Pierre Trudeau and the Alberta Premier Peter Lougheed as co-villains in the constitutional and energy deals. This makes the Tories very nervous, since they're acutely aware that three times in Alberta history, novel, protest movements have annihilated strong governments with little advance notice.

In 1921 the United Farmers of Alberta (UFA) crushed the Liberals; Social Credit blew away the UFA in 1935; and Lougheed's Tories virtually destroyed Social Credit in 1971. In each case governments that seemed secure one year were gone the next.

Western Canada Concept has all the markings of a new brush fire and the Tories are determined to bank it before it spreads. In an unusually direct attack on an opponent, Lougheed accused WCC of distorting the constitutional agreement and promised to argue his views forcefully.

"They (the separatists) are now public and high profile," he said. "I think it'll be important for the citizens to see what they actually stand for in terms of their separatist approach."

Kesler, striding down the main street of Olds in his 10-gallon hat on election night, had already told Lougheed what to expect in the Legislature: "I'm gonna look over at (him) and give him a wink and a smile and tell him I hope he has the courage to call an election, 'cause we're gonna lick him!"

That left former Socred Leader Bob Clark, who held Olds-Didsbury for 21 years but couldn't pass it on to his successor, to say what must have been foremost in Lougheed's mind.

"If I were the premier, I wouldn't give this group six months to get organized. I think he would be wise to go (with an election) right now."

Lougheed is surely tempted, because WCC is already lining up candidates, money and volunteers in at least a dozen central and southern Alberta ridings. Its enthusiasm, overpowering at any time, is now at such a pitch that members believe they can beat the slick Tory machine anywhere.

The Tories, even while they claim the upset was a by-election protest that will disappear in a general election, remember with dread the fate of earlier governments.

They must decide whether to move now, or wait to see if Alberta's new MLA hangs himself in the court of public opinion.

The last course seems most likely, if only because Kesler shows signs of the intemperance that flaws Western separatism. On election night he said: "If we're lucky, (Pierre Trudeau) will have a heart attack within the next five minutes."

That remark, a bit too strong even for Trudeau-hating Albertans, wasn't typical of Kesler's campaigning. He usually attacked Ottawa and bilingualism without attacking Trudeau and the French language.

He said he likes central Canadians, but feels sorry for them because they have to endure such terrible governments.

Yet his Trudeau remark proved that he can slip. The Tories, who would look rather foolish if they risked their huge majority — 73 of 79 seats — at the first sign of trouble, will probably hope for more of the same when the Legislature opens in the first week of March.

They may be disappointed, since Kesler, despite the powerful emotions that move him, is a shrewd and able politician. In his first campaign, he astonished veterans with his ability to win support without encouraging hatred.

When his supporters became too vocal, as they often did, he urged them to let the other candidates speak.

In fact, Kesler is much more subtle than his Americanized southern Alberta accent (vehicle, Trew-dow) makes him seem. He was educated in Utah, at Weber State College, and was a professional rodeo rider at 17. But he went back to school to earn a biology degree and a teaching certificate.

He worked in the African country of Zaire, an experience that cemented his anti-Socialist views, before returning to Canada to found his company, Wildcat Oilfield Scouting Services.

Now 37, the father of five and still a steer-wresler in occasional rodeos, Kesler is ready to give Western separatism its first official airing in a legislature that promises to be the most arresting in Alberta history.

☐ **Don Braid is the Edmonton Journal's political columnist.**

THE TORONTO STAR, FEBRUARY 20, 1983

Western separatists have birthday blues

EDMONTON — This is birthday month for Western Canada Concept, but our peculiar separatists are in no mood to celebrate.

They have skidded abruptly downhill since last Feb. 17, when rodeo rider Gordon Kesler sent them into euphoric fits by winning a provincial by-election in Alberta. Overnight, Kesler forced the rest of the country to take notice of Cowboy Power.

Today, WCC is groping to recover from election defeats, and trying to repair its image as a party of slapstick weirdos with a talent for throwing pies at each other.

But the separatists are a persistent lot. They're still burrowing away at the grassroots, and many are as determined as ever to lead their provinces out of the country.

Comfort in numbers

This might seem amazing, given the defeats, but like other political losers they take comfort in numbers.

They won no seats in Saskatchewan, but took 3 per cent of the vote even though the party barely existed when the election was called for last April 26.

The wild Alberta bunch, although shut out of the Alberta legislature on Nov. 2, won nearly 12 per cent of the vote.

In B.C., the party led by Victoria lawyer Doug Christie has nominated 19 candidates as it prepares for an election that may come this spring.

Christie's party is the most fiercely

DON BRAID
View from the West

separatist of the lot, but it's also the most practical.

President David Banister says he'll be delighted if the B.C. party wins two seats and 8 to 15 per cent of the vote.

"You don't take something like we're proposing and make it acceptable overnight," he says. "We're going to use our election as a training program."

Unlike the Alberta and Saskatchewan parties, the B.C. crew doesn't accept candidates who are soft on separatism.

"It's the only plank that the other parties can't steal from us," says one B.C. worker. "It's the thing that makes us different, the bat we can use on all the others."

Christie has been urging voters since 1980 to "Free the West," and he makes no secret of his contempt for wafflers, especially Kesler.

Christie calls the Alberta leader "gutless" on separatism.

Kesler says the Alberta party needs to reconsider its stand on separatism, because the election proved Albertans aren't ready for it.

Like another High River native, Joe Clark, Kesler has guaranteed a fierce scrap in his party by calling for a leadership convention, which may not take place for another nine months.

The Alberta WCC will probably split into two groups, one moderate, the other

hard-line, and each fighting the other rather than the Tory government.

The Saskatchewan WCC, led by driving instructor Ray Bailey, may also have problems at a party convention set for April 15 in Saskatoon.

Both prairie parties are plagued by dissension. Some members really want to separate, others simply yearn for more free enterprise, and a third group uses the party to express hatred for Pierre Trudeau and the Liberals.

Leave in a huff

On top of all this, many separatists hurt the party with their readiness to leave the country if they can't have everything their own way.

Most Albertans prefer leaders who won't leave in a huff if they happen to lose.

This problem will continue to haunt the separatists, because they often seem more attached to principles than to provinces. They are like true believers who search the world for a laboratory where they can apply their ideas in purest form. The location doesn't seem to matter.

Burdened with such queer notions, Western Canada Concept is doomed to be less a party than a pressure group that prods at governments from the right — and there won't be any happy birthdays for our peculiar separatists.

☐ **Don Braid is the Edmonton Journal's political columnist.**

Discussion Questions

1. What is sovereignty-association? Is it a practical alternative to our current federal arrangement? Does it not seek to create formal equality between two units that are manifestly unequal in economic and demographic weight? Is there any chance it will be adopted in the future?

2. What were the factors that led to the emergence of an independence movement in Québec? Can Québec's nationalist aspirations, as characterized by Solange Chaput-Rolland, be accommodated in the Canadian federal system?

3. Why have territorial particularisms in the Canadian federal system found expression almost exclusively through the provinces? Can regional and provincial interests have a share in central decision-making? How?

4. Is the federal form of government necessary in Canada only to deal with the so-called 'French fact' or is it also required to accommodate the diversity of English-speaking communities?

5. What factors account for the persistence and growth of regionalism in Canada? What binds populations to their provincial governments: the inadequacies of representation in federal institutions, social and economic differences, or other factors?

6. Are there any similarities between the Québec independence movement and Western separatist parties?

7. Which is a greater threat to Canadian unity: Québec nationalism or the growing economic strength of the Western provinces?

Suggested Readings

David Cameron. 'Dualism and the Concept of National Unity', in John H. Redekop, ed. *Approaches to Canadian Politics*, second edition. Toronto: Prentice-Hall, 1983, 233–50.

Susan Mann Trofimenkoff. *The Dream of Nation: A Social and Intellectual History of Quebec.* Toronto: Macmillan, 1982.

Paul W. Fox, ed. *Politics: Canada*, fifth edition. Toronto: McGraw-Hill Ryerson, 1982, 125–64 and 188–226.

Roger Gibbins. *Regionalism: Territorial Politics in Canada and the United States.* Toronto: Butterworths, 1982.

Anne Legaré. 'Canadian Federalism: A Marxist Theory', in *Studies in Political Economy*, no. 8, Summer 1982, 37–58.

David Cameron, ed. *Regionalism and Supranationalism.* Montreal: Institute for Research on Public Policy, 1981.

D.J. Bercuson and P.A. Buckner, eds. *Eastern and Western Perspectives.* Toronto: University of Toronto Press, 1981.

Garth Stevenson. 'The Political Economy Tradition and Canadian Federalism', in *Studies in Political Economy*, no. 6, Autumn 1981, 113–33.

David Elkins and Richard Simeon, eds. *Small Worlds: Provinces and Parties in Canadian Political Life.* Toronto: Methuen, 1980.

Roger Gibbins. *Prairie Politics and Society: Regionalism in Decline.* Toronto: Butterworths, 1980.

Donald V. Smiley. *Canada in Question: Federalism in the Eighties*, third edition. Toronto: McGraw-Hill Ryerson, 1980.

K. McRoberts and D. Postgate. *Quebec: Social Change and Political Crisis*, second edition. Toronto: McClelland and Stewart, 1980.

D.V.J. Bell and L. Tepperman. *The Roots of Disunity: A Look at Canadian Political Culture.* Toronto: McClelland and Stewart, 1979, 145–209.

John Richards and Larry Pratt. *Prairie Capitalism: Power and Influence in the New West.* Toronto: McClelland and Stewart, 1979.

c. Constitutional Reform

Ironically, a seemingly perpetual theme in Canadian politics is that of the quest for constitutional reform. This search has been marked by a number of serious and complicated attempts at revision that have ended in failure. (A central stumbling-block in the numerous rounds of constitutional negotiations was the absence of a workable amending formula. Until the 1982 version, the requirement of unanimity stymied most efforts.) Little significant revision has taken place in an area of overarching importance: the distribution of legislative powers between the two levels of government. In fact, prior to the 1982 Constitution Act, all formal amendments in this century affecting the division of powers operated in Ottawa's favour (unemployment insurance, pensions, and guaranteed income supplements). Over the past three decades, however, demands for reform—primarily from the provinces, and notably from Québec—intensified, largely as a result of rapid developments in the machinery of federal–provincial relations. The trend, after 1960, for the provincial governments to assert their jurisdictional authority by moving into new areas of government activity increased federal–provincial tension. Federal and provincial programmes often came to overlap and clash, creating considerable resentment towards Ottawa and giving rise to demands for regional input into the operation of central institutions.

The first ten articles in this section provide a representative selection of the commentary that followed the 1981 constitutional deal between Ottawa and the nine English-speaking provinces, and the final patriation (bringing home to Canada from Great Britain) of the constitution in the form of the Constitution Act. Press coverage was influential in the constitutional debate at several points—more so than it has been in many other areas. After the Supreme Court ruled in September 1981 that the federal government's unilateral constitutional initiative was not acceptable conventionally, the chorus of negative newspaper comment contributed to forcing Ottawa back to the negotiating table.

The constitutional deal finally achieved in November 1981 was the culmination of much manoeuvring in the wake of the defeat of the Parti québecois's sovereignty-association option in the May 1980 referendum. These activities were designed to reach some sort of accord in keeping with the promises made to the people of Québec during the referendum. But the lengthy agenda of issues only produced a stalemate, leading to the unilateral federal initiative on a much more limited set of proposals (patriation, an amending formula, equalization, and an entrenched charter of rights and freedoms). The key provincial demands for change in the division of powers were dropped from the immediate list of constitutional issues at this point and have yet to re-emerge. The federal government was forced back to the table by the Supreme Court decision, albeit with the potential sanction of unilateral action deemed legal but unconventional by the ambiguous ruling. Finally, a deal was struck on the restricted basket of issues, but it was with the regrettable absence of support from the Québec government.

The first six editorials and columns on the constitutional package are neatly divided on the basis of language. The francophone authors speak in pessimistic tones about the grave implications of the deal for Québec. By contrast, the English-speaking writers, though not jubilant, were satisfied in the main. One is left with the impression that they were above all relieved that a messy business had finally been brought to a close. *The Toronto Star* lambastes Prime Minister Trudeau for not having lived up to his previous initiative and for knuckling under to the provinces. That editorial, like those from *The Vancouver Sun* and *The Winnipeg Free Press*, makes no reference to any further constitutional changes and refers only to obstacles in getting the package through the British Parliament. Whereas the Québec writers believe that the deal barely touched the surface of renewed federalism, the English-language editorialists express a high degree of satisfaction with the modest changes—as if little had been in need of reform. Indeed, Frances Russell of *The Winnipeg Free Press* worries out loud about the possibility that the new amending formula may have given the provinces too much power.

The four editorials on the occasion of the constitution's patriation show the same language split. *The Globe and Mail* and *The Vancouver Sun* are satisfied with the accomplishments, but Michel Roy laments patriation in a touching and troubling way. In his view constitutional reform remains unfinished, and Québec's isolation from the rest of the country is a monumental deficiency. The editorial from the London *Times* presents a neat counterpoint to the others, providing quite a different perspective on the entire process.

A centre-piece of the ongoing constitutional debate was the inclusion of civil liberties in the constitution. With the Constitution Act, a limited range of civil liberties was entrenched as the Canadian Charter of Rights and Freedoms. Although the Charter's list of the liberties enjoyed by Canadians is by no means exhaustive, some measure of freedom is also guaranteed by the common-law tradition, various statutes (for example, libel laws), the restricted 1960 Canadian Bill of Rights, and the provincial bills of rights. The momentum towards entrenchment of rights derived from fears that these other protections were too weak, especially for minorities lacking popular support.

The demands for something more secure and permanent saw fruition in 1982. Jean-Louis Roy's two-part assessment of the Charter prior to its adoption in a modified form by the November constitutional conference re-examines the debate over constitutional entrenchment. Roy reviews the existing apparatus to protect rights and some of the consequences of entrenchment, especially the conferral of considerable power on the judiciary. In the second part he explores the shortcomings, ambiguities, laxities, restrictions, and omissions of the draft Charter. Gilbert Lavoie sounds a similar note of caution, suggesting that the Charter does not substantially alter existing rights or provide any guarantee that flagrant abuses can be avoided.

The final articles deal with specific aspects of the Charter. Linda Silver Dranoff digs into the implications of the 'notwithstanding' clause, and appeals for support for the opposition to this provision, widely regarded as the principal deficiency of the document. Unlike Jean-Louis Roy and Gilbert Lavoie, David Vienneau gives an optimistic account of the impending effects of the new Charter. He concentrates, however, on narrow legal and procedural questions, ignoring the broader political implications. Jeff Sallot discusses the preliminary reactions to the Charter by the courts. He observes that the Supreme Court has yet to rule on any case arising from the Charter, and that we will not learn exactly how it will be interpreted by the judiciary for several years.

THE TORONTO STAR, NOVEMBER 6, 1981

Trudeau's failure of nerve
A gutted constitution

Prime Minister Pierre Trudeau has broken faith with all Canadians — and with his own most cherished beliefs — by abandoning the key principles which he rightly maintained to be fundamental throughout the long and painful quest for constitutional renewal. And his ill-conceived bargain with the premiers has created the politically explosive situation of allowing the separatist government of Quebec to depict the province as the victim of a gang-up by Ottawa and the other nine.

There may be a sense of relief today that the long-elusive federal-provincial consensus has finally been found. Sadly, however, such relief would be misplaced. Before yesterday's historic but deplorable developments, we had a federal-provincial confrontation, but the prospect of a constitutional renewal package that would serve Canada and all Canadians well. Now we have accord between Ottawa and nine of the 10 provinces — but a hollow constitutional shell gutted of its purpose and efficacy.

Trudeau committed himself to giving the nation a charter of rights that would equally and effectively protect the basic rights of all Canadians from coast to coast. Instead, we are now to have a constitution under which even the most fundamental rights — rights such as freedom of religion, freedom of speech, or freedom of assembly — can be violated virtually at will by any provincial government. Any province will be able to bypass the so-called guarantees simply by specifying in any given piece of legislation that its action is being taken notwithstanding the charter of rights.

A 'checkerboard'

Legal rights — including protection against unreasonable search and seizure or arbitrary detention — are subject to the same opting out, as are guarantees against discrimination. Rights which should be fundamental to all Canadians may end up varying from province to province. It's even conceivable, in fact, that a province could exempt itself altogether from the charter, simply by routinely inserting a "notwithstanding" clause in all its legislation.

Trudeau committed himself to ensuring that future constitutional changes would be applied uniformly across the nation, to avoid the "checkerboard" phenomenon that would result from permitting provinces to opt out. Instead, we are to have an amending formula that will permit provinces to opt out from future constitutional changes they don't like.

The agreement is not entirely devoid of positive elements, though even these are tinged with uncertainty.

All nine English-speaking provinces have agreed to enshrine the right of francophone minorities to education in their own language where numbers warrant, without any opting-out provision. But it is not yet clear whether the same protection for English-speaking Quebecers will be imposed over the Levesque government's objections; if it is not, the resulting imbalance could produce a divisive anti-French backlash in some other provinces.

The right of Canadians to live and work in any province is also to be enshrined in the constitution, without opting-out as such. But provinces with employment rates below the national average will be free to undertake "affirmative action" measures that violate this guarantee of mobility rights. We could still find ourselves in a situation, for instance, where an Ontario construction worker would be barred from working in Quebec, while a Quebec construction worker would be guaranteed the right to work in Ontario.

Until yesterday, Trudeau himself was the most forceful critic of the flaws that are now to be built into the constitution.

"Rights are the common heritage of every Canadian. There is no place in Canada for second-class citizenship," he said in October of last year. Now he has accepted a constitution which will permit second-class citizenship where rights are concerned, a constitution under which a resident of Manitoba may be denied rights guaranteed to his fellow citizen in Saskatchewan.

Opting out, Trudeau said last April, "would permit special status not only for Quebec, but for all the provinces. It's an amending formula that would permit sovereignty-association not only for Quebec, but for all the provinces." Opting out, he said, would be a formula for "incremental separatism." Now he has accepted the opting-out formula he had so vigorously opposed.

Desirable as it is in principle to bring home the constitution, these deficiencies leave no room for rejoicing. Constitutional renewal is not, after all, an end in itself; the ultimate objective — which is unlikely to be met by yesterday's deal — must be to give ourselves a constitution which will well serve the long-term interests of national unity and the well-being of future generations. And a consensus that isolates Quebec alone may prove far more politically dangerous than would have proceeding over the objections of several, or even most provinces.

Had options

Trudeau had other options. He could have established the legitimacy of his initiative beyond dispute by taking his case to the people in a referendum. Or, his legal right to proceed despite provincial objections having been affirmed by the Supreme Court, he could have gone ahead with the resolution already before Parliament, accepting short-term continued controversy for the sake of an optimal constitution for the future.

Instead, as he had done earlier this fall in capitulating in the energy pricing confrontation with Alberta, he opted in the crunch for the path of least resistance. This time, that meant forsaking the one policy goal that he had regarded as most fundamentally important throughout his political career: As far back as the 1950s, in his writings in the magazine Cite Libre, he had called for "the essential step of a declaration of rights entrenched in the constitution which would be binding on all Canadians and on all our governments." Now, with the once-only opportunity for strong federal action relinquished, our nation may never see such a binding charter.

In the parliamentary debate on the constitutional package he has now emasculated, Trudeau quoted the late Governor-General Georges Vanier:

"The best time is always the present time, because it alone offers the opportunity for action, because it is ours, because on God's scale it is apocalyptic, a time when the lines between good and evil are clearly drawn, and each of us must choose his side, a time when there is no longer room for either the coward or the uncommitted."

Yesterday, Trudeau's courage failed him, his commitment proved insufficient, and we are all the poorer for it.

THE VANCOUVER SUN, NOVEMBER 6, 1981

The Canadian way

In the end it was quintessentially Canadian. It was a compromise acceptable but not perfect. It was complicated, abstruse, mysterious. It united enemies and it divided allies.

But it is our country, bound anew by a constitutional accord, after more than half a century of disagreement, reached by nine of the provinces and the federal government. As so often in history past, the tenth, the odd man out, is Quebec.

That is the hangover on the morning after. As the rest of the country comes together as never before, where does Quebec go?

That question, crucial to the future, cannot be answered hastily, and even Premier Rene Levesque, in his bitterness, promised, along with Prime Minister Pierre Trudeau, to try to negotiate a way in.

It was an astounding climax to four days of history in which Mr. Levesque was isolated from the seven other premiers who had dissented from the original federal constitutional proposals, first by Mr. Trudeau's tactical alliance with him against the rest, then when Mr. Trudeau swung over to join them.

The result is a compromise that fulfils the mandate prescribed by the Supreme Court of Canada—the convention of substantial agreement is upheld.

The agreement would make Canada truly bilingual and bicultural, and it was fitting that Ontario, hypocritically immune under the federal government's charter resolution, should waive exemption from language rights for its French-speaking citizens. That gesture, supported by all the other provinces, is one debt English Canada owes to the Quebec majority who voted to stay with them in one Canada in the provincial referendum on sovereignty-association.

The premiers got the amending formula they sought, with one very important change: any province that opts out of a future constitutional change will be penalized by being denied access to the federal portion of any shared-cost program with which it refuses to go along. Quebec and Ontario both lost the power of veto over any such changes, and the federal government gave up the idea of holding a referendum to decide on the amending formula, a notion that would fit very awkwardly into the parliamentary system.

There is one major disappointment in the charter of rights: it does not spell out the rights of native Indians. Exactly what happened in the final negotiations remains unclear, but it appears as if that controversial issue will be separated for discussion at a special conference and it might be some time before native rights are defined. The governments will have to do a lot of explaining to angry Indians.

The provinces won a legal technicality that permits them an override on some clauses in the charter of rights, but while that might be necessary as mere housekeeping in certain bills it is difficult to imagine anything more sinister. How could any provincial legislature risk outcry and ridicule, and any government defeat, by voting against freedom of religion, equality of the sexes, or fair trial?

The next step must be approval by Parliament of the revised resolution. The changes mean that debate can be opened up beyond the two-day limit previously agreed, but they should not be an excuse for mischief or filibuster by the opposition. Members are entitled to scrutinise the revisions carefully, but they should bear in mind that they represent an agreement signed by nine provinces, as well as the basic charter approved by them after extensive parliamentary committee hearings. The resolution should be passed with all deliberate speed.

It is even less conceivable that the package would be held up in Britain. Anything other than sympathetic interest and fast action would be regarded as colonialist.

The constitution as now devised may not be ideal but it is the best that nine premiers and a prime minister could do. It may be better than any country could do in these times.

At least today we have a country, still in one piece. Had the talks failed that would not have been so certain. Uncertainty remains, but it is the familiar, though no less unpleasant, uncertainty of what will happen in Quebec. And it is something that all the other provinces, united at last, can work with the federal government and Quebec to resolve.

THE WINNIPEG FREE PRESS, NOVEMBER 6, 1981

An agreement at last

The terse and cryptic document signed yesterday by Prime Minister Trudeau and nine of the 10 provincial premiers is hardly the stuff to inspire bonfires in the streets. Despite its pitfalls, however, it provides grounds for modest celebration.

The chief reason for celebration is the simple fact that it was signed at all. The clashes and confrontations of the past year had left Ottawa and the provinces on the brink of a constitutional crisis which could have been immensely damaging to the unity of the country. By finding an accommodation at the 11th hour, the prime minister and the premiers at least saved us from the strains on national unity that would have been created by unilateral action and from the international humiliation of having our domestic differences debated in a foreign Parliament.

In doing so, they came up with a package of constitutional changes which may well be more workable than it looks at first glance. It provides for the two immediate essentials, patriation and an amending formula. It provides a charter of rights which does not contain the ironclad safeguards its enthusiasts would like but which does go a good deal farther than most of the premiers have been willing to go for the past year or more.

The pitfalls in the agreement are obvious but, over time, they may turn out to be more theoretical than real. The most immediate concern is the angry rejection of the package by Quebec's premier, Rene Levesque, the resultant isolation of Quebec on the issue and Mr. Levesque's warning that the results of that isolation will be incalculable.

The initial reaction in Quebec, on the part of politicians, journalists and the intelligentsia, is likely to be sharp and hostile. Mr. Levesque is certain to use yesterday's events to prove to Quebecers that the prov-ince cannot count on the understanding of other Canadians and that the only way they can protect their interests is by independence.

When tempers cool, however, ordinary Quebecers may begin to notice that the accord, which their premier says is such a threat to their future, in fact makes little or no difference to their lives. It might force them to grant the educational rights to their English-speaking citizens that most of them, according to the polls, already agree should be granted. On the other hand, it might not even do that.

According to Mr. Levesque, Prime Minister Trudeau proposed informally that the clause covering educational rights would not be proclaimed until all the provinces agreed to it. The Quebec premier denounced that as blackmail. In fact, it is no different from the deal which Mr. Levesque offered the other premiers after his Bill 101 restricted the educational rights of Canadians moving to Quebec.

The clause which forbids provinces to give preference in employment to their own residents is misplaced in a charter which is supposed to guarantee fundamental rights, and the amendment which restores that power to provinces whose unemployment rate is above the national average, is an absurdity. The net effect in the foreseeable future, however, would be to leave Quebec's employment policies virtually untouched.

The scrapping of a provincial proposal that provinces opting out of constitutional changes which implement new national social programs should be reimbursed from the federal treasury strikes down a Quebec demand that goes back to the days of Maurice Duplessis. But, since there are no immediate plans for that kind of constitutional amendment, Quebec's loss there too is more theoretical than real.

The other potential pitfalls lie in the clauses which permit the provinces, one way or another, to opt out of various constitutional changes. The amending formula, which would permit provinces, if they choose, to reject changes which affect their powers, is the very one which Mr. Trudeau claimed would lead to a chequerboard Canada or to separatism by degrees. In fact, however, it would produce that result only in the event of a series of constitutional changes aimed at creating a vastly more centralized federation. No one at the moment is contemplating that sort of change and, if it were to come about, the result for Quebec would be separatism at one fell swoop, not by degrees.

The so-called "notwithstanding" clause, which would permit provincial legislatures to declare, for five years at a time, that they were not bound by some of the constitutional provisions guaranteeing fundamental freedoms, legal rights and equality rights could again, in theory, lead to a Canada in which rights enjoyed in one part of the country would be denied in another. In practical politics, however, it would take a bold government to ask its legislature to deprive its citizens of a fundamental right. The provinces see that clause chiefly as a form of protection against extreme or bizarre judicial interpretations of the charter.

In all, the agreement signed yesterday is a typically Canadian document, complicated, untidy and not terribly inspiring. It is the kind of compromise which has permitted the Canadian federation to muddle along for the past 114 years. As such, it reflects credit on all the political leaders who worked for it, and on Conservative Leader Joe Clark who, by stopping Mr. Trudeau's Juggernaut last spring, made it all possible.

LE SOLEIL, NOVEMBER 6, 1981

Agreement tragic for Québec

Gilles Lesage

As one might have foreseen, without wanting to, once again Québec finds itself alone. But it is too soon to draw any definitive or catastrophic conclusions from this fact.

To understand the drama that is tearing this country apart, it was enough to watch the televised conclusion of the constitutional marathon in Ottawa yesterday. On one side, Mr Trudeau and the nine anglophone premiers complimenting and congratulating one another on an historic agreement; on the other, Mr Lévesque, whose solitary 'no' resembles Mr Bourassa's in 1971, and what any premier of the province-not-like-the-others would have said in his place. In a single night of long knives, the common front of the eight provinces that were opposed collapsed like a house of cards. The two solitudes, the profound lack of mutual understanding between Québec and the rest of Canada, a gap that one might have believed to be healing, reopened in a dramatic, even tragic, fashion.

The drama is not to be found primarily in the fact that Québec does not agree with the ten other governments regarding the amending formula, freedom of mobility and settlement, and rights to minority-language instruction. With goodwill and flexibility, it would have been possible to smooth over these differences quickly, for while they are certainly important, they are not fundamental.

But a radical misunderstanding, which yesterday's agreement wipes clean, will still have to be surmounted: the terrible tendency to forget Canada's linguistic and cultural duality. Beyond the ten provinces and the four or five major regions, this country is made up of two distinct societies, two majorities that the Laurendeau-Dunton report spoke of nearly twenty years ago now: one anglophone, the other francophone. One may pretend to put them on an equal footing by ignoring this vital difference; one may ignore Québec's special status, but it persists in reappearing on important occasions. Like yesterday. And it will continue to haunt this country that should be dualist as long as there is no concrete recognition that Québec is the cornerstone, the home of francophones in North America.

* * *

Does this mean that Mr Lévesque comes out of this painful experience as clean as the driven snow, and that he can play on this failure to promote the cause of sovereignty? In my view, he has negotiated in good faith for a year and a half, even if he did make some strategic mistakes. Abandoning Québec's traditional right of veto last April was one of them, even if at the time Mr Lévesque was hoping to solidify the common front of the eight provinces. His premature praise for Mr Trudeau's 'interesting' offer, Wednesday, to submit the amending formula and the charter to a cross-Canada referendum in two years, was another mistake.

On the first point, Mr Lévesque should not have taken such an enormous risk, even if the eight had signed. Not only does Québec no longer have the right of veto, but if it withdraws from an amendment, it will no longer receive financial compensation.

On the second point, he revived the solidarity of anglophones who were worried about the 'French Mafia' and feared the referendum suggested by Mr Trudeau, to break up the impasse, as if it were the plague. Nocturnal negotiations did the rest, and once again Québec finds itself alone in its corner.

Mr Ryan spoke yesterday of Mr Lévesque's ambiguous and biased intentions, but the way he saluted the agreement as an 'important and significant breakthrough' is itself equivocal. For this agreement respects two of the three terms of the resolution adopted by the National Assembly on Oct. 2: that Ottawa renounce its unilateral action and negotiate with respect for constitutional principles and conventions. But it seriously contravenes the third term, by which the Assembly 'opposes any move that could diminish its rights and affect its powers without its consent'. The amending formula and the charter severely weaken the powers that Québec has gradually acquired over more than a hundred years.

* * *

Enthusiasm and jubilation elsewhere, anxiety and frustration in Québec: Québec's isolation gives no cause for celebration, except to those who advocate the worst form of politics. The times call for *sang-froid,* moderation, and level heads, not anger, fanaticism, and intransigence.

Bitter as he is, Mr Lévesque nevertheless said yesterday that this is not the end either of Québec or of Canada. Fortunately Québec has not yet played all its cards in terms of negotiation and legitimate appeal. All avenues must be explored without delay, including those of London.

The Assembly must take up the torch again to ensure that no such agreement is ever made without the essential consent of Québec.

THE WINNIPEG FREE PRESS, NOVEMBER 10, 1981

Provinces will rule Canada

By Frances Russell

South Carolina is too small to be a republic and too large to be a lunatic asylum.

So James Louis Petigru, South Carolina's leading federalist, described the secession of his state from the Union just prior to the onset of the American Civil War.

Were Petigru alive today, he no doubt would be wondering about the mental stability of an entire nation which could saddle itself with a constitutional opting-out clause and proclaim a great victory.

The April accord of the eight provinces opposing federal unilateral action on the constitution has become, to all intents and purposes, Canada's new amending formula. It permits up to three provinces to opt out of constitutional amendments affecting their rights by a simple majority vote of their legislatures. It will, as Ottawa has repeatedly warned, lead to incremental separatism and a "checkerboard" Canada.

The denial of financial compensation to opting-out provinces is a very small stick. Fiscal equivalents apply to shared-cost social programs. They have never involved constitutional amendments.

As Prime Minister Pierre Trudeau himself stated on the opening day of the conference, constitutional opting-out in essence denies the existence of a national will in Canada.

Further, it creates the possibility of the country being held hostage by one province. A province seeking to protect its rights over resources, for instance, now has a powerful new tool to use against the national interest. Should two-thirds or more of the provinces and Ottawa deem that a particular resource or resources should be placed un-

der federal jurisdiction, the province or provinces affected can merely opt out of the constitutional amendment, nullifying it. Similarly, a province can engage in a policy detrimental to other provinces and be insulated from remedying action. Since the provincial government concerned has no political accountability outside its borders, the remedy of defeat at the polls in a subsequent election is also precluded.

The argument will be made that Ottawa still retains its declaratory and emergency powers to handle such situations. But the use of those powers against an angry province, already in confrontation with the rest of the country for exercising what it justly regards as its constitutional rights, would be dangerous in the extreme. In any event, the implication that the national will can ultimately be expressed only through coercion is an odd, if not unique concept to place in a constitution.

The argument will also be made that such instances are likely never to occur in Canada. Unfortunately, the continuing tensions over resources and the current high tide of provincial rights gives no cause for such complacency. The concept of ultimate provincial sovereignty has now been constitutionalized. The provinces now reign supreme over the nation.

Parallel with the U.S.

Correspondents from the *New York Times* and the *Los Angeles Times* covering the constitutional talks wrote stories to their newspapers drawing parallels between Canada's new amending formula and the twin doctrines of secession and nullification which arose in the early 19th Century in the U.S. The doctrines stemmed directly from

the view of some states, particularly the south, that the American union was a pact. Since the states retained ultimate sovereignty, this position argued, they had the right to nullify federal law as it applied to them and secede as a last resort. Nullification attempts arose sporadically during the early history of the American union, and triggered the famous debate between Daniel Webster and Senator Robert Y. Hayne in 1830. Webster claimed nullification would eventually break up the American union and proclaimed: "Liberty and Union, now and forever, one and inseparable." Nullification and secession were never constitutionalized in the U.S. But neither were they finally laid to rest until the Americans had fought a bloody civil war.

The Canadian provinces, too, have advanced the doctrine of confederation as a pact between provinces. And now, they have succeeded in turning the concept of nullification into a constitutional amending formula.

The nullification aspect is not the only bad feature of the amending formula. The federal government has more restrictions on its ability to change its own constitution than do the provinces. According to the new formula, the provinces can change their own governmental structures at will, except for the office of the lieutenant-governor. However, Ottawa has been largely strait-jacketed in reforming its governmental structures. It cannot, for instance, introduce proportional representation in the House of Commons without the consent of two-thirds of the provinces.

Proportional representation, or PR, is one way for Ottawa to correct the fundamental weakness of Canada's federal system. That weakness is the absence of any provincial representation within the national government. Provincial premiers have filled that vacuum to become the sole voices for the provinces at the centre. However, the premiers are miscast in that role, because they are elected on provincial, not national issues. Earlier this year, when PR was again mooted by the federal government, several premiers, most notably Alberta's Peter Lougheed, railed against it, seeing it as a way to reduce and weaken the powers of the premiers. Now, the premiers have insulated themselves against any such change, and will be able to perpetuate themselves in an inappropriate role at the expense of balanced federal institutions.

The amending formula is perhaps the pre-eminent disaster inflicted upon the nation by the constitutional compromise of last week. But it is by no means the only one. Others are the "not quite entrenched" entrenched charter of rights and the limbo into which the native peoples of Canada have been placed.

There are now two levels of rights in Canada. Democratic rights, mobility rights and language rights, including minority language education rights, are to be entrenched, that is, they cannot be changed without formal constitutional amendment. However, in a move forecast by the initial Hatfield compromise (drafted by the federal government and introduced by New Brunswick Premier Richard Hatfield), the other important rights are all to be subject to a legislative override clause.

This means equality protections for women, the aged and the handicapped and all the fundamental le-

gal rights such as the protections against arbitrary search and seizure and cruel and unusual punishment can be abridged by Parliament or provincial legislatures so long as each act specifies that it affects the charter protections. There is a sunset clause of five years on all such laws, meaning that they have to be repeatedly passed if they are to stay in effect.

Protections removable

In interviews, several premiers, including B.C.'s Bill Bennett and Saskatchewan's Allan Blakeney, said they thought it would be politically difficult, if not impossible, for legislatures to abridge the charter protections. But the very time when it would be politically possible, even popular, for legislators to offend the charter, for instance, when there is a public outcry against a minority group or in favor of punitive measures, is precisely when the entrenched right is needed most. Ominously, the very week the charter was being discussed, the federal solicitor general publicly advocated returning to the use of writs of assistance, which amount to an open season for police to conduct arbitrary searches and seizures.

The concept of citizens having two levels of rights, some protected and others capable of being reduced, offends the very principle of entrenched rights. Now, indeed, Canadians can feel that the only rights they have are those their politicians have deigned to give them. Further, Canadians, who are among the most mobile people in the world, will have to live with a checkerboard of rights. This, in a sense, makes a mockery of mobility rights. Handicapped people, for instance, would hardly

wish to move to a province which had abridged their protections. For all this, Canadians have to thank the provinces' incessant and overweening concern about maintaining their own powers and rights.

The removal of the aboriginal rights of native people from the constitution, pending a constitutional conference, leaves Canada's original citizens in limbo. Their aboriginal rights have, at least in part, been protected by treaties under British jurisdiction. Once British jurisdiction has been removed in its entirety from Canada, the treaties could legally have no status until such time as Canada gets around to dealing with them. The fears of native people that this might never happen have a legitimacy based in long years of tragic experience.

The constitution was described in the self-congratulatory closing conference session as a "victory for Canadians." In reality, the most that can be said for it is that it was likely the best fudge of two irreconcilable positions on the amending formula and the charter of rights. Whether a good fudge is the best for Canada, or what the people of Canada would choose for themselves, is very much open to question.

It is significant to note that none of the 11 governments around that table had any real mandate to deal on the constitution. None had been elected on the constitutional positions they presented. The only two governments that could claim some legitimacy in the bargaining because their concepts have at least been known for some time were Ottawa and Quebec.

Quebec refused to sign the agreement. And Ottawa basically gave away the store.

LE DEVOIR, DECEMBER 5, 1981

Autopsy of a Crisis:

If Pierre Trudeau was right . . .

by Daniel Latouche

How to explain the behaviour of the seven premiers who signed an agreement with Québec and then took the earliest opportunity to tear it up? The tactical explanation suggests that the premiers never considered this agreement to be anything more than a basis for discussion with Ottawa. According to the strategic explanation, the Canadian premiers simply behaved as representatives of an English-Canadian society whose interests are inconsistent with those of Québec.

But is this the essential lesson to be drawn from their attitude? If so, Pierre Trudeau was right. Nowadays, obviously, this thought alone is grounds for excommunication. Yet some elements of his reasoning must be correct, because in the end he has won. At least it must be conceded that he knows English Canada better than most of us do. He cannot be cut off from both Québec and English Canada. He has to be somewhere.

For fifteen years, his approach has rested on the following premises:

a) *English Canada does not exist as a distinct society.* This would be a theoretical stance appreciated by Quebecers, especially since they themselves have proclaimed the existence of a Québec nation. If the English-Canadian Nation does not exist, there can be no interests that belong to English Canada. Thus one must expect the English-Canadian premiers to deny the existence of a Québec nation and the country's national dualism. This is what has happened.

b) *The premiers of the nine anglophone provinces are, above all, provincial politicians.* Mr Trudeau has never believed in the philosophic pretensions of Sterling Lyon, or Allan Blakeney's role as 'wise old man' of politics. He has always seen them as just so many pitiful little provincial politicians. It wasn't so long ago that he even included a Québec premier in the lot. Hence he gambled that such a group could never maintain its cohesion and hold discussions, equal to equal, with the only other head of State present, the premier of Québec. Having gambled that he could buy them one by one, he had no difficulty breaking the common front.

c) *The francophone citizens of Québec are, above all, French Canadians, not Quebecers.* From the beginning, Mr Trudeau has also gambled that Quebecers would react as a minority, and not as a nation. It should thus have been possible, according to him, to prevent a national, that is, a unifying, reaction among them. And this was precisely the outcome. The federal manoeuvre has multiplied the divisions among Quebecers: Péquistes *vs* Liberals, nationalists *vs* anti-nationalists, federal Liberals *vs* provincial Liberals, pro-Ottawa *vs* pro-Québec.

This gamble on minority behaviour may turn against Mr Trudeau, however, especially if the French Canadians of Québec can be persuaded that the federal plan *takes* something away from them. Didn't they vote 'no' in the referendum just because someone was threatening to take 'their' Rocky Mountains away? The next few months should thus see the emergence of a fierce competition between Québec and Ottawa to convince Quebecers that they are a minority, in the one case a threatened minority, in the other a minority that is at last protected. It promises to be lively.

One of these days we are going to have to reflect on the validity of Mr Trudeau's premises and draw from them the necessary conclusions. For instance, in the event that the majority of Quebecers decide to opt for sovereignty, they will have to negotiate not with English Canada, but with Ottawa. Moreover, the *Québécois* gloss seems to be pretty thin, barely covering fundamental French-Canadian divisions. If the Parti québécois had to launch itself into the federal arena, this gloss would not last very long. Apparently several in the party are toying with this possibility, thus surpassing the most secret wishes of Pierre Trudeau.

Except for the few minutes of the inaugural address when they take the lieutenant governor out of mothballs, no one in Québec reflects on the relevance of our political institutions. The British-style parliamentary system has its defenders here who would make Westminster blush with shame. Yet the present constitutional crisis has once again proved the enormous price we all pay for this blind attachment.

Certainly it is not a question of rejecting this system because it is English, old, imported, and in use throughout Canada. That would be childish. It must be revised from top to bottom because it constitutes an obstacle to the political development of Québec. That should be enough justification.

It is sufficient to examine the behaviour of Claude Ryan for the last few months to be convinced. He is the big loser in this badly understood parliamentary system. Obviously, the Péquistes will not fail to be delighted by this. What destroyed Claude Ryan is eating away the very heart of Québec's political identity.

It is this British parliamentary system that frustrates all Mr Ryan's intentions to support the government of Québec in its opposition to Ottawa. One may appeal to his conscience, beg him to forget the party line, it is still he and he alone who will pay the price for any support of the government. As head of the loyal opposition, he is paid to oppose everything the government does and says, a little like the defence lawyer whose job it is to thwart the plans of the Crown prosecutor.

The very spirit of our political system demands this permanent confrontation. And the question period is its everyday symbol.

Every day, government activity stops for several hours. In every ministry a list of possible questions is prepared, on which the minister is 'briefed'. He then waits an hour for someone to ask him the fateful question. During this same time, the members of the opposition and their researchers prepare an elaborate scenario aimed solely for television and the nightly news. Question period does not serve as a watchdog on government activities. No less than 80% of the questions are simple recapitulations of newspaper articles, the other 20% being a mixture of fabrications, rumours, and clever traps designed to make ministers lose their temper. How grown-up people can still lend themselves to this masquerade remains a mystery. There will be no valid reform of the parliamentarian's function until some of the foundations of our system are put to the question themselves. We could begin right away with secrecy and ministerial solidarity.

At present, even if the opposition does

not play the game of repeating *ad nauseam* questions as insipid as they are pernicious, it is still penalized. If they hope to win the next election, they must now set their sights as low as possible. The absurdity of the situation does not seem to have escaped Claude Ryan, who now has to choose between complete intellectual debasement and rejection by his party.

What is the government waiting for before undertaking an in-depth examination of our political institutions? Will we remain prisoners of this circus until the Great Day of independence arrives? It seems to me that, apart from the post of lieutenant governor, it would be possible to remodel these institutions to make them more responsive to our needs.

We have to stop waiting for everything to come from outside, from Ottawa, English Canada, the Supreme Court. To do so is to condemn ourselves to the mercy of someone else's strategy (for 'they' have no ideological reticence to adopt such strategies). For five years the Parti québécois government has chosen to be a 'good government' where agriculture, automobile insurance, and municipal finances are concerned. Why should it not now decide to be a good government in terms of our political institutions and our own constitution? As far as I know, this approach has been very profitable electorally.

Obviously, a debate over institutions is less intoxicating than one over social democracy. One of these days, however, we are going to have to hold this cursed debate. There is nothing to stop us from starting right away. For once we will be completely masters of the rules of the game.

The right to self-determination must be exercised as often as possible; otherwise it crumbles away. Until now we have used it only once, in the referendum. It must be entrenched in our institutions and political practice as soon as possible. Later, in a referendum or a referendary election, it will be easier to make others recognize this freedom if we ourselves have been careful to exercise it every day.

As well, a constitutional conference held exclusively among Quebecers would be a pleasant change. At last we would find out whether Minister Bédard is better than Claude Morin when it comes to negotiating special status for Saguenay-Lac-St-Jean.

THE GLOBE AND MAIL, APRIL 17, 1982

On April 17, 1982 . . .

Today the constitution of this country, after 115 years, will truly reside in Canada.

There is, in the enthusiasm for the occasion, a good deal of hyperbole to be reckoned with. People are saying this proclamation brings an end to our existence as a colony of Britain, that at last we are free of institutionalized intervention.

There is enough to celebrate without going to these distances.

We have for some decades been independent of Britain. Only our inability as Canadians to agree upon a formula for the functioning of the constitution has marooned it at Westminster all these years. We are now, in many ways, as uncertain as we were 40 years ago about how we can resolve constitutional differences. But we have succeeded in bringing the Act to Canada with a formula for amendment and with, we can hope, some determination to make that formula work.

The exercise of bringing the constitution home does not constitute one of the happier chapters of Canadian affairs. It is proper that we should acknowledge that fact, as we light our rhetorical bonfires on Ottawa's hilltops.

The Prime Minister deserves some credit for bringing it back. Had he not been seized with a sudden determination to achieve patriation, it is unlikely that we would be witnessing this week's ceremonies. But Pierre Trudeau's methods were divisive and left political scars that will not be healed in his lifetime.

His insistence upon proceeding unilaterally, upon having the constitution radically changed before patriation, plunged the country into one of the most bitter debates since Confederation. Those who opposed him were treated with contempt and, not surprisingly, heaped contempt on him. Few of the adversaries were left without reason for regret.

Leader of the Opposition Joe Clark, when all else failed, used parliamentary obstruction to halt the Trudeau express. Public opinion generated by the premiers, and expressed in poll after poll, forced the issue to the courts, and drove the Prime Minister back to the conference table. In the last days, the native peoples and the women of the country forced the negotiators to vital changes.

Quebec, unfortunately, was left unhappy. That, considering its Parti Québécois commitment to separation, was to be expected. Premier René Lévesque had to find a way out of any agreement, although it is a pity he was given grounds for claiming he was pushed. It would have been impossible for him to stand as one of the new Fathers of Confederation, and then turn about to slay the child.

In the end what was accomplished was considerable. At least we finally moved as a federal state. Some of us argued that we had labored and produced a typical Canadian compromise. It was nothing of the sort. It was an angry settlement, arrived at in the worst way to effect abiding change. It involved methods that, indulged in often, would leave us in danger of ceasing to be a country.

One thing we have assured ourselves is a guaranteed employment program for lawyers. Down the years they will be sorting out who governs Canada, the elected legislators or the courts. Down the years they will be determining who has what rights, notwithstanding the notwithstanding powers of Ottawa and the provinces.

We stand at a beginning, and that is why we will cheer the Queen, and perhaps cheer ourselves.

We will be buoyed by the belief that nothing ahead of us could be more difficult than the trials of passage that have put our feet where they now stand. Tomorrow is a lovely day!

THE VANCOUVER SUN, APRIL 17, 1982

Now let's work for tomorrow

Delesalle, Johnson, Hong, Pasquale, Hansen, Keiss. Today is for names like these.

Today is for the family, and these are young members of the family, invited from British Columbia, along with others whose names make up even more tiles of the mosaic, to dine with the Queen before she took part in the family party today — the day Canada comes of age, legally.

Some Canadians seem to find it easy to take a morbid or cynical view today. So much is wrong with the country and so many things are disappointing. But political failures, economic vicissitudes, and petty squabbling are only seasonal. Each spring, life is reborn. So is hope.

There is, in truth, so much to be thankful for in this great country that to cavil and quibble today of all days is misanthropic.

To be sure, the Constitution is mere words, and not very high words at that. We had no Jeffersons or Hamiltons to draft it, or even Lauriers and Macdonalds. But its importance cannot be denied and should not be obscured.

It is important for precisely the reasons that so much is wrong. It is important to the psychology of this nation. And it is a turning point in its history.

Canada has sheltered for 115 years behind the mother-skirts of the British North America Act, which was often the excuse for not doing anything about our national problems. But today we are making amends. We are taking care of history of which we have been negligent. It is still only the beginning. But it needs a will to begin, which our mere politicians must find or be shamed into finding by the people. Canada is beholden to no one, and Canadians can't blame others any more for their shortcomings.

The task for the future administrators of the Constitution is to make the nation work and to face up to its problems — especially its duality.

The naysayers and gloom-merchants of this country, the selfish and the bigoted, the greedy and the frustrated, the nitpickers and the petty and puffed-up have had plenty to say. They should now shut up and work for the country instead of against it. If they continue, they are not true-hearted Canadians.

The truth is that despite the rantings of separatists and the state of the economy (not unrelated) this is one of the richest and most beautiful places on earth. Compared to nine-tenths of the world, Canada is unspoiled paradise.

Enshrinement of a constitution is a starting point. It is a time at which Canadians might reflect where they are going and what it is worth. The answer must be that it is worth a very great deal, and worth more if we go together and not as ragged bands in different directions, not backwards into fortresses and fiefdoms, into intellectual ghettos, and political enclaves.

The Constitution, with its Charter of Rights, is imperfect. But instead of tearing it apart, Canadians should pull together to improve it, to make it work well and fairly. It is, in essence, despite the imperfections, a sound concept and a good foundation for a country.

The job will be terribly difficult and certainly beyond most of the politicians sniping at each other today. The disappointment of today is that the government of Quebec — not necessarily the people of Quebec — is not participating in the ceremony of patriation, of nationhood. But other leaders will come along. It is up to them to build on today's foundation and to ensure that Quebecers — the real Quebecers, not the ambitious politicians — sit at the family table. For they *are* members of the family.

There are other major tasks ahead. Having the Constitution in Canada means not only a given set of rights and division of powers. It also means being able to amend it, to let it evolve as the nation continues to grow. That, perhaps, is a greater opportunity for Quebec than its premier admits.

Other important legal and legislative reforms are needed, and some should be tackled quickly. But today Canadians should pause and reflect on their coming of age and how they will handle the responsibilities of maturity.

LA PRESSE, MONTREAL, APRIL 19, 1982

Requiem for an unfinished country

MICHEL ROY

With repatriation accomplished, Canada comes into possession of full sovereignty. But it was a mutilated Canada that celebrated that historic moment on Saturday, separated from a Québec whose absence destroys the federation's already precarious balance.

A sad weekend for this country that is forever searching for itself, that gives itself the illusion of a royal celebration, and is still waiting for its real spring to arrive! Just as sad as the rain on both the red tunics of Parliament Hill and the fleurs-de-lis of the Parc Jeanne-Mance.

As if to make everyone forget that the other half of the country was not there, it was Québec personalities from the federal level who led the ceremony: the prime minister himself, in his pocket the red colour of the Québec electoral map, flanked by Jean Chrétien and André Ouellet; Mme Huguette Labelle, Undersecretary of State, reading the royal proclamation with all the gravity of Antigone standing before Creon.

Anxious to reassure Quebecers, who saw among the dignitaries neither their lieutenant governor, nor their premier, nor the leader of their opposition, Mr Trudeau affirmed that 'Nothing of what makes Québec unique has been sacrificed' in the constitutional agreement. What a strange statement! Nothing has been sacrificed, except Québec's consent . . .

The Queen, whose remarkable dignity inspires admiration, in a few simple phrases recalled that Canada cannot attain its true greatness without the indispensable contribution of Québec.

In fact, Canada has not grown as a result of this long trial. Because the acquisition of complete sovereignty, a source of legitimate pride, remains a symbolic victory. The real challenge was to establish a constitution that would respect the complex reality of this difficult country, at the same time fulfilling the century-old hopes of Québec, the province that precipitated this reform of the fundamental law because it is not and will never be a province like the others. This challenge was not taken up. Because this agreement was made without Québec, which deprives the province of certain important means of defence, Canada has gained neither strength nor cohesion. So what happened between May 20, 1980 and April 17, 1982?

History will remember the implacable constitutional and political counter-offensive mounted by the Prime Minister following the Québec referendum. Mr Trudeau committed himself to renewing the federation if Quebecers reaffirmed their allegiance to Canada. He kept his word, to the point of absurdity: the federation is indeed in the process of change, but Québec is outside that movement, and its opinions no longer count. 'I did not commit myself to increasing Québec's autonomy', he told Québec's *Le Soleil* the other day. This is the truth. He did not say that renewal would mean more powers for Québec, since he never wanted that. But he did not announce that he would take powers away from the National Assembly without its consent. Nor did he specify that the principle of dualism would be flouted along the way. In May 1980, he did not let on that he would bolster centralist trends, nor that he would eventually deprive Québec, in economic and fiscal matters, of necessary means and resources. In those days, he was very careful not to predict the death of co-operative federalism, or to explain his strategy of unilateral action. He kept quiet about what fate had in store for his great ally at the time, Mr Claude Ryan, concerning reform. All in all, it was not far from fraud.

If Canada has not grown as a result of this battle, therefore, Québec is the sorrowful loser, and today finds itself not only in a state of political anaemia, but vulnerable to an economic crisis that affects it more severely than the other regions.

What does Mr Lévesque propose to do at this painful juncture? On the constitutional level, he is calling for resistance; in a pathetic speech Saturday, he celebrated in anticipation 'the independent country that will be the Québec of tomorrow'. In suggesting this perspective, the premier had better have a good idea of what he intends for us. Clearly he does not envision reopening the constitutional negotiations with Ottawa and the others, at least in the near future. The resistance referred to will no doubt express itself in judicial battles. Essentially, rather, the speeches of the last few days show the first signs of a renewed offensive in the fight for independence. This means that Quebecers will be called on in the coming months, perhaps in a year, to choose again whether they want a sovereign state. This is a coherent position. There will come a time when the PQ can no longer live in uncertainty and ambivalence within the federal regime. To protect both its *raison d'être* and its power, it will have to risk all to gain everything. A logical decision, but unrealistic, because the PQ government played the referendum card 23 months ago and lost. And it is doubtful, according to the latest polls, that opinion on this vital question has changed in the last two years. What good would it do to plunge Québec once more into the turmoil and division of another debate over its political future? Would it make us forget the recession and the budgetary impasse? The federal counter-offensive of May 1980 has pushed a weakened Québec into a political corner.

The situation is a mess for both societies. In the long run, it is not irreparable. The door remains open, writes Jean Chrétien. The constitutional package can be perfected, according to Léon Dion. Well and good. But if the same actors stay in place, every new effort is doomed to failure. We will have to wait for the epilogue. Meanwhile, the victory songs and formal ceremonies will have the sad tone of a requiem for an unfinished country.

THE TIMES, LONDON, APRIL 17, 1982

A CANADIAN CELEBRATION

It would be an impertinence to congratulate Canada on the attainment of its legal independence from the United Kingdom. In reality Canada has been an independent country for 56 years. The importance of today's ceremony in Ottawa, in which the Queen will sign a proclamation ending the constitutional link between the two countries, is not that it will make much difference to the Canadian government's freedom of action, either internally or in the international community, but that it puts an end to more than a half century of paradox. It removes an irritating, anachronistic and anomalous reminder of British colonial supremacy.

Canadian autonomy, and that of the other Dominions, was officially recognised by the Balfour Declaration of 1926, to which the Statute of Westminster of 1931 gave full legal effect. It was because Canada, alone of the Dominions, had been unable to provide for itself a workable machinery — acceptable to both the federal government and the provinces — for amending its own constitution that Westminster retained the sole right, and the obligation, to make amendments to the British North America Act of 1867. The fact that by convention it did so only at the request of, and in the terms asked for by, the federal government, did not provide a satisfactory answer to those Canadians who considered it both absurd, and to some extent humiliating, that one sovereign state should have to go to the legislature of another before it could pass certain laws.

The search for the amending formula, a constitutional Holy Grail, has been pursued intermittently and with varying degrees of vigour for more than a half century. That Mr Trudeau was finally able to find that formula, and to tack on a Charter of Rights in addition, is a tribute to his will, tenacity, negotiating skill and,

not least, when it mattered most, ability to compromise with the various and varying demands of the provinces. Only Quebec resisted to the end; and yesterday's statement by the Premier, Mr Levesque, reaffirming his party's demand for independence inserted a discordant note into the proceedings.

It is a question for debate whether Mr Trudeau would have been able to persuade Westminster to pass the required legislation at a time when his scheme was opposed by eight of the ten provinces. His initial insistence that Westminster must be no more than a rubber stamp for the Federal government's demands was not only couched in tactless terms, but was, some experts argued, constitutionally invalid.

The possibility of a constitutional crisis was averted by allowing the issue to go to the Canadian Supreme Court, whose decision managed to allow both sides to claim victory and also resulted in a new atmosphere of conciliation between the federal and all but one of the provincial governments. Westminster fortunately escaped having to adjudicate between bitterly opposing camps. Had it been forced to do so, the consequences for federal-provincial, and for Canadian-British, relationships might have been severely damaging. As it is, Westminster emerged with dignity from a difficult and sensitive episode. The serious attention it gave to the complex legal aspects involved, its reluctance to be used as a rubber stamp, and the interest and compassion which many members of both Houses showed to the cause of the Indian peoples, reflected well on Parliament.

Patriation of its constitution finds Canada in good shape, though not entirely free from problems. There will

continue to be difficulties over Quebec, the rights of the aboriginal peoples, and federal-provincial relations, especially over energy resources (the importance of which was demonstrated last week by the clear mandate which Newfoundland's electors gave its government to stand firm against federal claims to the lion's share of the rewards of offshore oil). These are all issues which were present before patriation, but Canada's new constitution has given them a new dimension.

Happily, the breaking of the constitutional link between Canada and Britain does not bring any other estrangement. The Queen remains Queen of Canada, all the easier for Canadians to accept because she will no longer be burdened by identification with the constitutional issue. Relations between the two governments, slightly (but only slightly) cooled when it seemed that Mr Trudeau would find Westminster less receptive to his demands than he might have wished, have already resumed their traditional warmth. Canada's prompt and active support of Britain over the Falklands dispute is current proof of that.

Canada is important as a friend and ally of Britain, as a senior and influential member of the Commonwealth, and as a democratic country with the same principles of conduct and ideals of freedom as our own. To claim that patriation will usher in a new era in Canadian-British relations would be to suggest that all has not been well between the two, and that would be incorrect. That Canada's constitution has, after 56 years, finally made its journey home, leaving no trail of bitterness behind it, should be a matter of great satisfaction to both countries, and can only cement the friendship between them.

LE DEVOIR, OCTOBER 30, 1981

Our rights and freedoms in the constitutional turmoil

1) *The political conditions and the new authority that is proposed*

by Jean-Louis Roy

Hours away from the constitutional conference, it seems increasingly obvious that the reconciliation or exacerbation of conflicts will depend on the fate of the plan for a Canadian Charter of Rights and Freedoms. This examination is imperative. The unthinking haste of the undertaking and the conflicts it has given rise to, have overshadowed the significant effects of this charter on the most important aspects of our lives.

Our rights and freedoms have become major political stakes in the past year. They are mobilizing parliaments, governments, political parties, and courts of law. They are arousing citizen's groups and professional associations, even the advertising agencies hired by the protagonists to deliver contradictory messages to us. This fever is as rampant in the media as in the marketplace of seminars and conferences. Never before has there been a parade of such highly abstract concepts across the public stage.

In another context, the civic and social appropriateness of such activities would have been great. In the present situation, however, our rights and freedoms have been reduced to objects of political haggling; they have become targets, rather than the fragile and indispensable foundations of the dignity and equality of individuals.

These intrigues and strategies, these compulsions, these ruses and all-or-nothing politics, severely threaten the essential objective: to assure the citizens of this country that they can live secure from any threat to or infringement of their fundamental rights, under the best possible conditions of knowledge, protection, and equality.

What reason should prompt an undertaking so essential to democratic societies joined together under a federal form of government? An examination of current political conditions, systems for the protection of rights, and the intrinsic value of the Canadian charter will allow us to arrive at some elements of an answer to this question.

The current constitutional war should not make us forget that some elements of a common understanding regarding rights and freedoms do exist in this country, despite the diversity of our cultural traditions and social values.

Fundamentally, voluntary associations, feminist associations, churches, unions, and public bodies, which pursue activities that draw attention to, promote, and defend rights and freedoms, all take their inspiration from the same international sources: the Universal Declaration of Human Rights, and agreements relating to rights or designed to eliminate various forms of discrimination. Even if the links among these groups are generally fairly loose, they have formed common fronts out of expediency from time to time.

Let us remember, too, that all the Canadian provinces, as well as the federal government, have created human rights commissions whose mandates are obviously limited to the jurisdiction of the governments that brought them into being. These commissions have statutes and powers that vary widely. Meetings and exchanges among these public agencies have recently multiplied. Moreover, they have banded together in the Canadian Association of Statutory Human Rights Agencies.

Finally, since the federal-provincial conference on human rights held in Ottawa (Dec. 11–12, 1975), the federal and provincial governments have developed mechanisms to ratify the treaties, conventions, and other international instruments relating to the rights of the individual for Canada. This conference also struck a continuing federal-provincial committee of civil servants responsible for pursuing discussions on all questions concerning human rights.

These joint mechanisms and the continuing committee are a result of the federal form of government in Canada. Before agreeing to any accord or international convention, the government of Canada must in fact consult the provinces and obtain their approval, since they alone can implement the provisions of accords and conventions in the areas for which they are constitutionally responsible. Only they can agree to incorporate them in their legislation, or to modify their own provincial constitutions in order to make them conform to the international documents if, on examination, such adjustments prove necessary. On Oct.

22, for instance, the government of Québec, through the Minister for Intergovernmental Affairs, Mr Claude Morin, notified the Secretary of State for External Affairs, Mr Mark MacGuigan, of its implementation of the convention on the elimination of all forms of discrimination against women. Canada, however, has not ratified this convention, since certain provinces have not yet answered the call.

As one can see from this brief summary, the knowledge, protection, and defence of rights, and freedoms have made real progress in Canada over the last few years. Pressure from citizens and groups, and the evolution of international efforts in regard to these questions, led legislators first to create public agencies to ensure the protection of rights and freedoms. Then they broadened the mandates of these agencies to respond to social evolution and the pressing demands of citizens.

In the last few years, in fact, the mandates of the human rights commissions have been broadened. In Québec, the charter adopted in 1975 has been amended three times and, as a result of the recent efforts of the Standing Committee on Justice, will probably be amended again in the next session. The governments of Ontario and British Columbia are currently revising the mandates of their human rights commissions. Saskatchewan, for its part, has recently broadened the mandate of its commission. Lastly, our governments have had to create an intergovernmental committee to ensure that the international conventions and accords are implemented.

Taking all of this into account, can the federal initiative be considered a significant step forward, as genuine progress in the protection of our rights and freedoms?

The question must be answered in the negative, owing to the political conditions of the initiative, the new system charged with this protection, and the very contents of the proposed federal charter. These three factors are inseparable.

The political conditions of the current initiative are known. Without their consent, the legislatures and governments of the provinces (with the exception of Ontario and New

Brunswick) find that a charter of rights has been arbitrarily imposed on them. Article 31 of the charter is very clear: 'This Charter applies to the legislature and government of each province, and to all matters within the authority of the legislature of each province.'

No justification can be advanced as grounds for resorting to this political coercion which, according to the Supreme Court, limits the powers of the provinces both retroactively and in the future. This concept of force is inconsistent with the accepted method of introducing international treaties into the domestic judicial order. It has been condemned by both opposition parties in the national Parliament, by eight provincial governments, and by a virtually unanimous resolution of Québec's National Assembly.

This initiative would derive legitimacy only from common consent given under conditions of full equality. Otherwise it is unreasonable, and a totalitarian option. It tips the balance of powers and rights over the edge and into an abyss. In fact, when we turn the weaving over to see how the threads are intertwined and knotted, another perspective emerges. Our rights and freedoms have become vulgar objects open to bidding, pawns on the chessboard of the crisis in the Canadian political system.

This denigration is both a function and a reinforcement of that crisis. It was neither necessary nor desirable to put the question of rights and freedoms at the very centre of the constitutional turmoil. This decision reflects a certain conception of the way the country works and of its political future. In designating it as indispensable, the federal government has taken a considerable risk.

It is not evident, in fact, that the new administration and articulation of our rights and freedoms that the Canadian prime minister is seeking to impose on us have been sufficiently tested by detailed analysis and exposure to public debate to become, tomorrow, the permanent foundations for the exercise of our rights and freedoms.

The haste to settle everything in a few weeks, the unthinking speed of

the initiative—which is, moreover, strenuously contested—and the conflicts that have arisen because of it, have unfortunately overshadowed the effects of the new administration and articulation of our rights and freedoms in the federal resolution.

If the political conditions actually undermine rights and freedoms, the system that would perpetuate these conditions does not necessarily provoke enthusiastic approval. The federal plan implies a massive transfer of power from the legislatures to the courts, that is, to non-elected judges. The consequences of this decision are difficult to predict. It does not constitute the universal panacea evoked by Jean Chrétien.

If the federal resolution were transformed, through the consent of the Canadian and British Parliaments, into a constitutional reality, the judges would acquire the very considerable power to determine, in a way, the structures of society. They would determine the concrete parameters of our rights and freedoms. They could literally dictate the limits of legislative powers to the legislature itself.

No one can foresee whether the courts as a whole would opt for a limited or a broad interpretation of the rights and freedoms that the constitutional charter would establish. We would thus be held hostage to the views of a few dozen people regarding the social and cultural evolution of our societies. These people are unassailable, and their decisions are definitive.

Is government by judges more democratically just than government by elected representatives?

Certainly we would be without any democratic instrument to contest the decisions of this group of rather isolated people, whose vision of the direction of our lives and of our aspirations would suddenly take precedence over any other power and all other forms.

The evolution of the extension and protection of our rights and freedoms has been quite spectacular in recent years, in Québec and in Canada. It is the result of the impact on legislators of the efforts and pressures of groups and citizens. A massive transfer of power to the courts in such matters would reduce this influence that has produced substantial, yet still insufficient, results.

We are facing a radical transformation in our ways of developing social consensus regarding rights and freedoms. Certainly we cannot refuse this new conception forever. However, in the current political war, has our society given enough thought to the consequences of such a conception to approve of it without further examination?

In matters as vital as this, the maturity produced by genuine social debate leads to more enlightened choices than ones made for us by politicians whose language and behaviour have fundamentally corrupted the very meaning of the enterprise of freedom.

Can one really believe that the citizens of Canada have made their choice among the various means of guaranteeing, on the judicial level, the protection of their rights and freedoms; that they have made their choice between parliamentary supremacy, which is in fact subject to electoral accountability, and judicial supremacy, which is in fact subject only to itself?

To entrench rights and freedoms in a constitution is to opt definitively for the supremacy of the judges.

It remains to examine the guide that the latter must decipher, the Canadian Charter of Rights and Freedoms. Even if the initiative is illegitimate, we must look at both sides of the question. Tomorrow, perhaps we will look at those documents that will gradually affect the most important aspect of our lives.

2) *Between memory and anticipation of failure*

The federal Parliament gave Canada the Bill of Rights in 1960. This was a matter of an ordinary law. By its nature it did not take any kind of precedence over other legislation, nor obviously, was it in any way a constitutional document. Its adoption was welcomed with enthusiasm, and these hopes soon evaporated. In point of fact, the courts responsible for interpreting this text, notably the Supreme Court, maintained the status quo regarding rights, citing the legislator's intention to conform to the declaration, and pointing out the shortcomings and omissions in the text.

Mr Alan Borovoy, president of the Canadian Civil Liberties Association, stated in October 1980 that Canadian courts have always manifested great reticence when it came to the protection of rights and freedoms. Indeed, he added, 'I do not see what difference it would make in judges' attitudes even if rights were enshrined in the constitution.' For his part, Mr André Morel, an eminent jurist, stated in October 1980 that 'the Bill of Rights has changed nothing in Canadian society from a practical point of view.'

Such is the paradox of the current situation. The transfer of power from the legislature to the courts, effected by the entrenchment of the charter of rights in the constitution, could mean maintenance of the status quo or even curtailment of our rights. Moreover, a 'constitutionalized' charter would be a monument made of lead, fixed for a long time to come. As a society we would lose some of the flexibility that at present allows us to respond relatively quickly to the demands of an ongoing evolution and, as a result, to modify or broaden the responsibilities of the agencies that protect our rights.

To modify a 'constitutionalized' charter, we would have to follow the narrow and risk-filled channels of constitutional amendment.

The dismaying experience following on the Canadian Bill of Rights, the assessment that numerous experts have made of it, and the rigidity of the charter's judicial status as part of a new constitution, make analysis of its contents imperative. Its actual scope, the precision or imprecision of its terms, their restrictive or limiting quality, will have a considerable impact on the work and the decisions of the courts that will have to refer to them, as well as determine the limits of this catalogue of rights and freedoms constitutionally recognized throughout the country.

Considered alone, without reference to the political aspects of the Canadian government's action or the anticipated effects of the new authority of the courts that it would establish, the text of the Canadian Charter of Rights and Freedoms is a document without scope, restrictive and largely deficient in relation to the equivalent documents in democratic societies comparable to our own.

Mr Gordon Fairweather is Chief Commissioner of the Canadian Human Rights Commission, and one of the country's most respected authorities on these questions. Last November, in front of the joint committee, he denounced the federal initiative's complete and unthinking neglect of some very useful data provided by the constitutions of several modern states, the European Charter of Rights, and the Universal Declaration of Human Rights.

In this regard, the report of the joint Senate-House of Commons Committee on the Constitution testifies to the haste and superficiality of the whole initiative. For weeks, parliamentarians of all parties listened to the testimony of dozens of organizations and hundreds of citizens. One might have thought that in these matters the forum presided over by Serge Joyal would have shown some sensitivity to diversity, and to minority and marginal perspectives. One might have thought that this committee would have been sensitive to the comparative dimensions of things, but it was predominantly a publicity exercise. It produced a three-page report, composed essentially of statistical tables smacking of partisan mathematics.

One must regret this loss of resolve, this infatuation with the quantitative and contempt for the qualitative. True, the bosses had given the orders. As with any advertising contract, after a certain date it was time to stop mulling it over—time to prepare the package for Mrs Thatcher.

A charter of rights, they say, is the concrete judicial formulation of the social consensus on the subject of rights. In this case, it was a fictional secondary character in a political novel. From this came the extreme weakness of the first draft and the mediocre quality of the final product. Under the guise of rights, its foremost aim is to impose a political conception of Canada.

Articles 6(2)b and 16 to 24, devoted to mobility of labour, and to linguistic rights both generally and in the schools, are typical of this regrettable initiative. Along the same lines, article 27, which raises to the rank of fundamental rights and freedoms the goals of promoting the maintenance and artificial preservation of Canadians' cultural heritage, borrows an electoral plank from our political parties, and is a political concession to distinct constituencies.

A strange conception of a country: in the balance of collective rights (a notion the federal apologists disparage, moreover, when it comes to Québec), cultural groups carry more real weight in the constitution than Québec does.

In recent weeks, the propaganda to extend the linguistic rights of Canadians and of minorities has become oppressive. At last, they announce, against a rustic back-ground scene, francophones outside of Québec will have the same rights as Québec's anglophones. Even if this vision were widely held, it would still be a dream that is contradicted by the very terms of the charter of rights.

Translating the dream into the cold prose of a legal text (article 20(1) (a) and (b)), the latter subordinates language use in federal offices to the volume of demand or to the office's function. Furthermore, minority groups will have the right to have their children taught in their own language 'where numbers warrant'. The phrase 'provided out of public funds', to quote the charter's jargon, is subject to the same criteria.

For a definition of this restrictive expression, the minister of justice refers us to the interpretations that the courts will eventually make. No doubt the minister is aware that the expression underwent a judicial test last December in Saskatchewan. One will remember that, at the time, they sent the francophones of the little village of Vonda to their school commission without deciding anything. Since the question is a political one, its resolution is a matter of political strength.

Finally, the new constitution imposes the obligations of article 133 on Manitoba and Québec. Only these two provinces, which New Brunswick has voluntarily agreed to join, find themselves forced to accept these nineteenth-century obligations, which are an unequal restriction on Canadian provinces.

The central part of the charter, which defines equality rights and outlines various forms of discrimination, although improved by the amendments of January 1981, reflects a hardening in the initiative. In 1981, one is entitled to demand a more exhaustive examination of the grounds for discrimination. The Québec charter lists five grounds for discrimination that we do not find in the federal text.

Even if the list of sources of discrimination is not exhaustive, surely protection would have been enhanced if the existing grounds had included marital status, political affiliations, language, sexual orientation, and social condition. More-over, the initial proposal should have been broadened to include a clear and unequivocal statement of the fundamental right to equality for women. The final version is basically the same as article 1–b of the Canadian Bill of Rights.

When tested before the courts, this approach provided to be ineffective.

There is a long list of ambiguities, imprecisions, and restrictions that have the potential to undermine the protection of these rights by the courts.

Article 1 speaks of 'such reasonable limits as are generally accepted in a free and democratic society'. The formula remains ambiguous and full of holes. This article conditions the application of the entire charter.

Article 2 enumerates fundamental freedoms in a highly restrictive manner.

Article 7 limits the right to life, liberty, and security to the principles of fundamental justice. This clearly is a serious mistake.

Article 12 depends on improvisation. Punishment must be 'cruel and unusual' in order to justify protection.

One could add to this list. But it is eloquent enough. The text is noteworthy for its ambiguities, its restrictions, and its omissions. The latter, it must be emphasized, define the whole field of rights and freedoms just as much as the restricted areas. One must in particular condemn the absence of any limitation on the exceptional power of the federal government in periods of crisis, and the omission of most economic and social rights.

In view of the preceding, can the federal charter be considered a significant step forward, as genuine progress in the protection of our rights and freedoms?

The political conditions of the current initiative and the paucity of reflection and analysis on the effects of the massive transfer of power from the legislature to the courts aside, the charter's contents themselves do not induce support. On the contrary, they are a trap to be feared, in the political area as much as in the determination and exercise of rights and freedoms.

Finally, for Québec, even from the point of view of maintaining the federal link, recognition of the right to self-determination constitutes a preliminary requirement for the real existence and exercise of rights and freedoms. Clearly we are light-years away from this necessary starting-point. To place this basic requirement in perspective, it is important to remember that the Canadian constitutional charter could serve as the constitutional reference document until well into the second millenium.

Intrinsically, the text of this charter is an expression of values and a carrier of hopes. These are, however, much more an expression of the past than they are a guarantee — firm, generous, and complete — of the rights and freedoms of a healthy federation and of societies resolutely committed, after agreeing freely, to the establishment of strict and binding rules that will assure an always-fragile counterbalance to constraint, violence, manipulation, and discrimination.

Less than two decades from the twenty-first century, the Canadian Charter of Rights does not assure the citizens of this country that from now on they can live secure from all threat to or infringement of their fundamental rights.

Based on political constraint, stripped of any exemplary value, mediocre, and stuffed full of secondary intentions — the most obvious of which is the imposition of a false model of linguistic equality — the Canadian Charter of Rights is a tragic expression of the limits of an abstract vision of the country, and of the repressive, short-sighted attitudes that Pierre Elliott Trudeau, that remarkably gifted and superbly obstinate man, has adopted towards francophone Quebecers. It is a paradox and an historical irony that it was Québec's referendary democracy that gave birth to the weighty initiative in question.

Next Monday, the participants in the constitutional conference will try to resolve the radical incompatibility between the federal system and the plan for rights and freedoms that is being imposed on us. To achieve this task, they will no doubt have to adjust, reduce, and limit the charter of rights: a troublesome operation and, in a sense, an artificial one. It would be better if they deposited this eloquent example of an initiative that betrays the very nature of this country in the archives. Perhaps then genuine negotiations could begin, with fresh teams. The latter would base their work on foundations other than memory or anticipation of failure.

Gordon Robertson, former Clerk of the Privy Council and long-time co-architect, with Pierre Trudeau, of the Canadian government's constitutional policy, recently summed up the question very clearly: 'How can one believe that a constitutional charter will command respect if its very birth is tainted with unconstitutionality? How can it be an effective instrument for the protection of rights if its birth depends on the suppression of constitutional rights recognized since 1867?'

LA PRESSE, MONTRÉAL, NOVEMBER 28, 1981

The charter will not prove to be a miracle cure

Gilbert Lavoie

Canadian citizens who have been sold the idea of repatriating the constitution in order to enshrine a charter of rights in it would be wrong to see this as a miracle cure for every case of discrimination that arises in their everyday life.

What the debates on the subject have neglected to point out is that the federal charter guarantees protection of its citizens' rights against government legislation, but does not apply in those cases of discrimination — infinitely more common — committed by individuals, groups, or corporations. With or without a federal charter, citizens' main recourse against these forms of discrimination will still lie at the level of the provincial charters adopted by the legislature of each province, which maintain respect because of such bodies as the Québec Human Rights Commission. The advantage of these commissions is that they assume the costs of judicial appeals when the offender refuses to make restitution. They also firmly prohibit all forms of discrimination between individuals.

Appeals

At what level should individuals who have been wronged appeal? It all depends on the injustice and, especially, the governmental jurisdiction involved. For example, an individual arrested for an infraction of the Québec highway code (provincial jurisdiction) would take his complaint to the Québec Human Rights Commission under the provincial charter. He could appeal under the federal charter only if the provincial legislation infringed on his constitutional rights, something which would very seldom occur. In the same way, a person arrested for an infraction of the penal code (federal jurisdiction) is in fact protected by the 1960 Canadian Bill of Rights. Once adopted, the charter of rights would provide another avenue of appeal against arbitrary action by the police, but the plaintiff would still have the opportunity to appeal to the Canadian Human

Rights Commission.

Where the new charter does offer an advantage is in connection with those institutions coming under federal jurisdiction, especially in linguistic matters. Various transportation (Air Canada, Via Rail) and communications (Bell Canada, CBC) organizations are good examples. Last winter we saw the directors of Crown corporations tell Parliament that their collective agreements with the unions prevented them from respecting the Official Languages Act. The question was whether the Official Languages Act took precedence over the labour code. This question will no longer arise with the new charter of rights.

The provinces

As far as provincial legislation is concerned, the main weakness of the charter of rights is that several of its articles will be subject to a 'notwithstanding' clause, allowing a legislature to adopt a law which specifies that it applies in spite of the charter. The articles subject to this constraint are the following:
• article 1: fundamental freedoms: freedom of religion, thought, belief, and peaceful assembly;
• articles 7 to 15: legal guarantees: right to life, liberty, and personal security, protection against improper search or seizure, protection against arbitrary detention or imprisonment, right to racial equality, sexual equality, etc. . . .

If we forget the language dispute between Québec and Ottawa, it is the 'notwithstanding' clause itself that creates the most controversy over the charter of rights. In his speech to the Commons on the subject, Justice Minister Jean Chrétien stressed that the clause constitutes a happy compromise between the powers of the courts and parliamentary supremacy. In short, according to him, there is no danger that the charter of rights will suffer the abuses of interpretation experienced in the United States, since the people's elected representatives can still overrule the courts.

Liberal Senator Eugene Forsey sounded another warning this week. The 'notwithstanding' clause negates the very principle of a charter, since it is in crisis situations, when majorities and their elected representatives swiftly agree to override the rights of minorities, that charters become truly essential, he said. The experts are divided on this point. According to Professors Gérard Beaudoin and Walter Tarnopolsky, who recently founded a Human Rights Institute at the University of Ottawa, Members of Parliament will think carefully before using such a tool. They recall that in 1977 the authors of Québec's Bill 1 (now Bill 101) quickly dropped their original plan to put this law beyond the reach of the Québec charter of rights. Despite this, the two acknowledge that the existence of such a clause does trouble them somewhat. In the same way, article 1 of the charter, which subjects basic rights to 'such reasonable limits prescribed by law as can be demonstrably justified in a free and democratic society', worries a number of people. Who will have the responsibility of showing whether a limit is reasonable or not, Prof. Tarnopolsky wonders.

All in all, the charter will not radically change the basic rights already guaranteed by the provincial charters and the 1960 federal law. And in the longer term, there is no reason to believe that it will prevent abuses such as the padlock law used against the Jehovah's Witnesses under the Duplessis regime in Québec. The only hope, as M.P. Céline Hervieux-Payette pointed out this week to *La Presse*, is that the very existence of a charter and the publicity surrounding it will make Canadians more aware of the fact that these rights exist, and of the means available for ensuring that they are respected. That is small consolation for the Japanese-Canadians who were interned and had their property sold by the Crown during the Second World War.

THE GLOBE AND MAIL, DECEMBER 23, 1981

Override: menace to basic rights?

BY LINDA SILVER DRANOFF

Linda Silver Dranoff is a Toronto lawyer, author and commentator on legal subjects.

BASIC RIGHTS and freedoms we take for granted are in jeopardy — fundamental rights such as freedom of assembly, religion, press, the right to liberty and security, equality without discrimination no matter what our color, religion, sex or origin.

The "Section 33 override," which

Canadians are being misled if they think the accord means fundamental rights can't be withdrawn without amending the Constitution.

those who govern us instituted last month, is the absolute power to unilaterally overrule the fundamental freedoms, legal rights and equality rights of every man, woman and child in society. This power is unfettered and unrestrained; use of the power need not be reasonable nor justified, nor must its use be proved appropriate in the context of a free and democratic society.

How much power are we willing to hand over to provincial and federal legislatures?

The Charter of Rights and Freedoms under discussion for the past year contained the following: "(1) The Canadian Charter of Rights and Freedoms guarantees the rights and freedoms as set out in it subject only to such reasonable limits prescribed by law as can be demonstrably justified in a free and democratic society."

Our Government therefore already had given itself the power to overrule by law our rights and freedoms, but only within justifiable limits, only within reason, and only within the context that we would continue to be a free and democratic society.

Since this kind of override clause could be used to justify the enactment of the 1970 War Measures Act, why do provincial and federal governments need the additional unlimited power of Section 33?

There is no limitation in Section 33 on the power of Parliament or a legislature to declare that an act of its legislature or any part of it shall be effective notwithstanding the provisions in Sections 2 and 7 to 15 of the Charter, which relate to the most basic and important fundamental freedoms, legal rights and equality rights taken for granted in Canada.

These include the fundamental freedoms of conscience and religion, thought, belief, opinion and expression, including freedom of the press and other media of communication, freedom of peaceful assembly and freedom of association.

The legal rights which are in jeopardy include the right to life, liberty and security of the person, the right to be justly treated, the right to be secure against unreasonable search or seizure, the right not to be arbitrarily detained or imprisoned, the right to be presumed innocent until proved guilty.

Equality rights are in jeopardy — the right to be equal before and under the law and to have the right to equal protection and equal benefit of the law without discrimination and, in particular, without discrimination based on race, origin, color, religion, sex, age or disability.

The accord that was reached in early November by the premiers and the Prime Minister spoke of an "acceptable consensus" which was to include "the entrenchment of the full Charter of Rights and Freedoms now before Parliament" with a "notwithstanding" clause.

Canadians are being misled if they believe that what the accord represents is "entrenchment," which means that fundamental rights, legal rights and equality rights cannot be withdrawn by any provincial or federal government without an amendment to the Constitution. Entrenchment is an assurance that if an individual's basic rights and freedoms are not recognized or are withdrawn, a case could be brought to court to seek a remedy.

For example, an entrenched guarantee to be secure against unreasonable search or seizure would allow an individual to question the use of the writ of assistance. This is a blank cheque given an RCMP officer to enter a private residence and search for drugs without a search warrant, and new writs have not been issued since 1976, because the McDonald Commission believed they represented unreasonable search and seizure powers. Solicitor-General Robert Kaplan has been quoted widely in the press recently as wanting to start issuing the writs of assistance again.

Without an entrenched charter, the Solicitor-General using the power given him in Section 33 of the Charter of Rights and Freedoms, could pass a law to overrule the Charter right to be secure against unreasonable search or seizure and start issuing the writs of assistance, without demonstrating that it's reasonable to do so within a free and democratic society.

Politicians have told us that if we remain vigilant, there will be little use of the Section 33 override. Vigilance will be possible only with an alternate bureaucracy to examine every act of Parliament or of a legislature. To lobby the Government to change a law is an enormous, expensive and frustrating task.

There is the possibility of abuse with any system, but the legislative override in Section 33 seems more dangerous than a court's power under an entrenched charter. Historically, courts have been better protectors of an individual's fundamental freedoms than legislatures. However, governments with one stroke of the pen can restrict the basic freedoms of all of us. And there is no appeal from an act of a legislature or the federal Parliament with an unlimited override.

With an entrenched charter, courts will be able to protect feedoms if legislators should abuse their power. And there is a right of appeal to a higher court from a judge's decision.

The accord was accepted to get approval for patriating the Constitution. But will it be worth patriating if we diminish basic rights and freedoms in the process? Patriating is only a symbolic gesture, a formality; it will not represent any change in laws that will affect Canadians in any real way. We know we are no longer a colony. The Queen and Governor-General and British Parliament no longer control our country, and Canada's decisions are merely rubber-stamped in England. The resolution that has gone to England confirms that "in the past certain amendments to the Constitution of Canada have been made by the Parliament of the United Kingdom at the request and with the consent of Canada."

No doubt if we were not to bring the Constitution home laws would continue to be passed in Canada and rubber-stamped in England and no one would be the worse for it. We were being pressured to feel a sense of urgency to bring the Constitution home, where no urgency existed. Especially if the price of patriation was a Charter of Rights that will diminish civil liberties, then the price is too high. If the price of getting a Charter of Rights was to include a clause permitting legislators to breach fundamental freedoms, legal rights and equality rights at whim, then the price is much too high.

Canadians have not had sufficient opportunity to understand that the effect of the accord is a diminution of rights and freedoms. We must express this view to the British Parliament, even though we may all be tired of the subject. Our legislators should remember that the text of the resolution, as it was introduced in the House of Commons Nov. 18, said "Canada has requested and consented" to the patriation resolution. How can it be said that Canada has agreed when Canadians have not absorbed the implications for denial of their rights? How can we say Canada agrees when Quebec is against it? The isolation of Quebec in the constitutional accord puts a stab wound into the heart of Canada and is contrary to the basis upon which Canada was formed at the time of Confederation, when every effort was made to satisfy the dual nature of this country and its French and English components.

THE TORONTO STAR, APRIL 19, 1982

New rights charter paves the way for changing way of life

"The difference between today and Friday is that then (basic human rights) could have been taken away from you. Now they cannot."

By David Vienneau Toronto Star

OTTAWA — Now that the Queen has returned to England, you may wonder how Her Majesty's signing of our new Constitution affects your life.

The answer, at least on the surface, is that it doesn't.

The Constitution won't have an immediate impact on you unless you're suspected of committing a crime or you move to Quebec and want your children educated in English.

The first legal challenges to the Constitution Act are expected to result from the legal and minority-language educational rights sections because they guarantee rights Canadian's have never before had.

Critical court role

Even so, it will probably take at least two years before either of these issues comes before the Supreme Court of Canada, which will play a critical role in interpreting the Constitution.

But Justice Minister Jean Chretien—the man largely responsible for Canada's constitutional success — says Canadians should not forget one very important thing:

Up until Saturday, rights they thought they enjoyed, such as freedom of conscience, religion and association, and freedom of the press, were guaranteed only by tradition — not by law.

"When you have rights, you use them," he told The Star

yesterday. "You're not in danger of losing them, as you were before. I don't say there were some governments that had any intention of limiting these freedoms so you might say it's not a problem today.

"But the difference between today and Friday morning is that then (those basic human rights) could have been taken away from you. Now they cannot. You can say it's immaterial because nobody wanted to take these rights away, but governments and moods in the country change.

"That is what we are protecting against.'

The Constitution's Charter of Rights spells out rights citizens have in their dealings with governments at any level. Previously, these rights didn't have constitutional status and could be legally overriden by Parliament or a provincial legislature.

Some of these rights may still be overriden, but legal experts say that is unlikely to happen, except in the rarest of circumstances. They argue it would be politically suicidal for any government to even attempt to override fundamental human rights.

Speedy trial

The charter's legal rights section includes the right to be secure against unreasonable search and seizure, the right to a speedy trial and the right not to be denied bail without a good reason.

Most of the court action resulting from the new Constitution will derive from this section. In fact, some lawyers are expected to make use of the new provisions in trials beginning today. Justice department officials say the clauses aren't intended to be retroactive.

This section will immediately benefit you if you're suspected of breaking the law. The key parts involve search

and seizure and arrest and detention.

Beginning Saturday, police across the country were — for the first time—legally required to read you your rights upon arrest. This includes telling you why you're in custody and informing you of your right to see a lawyer.

"I expect to see a lot of litigation in both these areas," says Marc Gold, an Osgoode Hall law professor. "I think we'll see a lot of cases challenging the admissibility of evidence when, in some sense or other, people feel their rights have been violated.

"In addition, a lot of people will claim they weren't informed of their rights. Equally, we'll see challenges from people who wanted to retain counsel but couldn't afford it."

A senior official in the justice department told The Star the search and seizure provision could be the most "contentious" part of the charter because now virtually any evidence obtained by police is admissible in court.

Hence, police will have to establish reasonable grounds for a search warrant, making it more difficult to use search warrants for "fishing expeditions."

Bathhouse raid

Some legal experts say the raid last year by Metro police on a Toronto bathhouse might well have been ruled unreasonable by the courts because of the force used.

If you feel your rights or freedoms have been infringed upon or denied, the charter says you may apply to a court for a remedy. This compensation clause is also new in Canadian law.

It means, for example, that a police officer who contravenes an accused person's constitutional right against unreasonable search or seizure may be ordered in a civil court

proceeding to pay damages as a remedy to the applicant.

Significant change

The charter also contains an"exclusionary rule," which means that for the first time courts may exclude illegally obtained evidence if it would bring the administration of justice into disrepute.

"This is a significant change because previously a court didn't have the power to exclude evidence, even if it had been illegally obtained," says Bill Black, a law professor at the University of British Columbia.

The clause is discretionary because the court has the power to accept evidence even though some people might consider it tainted.

But while the legal rights sections will eventually dominate the Supreme Court's agenda, Chretien says, the first test of the Constitution will likely arise from Quebec's language law.

Quebec's controversial Bill 101 determines who may attend an English school in Quebec. It restricts access to English-language schools to children whose parents received their primary education in Quebec's English system.

As a result, English-speaking parents moving to Quebec from Toronto don't have the right to send their children to English schools.

The charter's minority-language educational rights clause says that any child with a parent educated in English anywhere in Canada may receive an English education in the province.

Chretien predicts that the first case the Supreme Court will hear resulting from the new charter will involve the Quebec government's refusal to admit to an English school children of an English-speaking couple that has just moved to Quebec.

THE GLOBE AND MAIL, JANUARY 7, 1983

Judges reject liberal views in Charter cases

By JEFF SALLOT
Globe and Mail Reporter

OTTAWA — The new Charter of Rights and Freedoms is receiving a cautious welcome in the courtrooms of Canada.

A survey of cases from across the country suggests that, with some notable exceptions, lower court judges are declining the invitations of defence lawyers to lavish liberal interpretations on the Constitution's nine-month-old Charter or to declare portions of provincial and federal statutes unreasonable infringements of citizens' rights.

The Supreme Court of Canada has yet to pronounce on the Charter's most important qualifying phrase — reasonable limits. The first section of the Charter says that the new constitutional guarantees of rights and freedoms are "subject only to such reasonable limits prescribed by law as can be demonstrably justified in a free and democratic society."

Conservatism in lower courts

Legal observers believe it will take a series of Supreme Court decisions in the months and years ahead to establish rules and tests for determining whether the limits the lawmakers set on civil rights and liberties are reasonable.

Typical of the conservatism in the lower courts is a decision last September by Mr. Justice Thomas Zuber of the Ontario Court of Appeal. He ruled that the federal Criminal Code's requirement for an impaired driving suspect to submit to a breath analysis test was not a violation of the Charter's guarantee that an individual won't be required to give evidence against himself in court.

Judge Zuber took a narrow view, ruling that "the Charter does not confer a broad privilege against self-incrimination."

As a caution to exuberant defence lawyers, Judge Zuber said that the proclamation of the Charter by the Queen last April has produced some "bizarre and colorful arguments." In his view, however, "the Charter does not intend a transformation of our legal system or the paralysis of law enforcement. Extravagant interpretations can only trivialize and diminish respect for the Charter."

Judge Zuber's caution was quoted a month later by Mr. Justice Jean-Guy Boilard of the Quebec Superior Court. Judge Boilard turned down a request to declare unconstitutional portions of the Federal Income Tax Act that require taxpayers to submit financial records demanded by the Department of National Revenue.

The appellant, Albert Rolbin of Montreal, tried to argue that the demand was tantamount to an unreasonable search and thus a violation of the Charter.

Judge Boilard, however, interpreted the Charter literally. "A search is a search and a demand for information is a demand for information. To me the distinction is very clear."

In another of the initial Charter cases, Mr. Justice Edward Eberle of the Ontario Supreme Court said last May: "It cannot be thought that the intent of the provisions of the Charter that are in issue . . . is to undermine and bring to the ground the whole framework of laws and the legal system of the country at the stroke of a pen, even if it be a royal pen."

Judge Eberle ruled that the Charter could not be applied retroactively to aid a woman who claimed her rights were violated.

Karen Potma's lawyer argued that she had been denied crucial evidence from police that might establish her innocence in an impaired driving case. She wanted an ampoule that was used when she gave a breath analysis sample, but police said it had been discarded.

Charter victory shortlived

Although limited in their application to specific circumstances, a few cases in British Columbia have given defence lawyers reason to hope that some provisions of the Charter will protect clients who were charged with offences that allegedly occurred before the Charter was proclaimed.

In Ontario, there was a short-lived Charter victory in a lower court for a Chatham man facing a drug charge. Patrick Shea was charged with possession of cannabis for the purposes of trafficking. Police found the suspected drug in his apartment by accident. They were there with the landlord who wanted police assistance to enter the empty apartment in order to repair a leaking pipe.

An officer spotted the suspected drug and police later charged Mr. Shea. At the preliminary hearing, Provincial Court Judge C. E. Perkins ruled that the evidence was inadmissible because it had not been seized under the powers of a search warrant, and to allow its introduction would bring the administration of justice into disrepute.

Judge Perkins sidestepped the federal Crown prosecutor's argument that the Charter did not apply retroactively to the time of the seizure. The judge said that the Charter "is in effect today and it is today that the issue of admissibility of this evidence is before the court."

The federal Government appealed the decision and lost on an unrelated technicality. Mr. Shea, however, will have to make his Charter of Rights argument all over again at a trial next month. Federal prosecutors changed tactics and are now prosecuting Mr. Shea under what's called a preferred indictment. The manoeuvre skips the preliminary hearing stage and takes the case directly to trial.

In a case before the Federal Court last May, Mr. Justice Patrick Mahoney found fault with the weak evidence filed on behalf of a convicted criminal fighting deportation to his native Guyana. "If the Charter is to be respected, an alleged denial or infringement of the rights and freedoms guaranteed by it must be regarded as a serious charge and the court must insist that it be properly proved," Judge Mahoney said.

The man, who had lived in Canada most of his life, tried in vain to prove that deportation to Guyana was cruel and unusual punishment — prohibited under the Charter — because social and economic conditions in his native country were far inferior to those in Canada. Judge Mahoney ruled that deportation isn't punishment at all and the "reasonableness of the right of a free and democratic society to deport alien criminals is self-evident and, therefore, demonstrably justified."

Wheels of justice threatened

In a rape case in Sorel, Que. last year, Sessions Court Judge Paul Belanger said that it was reasonable to exclude the public from the courtroom during the testimony of the alleged victim, a 14-year-old girl, despite the Charter's guarantee to the accused of a "public hearing."

In a B.C. drug importing case, Mr. Justice John Bouck of the B.C. Supreme Court ruled last July that there was nothing unreasonable in Parliament setting a minimum seven-year sentence for the offence. He said that although one can argue the minimum sentence is arbitrary, "the Charter does not declare that arbitrary minimum sentences are contrary to the law of Canada."

In one of the most dramatic, and unexpected, developments since the Charter's proclamation, three judges of the Ontario Provincial Court have disqualified themselves from hearing criminal cases because the Charter guarantees an accused an impartial tribunal. The judges believe that they cannot guarantee impartiality, or the appearance of impartiality, when the same provincial Government that is prosecuting the cases sets the salaries, pensions and working conditions for the Provincial Court judiciary.

If the rulings are upheld by an appeal court, the wheels of justice in Ontario could come to a grinding halt.

However, in another case touching on some of the same legal issues, Mr. Justice Frank Callaghan of the Ontario Supreme Court ruled that a distinction could be made between provincial prosecutors and the provincial Government that administers the courts.

Judge Callaghan refused to throw out a case against a man who had been facing a charge for more than a year because of overcrowded courts. The Charter guarantees trial within a "reasonable time." The judge said the delays were the responsibility of the provincial Government, not the prosecution.

In a case last June in Thunder Bay, Ont., District Court Judge Stanley Kurisko interpreted the Charter as nullifying a section of the Narcotic Control Act dealing with drug trafficking.

The accused, Malcolm Hay, was caught in possession of six small bags of marijuana. The act says that if a court finds the accused in unlawful possession of the narcotic, it is up to him to prove he wasn't in possession for the purposes of trafficking, which is a more serious offence than simple possession.

Judge Kurisko ruled that this "reverse onus" provision of the act violated the Charter's guarantee that an accused is "to be presumed innocent until proven guilty."

Discussion Questions

1. How does the Constitution Act fit into the history of constitutional reform over the past few decades?
2. What factors have made reform imperative? Where have the demands for reform come from?
3. Does the Constitution Act disrupt the constitutional equilibrium between French- and English-speaking Canadians? Does it not violate certain historical understandings upon which the nation is based?
4. Is there a continuing momentum towards further constitutional reform? If so, in what areas is reform likely to be tried? Why do many suggested reforms concentrate on central institutions such as the Senate and the Supreme Court?
5. Will the new Charter contribute significantly to the protection of civil liberties in Canada? Are individual liberties and collective rights adequately protected? What are the advantages of their entrenchment?
6. Rights are often categorized as either political, legal, linguistic, egalitarian, or economic. Which of these categories deserve enhanced protection? What is the best strategy to protect each particular one?

Suggested Readings

Stanley M. Beck and Ivan Bernier, eds. *Canada and the New Constitution: The Unfinished Agenda.* Montreal: Institute for Research on Public Policy, 1983, two volumes.

Robert Sheppard and Michael Valpy. *The National Deal: The Fight for a Canadian Constitution.* Toronto: Fleet, 1982.

Paul W. Fox, ed. *Politics: Canada*, fifth edition. Toronto: McGraw-Hill Ryerson, 1982, 47–84.

Edward McWhinney. *Canada and the Constitution 1979–1982.* Toronto: University of Toronto Press, 1982.

Peter Russell. 'The Effect of a Charter of Rights on the Policy-Making Role of Canadian Courts', in *Canadian Public Administration*, vol. 25, no. 1, Spring 1982, 1–33.

W.R. Lederman. *Continuing Canadian Constitutional Dilemmas: Essays on the Constitutional History, Public Law and Federal System of Canada.* Toronto: Butterworths, 1981.

Thomas R. Berger. *Fragile Freedoms: Human Rights and Dissent in Canada.* Toronto: Clarke Irwin, 1981.

Donald V. Smiley. *The Canadian Charter of Rights and Freedoms.* Toronto: Ontario Economic Council, 1981.

Donald V. Smiley. *Canada in Question: Federalism in the Eighties*, third edition. Toronto: McGraw-Hill Ryerson, 1980.

Edward McWhinney. *Quebec and the Constitution 1960–1978.* Toronto: University of Toronto Press, 1979.

R. MacDonald and J. Humphreys, eds. *The Practice of Freedom.* Toronto: Butterworths, 1979.

3. Political Structures

a. Political Parties

A prominent political structure that did not exist at the time of Confederation, and is not mentioned in the British North America Act, is the political party. Parties are easier to identify than they are to define. The Elections Act, adopted in 1974, is one of the few official documents that provide anything resembling a definition of a political party. It refers to a registered party as a body that has either twelve seats in the House of Commons or candidates nominated in at least fifty constituencies. Political scientists, for their part, prefer a wider definition encompassing those groups organized to win elections, to operate the machinery of government, and to determine public policy. In this sense Canada has had a large number of political parties, even though only three or four are represented in the House of Commons at any one time.

Coverage of political parties in Canada is generally quite extensive and of high quality. Much information about party organization, strategy, policy positions, and effectiveness with voters can be gleaned from the press, although it is often subsumed in reports on elections. Of course, press attention towards all parties fluctuates according to the election cycle. On the negative side, reporters rarely provide any overall sense of the party system. The NDP, for instance, is usually treated as an equal competitor with the two major parties in the race to form the federal government, while its special role as the articulator of labour-union (and working-class) interest is neglected. Similarly, protest movements in the guise of political parties (for example, Western separatist movements) gain greater press coverage than their strength would justify, and the underlying causes of alienation are often overlooked. Journalists also have difficulties in interpreting the election mandates of the various parties: subsequent scholarly research often shows that the reasons they gave for election results were incorrect.

The first article in this section is the text of a speech by political scientist Blair Williams, a former national director of the Liberal party. Reviewing the changing status of political parties in recent years, he lists several factors that he believes have contributed to their decline: the parties' growing regionalization, the enlarged support apparatus for the parliamentary caucuses, the effects of technological change, and the rise of the bureaucratic state. He could easily have included a number of other causes: for instance, the rise of electronic journalism and investigative reporting, increased reliance on federal–provincial conferences to develop policies, the expansion of interest-group activities, and the long-standing dominance at the federal level of the Liberal party. Williams also neglects to consider the control of the party apparatus that party leaders have increasingly come to exert.

The next three articles assess the status of the three major parties between elections. John Gray's article on the Liberal party confirms the pivotal role played by the party leader, especially while in office. He shows that the party is rarely consulted for policy advice and that the leader concentrates instead on appealing to a wider public for support of his initiatives. The absence of internal Liberal party debates over leadership and policy questions contrasts sharply with the situation in the Conservative party. Gray's second piece, on Joe Clark's leadership prior to the review that prompted him to call a convention, describes a party consumed by the leadership question at the expense of debates on policy and ideas. (Only time will tell whether his successor, Brian Mulroney, will fare better.) The electoral difficulties of the NDP, outlined by Bob Hepburn, are especially surprising given the popular assumption that that party benefits during times of economic downturn. Clearly, the New Democrats face a public perception that they have little real chance of forming a government.

The remaining articles deal with party financing. John Fraser provides an excellent history of past practices, detailing the corruption and influence-peddling that were largely the result of heavy reliance on corporate contributions. The reforms instituted in 1974 introduced a new financing regime that has increased public confidence. In the trio of pieces at the end of this section, John Gray discusses the intentions of the reform legislation and the extent of its success. Although he does not deal with the shortcomings in the legislation—expenditure limits not adjusted for inflation, a relatively low level of costs paid from the public treasury, and disclosure provisions that discourage corporate contributions—he does illustrate the extent to which the fund-raising function has been decentralized. In the end, however, he acknowledges the overall soundness of the legislation.

THE GLOBE AND MAIL, JULY 4, 1980

The decline of political parties

BY BLAIR WILLIAMS

The following is excerpted from an address to the Liberal Party of Alberta. Mr. Williams, a professor of political science at Concordia University, was national director of the Liberal Party of Canada, 1973-75.

PARTIES IN Canada have suffered a loss of role. They have very little raison d'etre beyond the organization of periodic elections by which our legislators are chosen.

As policy-making institutions, our parties are almost certainly less effective and less important than they were 15 or 20 years ago. Even though full-scale policy conventions are relatively recent phenomena and are now a part of party constitutions, we should not be misled into believing that over the past decade parties have gained ground in terms of their policy significance.

For years freshman political science students were told that one of the major roles of political parties was to serve as national integrators — to be the vehicle of national reconciliation between regions, ethnic groups, social classes and so on. Recent writing has shown us, however, that if at any time this was the case, it certainly is no longer. Today, parties pursue regional strategies and reap the benefits that come from massive support in one region for one party and another region for a different party. Canadians simply do not look to political parties as the major means by which their interest can be accommodated and molded into a coherent national interest.

Further evidence of the decline in the importance of parties can be found in the extent to which the formal party apparatus has given ground to the Ottawa-based parliamentary apparatus. Many of the functions which were historically, and quite properly, performed by the elected executive and the national office of the Liberal Party are now performed by individuals hired to work on the Hill as assistants to the Prime Minister, ministers, members of Parliament and so on.

The result is that our party has dissolved into an election-oriented, leader-dominated, media-manipulated, marketing-machine. The role of the party today is to get organized every two or four years in order to return a government to power. The role of party militants is to supply applause for party leaders, to serve as background for the 11 o'clock television news.

This state of affairs is not the product of a malicious plot, or the result of the covert activities of a few (although there are a few who have worked diligently to assist this process). It is as much as anything else the product of the technological and communication revolution that we have undergone in recent decades. Like other institutions in our society, political parties have paid a price for the dominant role that television has come to play in our politics. We live in a world of image politics — long on style and short on substance — partly because we live in a world of instantaneous communications. We live in the world of the ever-present tube.

The second reality, which we must be aware of, is the rise of the bureaucratic state. We live in an era of big governments and massive government involvement in nearly all aspects of our lives.

The rise of the bureaucratic state in modern times has, among other things, resulted in the full flowering of political elitism. Nearly all the decisions taken on behalf of the community — on behalf of you and me as citizens — are taken by less than 5 per cent of the population interacting at the top. We have become an elite-dominated society, inasmuch as we are not really involved in any ongoing way in the most crucial decisions that affect our lives.

My first suggestion is that the party must become a focal point for the discussion of public affairs and for the involvement of citizens in the political process. The party must become a counterbalance to the bureaucratic state. In performing this role, it is important that the party become much more of a communicator and an educator with respect to public issues. By its very nature, the bureaucracy will tend not to communicate and not to educate.

What I am saying here, in short, is that the party has a vital role to play in the development of an ever more enlightened public.

Also, it seems to me that the time is right for the party to become a much more effective vehicle for the development and pursuit of good ideas. The fresh ideas that will guide public affairs in the 1980s will either come from the bureaucracy or from a self-asserting volunteer organization (such as the party). If we follow the pattern of the past two decades, these ideas will originate in the bureaucracy and they will be sprung on both the party and the people.

My second suggestion is that the party must become the leading edge or the vanguard of the age of voluntarism. The party should become the champion of public involvement. It should become a party that is prepared to move Canadians away from elitism and more in a direction of popular democracy. Those of us who are westerners by birth, or by adoption, should take the lead in this regard and demand what amounts to a populist revolution in the Liberal Party. I am more convinced than ever that the future — that the spirit of the 1980s — lies in the direction of populism and popular involvement in public affairs. As part of this process Liberals must learn to accept more dissent, more genuine debate within our camp. We must learn to defer less to our leaders, to expect less conformity from our colleagues and make the party into more of a realistic forum for the head-to-head debate of contentious public issues.

THE GLOBE AND MAIL, NOVEMBER 22, 1982

Grit policy awaits PM's parting

BY JOHN GRAY

Mr. Gray is head of the Ottawa bureau of The Globe and Mail.

OTTAWA

ALL THINGS considered, the Liberal party is not as dyspeptic today as might be expected. But there is about the Liberals an uneasiness which will disappear only with Prime Minister Pierre Trudeau.

The Gallup poll has induced a certain queasiness, to be sure, but they do not regard that as fatal. They nourish the conviction that their present indisposition will be cured with time and a change of leadership.

But their immediate problem is a certain collective aimlessness which has seemed to numb the senses of the Liberal Government for the past year, just as it numbed the senses of the Liberal convention delegates earlier this month.

For those who have talked with Liberals and watched them and their Government in action in recent months, the inescapable impression is that they do not really know where to go, and they do not know why.

Just one year ago the Trudeau Government won the agreement of the provinces and Parliament to a new constitution. That may eventually be seen as the triumph of the Trudeau years, but the achievement of that goal left the Liberals without an apparent focus for the future.

Since he took over the party in 1968, the direction of the Liberal party has been shaped almost exclusively by Mr. Trudeau. He made the Liberals the party of national unity, and from that flowed everything from bilingualism to the new constitution.

The only significant variation from that direction came during and after the 1980 federal election when the Liberals slipped into a new mold of nationalism. Whether this was a matter of conviction or convenience is irrelevant; for themselves and for others, the Liberal party acquired a new inspiration.

They would strengthen the Foreign Investment Review Agency; their new heroes were Herb Gray and, improbably, Marc Lalonde; they talked tough with the Americans; their miracle was the National Energy Program, and the ultimate Liberal cachet was a Petro-Canada credit card.

Presence of Trudeau continues to dominate Liberals' approach to new policies, as it has since he took command of the party in 1968 right up to convention in Hull this month.

The progress of that initiative in the intervening months has now been well documented. At the cost of a few modifications they managed to hold the National Energy Program, but they promised the Americans there would be no more; with calculated public eclat they trashed their promise to strengthen the Foreign Investment Review Agency.

Not surprisingly, when the Liberals got down to the national questions at their policy conference this month, they were splendidly schizophrenic. They voted solidly for increased economic independence and less foreign capital, and then they voted with equal determination to make foreign investors more welcome.

They show no such confusion on national unity. If foreign investment is a relatively new and uncertain concern, national unity has been at the very heart of the Liberal Government since Mr. Trudeau became Prime Minister. So on that there is no mistake; but there is no evidence of much passion.

The lack of passion is not from lack of trying. With more than a thousand Liberals as a captive audience, Mr. Trudeau did his best to be the Ottawa tough guy who was going out to beat up the provincial premiers if they were not good Canadians. There was no sign of ecstasy.

The Liberals are not ready to desert their commitment to national unity and the kind of strong central government which animates Mr. Trudeau. But they have the constitution, they have bilingualism, they won the Quebec referendum. Until a new crisis erupts or is provoked, unity is no longer the stuff of a crusade.

In the months since the constitution was approved the Liberals have, of course, embarked on new programs, but there is nothing which would suggest a new policy.

The six-and-five restraint program provided a short fillip, as did Finance Minister Marc Lalonde's more recent economic statement. They both came at a time when Liberal loyalists badly needed some reassurance that their Government in Ottawa was actually alive, and both initiatives provided that reassurance.

However, a twitch of life has not satisfied those who believe the party needs a genuinely new policy innovation. The Liberal equivalent of the New Jerusalem is not going to be constructed from patchwork programs and retreats from past mistakes.

Similarly the debate within the Cabinet about universality for social programs was hardly innovative. It reassured those whose commitment to the party is to small-l liberalism, but it gave no evidence of fresh thinking except about the necessity not to upset the voters.

Such thinking, of course, cannot be totally dismissed. More than other parties, the Liberals have a sure instinct for power. That instinct has been for them indispensable. But they have been a happier and more successful party when their instinct for power was allied with a sense of their own direction.

At the moment the Liberals are flailing on both counts. The controversial youth resolution condemning non-elected advisers and manipulative politics was, more than anything, a discreet ritual to tell Pierre Trudeau that they expect him to leave — not out of disloyalty, but out of realism.

Whether or not Mr. Trudeau shares their view is another matter, but the Liberals now seem to assume his departure is only a matter of time — after the Conservatives re-affirm Joe Clark as their leader, after the economy turns around, or after some other magical turning point within the next year.

From that change all else will flow. Until Pierre Trudeau takes his leave the party will simply mark time. Given the way such things happen with the Liberals, there will be no new policy determined until there is a new leader to make that determination.

So, for the moment, the Liberals are waiting, a bit uneasily, to see what kind of a party they want to be.

THE GLOBE AND MAIL, JANUARY 22, 1983

Determined to keep his job

Joe Clark: Tory with true grit

By JOHN GRAY
Globe and Mail Reporter

OTTAWA — When the members of the Conservative Party decided reluctantly seven years ago to make Joe Clark their leader, they were not sure what they were getting for their votes.

Their judgments varied. Most said he was bright and decent, if not inspiring. Some called him a Red Tory, others thought him quite conservative, newspapers called him Joe Who, and a caucus colleague called him a smart-ass kid.

Oddly they all missed the characteristic that has endured beyond all others. The man is stubborn. In his determination to hold his job as leader of the Conservatives, he has been as tenacious as a barnacle.

Others would have thrown up their hands in despair. From his first day on the job he has had to cope with those who were supposed to be supporters but who were sullen, resentful or rebellious. His solution was to endure.

Few leaders have had to suffer the public ridicule that has been Mr. Clark's daily lot. He was mocked for the way he walked and talked, the way he moved his hands, the shape of his hands, his chipmunk cheeks, his $200 haircuts.

Even when the Conservatives were up in the polls, as they are now, his critics gave him few marks for either his dignity or his competence in bringing any kind of cohesion to a party whose disunity seemed almost neurotic.

Joe Who became The Wimp, and when the Liberals wanted to sum up their scorn in the last election campaign they did it by talking about the Joe Clark Conservatives this, the Joe Clark Conservatives that. That said it all.

The scorn has come not only from the Liberals. Listen to Tory strategist Dalton Camp: "When Joe Clark comes into a room, Conservatives can't make up their minds whether to stand up or to send him out for a cup of coffee."

During that last campaign, when it was clear that Mr. Clark's brief government was sputtering to extinction, the Conservative Leader confessed during a television interview that he was frustrated by the voters' perception of him.

"I'm not sure that they like me personally. . . . I'd like to be liked, but it's not the sort of thing I lose sleep over."

In fact, Mr. Clark may be losing a little sleep these days. His supporters acknowledge that he is apprehensive

He has had to survive during a time when leadership was defined by Pierre Trudeau

about next week's national convention of the party in Winnipeg, where once more his leadership will be judged by secret ballot.

Over the Christmas break he went south for some sun, but he looks weary and strained, not like a man who is rested and relaxed after three weeks' holiday. In a way that he was not before the last leadership vote in 1981, he is uneasy.

But he remains as stubborn as ever in his desire to keep his job as leader of the party. You do not put up with what Mr. Clark has been through in the three years since the defeat of his government just to give up.

The surprise is that everyone remains so curiously surprised by just how stubborn Mr. Clark is. In fact, the stubbornness has been the constant of his life since he decided at 16

or 17 that he wanted to be prime minister.

It is not unusual that, years later, people remember vividly the fiery ambition of the school friend who has risen to great heights. That is in the nature of friendship. In the case of Mr. Clark, the evidence is more than just recollection.

The school friends all agree: He was skinny and awkward — always the last to be picked for a baseball team, as he admits — and alarmingly serious and increasingly informed about politics as he grew up in the Alberta town of High River.

The Parliamentary Guide lists the occupation of the 43-year-old Tory chief as "journalist," but that is a bit fanciful. He spent several summers working for newspapers, and then a full year, but that was two decades ago; since then he has been training to be prime minister.

The route was clear and relentless. Politics became his whole life, as he progressed from student leader through the ranks as special assistant, organizer, candidate, leadership organizer, special assistant, MP. When he ran for the national party leadership in 1976, everyone assumed that it was a trial run, that he was really running for the next time. That was not the last time they underrated him, failing to notice that stubborn streak.

Nobody, least of all Mr. Clark, would pretend that the intervening years have been easy. If he was not stomaching the public's perception of him, he was trying constantly to restrain the party, especially the parliamentary caucus.

It began with Claude Wagner and Jack Horner and it has continued through Elmer MacKay and Otto Jelinek and John Crosbie and David Crombie and the 38 other MPs who signed — but did not send — letters demanding his resignation.

On policy, he has been a total pragmatist, his cloth cut to suit either the perceived mood of the electorate or, perhaps more often, the fractious mood of his caucus colleagues.

The perfect example was the Conservative response to the Trudeau constitution package in the fall of 1980. The response was a reflection not of what the Tory MPs believed — because there was no agreement on that — but of the fact that the caucus would unite only in its opposition to Pierre Trudeau.

Such an escape from hard choice is not apparently offensive to Mr. Clark. Unlike most Conservatives, he is a man of little ideology and no passions. For him, being a Conservative is mainly being an alternative to the Liberals.

Personally, he has had to survive in an age when the understanding of leadership has been defined by Pierre Trudeau. There is no whisper of the new Athens about a man who likes his filet mignon well done, with fries and Coke.

For those without charisma, there is no alternative but to make a virtue in being ordinary. As Mr. Clark explained, "the age for seeking Messiahs is over."

Being ordinary turned out to be not as much of a virtue as Mr. Clark and the Conservatives might have hoped. After the Tories won the 1979 elec-

tion, the party's polling expert, Allan Gregg, went to the heart of it:

"The typical Canadian voter did not particularly dislike Clark (although over-all reaction to him was generally unfavorable), or disapprove of his performance as leader of the Opposition.

"In fact, the average, non-Liberal voter found very little risk with Clark. Rather, voters could simply not envision Clark as the prime minister. . . .

"He suffered primarily from being perceived as unqualified to assume the senior office of government, as uninformed and lacking strength. In fact, it may not be an exaggeration to suggest that a national leader has rarely, if ever, assumed office with lower expectations concerning his ability to govern."

In a sense, Allan Gregg identified the curse that has stayed with Mr. Clark like the Ancient Mariner's albatross. Conservatives fear that non-Conservatives will not vote for a party led by Joe Clark.

They point to the party's failure to win a majority in the Commons in 1979, the failure to retain power in 1980. Even MPs say publicly: Sure, but if there's a 15-point lead in the Gallup poll with Joe Clark now, think how high it would be without him.

They respect Mr. Clark, even admire him, and they say his government was not great but was certainly

better than Pierre Trudeau's has been in the past three years. But, they say, their neighbors won't vote for him; he's a liability.

The doubters tried two years ago to get rid of him, and they surprised themselves and devastated Mr. Clark by getting a third of the delegates to vote for a leadership convention. Mr. Clark decided the problem was not him but the party, and he stayed on.

The critics went underground for a while, but they had surfaced again within a few months. He faced them down a year ago, and they agreed to be quiet in the interests of the party. But then they started their letter-writing campaign.

And every time Mr. Clark appealed for unity, it was a reminder of the disunity. He was trapped in the dilemma best described by John Diefenbaker: "No leader can lead when he has to turn to see who is trying to trip him from behind."

The argument is circular and endless. The Clark side says the people will never elect a Conservative government if the Conservatives are always disunited and fractious. The anti-Clark side says party unity alone will do no good because the people will never elect Joe Clark, united or not.

And so it goes. With his political life in the balance, Joe Clark holds on, stubbornly.

THE TORONTO STAR, DECEMBER 18, 1982

NDP running hard just to stay even

Its support is ailing badly and the backroom boys can't find a cure

By Bob Hepburn Toronto Star

DARTMOUTH, N.S. — Like nervous, teenage wallflowers at their first high-school dance, they sit stiffly in chairs shoved up against the walls of the small meeting room. Dressed in their Sunday best, these earnest, stern-looking

young couples have braved a day-long blizzard that has handcuffed traffic throughout Nova Scotia to catch a glimpse of Ed Broadbent.

As he works the crowd of 75 loyal New Democrats, Broadbent stops to chat briefly with the wallflowers. Too timid even to stand, they tell him from

their seats how thrilled they are he drove through frightening whiteouts on the TransCanada Highway to see them.

His well-worked speech doesn't disappoint them either. It's a carefully crafted, memorized pitch designed to touch the right emotional chords: Jobs, more help for the fisheries and, for good measure, a little Trudeau and Clark bashing.

His best joke: The only difference between Pierre Trudeau and Joe Clark is it takes Joe less time to say nothing on television.

But despite the frivolity and Christmas cheer of this meeting in the bowels of a hockey arena, these are disappointing times for Ed Broadbent, the New Democratic Party and the loyal young couples and union activists who comprise the backbone of the party.

'In a crisis, people don't want to gamble . . . and the NDP is considered a risk'

Simply put, the NDP is in deep trouble.

It is losing—not gaining—support among voters and faces the distinct possibility its ranks in the House of Commons will be shattered in the next general election, expected in 1984.

"We've suffered a lot of bruises this year," one senior NDP official said this week. "Everybody is weak."

The signs are everywhere. The Gallup Poll indicates the party has plunged in popular support from 26 per cent in March to 20 per cent last month—exactly where it stood in the 1980 election.

In the October federal by-elections in Ontario, they finished third in Timiskaming, a riding they once virtually owned; in Leeds-Grenville a fringe party, the right-wing Libertarians, gathered more votes. Provincially, the NDP lost in Saskatchewan and, despite an extensive campaign, won just two seats in Alberta — and those by a handful of votes.

Mix in the lingering aftertaste of internal feuds, notably over the NDP's constitutional stand, which have eased but not disappeared.

What's even more worrisome for these NDP faithful in Dartmouth, as well as across Canada, is that they really don't know why they have failed miserably to capitalize on the anti-Trudeau sentiment sweeping the country.

Just as troublesome is the fact that

NDP insiders and strategists appear confused and baffled on just how to turn their sagging fortunes around in time to save their necks.

The result is a federal caucus that is flat, lifeless, grumbling in utter frustration among themselves, struggling to find an issue that will capture the imagination and the headlines.

For the rank-and-file NDP, the doorknockers, the envelope stuffers, the failure to gather support is just as frustrating. It's even disheartening to those die-hard ideologists, the ones who sell bran muffins and cookies at political meetings while handing out leaflets urging people to ban the Bomb, save the environment and baby seals, fight for abortions on demand.

Just once, they would like to talk about victory rather than seek solace in the knowledge they fought the good fight.

Broadbent, who has led the NDP through two general elections, also is in a little trouble. Although there is no question of his being seriously challenged for the leadership, he has detractors within the federal caucus from western Canada who charge the Oshawa MP pays too much attention to eastern issues.

And Broadbent still has fences to mend with the Saskatchewan NDP wing, some of whom are still resentful for his quick acceptance of Trudeau's constitutional package.

In personal interviews with The Star over the last two weeks, NDP strategists from British Columbia to Nova Scotia admit they are confused by what is happening to their party — and just as confused over what to do about it.

"We must face realities," Broadbent said, trying to find the right words to describe what is happening. "The get-Trudeau-out vote is going to the Tories."

At 35,000 feet, eating yet another Air Canada scrambled-egg breakfast as the jet slips from Toronto to Halifax last Sunday morning, Broadbent is surprisingly candid.

Voters are frightened, he says, fearful they will lose their jobs, their homes, their children's future. When they are scared, voters fear a massive change in their life. Thus, they will turn against the Liberals, but head straight for the Conservatives rather

than the NDP because their economic policies aren't that much different from the Liberals.

Gerry Caplan, NDP national secretary agrees. In tough times, people the world over seem to revert to parties they know, often conservative ones, rather than something untried such as the NDP.

"In a crisis, people don't want to gamble, and in most parts of Canada the NDP is considered a risk," he said.

Caplan also believes the Conservatives are exploiting the growing right-wing mood among voters, citing most Tories' anti-abortion and pro-hanging stances. And Broadbent questions whether the NDP has succeeded in explaining its programs to voters.

Or, more ominous, whether the message is getting through but is being rejected.

In addition, Broadbent doubts the party's preoccupation with jobs and nuclear disarmament, the top two public issues of the day, can be translated into votes on election day.

Several months ago, the federal Conservatives switched its attack in the House of Commons from the esoteric arguments over the size of the deficit to the more personal issue of jobs. Immediately, they cut the NDP off from being seen as the only opposition party that cared about unemployment.

'We must face realities, the Trudeau-out vote is going to the Tories'

"Voters may not see any clear difference between the priorities of the opposition parties," Broadbent said. "We're both talking about jobs."

At the same time, the NDP is fighting what party leaders call a "smear campaign" by the Conservatives to paint the NDP as being partners with the unpopular Liberals. It's a campaign that is working quite well in the West, where the NDP is the second party, far ahead of the faltering Liberals.

Only now has Broadbent and the NDP caucus launched an all-out attack on the Conservatives. Broadbent now spends more time in his speeches criticizing Joe Clark than he does Trudeau.

Pointedly, he claims the Tories have sided with the Liberals on every major economic issue, such as higher energy prices, since the 1980 election. In the past two years, the Grits and Tories voted together 70 times, he says.

Broadbent and Ontario NDP Leader Bob Rae believe the NDP needs an issue, not policies, to twist the party's fate around. Something like Petro-Canada or the 18-cent gasoline tax or the Israeli embassy location.

All were major issues in the 1980 election. All sprung more or less from Conservative actions, rather than long-held policies.

In an effort to tap this growing conservative mood sweeping Canada, Broadbent has gingerly tiptoed traditional NDP policy to the right. "There can be no increase in the federal deficit at this point," he tells a television audience. Several days later he talks about possible tax increases for certain income groups.

Both upset some hard-line party faithful. Broadbent insists more NDP members, especially union members, are now starting to say the same things so his remarks are not out-of-line. But one former top Broadbent adviser says the shift, albeit slight, is wasted on the general voter.

"People think of us as free-spenders anyway and we're not going to change that impression just by talking about holding the line on the deficit," he said. "The only thing we do is alienate some of our own supporters."

Broadbent has taken heed. In two major addresses last weekend to party workers, one in Toronto the other in Dartmouth, Broadbent never once mentioned the word "deficit."

Across the country, the NDP must run hard just to stay even.

The Atlantic provinces, where the party's hold is shutout federally and holds only two provincial seats, is a region of forever mounting hopes dashed at election time.

The area has a long small-c conservative tradition and many of its young people, the normal NDP base, go down the road to Toronto or western Canada in search of better times.

Also, there are major organizational problems. For example, six of the 14 NDP riding associations in the Halifax region failed to send out notices of the wine-and-cheese party Broadbent attended in Dartmouth until barely 48 hours before the event. The Halifax-Dartmouth NDP council has just $300 to its name.

'We have suffered a lot of bruises this year. Everybody is weak'

Quebec is a complete writeoff, with youths and union activists opting for the Parti Quebecois. Only a charismatic candidate, Broadbent suggests, will ever be able to win a seat for the NDP.

Ontario remains the key for the NDP. Broadbent is confident the party is doing well in southern regions, especially with labor, but is worried about northern Ontario. The Timiskaming riding may be a warning the party is out of touch with their concerns, especially with the perception, not entirely backed up by proof, that the party focuses too heavily on manufacturers at the expense of resource industries.

The Prairie provinces present the NDP's biggest problem. The Conservatives scored a resounding victory at the expense of the NDP government. Some observers claim part of the sweep was due to the Tories painting the NDP as bedpartners of the Liberals.

Broadbent discounts that theory, but admits he grossly underestimated the depth of feeling in the West over the constitution split. Now he is trying to rebuild personal contacts with Saskatchewan party workers.

All the while they are trying to heal the splits within the party, NDP strategists are watching the manoeuvrings within the Conservative and Liberal leaderships.

NDP insiders claim another Trudeau-Clark race would be disastrous for them, possibly reducing them to a handful of MPs as the Tories sweep the West. Even more than Clark, they fear the Conservatives ousting Clark in favor of Alberta Premier Peter Lougheed or Ontario Premier Bill Davis.

"The Tory support (now 46 per cent in Gallup Polls) is soft," one insider said. "The Conservative base is strong in the West, but Clark doesn't add anything to it. If Lougheed or Davis were leading the party, the Tories probably would be well above 50 per cent."

The best scenario, they say, would be a Clark-John Turner race. They believe Turner, the Bay St. lawyer and former Liberal finance minister now favored to lead the Grits whenever Trudeau steps down, would draw votes away from the Conservatives.

Also, Turner is perceived as being right-of-centre on many key issues, which the NDP claims will leave the left-leaning voters to them.

Next month, the NDP campaign committee will meet in Ottawa to analyze what is going wrong and how best to stop the slide. Most of the talk will centre on recasting the party's economic stance, trying to make their programs appear economically sound.

"We have long been bedeviled by the question in people's minds of where is the money coming from for our programs," Caplan said. "We need to address that perception."

It likely will take a lot more than fine-tuning some economic issues before the NDP starts to climb again in the popularity polls.

Broadbent keeps saying the party has a year to put itself together before facing another election. If it can't do it quicker than that, earnest young couples in Dartmouth and Vancouver may lose their enthusiasm and faith.

And if that happens, the NDP may see a repeat of the 1974 election when it plunged from 31 Commons seats to 16 the day after the votes were counted.

THE GLOBE AND MAIL, FEBRUARY 15, 1980

New breed
The bagman: no more taint of back rooms

By JOHN FRASER

In the realm of public esteem, the political bagman is right down there at the bottom where only undertakers and newspaper critics are fit company.

The word is an American generic term for a low-life creep who lurks around corners and back rooms scrounging cash in a bag in return for promises given and favors rendered.

The muck from the past inevitably sticks to the practitioners of today. But that's no reason to pity the guy who collects money to keep a party's electoral aspirations afloat — he can defend himself just fine.

In fact, fund-raisers for Canadian political parties may be coming into their prime in these days of cynicism, thanks in part to the Election Expenses Act of 1974 and in part to that cynicism itself. In a curious twist, it is party leaders and candidates who are under the most intense suspicion, while the bagmen end up sounding like high moralists fighting for democracy and the Western political process.

Since the passage of the Election Expenses Act, all donations above $100 must be publicly declared, and corporate and private donors have been enticed with tax deductions.

Political donations have been removed from the back rooms to the boardrooms. Companies now vie with each other for the mantle of good corporate citizen, giving donations of equal size to the government and opposition parties.

The move to this system came from a new generation of bagmen who were determined to get donations on a regular basis, unaffected by the number of elections held or which party formed the government.

Foremost among this new breed is Senator John Godfrey of Toronto, who was once chairman of the finance and treasury committee of the Liberal Party of Canada. He took on the task of collecting funds for the federal Liberals shortly after Pierre Trudeau became party Leader in 1968.

A spell as Ontario Liberal bagman had poisoned him on the business, but as a senior partner in a prominent Toronto legal firm he was at one point the only leading corporate establishment supporter of Mr. Trudeau. According to Senator Godfrey, he accepted the post on condition that the Liberals introduce reform in election expenses.

Although he has now retired from both his legal firm and the front ranks of bagmanship, the party has asked him to continue making his pitch to Canada's top 35 companies. He describes this as relatively easy work, where the ground rules are well established. Here, as elsewhere, he has always been a source of frustration to those who think of political fund-raisers as secretive and shady because he is so open and vocal on the subject.

Privacy right

He used to be more circum-spect about his list of donors even when he was lobbying for reform, because he felt they had a right to privacy. But two things changed his mind. Personal friends insisted that no company or individual would make a sizeable donation without expecting specific favors, and the Watergate scandal called political morality into question.

"Possibly I was being over-sensitive, but even my own children, after Watergate, seemed to me to be eyeing me quizzically at the dinner table as if they were wondering what dear old dad had been up to when he was raising money for the Liberals," Senator Godfrey says.

Disclosure of a secret donation by Fidinam (Ontario) Ltd., a development firm, to the Ontario Progressive Conservative Party in the early 1970s also confirmed him in the view that everything should be above board. Nevertheless, he is annoyed that the maximum amount of money any company or individual can donate anonymously is $100.

"There are lots of cases where someone would be prepared to make a donation of several hundred dollars to a specific candidate, even if the candidate was from a party the donor didn't want to be publicly associated with. Perhaps the candidate was an old friend or perhaps the donor has a small store and thinks it wise not to be associated with any party. I recommended that the maximum anonymous donation be $500. I had more faith in our MPs and candidates than

to think they could be bought for $101, but evidently they didn't, so who am I to argue?"

Senator Godfrey is a gregarious personality who has never fancied the traditional image of the bagman. After he saw the successful enactment of election expenses reform he went on the propaganda war-path, particularly inside the ranks of the Liberal Party. He notes that the younger and more idealistic Liberals always gave him a hard time about the source of party funds, but never hesitated to ask for more and more money to subsidize their campaigns. At one party rally, he suggested everyone stop calling him The Bagman and use the phrase "Great Provider," but, as he himself notes with a chuckle "it didn't catch on at all — I'm still the old bagman."

Although he is in semi-retirement, he hasn't lost his enthusiasm for candor or seizing the offensive. He tells new bagmen to pump companies for equal donations to government and official opposition parties, and he pushed that line even in the old days when it was standard to divide donations 60-40 to the Liberal government's advantage.

List donors

He notes with a wicked bit of a grin that the news media haven't taken much advantage of the Election Expenses Act by publicizing who has given what: "The Globe should print a whole page of donors. People like reading that stuff, but now that it's available no one seems interested. The Liberal

Party had a self-imposed limit of $25,000 from any one company, which was totally ignored by the press, so I have been pushing it up to $50,000 and there hasn't been a squawk from anyone.''

Part of the reason for pushing up the maximum was Watergate fallout. Most Canadian branch-plant firms were suddenly told by their U.S. parents not to make any political donations, Senator Godfrey said, and that hit both the Liberals and the Tories hard. ''IBM, for example, was all set to give us a donation a few years ago when the parent firm found out and forbade it. It certainly shows up the farce of a Canadian board of directors where autonomy is minimal if it exists at all.''

More than anywhere else, Senator Godfrey's convictions perhaps are rooted in his formative experience in raising party funds with those perennial losers, the Ontario Liberals. He was particularly riled when the Ontario Tories tried to get companies to divide donations on a 70-30 basis rather than 60-40. ''The Government party always has extensive opportunities to spread its message. It's opposition parties that need funds desperately in order to get a fair chance to present their sides to the public.''

Bitter experience

Down in St. John's, A.H. (Bill) Crosbie, uncle of Finance Minister John Crosbie and the youngest of Sir John Crosbie's legendary brood of sons and daughters, has a similarly bitter past experience. It's hard to believe now, but it wasn't so long ago that anyone in Newfoundland showing Tory tendencies could lose his job if former premier Joseph Smallwood took offence.

Collecting funds for the Tories was particularly bleak, since many Liberal donations were made in return for a specific *quid pro quo*.

Like Senator Godfrey, Mr. Crosbie is a colorful and vocal man. Both men share distinguished war records and believe passionately that in raising funds for their parties they are supporting the political process and democracy.

Mr. Crosbie's integrity is such that he was a natural for Tories, including his nephew, to lean on for help. In fact, it was this integrity that once rescued John Crosbie from political hot water.

In the late sixties, John Crosbie was not only a Liberal but a prominent Cabinet member in Mr. Smallwood's administration. On a point of principle he bolted the Cabinet, and Mr. Smallwood decided to embroil the entire Crosbie clan in a major scandal.

He accused Mr. Crosbie's businessman brother, Andrew, of trying to influence the Government for his personal benefit. Because the Crosbies are one of the richest and most influential families in Newfoundland, Mr. Smallwood knew much of the muck would stick in the public's mind whether it was true or not.

One mistake

The premier made one mistake. Outside the provincial House of Assembly and its privileged immunity, he also accused Bill Crosbie of influence-peddling. In those days John Crosbie was a tongue-tied and insecure public figure who seemed overwhelmed by the enormity of Mr. Smallwood's attack. Consequently he fudged his defence badly. But Bill Crosbie knew he had won when he was named outside the Legislature.

Within hours, Mr. Crosbie — a meticulous man in business dealings — had collected his notes on the incident the premier referred to. He had also checked all the main participants and then had his lawyers present Mr. Smallwood with an ultimatum: a specific public apology or a libel suit. Later, Edward Roberts, special assistant to Mr. Smallwood (and later provincial Liberal Leader), phoned Bill Crosbie and said: ''We're trying to make this easy on the Skipper, so. . . .''

Public apology

Mr. Crosbie cut him off cold. ''You tell that son of a bitch if he doesn't make a loud public apology, I'm suing.'' He slammed down the receiver.

I was a university student in St. John's in those days and was in the Crosbie house when that call came. I also went to the Legislature the next day to hear Mr. Smallwood's full apology.

The last days of Joey Smallwood were a signal lesson in the corruption of power. That experience, as well as trying to keep the Tories from disappearing altogether, color Mr. Crosbie's approach to raising funds for his nephew's campaign.

''The Election Expenses Act had a positively revolutionary effect, at least on Newfoundland politics,'' he says. ''One of the principal beneficiaries has been the NDP, which can now mount major campaigns here. But it was most important in helping to change the nature of how politics operated. Things went from the covert to the overt and that was revolutionary.''

Deposit money

Still, and not just with the big parties, the legend of the bagman persists. Earlier in this campaign I was talking to Mel Doig, a candidate for the Communist Party of Canada (Moscow-aligned), who wondered how the Marxist-Leninist Party (Albania-aligned) came up with deposit money for its 176 candidates — which at $200 each comes to $35,200. ''It makes you wonder where the money comes from, doesn't it?'' Mr. Doig said.

Since I wasn't quite connecting, I asked wildly if he meant the funds came from Albania. Mr. Doig snorted the kind of snort reserved for the most naive. Bagmania, clearly, has global implications.

THE GLOBE AND MAIL, NOVEMBER 29, 1980

Parties richer, but democratic dreams fading

Financing law, six years later

By JOHN GRAY
Globe and Mail Reporter

OTTAWA — When the government of the day decided it was time to take political financing out of the smoky back rooms and make bagmen into something close to government agents, the talk was about democracy.

Allan MacEachen, the man responsible for the new law, said it would "encourage more Canadians of average means to contribute to the party of their choice and become more actively involved in the political process."

Mark MacGuigan, then a parliamentary secretary and now External Affairs Minister, talked of parties being able to make the broadest possible appeal: "The man who contributes as little as $2 or $5 to his party will be able to have credit for that, and this will provide an incentive for parties to go to people in great numbers, in the thousands or maybe in the tens or hundreds of thousands, to make contributions to the political party of their choice."

More than seven years and two elections later, it is clear that matters have not worked out quite as expected since passage of the legislation to control and subsidize the spending of political parties.

Statistics provided by the office of the Chief Electoral Officer demonstrate that, in spite of the legislation, the essentials of political financing have not changed.

Even with the attraction of a tax credit worth up to 75 per cent of what a person contributes, only about one-half of 1 per cent of Canadians contribute personally to political parties. Corporate donors are still the bulwark of financial support, as they always have been, for the two older, larger federal parties.

The election-expenses legislation was passed in 1973 but did not take effect until Aug. 1, 1974, just 24 days after the federal election that returned Pierre Trudeau to power with a majority.

Before that, no political party kept records of donations, or at least no records a party was prepared to make public. The law changed that.

In the first full year for which the parties have records, slightly more than 75,000 Canadians contributed to either the Liberals, Conservatives or New Democrats. Last year, 111,632 contributed to the three parties — a 48 per cent increase in individual donations over five years, but in terms of actual numbers hardly manic democracy.

In the first full year under the election-expense legislation, individual contributors accounted for 89 percent of New Democratic Party revenues. In the intervening years the role of individual contributors has declined marginally as trade unions increased their financial commitment to the party, but the NDP's 63,655 contributors last year was almost double the Tories' 34,952 and many times more than the 13,025 for the Liberals.

The Conservatives, mainly on the strength of a determined direct-mail campaign, have made the most spectacular progress in broadening the base of their contributions. There were six times as many donors as the mere 6,423 in the first 12 months under the act. The Liberals were far less successful. They had 9,882 donors in 1974, rose above 20,000, and then sank back to 13,025 last year when they were out of power.

And far from becoming more democratic, the Liberals have become even more dependent on corporate contributions. In the first year of the act, corporations accounted for 46 per cent of Liberal revenue; by last year that had risen to 74 per cent. The Conservatives started with corporate donations totalling 53 per cent of revenue, pushed that down to below 50 per cent, then saw the corporate share rise again last year to 60 per cent.

Corporations contributed $170,000 to the NDP last year, 6 per cent of its revenues, compared with $3.8-million for the Liberals and $5-million for the Tories.

But the bottom line for party organizers is less how many donors they get than how much the donors contribute and how regularly. In that respect, the parties have never been better off.

As John Laschinger, former national director of the Conservatives, said: "What is significant is that the pie has become larger."

Another factor cited by Mr. Laschinger and senior figures in other parties is that the new legislation has imposed a discipline on political parties and their electioneering that was previously quite alien.

NDP national secretary Robin Sears: "It has forced a sense of fiscal responsibility on all of us — which was not common among political parties before."

The same point is accepted by Torrance Wylie, chairman of the Liberal Party's fund-raising agency, but he is convinced that parties can go even further: "There's still quite a bit of slack to be picked up."

Flesh going unpressed, but mails a bonanza

OTTAWA — In the mythology of politics, the bagman is not a lovable creature.

Dark suit, a vaguely menacing manner, and a shiny briefcase in which he carries massive quantities of money from other men who are notable for their dark suits, vaguely menacing manners, and shiny briefcases. Vast amounts of money.

The modern counterpart of the bagman is a $150,000 computer.

Direct-mail fundraising by computer did not originate with the Conservative Party, but the Tories adopted the system with enthusiasm in 1974, spurred by the memory of a large and embarrassing debt, the inevitability of another debt and one more period in opposition.

The Conservatives were particularly inspired by the example of the Republican Party in the United States. Even at the height of Watergate, when Richard Nixon was halfway between a curse and a joke, the Republicans were rolling in money.

Robin Sears, federal secretary of the New Democratic Party, has a theory that only right-wing and left-wing parties can go to direct-mail advertising. His idea is that the mail pitch must be based on ideas and values, so that only New Democrats and Conservatives could use the system in Canada.

Liberals interested in expanding use

That's not a theory that has made much impact on Torrance Wylie, chairman of the Liberal financing agency, because, although he does not really like the idea, the Liberals have used the device to some degree and are interested in expanding its use.

Mr. Wylie's complaint is that fundraising by mail is too technological; the Liberals have preferred to raise money by traditional means that, at the same time, reinforce the organizational base of the party. But the bottom line for Mr. Wylie may turn out to be that his Liberals managed to raise only about a third of the amount raised by the Conservatives last year, with about a third the number of donors.

Just the other day the Conservatives put their trusty computer to work on a list of 50,000 names, all of them people who have contributed to the Tories in recent years, and sent them a letter from national director Paul Curley. By the measure of past success, Mr. Curley estimates that about 7 per cent of those who get the letter will send back money, and it will amount to about $500,000.

The only immediate cost was printing and postage — much cheaper than the massive phone campaign the Tories organized a few months ago. They phoned just about everyone who had contributed in recent years and it netted them $340,000, but the cost of the phones and the people to man them came to about $75,000, and several irate people across the country wanted to know why they were wasting their money.

The man who pioneered the Tory fundraising-by-mail system is David McMillan, now a private consultant, who moved into the operations of the depleted and depressed Conservative Party in 1974 as it headed for yet another election defeat.

Inspired by the example and the advice of the Republicans, their ideological cousins in Washington, the Tories bought a computer and began the long and exacting task of ''prospecting'' — sending letters appealing for money to people whose names appeared on various subscription lists that are for rent.

To their surprise, and quite contrary to the experience of most direct-mail fundraising, they actually made a profit in their prospecting ventures. Usually such operations break even at best; they provide a low percentage of positive respondents, which can be given concentrated attention later on.

After a few efforts at prospecting, direct mail becomes a dream for those with a taste for computers. The variables all come together—the message, the donor's past record, the region, current politics, the source of the name.

Without much effort an analyst can figure out whether a Maritimer who reads Playboy is more or less likely to give a greater amount to the Tories in response to a direct attack on Pierre Trudeau than an Albertan who has never contributed before but whose name comes from Reader's Digest.

Whatever the answer, the system worked. And it worked, as Mr. McMillan says, at a period when it was proving difficult to recruit people to go door to door to ask total strangers for money. National headquarters was finding it could not rely on the volunteer efforts of untrained, sometime canvassers when there were bills to pay.

The bonus of the mail system, he says, is that it reached people who had never previously contributed to any party: ''The principle was to go where the money was rather than the politics.''

Mr. McMillan calculates that the party would be lucky to make even $3 for every $1 spent in the ''prospecting'' phase of refining lists; but once donors are identified, the expectation is donations of $25 for every $1 cost.

Although they are cagey about precise figures, it appears that more than a quarter of the money contributed to the Conservatives by individuals comes through direct mail. If that estimate is correct, the mails brought the Tories close to $1-million last year.

The Conservative success has convinced the New Democrats that, despite their preference for a more personal pitch, they must turn to some degree toward the mail system. The NDP is also trying to secure monthly long-term commitments rather than one-shot contributions.

Parties find money rolling in, control of ridings trickling out

OTTAWA — Canada's politicians began to think seriously about election-expenses legislation when they realized that the old system could not meet the demands of modern electioneering.

The cost of jet travel and television advertising were too much for the handful of discreet bagmen who had customarily plied their trade in the boardrooms of Bay Street in Toronto and St. James Street in Montreal. The parties needed more money, and also needed to clear away the odor that had always haunted political fund-raising in Canada.

The legislation finally passed more than six years ago has given them money beyond their dreams, and respectability beyond their hopes. But it has also created by accident a chain of feudal fiefdoms that the parties find increasingly alarming — powerful riding associations that, from the parties' point of view, could turn into political Frankenstein's monsters.

The legislation finances the political process in two streams. The most visible financing is paid to the taxpayer, whose contributions, whether individual or corporate, are rewarded with a tax credit on a sliding scale of up to $500.

Parties get back half expenditures

The other branch of Government financing goes to the politicians, either individually or to their parties. The parties, which get back half the money spent during campaigns on radio and television ads, are all delighted with the idea of spending dollars that cost them only 50 cents (although they complain this effectively prevents advertising in other media). But they are less delighted with the rebates that go not to the party but to the candidate.

Candidates who get at least 15 per cent of the vote qualify for a rebate that can be as high as their campaign spending. For example, in the 1979 federal campaign New Democrat Leo Heaps spent $11,141 in his unsuccessful campaign in Eglinton-Lawrence. The full $11,141 was rebated, and so the modest $6,319 he had raised for the campaign goes into the local riding association kitty.

The whole system takes on a quite different dimension when the numbers get bigger. In Etobicoke Centre, for example, the encouragement of a tax credit prompted $60,603 in contributions to Conservative Michael Wilson for his hard battle against former Liberal minister Alastair Gillespie in 1979. Mr. Wilson spent $28,950, close to the legal limit, and got a rebate of $16,534 from Ottawa. Contributions plus rebate minus expenses equals a bank balance of about $48,000 for the local Conservative association.

That riding is not unique. Almost at random, Liberal fund-raising chief Torrance Wylie points to a Northern Ontario riding where the Liberal association is sitting on a surplus of about $85,000 after two elections, and a fast glance through the report of the Chief Electoral Officer suggests there are riding associations like that all over the country. In areas where it is a major competitor, even the NDP is developing fat-cat riding associations.

Conservative Leader Joe Clark estimates his party has "something like $2.5-million salted away in constituency funds across the country," with one constituency controlling $100,000 by itself. Warning that the national party must get hold of some of those funds, Mr. Clark said too much money locally removes the incentive to raise more funds. And however rich the local association may be, the national party still needs money.

All parties acknowledge they are concerned over the thought of fat election funds controlled in only the most nebulous way by either the parties or the law. Suddenly they face the spectre of candidates and their local associations being waywardly independent.

Headquarters has no local control

Party headquarters in Ottawa have no control over the local money and how it is spent. As one Conservative said: "Individual candidates will need the party less and less. The local guys don't need the national headquarters. . . . In fact, they are far more solvent than headquarters."

The various headquarters, however, are far more solvent than they used to be in the days before the election-expenses legislation when, after a decade in opposition, the Conservatives swallowed their pride and begged the major banks to write off more than $2-million in debts. Under the new act, the Tories managed to repay $1.1-million in debt from the 1974 election campaign within 18 months, just in time for Joe Clark to take over the leadership with the books in balance.

Still, the financing picture is not entirely rosy. Although the growth of political contributions in recent years has been spectacular, NDP federal secretary Robin Sears insists that political costs have gone up even faster. More serious is the evidence in the reports from the Chief Electoral Officer that the rate of growth in contributions seems to have levelled off.

Discussion Questions

1. What aspects of politics do parties continue to influence? How significant is their function in determining who occupies the government benches in Parliament (the pool from which Cabinet ministers are selected)?

2. Why are an increasing number of people seeking to participate in politics and public life outside the framework of political parties?

3. Given the dominance of the Canadian political system by the three major parties, are Canadians provided with a meaningful choice? Under what circumstances would the rise of a new party be likely?

4. Are political parties amalgams of their historical traditions, ethnic and religious loyalties, and particular political interests, or are they vehicles for their leaders?

5. What functions are political parties expected to play in the Canadian political system? How well do the current parties perform them? How might their performance of these functions be improved?

6. Can the major political parties in this country be described as anything other than 'moderate'? Is it fair to say that the major parties reflect the middle-class values of a middle-class nation? What role has ideology played in Canadian parties?

Suggested Readings

Frederick C. Engelmann. 'Canadian Political Parties and Elections', in John H. Redekop, ed. *Approaches to Canadian Politics*, second edition. Toronto: Prentice-Hall, 1983, 207–32.

Paul W. Fox, ed. *Politics: Canada*, fifth edition. Toronto: McGraw-Hill Ryerson, 1982, 292–350.

Christina McCall-Newman. *Grits: An Intimate Portrait of the Liberal Party.* Toronto: Macmillan, 1982.

Richard J. Van Loon and Michael S. Whittington. *The Canadian Political System: Environment, Structure and Process*, third edition. Toronto: McGraw-Hill Ryerson, 1981, 304–69.

Joseph Wearing. *The L-Shaped Party: The Liberal Party of Canada 1958–1980.* Toronto: McGraw-Hill Ryerson, 1981.

David E. Smith. *The Regional Decline of a National Party: Liberals on the Prairies.* Toronto: University of Toronto Press, 1981.

M.J. Brodie and J. Jenson. *Crisis, Challenge and Change: Party and Class in Canada.* Toronto: Methuen, 1980.

Donald V. Smiley. *Canada in Question: Federalism in the Eighties*, third edition. Toronto: McGraw-Hill Ryerson, 1980, 120–57.

Hugh G. Thorburn, ed. *Party Politics in Canada*, fourth edition. Toronto: Prentice-Hall, 1979.

R. Schultz, O. Kruhlak and J. Terry, eds. *The Canadian Political Process*, third edition. Toronto: Holt, Rinehart and Winston, 1979, 117–223.

George Perlin. *The Tory Syndrome.* Montreal: McGill-Queen's University Press, 1979.

b. Elections

Perhaps the most exciting spectacle in Canadian politics is a general election. For the majority of citizens it is the most conspicuous feature of their democracy and, by and large, one of its more interesting and entertaining aspects. For most, as well, voting is the only means by which they participate in the political system. (Election turnouts, although not as high as in some countries, generally hover around 75 per cent of those entitled to cast a vote.) People feel more inclined to identify themselves with the process or to participate more actively when they have a chance to become involved in helping to choose who will hold political office. Thus elections not only select particular governments, but encourage a broad base of public support for the political process itself.

As the most closely observed political events in the country, elections necessarily draw an extraordinary amount of press attention, and newspapers expend considerable resources on covering them. An exceptional range of public issues is raised during an election campaign— more than at any other time. In fact, contemporary campaigns are basically staged as media exercises. Today the pivotal role that newspapers once played in elections has been largely taken over by the electronic media. The influence of editorial endorsements —once a key barometer of party fortunes—has dissipated. Other forms of press coverage and commentary also appear to have a limited direct impact. Instead, such coverage operates indirectly by reinforcing voting decisions, forming images of leaders and parties, and influencing the selection of issues and the tone of the campaign itself. In addition, newspapers help to identify serious candidates, declare the winners in whatever debates may be held, and define the criteria for assessing campaign activity and reviewing party strategies and policy positions. Whether press coverage actually affects the outcome of an election is open to question—it largely depends on how close the race is and what other factors come into play—but there is no doubt that it does help to determine what people know about the campaign.

Most newspapers follow a roughly similar pattern in election campaigns, carrying candidate and riding profiles, interviews, and analyses of issues, along with reports on public-opinion polls and election meetings such as all-candidates forums. By contrast, the first six articles in this section represent a relatively new phenomenon in election coverage: they are critiques of the coverage itself. Ben Tierney and Charles Gordon examine the question of leadership in the 1980 campaign and assess the extent to which the media can shape leader images. They also provide insights into the centralization and homogenization of reporting during elections. Attention is now increasingly focused on the national level to the detriment of local and regional campaign efforts, as Gordon observes. Both he and Murray Goldblatt note the media's preoccupation with the leaders, but they differ on whether newspapers have given adequate treatment to campaign issues. As well, Goldblatt comments on the heavy media use of polls during campaigns, underscoring the horse-race focus of much of the coverage. He also points out that the media rarely examine polls in the depth they deserve, using them for little more than forecasting results.

In recent elections the principal, if not only, theme of importance has been leadership. Paul Moloney observes that the parties tend to use the leaders' tours to direct media coverage, and recognizes that such exploitation is inevitable. Because the costs of this form of reporting are so high, only large media outlets can afford to send people to cover the leaders full-time. Geoffrey Stevens takes up this question at the more general level of image-making and places much of the blame on television. Certainly television has taken priority as a medium for politicians — in 1980, the Liberals boldly declared that they did not care what the print medium carried as long as they received regular and equal television coverage.

The next group of articles provides an extensive cross-section of newspaper editorials and columns evaluating the 1980 election. The press reaction ranged from enthusiasm to cynicism depending, to a certain extent, on the editorial endorsement of the paper. Before the election, *The Toronto Star* was the only major English-language paper to support the Liberal cause editorially. The day after, its headline was triumphant: 'Encore! Pierre's Back In With a Majority.' *The Globe and Mail* had come down on the side of the Conservatives, largely for negative reasons, characterizing the Liberals' policies as skimpy and ambiguous; by contrast, the Tories had tried 'to set our country on a course of recovery' using long-range planning. In the wake of the Liberal victory, the *Globe* printed a rare front-page editorial cartoon of a smug Trudeau sitting comfortably in an easy chair, a rose in his hand, stating, 'There was nothing to it. . . . ' The French-language press, on the other hand, had been almost uniformly behind the Liberals,

and its enthusiasm over their win was unrestrained.

A dominant theme running through the English-language commentary was the lopsidedness of the outcome and its implications for federal–provincial relations. Many editorialists proposed schemes to increase the number of Westerners in the government and the Cabinet, including proportional representation and the drafting of Western Senators into Cabinet service. The final four articles discuss the question of electoral reform. The articles by Vincent Prince and John Gray , which focus on regional representation, underscore the fact that the current electoral system encourages parties to adopt regional strategies that can only exacerbate conflict on those grounds. This system exaggerates parliamentary representation from the strongest party, penalizes second parties, and devastates third parties with support spread thinly across the country. Political scientists William Irvine (1979 election) and Dale Thomson (1980 election) advocate the adoption of proportional representation (P.R.) — which the *Gazette* headline confuses with the historical doctrine of representation by population. In summary, these articles argue that our first-past-the-post (or plurality-vote, single-member constituency) system leaves those voting for minority parties (Liberal in Alberta, Conservative in Québec) unrepresented. Under P.R. their votes would elect some MPs, thereby improving regional representation as well. Among the disadvantages are the possible emergence of splinter parties and stimulation of political extremism (because the system encourages small parties); difficulties in gaining majority governments; and the breaking of the link between the individual MP and a specific constituency (since members are elected from party lists in most systems of P.R.).

THE CITIZEN, OTTAWA, JANUARY 29, 1980

Joe, the journalists' gaff, but had it been Pierre . . ?

Ben Tierney

Southam News

In recent days Tory staff travelling with Joe Clark have been increasingly inclined to suggest their man is not getting a fair deal from the nation's press.

Their complaint is not without justification.

Canadian newsmen — particularly columnists who are as much interested in entertaining as in informing — have devoted a not inconsiderable amount of time and talent in this election campaign to underlining the failings of Clark while overlooking those of Pierre Trudeau.

The Canadian public has been told that Clark is a wimp — whatever that is.

They've been led to believe that he's scarcely capable of walking and talking

at the same time, that he doesn't understand much of what is happening around him, that he is an embarrassment to Canada the moment he sets foot outside the country, that he is, in short, a total disaster — an accident determined to happen.

At the same, Trudeau has been sketched as a divinely inspired leader of men capable of doing everything right when the mood is on him — a blessed creature who can hardly be blamed for the fact that

there are but 24 hours in each day for him to scatter his pearls among us.

The facts are somewhat different.

Clark, in fact, is a bright young man — who combines an even and stable temperament with a keen and quick wit. Trudeau these days is an old and a quite evidently tiring individual whose human side (never easily discovered) is increasingly obscured by crankiness.

The misrepresentation of Clark is nothing new. From his earliest days as a national figure, when he sought the leadership of the Conservative party, he was the subject of mindless mirth. Then, he was Joe Who? And when he set out to acquire a touch of international stature by touring the world, he fell victim to a number of ordinary mishaps that translated into unfavorable headlines back home.

But these are not the early days of Clark's career. Canada is in the midst of an election campaign, Clark is campaigning as the prime minister of the country (having convinced many voters, if not the majority of newsmen, that he is capable), and the time may be overdue for a basic level of fairness to be applied to the events being reported.

Asked to provide examples of what they think is unfairness, Clark's aides are loathe to oblige.

But they will, when pushed, and after stressing that they are not asking the press to "take it easy" on Clark, point out a number of incidents on the Trudeau tour that, had they taken place on Clark's tour, would have been quickly gathered up and offered to the Canadian public as further evidence of incompetence.

The most obvious example of this was Trudeau's madcap notion to twin the CN railway track between Winnipeg and Vancouver — a totally unnecessary proposal that would cost Canadians hundreds of millions of dollars and require the demolition of at least three rather majestic mountains.

Had Clark made the proposal, one suspects, jokes about the Joe Clark's Loopy Line would have been in columns coast to coast within 24 hours, and the

boys on the press bus would have required scarcely more time to compose yet another campaign song, beginning, inevitably: "Joe's been workin' on the railroad . . ."

As it was, the railroad proposal was examined briefly (if somewhat critically) and allowed to vanish as an issue.

Trudeau's performance on a dairy farm early in January is another case in point. Watching a milking operation, the former prime minister asked a number of questions so banal (would dumb be a better word here?) that reporters could scarcely believe the man was not trying to be funny.

But the episode was not subtracted from Trudeau's supposed level of brilliance as, one suspects, it would have been added to Clark's alleged level of incompetence.

There are other examples.

What, one wonders, would the press coverage have been like if Clark had announced that, yes, his party did have an oil pricing policy, but that, no, the people of Canada couldn't be told of its details now . . . that they would learn the "algebra" of it eventually?

What would the coverage have been like had Clark announced that he would hold the line on Canada's deficit, then taken the following week to announce projects (including the Loopy Line between Winnipeg and Vancouver) bound to cost billions?

What would reporters have said had

Clark, after weeks of refusing to campaign more than absolutely necessary, told them: "I'll talk to the press when I want to, not when you guys want to"?

And, finally, what would have been said if, after weeks of transparent excuses, Clark had finally offered the proposed presence of journalists on the set as a final reason for not taking part in a TV debate?

We'll never know for sure. But one has the uneasy (not to say guilty) feeling that, if even half of these episodes had involved Clark instead of Trudeau, Clark's campaign would be in utter ruin by now, instead of sailing on, as is Trudeau's, 20 points ahead of the opposition.

This is not to suggest that the nation's journalists will be responsible for the defeat of Clark and the re-election of Trudeau on Feb. 18, if that is the eventual outcome of this campaign. There are other forces at work in this and other campaigns that lie beyond the influence of journalists.

Nor is it to suggest that there is any conspiracy among journalists to assassinate Clark. Journalists are inherently incapable of conspiring to do anything.

But it *is* meant to suggest that on examination of the record of recent weeks, one could make the case that the journalists have been somewhat less than evenhanded in their treatment of the two leaders.

THE CITIZEN, OTTAWA, FEBRUARY 18, 1980

Has election coverage been fair to Clark?

A few final rhetorical questions on election coverage:

Has the press been fair to Joe Clark? The question was raised by Southam's Ben Tierney in *The Citizen* Jan. 29. Canadian newsmen, Tierney wrote, "have devoted a not inconsiderable amount of time and talent in this election campaign to underlining the failings of Clark while overlooking those of Pierre Trudeau."

Tierney said that had such things as Trudeau's double-tracking the CNR proposal received the kind of scathing coverage given to such things as the Joe Clark

Media Watch

Charles Gordon

world tour, Trudeau would not be enjoying a comfortable lead in the polls.

Tierney concluded that "on examination of the record of recent weeks, one could make the case that the journalists have been somewhat less than even-

handed in their treatment of the two leaders."

Some of Tierney's colleagues take a diametrically opposite view. The *Vancouver Sun*'s Marjorie Nichols quoted a member of the Clark inner circle who "thinks that roughly 90 per cent of the press are in the Clark cheering section."

Douglas Fisher, in a column carried in *The Citizen* Jan. 23, said that "most print journalists are dismayed at the prospect of Trudeau as prime minister again."

Dalton Camp, once a member of the Tory inner circle, now a columnist for the *Toronto Sun*, has a similar view:

"I have not met anyone in the media business who is not alarmed at the prospect of the destruction of a government which was never given an opportunity to prove either itself or the worth of its purpose and the return to power of a party that, at this point in its history, represents a legacy of failure and the desperation of a mere handful of survivors."

If Tierney is wrong about coverage of the 1980 election, what about another school of thought: that the damage had been done before the campaign started?

This is a view held by Lubor J. Zink, the doggedly anti-Communist *Toronto Sun* columnist. Zink says the numerous editorial endorsements of the Tories this time are too late. They "came *after* the damage the image-making machinery can do had been inflicted."

After an intriguing reference to the *Toronto Star* and the Ottawa *Citizen* as "the sort of *Pravda* and *Izvestia* of our lib-left establishment," Zink blames the damage done to Clark on the electronic media, which he says are "manned by a mutual admiration fraternity of messianic 'leftists'."

Zink's characterization of the electronic media as "tone-setting Jaguar socialists" may seem extreme, but his point about image politics is backed by William Johnson of the Toronto *Globe and Mail*. Johnson stresses the media's insatiable lust for "color", an urge that is strongest when the campaign output of real news is lowest.

"If Joe Clark has been established as prone to trivial bungles, then every instance of a trivial bungle becomes a fit subject for a color piece. But a trivial bungle by Pierre Trudeau will not be suitable material because, in the simple scenarios of the trade, Mr. Trudeau has not been established as the character who bungles. He is the arrogant one: vignettes which show his arrogance will be sure-fire color pieces."

Well, what to make of all this? First, it would be difficult to convince any of the journalists who covered the Clark world tour that the things they wrote about did not happen.

Second, it would be difficult to convince anyone that Clark has not bungled at least a few times since then. Third, many journalists wrote favorably of Clark, after the initial fiascos, particularly with regard to his performance in the House of Commons.

Fourth, the coverage of Clark's campaign this time has been, on balance, kinder than the coverage of Trudeau's. Reporters who pride themselves on their objectivity would say this is simply a re-flection of the way the two campaigns have been run.

We are left with the ominous possibility of a lag in public perception: the so-called Wimp Factor looms largest in the public mind at a time when it has ceased to be a reality for the journalists.

* * *

Has coverage been too leader-oriented? Unquestionably, yes. The media generally used the techniques of the 1979 campaign, which *was* leader oriented, to cover a 1980 campaign which was, at least, not supposed to be.

If the Liberals were running a team campaign, as they claimed to be, where was the coverage of the team? Jean Chrétien, for example, logged thousands of miles, yet received virtually no national coverage. On the other hand, if the judgment was that there was no Liberal team, that fact itself was worth more coverage than it got.

The leader-oriented coverage may in fact have hurt the Tories.

John Crosbie's abilities as a campaigner are legendary by now, and Crosbie did a lot of travelling. While the wire services staffed his appearances, stories about those appearances made the newspapers only when Crosbie happened to be in town. More damaging still, Crosbie hardly ever made the network television news.

* * *

What about coverage of local campaigns? It is an impressionistic judgment, but a strongly-held one that large papers do a bad job of covering local campaigns. Perhaps this is because there are too many ridings, too many candidates. But the tendency is to cover a few all-candidates meetings, write a riding profile, put out an election supplement and call it a day.

This is not enough. There is little room in supplements for any kind of give and take among candidates. The same goes for riding profiles, which one parliamentary reporter has referred to as "bubble-gum cards". In fact, local television and radio debates are far more helpful.

As for all-candidates meetings, coverage inevitably focusses on audience response, as opposed to what the candidates are saying. When you think about it, this is ludicrous.

Candidates pack the crowd, and if one candidate gets a good round of applause on a statement, it means only that he has more friends and relatives in the hall than another candidate has. The way to cover candidates is to spend some time with them, something big-city newspapers do not seem willing to make the commitment to do.

There is, to be sure, thorough coverage in both newspapers and television of the races in glamor ridings, such as Vancouver Centre or Halifax. The somewhat ironic result is that voters in a Toronto or Ottawa riding may know more about the candidates in Vancouver Centre than they know about their own.

* * *

Are TV and radio too good? At certain things, yes. The television networks have become so adept at matching pictures to words that the words become impossible to follow in the rapid shifting of images.

An example: Thursday night's CBC coverage of Joe Clark lasted one minute and 45 seconds. In that minute and 45 seconds, there were 18 different images on the screen. Among them: crowd shot, Clark at podium, crowd shot, crowd closeup, Clark talking, standing ovation at another rally, reporter in front of crowd, Flora MacDonald waving, David Crombie shaking hands, Bill Davis making an introduction, Clark climbing on stage, crowd, Clark talking, signs in crowd, Clark at a different angle, balloons falling from ceiling, closeup of Clark in crowd.

All the time this is going on, words are coming out of the set and the viewer strains to comprehend them at the same time as he wonders whether that is Uncle Harry in the tenth row, admires Crombie's tie, watches the balloons and tries to find Clark in the mob.

Someone, it is feared, has decided that TV news clips should move as quickly as television commercials.

The audio equivalent happens on radio, most drastically on CBC's *Sunday Morning*, where as background noise to a report on Pierre Trudeau's week ending Jan. 27, we hear the following:

A snowmobile, the voices of Indian children talking to Trudeau, a band playing '60s music at a rally, the University of Manitoba marching band, violin music in St. Boniface, people singing *Hail, Hail the Gang's All Here* in Sydney, N.S., the Scotia Square office of the Halifax Board of Trade (which sounds like most office buildings) and cars going by somewhere.

By contrast, CBC's *The House*, which is carried on Saturday mornings, gives a thorough and undistracting report read by reporters in a studio. It is a terrific wrap-up and any day now someone will tell them to liven it up a bit.

THE GLOBE AND MAIL, FEBRUARY 8, 1980

MEDIA NOTEBOOK

Record on issues still below par

BY MURRAY GOLDBLATT

Mr. Goldblatt is associate professor in the Carleton University School of Journalism.

OTTAWA

ENGLISH LANGUAGE media performance in this election continues to be strong on the specifics of hard news coverage and weak on background-interpretive material.

Take the case of public opinion polls. In the current campaign, polls are in the forefront of the news, although some politicians regard them as poison. It was the results of public and private polling last fall that dictated, at least in part, Liberal party thinking in moving to upset the Tory Government in December.

Despite the importance of polls and the headline play given them, there has been little effort to demystify the polling process.

Canadians know through polling by three major organizations in the past six weeks that the Liberals have maintained a substantial lead over the Tories, with the NDP at or near their traditional third-party level. In the past week, that Liberal lead has narrowed to some degree—the polls disagree as to how much. And they differ too on the size of the undecided vote.

What is normally published in the media are national figures and percentages with some regional breakdowns (British Columbia, Southern Ontario, Metro Toronto). But the stories rarely assess the bias between votes and parliamentary seats — in Canada one doesn't parallel the other.

Nor do reporters examine the sample used in the polls. They don't explore other questions put to voters. (The CBC-sponsored Carleton University School of Journalism poll was an exception here.) They don't analyze how the sample was weighted in terms of sex, age and region. They often ignore the definitions for such key categories as the undecided and whether those definitions have been revised. And they rarely trace voter patterns in samples used.

Roger Smith of The Canadian Press did make a creditable attempt to discuss the implications of opinion polls in a piece published in the Calgary Herald. Geoffrey Stevens, Ottawa columnist for The Globe and Mail, turned out a careful comparative study of current polling results in a two-part series. And in the Toronto Star's Insight Section, Pamela Wallins tackled some of the variables involved in polling.

When foreign affairs intrudes in Canadian electioneering, it is scarcely at a high level — often it is merely a mixture of posturing, flimflam and cynicism.

This campaign has been no exception, with the response of Canadian parties to the Soviet invasion of Afghanistan, the threatened Olympic boycott and the spiriting of six Americans out of the Canadian Embassy in Iran. Party leaders, led by the Hawk of High River (to use columnist Allan Fotheringham's phrase), have vied for the crown of who will be first to bell the Soviet cat.

As usual, media coverage has been about as shallow as the politicians' debate. Perhaps the best backgrounder was produced by Stephen Handelman of the Toronto Star's Ottawa bureau — a well-researched review of foreign policy positions of the major parties. Ron Collister, now editor-at-large for the Edmonton Journal, tried his hand at the same thing in a more lighthearted vein. Syndicated columnist W.A. Wilson scanned Pierre Trudeau's much-touted record as an elder statesman of international affairs. In Mr. Wilson's eyes, the record was patchy—misguided on NATO, "fuzzy" on the link with the European Economic Community.

Beyond these contributions, there was almost nothing in the press about larger issues of foreign policy in the light of events in Iran, Afghanistan and other parts of Southwest Asia. What about an assessment from Canada-based journalists on general Canadian policy in Iran, about Soviet aims in Afghanistan and Pakistan? What about an analysis of the Moslem upsurge in a wide band of nations around Iran? What about an update on Canadian defence policy and foreign aid objectives? The situation called for more backgrounders and fewer stories based on Fortress Canada speeches.

There has been a steady escalation in the sniping directed at party leaders by roving reporters and columnists. It seems to be a case of substituting invective for invention.

The NDP's Ed Broadbent escapes with a minimum of damage in this kind of exercise. Both Prime Minister Joe Clark and Opposition leader Pierre Trudeau, however, are subjected to it daily.

Since the early days of the 1979 election campaign Mr. Clark as Joe Who or Joe Where has been tested regularly for image acceptability. Mr. Clark told Ben Tierney of Southam News Services and others that if he were beaten, it would be because of an image problem. Bruce McLean of the Vancouver Province spent most of a newspage discussing "Joe's Wimp image" and how it could be dispelled (not enough time, said the ad and PR experts). Ron Collister labelled him Gunboat Joe in the Edmonton Journal. Syndicated columnist Doug Fisher in the Toronto Sun concluded that many of his readers found Joe indecisive, a flip-flopper, "a tinker, not a thinker. . . ."

For Mr. Trudeau, the dose of vitriol is stronger this time. Richard Gwyn of the Toronto Star, writing when Mr. Trudeau made his decision to reassume the Liberal leadership mantle, found the performance sad, "also a little bit sickening — nothing the speaker says needs to be believed . . ." One reporter described his campaign speeches as "a few minutes of canned rhetoric." Columnist Allan Fotheringham, F.P. Publications' sophisticated version of The Oatmeal Savage, suggested Mr. Trudeau's approach to the campaign represented "the phoniest bit of packaging since Evel Knievel . . ." Mr. Fotheringham raked Mr. Trudeau at a press conference for stalling, obfuscating, stonewalling. The Toronto Sun's Robert MacDonald, in typical shoot-from-

the hip fashion, dismissed Mr. Trudeau as "a burnt-out leftist revolutionary".

The media have been indicted in recent campaigns for being obsessed with political leaders and their images at the expense of key issues.

This time journalists and their editors have tried to fend off this charge. CBC-TV assembled its issues team to examine such complex questions as the federal deficit and high interest rates. CTV and Global have followed suit to a lesser degree; CTV, for example, did a conscientious job on the tangled Petrocan issue. All have used graphics more successfully than before. Papers in major urban areas have assigned political reporters on a rotating basis to do backgrounders.

Energy issues have received especially thorough and sensitive treatment in the Montreal Gazette, Globe and Mail and Toronto Star. David

Crane supplied a particularly penetrating analysis of energy pricing in the Star. James Rusk contributed a useful review of the recycled Liberal party program in The Globe and Mail. And as in the last campaign, CBC Radio's two public affairs shows, The House and Sunday Morning, provided a consistently high level examination of such issues as energy, the economy and federal-provincial relations.

But the media record on issues was still below par. Except for measuring the impact of the energy elements in the Tory budget, the broad questions of unemployment and inflation were bypassed. Reporters skipped social welfare matters as well, apart from a brief flurry over Liberal proposals to increase the guaranteed income supplement for the needy aged. There was almost no discussion of the dangers to the federal-provincial medical care insurance scheme, although the NDP tried to keep it alive.

THE CITIZEN, OTTAWA, FEBRUARY 13, 1980

Four ways of covering the issues
TV CAN BE FAST, NEWSPAPERS THOROUGH

Of the English media seen here, only the *Toronto Star* and *Globe and Mail* have consistently produced blockbuster issue stories. But there are other ways to cover issues.

Five, in fact: the instant analysis; the comparison of party positions; the blockbuster feature, which discusses the issue at length before comparing the party positions; questionnaires and interviews, in which the parties speak for themselves, unfiltered; and the political column.

This last will be discussed later this week. • • •

Instant analysis: Television can do this well and there are several instances of the networks jumping right on an issue as it breaks, summing up party position and quickly placing it in context.

Media Watch
Charles Gordon

A good example: when the U.S. decision on pipelines was announced Jan. 18, CBC had maps of all the proposed routes and a discussion of the impact of the American election campaign on the decision. CTV focussed on the oil tanker aspect, interviewing B.C. fishermen and getting reaction from Premier Bill Bennett.

It is fair to say of television that there was not enough of this kind of thing. During the later phases of the campaign, attention has shifted to who's-winning pieces. In CBC's case, time was wasted

in a series of glorified man-in-the-street interviews.

The *Globe and Mail* has used the instant analysis frequently, with pieces on the Liberal platform (in which little new was found) and the Trudeau oil price plan (found by the *Globe* to be similar to one he rejected four years ago).

The instant analysis approach also works well for a newsmagazine, which can focus its weekly campaign coverage on a specific issue, as Robert Lewis of *Maclean's* did with foreign policy last week. • • •

Party comparisons: Voters are helped by comparisons of party stands on issues as they arise. The *Toronto Star* has been running weekly roundups of the issues discussed each week, setting out in point form the positions taken by the various parties. Sunday's, for example, covered energy, opinion polls, leadership, the deficit and federal-provincial relations. The weakness of the *Star*'s technique is that the party comparisons consist of quotes from the party leaders that are often not strictly comparable.

The *Montreal Gazette*'s Saturday weekly review section has contained a number of solid comparative pieces by John Saunders, among them studies on the economic and energy platforms of the parties, and the *Globe and Mail*'s Wayne Chevaldayoff wrote an excellent summary Jan. 23 on the three parties' approaches to interest rates.

News services have also done issue wrapups. Southam News' issue pieces began this week with an article in *The Citizen* yesterday by Jo Ann Gosselin on defence spending. Those who think voters make up their minds before the last week will feel that Southam started too late.

Carol Goar of FP News Service wrote a comparative wrap-up of party views on energy pricing, pensions, government spending, interest rates, oil tankers and Afghanistan. It ran in the *Winnipeg Free Press* Jan. 26 but was not seen here.

(Other news services, particularly Canadian Press, face similar difficulties. The stories are written but not used. There is in fact more being written about issues than meets the eye.)

• • •

The blockbuster: The blockbuster also compares party positions. But it looks in greater detail at the issue itself. It is long, in other words.

The *Toronto Star* has been most impressive here, with a series of what it terms "position papers" on such subjects as the deficit, Petro-Can, industrial strategy and energy, as well as lavishly displayed features on party promises, foreign policy, offshore resources and federal-provincial relations.

An example of the *Star* approach is a Jan. 26 feature on the deficit, by John Honderich. The article began on page one, then took a whole page inside, with pictures of John Crosbie and the party leaders, as well as a graph comparing Canada's budget deficit with those of other countries. In addition to the main article, there were shorter pieces on the party positions and where Canada's deficit stands in relation to that of the United States (smaller, on a per capita basis).

The main article contained interviews with economists, most of whom said the deficit is not bad in itself or, to put it more precisely, is bad when businessmen think it is bad and translate their pessimism into decisions that work against economic growth.

As for the national debt, Honderich draws the analogy of a family, the members of whom owe money to other members of the family. There is debt within the family, but the family itself is not in debt.

Where danger arises is in the interest on the debt which, as it mounts, weakens the federal government's ability to redistribute income.

All of this takes several thousand words, which is where print has an ad-

vantage over the electronic media. On CBC Feb. 4, Ken Colby did an excellent job of summing up the party positions on the deficit, where they would spend money, where they would raise it. But television allowed less time for thoughts on the deficit itself, whether it's bad or good, and if bad, how bad?

Energy was the issue at which most of the media blockbusters were aimed. CTV's Jim Munson examined, on Jan. 19, the question of whether oil prices should be allowed to rise to world levels and summarized the party positions.

The CBC's Colby, in a Jan. 25 report, focussed on the balancing act between avoiding the inflation caused by higher prices, on the one hand, and using higher prices to bring about energy self-sufficiency on the other. A comparison of party positions rounded out the report.

The *Globe and Mail*'s James Rusk dealt at length on Feb. 8 with the question of higher oil prices versus higher oil import compensation. Lower prices, wrote Rusk will lead to greater consumption, thus larger imports and more money spent on compensation.

Four days later, Rusk wrote about the Liberal "blended" oil price and the possible effects on federal-Alberta relations of a price increase below the $4 level. A companion piece, by Ross Laver, quoted economists as disagreeing on whether higher prices cause decreased consumption.

In contrast to the *Star*, which trumpets its features, the *Globe*, in a kind of reverse vanity, tends to hide them. The Rusk-Laver pieces mentioned above ran at the bottom of page 9, unillustrated. Worse fates have befallen other articles, such as a thorough piece by Wayne Chevaldayoff on prospects for job creation and party job creation proposals. It ran yesterday on page 10, unindexed, unillustrated and right next to an ad for Trans-Canada Liquidations Ltd. Issue stories can be heavy going and the reader (not to mention the writer) deserves a more alluring treatment than that.

Well used, illustration can help the reader or viewer, as in the case of the *Star* deficit story. Badly done, it is more trouble than it is worth. *Maclean's* biggest issue piece of the campaign has been an examination of the coming federal-provincial battle over resources, sparked most recently by the discovery of Newfoundland oil. Robert Lewis examined the party positions and set out the views of the provinces, including especially Newfoundland's Brian Peckford.

Interspersed with Lewis's text are pretty little three-color charts that combine to make such matters as federal transfers, government expenditures and

degrees of centralization even less comprehensible. One chart features scissors, smokestacks and a dollar bill. Another has a piggy bank marked "tax" sitting between a hand with money in it and a cash register with the Parliament buildings printed on the side. Dates and numbers are scattered around in what seem to be a random way.

The use of charts to simplify a complicated story can also run the risk of oversimplifying it. A Saturday *Toronto Star* story on the cost of party promises makes it clear that the NDP would phase in its $6-billion worth of promises over a period of years and that unspecified corporate tax increases would make revenues higher than the $1.25 billion previously accounted for. But the table accompanying the article displays no such subtlety. In bold type it totals the promises: $6,724 million. And the revenues: $1,250 million. A voter looking at the chart and not the article could be severely misled. The New Democrats are angry, and have a right to be.

• • •

Questionnaires and interviews: The parties love questionnaires. If you like answers unfiltered by the views of beastly journalists, you will love them too. The device, used in *The Citizen* last Saturday and in the *Globe and Mail* today consists of asking the parties an identical list of questions and printing their replies. It enables a comparison of their positions.

Whether their unfiltered nature is a strength or a weakness depends upon your view of the journalist's role. If you think the role of the journalist is to point out contradictions, you will miss him. If you think the parties should speak directly to the voter without heckling, you will be just as glad, and we'll all be out of work.

The interview is similar, except that a skilful interviewer can shed light on the subject where light needs to be shed and direct the interview to bring out the issues. CBC has had Patrick Watson interview the leaders, and programs such as *Sunday Morning* and *The House* have interviewed leaders and featured debates among party spokesmen. For Global, Peter Desbarats has interviewed the leaders, and CTV is featuring short interviews with the leaders at the end of newscasts, plus press conference settings for Clark and Broadbent (Trudeau declined to appear) on *Question Period* and interviews with party spokesmen on *Canada A.M.*

The *Toronto Star* in a print version of the TV interview has been running verbatim transcripts of interviews between reporters and the leaders. The advantages of television in this context is that you can see whether the leader keeps a straight face.

THE WINNIPEG FREE PRESS, FEBRUARY 14, 1980

Touring with Trudeau (but why?)

Reporter Paul Moloney of the Free Press *travelled with Liberal Leader Pierre Trudeau's campaign across Western Canada for four days last week. Here he reflects on Trudeau's icy handling of newspaper reporters and how they respond to it.*

By Paul Moloney

news'man, n. 1. A bearer or collector of news. — *The Shorter Oxford English Dictionary.*

A simple chore, and one would think it could be easily accomplished by 50 senior newsmen travelling in close proximity to Pierre Trudeau, the man polls suggest will be prime minister when votes are counted Feb. 18.

But during the Liberal party leader's four-day swing to five Western Canadian cities last week, I found it wasn't easily accomplished — in fact, it wasn't really accomplished at all.

Pierre Trudeau doesn't talk to newspaper reporters and he talks to television and radio reporters only under conditions carefully managed by his aides.

The print media, prevented from asking Trudeau specifically what he would do as prime minister, turn to summarizing what he says in his speeches — speeches that are full of generalities and are essentially the same in each city he visits.

Many and varied

And they cover the things that actually *happen:* an elderly man suffers a fatal heart attack after shaking Trudeau's hand in Kamloops; Trudeau masterfully puts down a heckler at a speech in Prince George; Trudeau's visit to a sawmill is cancelled because his plane is fogged in.

The television media, for whose benefit these flashy but fleeting campaign visits are really intended, capture the style of the campaigner in 45-second film clips.

This is often distortion. Because of his commanding television presence, Trudeau can appear to be delivering impressive oratory when in fact his partisan audience is beside itself in dis-

appointment that the man they respect so much is speaking with shallowness, in terms of both style and substance.

One of the reasons Trudeau eludes the media is because they let him get away with it.

Perhaps after all this time they are still intimidated by the man, his personality and his intellect.

What would happen if a reporter simply approached Trudeau during a free moment on the campaign plane, and asked for permission to ask a question?

"He'd probably say to get lost, I don't know," said one member of the parliamentary press gallery, in a tone suggesting nobody has ever tried it.

Trudeau *is* an imposing figure, and his almost-total disdain for journalists does seem to humble, rather than challenge, reporters.

Imagine the Washington press corps, for example, standing meekly by while President Jimmy Carter brushes past, saying angrily: "I talk to the press when I want to, not when you want to."

But that's exactly what veteran journalists, and the newspapers they work for, are allowing the candidate for prime minister to do.

If Trudeau feels, as he obviously does, that he can win this campaign through a strategy of keeping Canadians in the dark, shouldn't this be an issue in itself?

It's not as if Trudeau is hurting himself by refusing to speak to voters through the media. His handlers are deliberately shielding the leader, on the apparent premise that he can win without having to say anything or commit himself to specific policies. And the polls show this reign of silence is working.

Take energy. In each city he visited last week, Trudeau slammed Joe Clark's energy policy, saying it would add hundreds of dollars to the annual cost of heating a home and driving a car. But the Liberal leader seems destined to go to the voters next Monday without stating what his own energy price would be, in order to allow voters to compare the two prices.

All the voters are left with is Trudeau's eloquent conviction that his energy is better, even though he won't

tell them how much better.

This situation isn't all the media's fault.

For nowhere do the voters seem upset that they are being asked to go to the polls without a clear knowledge of what a Liberal government would do about many major economic and social questions.

Nowhere is it made crystal clear to reporters that people feel strongly that it's not good enough for a major political leader to try to seek office while operating from within a cocoon.

Perhaps the media's timidity isn't really timidity, but simple acceptance of the fact that, after all, no one can make another human being speak, short of torture.

It's clear that many journalists, while putting up with Trudeau's silence, don't like it. And at times they make their discomfort known.

Last week, in a press room set up in a hotel so reporters could file stories back to their papers, a columnist who contributes to *The Vancouver Sun* confronted a Trudeau aide, Jim Coutts, with a *Sun* editorial slamming the leader for campaigning in what's been called a box of mirrors.

Another columnist for the *Sun* had been turned down for an interview and the editorial was critical of Coutts for shrugging off the request by saying: "Mr. Trudeau does not give interviews to the regional press." (The *Sun* has an average daily circulation of about 240,000.)

Coutts appeared slightly taken aback by the editorial and it moved him to sit down at one of the typewriters in the press room to hammer out his reply, which essentially said that in his opinion the *Sun* should go jump into English Bay.

The columnist offered to relay this message to the newspaper, but Coutts declined. He put it in his coat pocket, saying: "It needs editing."

It was the only time during the four-day trip that a member of Trudeau's entourage appeared the slightest bit uncomfortable with the idea that newspapers have very little role to play in a federal election campaign.

THE GLOBE AND MAIL, FEBRUARY 23, 1980

A case of image over reality

Starting with the mass media, television is chief villain

BY GEOFFREY STEVENS

IT WAS LAST Saturday, two days before the election, and Joe Clark was campaigning through some of the small towns north of Montreal. Marcel Masse, one of the Conservatives' star candidates in Quebec, takes time for a quick lunch in a motel restaurant. Mr. Masse, once a senior provincial cabinet minister is flying his second suicide mission (the first was in 1974) for the Tories in the federal riding of Labelle.

A reporter inquires casually, how is the campaign going? The candidate's reply is vehement:

"How should I know? I'm just a local candidate. I'm irrelevant. The only things that matter are the image of the leader, the national campaign, the national polls, the national issues and the national media coverage. I've always been a constituency guy, but there's no role for me any more."

Marcel Masse was dead right.

By some sort of perverse genius, Canadian politics has managed to pick up the worst, most inappropriate aspects of American presidential politics and to marry them to an incompatible parliamentary system. Much of the strength of the parliamentary system is the direct, daily connection between the minister and the grassroots. A minister is not only responsible to Parliament, he is accountable to his own constituents. He may, if he is the member of a majority government, be able to get bad policies through Parliament. But if his constituents don't like them, or him, he will find himself an unemployed former MP — or, if

fortune smiles a senator.

That's the theory. The practice is quite different. Individual accountability to one's constituents has become largely meaningless. The way Joe Clark walks, or what Pierre Trudeau shouts at a heckler is far more crucial to the election of a local candidate than the campaign the candidate wages, or the work he may have done as an MP.

Obviously an exceptional candidate — a David Crombie or a Michael Wilson in Toronto or Lloyd Axworthy in Winnipeg — can make enough of a difference to withstand a national or regional trend. The average candidate, however, might as well spend the campaign on a beach in Florida for all the difference he makes.

Most MPs won't admit this. They like to think they got elected by dint of hard work or personal appeal. The backroom boys, however, say that the national party, its policies and its organization, count for nearly half of a candidate's support and that leadership or the image of leadership also counts for close to half.

Not the system, just blind luck

A typical candidate is worth between 3 and 5 per cent — no more. For proof of this proposition one looks no farther than the fate of the entire Social Credit caucus, the most constituency-oriented of all MPs, or the defeat in Prince Edward Island of Secretary of State David MacDonald, who was as good an MP as Ottawa has seen over the past 15 years.

Surely, a local member should

be worth more than 3 or 5 per cent in the political equation. Self-interest demands it. If voters don't elect good MPs, they won't get good government.

We may get good government out of the sort of election campaign from which the country has just emerged. But, if we do, it will be the result of blind luck rather than the product of an adequately functioning system.

The election was a triumph of image over reality. Mr. Trudeau did not win it, Mr. Clark lost it. His Government made some mistakes, but they were no more serious than, say, the mistakes that the first Pearson administration made in 1963 (anyone remember Walter Gordon's first budget?). They were the mistakes one would reasonably expect an inexperienced group of ministers to make upon taking office after 16 years in Opposition.

Mistakes didn't kill Prime Minister Clark, but they did reinforce the image of incompetence and inadequacy. The image was already there in the 1979 election, but Mr. Clark won anyway because Mr. Trudeau's negative image was even stronger. This time, by keeping himself and his campaign under tight control, Mr. Trudeau was able to minimize the negative and to persuade voters — those east of Manitoba, at least — that he was no longer the man they used to love to hate.

It would be bootless to blame the public for not seeing through the distorted images of the leaders. The responsibility starts with the mass media. The media may not have invented the images, but they nurtured and fed them.

Television is the chief villain. It is both the most compelling, believable medium and the most superficial. Television is the perfect vehicle for reinforcing images, for showing a politician to be what the public has been conditioned to expect him to be. Television is a terrible vehicle for contradicting conventional wisdom, for revealing how a politician really thinks and what he really believes.

Because television is the most powerful medium, all parties geared their election campaigns to exploit it — the Liberals differing from their opponents only in the degree of their success.

It is a truism that television brings individuals and communities closer together, that it breaks down the boundaries of geography, language and race. Its impact on the Vietnam war was enormous because, for the first time in history, it brought war and death — Vietnamese deaths, American deaths — in gory color into the living rooms of the American people.

But when ideas, not physical action, are in conflict, television can have the opposite effect. It can set people farther apart. Thanks to television, more voters today are exposed to political leaders. But the leader on the television screen is more remote than leaders used to be when they stood on the back platform of a train or walked down Main Street, shaking hands, chatting, and chucking babies under the chin.

Canadians have less opportunity to see a leader in person, to touch him, talk to him, question him, appraise his demeanor and assess his credibility — in other words, to form a personal impression.

Instead, it is the impersonal impression of the television camera and producer — the image — that the voter is left with. Television, and this is both the power and the danger of the medium, seems so believable. The viewer assumes that what he sees on the screen is more reliable, more truthful, than what he reads in the newspaper.

How significant the TV clip?

He assumes he is hearing and seeing what the politician is actually saying, without passing first through the filter of a reporter and an editor.

It's simply not true. There are more filters in television than in any other mass media. The 30-second clip on television probably came from a 30-minute speech and, in all likelihood, it wasn't the most significant 30-second segment. They were the 30-seconds the television reporter wanted to illustrate the point he, the reporter, was anxious to make in his nightly report.

Most of the time, the viewer doesn't even get 30-seconds of the leader. How many times have you turned on the television and seen a leader talking inaudibly in the background while, in the foreground, the television reporter reads his script, a script he may have written hours before the leader arose to make the speech the reporter is commenting on?

To return to Marcel Masse's point, there is almost no place for a local candidate in a made-for-television national campaign. If a leader comes to his riding, the candidate may (if he's lucky, as Mr. Masse was on Saturday) get to introduce him to his constituents — but the introduction won't get on television. Most of the time, the candidate's function is to smile, applaud at the right time and stay out of the way of the cameras.

There's nothing much that can be done about television coverage of campaigns. But we can do something about the worst exploitation of the medium by political managers and manipulators. This is the objectionable, offensive little television commercial, which strives to build up one leader by tearing down his opponents.

Under the Election Expenses Act of 1974 every broadcaster was required to make 6½ hours of air time available for sale to national parties. To enable all parties to exploit this powerful medium, half the cost of the time purchased is reimbursed from the federal Treasury. This compensation made it possible for the Liberals and Conservatives to spend roughly $2-million each, or nearly half their total election spending, on media advertising. The New Democrats were not far behind.

In retrospect, these provisions in the Election Expenses Act were a mistake. The electorate would be better served if paid political time were eliminated, if it were illegal for broadcasters to sell or political parties to purchase radio and television time. It would be better to require every broadcaster to provide a generous amount of free time—in segments no shorter than five minutes.

This might force the parties and the leaders to talk to the voters intelligently, to address themselves to issues and policies, rather than, as at present, fill the air with slick, superficial 30- or 60-second spots which tell us nothing about what's right about the party sponsoring the commercial, but a great deal about what's wrong, or alleged to be wrong, with the other fellows.

Another useful innovation would be to amend the Broadcasting Act and the Canada Elections Act to provide that the networks set aside, say, two hours during the final two weeks of each general election for a television debate among the leaders of parties which got 15 per cent of the popular vote in previous election— with the Canadian Radio-television and Telecommunications Commission to act as arbiter if the parties were unable to agree on the format. No leader would be compelled to take part, but it would be risky, politically, for anyone to refuse to debate if it were institutionalized in the law.

The opinion polls — always influential, frequently misleading, too often wrong — are a problem that will require action at the federal level. Even community colleges are getting into the act. In British Columbia the taking and publishing of polls is banned during provincial elections. That remedy, however, poses serious questions about freedom of expression and freedom of the press.

Federal action against the polls

A better solution would be national standards and a system of voluntary or delegated regulation. A National Polling Council, or some such body, could do for the proliferating public opinion industry what the Ontario College of Physicians and Surgeons and the Law Society of Upper Canada do for the medical and legal professions in Ontario. If a polling outfit did not choose to join the national body and subscribe to its standards, its surveys could be assumed to be unreliable.

Anything which limits or lessens the influence of television and opinion polls will enhance the role of the local candidate and increase his value in the political equation.

It would be worth the effort.

THE CHRONICLE-HERALD, HALIFAX, FEBRUARY 21, 1980

Canadian newspapers editorialize on election outcome

By THE CANADIAN PRESS

Following is a selection of excerpts from editorials in Canadian newspapers on Monday's general election:

His greatest challenge

Montreal Gazette: Pierre Elliott Trudeau's achievement of a majority government, only nine months after his decisive rejection by the electorate last spring, is a historic accomplishment . . .

Mr. Trudeau was, of course, helped by the unfortunate public perception of Prime Minister Joe Clark, who has been consistently under-rated. But Mr. Clark's problems alone would not have been enough to rehabilitate most politicians who fell from power after 11 years of office. What the voters chose, in the end, was Mr. Trudeau's leadership . . .

Mr. Trudeau now has four crucial tasks.

First, he must deliver his promised new team . . . Second, he must avoid the temptation to view the Conservative interregnum as a mere accident. The Clark government, for all its blunders, set some good new policies . . .

Third . . . he must continue the drive to bring federal finances under control.

Fourth, Mr. Trudeau must now address himself once again, and in a more urgent context than ever before, to national unity . . .

Canadians have given Mr. Trudeau a rare chance to end his career on a high note of accomplishment, rather than the sour anticlimax of last spring's defeat. It is his last and perhaps his greatest challenge; we wish him well as he prepares to meet it.

Complicate Ryan's task?

Montreal La Presse: Quebecers have once more supported one of their own. One can't hide the sentimental side of this vote. People may even have gone to the rescue of Mr. Trudeau all the more since they had trouble accepting the Liberal defeat last May 22, a defeat attributed of course to English Canada.

The Conservative party, under its last two leaders, has made real efforts to make itself accepted in Quebec. . . . The least that can be said is that the Conservatives will have to undertake a serious re-examination in the months and years to come. It is unhealthy that there is not a serious alternative in Quebec.

The most noteworthy result of the election in our province is probably the wiping of the Social Credit party off the electoral map. And despite the good that can be said of certain candidates who were running under this banner, their disappearance shouldn't impoverish the federal scene too much. In fact, they had become something of an anachronism . . .

Mr. Trudeau's sweeping victory could lead him to want to play a greater role than had been foreseen in (next spring's) referendum. This could complicate Claude Ryan's task as leader of the no forces . . .

It is certain that the Parti Quebecois will want to look closely at the consequences of Mr. Trudeau's triumph on the referendum debate . . . Mr. Levesque and his colleagues will have difficulty forgetting that Mr. Trudeau has immense popularity in Quebec and there could be danger in attacking him too strongly and too directly.

East against West?

Montreal Le Devoir: English Canada . . . clutches now to the Liberals, like a return to the cradle . . . Last May, only Quebec remained totally faithful to the Liberal regime, which illustrated the linguistic and ethnic division of the country. . . . Now the polarization from now on may be East against West. That will be the challenge for Mr. Trudeau. . . . Thanks to him, as well as to the weakness of the Conservatives, the Liberals take power again without having taken advantage of the lessons learned in their defeat of 1979. (Trudeau's) resources are limitless, and his ability to accept setbacks and overcome obstacles force our admiration. Quebec gave him a plebiscite Monday, at the same time as it signaled the end of Social Credit, a party with no place in the 1980s. But at a time of critical choices—the referendum, the election, the political future — will Pierre Trudeau be the spokesman that Quebec needs?

Must work with resolve

Ottawa Citizen: Pierre Trudeau has been resurrected but not yet rehabilitated. His majority victory . . . places on him a greater moral obligation than he has ever borne after any previous election to prove that the voters' faith has not been misplaced. He must work with resolve to allay the fears of westerners who will have no significant representation in the government.

Trudeau will have to make good on his promises, most of which came at the tail end of the campaign and most of which seemed little more than a ploy to steal enough votes from the NDP to win a majority in the Commons.

Trudeau will have to work equally hard to prove worthy of the public's trust in two other areas — economic management and energy.

Both policy areas were given the most superficial treatment by Liberal campaigners, both were couched in glowing motherhood phrases like "energy security at fair prices" and "balance objectives in setting interest rates."

There is no indication from their campaign posture that the Liberals believe that the government's huge deficit demands priority attention in the budget that must come soon. There was no immediate policy to control inflation except for a gradual reduction in the rate of growth of the money supply.

While Pierre Trudeau may be tempted to lapse back into his preoccupation with Quebec and the forthcoming referendum on sovereignty-association, the even more pressing constitutional problem is that of energy revenue sharing with the West, especially Alberta.

But a new energy policy must be in place soon, because Canada's dependence on foreign oil is not diminishing while the cost of offshore purchases is rising.

The confrontation with Quebec is already a shadow of its earlier self. The Rene Levesque of 1980 is not the Levesque of 1976. The referendum seems doomed to defeat, and Claude Ryan will be making Quebec's constitutional demands some time after the provincial election that must come by November, 1981.

That issue can afford to wait while Pierre Trudeau cleans up the house he himself left in such disarray just nine months ago.

Country polarized again

Ottawa Le Droit: The Liberal party's gamble in siding with Ontario in the energy confrontation between (Ontario Premier Bill) Davis and (Alberta Premier Peter) Lougheed paid off (Feb. 18).

But the country is polarized once again . . . we must seriously worry about the image that the apparent unanimity in Quebec will project on the federal scene. . . . The Liberal victory in Quebec is clean as a whistle but is it as beneficial as we might think?

Ontario fashioned the government by simply switching to Liberal last May 22's Conservative vote. What this province's results show is how imperfectly the Canadian electoral system translates the true allegiance of the majority of Ontario citizens because a small variation of five or six per cent of the votes are enough to defeat the government.

At the frontier between East and West of the country, the picture changes: The New Democrats spread their wings. . . .

In short, Canada has just shown more of a reaction against the Clark government rather than a real commitment to the Liberal way. If the latter had aroused the allegiance they are taking credit for, we wouldn't have this division in the country between the East and the West, but instead a vast sweep in their favor. This is what we must learn from this election which has perhaps given Canada a majority government but which failed to bring the yearned-for stability.

Grave decisions ahead

Toronto Globe and Mail: The Liberals are not without knowledge of the problems facing the country. They created them, and those problems will not go away simply because the country has rejected the government of Joe Clark and its efforts to solve them.

The price of oil will have to rise to world levels if we are not to put at risk our future energy supplies. The interest rate will have to rise if we are not to put at risk the value of the Canadian dollar. Taxes will have to rise if we are not to put at risk the entire economy of the country, burdened as it is with a succession of crippling budget deficits and a record public debt.

There are grave decisions ahead that will determine what kind of a country we are going to have . . .

. . . It is obvious that the Canadian people, by sending a majority Liberal government to Ottawa, have greater faith in Mr. Trudeau and his Liberal team . . . than they do in the government of Joe Clark.

Such a vote of confidence offers great opportunities. We hope those opportunities will be recognized.

We'll get what we deserve

Toronto Sun: It's as if last May 22 never happened . . .

For those who are appalled at the reality (spectre?) of four —make that five—more years of Pierre Trudeau—better get used to it . . .

Love him or loathe him, he's a remarkable politician. Sort of combination Muhammad Ali and Lazarus: coming back from a beating and rising from the near-dead, campaigning like a zombie.

But the country has spoken, and those who believe in our democracy must accept it. And fight on another day . . .

The Clark government will be remembered as an aberration; something to recall at future elections (if there are future elections!). Maybe then they'll appreciate Joe's team.

But that's our system — we will get what we deserve, for better or for worse. . . .

Poor gutsy, awkward, nice, ineffectual Joe. He deserved better . . .

Looking back, virtually the only positive thing the Clark government achieved was the Order of Canada for Sir William Stephenson, the Man Called Intrepid. Not much to show for seven months in power.

A priceless opportunity

Toronto Star: Canadians have given Pierre Trudeau, the Liberal party and the nation a chance for a new beginning.

For Trudeau, Monday produced a personal triumph of spectacular proportions; his fourth national election victory —and third majority—assures his place as a towering figure in Canadian history.

The electorate has given him a priceless opportunity to still fulfill the enormous potential he brought to our national leadership.

Circumstances have now left Trudeau free to pursue that fulfilment and makes his hold on his party unassailable. And because he intends this to have been his last election, he has the freedom to do what he believes is right, without succumbing to political timidity or electoral calculation.

The Liberal party has also been provided with the opportunity for a new beginning. In the past few years, the Liberals had become increasingly lax, complacent and lacking in policy commitment or fresh ideas; in a misguided search for a shortcut to the electorate's favor, they had begun to drift toward the political right.

But the defeat last May reminded them they aren't invincible and the spell in opposition forced them to re-examine their reason for existing.

The nation needs an immediate, dynamic start on doing what must be done. Trudeau has indicated he is still able to command the confidence of a great many Canadians. And he still possesses the attribute of leadership, the ability to stir the spirit.

What he makes of this golden opportunity will determine not only his place in history, but also Canada's future.

Faith wasn't justified

Winnipeg Free Press: The results of the federal election represent an immense act of faith in Pierre Trudeau by voters in Eastern Canada. That faith was not justified by the campaign which preceded the vote. All Canadians can only hope that it will be justified by the performance of the Liberal government in the months to come.

The swing to the Liberals in the east was clearly stimulated by two factors: The reality that Mr. Trudeau looks more like a leader than Joe Clark and the illusion that Mr. Trudeau and a Liberal government can deliver cheaper gasoline than the Conservatives.

It's back to square one

Winnipeg Tribune: Well, it's back to square one. Indeed, for many people it must feel as though the past seven months never were. And many others must have a strong feeling of deja vu as the Liberals stormed back into power, ending the short reign of Prime Minister Clark and his Conservatives.

It is apparent the election was fought and won on two issues: The personality of Mr. Clark and Mr. Trudeau and energy. Obviously, Mr. Trudeau won on both counts.

Difficult to understand

Regina Leader-Post: Ontario and Quebec Liberals gave Pierre Trudeau a largely regional majority. The antagonism of Quebec and Ontario voters to the Clark budget of last December and the leader himself is difficult for many Westerners to understand and a great deal of it, sadly, was based on the personal image of Prime Minister Clark. He was not an Easterner, he did not look and act like an Easterner and Easterners would not accept the political courage, honesty and realism that was projected in the December budget — and they threw him out of office.

Trudeau said he was determined to improve his party in the West, but "We saw little of Trudeau in Western Canada during the campaign and heard little, other than his suggestion to doubletrack the Canadian National Railway . . ."

There is an immediate need for a new agreement on oil prices and the premiers of Alberta and Saskatchewan will be no less firm in negotiations than they were with Clark. Strong regional leaders of all parties will have to assume additional national responsibilities in their dealings with the still unknown central government and its cabinet leaders. Saskatchewan Premier Allan Blakeney will face additional pressure to assume a national role in the NDP, and the leadership is his nationally if he wants it when the review of Ed Broadbent's performance is made by the party.

Canada's ills may deepen

Calgary Albertan: . . . We cannot know with certainty what brought about the Clark government's defeat . . . But if the electorate was saying that it wanted no part of the budget's stern objectives, Canada's ills may deepen instead of easing. They will, should the Liberals attribute their victory to such ostrichism and pander to it. The 18-cents-a-gallon increase in the gasoline tax was not, in itself, essential to a responsible program. But it is vital that energy prices be raised to more realistic levels and that the budgetary and balance-of-payments deficits be reduced as quickly as possible. If the Liberals are to earn their return to power, they will relegate naked political calculation to second place and commit themselves to these goals.

The ball over for Canada

Edmonton Journal: The paradox of Joe Clark is that his stature grew as his government fell in ruins around him.

His performance in what was clearly a lost cause from the moment his 18-cent excise tax swept him from office last December should lay to rest all those cruel jokes and estab-

lish him as a man of character, of honesty and hidden steel.

But the immutable reality is that he came of age in defeat . . . The Progressive Conservatives, with those solid 70 Liberal seats in Quebec always to overcome before a vote is cast, know that they have to find a new leader . . . and some means of offsetting the win-at-any-costs professional cynicism of what must surely be the most power-hungry aggregation of Liberal hucksters and vote-catchers in Canadian history.

In 1980, the Liberals have fooled the voters into believing that the days of cheap energy are not gone. The ball is over for Cinderella Canada — only this Cinderella never had a glass coach, just the mirage of Trudeauvian magic that fades with the dawn.

In his victory speech, Mr. Trudeau declared he had a mandate to speak for all the people of Canada. Something must have got lost in the translation in the West . . .

Alberta overcame worse

Calgary Herald: Albertans . . . deserve the understanding of other Canadians when we feel and express a sense of unease and sadness over still another unevenly distributed national vote that results in inexact consensus from which entire regions are left out . . . But let not gloom pervade . . . Despite ominous economic and international overtones, Canadians can overcome much with a properly functioning Parliament. And if not, there are always the words of Alberta's own William Aberhart nearly 45 years ago: "If the public of Alberta has not suffered enough, it is their God-given right to suffer some more." We overcame worse, back then . . . It would be unrealistic to expect Trudeau to be unwilling or unable to work out (an energy-pricing deal with Alberta). After all, Trudeau and Lougheed concluded energy-pricing agreements before and they can be expected to do so again. There will be a lot more political noise made during the course of bargaining than there was with a Tory prime minister, but the bargaining will go on and a deal will be struck.

East rejected reality

Kamloops Sentinel: Western Canada expressed its feelings as definitely as the east. The majority of battles were between the New Democratic Party and the Tories. The philosophies of the eastern-based Liberals, weak on policy and strong on charisma, sit poorly in the West.

In contrast, eastern Canada rejected the reality of higher energy prices and a tough but realistic budget which combined spell trouble for the manufacturing-based provinces of Ontario and Quebec. They opted instead for a party that said it would create another bureaucracy to study energy policies and a man who said he would quit in two or three years if elected.

Possibly this, more than anything is what the Feb. 18, 1980 election will be remembered for. The election, more than the Quebecois or old rivalries, showed that Canada is a divided nation. Until Canadians begin thinking as a nation instead of easterners or westerners, the future will be rocky. That day appears to be a long, long way off.

Relations won't be easy

Vancouver Sun: Pierre Trudeau, who accomplished one of the most amazing comebacks in Canadian political history, spoke movingly in his victory speech of a united Canada and he can certainly take heart from the huge support he received in Quebec, of a magnitude to make Premier Rene Levesque and separatists shudder.

But he also recognized the great danger posed to Canadian unity unless his majority government can represent the West.

Relations between the new government and the West won't be easy, especially in the crucial new debate about energy resources that must now take place, pitting the rich West against the hungry East. The Liberals did not articulate their energy policy clearly in the campaign and still must demonstrate their good faith. This will be all the more difficult because of the demands that will be made by Ontario, which gave the Liberals their majority.

But the onus is not all on the new government. We in the West are going to have to remember, as is Mr. Trudeau, that we are all Canadians first.

West will feel shut out

Vancouver Province: Pierre Trudeau's return from the dead Monday night in the most astonishing political turnabout in recent Canadian history has endowed both him and his resurgent Liberals with both a powerful mandate and an awesome responsibility.

With these election results, Ontario has teamed with Quebec in an assertion of Central Canadian interests against those of the West. The West, particularly the economically aggressive provinces of Saskatchewan, Alberta and B.C., will feel shut out from the decision-making processes of the central government and may therefore lose some confidence in the federal system.

To some extent it (Liberal government) will have to ignore the obvious fears of Central Canada, particularly Ontario, in developing new energy and economic development policies.

Mr. Trudeau is obliged now to be much more precise in defining his policy options than he was during the campaign. He is unhindered by promises.

Division is worrisome

Lethbridge Herald: The way the country is divided politically with the Liberals strong in Central and Eastern Canada while weak in the west is worrisome. Trudeau will have to show unusual sensitivity to prevent this situation from making the country unworkable.

A conception of Joe Clark as inept seems to have had a good deal to do with the defeat of his party. Although inexperienced, Clark has greater competence than has generally been conceded . . . Any move on the part of the Conservatives to dump their leader would surely be a mistake.

Despite the gain in seats by the New Democratic Party, they have lost in power. Only in a minority government situation would they have had influence of a satisfying kind.

The disappearance of the Social Credit party from Parliament is a good thing. There is one less party to confuse the situation now. Henceforth, any candidates who might get elected under that label will be seen as independents rather than as representatives of a national party.

THE NEW YORK TIMES, FEBRUARY 20, 1980

Mr. Trudeau, Too, Has to Save Gas

Let Americans not be misled: It wasn't just the gas tax. Canada's Pierre Trudeau had a lot going for him in the election that resoundingly restored him to power. His Liberal Party has only intermittently faltered in Ottawa; as it did last May when the Western-based Progressive Conservatives won a narrow plurality. And the street-smart Mr. Trudeau was pitted against a tyro, Joe Clark, who proved more adroit at rescuing Americans from Teheran (*merci encore, Canada*) than in defending a sound desire to conserve oil.

Even so, Mr. Trudeau's leap from the political grave has a Lazarus touch. Just three months ago, he was bidding adieu to national politics; his successor in the party was to have been chosen next month. When Mr. Clark misplayed the gas tax, and his minority Government fell in December, Mr. Trudeau was providentially recalled to life and given a few years more to deal with a formidable array of troubles.

The most serious trouble was spelled out in the voting returns; the Prime Minister-elect is a national leader with a regional base. He owes his victory to a Liberal surge in Ontario, the industrial heartland, and gains in the Maritime Provinces. Not a single Liberal was elected west of Winnipeg, nor is there a Liberal premier in any of Canada's 10 provinces.

Mr. Trudeau needs to grapple — still — with ethnic separatism in Quebec, where a referendum on autonomy will be held in late spring. He must also contend with regional economic jealousies, especially in oil-producing Alberta. As Albertans see it, they are buying dear in a tariff-protected market but selling oil cheap, to Ontario's benefit. (Regular gasoline still costs from 60 to 84 cents a gallon in Canada.)

Canada has only begun to weigh the high costs of cheap energy. Canadians have yet to endure the agonies of lines at the gas pump; about three-fourths of their petroleum is produced domestically. Mr. Clark's 18-cent-a-gallon tax increase was sprung on the voters hastily and without adequate explanation and his minority Government could not withstand the revolt.

Now Mr. Trudeau — whose campaign statements on energy were Delphic—inherits the politics of petrol. How well he balances national and regional interests could well determine the value of the mantle he plans to yield to a new party leader before his five-year term ends. In this sense, Mr. Trudeau's restoration may be a national gain for Canada; he can worry more about the next generation than the next election. If he does, he will have to embrace the same cause of oil conservation that brought him this chance.

THE WINNIPEG FREE PRESS, FEBRUARY 19, 1980

Lack of strong people led to Clark's defeat

Allan Fotheringham

OTTAWA—The major misjudgement of these final few weeks is that Joe Clark somehow has been unfairly defeated because of his "image."

The theory—pushed strongly by Clark people and almost accepted by the guilt-ridden media — is that the arrogant Trudeaucrats are back in the throne room because too much emphasis was placed on the way Clark walked, talked and waggled his spindly fingers.

It's not true. It's not true because the defeat of Joe Clark signals that not for a long time will the Canadian public accept as prime minister a person who really has no reason for being there other than that he has mastered the arcane mechanics of party politics.

Joe Clark, a very decent fellow who won a lot of fans among formerly derisory reporters because of the dignified, courageous way he faced his obvious defeat in the final days, is not really a leader.

He is — as one would expect of any 40-year-old whose sole and abiding interest since high school has been party politics — a diligent organizer, a shrewd analyzer of necessary tactics, a synthesizer who, as he confesses, has spent 15 years of his life in meetings.

That combination, while very useful in climbing the party ladder, does not make a leader.

Probably the number one reason why Joe Clark, not being a natural leader, was resoundingly defeated last night is that he does not attract strong people around him.

It's a cruel thesis of the Harvard School of Business Administration that first-class men attract first-class people around them; second-class men attract fourth-class people.

It has never really been grasped (except by the voters last night) that the celebrated foul-ups on Clark's disastrous world tour had nothing to do with the meaningless loss of his luggage.

The significance was that Clark had somehow surrounded himself with a staff that could neither read an airline schedule nor react to it.

Those very same people are with him today. He has not changed one. The same people who saw (and nurtured) him through Jerusalem, Petrocan, the budget — and the decision not to delay a vote on Dec. 13 when it was obvious they would lose it.

The prime minister in the final, fatal days allowed that someone had "done a number on me." As if he were some neighborhood virgin complaining of a pristine reputation being besmirched.

It's as if a completely phoney, invented image could be created for such a public person. No such animal exists.

Every politician has an "image" — and is responsible for it. A wise man once said that every man at the age of 40 is responsible for his own face. So is any politician who ventures into public life.

An image is made up of many things. Clark's twitchiness in public, his nervousness, came across to the public as indecisiveness. His ludicrous stand on Jerusalem was viewed as pure Toronto expediency — and indicated to the public that a nervous young man of not great self-confidence had — despite a journey to Israel — absorbed neither religious, cultural nor historical insight into that area.

All politicians live on image. Churchill used image to devastating effect with the means of his day — radio, newsreels, cigar, bluster. Dief had an image of dynamism before the public perceived that he was a ditherer.

It was never clear to the public after May 22, that Clark stood for anything but expediency. (Trudeau, who has run possibly the most arrogant and cynical, empty campaign of modern times, at least in the public mind is known for his resolute views on Quebec and national unity.)

The nasty jokes about Clark — which originated among politicians and press close around him — filtered down to the voters and the schoolyard. But jokes merely confirm the public's impression of a politician.

Robert Stanfield was not done in by the football-fumble photograph; it just reinforced the electorate's opinion. A dim-witted Gerald Ford *appeared* as someone who would bump his head. Trudeau didn't lose votes by going to a New York disco. He gained them.

Joe Clark won a lot of Brownie points in the end with the gutsy way he faced obvious defeat. But no one did a number on him. He did it to himself.

Sorry. Because he deserved — compared to the other guy — to win.

THE CITIZEN, OTTAWA, FEBRUARY 19, 1980

Grim prospect

Trudeau may be around a long time

Charles Lynch
Southam News

For those of us of the Trudeau generation, there is some comfort in the fact that the old guy beat the young one.

But as one who had hoped in a lifetime to observe something other than Liberal governments, the prospect of permanent Grit rule casts a pall.

The Tories were in power for such a short time we scarcely got to know them, though obviously the vast majority of voters felt they had seen enough.

Galling experience

Seen enough of Joe Clark, his style and his policies.

Seen enough of Ed Broadbent, who had the galling experience of moving the motion that brought Clark down, only to draw Pierre Trudeau back into politics and project him once again into the prime ministry.

And seen enough of pain through taxes. The Clark government was forced to run on its tough budget and it couldn't be done, any more than Robert Stanfield could win on wage and price controls in 1974.

Once again, "Lucky Pierre" was blessed in the nature of his opposition — and in doing so stands tall in the pantheon of great prime ministers, just as he stands alone, among democratically elected leaders, in terms of durability.

The irony of the election outcome is that the Liberals, with their majority, can proceed to introduce the tough measures the economy needs — and nobody need doubt that Trudeau can be tough.

The difference is that Trudeau can ram his measures through Parliament early in his new mandate, without fear of meeting the fate dealt to Clark.

Voters may have turned to Trudeau hoping for lower taxes and lower gasoline prices than Clark was proposing, but almost certainly they will be disappointed. Unlike Clark, however, Trudeau can count on a full term, giving him time to sweeten the pot before he or his successor faces the voters again.

Trudeau has said repeatedly that he does not propose to serve a full term — but the size of his victory, wiping out the ache of last May's defeat, may give him renewed appetite for the work, confident as he is that nobody could do it better.

Joe Clark, who won his party's leadership with no personal power base anywhere in the country, winds up with no solid ground to stand on as he contemplates the wreckage of his young government.

Nothing helped — his young wife fought hard by his side, whereas the aging Trudeau was forsaken by Margaret, who did him the favor of her silence during the campaign.

The election vindicated the public opinion polls, and proved once again that the editorial support of newspapers — heavily for Clark — counts for nothing in an election.

Media-bashing

Trudeau not only put the editorialists to flight, he also outflanked the working reporters who felt he was treating them with contempt. Trudeau has never lost public esteem by bashing the media, and prospects for press-government relations in the new Parliament cannot be called bright.

"It's certainly going to be a different Parliament," said Tory House Leader Walter Baker, in one of the understatements of the evening.

It certainly is!

Not only different, but longer — maybe five years of Liberal rule. Take a deep breath, and start counting. The Old Guy could last until he's 90.

LA PRESSE, MONTRÉAL, FEBRUARY 19, 1980

Trudeau Starts Again With a Free Hand

Paul Longpré

Liberal leader Pierre Trudeau has just pulled off the greatest 'comeback' in the history of Canadian politics, at the end of a campaign that was above all a trial of the short-lived administration of Mr Joe Clark.

Since Confederation, only two other defeated prime ministers have succeeded in moving back into the official residence of the prime minister. Mackenzie King even did it twice in the course of his 21-year regime, in 1926 and 1935. The very first prime minister, John A. Macdonald, made a comeback in 1878.

But neither of these two giants of Canadian politics had resigned as head of their party,

as Pierre Elliott Trudeau did last November 21, provoking dismay in his Quebec troops and firing desires in several leading Liberal understudies, among them John Turner and Donald MacDonald.

As for Mr Clark, in his way he too broke a record, for he will have served the shortest time of any prime minister to have obtained his mandate in a general election. Two other prime ministers had briefer 'reigns'—Meighen and Tupper — but both of them came to power by succeeding a prime minister in office, following a leadership convention.

Quasi-president

The man who, in a few days, will move into the offices in

the Langevin Block, across from Parliament Hill, will in fact sit in a presidential chair. He was enticed by his caucus, literally on its knees, in the hope put to him by party strategists (Graham, Davey, Coutts, and company) of bringing down the young Clark government with its first budget, an austerity budget that was extremely unpopular except in high-finance circles, notably Bay Street.

On the policy level, Prime Minister Trudeau, second edition, will have a free rein. On one hand, he made very few promises during the electoral campaign. On the other, since he does not need to ensure his re-election because he solemnly promised not to run

again except to gain a mandate, he can direct his policies along the lines suggested during his last months in power in 1979: neo-conservatism in economics and 'centralism' in constitutional matters.

At the head of a team that has been dangerously disintegrating in recent years, the new prime minister will now have the opportunity to draw on the ranks of newly elected Liberals or turn to the numerous personalities who have been cooling their heels on the back benches, to build a cabinet more impressive than the one that was decimated in the catastrophic May elections. One thing is certain: there will be plenty of action in Ottawa in the coming months.

THE CITIZEN, OTTAWA, FEBRUARY 25, 1980

Accept verdict of the voters

The Liberal party has been out of power just a few days short of the time considered medically normal for the gestation of human life. To many people, it seems an indecently swift rebirth.

It's not surprising that feelings are running a little high among those who tasted power so briefly, their supporters, families and friends.

For example, take John Fraser, departing postmaster general, a Vancouver lawyer of serious mind and notable dedication to public service. He produced this gloomy valedictory following the Clark cabinet's last meeting:

Christopher Young

Southam News

"If Mr. Trudeau conducts himself the way he did during the last 11 years, it will take all my responsibility and the responsibility of those who represent the federal political system from the West to keep the situation under control."

A telephone caller previously unknown to me insisted that the Liberals had "no right" to take over the government.

My old friend and colleague Charlie Lynch, in typically vivid prose,

called the Liberal victory "a cynical Mafia-type job staged by a crowd of hit artists in stocking masks, bent on giving Clark the cement overcoat treatment under the cover of law."

Calm down, fellows

Well come on, fellows, let's all just calm down a bit.

Like it or not, the Liberals won the election quite decisively. It was far short of the 20-point landslide forecast by the Gallup poll, but there was no doubt about the winner. Liberal candidates won 43.9 per cent of the popular vote to the Tories' 33 and 19.8 for the New Democrats. (These figures were reported with 98 per cent of the ballots counted.)

In our system, however, victory is not decided by popular vote but by seats in the House of Commons. Usually, but not always, the same party wins on both counts.

On that test, the Liberals did better in 1980 than the Conservatives did in 1979, winning a clear majority of the 282 seats in the House of Commons. Liberals won 146 seats to the Tories' 103 and the NDP's 32, with one deferred.

In 1979 the Tories won 136 seats to the Liberals' 114, but they did it with 35.9 per cent of the popular vote to 40 per cent for the Liberals. This was possible because of the massive ''wasted'' vote for the Liberals in Quebec.

So if anyone had cause to cry robbery, it would have been the Liberals last May, not the Tories this February.

Potentially dangerous

Of course from a non-partisan national point of view, the shutout of the Liberals west of Winnipeg is unfortunate and potentially dangerous. So was the near-shutout of the Tories in Quebec last year. But through Prime Minister Clark's moderate and cool approach to Quebec, and the Quebecers' understanding of their own responsibility for what they had done in the voting booths,

no terrible consequences flowed from the 1979 result.

Obviously the Clark government would have been better and stronger if it had included strong ministers from French Canada. French Canada, not Clark, made that impossible.

Now the three most westerly provinces find themselves in that position with respect to the fourth Trudeau government. Western voters made that decision collectively and deliberately in their own best judgment of what was good for them and for the country. Had they wished to climb aboard the Liberal bandwagon and elect a few potential cabinet ministers as insurance, they could have done so.

It's rather striking that despite all the talk about the polls and whether they should be banned for stampeding people, the evidence is hard to find that this is a real threat.

If they believed the polls in this last election, Westerners knew we were heading for another Liberal government. They voted Tory and NDP regardless.

If Quebecers believed the polls in 1979, they knew that English Canada was likely to elect enough Tories to make Joe Clark prime minister. They voted Liberal anyway.

Where was the bandwagon effect?

No stampede

Quite properly, it seems to me, the mass of voters in both these elec-

tions and in these two widely-separated regions of the country, stuck to their own convictions and refused to be stampeded by polls, pundits or political blandishment.

To propose the opposite is to say that voters ought to decide on the basis of ''a piece of the action'' rather than on their perception of candidates, parties, policies and leaders.

As for the Fraser view that the West may run out of control as a result of its exclusion from the inner councils of the new government, that suggests a degree of political immaturity that is hard to accept. There seems no good reason to assume that the West will react less wisely to its temporary exclusion from power in Ottawa than did Quebec under the outgoing government.

In any case, we have now had two-and-a-half years of more or less continuous electioneering. A new government (or the old one reborn) is about to take office with a small but stable majority. There are legitimate concerns about its weakness in the West, and about the Liberals' longevity in power, but there is nothing to be done about those problems for the time being.

The theory and practice of democracy, it seems to me, now require that we settle down to work and live with the verdict of the voters, while retaining the necessary vigilance against the follies of the newly mighty.

LA PRESSE, MONTRÉAL, FEBRUARY 27, 1980

Does the Electoral System Need Review?

The problems now confronting Prime Minister Trudeau in forming his cabinet are analogous to those that confronted his predecessor, Joe Clark, when he was putting together his own nine months ago. If Mr Clark had to look into ways of ensuring representation for a Québec that had rejected his party, Mr Trudeau now has to do the same in regard to the Western provinces, where he has only two members.

For the moment it seems that the prime minister-elect will follow his predecessor's formula, with a few adjustments. He could name some western personalities as ministers in his cabinet by way of the Senate. However, these ministers would not be entrusted with portfolios, contrary to the case in the Clark administration. Thus we would return to the parliamentary tradition in which the heads of departments are able to answer for their management to those elected by the people — in other words, they sit in the House of Commons.

But in several sectors this arrangement is felt to be somewhat artificial and therefore unsatisfactory. Thus more and more people across the country are demanding revision of the electoral system instead. In the wake of the Pépin-Roberts report, they are demanding the addition of a proportional element to our current voting procedures.

Their arguments are quite convincing. The Conservatives in Québec elected only one member, but if the recommendations of the Pépin-Robarts Commission had been applied, they would have had approximately ten. The same situation would have been reversed for the Liberals in the West, where they would have gained nine members in B.C., six in Alberta, three in Saskatchewan, and four in Manitoba. The NDP would also have increased its representation, thanks to the proportional factor.

Certainly the addition of some proportional element would give a clearer picture of the political situation in Canada. Following the election of May 22, 1979, just as after the election of last February 18, the talk was of a country profoundly divided, one in which the West rejected the Liberals and Québec turned its back on the Conservatives. At the very least, the reality reflected by proportional representation would be far more accurate.

The leader of the NDP, Ed Broadbent, wants Prime Minister Trudeau to move quickly on changes in the election law as soon as Parliament reconvenes, to correct the distortion in regional representation. If Mr Trudeau were to go along with this request, it seems all he would have to do would be to put together a provisional cabinet which he could very soon remodel by adding some genuine members from the prairies, that is, those that the proportional factor would have allowed him to add.

If this is indeed the intention of his proposal, it seems difficult to accept. In effect, it would mean changing the rules of the game after the match is finished. People could have voted differently if they had known the proportional element would apply.

But in the longer term, surely there are grounds for studying the possibilities that some form of proportional representation might offer to help resolve the problem of alienation in certain regions of the country, depending on the political stripe of the government. And while we are studying possible changes in the electoral system, we could take advantage of the chance to examine other avenues, such as the "run-off" form used in France.

But confining ourselves to the proportional factor — and it matters little which formula could achieve a consensus — it would certainly provide a clearer expression of the variety of opinions across the different regions of the country, and would allow third parties a better chance to assert themselves on the national chessboard. All political currents would have a chance of being represented, however weakly, at the centre where decisions are made. Democracy would probably benefit.

In this context, before committing ourselves definitively in this direction, it is important to point out the disadvantages of such a formula: two categories of members instead of one, the virtual impossibility of a parliamentary majority, the risk of almost constant coalition governments, etc.

In other words, we would have to be sure that the advantages of some kind of proportional representation really did outweigh the trouble it could cause.

We would also have to ask ourselves if the evils of the present formula have not already been partially corrected by the numerous mechanisms of consultation and collaboration that make up the various kinds of summit conferences on the level either of first ministers or of the heads of various departments. There would also be grounds for asking whether the creation of a House of the Provinces, suggested in several proposals for constitutional reform, would not be just as effective a remedy for the caprices of regional representation in the House of Commons.

Vincent Prince

Clout is a numbers game the West can't win

By JOHN GRAY
Globe and Mail Reporter

OTTAWA — When he emerged uncertainly from his short-lived retirement a little more than a year ago, Pierre Trudeau promised to launch "a special effort to gain supporters in Western Canada.

"In my decision to lead the Liberal Party once more, I very much want Western Canadians not only to feel, but to be fully involved in the continuing nation-building of Canada.

"I want to form a government with good people and good representation from Western Canada."

That lofty ideal landed with a crash on election night, of course, with the Liberals winning just two seats in the region, despite gaining a majority Government overall.

Those two MPs, both from the Winnipeg area, form a tiny minority in the 146-member Liberal caucus, barely more than 1 per cent. So, again, the voice of the West in the corridors of Government is thin and reedy; once more the West is out of power.

The results of the 1980 election seemed worse for the West because the Conservatives, the party favored by voters there, had been rudely thrown out of power by a shift of votes in Ontario.

When Joe Clark's Tories were in power, Western MPs had a strong voice in the government caucus (57 of the 136 Conservative MPs), but with defeat they were back to familiar isolation.

Westerners will tell you that "we don't have the numbers," and they're right. Western seats account for just a quarter of the national

total and now, as it turns out, just above 1 per cent of the Government caucus.

By contrast, and with only one exception in the past 35 years, Ontario and Quebec have accounted for more than half of the seats in the ruling party caucus. Usually, as in the present House of Commons, it's closer to 80 or 85 per cent of the seats.

So Westerners do not have the numbers, even when they vote for the winning side. Small wonder that, as Joe Clark said recently, there has been a sense in the West that they were being governed against, that their interests were not reflected in national policy.

"That might have been right, it might have been wrong; its merit doesn't matter. Its force is what counts. Its force was real in Western Canada, and that tradition is in the air."

Pauline Jewett, an Ontarian and a Liberal by upbringing, a Westerner and a New Democrat by later persuasion, has a theory about what happened to Mr. Clark and what lies in store for Western leaders in general.

"Ontario and Quebec have never, in their deepest hearts, never accepted a Western leader. . . . It was Southern Ontario which turned against Clark. They are not happy when a Westerner becomes a leader or reaches a dominant position. . . .

"There's no way yet, particularly in Southern Ontario, that a Westerner will be allowed to stay too long in power, particularly if it looks as though they are going to take away something from the people of Southern Ontario."

(Although Ontario was the key area for lost Conservative seats, the party also lost seats in the West and the Tory vote declined in each of the Western provinces.)

Miss Jewett believes that the political leadership, which, with a few notable exceptions the West has so sadly lacked until now, may come as a result of the region's growing economic power.

She may be right, but the theory runs counter to the instincts of the West in the past. As authors Larry Pratt and John Richards have written, the West lost its identification with the conventional loyalties of federal politics:

". . . Westerners of all classes came to perceive Ottawa as an imperial government, a complex of institutions organized by Central Canadian elites for the purpose of dominating and plundering the hinterlands.

"The provincial administration, whatever its political coloration, became the indispensable agent for attacking political colonialism and bargaining with external economic interests."

Other Western politicians have different perceptions about the nature of the problem.

Alberta Conservative Harvie Andre says that "to win in this country you have to have a visceral understanding and an ability to communicate with the power base, and that power base is right here (in Central Canada) because this is where most of the votes are. If a leader is from Ontario or Quebec he will have a better understanding. As simple as that."

Saskatchewan New Democratic

MP Lorne Nystrom says that the Liberals have come to be seen as the symbol of power, specifically Eastern power, and the focus of Western anger over just about everything.

Mr. Nystrom also cites the numbers. Any government is going to be guided by the political effects of its decisions, and in any government the numbers lie in Central Canada.

Provincial governments seen as most legitimate

The relative lack of representation in the Government in Ottawa has had varied effects on the West. Westerners have looked to their provincial governments rather than to Ottawa to protect their interests. In the process, as the Canada West Foundation noted recently, the legitimacy of the federal Government has been undercut.

Two British Columbia MPs, a Conservative and a New Democrat, both see the federal Government as indifferent, but do not agree on why this has occurred.

New Democrat Jim Fulton compares the attitudes of the liberal Government with the approach of the short-lived Clark Conservative government. At least the Clark ministers went out of their way to try to respond immediately to problems, he says.

The pattern among the Liberals has been delay, "hoping in many cases that it will go away . . . It's only when there is profound long-term pressure that they respond . . . . It comes with the length of time they've been in power. Their instinct is to delay."

Conservative John Fraser, a minister in the Clark government, blames the Liberals' over-riding interests in Central Canada, especially Quebec, for their failure to win seats in the West.

His voice rising with excitement, he lists a succession of unresolved Western sore points, such as oil-tanker traffic down the Pacific Coast, the proposed extension of Vancouver airport, demands for new port facilities at Prince Rupert, the flooding of the Skagit Valley and federal support for Montreal rather than B.C. Olympics.

The grievances and the rage cover more than a decade. "They couldn't see what the fuss was all about. We just thought they didn't want to listen to us at all . . . . We'd get a lot of nodding and a lot of sympathy, but nothing ever happened."

Although Mr. Fraser sees such things, not surprisingly, in partisan terms, others see the failure extending beyond a single political party.

Queen's University political scientists Richard Simeon and Jeff Evenson point to one-sided political representation, whether Liberal in Quebec or non-Liberal in the West, in terms of broad institutional failure in the political process: "The classic model of 'brokerage politics' in Canada suggested that the critical integrative institutions were to be political parties, winning support across the country.

"As coalitions of regional interests, the parties would need to formulate policies with broad national appeal . . . . This model no longer corresponds to reality."

The system, in other words, is no longer working.

In political terms, the West began to fall out of step with the rest of the country 60 years ago. The two-party system that had comfortably dominated the country since Confederation collapsed in 1921 in the face of rising discontent, and the two-party system has been dead in the West ever since.

First there were the Progressives, who swept 40 Western seats in 1921. As the Progressives declined the United Farmers of Alberta rose up; then came Social Credit and then the Co-operative Commonwealth Federation, now the New Democratic Party.

Whatever the sporadic incursions of the newer parties, which, in their time, seized power in each of the Western legislatures, the Liberals remained the dominant federal party throughout the long reign of Mackenzie King and then Louis St. Laurent.

The Conservatives were the fat cats of Bay Street, the banks and the CPR, so generations of Liberal politicians benefitted from Western satisfaction with the Liberal immigration policies that brought their ancestors to Canada.

But time and John Diefenbaker changed all that. In Mr. Diefenbaker's first election as Conservative leader, in 1957, the Liberal grip on the West was severely shaken. In 1958 the party was wiped out in the region.

The collapse of the Liberals in the West — especially when measured against their continued dominance in Quebec — has been the critical fact of political arithmetic ever since.

14 Westerners sat in Trudeau Cabinets

It's not as though the Liberals have not tried, nor is it that the West has not been represented around the Cabinet table. During the period of Trudeau government 14 different Westerners have been Cabinet ministers.

To assuage the West over the years, Mr. Trudeau called the Western Economic Opportunities Conference, pried Jack Horner loose from the Tories, tried on several occasions to persuade the NDP to join a coalition, and recently instituted the Western Development Fund.

These efforts have done nothing to halt the decline in the standing of the party — and apparently that of federalism — in the West.

But the vagaries of politics and the West are not Liberal alone. Joe Clark likes to boast that he is the only native-born Westerner to have become prime minister. He is, although R.B. Bennett and John Diefenbaker, also both Conservatives, were Westerners by adoption.

The fate of all three may be instructive about the nature of Canada and the place of the West in Canada. Mr. Bennett lasted one term in office. Mr. Diefenbaker won three terms but two were with minority governments; and Mr. Clark lasted a minority term of nine months.

THE GLOBE AND MAIL, JANUARY 14, 1980

The need for election reform

BY WILLIAM P. IRVINE

Mr. Irvine is associate professor of political studies at Queen's University.

FROM THE Task Force on Canadian Unity to post-election commentaries last May, there has been interest in changing the electoral system. The present one over-represents parties in some regions and under-represents them in others.

There is another consequence. The present system encourages electoral adventurism. It undermines the stability of parliaments. As our campaigners trudge through the snow they might reflect on this.

Why are we having an election now? Was the Government unrealistic in framing its budget? Were the Liberals and New Democrats opportunistic in the light of the November Gallup Poll? It will be up to each Canadian to assess the blame.

Before trying to do so, he should recognize that there is some truth in both. Both kinds of actions are encouraged by the electoral system. If a government has an unpopular policy, it will try to get it through early in its mandate, or when its opponents are disorganized. It only wants popular measures in the voters' minds when it goes to the polls. If an opposition finds that it is especially popular, it does everything to make life miserable for a government.

The electoral system exaggerates the swings in the popular mood. Last May, the mood was anti-Liberal, at least in English Canada. Outside Quebec, its vote fell from 39 per cent to 32 per cent. The party was savagely punished in terms of seats. Again outside Quebec, its seat share fell by 20 points, from 43 per cent to 23 per cent. The Progressive Conservative Party improved its popular support between 1974 and 1979, at least outside Quebec. The gain was fairly modest, however, from 42 to 45 per cent. The PC seat gain was more impressive, going from

48 per cent of the seats outside Quebec in 1974 to 65 per cent in 1979. The vote shift in their favor was amplified more than five times by the electoral system.

One can't call "foul" over any of this. It's the way the system works. The Progressive Conservatives paid their dues to the system many times over in the preceding period of Liberal strength, and still do as far as votes and seats in Quebec are concerned. But there is a simple moral to the story: Call (or provoke) elections when opinion tides are going your way.

If the Liberals and NDP seem to have been opportunists on Dec. 13, they were acting according to the politician's Golden Rule: Do unto others before they do unto you. The

Government would have preferred to time an election after people collected their 1979 mortgage tax credits and before they had to pay the full 1980 oil price rises.

Under a more proportional electoral system, the incentive to act this way would not be there. A five-point gain in popular support, as the Liberals received in the last Gallup Poll, would translate into only 5 per cent of the seats, hardly enough to justify provoking an election.

Proportional electoral systems have a bad press. Don't they lead to minority parliaments of the kind that

There is no evidence minority or coalition governments are irresponsible

has just acted so irresponsibly? They do, but they do encourage responsible behavior. Parties cannot count on exaggerated swings in seats. They have more incentive to make a parliament work.

Don't they lead to coalition governments? Wouldn't coalitions fail to act decisively to deal with the serious problems confronting Canada? "Yes" to the first question; but "No" to the second.

Whatever the Progressive Conservatives may say about this Parliament in the next two months, there is no evidence that minority parliaments or coalition governments are irresponsible. The German and Swiss currencies are among the strongest in the world; their inflation rates and budgetary deficits are among the smallest. Both have proportional representation electoral systems and broadly based governments.

I believe we must turn the conventional wisdom around. Countries facing grave economic or constitutional challenges need broadly based governments. They need electoral systems that encourage those governments and discourage parties from taking cheap advantage of the troubles of other parties.

Budgets in any country are coalition documents. If we feel that European coalitions take a long time to form themselves and to develop policies, the past government was no speedier. Its budget was in the gestation stage for four months. It was not completely fleshed out even by Dec. 11. Alberta and Ottawa had not yet agreed on the precise sharing of energy funds. The Clark Government was seeking a policy package that would have been acceptable to Alberta, Ontario and the Atlantic region. Now it hopes that it really had done so.

However that may be, and we will only know the answer on Feb. 18, it was a coalition budget. I can't believe that it would have taken much longer to fashion a budget that could command a parliamentary majority as well. Nor would such a budget have been worse for the country. But the Clark Government didn't seek that kind of agreement.

That is a pity. It is clear that the following years will demand sacrifice from everyone. Sacrifice is easier to accept if it is equal sacrifice. Its backing must be politically broad. The nature of the sacrifice was not made clear in the last campaign. It was not bargained widely in Parliament after the election. Nothing in the incentives of the electoral system would have encouraged that, and the Clark Government did not rise above the system. None of the parties did.

The first argument for electoral reform should not be lost from sight. The only thing we can predict in the early weeks of this campaign is that

Feb. 19 will see another regionally fragmented Parliament. The Liberals can expect no breakthroughs in the West. They have had too little time to change their leadership or policies or to build up their organizations. And although the Progressive Conservatives needn't worry about the West, one can also predict that they will take care to paint the Liberals and NDP as the parties that robbed westerners of their rightful oil and gas revenues. That is also a rule of the system: Make a regional appeal wherever you can.

The Progressive Conservatives will also have their troubles in Quebec. Quebeckers will find their leadership, policies and organizations there as unappealing as westerners find the Liberals. The Clark Government could have wooed Quebec if it had given itself time to do so. But its economic policies, purchasing policies and constitutional policies for Quebec will remain unknown in this election. They have not been acted upon so cannot be felt. There is little organization to carry the message.

little prospect of getting as many seats as their votes would justify. In the last Parliament, every party was a "third party" — in at least one crucial region of the country. The Liberals are the third party in the West. The Progressive Conservatives are third in Quebec. The NDP is third in the rest of Canada. All suffered the ravages of the electoral system some place. Surely all could see that they had an interest in changing it.

The next Parliament, too, will find every party weak and underrepresented in some crucial region of the country. That is the kind of Parliament that will have to steer the country through a tough economic and constitutional period.

What kind of reform should we seek? The Pepin-Robarts Task Force on Canadian Unity proposed a reform that would go a long way toward correcting regional underrepresentation. The Progressive Conservatives could count on a good number of Quebec seats; the Liberals would elect spokesmen from the West. That system would

Canada should go beyond the Pepin-Robarts report to proportional representation

The second election in nine months will produce one of two governments: a government from which French Quebeckers are largely excluded or a government which they dominate. We can't afford it. After the hard economic choices come the hard constitutional choices.

Hard choices need broadly based governments and stable parliaments. These in turn can only stem from the electoral system that is more responsive to broad opinion trends than to short-run moods. When the 31st Parliament was elected, it seemed to be one which might reform the present electoral system.

There is another operating characteristic of that system. Third parties tend to do very poorly, and have

still exaggerate the consequences of opinion swings. It would still encourage parties to call elections on the basis of private polls. It would encourage them to infiltrate economies just before the election. Governments would still time all the harsh economic measures for early in their term of office whether or not that was the most economically appropriate time.

For that reason, we should go beyond the Task Force proposals toward a fuller system of proportional representation. Only that way will we get governments that can speak for at least half the population. Only that will produce governments motivated to dole out both harsh medicines and happy bonuses in more even-handed ways.

THE GAZETTE, MONTREAL, FEBRUARY 26, 1980

'Rep-by-pop': Prescription for minority government

By DALE C. THOMSON
Special to The Gazette

With the federal elections out of the way, a majority government in place and the Quebec referendum not yet officially under way, the media have rediscovered western alienation as big news. And their preferred solution? — proportional representation.

Western alienation has been around a long time, in fact about as long as the western provinces have existed. In Alberta in the 1920s and 1930s, young people were raised not as young Grits or Tories as in the "East" but as western radicals, or more exactly western nationalists. Notwithstanding their ideological differences, both the CCF/NDP and Social Credit built their original power bases on that sentiment.

Eastern image

If the Liberals were weak in Alberta, the Conservatives were virtually non-existent at the provincial level. John Diefenbaker and Peter Lougheed turned that situation around by disassociating the party from its eastern image, and making it the party of western interests, as well as a national party.

One of the reasons that was possible was that the electorate · was changing. It was more prosperous and less parochial. It was not turning its back on Ottawa as much; it was demanding more effective participation in the federal government. That is the real sense of the current tension between the West and Quebec, the competition for influence in Ottawa rather than rejection of federal government leadership.

The western Canadian electorate continues to change, and in a direction that is making it less rather than more alienated. In the cities, the Liberal and New Democratic parties garnered together a majority of votes, and neither is today a party of western interests.

To seek solace from fellow Tories after Feb. 18, columnist Charles Lynch had to flee from Edmonton to rural Alberta. But even there he found little alienation. "It would be exaggerated to suggest Albertans brood overmuch about these things," he reported (*Gazette*, Feb. 22), "absorbed as they are with the garnering of goods and the reaping of riches."

The fact is that those western Canadians who sent a solid phalanx of Tory MPs to Ottawa again were voting with their pocketbooks — don't we all? — and for or against certain personalities. It is fair to speculate that if either of those considerations changed, so would the voting pattern.

Three or four years ago, public opinion soundings indicated that, as Liberal leader, John Turner could have made significant gains right across the West. Who is to say that, three or four years from now, a westerner like Lloyd Axworthy can't do even better? The tide is running in favor of national consciousness, not increasing alienation.

In these circumstances, the proposal for partial proportional representation seems almost quaint. It would encourage regional bloc voting since every party would get a number of seats in Parliament proportionate to the numbers of votes it garnered in a region. There would be less concern about "wasting" a vote by opting for a party that had less chance of winning a clear majority.

Proportional representation, either total or partial, would virtually guarantee minority government in Canada. The Feb. 18 vote, had it been totally based on proportional representation, would have given the Liberals 124 of 282 seats, the Conservatives around 100, the NDP 56: in other words a minority Liberal government. And if there is one lesson Canadians — except some NDP adepts — have learned in the past couple of decades, it is the high cost of minority government, as politicians engage in a frenzy of bribing the citizenry with its own money instead of providing sound administration.

Hardly edifying

The example of countries where proportional representation is applied is hardly edifying. What European system would Canadians wish to emulate? The Italian? The French? Or even the West German, which has watered down the principle of proportional representation to make it somewhat more workable? It should be noted that, in all these countries, the percentage of citizens that feel alienated from the councils of power is as high or higher than in Canada.

For would-be reformers, a proposal exists that is much more realistic and much more in keeping with Canadian traditions. That is a federal House of the Provinces.

Some regions feel left out of national decision-making? Some provincial governments feel that their views are not heard in Ottawa? Canadians feel — and oh how rightly — that the Senate has failed miserably in its function of spokesman for the regions? Then create a "House" where provincial views can be heard as an integral part of Parliament's processes.

Let each legislature designate that province's representatives after provincial elections, and let provincial cabinet ministers, including premiers, be included among those representatives. In that way, the voices of the regions would be heard on the national level in keeping with the concept of parliamentary democracy that the Fathers of Confederation had in mind when they created the Senate.

Of course, many modalities would have to be worked out to ensure that the provinces didn't ride roughshod over the House of Commons. But if the principle is accepted, the rest is largely housekeeping. And the principle has become acceptable in recent years to the former Trudeau government and to a majority of provincial governments. Each has included it in some form in constitutional proposals, as has Claude Ryan in his alternative to sovereignty-association.

Objections have been raised to such a plan as well. Senators wax eloquently indignant. Proponents of parliamentary ''sovereignty'' fear that the authority of cabinet and the House of Commons would be diminished in a continual power struggle between the two Houses.

National statesmen

This concern could be met by carefully circumscribing the powers of the House of the Provinces. And anyway, the power struggle would not likely be any more damaging than the one carried on between Ottawa and the provinces at the present time through the media. The West German experience shows that such a two-house Parliament is a very suitable setting for working out a consensus. And it has the additional benefit of turning regional politicians into national statesmen.

Significantly, the main provincial opposition to House of the Provinces comes from Premiers René Lévesque and Peter Lougheed. With regard to the former, little comment is needed; what is good for Canadian unity is bad for his party. As for Lougheed, his objections are largely personal: he doesn't see himself commuting back and forth between two legislatures, and even less delegating his power to deal with Ottawa to colleagues. He prefers, in his own words, to deal ''one on one'' with the prime minister of Canada.

But the sands of time are running against him as well. As indicated above, Albertans are changing, and they are thinking more and more in terms of the post-Lougheed era.

He has indicated that he has run in his last election. So unless he ''does a Trudeau,'' a fresh and quite possibly more national-minded person will be speaking for Alberta before the present constitutional debate is concluded.

In assessing proposals for constitutional change such as proportional representation and a House of the Provinces, the question has to be asked whether the cure is worse than the disease. In other words, is regional alienation so serious as to justify such structural changes? Or will Canadian parties and voters take the necessary corrective measures in a more pragmatic way?

There are solid indications that they are moving in that direction. But is that enough? The answer to that question depends in part on whether western and other regional alienations are perceived as media hype or a genuine threat to Canada.

- *Dale C. Thomson is a political science professor at McGill University.*

Discussion Questions

1. Do elections make our political parties accountable to the people?
2. Is there any value to the plurality-vote, single-member constituency system other than the fact that it improves the chances of one party's winning a majority of parliamentary seats, and therefore promotes the effective working of parliamentary government?
3. Does the current electoral system prevent the emergence of a truly successful social democratic party?
4. Should proposals for the reform of the Canadian electoral system based on proportional representation be advanced on the basis of social justice—making each vote count equally—or on considerations of regional representation in the governing party?
5. Following is a proposal for reform of the present electoral system, designed to provide greater regional balance in the major parties' parliamentary representation without producing any more than the usual number of minority governments.

    An additional twenty-eight seats (10 per cent) would be added to the House of Commons. These additional members would be full MPs chosen by the party leaders on the basis of their parties' proportion of the total popular vote, but they would be without specific constituencies. If the plan were put into effect, according to the 1980 election figures the distribution of seats would be as follows:

current seat distribution		+	10% by P.R.	=	new seat totals
Liberals	147		13 (West)		160
Conservatives	103		9 (Québec)		112
NDP	32		6 (Québec and Maritimes)		38
	282		28		310

What general problems present in the Canadian political system would such a reform address? What are its strengths and weaknesses?

Suggested Readings

William P. Irvine. 'Does the Candidate Make a Difference? The Macro-Politics and Micro-Politics of Getting Elected', in *Canadian Journal of Political Science*, vol. 25, no. 4, December 1982, 755–82.

Harold D. Clarke *et al*. 'Voting Behaviour and the Outcome of the 1979 Federal Election: The Impact of Leaders and Issues', in *Canadian Journal of Political Science*, vol. 25, no. 3, September 1982, 517–52.

Paul W. Fox, ed. *Politics: Canada*, fifth edition. Toronto: McGraw-Hill Ryerson, 1982, 351–425.

Howard R. Penniman, ed. *Canada at the Polls, 1979 and 1980: A Study of the General Elections.* Washington: American Enterprise Institute, 1981.

Richard J. Van Loon and Michael S. Whittington. *The Canadian Political System: Environment, Structure, and Process*, third edition. Toronto: McGraw-Hill Ryerson, 1981.

Jon H. Pammett. 'Elections', in Michael S. Whittington and Glen Williams, eds. *Canadian Politics in the 1980s*. Toronto: Methuen, 1981, 206–20.

Harold Clarke *et al. Political Choice in Canada*, abridged edition. Toronto: McGraw-Hill Ryerson, 1980.

John C. Courtney. 'Reflections on Reforming the Canadian Electoral System', in *Canadian Public Administration*, vol. 23, no. 3, Fall 1980, 427–57.

William P. Irvine. *Does Canada Need a New Electoral System?* Kingston: Institute of Intergovernmental Relations, 1979.

c. Interest Groups

David R. Hayes, 'A Word From the Wise', *Globe and Mail*, February 12, 1983 : *207*

Deborah McGregor, 'Business Lobby Splits on Strategy', *Financial Times*, March 22, 1982 : *209*

Les Whittington, 'Lobbying Ottawa', *Financial Times*, June 22, 1981 : *211*

Vianney Carriere, 'Bulloch Means Business on the Budget', *Globe and Mail*, May 13, 1982 : *212*

'Bank Act Successes Won by Guerrilla Lobbyists', *Globe and Mail*, October 28, 1980 : *214*

Interest groups are entities whose members hold views and objectives in common and actively seek to influence the determination of government policies that may directly or indirectly affect them. Corporations, labour unions, and professional associations are all interest groups, even though their primary functions are not political. Group activity has increased substantially over the past two decades. This development can be explained by a variety of factors, including the substantial growth of government itself; the extension of a significant regulatory structure; rational decision-making exercises within government that force groups to seek professional knowledge of the political process; and government financial support for a wide variety of groups in the name of participation. That interest groups are deeply embedded in the political system must be accepted as a given.

Press coverage of interest groups tends to be sparked by their actions, which may vary from public demonstrations to the presentation of briefs to the Cabinet. Adequate reporting on groups is severely impeded, however, by the fact that most of their interactions with government take place in private. Groups seldom try to influence legislators; they concentrate on civil servants and Cabinet ministers. The cases they present to persuade and educate these officials often include technical data, group-conducted polls, or other information not released to the press or the public. In addition, the sheer size and complexity of government today prevent reporters from gaining a broad perspective on the extent of group interactions with it. More than 200 associations have their headquarters in Ottawa, and an increasing number of corporations have set up public-affairs departments there to handle government relations. Finally, press coverage is skewed towards the established, highly legitimate groups, especially business associations; it is no accident that four of the five articles in this section are about business groups, nor that they come from *The Financial Times* and *The Globe and Mail*.

The piece by David Hayes is a rare example of an overview on interest-group activity. He correctly notes that the key to influencing policy is the successful persuasion of civil servants. Many groups tend to overemphasize the importance of Cabinet ministers. This is not to say that ministers are unimportant in the policy-making process; but by the time their intervention is solicited, it is usually too late. Hayes fails, however, to examine the reasons why some groups are more successful than others. Success depends on many factors, not the least of which is the group's 'clout'. Clout is based on such factors as size, informational resources, contacts in government, and, most important, legitimacy: the capacity to speak credibly for a significant element of society. The question of effectiveness is more accurately dealt with by Deborah McGregor, who outlines the intensity of competition among business groups. Les Whittington's article shares many of the deficiencies of the one by Hayes. Foremost among them is an inaccurate perception that access to government is always necessary and equal across the board.

There are substantial obstacles to group activity in Canada, including government secrecy, the shared jurisdiction in most areas, and the concentration of power in the hands of the executive. Vianney Carriere's article on John Bulloch's Canadian Federation of Independent Business (CFIB) suggests how difficult it is to influence governments directly. Bulloch's organization has had a degree of success applying tactics familiar in the United States to gain a more prominent place for small-business issues on the public agenda. Other groups have not been nearly so effective in their use of the same tactics.

The *Globe* article on the passage of the Bank Act presents a concrete example of group activity. The case itself is unusual because the extensive lobbying undertaken by the Canadian Bankers' Association prior to the introduction of the legislation was ineffectual. Groups tend to lobby parliamentarians only when they have failed to persuade the executive. Although lobbyists have paid more attention to legislators in recent years, they have traditionally resorted to this activity only when they could not get a hearing by the government or had failed to influence policy at an earlier stage.

THE GLOBE AND MAIL, FEBRUARY 12, 1983

A WORD FROM THE WISE

There are no lobbyists, only euphemisms for same

ASK anyone who deals with the government how important lobbying is these days and they'll chuckle and give you a case in point of what happens without it. After the first OPEC oil crisis in 1973 shocked the Canadian public, and Marc Lalonde, then minister of Energy, Mines and Resources, stated clearly his intentions to intrude upon virtually every significant industry activity as well as the laws of supply and demand, the oil industry refused to play ball. Negotiations between the oil barons and the bureaucrats stalled and were frequently stalemated, the customary presentation of private sector interests, information exchange, and orderly bargaining process was short-circuited. In essence, the industry broke unwritten Lobbying Rule Number One: never stonewall a government when the odds are stacked against you. When the NEP was finally introduced in October, 1980, its effect was dramatic—even tragic from the oil industry's point of view. A senior official of the Canadian Petroleum Association recalls: "We just didn't believe it was going to happen."

NEP cut deep into the heart of the industry, far more so than necessary, adds Bill Neville, vice-president and assistant to the chairman at the Canadian Imperial Bank of Commerce. Neville, a former journalist, founding partner of one of Ottawa's established public affairs consulting firms, and later chief of staff in the office of Opposition Leader Joe Clark, has played every position in the game and understands the rules thoroughly.

"The key to successful lobbying is realizing when a general objective has widespread public support, associating yourself with that objective, then trying to alter how it is eventually expressed as public policy," says Neville. "This was a classic example of what can happen when you misread the political climate."

The term lobbyist, coined in honor of seventeenth cen-tury favor-seekers who loitered in the lobbies of the British parliament, has traditionally had nasty connotations. It conjures images of sleazy deals struck over boozy dinners, of bribery and furtive negotiations. Although this sort of pork-barrel politicking has, at least in principle, disappeared, lobbying has not. The size and complexity of all levels of government, an $80-billion federal budget, and state intervention into the economy has all but forced the business community and just about everyone else with a stake in influencing government decision-making to ensure their particular interests are being represented. Those who do so with the most skill—and, cynics would add, the fattest wallet—benefit when government policy is enacted. The proliferation of interest groups and their representatives in Ottawa has become so large and well-organized that lobbyists almost constitute an arm of government itself.

Talk to individual lobbyists — they prefer more dignified job titles such as Public Affairs Specialist or Government Consultant — and they'll tell you they constitute a legitimate part of the democratic process. The catchword in lobbying circles is credibility. It is acknowledged on all sides that an effective lobbyist provides the government with relatively unbiased information as a quid pro quo for the privilege of being taken seriously when he tries to nudge the system in his direction.

"There is sometimes an impression that lobbying is dirty or immoral," says Herb Perry, executive director of the Insti-tution of Association Executives in Ottawa. "Every time a voter phones a school trustee he's lobbying. When the Society for Crippled Children asks for larger doorways on washrooms, it's lobbying."

A classic success story lobbyists like to cite was the fierce battle for the Mackenzie Valley pipeline contract. Canadian Arctic Gas Pipeline Ltd., was generally seen as the more attractive applicant, with extensive technical resources and a solid financial base. But its competitor, Foothills Pipe Lines Ltd., orchestrated an exhaustive lobbying campaign that took into consideration even the most marginal participants. By identifying the public interest early in the game and adjusting its corporate strategies to match, Foothills won the contract in 1977.

When a client solicits the services of a lobbyist, he is usually paying for technical advice and guidance through the bureaucratic labyrinth. A lobbyist may also open a door into a cabinet minister or senior bureaucrat's office, but it is the client himself who engages in face-to-face meetings and other acts of direct diplomacy. Most lobbyists insist a firm's reputation would be shattered if it routinely made sales pitches on the many, often conflicting, interests in Ottawa. Bill Lee, who with Bill Neville formed Executive Consultants Ltd., in 1968, says: "We provide a strategy. We tell our clients who to see, what to say, and how to say it.

"It's very insular here in Ottawa," adds Lee. "People play squash together, have dinner together, and their sons and daughters marry each other. If you are in Vancouver or Calgary and don't put your message across by taking an active role in government, you have no one but yourself to blame."

Some say the lobby system is one that typifies a root problem in society itself. Bigger is better when it comes to interest groups, and the public interest, often under-represented and inadequately financed, suffers as a result. Although the old-boy network is said to have been dismantled years ago and backroom palm-greasing is rare, money still has a way of making itself heard.

Andrew Roman is an outspoken lawyer with Toronto's federally-funded Public Interest Advocacy Centre, famous for taking on Bell Canada's rate increases on behalf of the consumer. He points out that interest groups with the resources to hire a top-flight lobbyist enjoy a distinct advantage over smaller operations. Even if the client does the talking, as Bill Lee suggests, there is scant difference in Roman's mind between a lobbyist chatting to a friend in a government department on behalf of his client and the client walking through a series of already opened doors to read from a prepared script. Professional lobbyists even have to tell well-tailored Bay Street-types how to dress, laughs Roman. "Anyone in Ottawa wearing a suit that fits is either a pimp or a fashion model."

Roman thinks most smart lobbyists separate their advocacy roles from their information-providing function. Information should be balanced and accurate, but when you are asked to comment on a matter of policy, it is possible to exercise your bias. Often it is a question of focusing the energies of a public interest group in a direction that can be applied to policy. If he had been asked by women's groups for a strategy to attack Playboy programming on Pay-TV, for example, he would have advised them to challenge the definition of obscenity under the Criminal Code rather than cutting up credit cards.

Gordon Floyd, president of Toronto-based Public Affairs Management Inc., shares the belief of most lobbyists in the integrity of their profession. And like most lobbyists, he is uncomfortable with the term — Floyd's particular euphemism is "political strategist" — but he happily describes his role as that of a translator and middleman.

"I came to this job with an idealistic streak," he says over lunch in a downtown restaurant. "My political experience (as an aide to former Liberal leader Stuart Smith) revealed a communication problem and a complete sense of distrust between politicians and the business community."

Fees, he explains, vary greatly. On a project basis, a clearly-defined brief alone would run $2,500 ("for a short, simple one") up to $15,000. An onerous, time-consuming assignment, like helping a firm lobby for a legislative amendment or other significant change that might take a year, would average $60–75,000. Clearly the marginally funded public interest group would have to rely on some very creative lobbying — perhaps buttressed by divine intervention — to compete in this league.

Some public interest groups do manage to remain effective despite limited funds. Energy Probe receives 70 per cent of its funding from donations. Despite its low-budget status, it manages to mount scrupulously researched attacks on, most notably, Ontario Hydro. In 1980, Energy Probe took the utility to task over its $3-million-a-year public relations department, accusing it of misleading and manipulating its customers on energy issues. The campaign was sufficiently persuasive that the usually reticent Ontario Energy Board instructed Hydro to re-examine its PR department, at least a partial victory for Energy Probe.

But officials at Energy Probe say they are frequently unable to represent themselves because of costs involved. When hearings on Ontario Hydro's proposed additional transmission lines into the Bruce Nuclear Station were held in Stratford, a staff representative was able to commute only on days when priority issues were being discussed. Because these hearings fell under the new provincial Consolidated Hearings Act, the regulatory board involved could award costs to participants deemed to contribute sufficiently to the hearings. Energy Probe was awarded $3,875,

but payment comes after the fact and is not guaranteed. Energy Probe lawyer David Poch argues that the cost of adversarial public interest groups should be borne by the company involved.

"The public hearing process should be seen as a necessary cost of any project," he says. "The participants should be paid, just as a lawyer is paid for a zoning change or an engineer for his services. If it is an important project that needs a public hearing but the proponent is not large enough to bear the costs, then let it come out of the public purse."

A 1981 report for the Economic Council of Canada written by two Toronto lawyers recognized the inherent imbalance on the public interest side of the lobbying trade, and identified an eternal bugbear in the process — "free riders" — the majority of people who, although they do not contribute to a group, will happily share the victor's spoils.

The report catalogued possible solutions to the plight of public interest lobbyists: greater direct government funding will improve finances but carries with it the danger that political independence could be eroded; a cost awards system, like the one that reimbursed Energy Probe, does not

help pay the bills between hearings. The report recommended that the cost awards system be officially established, along with a system of tax credits to attract "free rider" support and broaden the funding base of under-financed public interest groups.

Critics point out that it is exceptionally difficult to pinpoint impropriety in the huge grey area between patronage and friendship. It would be hard to prove a casual stock market tip mentioned over lunch was a payoff, or prove that an ambassadorship came about as a result of a whispered promise to return a favor done years earlier. At various times a private bill has been unsuccessfully raised calling for a parliamentary registry for lobbyists, but a similar U.S. system is generally dismissed as ineffective. Public Affairs consultants agree with the idea in principle, but patiently explain that they do not indulge in *lobbying*, so they wouldn't register even if a bill was passed.

"It's sort of like adultery," Andrew Roman says of the notion that government affairs professionals in Ottawa are not lobbyists. "It's not the sort of thing the successful ones will talk about."

David R. Hayes

Anatomy of a successful lobby

GORDON FLOYD outlines a successful lobbying effort on behalf of a U.S. client. Roadway Expressway Inc., a trucking firm based in Akron, Ohio, wanted to acquire Harkema Express Ltd., a small company in Brampton.

The federal Foreign Investment Review Agency had considered many similar propositions and turned them down.

"As an economic nationalist, I winced at the prospect of helping a U.S. company," Floyd admits. "But I had no qualms after I looked at the firm, saw the purchasing it planned to do in Canada, the research and development and the employment it would create."

Floyd's first step was a thorough researching of FIRA's pre-disposition and identification of all likely opponents and supporters. He lobbied local, provincial and federal members of parliament and

asked them to make representations to FIRA. He directed the same campaign at Herb Gray, federal Minister of Industry, Trade and Commerce, by enlisting provincial Ministry of Transport and Industry, Trade and Commerce officials, local MPs, the Ontario caucus of the Liberal Party, and especially Ross Milne, president of the federal Liberal Party's Ontario branch and a man likely to run in the Brampton riding in the future. Floyd also approached the opposition critics for assurance that they supported the idea and would not be likely to roast Gray afterward.

An additional feature of the Roadway Expressway lobby was Floyd's discovery that a U.S.-Canada trucking war might be relieved by a successful resolution of the FIRA application. Deregulation of the U.S. trucking industry meant that Canadian truckers were free to buy

licences and to operate south of the border, but FIRA effectively kept American interests out of Canada. Floyd realized the U.S. might regard FIRA approval of Roadway Expressway a sign of Canada's flexibility on the issue. It might even result in a lifting of the current moratorium on sales of trucking licences to Canadians.

Floyd acquainted the American authorities with the situation via the U.S. ambassador and the Canadian embassy in Washington, and got the message to Gray in what Floyd describes as "an authoritative yet non-threatening way."

Floyd's strategy was successful. Roadway Expressway's purchase was approved last November — 14 months later — and four business days after the decision, the U.S. lifted its moratorium on Canadian truckers.

THE FINANCIAL TIMES, MARCH 22, 1982

Business lobby splits on strategy

Debate centres on confrontation

By Deborah McGregor

OTTAWA — The usual murmur of organized business voices in the government's ear is rising to a deafening roar. Seldom have business and government been so polarized in their views about how to attack the country's economic problems. Seldom have business groups played so loud and visible a role in trying to sway the federal policy-makers to their points of view.

The noise raises two crucial questions:
• How effective are these groups — ranging from the broadly-based, big-business-oriented Business Council on National Issues to the narrow special-industry groups such as the Life Underwriters' Association of Canada?
• How well do they represent the views of the thousands of businessmen they claim to speak for?

Categorical answers simply do not exist, but the questions have become so vital in these times of financial hardship that they can turn a business group inside out.

A recent example is the sudden resignation of Stanley Roberts, 53-year-old president of The Canadian Chamber of Commerce. The chamber is the country's largest business group, with 140,000 members. The events leading to the Roberts resignation make one of the more dramatic examples of how divided and unsure some business groups have become about how to present the business position so it will be heeded by government.

In the weeks before the resignation, Roberts, Chamber president for just over a year, had been locked in an internal wrangle with his board of directors. The problem: his high profile and strongly political style. Roberts was making six to eight speeches a week. He spent most working days on the road. A lifelong Liberal, he had become disenchanted with the current regime in Ottawa. He pulled no punches in criticizing the policies and orientation of the federal government on behalf of the Chamber.

Roberts' 42-member board was decidedly uncomfortable with the controversy and publicity. But that wasn't all.

Roberts' outspoken political style was judged by many on the board to be generating an ominous side-effect. They said doors in Ottawa were slowly closing to the Chamber. Sources say Prime Minister Trudeau's top advisers were rapidly cooling. They saw a political enemy masquerading as a business spokesman. Roberts does not acknowledge this, although he concedes there were some "intense" meetings with his board of directors over his unwillingness to be a "stay-at-home administrator."

For the Chamber, a group that has prided itself on excellent government contacts and on carrying a broad business view to government, the Roberts resignation resolved the immediate problem but left the chamber facing some tough soul-searching on future approaches to government relations.

For other business groups, this affair has been a fascinating lesson in strategy at a time when they are deeply divided over how strident they should be in opposing a government considered by many to be out of touch with their world.

Some groups — notably the small businessmen and life insurers — have opted for turning the decibel level right up. They have plunged into all-out public war with Finance Minister Allan MacEachen over his highly controversial tax changes.

It has degenerated to "political hardball," says John Bullock, president of the Canadian Federation of Independent Business.

Both Bulloch and the life insurers have long concentrated on mobilizing public opinion to try to win their cases.

Last week, for instance, Dominion Life Assurance Co., one of the most militant of the life insurers, provoked a swift and angry response from the usually implacable MacEachen when the company sent letters to 7,000 mortgage-holders urging them to oppose a supposed government intention to impose a tax on homeowners.

Tax denied

MacEachen quickly and firmly denied he has any intention of imposing such a tax or that it has ever been considered. He accused the company of being "mischievous," trying to frighten and confuse people as a way of gaining support for a narrow change the life insurers want to achieve in the government's proposed taxing of accrued income on life insurance policies.

Will the new style, the high-profile, combative approach chosen by the small businessmen and life insurers succeed in swaying the policy-makers where traditional methods have failed?

"I am impressed by logic, argumentation, the strength of the argument, rather than by hastily arranged coalitions, press conferences and rhetoric," MacEachen told the *Times* in an interview.

Put more bluntly, "Do you listen to people when they scream at you? Absolutely not," says John Evans, MacEachen's former parliamentary secretary. He has been meeting with several business groups on budget issues in recent months.

Evans gives high points to the broad-based business groups such as the Business Council on National Issues and the Canadian Manufacturers Association for what he calls a "more balanced approach."

"They don't drag it down into the mud with far overblown statements designed to inflame public opinion," he says.

Jean-Jacques Gagnon, a vice-president with Alcan Aluminium Ltd. and chairman of the CMA, who also sits on the policy committee of the BCNI, believes a quiet, consistent offering of views to government is more useful than public fanfare and emotional appeal. Yet, endorsement from politicians is not considered entirely a boon by the rank and file of many business groups. The "reasonable" approach praised by the politicians appears too soft to many of the groups' members.

Part of the Stan Roberts dilemma at the Chamber, for example, is that he was accused by some members of not going hard enough on the government over the budget.

Under criticism

"I was under criticism for not speaking out strongly enough on that one," he recalls.

At the Business Council, composed of 140 chief executives, president Thomas D'Aquino has been urged by at least one member to take a harder line. In yet another revealing example of how associations are forced to juggle internal politics, the Prospectors and Developers Association came out publicly swinging at the recent mineral strategy paper released by Mines Minister Judy Erola after having praised her privately for consulting it closely through the paper's formation. When confronted by an angry Erola after all the negative headlines, the PDA's somewhat sheepish response was that it simply couldn't be seen by its members to be agreeing with the government.

Methods vary among groups for keeping in touch with members' views. The CFIB, for instance, does regular and thorough surveys of its 64,000 members, providing background on an issue and asking for a member's position on it. The CMA has a telephone call-in service through which it keeps tabs on what issues are of primary concern to manufacturers.

In most associations, single-issue committees made up of executives from several member companies thrash out a position and conduct research on a particular subject. The results are then funnelled through for endorsement by an executive committee and board of directors.

However, the particular style of an association president can be just as much if not more of a factor than the group's official position. Bulloch of the CFIB, for instance, has become a controversial and outspoken figure, a kind of celebrity in his own right.

Not all presidents see their role as that of public figure. George Fleischmann, an ex-civil servant who knows his way around most of Canada's bureaucratic corridors, is one. As president of the Grocery Products Manufacturers of Canada, one of the more effective lobby groups in Ottawa, Fleischmann sees his job as one of introducing the executives of GPMC's 142 member companies to Ottawa's senior powerbrokers. "I am trying to get my guys to look ministers and deputy ministers right in the eye — I don't even want to be in the middle," he says. Fleischmann arranges monthly breakfasts for 20 or 25 of his member presidents and invites a senior bureaucrat or politician as guest.

A main responsibility of a trade association is to let government know of the consequences of taking an action that has adverse effects, he says. "But it doesn't mean that we are going to get what we want all the time."

A point of weakness, one acknowledged by many of the groups, is the lack of sophistication in briefs they routinely submit to government on specific policies. An increasing number of groups are hiring economic consulting firms to prepare technically convincing briefs.

The need for a business group to do its homework thoroughly on an issue is stressed by the Business Council's D'Aquino: 'Fundamental to the quiet and reasonable approach is the need to do incredibly thorough homework, equal to that done by the officials themselves. To not do that homework is to go in with one hand tied behind your back."

And yet, as CMA president Roy Phillips has observed, even the best briefs don't always get acknowledged. Phillips says the government should give business a better idea of how their submissions are received. "When we make a representation, we find we always have a good hearing, no difficulty getting access to ministers or officials. The difficulty is we don't get feedback as to their appreciation of our submission."

To many business spokesmen, this is a clear symptom of the fundamental rift between the two sides. While not all share Stan Roberts' political views, most seem to feel, as Roberts does, that: "No organization can claim that it has the ear of this government. This government is not co-ordinating its activities with those of the private sector. And it's missing a lot of bets because it isn't including the business community in its policy formulation."

Whether a stronger business lobby will do anything to alter that relationship remains to be seen.

Number of members	Some major lobbyists	Annual budget $ millions
140	Business Council on National Issues	1.0*
140,000	Canadian Chamber of Commerce	2.4
14**	Canadian Federation of Agriculture	8
64,000	Canadian Federation of Independent Business	6.0
8,500	Canadian Manufacturers' Association	3.5
70	Canadian Petroleum Association	8.0***
24,000	Canadian Real Estate Association	1.4
100	Mining Association of Canada	2.2

*BCNI draws heavily on resources of members for preparation of briefs, etc.
**includes 10 provincial federations plus 4 national commodity organizations.
***includes a $4 million advertising budget.

THE FINANCIAL TIMES, JUNE 22, 1981

Lobbying Ottawa

It can be relatively easy if you know all the rules

By Les Whittington

Special to the Times

Ottawa—Throughout the spring and summer of 1980, glimpses of what the federal government was planning for its hard-hitting national energy program sprang up repeatedly in the business press and in investment house newsletters.

Yet oil industry executives howled with indignant surprise when Energy Minister Marc Lalonde released the details of the nationalistic program last Oct. 28.

The waves of shock heard from Montreal to Calgary underscore a simple fact: Many corporations, for all their extensive marketing and production knowledge, are still in the Dark Ages when it comes to the decision-making process in Ottawa.

"You'd be amazed the number of oil and gas companies who either didn't understand what was happening in national energy policy before the NEP came out or didn't believe what they were hearing would really happen," says David MacNaughton, president of Ottawa-based Public Affairs International Ltd.

"The reason was that the companies didn't understand the motivation of those in the government who were involved," says MacNaughton.

His firm, which advises corporations on federal policy, is part of a vast lobbying industry that has grown up in Ottawa in the past three decades to help business and other

groups better understand—and influence — what the government does.

At the centre of this effort are the associations, an estimated 300 of them representing professional and trade groups in Ottawa. They employ 2,000 people here and spend an estimated $100 million-plus a year getting their messages across to ministers, MPs and bureaucrats.

There are also the lawyers and other freelance lobbyists with good connections, policy consultants whose collective experience covers every area of public policy and government relations specialists. These last experts supply information on where the government is going and help companies write briefs — but refuse to actually represent clients.

Generally, in serving business, the aim of all these high-paid representatives is twofold: To alert companies in advance to decisions that will

influence corporate planning or to press the government for changes in existing or proposed legislation.

"Lobbying" tosses up shopworn images of well-heeled insiders cornering the powerful at exclusive cocktail parties or senior executives slipping into a minister's office for a quick chat after some lawyer with the right connections has managed to pry open the door on short notice.

No doubt that sort of thing goes on. But the real business of lobbying today is a sophisticated, professional endeavor that relies on much more than knowing the right person.

To begin with, a company with a problem has got to know exactly who to see. For instance, says one lobbyist, you shouldn't start with a minister. If he turns you down, then there's no one to whom you can appeal.

Bill Lee, who directed Prime Minister Trudeau's 1968 election campaign before forming Executive Consultants Ltd. in Ottawa, insists that 85% of all government decisions are taken by officials.

"There's no point in sending a businessman in cold to see a minister who may not 'care less' what the businessman is talking about," Lee says.

Door-opening

"In many cases, the minister's not the guy he should be talking to. If the businessman can talk to a public servant and convince him that what the government has in mind is detrimental to the public interest— that it may cost jobs or trade opportunities, for example — the public servant likely will not do it."

For these reasons executives should be wary of "door-opening," a special intervention to set up an appointment with a minister.

Besides providing reports to business on government policy, what to expect in federal budgets, problems with emerging legislation, analysis of competition legislation and

so forth, Executive Consultants also gives its clients a hand in preparing briefs to be presented to officials or to committees.

"One thing you definitely don't want to do if you're going to go in and see a minister or deputy minister or parliamentary committee is to prepare a one-inch-thick brief that nobody's going to have time to read. You have to boil it down to one or two pages," says Lee.

Corporate representatives should also develop some understanding of policy that includes the public interest as well as the business interest and to make suggestions that will solve the problem from both points of view.

Some points

Here are a few other points to keep in mind when dealing with the government:

• In discussion with an official or MP, don't forget to consider where he or she stands in the policy-making process. Otherwise your evaluation of what was said may prove faulty.

• Look at government dealings as you would any corporate problem. "Many companies' difficulty is one of approach," says MacNaughton. "Companies don't use the same skills they have learned in marketing or finance or whatever when it comes to dealing with government. They think government is weird and wonderful and something you approach differently."

• Be factual and reasonable. A well-researched brief is much more effective than tough talk.

• Find out what theories and information are guiding officials. Don't assume they know more or less than they actually do.

• Stress general issues. Politicians in particular are inclined to grasp "the big picture" rather than the small details.

• Monitor and follow up all submissions.

There's plenty of room for imagination. Witness the

Canadian Federation of Independent Business, which in 10 years has established itself as the most successful pressure group ever to hit Ottawa.

In its first decade, the federation boasts, it has reduced the annual taxation burden on small and medium-sized businessmen by more than $1 billion.

The CFIB, whose national affairs director and front-line operator in Ottawa is Jim Bennett, has won points by providing information about its members that politicians can't ignore.

Recently, the CFIB conducted a poll on the federal government's employment tax-credit system, then presented Employment and Immigra-tion Minister Lloyd Axworthy with the stunning knowledge that half of the respondents spurned the plan. This led Axworthy to bypass his own officials and ask the federation to conduct another survey to find out what small business-men thought was wrong with the tax credit system.

"When dealing with politicians," says Bennett, "you've got to talk in terms of short-term politics as well as long-term economics. They want to know what's going to get them elected."

In addition to the CFIB, some of the other groups considered among the most effective in federal circles are the Chamber of Commerce, the Canadian Federation of Agri-culture, the Canadian Manu-facturers' Association, the Consumers Association of Canada and the Canadian Labor Congress.

The lobbying game never holds still, even for the most powerful. Many observers be-lieve Canadian bankers, who have always wielded consider-able clout with government, found themselves badly out-manoeuvred in the fight over the new Bank Act.

Feeling threatened by the early proposals for Bank Act changes forwarded by the fed-eral finance department, the near-banks, such as trust com-panies, leasing companies, credit unions and caisse popu-laires, left no stone unturned in a furious lobbying effort that led to extensive alterations be-fore the legislation was finally approved.

The banks' competitors ap-plied relentless pressure on federal MPs, both at the grass-roots levels and in innumera-ble interviews in Ottawa, and sought help from provincial governments in getting certain aspects of the proposed legisla-tion altered. What the banks, through their organization, the Canadian Bankers' Associa-tion, seemed not to realize was that lobbying had become much more complicated since the previous Bank Act changes way back in 1967.

Les Whittington is an Ottawa freelance writer.

THE GLOBE AND MAIL, MAY 13, 1982

Bulloch means business on the budget

"I feel like I've been the Minister of Finance and the Minister of Industry, Trade and Commerce for 10 years now." — John Bulloch, president of the Canadian Federation of In-dependent Business.

By VIANNEY CARRIERE

Billy Graham berating the devil might be a mild-man-nered diplomat compared with John Bulloch as he rails against the fools and incompetents, the technocrats, bureaucrats and politicians who have given us The Budget.

Not in 10 years, since the anathema of E.J. Benson's white paper on taxation — a document that was eventually junked and the most lasting ef-fect of which may well have been the creation of John Bulloch — has the self-styled champion of small business been as evangelically aroused.

After an hour's conversation with him — he is still warming up at this point — contempo-rary problems begin to assume Biblical proportions as one awaits his injunction to gird up one's loins and join him in battle.

In the course of a kaleido-scopic interview during which The Budget is the glue that holds the collage of philoso-phy and anecdotes together, he rolls his eyes, punches invisi-ble demons in front of him, slaps his thighs and occasion-ally breaks into childlike gig-gles as he pontificates on the absurdity of it all.

He will say, eloquently, tire-lessly and never-endingly, that he is sad, angry, worried, ap-palled and dismayed and that today he roams the country with a heavy heart because of the economic despair he sees.

He goes on and on, an oil-and-water mixture of passion and logic, in a series of dia-tribes that trickle at the source and grow into a verbal Niagara as the morning progresses.

In the end, the sum total of it all, inescapably, is that John Bulloch, 48, founder and president of the Canadian Federation of Independent Business, loves the fray and craves the political dust that swirls around him as he does what he does best: lobby, cajole, exert pressure.

In the years since that first great victory over Mr. Benson he has, to a large extent, been consigned to a limbo of impor-tant but low-key and low-pro-file skirmishes, the results of which were often recorded, he points out, in two-para-graph items in the Report on Business.

Those years have also seen bitter intramural squabbling in the federation, and the quel-ling, not without bloodshed, of a staff revolt that gave Mr. Bulloch "a lot of scar tissue" and a new, more subdued role in his organization.

The Battle of the Budget, on the other hand, 10 years after the victorious joust with Mr. Benson, has revitalized the man even as the constant travel and the endless lobbying have drained him.

"I'm front and centre on the budget and this is a four-year war," he says without a hint of trepidation that in war those front and centre face the most lethal volleys.

He has made enemies. He is no longer invited to state dinners, he says, and he has not had his picture taken with the Prime Minister in recent months.

But that, Mr. Bulloch is quick to point out, is all part of the game he and politicians play, a game in which, depend-ing on one's causes, yester-day's ally is today's foe and today's enemy may be tomor-row's elbow-mate at the head table of an Ottawa dinner.

In the decade since Mr. Benson's white paper was withdrawn, Mr. Bulloch's clout has evolved from his position as founder and leader of the fledgling Council For Fair Taxation to where he sits today, in the just-short-of-luxurious new headquarters for the 64,000-member Canadian Federation of Independent Business on north Yonge Street in Toronto.

The organization has grown from the embattled, angry people who were galvanized into vociferous protest by Mr. Benson's tax proposals, to a powerful national institution and lobby whose stated aims are "to promote and protect a system of free enterprise in Canada and give the independent a greater voice in laws governing business and the nation."

In his own analysis, when Mr. Bulloch says Allan Mac-Eachen's budget is the most flawed and detrimental policy paper ever to swat small business, the politicians and civil servants must perforce hear him because of the constituency he has created and the federation's credibility.

"The budget," Mr. Bulloch says, "is an attack on small business." He pauses before completing the statement in a way that goes far in providing the key to John Bulloch: "And an attack on small business is an attack on my father."

John Bulloch Sr. was, for 30 years, a Bay Street tailor who built a business by flouting conventional practices, and in the process pioneered advocacy advertising in a regular series of frequently reactionary and always outrageous newspaper ads.

His ghost, two years after his death, is the other leitmotif in an interview with John Bulloch Jr.

When he was 10 years old, today's lobbyist was an occasional business apprentice and sometimes helper at the tailor shop. Two blocks away on Yonge Street was Bassel's Lunch, where father and son occasionally escaped for rice pudding. The memory, be it of the pudding, or of the father-and-son closeness, has Mr. Bulloch silently closing his eyes in nostalgic ecstasy.

Mr. Bulloch's politics and his iron will were being shaped by that relationship.

"Later, I was a teacher of business at Ryerson," Mr. Bulloch recalls, "and I was still watching the living experience of my father running his business. I've always had problems with all those conventional theories of capitalism because what my father did just didn't fit into the theories. To me, the marketplace has always been half a million people like my old man."

Bulloch says he feels indispensable

Mr. Bulloch feels he is indispensable to the federation and in a uniquely appropriate position to speak for all those who are trying to make ends meet in the marketplace because of what he learned from his father, to him the epitome of the small businessman.

"No one around here has the instincts I have," he says. "My dad was typical. My staff is not typical. I am more typical."

This conviction, he says, is reflected by Mandate, a continuing series of member surveys the federation undertakes to canvas views on a wide range of business and government-related topics.

"My staff are buffaloed all the time when they see how members vote on Mandate," Mr. Bulloch says. "But I'm not, because I can always say that's the way dad would have voted."

Mr. Bulloch relates a telling anecdote about his father. It seems that, years after he was established as a tailor on Bay Street, the old man would come to work in the morning and his first chore would be to inspect the washroom and clean and polish the sink and toilet bowl if he found them less than spotless.

"I learned that when you're the boss, you clean the toilet," his son says.

Or, by analogy, the boss does everything because in the end no one can do it as well as he can. It's not the best way to instill confidence in employees.

The son learned his lesson well. "I'm the only one who can do all the jobs around here. I'm still the only one here who could start this whole thing all over again . . . . The policy people I have around here, they are professional managers. They are not entrepreneurs."

But in spite of that belief, Mr. Bulloch no longer behaves as if the essence and survival of the federation were linked intrinsically to his personality and intellect alone.

It took a staff walkout and near coup d'etat in 1979, prompted by an attempt by Mr. Bulloch and Ray Sherk, his right-hand man at the time, to reorganize the federation's field staff, for the federation's founder to realize that his child was growing and could now wallop daddy.

"It was strictly a two-man show between Bulloch and Sherk," says Daniel Horigan, a federation pioneer who left at that time and founded the competing Canadian Organization for Small Business. "I had always believed in participatory management, but Bulloch and Sherk consulted nobody."

The federation survived the blood-letting, but in the aftermath, the organization and Mr. Bulloch's role in it had changed. "I now have a board of directors and a contractual arrangement with them," he says. "So they can come after me if I cease to be effective or if I'm acting dumb."

As Mr. Bulloch explains it, his role changed from that of an entrepreneur to that of a manager. His language is revealing when he contrasts the two.

"Entrepreneurship is a high. It is total exhilaration and total exhaustion. There is nothing like the high of getting something started and watching it take off. During those years, you make it because you just can't handle the thought of failing. Every time you come close to failing, you brace yourself and give it another shot . . . .

"There are different kinds of pleasures now. My pleasure now is the same kind of pleasure I get watching my teenagers become adults. I've had my years of chaos. Now I sleep more, and I take holidays . . . ."

If Mr. Bulloch displays more eloquence for his previous incarnation as autocratic entrepreneur than he does for his role as manager, it is because he is more of a fighter than an administrator.

The federation was born out of anger, a collective anger channelled through the evangelical Ryerson teacher who, despite today's change in roles, jealously preserves what he describes as "the mystique of the founder."

It has been said that Mr. Bulloch, to his detriment, has never outgrown the confrontational approach that once forced him to beat down doors to be heard.

"He was the right man for the right time," says Stanley Roberts, president of the Canadian Chamber of Commerce. "No one else could have broken down those doors. But there is a need today for a man who can dialogue and persuade and John might no longer be the right man, because he does tend to flare up . . . ."

Horigan is less persuaded

Mr. Horigan is less persuaded of Mr. Bulloch's effectiveness over the years. "He's certainly been highly visible," he says, "but if you look at where we are now as opposed to where we were 10 years ago, you see more taxes, more government intervention, more regulation . . . ."

Mr. Bulloch responds, "The places where I haven't been effective is where no one's been effective."

His approach has left the federation a fiercely independent body that speaks to all governments and all political parties, but that will get into bed with none.

But Mr. Bulloch has a future vision, with thinly disguised political overtones, of leading the federation down a more ideological path.

Within a year, he says, he hopes the federation, which he describes in this context as "a political action group," will "articulate a position paper, a manifesto on the federation's political and economic philosophy. We would have to put our philosophy in relevant Canadian terms, not Southern Baptist terms, in a way Canadians would accept it and hopefully unify the country."

But so long as he is wanted, useful and effective, he says, he will stay with the federation because of the parental feeling he has for the organization and because, undeniably, the federation has clout and John Bulloch revels in having clout.

The pleasures of being a manager, as he says, are different, but no less intense.

And yet, in his just-short-of-luxurious office, at no point in his recounting of the history, battles, tribulations and victories of the federation does his face light up quite so brightly as when he describes the day it moved into its first dumpy office on Mount Pleasant Road.

The first thing Mr. Bulloch did that day, he recalls, was scrub the toilet.

THE GLOBE AND MAIL, OCTOBER 28, 1980

Bank Act successes won by guerrilla lobbyists

From the Ottawa Bureau of The Globe and Mail

OTTAWA — Robert MacIntosh, president of the Canadian Bankers Association, is singing the Bank Act blues these days because the banks have been out-lobbied by various other interest groups, such as credit unions and trust companies.

It's an ironic situation, because MPs on the Commons finance committee believe the CBA, representing Canada's dozen or so chartered banks, has used its resources, staff, access to private planes and key connections at the top in Ottawa to mount the most organized and effective lobby on pending changes to the Bank Act.

But Mr. MacIntosh doesn't agree: "We haven't been effective, because from the time of the white paper (on banking in 1976) through to today, the Government has on almost every issue made concessions to the competitors of the banks."

On such things as leasing and mortgage lending, the trust companies and the automobile dealers have put themselves

Trust companies seek protection

forward as the little guys who need protection from the big guys (the banks), and the members of Parliament have by and large bought that line.

So much so, Mr. MacIntosh says, that the Commons committee has voted to restrict the banks in these fields, even though that would be detrimental to consumers who could expect lower interest rates on car leasing and mortgages to result from the extra competition from banks.

Dismayed by the Commons committee's attitude, the bankers are now lobbying hard at the Senate banking committee, whose members have historically been more receptive to the arguments of the large chartered banks.

The big lobbying efforts on the Bank Act—though mostly carried out behind the scenes — have been the most active and heated of any directed at a piece of federal legislation concerning business in several years.

The Bank Act governs what type of financial business the chartered banks can or cannot do. The current Bank Act keeps the banks out of such businesses as leasing, and puts a ceiling on their mortgage lending to give protection to other financial institutions.

Various forces have come into play — not just the vested

Equality principle has been eroded

interest groups in Canada but also foreign banks and provincial governments.

The original intention of the federal Finance Department, as expressed in the white paper, was to have all financial institutions in Canada compete on an equal basis, although with some limit on the over-all slice of the pie going to foreign banks.

Notwithstanding the Finance Department, this principle has been eroded so much during the past four years that it no longer exists in Bill C-6, the latest version of the Bank Act that is currently being considered by the Commons finance committee and is supposed to pass Parliament completely later this year.

How did this happen? Lobbying.

It was lobbying, in the sense of vested interest groups putting forward positions on vital issues, that did the trick.

It all started years before the 1976 white paper on banking. The CBA and individual bankers met Finance Department officials, submitted briefs and made numerous speeches advocating the principle of the banks being on the same footing in competing with other financial institutions.

The banks no longer wanted a ceiling on mortgage lending and the numerous restrictions on what business they could do, such as leasing and factoring, that other financial institutions, including foreign bank subsidiaries, were allowed to pursue.

Furthermore, the banks did not want to be saddled with the requirement to keep cash on hand when other financial institutions did not have to do so and, consequently, had lower operating costs.

The Finance Department agreed, and the white paper outlined a system whereby the banks would be allowed to do virtually anything, the foreign banks' subsidiaries would become banks and have to compete as such, and all financial institutions would have to belong to a Canadian cheque-clearing system and also hold cash reserves.

This was equivalent to reading the riot act to the near-banks, such as the credit unions, caisse populaires, trust companies and leasing companies, which had all had some protection from competition from the banks and which all feared they would be out-gunned in the market-place.

That is when the lobbying began in earnest.

Seeing that the proposal would cost them more money, the Canadian Co-operative Credit Society (representing credit unions), the Quebec-based Caisses Populaires Desjardin and the trust companies began feverishly to lobby the Finance Department and Finance Minister.

When they saw they were not getting anywhere in Ottawa, they then turned their attention to the provincial governments, which tend to be more sensitive, particularly in Quebec, Saskatchewan and British Columbia, to the needs of the credit unions and other near-banks, the alternative to the banks.

Provincial politicians urged to use clout

The credit unions and caisses populaires (with nine million members) sent out information to local managers across the country, who usually knew the local MP and member of the Legislature and found it easy to put their case to the politician on his home turf. The provincial politicians were asked to use their clout in federal-provincial relations to squelch the proposed mandatory-cash-reserve requirements.

Forces combined, the provincial governments voiced their opposition to the federal proposal, and the lobbying effort worked. The federal Government announced soon afterward that it would not require all financial institutions to be members of the cheque-clearing organization and only the banks would be forced to maintain cash reserves.

Was it the right thing to do? Never mind. With one stroke, the Finance Minister was able to get the credit unions, caisses populaires and provincial governments off his back.

Thus, the federal Government dropped its intention to maintain some competitive balance in the Canadian financial system. But this wasn't enough to satisfy all the other vested-interest groups.

When Bill C-57 was introduced in May, 1978, the Commons and Senate hearings heard a variety of shrill complaints: The trust companies wanted to keep the ceilings on bank mortgage lending: the Canadian Association of Data Processing Companies wanted to keep the banks out of the computer field; the Investment Dealers Association wanted restrictions on banks in security underwriting; the Cattlemen and Canadian Agriculture Association were after special favors; and so on.

Bankers succeeded in several battles

All claimed they would be run out of business by the banks. In other words, they all wanted to protect their bread and butter from the allegedly greedy banks.

The Senate and Commons committees complied by and large with these requests, giving greater protection to investment dealers, data processors, trust companies and leasing companies.

The banks also won some battles, talking down the new provision to prevent bank officers from holding non-bank directorships and retaining their right to do mortgage lending (although still with a ceiling), to do banking-related computer work, such as payrolls, and to do leasing through subsidiaries.

The short-lived Conservative government introduced a revised Bank Act that accepted many of the Commons committee recommendations. When the Conservatives were defeated and the Liberals took over once again, Finance Department officials thought that finally, they had a Bank Act that both major parties accepted and would receive quick passage.

It was not to be. During the past summer, the vested interests have again put their lobbying efforts to work on the Commons finance committee and have won further concessions, much to the chagrin of the bankers and the Finance

Department, including Pierre Bussieres, the Minister of State (Finance), who was assigned by Finance Minister Allan MacEachen to shepherd the bill through Parliament.

During the past few months, the Automobile Dealers Association, getting its members to nab MPs at their constituency offices, have managed to get the committee to agree to restrict the banks from leasing for all vehicles under 46,000 pounds. Thus, the auto dealers retain their monopoly on car and truck leasing.

The Canadian Cattlemen's Association won a special clause giving preference to farmers in certain agricultural-products loans.

And the trust companies won a major concession when the committee set aside a provision which removed the cash-reserve requirement for banks on term deposits with a maturity of more than one year. (This gave the trust companies, which are not required to keep such reserves, a competitive edge on the banks.)

It showed up the fact, one Finance Department official said, that the banks have largely been ineffectual during the latter stages of the Bank Act review, and other vested interest groups have learned quickly how to muster support for their positions. (The exceptions to the rule were the finance companies, which are of diminishing importance on the financial scene, and to some degree the trust companies, which failed to agree as a group on many issues and left much of the lobbying to individual companies.)

The erosion of the banks' initially strong position took place at the level of the MPs, who always tend to favor the little guy. There were even cases when Liberal MPs voted against the advice of the Liberal minister in charge, Mr. Bussieres — a blow to party solidarity.

All this leaves the CBA's Mr. MacIntosh licking his wounds in Toronto, wondering what went wrong.

He is also a little bitter about

the way the committee system of Parliament works. There is no requirement for consistent, deliberate consideration of the bill clause by clause; instead, MPs wander all over the place. Furthermore, he said, the composition of the committee can change at any time, with some MPs arriving to vote on changes without even having been present for the discussions.

Mr. MacIntosh said in an interview that lobbying over the Bank Act has changed dramatically since the act was last changed in 1967, when contact with the Minister of Finance and Finance Department officials was more important than lobbying individual MPs.

The banker hinted that the CBA has watched with admiration the way the credit unions have made their problems known to their members and have thereby increased support in the community at large for the credit union position, knowing that the MPs would have to respond to it.

Banks are expected to seek staff support

Mr. MacIntosh said the banks will be doing more of the same, informing their 154,000 employees across Canada about bank problems and try to get the staff to help out.

In the communities, he said, the bank manager comes and goes, while credit union managers and car dealers are usually permanent residents and know the politicians much better.

"We also have problems with our image. When we go to lobby, we have an unsympathetic ear at all three parties."

As Mr. MacIntosh put it, the banks "feel that they have to get politically hard-nosed in putting our case to the public. MPs reflect the public perceptions, and if we're going to get through to the politicians, we have to get through to the public.

"It's a whole new ball game in some respects."

Discussion Questions

1. It has been claimed that the CFIB is the most successful business lobby in the country. Can we tell from Carriere's article whether this is true? How do we measure the success of an interest group? What are the characteristics of a successful group?

2. Does the success of the CFIB depend on the personality of John Bulloch? Would the organization survive under different leadership?

3. Neo-marxist analysis claims that government operates more or less as an agent of the bourgeoisie or big business. How valid is this argument in the case of the Bank Act revision? Assess this argument also on the basis of McGregor's article.

4. From a pluralist perspective, there is nothing inherently undemocratic about the existence of powerful interest groups in society. What conditions have to be met in order for this pluralist democracy to be realized? Does the pluralist model adequately describe interest-group activity in Canada?

5. All the articles in this section dwell on the most visible interest-group activity. Is this preoccupation with the 'tip of the iceberg' a reflection of how inadequate press coverage is, or of how effective the best interest-group techniques are? What techniques are not examined?

6. Is ours a government of special interests?

Suggested Readings

Mildred A. Schwartz. 'The Group Basis of Politics', in John H. Redekop, ed. *Approaches to Canadian Politics*, second edition. Toronto: Prentice-Hall, 1983, 313–36.

'Governing Under Pressure: The Special Interest Groups', in *Canadian Public Administration*, vol. 25, no. 2, Summer 1982.

Richard J. Van Loon and Michael S. Whittington. *The Canadian Political System: Environment, Structure, and Process*, third edition. Toronto: McGraw-Hill Ryerson, 1981, 406–43.

A. Paul Pross. 'Pressure Groups: Talking Camelions', in Michael S. Whittington and Glen Williams, eds. *Canadian Politics in the 1980s*. Toronto: Methuen, 1981, 221–42.

Fred Thompson and W.T. Stanbury. 'The Political Economy of Interest Groups in the Legislative Process in Canada', in R. Schultz, O. Kruhlak, and J. Terry, eds. *The Canadian Political Process*, third edition. Toronto: Holt, Rinehart and Winston, 1979, 224–49.

A. Paul Pross, ed. *Pressure Group Behaviour in Canadian Politics*. Toronto: McGraw-Hill Ryerson, 1975.

d. Public Opinion

Rosemary Speirs, 'Tracking the Voters Right to the Polls', *Globe and Mail*, April 17, 1982 : *218*

Joe O'Donnell, 'Pollsters Set Priorities for the 1980s', *Toronto Star*, August 15, 1982 : *221*

Bryan Johnson, 'Self-Promotion Ottawa Style: Spend Money', *Globe and Mail*, May 8, 1982 : *224*

Lindsay Scotton, 'Ottawa's Advertising: Persuading Us With Our Own Money', *Toronto Star*, March 27, 1982 : *226*

Government policy is determined not only by objective conditions present in the country, but also by public desires. This is not to imply that decision-making slavishly follows public tastes; nevertheless, public opinion is a crucial element of the environment within which decisions are made. Political leaders have always carefully followed shifts in public attitudes, and they have increasingly come to rely on formal opinion surveys to guide their decisions. In fact, people in non-governmental organizations who seek to influence policy also commission public-opinion polls to discern public preferences. Changing values and policy preferences have played a key part in the determination of policy trends and future policy development.

Press use of public-opinion data has been extensive in recent years, especially during elections. The 1979 and 1980 federal campaigns saw the publication of, respectively, eight and ten national polls and innumerable local ones. Polling was particularly heavy in Québec in the months preceding the May 1980 referendum: nine surveys, some quite contradictory, were reported from December 1979 to the day of the vote. But if a few polls, notably those taken between elections, have contributed to the democratization of public-affairs coverage by drawing attention to public preferences, most have simply served to intensify the horse-race atmosphere of elections. And although the reporting of surveys has improved and the range of information generally included is wider now than it was, news reports still emphasize the attempts to forecast outcomes, ignoring the data that helps to explain voter preferences and changes in issue orientations. Even between elections, journalists tend to pounce on the monthly party standings in the Gallup poll. The numbers are used

uncritically, and it is rare to find a journalist who will examine such questions as the strength of voting commitment, the part played by the undecided portion of those surveyed, and the link between public preferences regarding leaders and regarding issues.

The articles by Rosemary Speirs and Joe O'Donnell do not focus on public opinion as such but on two prominent pollsters, not coincidentally Toronto-based. In fact, the similarities between the two pieces indicate a certain lack of creativity on the part of the newspapers in dealing with this subject. Rather than examining the strengths and weaknesses of the polling organizations, both resort to the standard approach for covering an intangible, amorphous issue: the personality profile. Curiously, neither article provides any hard data to assess the work of the subject; both rely exclusively on the opinions rendered by the pollsters themselves. The absence of any independent verification of the facts makes it possible to present the views of partisan pollsters without critical comment. Generally speaking, even when data are provided (usually in polls commissioned by the news organizations themselves), reporters neglect to pass on the appropriate qualifications issued by the polling agencies. Adequate information on sampling techniques, sample size, and question wording is rarely provided. As a result, reporters often give misleading accounts of surveys or exaggerate the importance of small differences between one poll and another. Reporting such mistaken impressions — for instance, that various polls contradict one another, when in fact they are in broad agreement — undermines the credibility of polling.

The final two articles deal with a different aspect of the public-opinion question: the efforts of governments to influence public attitudes. Recent evidence indicates that government leaders now make extensive use of public-opinion surveys as aids in decision-making. Indeed, it seems that many confidential surveys commissioned by government are more detailed and sophisticated than most in the public domain. As Bryan Johnson points out, governments use this information to structure advocacy advertising campaigns. What he neglects to note is how recent this trend is. Government advertising used to consist of consumer information promoting tourism, drawing attention to various public services, or explaining new laws such as seat-belt legislation. But the 1980 Québec referendum on sovereignty-association pushed governments into practices formerly used only by private corporations. Lindsay Scotton of *The Toronto Star* is properly exercised over the use of public monies for advertising. Although she does not specifically discuss the issue of advocacy advertising, she does correctly differentiate between the advertising of products by private companies and the marketing of ideas or concepts. According to Scotton, governments' use of the manipulative techniques associated with product selling is against the public interest.

THE GLOBE AND MAIL, APRIL 17, 1982

Tracking the voters right to the polls

He's the Conservatives' answer to the Liberals' Goldfarb. The Clark Government ignored the warnings. Bill Davis knew better.

BY ROSEMARY SPEIRS

Rosemary Speirs is the Queens Park bureau chief of The Globe and Mail.

THE FORMER prairie punk kid, his long hair trimmed, one earring still in his ear and the tattoos hidden under his shirt sleeves, moves comfortably these days in the discreetly posh ambiance of the Albany Club. Allan Gregg says he's a shock to other denizens of Toronto's Conservative Party watering hole, but insiders are indulgent about the mild eccentricities of this rising star of the Tory establishment.

As the party's official pollster, Mr. Gregg regularly reads the entrails for Bill Davis, Joe Clark and other Conservative leaders across the nation. Joe Clark's short-lived government ignored what Mr. Gregg's polls were saying, and fell from power. Mr. Davis listened carefully and won back his majority.

"He's a very bright young man," says Ontario Conservative strategist Norman Atkins. At age 30, Mr. Gregg is being touted as a Tory secret weapon, the party's answer to Martin Goldfarb, the Liberal Party of Canada's pollster and backroom strategist.

"He's pretty good competition, I'll say that," Mr. Goldfarb concedes, but he hastens to add that any party rich enough could buy the same sort of detailed voter information that Mr. Gregg supplied to the Ontario Tories in last March's campaign.

'Voters are worth different amounts. So you identify the votes'

While they compete at election time, as Mr. Gregg's polling house Decima Research Ltd. pits its computer hardware and Mr. Gregg's prognosticating skills against Goldfarb Consultants, in between elections there is a certain comfortable carving up of the territory. The Ontario Tories acknowledge some conflict in hiring their political pollster to do government survey work: they farm government policy polling out to Mr. Goldfarb. At the federal level, in return, Decima Research has started picking up a share of Mr. Goldfarb's leavings.

"In Ontario, he does the party polling and I do the government work," says Mr. Goldfarb. "In Ottawa, it's the reverse."

The two pollsters are an interesting contrast in styles. Mr. Goldfarb constantly plays down his influence, concerned by the perception of his role that has led Opposition members to complain of "Government by Goldfarb." Mr. Gregg has no compunction about being a manipulator of public opinion. His conversation occasionally lapses into the jargon of the political backrooms where the "handlers" plot strategy for "the body."

"A lot of people find what I do frightening," he concedes. "I don't. A businessman starts with the philosophy that a dollar spent wisely is better than a dollar spent poorly. In the same way, votes are worth different amounts. So you identify the votes that can be swung and you allocate your resources there."

The important change in modern political polling is the switch from nationwide opinion surveying to a type of detailed tracking of opinion on a local basis. Decima Research goes in well before an election is called to survey voters down to their toenails. Party strategists now use polls to tell them what type of candidate can most likely win a riding, or where to place their signs, what to say while canvassing and what to put in brochures for distribution on a certain block.

"We can target not just the possible swing ridings, but the swing polls within those ridings, and key voters within those polls," Mr. Gregg says. "We can identify on a block by block basis their historical voting behavior, their demographic profile, their inferred preference and reach them, not by the old mass media techniques, but by telephone and direct mail. In last year's provincial election, we identified 25 volatile ridings where we went in. Of those 25 ridings, six were Tory when we started and 19 were Tory when we ended."

At Decima's Yonge Street headquarters, Mr. Gregg sits in grey corduroys, white shirt and suspenders, framed against the plate-glass wall of his office that looks out on an atrium with trees and goldfish pond. The long hair and gold earring are incongruous in this setting. In a perverse way, he says, that can be an advantage. "People's expectations are so low that when you open your mouth they think you are a genius."

He was born in Edmonton, the son of a suit salesman. His youth, he concedes, was marked by a certain amount of drinking in bars and rough behavior. His first tatoo, a spider on one shoulder, is the result of teenage bluster when a trucker dared him to stand up to the needle to prove he was no sissy. "Allan is a bit of a romantic," says Nancy Jamieson, a friend who also works in Conservative Party circles. "The earring was part of being a prairie punk kid from north-end Edmonton. It's his way of saying he's still himself."

Mr. Gregg was studying for his Ph.D in political behavior at Carleton University when he started doing contract research for the Tories in 1975, as a way of earning money now that he was married with a baby son. The Conservatives were using American pollster Robert Teeter's firm, Market Opinion Research and, while happy with his technological expertise, felt there were difficulties in polling Canadians on the basis assumptions developed from the U.S. political scene. Mr. Gregg began running the Conservatives' in-house polling, an unsophisticated operation using Carleton computers. It was fun, but too slow for election purposes.

During the 1979 campaign, he went back to Market Opinion Research for the technology, but did the interpreting himself.

Meanwhile, Mr. Gregg and the Conservatives discovered the kind of in-depth polling being done by Decision Making Information, the firm of Ronald Reagan's pollster Richard Werthlin. In by-election work for the Ontario party, DMI provided detail, not only on how people were intending to vote, but where they'd go if they changed their minds, and what were the issues that might cause the shifts. "Allan had done so well and been so helpful to Clark that there was a push among Ottawa and Toronto Conservatives to see if we could establish a Canadian polling concern with a Conservative affiliation," says Hugh Segal, political aide to Mr. Davis. "It was to be the Conservative answer to Goldfarb."

In the spring of 1979, Mr. Gregg formed Decima Research, in partnership with DMI and Sherwood Communications, the parent company of Foster Advertising, the Ontario party's advertising house. (Recently, the other two partners sold out their interest in Decima to Kinburn Capital, a venture capital company.) As president of Decima, one of Mr. Gregg's first jobs was to provide a critique for Mr. Clark's federal strategists. It was a devastating assessment. The final paragraph read: "Clark's image problems at the end of the campaign, by and large, were the same as at the beginning. He suffered primarily from being perceived as unqualified to assume the senior office of government, as uninformed and lacking in strength. In fact, it may not be an exaggeration to suggest that a national leader has rarely, if ever, assumed office with lower expectations concerning his ability to govern."

'I'd been thrown to the dogs. I was to tell them not to give up on us'

Mr. Gregg's assumption was that since the Conservatives had obtained

power largely on a negative anti-Trudeau vote, much work remained to be done to win Canadian voters' positive approval. "It was a funny time for the Tories nationally. The Conservatives were so convinced that the people had wanted them that polls were non-issues. They'd been a tremendous consumer of polls before the 1979 election. But they went into the '80 election with almost no soundings. Everyone was consumed with the idea they had a job to do — that it was right and what people were thinking was secondary."

The federal strategists even ignored one poll Mr. Gregg did late in 1979, warning that Mr. Clark was in trouble with Ontario voters for his energy policies. By this time, Mr. Gregg had met Norman Atkins, the president of Camp Associates Advertising Ltd. and a close adviser to Mr. Davis, and had begun working for the provincial party as well. He was in an uncomfortable position, occasionally dispatched to Ottawa to explain the provincial government's opposition to Mr. Clark's energy proposals.

As the federal election campaign drew to a close, the federal Conservatives were dismayed by publication of a Gallup poll showing them 21 per cent behind the Liberals. Mr. Gregg's last poll for them weeks before had showed a gap of only 12 per cent; recent trackings in key ridings showed the party moving up. Party strategists decided to use Mr. Gregg to persuade the press the Conservatives still had a chance.

"I was having dinner with friends at my house when Bill Neville (Clark's aide) called from the plane saying the media wanted a backgrounder on my figures. I was reluctant but I went down to the Hotel Toronto. I looked terrible — dressed in old clothes and I'd cracked a beer, figuring it was just a backgrounder. Suddenly the cameras and the microphones were in front of me and reporters were asking 'will you win?'

"I'd been thrown to the dogs. I was there to tell them not to give up on us. I had to tread very carefully between gilding the lily and telling a lie."

The media took Mr. Gregg's careful footwork at face value — then ended up saying he had egg on his face when the next day's results were much worse than the "best scenario" he'd given them. It was an incident that hurt, because Mr. Gregg's figures for party insiders had actually been dead on. He resolved never again to let himself be used to put a good face on the data.

While Mr. Gregg talks, supervisors at Decima Research are setting up questionnaires on the phone banks a floor below, where the action starts after 5 p.m. with the arrival of the part-time housewives and university students who do the actual telephone polling. They say they are calling for Summerhill Research Centre, rather than use Decima's name, in case interviewees identify the research as being done for a Conservative house. "During Mr. Davis's campaign last March, we did 900 interviews in 14 hours," Mr. Gregg says. "We would start at 5 p.m. and by the time of the morning breakfast meeting (of campaign strategists) I'd have the results."

The Ontario Tories made effective, if somewhat unsavory, use of Mr. Gregg's polling techniques in the November, 1980 by-election in Carleton, the testing ground for the provincial election that was to follow. The polling confirmed what the newspapers had been saying: that there was slippage in the Tory core vote because of Mr. Davis's support for Liberal Prime Minister Pierre Trudeau on the constitution. Still, the polls showed the seat was winnable.

Hugh Segal, aide to Mr. Davis, says Conservative strategists decided to show the voters that if Mr. Davis was soft on the constitution, he was still "holding the line on some things."

The Conservative campaign distributed a pamphlet accusing Liberal Leader Stuart Smith of favoring "official bilingualism" for Ontario, while Mr. Davis had "caused the federal Government to back away from a blanket bilingual policy in favor of Ontario's existing policy of providing French language services where numbers warrant." The pamphlet led to Opposition charges in the House that the government was trying to win votes by stirring anti-French sentiment.

Although Mr. Gregg's polls provided the data for this appeal to

reaction, he says he didn't know about the pamphlet and wouldn't have approved.

A year before the March election, Mr. Gregg's firm had begun tracking 25 ridings that Tory strategists identified as bellwether ridings for the election. Mr. Gregg was able to tell them what kind of candidates to run in each riding — in general strong local candidates, not identified as Big C conservatives, who could appeal to the moderate middle vote as well. "He helped us to understand that these days you can't just run good old Bob because he has been on the local Conservative executive for years, and come up with a winner," Mr. Segal says.

Once the election was under way, Decima did daily trackings in each riding. People identified as key voters in swing polls received personal phone calls inviting their views on current issues, or were mailed something called "the Premier's policy survey," which purported to be a letter from Mr. Davis, who wanted their individual opinions to assist him in policy-making. Campaign headquarters actually dealt with the results, using the survey for election purposes. Mr. Gregg still won't talk about the details of how the survey worked, because he doesn't want the opposition catching on. "There are people in the party who consider it a competitive advantage."

The aim of all the polling was to sound out the questions in voters' minds, then get them going to the polls believing "the question they are answering is the question most to your advantage."

The real issue, the polls found, was the erosion of Ontario's manufacturing base: de-industrialization. "Nothing scares Ontarians more than the prospect of being a have-not province," Mr. Gregg says.

Stuart Smith had taken up this theme that Ontario now was Number 10 in the country in terms of economic growth. The Conservative response was the classic advertising man's trick — to play on the voters' fears and hopes. Dr. Smith, whose ratings had been high before the election, began to tumble in popularity as Premier Davis tagged him "Dr. Negative."

The Tories kept insisting that the

'We know from our polls the criterion for voters is Does it work?'

economy could revive, and that the key to this revival was good administration. Dr. Smith was pictured as too erratic to manage the province; Bill Davis and his team were the only safe answer.

Mr. Gregg's polls had also shown that over-riding issues were not the only key to the election. People would also vote locally on issues that affected them personally. So when Mr. Gregg's trackings began showing the NDP was making gains by suggesting the Tories would drop rent controls, the Conservatives knew just where to drop their pamphlets promising to keep controls and what areas to avoid with the message. They even knew that tenants listen more to the radio than do householders, so that radio was the medium to choose for rent control ads.

Tracking the success of this campaign, Mr. Gregg predicted that with a 68 per cent voter turnout, the Conservatives could expect 13 new seats. In fact, the turnout was 58 per cent, and the Government won 12 seats.

His accuracy in the election has given Mr. Gregg new clout within the Ontario party. He is using it, Mr. Segal says, to be an influence for moderation in the struggle between Mr. Davis and more right-wing elements of the party. When the issue is in doubt, Mr. Gregg can be called in with his statistics. He was there at the party's London policy conference, armed with slides and self-deprecating jokes, to persuade the faithful that the way to remain in power was to occupy the "moderate middle."

"Extremism scares the hell out of Ontarians," Mr. Gregg says. "We know from our polls that the criterion for the voters is not philosophy or ideology, but 'does it work?' . . . There are those in the party who say the pragmatic approach is a cop-out, that it is not leadership. But it is the reason for this government's longevity in Ontario."

THE TORONTO STAR, AUGUST 15, 1982

Pollsters set priorities for the 1980s

By Joe O'Donnell Toronto Star

George Gallup, the grandaddy of pollsters, called it "the pulse of democracy."

And though the science has undergone revolutionary changes from the more primitive days of man-on-the-street interviews to incorporate the most sophisticated hardware of the computer age, the basic objective hasn't changed.

Pollsters are still paid — albeit in megabucks nowadays — to tell us how we feel, what we think, and why. They're hired by clients ranging from politicians to corporate superstars to find out what sells, what to do and not to do. Or, to put it another way, how to win.

In Canada, the field is dominated by two Metro gurus: Martin Goldfarb of the prestigious firm, Goldfarb Consultants, and Allan Gregg, president of three-year-old Decima Research. Among their major clients are the nation's two senior political parties. Goldfarb works for the Liberals and Gregg is the pollster for the Progressive Conservatives.

Goldfarb, 44, who was educated in anthropology and moved on his own into public opinion research in the 1960s, says the pollster's most important job is interpreting the results of surveys.

"It's one thing to ask the right questions and to get some answers," he says. "It's quite another to know how to use that information, how to explain to a client what it all means and then, as a result, to give the right advice."

Even the authoritative Gallup polls allow themselves a small margin of error. They say they're accurate within four percentage points 19 out of 20 times.

So how often do the pollsters really blow it, as in the 1948 U.S. presidential election? All the experts predicted that Harry Truman would be slaughtered, yet he easily won re-election.

Goldfarb says that while the numbers are rarely, if ever, 100 per cent accurate, the advice has to be bang on: "My clients don't pay me to be wrong."

Gregg says bluntly: "We're paid to make winners. That's the job." The 30-year-old Alberta native, a social scientist by training with a PhD in political science, says pollsters "have no propensity for predicting behavior," just explaining it.

"We take snapshots of public opinion and then try to explain what it all means . . . Polling is really one-part science, one-part logistics and one-part art." And perhaps the most important ingredient, he says, is just a good gut sense of the world: "It's a very touchy-feely kind of experience. I think you need to be a very astute social observer to be a successful pollster."

Goldfarb and Gregg both agree that the mood of Canadians today is just plain rotten.

According to Goldfarb, after a refreshing period of national self discovery — the Expo celebrations and our euphoric (at the time) gamble on a youthful and charismatic new prime minister — Canadians have gone through a turbulent decade. There was Quebec's threat to bail out of Confederation, constant bickering between Ottawa and the Western provinces over an oil-pricing agreement, and most recently, an economic slump so severe it's affected virtually every Canadian's lifestyle.

The result, say the pollsters, is a public that's angry, frustrated and, most importantly, confused. Simply put, we're in a foul, foul mood.

"Canadians have gone through a long period of introspective analysis," Goldfarb explains, "without coming up with any clear answers . . . The jury is still out."

He says the difference between the public mood in the U.S. and Canada is that Americans have a sense that the economic policies of President Ronald Reagan may work, while Canadians don't believe the federal government is doing anything at all.

But Goldfarb says if the Liberal government's wage and price restraint program pans out, public faith could be restored sooner, rather than later.

Gregg doesn't buy that. The problem of public disenchantment runs far too deep for the Liberals to turn things around in time to survive the next federal election, he says. "The credibility problem for them (Liberals) is far too serious. Canadians are far too pragmatic these days. They're not motivated by ideology. All they want to know is: What works?"

And he insists that only a change of government will restore Canadians' faith that there's something left to believe in, that there's some way out of our economic doldrums. "Canadians still believe that governments can solve problems and that things will eventually get better," says Gregg. "They've just lost all faith in the government of the day."

While the two pollsters' loyalties are at odds, they agree that any party in power has a tough job ahead in the 1980s, what with an economy still deeply mired in recession and no end in sight.

So The Star asked them to map out their own eight-point Agenda for the Eighties, priorities and issues the nation and its governments — provincial and federal — will have to tackle.

For if the issues are ignored, says Goldfarb, Canadians will remain for some time in what he calls the dangerous state of "attitudinal purgatory."

Here are their reports:

Politicians must show they are taking charge: Martin Goldfarb

1 The economy and the myriad issues and problems it represents will continue to dominate Canadian politics in the 1980s.

Even opposition parties and victims of the deep and prolonged recession acknowledge that there are no easy solutions to bail us out of the mess we're in. So the key challenge to governments is to show Canadians they're doing something about our economic problems, that they are taking charge, to convince Canadians that we are on the road to recovery. If we continue to believe that things are out of control, the country will remain in attitudinal purgatory for years to come.

2 Jobs, jobs, jobs are needed to put this country back to work. With national unemployment hovering at post-Depression record levels of nearly 12 per cent, it remains our most critical and crippling problem. If we're to escape the current doldrums and emerge from the 1980's as a thriving, vibrant country, then a top priority for governments is to take bold and creative measures in all sectors of the economy that will not just stabilize existing employment levels, but create new job opportunities.

During the 1970s, we squandered opportunities to rejuvenate such crucial industries as forestry and mining. Rather than just licking our wounds, we must concentrate on pouring money into research and development of industries with the greatest potential in the international market. We must exploit our natural resources and develop our tremendous potential to compete in the world market, particularly high technology.

3 All Canadians, not just politicians, must share the blame for the malaise we're in today. And we must be active participants in the search for effective answers to our troubles.

During the 1970s, the Canadian workforce seemed to operate under the code: The less you do and the more you got for it is the objective. That was considered smart. That was considered beating the system. But if we're going to get this country back to work, all Canadians must adopt a stimulative and productive work ethic. It's not good enough to place all the responsibility on governments for rejuvenating our economy.

Collectively, Canadians must become more productive if we're to compete in the world market. We can't afford any longer to ignore long-term economic health for short-term gain. That's one of the main reasons we got into this mess in the first place.

4 Restraint is going to be another crucial element of economic recovery and must be on the Canadian political agenda of the 1980s.

Despite significant signs during the 1970s—such as the world-resounding OPEC crisis — that the well can run dry and that even our own vast resources aren't unlimited, it was a decade marked by enormous government spending. It was like a big, long party and now we're paying for it.

Governments must show leadership with genuine restraint measures to show they mean business and all Canadians must be willing to not just support those measures, but to participate in a national program of restraint. Unchecked and inflationary wage demands can't continue if we're to get the economy back on track again. Canadians have indicated they're willing to lower their expectations, provided we're all involved equally in the process.

5 Organized labor will also have a key role to play during the 1980s in the process of economic revitalization. During the past decade, this country has been seriously plagued by labor-management disputes resulting in some lengthy and sometimes-devastating strikes. High on the agenda for the 1980s must be a new role for organized labor, a commitment to a healthy industrial climate that will provide the framework for aggressive international competition with Canada as a key player.

We can take a valuable lesson from, for example, the Japanese, who have joined together — government, management and labor — in a commitment to quality production, job security and national economic stability. We can not only incorporate those goals, but even take them a step further.

6 Co-operation is also required at the federal-provincial level. As the oil-rich western provinces began to flex their muscles and eastern offshore oil discoveries gave two Maritime provinces a new raison d'être, not to mention unparalleled political clout, the whole nature of federal provincial relations changed dramatically during the past decade.

Despite some breakthroughs more recently with federal pacts in three provinces, the mood continues to be largely unsettled and volatile. Resource-rich provinces want a fair slice of their own wealth, but a commitment to sharing for the national good must have ascendancy in further negotiations during the 1980s.

This country will not survive if federal-provincial disputes pit region against region indefinitely. Canadians, by their nature, believe in fairness and they're willing to share. Governments can, and must, capitalize on that willingness for the sake of a healthy, united future.

7 While the economy will continue to dominate the political agenda in the 1980s, social issues cannot be ignored. Economic recession is no excuse for governments to ignore our mounting needs in education, and equal opportunity in the workforce.

Free education and universal access to our universities and a quality system geared to the real employment needs of our country remain vital goals for Canada as do universal medicare, sound health care services and social security for an aging population. And finally, women must be recognized — and not just in platitudes and study groups — as equal partners in the workplace. Women continue to be senselessly and unfairly shafted so it's time to put an end to that injustice once and for all.

The Constitution and federal-provincial disputes have tended to dominate the political agenda for the past decade, the undercurrent of some major social issues cannot—and must not — be ignored during the 1980s.

8 In addition to those pressing needs, perhaps the other most important item on the political agenda for the 1980s is for governments to restore their integrity — and not just for their own sake, but also for ours.

Canadians don't so much distrust governments today as dislike them. It's not that we don't still believe that governments can solve our problems. We do. We haven't yet totally lost faith.

Our greatest fear isn't that we may have to accept less, it's that we don't know where we're headed. What we don't see is government leading the way and that's why we feel our governments are failing us.

These are tough times and governments must make some tough decisions. Political parties too have an important role to play by providing the electorate with a clear sense of their philosophy, objectives and identifiable platforms and policies. They must, in effect, take control of the process of policy development instead of leaving it just to the elected officials.

Canadians want change but are worried about it: Allan Gregg

1 Canadians on a precipice: The public continues to embrace many traditional values—stability, progress, achievement — yet feel they are less attainable because of the many and growing problems they see us facing as a country and they face as individuals.

Thus, we see a public that is increasingly willing to accept public policy options and propositions that are in basic conflict with their traditional value assumptions.

Canadians see their, and the country's, current situation as unstable. So we see a culture that values stability calling for change — to redress instability. But, Canadians also fear change because so many feel that they personally cannot accommodate any change that might produce instability.

The same ambivalence holds true when the commitment to progress is examined. Canadians value progress and continue to measure progress through consumption. But because they also recognize that it is increasingly difficult to measure progress through these traditional means, they are more than prepared to protect themselves through retrenchment — in effect, equating progress with the curtailment of their lifestyles.

2 Growing demands for solutions: Our research also reveals a continuing and consistent belief that these readily recognized problems are imminently solvable. The tenuous nature of the public beliefs therefore makes it impossible to predict a single and consistent set of demands from the electorate.

It is equally impossible to predict that the public will move drastically to the right or left. Moreover, it is impossible to predict a single and consistent set of demands because demands are unlikely to be either single and consistent, and ideology is unlikely to be the motivator that produces these demands.

But because people believe our problems can be solved, the one thing we can safely predict is that demands on systems will be forthcoming from the public. We cannot anticipate a passive electorate. Rather, we should expect a public that is increasingly solution-oriented and who places an increasingly high premium on decision-makers who bring forward solutions.

3 A new political style: The agenda for the 1980s then is likely to be turbulent and highly diverse. And the public itself will not actually set this agenda. The public will place many different and often diverse demands on the system and decision-makers for solutions, but the agenda itself will have to be set by the decision-makers.

Genuine political leadership will be in more demand in the 1980s than in the past two decades.

4 Leadership: Canadians are more likely to evaluate leadership on one criterion: "Does it work?"

The successful politicians of the 1980s need not be either charismatic nor ideological. Pragmatism and problem-solving ability will be two characteristics of leadership most demanded by the electorate.

Those areas where the problem-solving capabilities and pragmatism of the 1980s decision will be in most demand include:

5 A new industrial order: Canadians recognize that the "old rules" are not working. Therefore in the face of increasing anxiety over the prospect of unemployment, we are witnessing a public that is also increasingly reluctant to see government bailing out industries that are not financially viable. It is almost as if Canadians know that jobs cannot be produced through the old industrial order because the old industrial order has dominated their concerns as unemployment increased. Political leaders of the 1980s therefore will have to define this "new economy" that will produce sought-after jobs.

6 A new educational order: While Canadians demand a change in our industrial base and anticipate that change will come they also fear that change. This fear of change, in turn, is rooted in a belief that our educational system has not produced sufficient skills to accommodate change.

For this reason, manpower training will grow as an issue and the role of our educational system in the new industrial order will be questioned.

7 A new political order: Political conflict is seen to be at the heart of many of our problems and as a major barrier to their solution.

In the past it has often been in decision-makers' political interest to generate conflict in order to demonstrate "toughness in leadership" or to mute larger issues. In the 1980s, the premium will be placed on consensus building and a more "corporatist" approach to government, business and labor relations. New structures to accommodate this consensus building will also be in demand.

8 The role of government: Discussions on whether the role of government in the economy and in our life will expand or contract in the 1980s fails to take into account the pragmatic basis of Canadians' demands.

Government intervention designed to produce publicly approved results will be accepted. Government intervention that does not produce these results will be rejected.

The same holds true for issues such as deficit spending. Canadians only reject deficit spending when they see themselves receiving no benefit for that spending.

THE GLOBE AND MAIL, MAY 8, 1982

Self-promotion Ottawa style: spend money

BY BRYAN JOHNSON

Mr. Johnson is a feature writer for The Globe and Mail.

THE NEAT, bespectacled young man in the billboard peers down on the Greek restaurants, Chinese grocery stores and Italian supermarkets of Danforth Avenue, in Toronto's east end. Behind him are three picture tubes that might belong to computers, TV sets or even video games. Above him stands the message: "Canada au travail."

Huh?

The confusion should be cleared up a block farther east, where an identical billboard is plastered with the English slogan: "Helping Canada Work." But passersby can still be forgiven for wondering what it's all about. *Who*, if anyone, is helping Canada work—especially at a time when the unemployment rate has reached a 40-year high? Who is this young man; why is he smiling in two languages; how on earth is he helping us?

There is no direct answer to any of those questions. Clearly, *nobody* is having much luck in putting this country to work. The guy in the picture is just a model, paid to smile and look vaguely productive.

The red maple leaf in the corner of the ads, however, gives the game away. The billboards were tacked up by the federal Department of Employment and Immigration, part of a $5-million ad campaign that has drawn denunciations from labor groups as an open insult to the unemployed, and left the Consumers' Association of Canada "appalled and outraged." The signs, it turns out, are meant to promote a federal job-training program — regardless of how puzzling their message might seem to passing motorists.

The campaign is one example of a Government ad explosion that has reached near manic proportions at both the federal and provincial level in the past few years — and will zoom this year's total public advertising bill to an estimated $200-million.

Unlike the United States, Canada's largest national advertiser is not Procter & Gamble or General Foods. It is the federal Government, which last year pumped at least $65-million into direct ad campaigns and more than doubled its nearest competitor in the private sector. Two provinces, Ontario and Quebec, also ranked in the top 15 big spenders. Even at that, the totals don't begin to count the advertising megadollars spent by such Crown corporations as CN and PetroCanada. And they are separate from the vast sums, also in the hundreds of millions of dollars, which Canada's 11 Governments routinely spend on promotion, public relations and "information publications."

By contrast, the U.S. Government ranks 24th on that country's list of advertisers, with a per capita expenditure less than one-quarter of what is spent on every Canadian.

"The excess is just unbelievable," complains Thomas Reid of Toronto's Reid Management. "For example, Procter & Gamble is second on the list. They have to sell Tide and Crest and all those other products. They've got their Crisco oils and their cake mixes. They've got this whole line of products which they're advertising in a concentrated way all across the country . . . and they're still only able to spend *half* the money. How in hell does the Government waste so much money? It's shocking to me. It's excessive to the point of being obscene."

The federal Government, of course, doesn't see it that way. Secretary of State Gerald Regan, the man responsible for federal advertising, is unperturbed by the huge spending gap between Ottawa and Washington. "The basic difference," he informed the House of Commons this week, "is that this is a Government that has very important social programs that do not exist in the United States. People on this side believe those programs must be communicated."

It is true the swollen ad budgets include essential information which Canadians demand from their governments, and the standard foreign advertising all countries use to attract tourism and investment. But as the spending mushrooms, the real growth industry is "image" or "advocacy" advertising — modern terms for old-fashioned propaganda.

The 1980 referendum in Quebec launched the flood of outright hardsell, as Ottawa banged heads with the Parti Québécois Government on billboards and airwaves across the province. Even the federal anti-alcohol ads were dragged into the fray, with the double-edged slogan: "Non, merci."

Provinces such as Ontario (where the ad budget has quadrupled in the past four years, to more than $25-million annually) were quick to follow suit. When a provincial opinion survey found that many residents felt their Government wasn't doing enough to protect the environment, Bill Davis's Tories took immediate action. No, they didn't start a clean-up drive; they simply launched a TV ad campaign showing deer lapping clean water, a beautiful girl emerging from a lake . . . all with the message that things are fine, the water is great.

"There was no information provided at all," recalls one Queen's Park researcher for an opposition party. "They just told us the lakes were clean, spent a lot of money, and put a Tory ad agency to work."

Such tactics were honed to a fine edge, on both sides of the debate, during the recent constitutional wrangle. The federal Government's Canadian Unity Information Office (CUIO) — prime mover in the billboard battle of Quebec, and dubbed by the Opposition as a "tax-funded propaganda arm of the Liberal Party" — was hastily refitted with a $32-million budget to fight opponents of the Trudeau patriation scheme. Soon, geese were winging across the nation's TV screens in ads about the "freedoms" we had to fight for; trees were sprouting in "common soil." In provinces such as British Columbia and Alberta, meanwhile, Canadians had the great privilege of watching *two* different Governments using their own money to send them a message. B.C. handed out a million copies of an eight-page tabloid that accused Ottawa of trying to take "real control of any province away from the people who live and work in it, and hand it over to a Government mainly elected by . . . central Canadians."

"We reduced the constitutional debate to a war between competing advertising agencies, all financed out of the public purse," snorts Tory MP Perrin Beatty, who directed Government advertising during his party's brief tenure in power. "And I think that's a pretty squalid level to reduce an issue as important as the future of Canada." Mr. Beatty is equally offended by the $8-million confection of patriotic ads the CUIO is currently pumping out to greet the new Constitution.

"You can't contrive a sincere, deep-felt emotional outpouring just because you'd like to see it," he says. "And yet that's what this advertising is trying to do, in the most vacuous, artificial and manipulative way." Like many opposition members in Parliament, Mr. Beatty verges on apoplexy when he speaks of the Unity Office, which he feels should have been scrapped after the Quebec referendum and has now become "potentially, a very dangerous rogue elephant."

It is virtually impossible to miss the CUIO's radio ads; they boast that "today we can truly say, the future belongs to us" and employ a pseudo-documentary format to recreate every Canadian triumph from Alexander Graham Bell to the Columbia's space arm. They also include the rather unfortunate phrase:

"Canada now has its own Constitution with the traditional rights and freedoms we once took for granted." We are not, apparently, able to take them for granted any longer.

The Sparks Street offices of the CUIO, which distributed more than seven million "pieces of information" last year, are positively redolent of nationalism. The red maple leaf and miniature copies of the new Constitution are everywhere, along with posters shouting "It's All Ours!" and pamphlets with titles like "Federalism and decentralization: where do we stand?"

"Actually," says interim director Daniel Gagnier, "the name Unity Information Office is misleading now. There was a time when it applied strictly and religiously. But now, we're doing much broader things." That may be why the office uses the mailing name 'Publications Canada,' but Mr. Gagnier is quick to disclaim any parallels with the now defunct Information Canada. "This is not Information Canada," he says firmly. "They had rigid control; I don't have that kind of mandate."

The CUIO was formed in 1977 for the specific purpose of combatting Quebec separatism, he explains, "and has just evolved." At $25.4-million (with $9.5-million earmarked for advertising), its

current budget is larger than during the Quebec referendum, and its new mandate is vaguely described as "flexible." Aside from the advertising, the CUIO now sends travelling exhibits all over Canada, operates booths in places such as the Canadian National Exhibition, and mails out pamphlets and posters by the million.

The Unity Office has often been a target of opposition barbs. (One small scandal erupted when it was discovered that the CUIO was having local newspapers flown in at $95 each, when at least one of the papers was available for $1 at a nearby newsstand. Another fight was touched off when the office spent $61,000 on a public opinion survey, but refused to make the results public.) Thus officials are sensitive to any criticism of the current constitutional ad blitz. It was "pre-tested in advance," says Mr. Gagnier, and has been very successful all across Canada.

None of that, however, cuts much ice with opposition critics. Perrin Beatty sighs, "The very point of these ads is to get people to write in. They (the CUIO) say, 'look how many people are asking for Government bumpf! That proves we're filling a demand.' What they're really doing is advertising to create a need for their own existence . . . It's all unbelievably manipulative, and wasteful."

And it's all from the public purse

The federal Government has adopted a curious dual stance on so-called "advocacy" advertising. On one hand, Secretary of State Gerald Regan informed an advertising conference last November that such ads "cut no ice" in influencing Ottawa. In the same speech, however, Mr. Regan strongly defended "persuasion" as the "essence of democracy" and admitted flatly that no Government of Canada has ever been "more determined . . . to make visible the work and worth of the national Government."

The man in charge of Ottawa's advertising also revealed a new principle of the Trudeau Government's ad policy: "The Government," he told the conference, "has a duty to inform the public of its proposals before they have been decided by Parliament."

The Liberals, in other words, reserve the right to publicize their policies, at public expense, before the Tories and NDP have any chance to debate the issues in the House of Commons. Should the opposition parties wish to advertise their own policies, of course, they would have to pay the bill themselves.

Not surprisingly, that policy enrages Perrin Beatty, the Tory MP who directed Government advertising during his

party's brief term in office. "There's a tremendous potential for this to be extremely dangerous," he fumes. "But fortunately, people like the Canadian Unity Information Office (CUIO) have been unbelievably inept with all their 'image' ads. People take a look at it and say 'isn't that a cynical bit of manipulation?' It just angers people.

"So far, it (the federal advertising) has only managed to be wasteful. It hasn't succeeded in the role the Liberals want."

Mr. Beatty and other critics are particularly angry at what they see as "image advertising"—geese flying "free" across TV screens; such slogans as "We've got a lot to be thankful for" — and charge that agencies like the CUIO do not promote the Government of Canada, but merely the Liberal Party.

Mr. Reagan, however, has consistently denied the Government uses "advocacy advertising" at all, claiming that Ottawa is obliged to "inform the public of its policy proposals" and "provide access to information on an equal basis in all regions of Canada."

He described the controversial constitutional ads as "innocuous," and soon after the policy speech told a TV interviewer that they "didn't try to sell the federal

side of the debate . . . What that advertising was intended to do was to make people think about the Constitution."

When the interviewer suggested many Canadians did not approve of the Government spending money for that purpose, Mr. Regan replied, "I guess we'll have to disagree in relation to that."

The Secretary of State also described himself as "a strong advocate of Government advertising" and said he didn't think the use of public funds to promote Government policies was "unfair in any sense."

Tory spokesman Beatty does not accuse the Government of violating any specific laws with its ad policy, but clearly hopes to embarrass the Liberals into putting their own limits on self-promotion.

"I don't know how you'd write rules to say Government advertising can't be self-serving," he says. "Ultimately, you have to count on the sense of decency and judgement of the people in power. The Liberals have taken the attitude that, if there's nothing in the law which restrains them in the use of public funds this way, then there simply *are* no restraints.

"That's just how it is. There are no checks and balances in (the Canadian) system."

THE TORONTO STAR, MARCH 27, 1982

Ottawa's advertising: Persuading us with our own money

By Lindsay Scotton
Toronto Star

Ottawa — When Canada's constitution comes home next month, the people of this country will be deluged with a flurry of publicity proclaiming how wonderful it is to have a home-grown constitution, and by extension, how wonderful the Liberal government is to have achieved this marvel.

Canadian taxpayers will be shelling out more than $4 million to pay for this publicity campaign, which is additional to the millions that will be spent on "information" — printing up the charter of rights for distribution in schools and to the public, for instance.

Drop in the bucket

And this lavish display of government congratulating itself at taxpayers' expense is just a drop in the bucket in terms of the Liberals' ongoing romance with "concept" advertising.

The federal government is the nation's single largest buyer of advertising.

According to the department of Supply and Services, advertising contracts worth more than $65 million were handed out by the government between April of 1981 and March of 1982: estimates from the same department indicate that the government has plans to spend more than $70 million on advertising within fiscal 1982–83. The minister responsible for government advertising, Gerald Regan, says this will allow the government to "see to it that the public knows of government programs, of government proposals, and of government policies."

His boss, Prime Minister Pierre Trudeau, put it more succinctly when he said that governments use advertising to promote the "policies, advantages and glories" of their jurisdictions.

The traditional role of government advertising is to provide information on services or to advise of changes in regulations. But the current thinking of the ruling Liberals on advertising and its uses is somewhat more sophisticated. Its publicity campaigns have taken on the noxious odor of propaganda.

Take, for example, a series of full-color newspaper advertisements promoting the federal government's contribution to agricultural research. The ads point out that research is important in agricultural enterprise (a message that really must give Canada's growing population of bankrupt farmers a thrill) and that the federal government knows it. The mellifluous copy, set against a golden pastoral landscape, goes on to inform us that those hard-pressed farmers are "working together, and with the help of government, helping Canada grow."

"What's conveyed here?" asks a frustrated Perrin Beatty, Conservative communications critic. "What's conveyed? Nice country we've got here. Nice government we've got here."

The wonderful ways

On November 11, 1981, an ad placed by the cabinet committee on economic development listed all the wonderful ways in which the government was pumping cash into a tired economy. Recognize the date? Finance Minister Allan MacEachen delivered his tight-fisted budget the following day.

Of course, we all remember the controversial government ads promoting constitutional reform in the midst of federal-provincial negotiations on the issue, and ads from the Department of Energy promoting the federal stance during oil-pricing talks with Alberta.

And the beat goes on. Along with the constitutional hoo-ha, there is a major advertising campaign in the works to lend credibility to the thin package of job creation programs announced this week by Employment and Immigration Minister Lloyd Axworthy. A similar campaign will soon inundate Western Canada with the federal government's arguments on why the Crow's Nest Pass freight rates should be hiked.

These campaigns, and others, come to us after approval from the government's Advertising Management Group (AMG), a collection of marketing experts plucked from the private sector 18 months ago to give government advertising the same gloss and impact as ads for toothpaste or orange juice.

Peter Zarry, responsible within AMG for central Canada, laughs uproariously when reminded of the strong controversy over last summer's constitutional ad campaign — the ones that starred geese winging across television screens, and trees growing out of "common soil." As far as he's concerned, the ads were a tremendous success.

"Every time anyone complained about it, they did just what we wanted — they talked about the constitution. They screamed, they hollered, oh, it was beautiful!" Zarry, with 25 years of experience with ad companies in the private sector, is known as one of the shrewdest marketing strategists in the country. He's well-versed in overcoming consumer resistance to certain products, and in targeting and developing new "product image" — as he did in his successful campaigns for "FDS" Feminine Deodorant Spray and Labatt's 50 Ale.

Bombard the public

Nor is the federal government satisfied with merely advertising programs and services devolved from legislation that has been passed in the House of Commons. The Liberals have decided that is their responsibility to bombard the public with their point of view on a particular piece of legislation — before it is passed by the Parliament of the land.

"I don't think that the government should have to wait until a bill is passed in the House," says Gerald Regan, chairman of the cabinet communications committee that assesses the need for advertising in a particular area.

Does that mean the government is indulging in advocacy advertising, by pushing a single, and often controversial, point of view on the public? "I don't think I could define it with any degree of exactitude," says Regan, "What's unacceptable is advertising that is obviously politically partisan."

That must mean that subtle political partisanship is okay, because that's exactly what's going on. The Liberal government has decided that advertising is the best way to keep and expand its market share of voter support, and is as determined as any soft-drink manufacturer to keep 'em coming back for more.

□ **Lindsay Scotton is a member of The Star's editorial board.**

Discussion Questions

1. What role do public opinions play in the Canadian policy process? Are there effective means by which citizens can influence government policy decisions? Do public opinions have a more or a less significant impact on politics than political parties and interest groups do?
2. Do pollsters such as Martin Goldfarb and Allan Gregg play a politically significant role, or are they neutral messengers bringing public preferences to light?
3. Should polls be published during election campaigns? Given that the outcome of an election may hinge on the swing of a few percentage points, and that the acknowledged margin of error in most polls is so high, do election polls simply muddy the waters?
4. Are elections just large-scale public opinion polls?
5. Is it legitimate to spend taxpayers' dollars to promote what could be construed as politically partisan positions?

Suggested Readings

Duncan McDowall, ed. *Advocacy Advertising: Propaganda or Democratic Right?* Ottawa: Conference Board of Canada, 1982.

Paul W. Fox, ed. *Politics: Canada*, fifth edition. Toronto: McGraw-Hill Ryerson, 1982, 229–70.

Kenneth Bryden. 'Public Input Into Policy-Making and Administration: The Present Situation and Some Requirements for the Future', in *Canadian Public Administration*, vol. 26, no. 1, Spring 1982, 81–107 *or* in Fox (see above), 258–68.

Richard Simeon and Donald E. Blake. 'Regional Preferences: Citizens' Views of Public Policy', in David Elkins and Simeon, eds. *Small Worlds: Provinces and Parties in Canadian Political Life.* Toronto: Methuen, 1980, 77–105.

M.D. Ornstein *et al.* 'The State of Mind: Public Perceptions of the Future of Canada', in R.B. Byers and R.W. Reford, eds. *Canada Challenged: The Viability of Confederation.* Toronto: Canadian Institute of International Affairs, 1979, 57–107.

F.J. Fletcher and R.J. Drummond. *Canadian Attitude Trends, 1960–1978*, Working Paper No. 4. Montreal: Institute for Research on Public Policy, 1979.

G.B. Doern and A.M. Maslove, eds. *The Public Evaluation of Government Spending.* Montreal: Institute for Research on Public Policy, 1979.

M.D. Ornstein *et al.* 'Public Opinion and the Canadian Political Crisis', in *Canadian Review of Sociology and Anthropology*, vol. 15, no. 2, May 1978, 58–205.

L. Leduc. 'The Measurement of Public Opinion', in Howard Penniman, ed. *Canada at the Polls: The General Election of 1974.* Washington: American Enterprise Institute, 1975, 209–41.

Notes